THE LETTERS
OF
THOMAS WOLFE

BOOKS BY THOMAS WOLFE

Look Homeward, Angel
Of Time and the River
From Death to Morning
The Story of a Novel
The Face of a Nation
The Web and the Rock
You Can't Go Home Again
The Hills Beyond
Letters to His Mother
A Stone, a Leaf, a Door
The Letters of Thomas Wolfe

*My whole effort for years might be described as an effort to fathom
my own design, to explore my own channels, to discover my own ways . . . .
I have at last discovered my own America, I believe I have found
my language, I think I know my way. And I shall wreak out my vision
of this life, this way, this world and this America, to the top of my bent,
to the height of my ability, but with an unswerving devotion, integrity and
purity of purpose that shall not be menaced, altered or weakened by anyone.*
From the Letter of December 15, 1936 to Maxwell E. Perkins.

52723

ACKNOWLEDGMENTS

GRATEFUL ACKNOWLEDGMENT is here made

To William B. Wisdom for making available the major portion of Wolfe's own letters and other papers, which he purchased from the Wolfe Estate and presented to Harvard University;

To Houghton Library, Harvard University, and to the following members of its staff: William A. Jackson, William H. Bond, Carolyn E. Jakeman, Mary Shea Goulart, Jean Briggs, Mary K. Daehler, Julie P. Johnson, Marilyn S. Schultz, Winifred Cadbury Beer, Arnold Weinberger, W. B. Van Lennep, Mary J. Reardon, George W. Cottrell, Leslie M. Oliver and Thomas Mathews; also to Widener Library and Thomas Little, and to the Poetry Room of Lamont Library and Mrs. Lydia Roberts and Robert O'Clair;

To Mabel Wolfe Wheaton and Fred W. Wolfe for making available letters written by Wolfe to them and other members of the family, for permitting quotations from letters of their own, and, in general, for their tireless and devoted aid;

To the University of North Carolina Library for making available the letters and other material by or about Wolfe in its possession; also to Charles E. Rush, Director, and to Mary L. Thornton, Librarian of the North Carolina Collection;

To Charles Scribner's Sons for making available their own correspondence with Wolfe and their records concerning him; also to the following Scribner employees, past or present: Irma Wyckoff Muench, Marion Ives, W. Gilman Low, S. Elizabeth De Voy, Whitney Darrow, Robert Cross, George Merz, David Randall, Wallace Meyer, Elizabeth Youngstrom and Fidelia Stark; and to John Hall Wheelock and the late Charles Scribner III for their sympathetic encouragement and affectionate paternalism;

To the late Aline Bernstein for making available certain letters written to her by Wolfe, for providing much background material, and for giving unstintedly of her own recollections concerning Wolfe;

To Pack Memorial Public Library, Asheville, and to Myra Champion of the Reference Department for her energetic and enthusiastic help;

To the New York Public Library and to Paul North Rice, Chief of the Reference Department;

To Newberry Library, Chicago, and to Stanley Pargellis, Librarian, and Amy Nyholm, Manuscript Cataloguer;

To Mrs. Sherwood Anderson for allowing the quotations from Anderson's letters to Wolfe of April 23, 1935 and December 17 and 18, 1937, and for supplying background material. Also to R. L. Sergel;

To New York University for making available the letters of Wolfe to Homer A. Watt and the records concerning Wolfe's employment at the University; also to Thomas Clark Pollock, Oscar Cargill, LeRoy Kimball, and Jean Webster;

To the Princeton Library and to Julian Boyd, Alexander Clark, and Alexander D. Wainwright, and to Mrs. Samuel J. Lanahan, daughter of Scott Fitzgerald, for allowing the quotation from Scott Fitzgerald's letter of July 19, 1937 to Thomas Wolfe.

To Mrs. George P. Baker for allowing the editor to examine Professor Baker's own correspondence, and for supplying background material;

To the late J. M. Roberts for allowing the quotation from Mrs. Roberts' letter of May 11, 1936 to Wolfe, and of her commentary on the letters which Wolfe wrote her;

To Robert N. Linscott for permission to quote from his letters of October 22 and November 17, 1937 to Wolfe, and for his recollections of the negotiations between Wolfe and Houghton Mifflin;

To Melville H. Cane for his encouragement and advice;

To Richard S. Kennedy for allowing the editor to read his "Thomas Wolfe at Harvard" and other writings concerning Wolfe before their publication, and, in general, for making available to her the results of his own research;

And to Edward C. Aswell, Administrator C.T.A. of the Estate of Thomas Wolfe, for his loyalty and devotion, and for his self-sacrificing expenditure of patience, strength, and time.

GRATEFUL ACKNOWLEDGMENT is also made to the following for letters by Wolfe, or information concerning him, or both:

Milton A. Abernethy, George Matthew Adams, Phoebe Adams, Walter S. Adams, Mrs. Charles S. Albert, Ruth and Maxwell Aley, Elizabeth Ames, Anne W. Armstrong; *The Atlantic Monthly:* Edward Weeks and Charles W. Morton; Caroline Bancroft, LeBaron R. Barker Jr., Stringfellow Barr, Hamilton Basso, Ralph A. Beals, Gweneth P. Beam, Alice Beer, Richard C. Beer, Alladine Bell, Pincus Berner, Arthur F. Blanchard, LeGette Blythe, Charles S. Boesen, Dr. Walter Bonime, Hilda Westall Bottomley, Mrs. James Boyd, Nancy Hale Bowers, Donald Brace, E. N. Brandt, M. A. Braswell, Joseph Brewer, the late Herschel Brickell, H. Tatnall Brown Jr., John Mason Brown, Mr. and Mrs. Struthers Burt, Witter Bynner, Gwen Jassinoff Campbell, Henry Seidel Canby, Henry Fisk Carlton, William D. Carmichael Jr., Mrs. D. D. Carroll, John Carswell, Lenoir Chambers, Harry Woodburn Chase, John W.

Chase; The Chatham, and Fred F. Holsten, General Manager; Richard S. Childs, Albert Coates, William J. Cocke, Allan C. Collins, Benjamin Cone, Pascal Covici, Ray Conway, Kyle Crichton; The North Carolina Historical Society, and Christopher Crittenden, Secretary; E. A. Cross, B. Crystal and Son, Mina Curtiss, Jonathan Daniels, Alfred S. Dashiell, Edward Davison, Mrs. Clarence Day, Frederic L. Day, L. Effingham de Forest, George V. Denny Jr., Byron Dexter, Robert B. Dow, Olin Dows, Dr. A. Wilbur Duryee, Dr. Eugene F. DuBois, Max Eastman, Duncan Emrich, Morris L. Ernst, Evangelical United Brethren Church, W. Ney Evans, Mrs. Raymond C. Everitt, Mrs. Marjorie C. Fairbanks, Dr. Achilles Fang, Thomas Hornsby Ferril, Mrs. Arthur Davison Ficke, Kimball Flaccus, Dr. John C. Frothingham, A. S. Frere, Daniel Fuchs, Charles Garside; Genealogical Society of Pennsylvania and John Goodwin Herndon, Executive Director; General Alumni Association of the University of North Carolina: J. Maryon Saunders and William M. Shuford; Charles Goetz, J. Lesser Coldman, Henry Gollomb, Edward Goodnow, Mack Gorham, Mr. and Mrs. Douglas W. Gorsline, Elaine Westall Gould, Frank P. Graham, Hans J. Gottlieb, Mrs. W. W. Grant, Paul Green, Kent Roberts Greenfield, Ferris Greenslet; The John Simon Guggenheim Memorial Foundation: Henry Allan Moe, Josephine Leighton and James F. Mathias; James J. Hankins, William E. Harris, Henry M. Hart Jr., Rupert Hart-Davis; Harvard University Archives: Miss Florence K. Leetch and Clifford K. Shipton; Charles M. Hazlehurst, George W. Healy Jr., Theresa Helburn, Dorothy Kuhns Heyward, Greta Hilb, Betsy Hatch Hill, Helen Train Hilles, Clayton and Kathleen Hoagland, Mr. and Mrs. Terence Holliday; Houghton Mifflin Company: Paul Brooks and Mrs. Dorothy de Santillana; James S. Howell, Arthur Palmer Hudson, Louis C. Hunter, Katherine Gauss Jackson, Dr. A. C. Jacobson, Belinda Jelliffe, Edith Walton Jones, The Rev. Arthur Ketchum, Donald W. Keyes, Kenneth J. Kindley, Freda Kirchwey, Mary Mathews Kittinger, T. Skinner Kittrell, Blanche Knopf, Mrs. Frederick H. Koch, Charlotte Kohler, Eleanor Lake, Dr. Else K. La Roe, H. M. Ledig-Rowohlt, Dr. Russel V. Lee, Elizabeth H. Lemmon, Edgar Lentz, Dr. Isaiah Libin, G. Linnemann, Louis Lipinsky, Marian Smith Lowndes, Mabel Dodge Luhan, Ralph E. Lum, Percy Mackaye, Dr. J. Donald MacRae, George W. McCoy, Thomas McGreevy, Lura Thomas McNair, Gertrude Macy, J. Carroll Malloy, Arthur Mann, Sam Marx, Mrs. Edgar Lee Masters, Robert D. Meade, Nina Melville, Mr. and Mrs. Edward M. Miller, Fred B. Millett, Cornelius Mitchell, Nathan Mobley, Doris Moskowitz, Anne Arneill Mueller, Herbert J. Muller, James Buell Munn, Hugo Münsterberg; National Institute of Arts and Letters, Felicia Geffen, Secretary; The New Yorker, and Mrs. K. S. White; Marcus C. S. Noble Jr., Paul Nordhoff; Northwestern University Alumni Association, and G. Willard King, Executive Director; Donald Olyphant, Paul Palmer, Hortense Roberts Pattison, Wendell L. Patton,

Charles A. Pearce, Marjorie N. Pearson, Norman H. Pearson, Bessie Peretz, Mrs. Maxwell E. Perkins, Frances Phillips, James Poling, William T. Polk, Garland Porter, Desmond Powell, George R. Preston, Henry F. Pringle; *The Raleigh News and Observer:* Mrs. Harry W. McGalliard, Librarian; Dr. James G. Ramsay, Mr. and Mrs. Robert Raynolds, Filomena Ricciardi, Mrs. Lillian W. Richards, Mrs. Lennox Robinson, Barnet B. Ruder, Phillips Russell, Thomas Sancton, Mrs. Dorothy Greenlaw Sapp, Mrs. A. P. Saunders, Mrs. Bradley Saunders, Mark Schorer, Edgar Scott, George Seldes, Mrs. Mary Shuford, Luise M. Sillcox, Mrs. Lora French Simmons, Beverly Smith, Harrison Smith, Mrs. Stella Brewster Spear, Mrs. Catherine Brett Spencer, Corydon P. Spruill, Stanford Alumni Association, Marion L. Starkey, George M. Stephens, Mrs. Martha Dodd Stern, Mr. and Mrs. James Stevens, George Stevens, Donald Ogden Stewart, James Stokely, Edward Stone, Jesse Stuart, Mr. and Mrs. James Sykes, Nathan R. Teitel, Arthur Thornhill, William Y. Tindall, Perry Tomlin, Mrs. Susan Hyde Tonetti, Jean Toomer, William Troy, S. Marion Tucker, U. B. Publishing Estab., Inc., The late Carl Van Doren, Mark Van Doren, Willard Van Dyke, Henry Volkening, Frank K. Wallace, Mrs. George Wallace, Margaret Wallace, Nathan Wallack, The late Dixon Wecter, Mrs. Emily MacRae West, Bruce William Westall, Caroline Whiting, Mrs. Dorothy F. Wiley, Mrs. Jeannie Colvin White, Mrs. Lenore Powell Whitfield, Max Whitson, John Hay Whitney, James Southall Wilson, Ella Winter, Edgar E. Wolf, Olivia Saunders Wood; Yale School of Fine Arts: Maude K. Riley, Registrar; Stark Young.

CONTENTS

INTRODUCTION

BY ELIZABETH NOWELL

SOME of Thomas Wolfe's most interesting letters were the ones he never mailed. Among his papers, now preserved at Harvard and the University of North Carolina, there are many of these letters, written with his typical wholeheartedness and eloquence and verve, but simply never sent. For this, there was a variety of reasons. For one thing, Wolfe was usually too absorbed in his own creative world to perform the routine acts of life, such as buying envelopes or stamps or pen and ink, let alone remembering to take a letter to the mailbox. For another, his life was a series of engrossments and of interruptions: if something intervened to prevent his completion of a letter, he would seldom have the time or inclination to go back to where he had left off. For still another thing, his utter trustfulness and lack of reticence were sometimes superseded by fits of caution, or even of suspicion: he might suddenly get a hunch that what he'd written was too indiscreet, and break off in the middle of a sentence. Then he would stride up and down his room in indecision, meditatively suck his upper lip inside his upthrust lower one, rub the nape of his neck or the back of his head, or thrust his hand inside his shirt and rub his chest, and say: "Well, I don't know . . . ," and turn to other things. Sometimes, if repeatedly goaded to anger or perturbation by the matter dealt with in his letter, he finally would grab it up and finish it and mail it and be done with it. Or sometimes he would rewrite it, over and over, until the version which he mailed was only a brief and non-committal note. But he had a chronic difficulty in arriving at decisions, so for the most part, he would never "get around" to doing any more about a letter, but would simply leave it lying on his writing-table.

Also, many of his letters were not written for his correspondents as much as for himself. He maintained that "a writer writes a book in order to forget it," and he might have said the same about a letter. From his youth, he had the habit of pouring out on paper all his thoughts, emotions and experiences, either in rough-draft notes for possible creative work, in diaries or letters—and the dividing line between these different forms of writing was often very thin. This outpouring was a psychological necessity: it was a solace for his loneliness, an apologia for the errors and confusions and difficulties of his life, and a safety-valve for his intense emotional reactions. Once off his chest and down on paper, "for the record," as he called it, an emotion or experience lost its first compulsive force and could be stored away and half-forgotten. It had had its primary effect on Wolfe himself: the communication of it to other people was a different, secondary thing.

Therefore, for one or several of these reasons, his letters might lie discarded on his table, together with manuscripts, bills, timetables, empty envelopes, shopping lists and other papers, till the accumulation grew so large as to leave no room for him to write, whereupon he would grab it up and move it to his mantelpiece, bookcase, bureau, chairs, or, lacking any other space, the floor. There it would remain for weeks or months or even years, growing grimy with the coaldust of New York, Brooklyn, London, or wherever he might be, until the time came for him to move into a new apartment, or to embark upon the feverish travels which were for him both a rest and a renewal. At the last possible moment, he would plunge into the dreaded task of packing, and would jam the entire hodgepodge mass of papers into battered suitcases or the big pine packing-boxes which he got from Scribners for this purpose. From that moment on, it became part of the vast accumulation of manuscripts and other papers which was his carefully-hoarded possession, in fact the only permanent possession which he had.

In *Of Time and the River,* Wolfe describes Eugene Gant's belongings: "the notebooks, letters, books, old shoes, worn-out clothes and battered hats, the thousands of pages of manuscript that represented the accretions of . . . years—that immense and nondescript collection of past events, foredone accomplishment, and spent purposes, the very sight of which filled him with weariness and horror but which, with the huge acquisitive mania of his mother's blood, he had never been able to destroy." Wolfe himself was no string-saver like Eliza Gant, but he had a strange reluctance to throw anything away, and this increased to blind possessiveness when the thing was a piece of paper—any piece of paper—with his writing on it. And so, just as Eliza slept in a room "festooned with a pendant wilderness of cord and string," Wolfe lived and worked, for the great part of his adult life, in a succession of small two-room apartments, encumbered with his battered suitcases and huge pine packing-cases full of manuscripts and other papers. Moreover, when he travelled, he either had to take this vast accumulation with him, or had to store it with his publisher or with some trusted friend. He would complain half-humorously about it—"This business of being a vagabond writer with two tons of manuscript is not an easy one," he said. However, if any of the well-intentioned friends who were always trying to bring order to his life suggested that he dispose of anything, he would become as desperately tenacious as Eliza Gant. "Here, give me that!" he'd cry in outraged panic. "I might need it! I might find a place to use it some time!"— and back into its crate the paper would immediately go. The fact was that he considered all of his vast hoard of papers, whether manuscripts or random notes or letters, as part of "the fabric of his life" from which his books were made. "It is, so far as I am concerned, the most valuable thing I have got," he wrote in 1937 to his brother Fred. "My life is in it—years and years of work and sweating blood."

This accumulation of Wolfe's papers, now preserved in the William C. Wisdom Collection at Houghton Library, Harvard, and at the library of the University of North Carolina, has been the chief source of material for this volume of his letters. The unmailed or rough-draft letters found scattered among his manuscripts have, for the most part, been included, and when there have been various versions of a letter, the most revealing has been chosen, regardless of whether it was the one actually mailed or not. In these letters, Wolfe seldom bothered to write in any heading of place or date, or even any salutation. This data has been guessed at after a study of Wolfe's diaries and other sources of information concerning him: when it is probably correct, it has been marked with brackets: when dubious, with both brackets and question marks. The same designations have been used for words which were illegible, either because of the tearing or decomposition of the paper, or because of Wolfe's too-hasty handwriting. Words always came boiling, pouring from Wolfe's mind too fast for him to get them down on paper, and because of this, his writing was a kind of shorthand: he would form the salient letters of a word with some degree of legibility, but would indicate the less important ones by a series of hasty undulations or by simply a straight line. As a result, one cannot read his writing by deciphering it, letter by letter: one must take a bird's-eye view of it through half closed eyes, get the general gist of it, and then be guided by one's intuition of what he meant, rather than by what his hasty hen-scratches may actually seem to say.

Also included in this volume are carbon copies of many letters typed by the stenographers who worked for Wolfe during the last eight years of his life; also letters from the files of Charles Scribner's Sons, and from those of his friends and other correspondents whose names are listed gratefully at the conclusion of Acknowledgments. Wolfe's letters to his mother have been omitted, since they have already been published in a separate volume:* also his more personal letters to Aline Bernstein have been excluded from this volume at her request since it was her intention to edit them herself. Also omitted are form letters written in reply to fan mail, legal or routine business letters, letters which repeat, almost word for word, material written to other people, or letters which concern the affairs of the people to whom Wolfe was writing, rather than those of him himself. In other words, the letters published here have been selected from the huge bulk of Wolfe's

* *Thomas Wolfe's Letters to His Mother,* edited by John S. Terry, Charles Scribner's Sons, 1943.

correspondence to tell the story of his life, with the immediacy of its successive moments.

As might be expected, many of Wolfe's letters deal with the personal relationships which influenced him strongly and also caused him bitter disillusionment during a great part of his life. For instance, there are letters expressing his early adoration of and subsequent compulsion to break away from, first, Professor George P. Baker, then Aline Bernstein, and finally Maxwell Perkins. Wolfe has been accused of "turning against" these influential people in his life, and even, by one somewhat sensational writer, of "betraying" them. However, there is no law which compels a man to enroll for the same course at Harvard for more than three successive years, nor to love eternally a married woman nineteen years his senior, nor to remain forever with one publisher, especially if he feels that his general reputation and his creative talent are suffering therefrom. A calmer, more judicious description of what happened would be to say that Wolfe "turned *away*" from these people, or outgrew them and their dominating influence upon his life. But it is hard to be calm or judicious about Wolfe: his own emotional intensity tends to be reflected by everything and everyone concerned with him.

Wolfe constantly became involved in these too-constricting personal relationships and these subsequent struggles to break free from them as a result of what he called "the search for a father." "The deepest search in life, it seemed to me," he wrote in *The Story of a Novel*, "the thing that in one way or another was central to all living, was man's search to find a father, not merely the father of his flesh, nor merely the lost father of his youth, but the image of a strength and wisdom external to his need and superior to his hunger, to which the belief and power of his own life could be united." This quest of his has been attributed to various causes: to a nostalgia for the security of his early childhood which was disrupted by the partial separation of his parents; to a simple feeling of bereavement at his father's death; to a desire to escape from the domination of his mother; to a subconscious yearning for her; and to a search for the God-the-Father of a religion which he intellectually could not accept but for which he still had need. There is something to be said for all of these interpretations, but it must also be remembered that the normal impulse of all adolescents is to attach themselves to people they admire, and that Wolfe retained many adolescent traits until comparatively late in life.

At any rate, in both his letters and his novels, he repeatedly described this search, and the disillusionment it inevitably led to. "Why was it? What was this grievous lack or loss—if lack or loss it was—in his own life?" he wrote in *Of Time and the River*. "Why was it that, with his fierce, bitter and insatiate hunger for life, his quenchless thirst for warmth, joy, love, and fellowship, his constant image, which had blazed in his heart since childhood, . . . that he grew weary of people almost as soon as he met them? Why was it that he seemed to squeeze their lives dry of any warmth and interest they might have for him as one might squeeze an orange, and then was immediately filled with boredom, disgust, dreary tedium, and an impatient weariness and desire to escape so agonizing that it turned his feeling almost into hatred? Why was it that his spirit was now filled with this furious unrest and exasperation against people because none of them seemed as good as they should be? Where did it come from—this improvable and yet unshakable conviction that grew stronger with every rebuff and disappointment—that the enchanted world was here around us ready to our hand the moment that we chose to take it for our own, and that the impossible magic in life of which he dreamed, for which he thirsted, had been denied us not because it was a phantom of desire, but because men had been too base and weak to take what was their own?"

Occasionally he would find a man or woman, such as Professor Baker, Mrs. Bernstein or Maxwell Perkins, who was remarkable enough to withstand this first onslaught of his scrutiny, and to seem to be a fitting "image of strength and wisdom . . . to which the belief and power of his own life could be united." Then he would be swept up on a great surge of strength and joy and certitude: he would literally idolize his friend, would proclaim his or her excellence to all the world, and would lay the entire conduct of his life into his hands, or hers, repeating, like an incantation: "If you'll just stand by me, everything will be all right." However, he could never rest content till he had probed deep into a person's character and decided what the very essence of it was: he seemed always to be searching for a flaw, although hoping fervently that he would fail to find one. But the men and women whom he worshipped were only human, after all, and when he finally did find faults in them, he felt a bitter disillusionment and a sense of having been betrayed. "I see every wart and sore upon them," he wrote in an unpublished passage from *Of Time and the River,* "every meanness, pettiness, and triviality . . . and I hate these mutilations in them ten times more cruelly and bitterly than if I saw them in people that I did not know, or cared nothing for."

Then would begin the period of his trying to break away which caused so many wounded feelings. Because of his emotional intensity, Wolfe could not drift casually away from an outworn friendship, as an ordinary person does. Instead, he felt a moral compunction to explain the causes of his disillusionment to his defective friend. Sometimes, as with Professor Baker, he merely wrote out his complaint in letters which he never mailed: sometimes, as with Mrs. Bernstein, he delivered it face to face in scenes of violent recrimination: sometimes, as with Maxwell Perkins, he both wrote and talked about it, endlessly, until the latter cried out in exasperation: "If you have to leave, go ahead and *leave,* but for Heaven's sake, don't talk about it any more!"

However, in spite of all these endless explanations and accusals, Wolfe's friends, as for instance Mrs. Bernstein and Maxwell Perkins, were usually thrown into a state of bewilderment and shock by his decision to break free from them. They were still devoted to him, and after constant contact with his vitality, emotion, humor, his enormous talent and his basic goodness and nobility, the prospect of life without him seemed intolerably drab and thin. But if they tried to cling to him, he would be overcome by a sort of claustrophobia of friendship and "a desire to escape so agonizing that it turned his feeling almost into hatred." To quote his favorite words from Martin Luther, he had to leave them, he "could not do otherwise." It was not until he had achieved his freedom from these too-close relationships that they could be reduced to any sort of norm, the first excessive hero-worship and the subsequent too-violent disillusionment balanced evenly against each other, and a final statement made of detached, nostalgic gratitude and love.

For stronger than "the search for a father" and entirely superseding it in the last year of his life, was Wolfe's need to grow, and to grow in complete freedom. "My life, more than that of anyone I know, has taken on the form of growth," he wrote in his "Credo" at the conclusion of *You Can't Go Home Again*. And again, in his letter of December 15, 1936, to Perkins: "My whole effort for years might be described as an effort to fathom my own design, to explore my own channels, to discover my own ways. In these respects, in an effort to help me to discover, to better use, these means, I was striving to apprehend and make my own, you gave me the most generous, the most painstaking, the most valuable help. . . . As for another kind of help—a help that would attempt to shape my purpose or define for me my own direction—I not only do not need that sort of help but if I found that it had in any way invaded the unity of my purpose, or was trying in any fundamental way to modify or alter the direction of my creative life—the way in which it seems to me it ought and has to go—I should repulse it as an enemy, I should fight it and oppose it with every energy of my life, because I feel so strongly that it is the final and unpardonable intrusion upon the one thing in an artist's life that must be held and kept inviolable. . . . I have at last discovered my own America, I believe I have found the language, I think I know my way. And I shall wreak out my vision of this life, this way, this world and this America, to the top of my bent, to the height of my ability, but with an unswerving devotion, integrity and purity of purpose that shall not be menaced, altered or weakened by anyone."

This collection of Wolfe's letters tells, in his own words, the story of his growth and his discoveries. The tragedy, of course, is that the story is unfinished—that his death at the age of thirty-seven has left us only to speculate on what he might have come to, had he lived,

THE LETTERS
OF
THOMAS
WOLFE

I

CHILDHOOD AND CHAPEL HILL

1908–1920

The earliest existing letters written by Wolfe are to his eldest sister, Effie, who had married Fred W. Gambrell and moved to Anderson, S.C.

To EFFIE WOLFE GAMBRELL

Asheville, N.C.

October 23, 1908

Dear Effie:

I am sorry to hear you are sick.

Mabel [1] went to Anderson this morning.

It has been raining here for two or three days.

I got your letter the other day. If you don't get any better, write us and we will come down to see you. I am getting off to school in time every morning, and I am never late.

I want to see you very much.

We have got the house cleaned fine down at 92.[2]

But we can't get papa to go. But mama says soon as it stops raining she is going to move us down there any way.

I had better close my letter now.

It is time for me to go to bed.

Good by,

Your little brother,

Tell Fred [3] I will write him a letter next time.

---

[1] Mabel Wolfe, now Mrs. Ralph H. Wheaton, Wolfe's other sister.

[2] 92 Woodfin Street, Asheville, where Wolfe was born. In 1906, Mrs. Wolfe had bought her boarding-house, The Old Kentucky Home, at 48 Spruce Street, with the result that the children lived sometimes at one house, sometimes at the other.

[3] Fred Gambrell.

To EFFIE WOLFE GAMBRELL

Old Kentucky Home
Mrs. Julia E. Wolfe
Owner and Propr.
No 48 Spruce Street
Asheville, N.C.

May 16, 1909

Dear Effie:

How are you feeling?

I am selling Post [1] and won a prize last month and think i am going to win one this month. I sold 61 Post this week.

Fred is going to give the boys who sell the most Post this week 50 cents, but i ain't in it, if i was i would beat them all to pieces. So he don't want me in it. The boys would not feel like working if I beet them.

We are going to have a pretty good crop of fruit this year. We will get out of school in two or three weeks.

Good by,
Your brother

The following letter to Ralph H. Wheaton, the husband of Mabel Wolfe Wheaton, was written by Wolfe just before he entered the University of North Carolina. At this time Wheaton was a salesman for the National Cash Register Company with an office in Raleigh, N.C. He had offered to drive Wolfe out to the University at Chapel Hill and to help him enroll there.

To RALPH H. WHEATON

48 Spruce Street
Asheville, N.C.

September 10, 1916

Dear Ralph:

Mabel received your telegram saying you would meet me Tuesday. I realize this is an imposition on you, but I think you could better arrange matters at Chapel Hill than I, that is, if it is possible for you to leave your work. I arrived at my decision to attend our state university last Wednesday night. Perhaps I should say *forced* instead of arrived. For that was

[1] Wolfe was selling the *Saturday Evening Post* on the streets of Asheville under the direction of his brother, Fred W. Wolfe, who held the local agency for it.

what it amounted to. For I had held out for the University of Virginia in spite of the family's protests. But when no reply came from the University of Virginia, I consented to go to Carolina. Two days later a letter did come from Virginia telling me to come on. However, it was too late. But, nevertheless, Carolina is a good school, and perhaps everything is for the best. Will at least be near you and Mabel. If it is possible for me to connect with a train at University Junction, I think that would be best. However, do as you judge right. Will be on the lookout for you at University Junction, which is, I believe, a few miles from Durham. Will leave here Tuesday morning at 8:00. Expect to reach Durham about 5:30. Mabel will not be on until Saturday.

As to the news, there is none of importance. All the home folks are well. The town is emptying itself of summer visitors fast. Monday will see nearly everybody gone from this house. Hope you are well and enjoying a good business.

To FRED W. WOLFE

[Chapel Hill, N.C.]

[September, 1916]

Dear Fred:

I wrote you a letter a while ago. Received your other postal. I was unable to know where you were living.[1] I wrote home and just received your postal, with a notation on top of it. You mentioned money matters in your postal. Please don't worry about it and take your own time as I have plenty.

Papa has been most kind in regards to everything. I have made only one mistake so far. Am located at ——'s, an Asheville lady. The food is splendid and costs $15 a month. This is cheap enough, as cheap as may be had in town, although Swain Hall, run by University costs only $12.50 a month. I room also at ——. This is where I am being "stuck." My half of the room costs me $7.50 a month which is exorbitant. The University Dorm. costs only $3. Papa sent me a check soon after my arrival and advised me to pay board and room two months in advance. If I'm held up here until November, I will then seek cheaper quarters. Have met all my "profs" and they are fine fellows. I hope I will do well in all my studies and my guess is I'll have to "bone" on math.

Have met and made many friends. I have enrolled a week ago with a frat whose membership is 137.[2] It's the custom of older members of this

---

[1] Wolfe's brother Fred was working in Dayton, Ohio at this time.

[2] The Dialectic Literary Society, which was really not a fraternity at all. In *Look*

society to put the freshmen through a mock initiation in which they try to get their "goats." They have instruments to shave our heads, etc. After the poor freshman is frightened half out of his wits some "soph" calls on him for a speech. I was the first called on. The society hall is lined with the pictures of the distinguished men once belonging to this society. The portrait of Zeb Vance hangs right over the rostrum. In my little talk I told " 'em" I was both happy and proud to be in such distinguished company. I ended by telling " 'em" I hoped they would have the pleasure some day of seeing my picture hang beside Zeb Vance's.

Just address mail c/o University Post Office, Chapel Hill and I'll get it.

The following letter to James Holly Hanford, a professor of English at the University of North Carolina, indicates that Wolfe's desire to go to a larger and more distant college than the University of North Carolina had persisted through his freshman year. In a previous letter, now lost, he had evidently asked Professor Hanford to recommend him to Princeton, which Professor Hanford had agreed to do. Wolfe's father refused to let him make the transfer, however, and he remained at the University of North Carolina for the full four years' course.

To JAMES HOLLY HANFORD

> 92 Woodfin Street
> Asheville, N. C.
> August 15, 1917

Dear Professor Hanford:

I received your letter yesterday and I can't begin to tell you how much your writing it is appreciated. But that is what I expected you to do. Not "feeding you taffy," sir, but I knew that you would direct me impartially as "a friend and not as a professor." That is why I wrote you instead of anyone else.

I have not brought the matter before Father as yet. I am collecting my forces in order to deliver a crushing blow. My sister [1] has enlisted in my brigade and her influence will count. Have two letters from the registrar at Princeton and when I receive a third in a few days, I will make the attack. If I am repelled it will not be due to defective generalship. But if Father

---

Homeward, Angel, Wolfe describes this incident with embarrassment: "He was the greenest of all green freshman, past and present: he had . . . been guilty of the inexcusable blunder of making a speech of acceptance on his election, with fifty others, to the literary society."

[1] Mabel Wolfe Wheaton.

should refuse, nevertheless, a beginning will have been made and, I have no doubt, I will be able to finish my last two years at Princeton—a proceeding upon which I am now decided.

I do not know if what you said in the letter concerning myself is true. I hope so and I have tried to be a boy of "honor and ideals." At any rate, it's not so very hard to go straight as long as you have friends who say these things. I sincerely hope the boy will one day become a man who is a man, and thereby justify the faith of his friends.

I have just returned from the depot. A crowd of young officers from the camp at Oglethorpe came in this morning. They were a fine looking set of men. Among them I saw "Nemo" Coleman—last year's football manager, Leicester Chapman, who, as you remember was in English I last fall, and "Cy" Parker, the cheer leader.[2] I believe the old University, if personified, would feel proud of her sons who have stood up to their work so well. I am a little envious and wish that I were older.

By the way, my uncle, Mr. Henry A. Westall,[3] lives in Boston. His residence is in one of the suburbs, I think. He is Harvard, '79, having graduated for the ministry, but went into real estate business because it paid better. He is very eccentric but interesting. If you have the time or the inclination, look him up.

I will write you shortly and inform you how matters turn out. If I get to go, I suppose poor old U.N.C. will in time manage to lift its drooping head and bear up under its loss. If I don't go, I'll be back next year and work like fury.

Wolfe's brother Ben has been immortalized in Look Homeward, Angel. *The following letter to him was written soon after he had taken his father to Johns Hopkins Hospital for treatment of the cancer which caused Mr. Wolfe's death in 1922.*

To BENJAMIN H. WOLFE

Chapel Hill, N.C.
February 18, 1918

Dear Ben:

I have intended writing you for some time but exams have kept me busy until recently and even now various activities are taking up my

---

[2] James M. Coleman and Samuel I. Parker were members of the Class of 1917 at the University of North Carolina: Leicester Chapman was a member of the Class of 1918 but left the University to enlist in 1917.

[3] Henry A. Westall was Mrs. Wolfe's brother.

time. I hope you enjoyed your stay in Baltimore and that you left Papa progressing nicely. It is indeed fortunate that he was persuaded to go and the whole outlook is much more cheerful now.

I am happy to say that my year so far has been most successful (I averaged 91% in work) and I look forward to an exceedingly busy Spring. I go out to-morrow for track and will try to make the quarter mile. I have only one competitor and he has the advantage of having had more experience. However, I have the strides on him and if I can get away at the beginning I see no reason why I shouldn't make the team and perhaps my letter this spring. This quarter mile is a very devil of a race. It is just long enough to be tiresome and just short enough to keep you sprinting all the way. If I don't make it, the other fellow's going to know he's not had any evening stroll. I've found out one thing down here that ought to be invaluable to me some day when I get out and root for the shining shekels. You don't get anything handed to you on a silver platter. The man that is most popular and the best-liked is the man that goes out and takes what he wants by his own efforts.

I have received a card and a letter from Fred. He seems a little raw just now but I'm sure he's going to like it immensely when he gets more accustomed to surroundings. Think he did the wisest thing. He didn't have a chance in the army.[1]

They're giving us blazes in this military stuff. Military engineering, bomb throwing, trench warfare, bayonet fighting are a few of the things we are doing. By the way, we're going to have a big summer camp at Bingham. Quite a number have signed up already.

I believe you mentioned Christmas that you had an old suit of clothes you were not using. Of course, I wear my uniform on drill days, but Tuesday, Thursday and Saturday afternoons we have no drill. Most of my stuff is getting frayed except the new suit, so if you don't need this particular suit I would be more than thankful to get it. But please don't send it if you need it at all.

Write and let me know how you are getting on and I will send you all the news down here. I hope you are in good health and enjoying a good business.

The following letter from Wolfe to his father was written on a page of the March, 1918, issue of The University of North Carolina Magazine, *in which appeared a poem by Wolfe called "The Challenge" and a story by him called "A Cullenden of Virginia." In a speech made at Purdue University in May, 1938, Wolfe says that these were his first creative efforts to be published.*

[1] Fred Wolfe had enlisted in the navy.

To WILLIAM OLIVER WOLFE

[Chapel Hill, N.C.]
Wednesday, March 27, [1918]
2:00 P.M.

Dear Father:

I have just received your letter and your check for $40.00. Please receive my thanks. I was initiated into the Pi Kappa Phi Fraternity Monday night after taking a 12 mile march in the afternoon. It is the greatest thing I ever did and will mean much.

Through my work for the magazine *Tar Heel* [1] I have just received a bid from Sigma Upsilon, the great national literary fraternity. See Hiden Ramsey [2] and he'll tell you about it. The expense is small and it is a big honor to belong to it, only about 15 members in school.

Will write later.

Wolfe's letter of May 17, 1920, to Lora French was written one month before his graduation from the University of North Carolina. Miss French, now Mrs. Clarence R. Simmons, had met Wolfe when she spent a few weeks in Asheville during the summer of 1919, and had soon afterwards moved to Los Angeles.

To LORA FRENCH

Chapel Hill
Monday, May 17, 1920.

My Dear Lora:

. . . I haven't been working a "hold out" game on you, waiting for you to write, but I wanted some definite information as to your residence. Hereafter I'll communicate direct to Los Angeles. Do you mean to say that you have received only *one* issue of the *Tar Heel* and *three* of the *Baby?* [1] Something must be sadly amiss and I'll go gunning for my business manager immediately. I'm sending you a copy of our latest *Tar Baby*—the

[1] The student paper at the University of North Carolina. Wolfe became managing editor of it in his junior year (1918–1919), and editor-in-chief in his senior year (1919–1920).

[2] The general manager of *The Asheville Citizen and Times.*

[1] *The Tar Baby*, the undergraduates' humorous magazine at the University of North Carolina. Wolfe was Guest Editor of the April 10, 1920, issue which burlesqued the *Raleigh News and Observer.*

burlesque on the *Raleigh News and Observer*, Josephus Daniels' paper. Jo is an old Carolina man and he took it with a grin, although we treated him rough at times. I edited this issue and, in fact, wrote most of the stuff. The *News and Observer* gave us a good write-up in its Sunday edition, which I'm sending you. Tar Baby, Inc. wants me back next year to edit the issues. May accept. Graduate in another month.

I hate to leave this place. It's mighty hard. It's the oldest of the state universities and there's an atmosphere here that's fine and good. Other universities have larger student bodies and bigger and finer buildings, but in Spring there are none, I know, so wonderful by half. I saw old Carolina men home Christmas who are doing graduate work at Yale, Harvard and Columbia. It would seem that they would forget the old brown buildings in more splendid surroundings, but it was always the same reply: "There's no place on earth can equal Carolina." That's why I hate to leave this big, fine place.

The seniors are going to have a glorious time Commencement. One of our features will be a "Dinner Dance." We'll have girls down and between courses pull off a cabaret stunt between the tables. Also a program of the Playmakers and a Senior Stunt, which I'm working up at present.

I've read about the Los Angeles moving picture craze from such infallible authorities as the *Saturday Evening Post* and others, but this is my first experience with a young lady who has been hypnotized or, shall I say, Los Angelized? Don't sign a contract, please, for less than a thousand a week. After reading the *Post*, I am sure that even the bathing girls get that much.

It's good to know that you've missed me. I miss you also, and I know that this summer will only bring back the memory of the short days I was with you in Asheville. I can only hope that time and space (some three thousand miles of it, I believe) will be generous to me and that we will soon meet on that beautiful shore (Los Angeles, of course, if it's on the shore; if not we'll move the ocean).

II

HARVARD AND THE 47 WORKSHOP

1920–1923

The following letter, giving Wolfe's first impressions of Harvard, was written to Professor Frederick H. Koch, the founder and director of The Carolina Playmakers at the University of North Carolina, under whom Wolfe had begun his career as a dramatist, and on whose recommendation he had enrolled in Professor George Pierce Baker's English 47 at Harvard.

To FREDERICK H. KOCH

[48 Buckingham Road]
Cambridge

Friday, Nov. 26, 1920

Dear Prof:

I wonder if you'll accept a letter written on the leaves of a note book and with a pencil, the ink having fled from my pen. When I get through I'll go back and write a gloss (à la Coleridge) with suitable annotations, in the margin. Out of the chaos of interesting things that come crowding forward to be told, all of which, I know, won't go into one letter, I want to tell you first of the joy with which I received news of your glorious success in the Raleigh pageant.[1] Coates [2] and I are waiting now for the book which, like the production, is said to be "a thing of beauty and a joy forever." I hope you don't get a foot taller and with a softly modulated accent tell the world that "I'm a creative artist"—the last being quoted from some of my "Neat Particular" "ass"-ociates in English 47. And now

[1] *Raleigh, the Shepherd of the Ocean,* a pageant drama written by Professor Koch for the Tercentenary of Sir Walter Raleigh, was produced on October 19, 20, and 21, 1920, at the amphitheatre of Baseball Park, Raleigh, N.C. It was published in 1920 by the North Carolina Historical Commission.

[2] Albert Coates, a graduate of the University of North Carolina, was studying at the Harvard Law School and had a room at 48 Buckingham Road, as did Wolfe.

to tell you about Eng. 47, Prof. And about Mr. Baker who is one of the best friends you have. He is enthusiastic about you and the work you're doing (I had a half-hour conference with him this morning) and he has suggested putting on some of the plays you sent him. He likes my "Buck Gavin" and says it is a more finished piece of work than my "Third Night," [3] which he said absorbed him at first but lost in interest as he went on.

I'm happy since my talk with him this morning, Prof, because I don't feel quite so useless. I wrote a letter to Horace [4] the other day when I was in a gloom that covered me "deep as the pit from pole to pole" but, with startling swiftness, my attitude has changed again. And the reason, to wit: Mr. Baker's first task for the budding Pineros is to put them to work on an adaptation of a current short story. My first attempt was rotten; I knew it when I handed it in. It followed the story up bit by bit and ended with many tears in the last scene where the father conveniently dies of heart failure offstage. I was completely lost at first, Prof; didn't know where to turn. My associates in this class (there are a dozen of us) were mature men, eight, ten and in one case twenty years older than I am. When they criticize, it is as follows: "Sir Arthur Pinero takes that scene and treats it with *consummate art*." or "The remarkable literary charm of this play seduces my admiration." Prof, so help me, God, these are direct quotations. Imagine a raw Tar Heel who, with native simplicity has been accustomed to wade into a play (at Chapel Hill) with "that's great stuff" or "rotten"—simple and concise. Why, one man the other day made a criticism of a play as follows: "That situation seems to be a perfect illustration of the Freudian complex"; and it gladdened me when Mr. Baker, the most courteous of men under very trying conditions, replied: "I don't know about the Freudian complex; what we are discussing now are the simple human values of this play." At any rate, you understand the atmosphere, and they are all sincere earnest people at that, but with that blasé sophistication that seems typical of Harvard.

At any rate, Prof, I went through hours of bitterness and self-condemnation, finally drawing into myself and trying to forget the others. On the revision of my adaptation I cut loose from the story and made my own play, which now is not at all like the story. Mr. Baker read it the other morning and likes it. He says I've struck a keynote greater than that the short story author thought of, and that I have the beginnings of one of those curious comic tragedies. In the meantime, Prof, I'm at work on my

---

[3] Professor Koch had sent to Professor Baker the manuscripts of Wolfe's two plays which had been produced by the Carolina Playmakers: *The Return of Buck Gavin* and *The Third Night*.

[4] Professor Horace Williams, head of the Department of Philosophy at the University of North Carolina.

original one act play [5] and I'm exalted—that's all—pure exaltation. It's a North Carolina play and, Prof, I believe I've struck gold, pure gold. Of course it may turn out rotten in Mr. B's estimation, but now I think I've got something. He asked me this morning what kind of plays I wanted to write and I told him promptly that what I didn't want to write were these blasé, high society dramas (à la Oscar Wilde) in which divers wise epigrams are flourished about the differences between man and woman, etc. I hit the bullseye, for he " 'gins to be aweary of the puns" and tells me he has too many "high society" plays now by authors who know nothing of high society. Prof, I'm going to play fair with myself and I'll make a go of it, I think. This thing has seized me with a deathlike clutch, with few friends to take my time away, with no more delightful "bull sessions," I have turned to work and I'm really working, Prof. I'm reading voraciously in the drama, stocking up with materials same as a carpenter carries a mouthful of nails: I am studying plays, past and present, and the technique of these plays, emphasis, suspense, clearness, plot, proportion and all the rest, and I've come to realize that this doctrine of divine inspiration is as damnable as that of the divine right of kings. Coleridge, certainly one of the most inspired imaginatively of the poets, did more research work for "The Ancient Mariner" than does the average chemist in writing a book. I had almost got to the point of sneering at the Facts, and laughing at those who grubbed for them as little worms, and of course this is true if you submerge in a sea of Facts. But to paraphrase Kipling, "If you can dig and not make Facts your master, You'll get along in writing beaucoup faster." This is rotten, I know, but I couldn't resist it.

But when all's said and done, Prof, what you said last year is pretty true: "Harvard teaches you to appreciate the Hill more." This is a great place, no denying it, but Chapel Hill holds much that Harvard doesn't. Vice versa, also. You can get what you want if you want it: if you don't, nobody worries. In the graduate schools one finds real men fit to be classed with our Tar Heels on the Hill. As to that species of knickerbockered, golf-stockinged, Norfolk-jacketed, lisping ass that is turned out with machine-like regularity by the college, the species for which Harvard receives much odium everywhere now—to those I say: "Why don't you get a college education instead of coming to Harvard?"

Prof, I've hurled myself at this letter viciously to relieve myself, and if you can read it, you have one on me. I realize that, to a certain measure, the fair name of the Carolina Playmakers at Fair Harvard rests with me, and the Carolina type of play is what I'm going on with. But, Prof, realize that Mr. Baker welcomes this, he wants me to do it, he sincerely admires you and your work, and he says your plays are remarkable. The man is

[5] *The Mountains.*

tired, I'm sure from what he said this morning, of an excess of light froth—
a class of stuff the embryos around here dote on.

For heaven's sake, what do we go to the theatre for? I go to be lifted out
and away, and if that sensation leaves as soon as the curtain falls I don't
think the play worth a single curse. It's a species of fairyland, I think, this
theatre, and I want fairyland to last with me even after the players have
passed off the stage. I don't think we go to see life as it is in all its minutiae
—to h— with all the "realists" as they style themselves (pardon my
French)—if a play hasn't some lifting quality besides bare, sordid realism, then it becomes nothing but a photograph of life, and what place has
a photograph in art? I don't mean that it has to end happily, or that you
have to use any cheap trick at all to please your audience, but just as
"Macbeth" and "Oedipus the King" become something bigger than men,
they become monuments of Gigantic Ideas—so should the play become
something bigger and finer than drab, sordid, commonplace, everyday
life. And in spite of all our pathetic optimism, Prof, that's just what everyday life is—drab, sordid, and commonplace. And I'm not posing as one
who has lived and suffered either. At any rate, that's my ideal for the
theatre—it lifts you up just as a great picture lifts you. A great landscape
artist one time remarked when looking at a beautiful sunset that "it was a
pretty good imitation, but you should see one of mine." Voilà—there you
are, Prof. And I'm going to keep that in mind. Write and let me know
what you think about it.

This has been a feverish, wild letter, hasn't it? I've written at terrible
speed, as you've found to your sorrow, I suppose, and for startling beginnings and tame endings, my epistle has all the qualities of that amazing
grammatical construction: "The man threw the horse over the fence some
hay"! I groan for Chapel Hill at times—many times—but I know my bolt
there is shot. I got away at the right time. Here, as there, I am a Carolina
Man, learning with sorrow to-day that Va. beat us. It's the greatest place
in the world, Prof. That sums up all my findings.

Mr. Baker took me into his course even before you sent the plays, solely
because I had worked under you. I use "work" here with poetic license.

Please forgive my laxness in writing—I've really worked hard—and
write me a good letter. Give my regards to the Class, tell them I'm a sadder,
and I hope wiser man, and that I no longer wade in with glittering eye and
inflated nostrils to flay the quivering brain-child of some hopeful author. I
have mellowed and grown sweet under adversity—a great example of
chastened pride. But tell them—for I can even now see the eagerness on
their bright young faces when hearing of me—that my spirit is high, my
head, though "bloody is unbowed," and though a tadpole with 6000 others,

I cannot refrain from 'aving 'opes. And if they bear up bravely under this, give them, the male members, my continued felicitations.

Love and Kisses for the Co-eds. (More Power to 'Em.)

Your whilom loafer,

The first and last parts of the following letter have been lost, but it was evidently written to Frank C. Wolfe, Wolfe's eldest brother, in the early summer of 1921.

To FRANK C. WOLFE

[Cambridge, Mass]

[Early Summer, 1921]

. . . Personally I'm always ready to root for the spectacular, the running, twisting slashing teams,—but Harvard is out to win.

All that has been said of *some* Harvard under-graduates is true and more, but I wish you could have been here with me Commencement, and seen the old grads back to their class reunions. They were the finest looking group of men I ever saw. The real thing. Something must happen to them after they leave.

I suppose Asheville is again overrun with pretty girls. They're all right if you can just look at them without having to talk to them, but when they open their mouths all is lost. I am convinced that the average girl around Asheville (aged 20 or over) has the brain capacity of a fourteen year old child.

There's one thing we're deadly afraid of in North Carolina and that is appearing highbrow. If you use a word of more than one syllable around an Asheville girl she will roll her eyes, look up to heaven and say, "Look it up in the dictionary." If you happen to know the year Columbus discovered America you're a bookworm. This is slightly exaggerated but it's true in its essence.

And the hell of it is that the damn-fool boys pander to the girls, deal with them in their own silly childish talk and in time become empty vessels themselves. Consider what a vacant life young people around Asheville lead. Five dances a week throughout the summer at night and Patton Ave. all day. What imbecilic slop this is! I don't want to make professors out of everyone but it is possible to mix a certain amount of purpose and pleasure in life and be better for it.

If I get home and use a new word and the boys look at each other and wink and say, "Aha—Harvard did that," I'll tell them to go to hell. The biggest crime one can commit is to check their own development because of some weak-kneed desire to appear as vain and shallow as the rest.

We've boasted about our Southern beauty long enough. It's foolish! There are pretty girls everywhere, thousands of them here who prove it is possible to have brains as well as beauty. I am not speaking of education but of intelligence—an entirely different matter. Shop girls here are more intelligent, I believe, than most Southern girls. They have definite ideas and show they have done some thinking for themselves. Personally I don't believe the presence of brains in a female detracts from her charm although many down South fear it more than they do a double chin.

Every town has a definite personality. I sometimes wonder if that little town of Asheville has a soul or if it is like its young people, shallow, vain, inconsequential. There's a good play in Asheville—a play of a town which never had the ordinary, healthy, industrial life a town ought to have but instead dressed itself up in fine streets and stuck hotels in its hair in order to vamp the tourist populace. There's a good play in the boy who lets the town vamp him, who sees the rich tourists and their mode of life and thinks he must live that way, who gets a job without enthusiasm or ambition in order to pay his way around at night and who finally settles down a dull, plodding, month-to-month fellow till he dies. The town got him. The octopus drew him up. It sucked away his youth, hope, ideals, ambition and left a clean shirt front. You and I have seen that fellow—dozens of times. I believe there's a play there. There's a play in everything that lives if we only had the power to extract it. . . .

To FRED W. WOLFE

42 Kirkland Street
Cambridge, Mass.
[July, 1921]

Dear Fred:

. . . My transatlantic steamer plans fell flat due mainly to the fact that employment is given out mostly at the New York offices of the steamship lines operating from here.[1] I wish you could have come to Mass. Tech for your summer course [2] . . . At any rate Atlanta will prove no hotter than Bean Town which, despite its northerly location, is quite an inferno in summer. It's the humidity more than the heat, the humidity that doesn't

[1] Wolfe had considered trying to work his way across the Atlantic on a steamer during summer vacation, but had finally enrolled in Summer School instead.

[2] Fred Wolfe had enrolled for a summer course at Georgia School of Technology.

allow the sweat to evaporate and keeps one sticky and uncomfortable. You should hear our Uncle Henry curse Yankee weather, Yankee honesty and everything Yankee in general.

He and Aunt Laura [3] are a great pair; they are giving me materials for a great play which I shall write some day. Each waits till the other is out of the room and then asks if you've noticed how childish he (or she) is getting. Isn't that a pure, 100% cross-section of human nature for you? They have been very kind to me, however, although Aunt Laura spends a great part of the time in telling me what a fearful handicap it is to be born a Westall, how I must watch myself at every point to keep the family traits from cropping out, and what an unbalanced, lopsided clan we are in general.

I got a card from Frank when he was home. About all he said [was] nerves and pus under a tooth. . . . I don't see why nature doesn't fit us with durable cast iron teeth and do away with all this damned business of cavities, nerves, pains, aches, which haunt us from the cradle to the grave.

I hope you won't wait as long to answer this as I did to answer yours. Give my kindest regard to all my friends who inquire about me.

To WILLIAM OLIVER WOLFE

[Cambridge, Mass.]

[August, 1921]

Dear Papa:

I got your letter along with Mama's this morning, and coming in the midst of my lonesomeness, it was thrice welcome. I put in five weeks of hard study in the Summer School which closed August 13, and although I have heard nothing yet as to my grade I am reasonably certain it is high—a B plus at any rate.

Do not think I feel no call from home, that I have no desire to go back to see my people and my home town. That call has been loud and long ever since Christmas, and this summer when my friends were gone and I was alone here in a big city—and, as you know, even the solitude of a desert is companionship when compared with the loneliness of a city— during this time in particular have I thought of you all and wanted to see you. My friends and you and Mama have had such faith in me that you can hardly realize how powerful the will within me is to justify your faith: so strong is that will that I believe I would use the last rasping breath. . . .

[THE LETTER BREAKS OFF HERE, OR THE REMAINDER OF IT HAS BEEN LOST]

[3] Mr. and Mrs. Henry A. Westall.

The following letter was written in answer to one from Margaret Roberts who, with her husband, J. M. Roberts, had conducted The North State School in Asheville where Wolfe had been a pupil from 1912–1916. Mrs. Roberts had written Wolfe to ask if he would recommend her for a teaching position to Frank Wells, Superintendent of Schools in Asheville. Wolfe's letter to Wells is chiefly a repetition of what he wrote to Mrs. Roberts, and has therefore been omitted here.

To MARGARET ROBERTS

Cambridge, Mass.

Sept. 2, 1921

Dear Mrs. Roberts:

Your letter finally came a day or two ago and I am getting a glowing testimonial under way to Mr. Wells. *Glowing* I say, and the term is mild: if I didn't restrain my leaping pen it would be a red hot paean. And I find the difficulty in writing such a letter is the tempering it down to a point where the man won't think you hired me. I know you were joking when you asked me if I would do this as a *favor* but I wonder if you really have any idea what a joy and a privilege and an honor I esteem it. I only fear I may hurt your own cause by my own fervor. Under any condition I fear the letter will have an over-eulogistic flavor to one who doesn't know me—or you. I am therefore making the letter informal, as I know Mr. Wells slightly, for I feel I will better create the impression of utter earnestness I am so desirous of creating.

But I shall certainly tell him that I have had only three great teachers [1] in my short but eventful life and that you are one of these. Harvard, fine as it is, has as yet been unable to submit any candidates to my own Hall of Fame though I hope within another year to nominate and elect a fourth.

This 'point system' of selecting teachers is a relic of barbarism—when I compare you not only in actual culture but in the more vital quality of stimulating and inspiring the love of fine and beautiful literature in the heart and mind and soul [of] that boy lucky enough to claim you for a teacher (my sentence is becoming attenuated; I'll have to get a fresh breath)—when I compare you in these respects to the average college grad, comparisons, as Mrs. Malaprop says, become odorous.

Mrs. Roberts, there's no estimating the influence you've had on me and the whole course of my life; what's done is done, each day causes me

---

[1] The other two were Horace Williams, head of the Department of Philosophy, and Edwin Greenlaw, head of the Department of English, at the University of North Carolina.

to see more plainly how tremendous an influence that was, and I know I shall be even more emphatic on this score the last day of my life than I am now.

Your friendship, and that of Mr. Roberts, and your faith and hope in me, one of the most cherished possessions of my life, causes me ghastly suffering at times when I doubt myself and wonder if you are fooled in me. Yes, I have actually writhed in my sheets in the dead dark night thinking of this and this alone. It has been my yoke and will. . . .

It goads me to fury to hear the cant and the clap-trap daily bandied about which would divorce a man like Shelley from Life and Reality and call him a cloud-gatherer, and laud a writer of debauched plays such as Wycherley or Congreve for his *infinite* knowledge of life. What rot! Those who spend their lives searching around pigsties, bask in the favor of the unthinking, while those who take a [——?] view of things or, as Shelley did, identify themselves with the wind—"timeless and swift and proud" —are hooted at because they won't stay to be shod!

Francis Thompson was a unique figure and had a good deal of the Coleridge mysticism about him. I have read his "Hound of Heaven" and some of his other poems. He too was a drug addict and a street waif, the people who finally unearthed him and supported him finding him almost barefoot. I suppose he could have satisfied the utmost desires of the worldly with "knowledge of life" if he'd cared to exhibit that "knowledge" but fortunately the glory and significance of things struck him as more important.

Well, I mustn't rave any more or I'll be at it all night. I am desperately tired and weary of limb. We are having another hot spell—it was almost 100 to-day. I want to go home. I've *got* to go somewhere, but I'm afraid they [2] won't want me to come back next year and I've got to do that also. Give my kindest regards to Mr. Roberts.

To HORACE WILLIAMS

[42 Kirkland Street]
Cambridge, Mass.

Sept. 9, 1921

Dear Mr. Williams:

As I write this I suppose you are preparing for another busy and fruitful year and, in order to wish the thing that will bring you most happiness, I

---

[2] Wolfe's parents, who had agreed that he should go to Harvard to "try it for a year" but who, at this time, had not consented to his demands that he be allowed to re-enroll for 1921–22.

hope that Logic [1] is filled with the most disputatious, questioning crew ever.

I had a good year at Harvard and am about to return for a second under the urging of my professor of dramatics, Mr. Baker, who has strongly encouraged me and thinks that now is the time for me to continue. I didn't go home this summer but stayed to the summer session where I took another course toward my master's degree. Since then I have done nothing but rest but I rather regret not having gone home as I feel it would have rested me more.

I have tasted to the full this summer the philosophic sweets of solitude but I find it not an unmixed blessing. It is something one enjoys, I think, when one has friends to run from; but when enforced, it loses much of its charm. The poet seems to find communion with nature; I could imagine Wordsworth having a lively time on the Sahara desert but in a city where he knew no one, never! There one finds not solitude but loneliness. But I am not at all as melancholy as I sound. I am quite cheerful, indeed, and as school draws on I don't regret the summer a bit, for it was inevitable that a restless fellow like myself would do considerable thinking in that time to keep himself company. That I have done with some profit, I believe, and never have I been in more need of such a period of contemplation, for last year, as you would know, was a great seed-time to me, filled with new questionings, new surveyings, new and varied attempts to penetrate and devise. All of which left me in a muddled state. It has been said that men desire order before freedom, and indeed, human experience seems to argue this. To some small degree perhaps I have achieved order: now we shall see . . .

Mr. Williams, at times my heart sickens and sinks at the complexity of life. I know I haven't looked through yet; I am enmeshed in the wilderness and I hardly know where to turn. Your words keep haunting me almost even in my dreams: "How can there be unity in the midst of everlasting change?" In a system where things forever pass and decay, what is there fixed, real, eternal? I search for an answer but it must be *demonstrated* to me. Merely saying a thing is not enough. The other night I was reading "Adonais" by Shelley, a really great poet, I think. The beauty of his lines . . .

[THE REMAINDER OF THIS LETTER HAS BEEN LOST]

Wolfe's one-act play, The Mountains, *was produced at the Agassiz Theatre at Radcliffe on October 21 and 22, 1921, and was received unfavorably. The*

[1] One of Professor Williams' courses at the University of North Carolina.

*following two letters, found among Wolfe's own papers and perhaps never
sent to Professor Baker, show Wolfe's reaction to the criticisms of the play
which, according to Workshop custom, were written by the audience.*

To GEORGE PIERCE BAKER

[Cambridge, Mass]

[October 23 (?), 1921]

Dear Professor Baker:

After reading the numerous *remarks*, euphemistically called criticism,
on my play, and some few criticisms which I consider worthy the dignity
of that title, I feel compelled to make some rejoinder in defense of my play.
It is useless, of course, to try to argue my play into popular favor; if the
people didn't like it I shall play the man and swallow the pill, bitter as it
may be.

Many of the audience seem to be of the opinion that I conspired to
make them as uncomfortable as possible for thirty-five minutes. One of
the catchwords which these people are continually using is that a play is
"depressing." My play has been called "depressing" so many times in the
criticisms, and with so small a store of illuminating evidence that I am
even now in doubt as to just what has depressed these gentle souls.

My play is wordy, I admit [but I] take it they didn't mean exactly this.
The play itself, the theme, more than the manner and the execution, depressed them.

Now let us analyze the cause of this depression. Is it due to some
monstrous distortion of character? I think not. Richard, as he now is, may
be a little the prig but he is not unworthy of sympathy. Dr. Weaver, a
tired, worn, kindly man, is surely deserving of a warmer feeling. Can we
feel nothing but repugnance and dislike for a poor ignorant devil like
Tom Weaver, who feeds on hate because he's never known anything else?
Do Laura and Mag and Roberts turn us to loathing? No, I think not. The
thing that shocks these good people is the ending. It is such a pity that
Richard must go the way of his fathers. One can understand it of his
Uncle Tom, but Tom hasn't got the fine understanding about these
matters that a Harvard man would have. But to see Richard, whom they
continually dub "the idealist" (because, I suppose, he preferred to practice
his profession rather than go out and shoot his neighbors—surely a normal
desire)—to see him crack after all his fine talk, is more than they can bear.
Dear me!

All I have to do to please these people is to change the ending slightly.
Richard can go out with Roberts instead of with his father. Tom Weaver
can slink off with a beaten look on his face, and the curtain speech can be

given to Dr. Weaver, who might look upward and say: "Thank God! He wins where I have failed." The cause of depression having been thus removed by these slight changes, the curtain can descend leaving an audience to go home in a happy frame of mind, knowing that virtue and the higher education has triumphed, and myself—to go out and jump in the Charles River. This can never be! My show is over, they will not have to suffer again, but, even now, they can't egg me into changing the ending.

If the audience is depressed over my play, I am depressed over my audience. Good God! What do they want? What would they have me do? Are these people so wrapped in cotton-wool that they are unwilling to face the inevitable fact of defeat in a struggle like this? Let me write a contemptible little epic to small-town mean-ness (a favorite theme nowadays) in which the principal goes down to defeat from the parlor-and-gate slander of spinsters, and they will applaud me to the echo: "This is life! This is reality! This is a play of great and vital forces!" But let a man go down in a monster struggle with such epic things as mountains, and it is merely depressing and sordidly realistic. They can see no poetry to such a fight.

Why should I bother myself about all this anyway? I would like to be lofty and above such criticism, to feel like a statue attacked by a swarm of wasps, but these things [——?] and goad me. I sweated decent honest blood on what I thought was a decent, honest play. If my motive was that, I at least deserved a decent, honest criticism. I'm no pachyderm.

There was also considerable talk about my "psychology" and my "philosophy" in this play. If I've got to deal with this jargon, let me make my peace with all the "subtle-souled psychologists" straightway. Must I be accused of expressing my own personal philosophy in every play I write? Must an opinion uttered by one of my characters be taken from his mouth and put into mine, as an official credo? One critic found fault with a statement of Richard's to the effect that "a man may leave the sea or the town or the country, but it isn't often he leaves the mountains." Why blame me for such a statement? I didn't say it. Richard said it. Yet the critic would debate with me regarding the truth of an opinion uttered by a person with an antipathy toward his environment occasioned by what he believes to be the very holding power of that environment. Richard said he hated the mountains. I've never said any such thing. Weaver saw no beauty there. I see great beauty. Tom Weaver expressed faith in the curative quality of gun-shot to heal inter-family disorders. I hope I may be accused of no such "philosophy" for it seems that every stray observation is sure to be dignified as philosophy.

Others don't understand what they call the "psychology" of Richard. They can't understand how he could express the opinions and convictions he had, and yet give in at the end. If we must fool with "psychology" here, let me say that Richard's giving in has not to do with the psychology of an individual. It has to do with the psychology of a circumstance and a situation. To listen to such criticism, one would think that Richard was free to do as he chose, yet the whole struggle of the play is the struggle between his inner conviction and the outer pressure. And the outer pressure wins.

If even this is lost on them—this, the one vital thing in the play—then indeed I am the most wretched and miserable of bungling pen-pushers and should know enough to quit now before I get to the point where people will say: "You had better have died when you were a little boy."

I don't know whether it be ungracious and unbecoming to fly my colors in the faces of my critics, but if they expect me to sit quietly by and chew the cud in the face of such nincompoop criticism, they are far wide of the mark. The crowning insult of all came when my play was put in the same category with "Time Will Tell." I thank God that the far-reaching wisdom of the founders [1] saw fit to remove the names from the criticisms, for if I knew who wrote that, I would no longer be responsible for my actions.

The following letter was probably written to Gladys B. Taylor, whom Wolfe had evidently met at Harvard. It was found in rough draft in his own files and may or may not have been rewritten and sent to her.

Probably to GLADYS B. TAYLOR

> 208 Craigie Hall
> Cambridge, Mass.
>
> Sunday Morning, Nov 13, 1921

My dear Gladys:

I was about ready to write you and tell you that if you were waiting for me to write twice to your once you had the victory, and I wish you joy of it. Last night, however, I slept at 42 Kirkland for the first time in six weeks and I found a most welcome letter from you which the good landlady had saved for me for over a month. You will therefore be able to forget and forgive.

I did not go home at all. But just as school started I got a call to go to Baltimore; my father and mother were there. He is sick, you know, and

---

[1] The founders of the 47 Workshop.

goes to Johns Hopkins every year or so. I went to Baltimore and stayed there two weeks. My father is feeble but in better condition, the doctors say, than he was two years ago.

I stopped in New York long enough to see several shows:—"Liliom," "The First Year," "Daddy's Gone a-Hunting," and a revival of "The Return of Peter Grimm"—which someone suggests should be called "Daddy's Gone A-Haunting." Not bad. I saw the Follies when I got back to Boston. Fanny Brice is an artist.

There have been several good shows in Boston. Lionel Barrymore does a wonderful piece of acting in "The Claw"—a French play of Bernstein's. I also saw sister Ethel in "Declassée," an artificial play but enhanced by lovely and touching acting on her part. Saw Holbrook Blinn in "The Bad Man," a subtle and very funny satire, and Margaret Anglin in "The Woman of Bronze," the world's worst play (including those I myself write or try to). If you get to New York try to see "A Bill of Divorcement" and "The Circle." Both are highly recommended by no less an authority than our own Professor Baker.

Boston has two capable stock companies now, one engaged in producing English plays, the other American. I manage to see their programs quite often and have regaled myself with "The School For Scandal," "A Woman of No Importance," Galsworthy's fine new play "The Mob," "Three Faces East," and "A Cure For Curables."

We also have an Experimental Theatre which has planned a most ambitious program for the year (if they can only carry it out). Last night I saw them present what is probably our greatest native play, Eugene O'Neill's "Beyond the Horizon" and it is seldom I have been so stirred and moved. The play has somewhat of the spirit in it of my own one-act play, "The Mountains," which, by the way, ran here for two consecutive nights on Oct. 21 and 22, just a day after I returned. I have been reading a batch of the criticisms which an ironic Fate has deluged me with and I feel much as the tailor must have felt when requested by the tramp to "please sew a suit of clothes on these buttons." However I think my play was successful. It made either friends or enemies which speaks volumes for it, and I hope the friends outnumbered the enemies. I am setting to work to make a three act play of it. . . .

C. is going to see a girl in Brookline that he met in the bank last summer and it seems the Ohio girl has been ditched and after all his fine talk about the true delight of connubial relations and so on! These young fellows never learn. I, myself, am, as usual, a free-lance and will continue so, I fear. Cambridge has some fearful and wonderful women. They call me up on the telephone without divulging their identity, show the utmost familiarity with all the family skeletons and then ring off with a mocking laugh.

I am comfortably located at #208 Craigie Apartments but I am preparing to move again. My room mates are nice boys—when they're sober—which is about twice a week. I can't get my intellect to functioning properly with the fumes of alcohol and girlish shrieks of laughter coming to me from other parts of the apartment. However, I must fold up my tent like the Arab (I believe it was the Arab who folded up his tent).

I hope you're meeting success in conveying knowledge to your classes and I believe you will. I went out to Columbia while I was in New York and visited all your old haunts (if you did much haunting there this summer).

I want to hear from you and I don't want to wait the time I have kept you waiting—for reasons which I have satisfactorily explained, I hope.

You may write me here: if I'm not here the mail will reach me.

Yours in the bonds of Amity,

To MARGARET ROBERTS

[67 Hammond Street]
[Cambridge, Mass.]

Sunday night [February (?), 1922]

Dear Mrs. Roberts:

I am still paving the infernal road with my good intentions. Yet failure to answer promptly letters from one who never fails to send hope and to invigorate me with new strength is not merely bad manners but bad judgment. If the press of work and examinations recently ended cannot come to my aid by way of excuse, nothing else can.

Yesterday the secretary of the Graduate School sent me a note saying he was "happy to inform" me that I would get my M.A. with distinction upon removing the French requirement.[1] I am sure his happiness cannot equal mine. I have heard from only one course—but that is the one course I need. By their generosity my grade was A, although I would hardly have dared to mark myself so well. So far, I have made but one B and that was B plus last year in the Workshop. The rest have been A's. When the year is over, I will not only have completed the four courses required for the

[1] Wolfe had come to Harvard with no credits in French, and was therefore obliged to take French A or to pass the elementary French admission examination with a grade not lower than C before being eligible for his M.A. degree. He took the examination in June, 1921, but received a grade of only 60. He therefore took it again in May, 1922, and passed it satisfactorily.

degree but will have received credit for two more as well.[2] Six in all. This does not include the French. My second year in the Workshop didn't count for the degree, since not more than *one* composition course may be counted and, of course, 47 last year went down for that.

I am reading heavily. I will give you some idea of my labor for I take a great delight in counting the victims of my insatiable bookishness, though I despair at ever really knowing anything. To-day is Sunday. This morning I finished Wells' "Undying Fire," which I began last night. This is one of the few moderns I have had time for, but rarely have I been more stimulated. He's not a profound man, but he's a very sound man. Not, i.e. what Emerson would call a "primary man" but one who is a living proof of the benefits of a broad and intensive education applied to the training of a first-class mind. But to go on with the tally: this afternoon I took a walk and read half through Swift's "Tale of a Tub." Tonight I have read two essays of Emerson's and will finish Leslie Stephens excellent life of Pope before I retire. I suppose I make a mistake in trying to eat all the plums at once, for instead of peace it has awakened a good-size volcano in me. I wander throughout the stacks of that great library there like some damned soul, never at rest—ever leaping ahead from the pages I read to thoughts of those I want to read. I tell you this in all its monotonous detail because it is illustrative of the war that is being waged within me now— between what forces? For it brings me acute discomfort even in my writing. Still, as ever, I am seized with these desires to scribble, but this thing wiggles at me like some demon and says: "not yet, not yet. In two, three, or five years! Then you'll be ready." But this is folly! If it continues, the weight of my ignorance will fall on me like a stone, to crush me.

There is something in that splendid serenity of Emerson that gives me courage. I reread for the second time to-day his essay on Books. . . .

[A PORTION OF THIS LETTER IS MISSING HERE]

. . . with death" The reference, of course, is plain, namely that the drama cannot deal successfully with the supreme moment. But is not this a little unfair? I know of no other art form which can treat the subject with more truth. The interesting thing about "Liliom" is that this play gets off to a new start in interest after the hero kills himself. The next scene is the suicide court in Heaven (as he thought it would be). But I will tell you no more. There is humor, even farce comedy, while he dies; there is comedy almost of a slapstick variety in the Heaven scene; but all the time one says "Why not?" For if we look at life intelligently, we realize what a curiously woven fabric it is. The calloused police officers in "Liliom" drag the body

[2] He had taken the other courses necessary for his M.A. in 1920–21 and in Summer School.

of the dying man out to an open place, and while he lies there groaning his life away, talk about the heat, curse the mosquitoes, the new wage-scale, etc.

Let me add a gruesome touch of my own. When my brother died a few years ago, I went around to the undertaker's with Fred to see him. The particular undertaker who met us, a pious, mealy-mouthed man, took us back, asked us to wait a moment, as an artist would ask his friends to wait until he got the light adjusted on his picture. Then he called us back and showed us Ben's body. As we stood there watching, filled with emotions and recollections of indescribable pain, the man began to talk. He was proud of this job. It was one of the best he had ever done. No other undertaker could do a better one. Then, with true artistic pride, he began to point out the little excellencies in his finished work that showed the hand of the master. It was too much for me. I went into howls of uncontrollable laughter. It was no doubt a reflex of my condition at the time, but to this day I think of the incident with a smile.

That is one reason I defend Sir J. M. Barrie whenever he is criticized. I think Barrie is the most significant dramatist in the English-speaking world to-day because he really is carrying on the great tradition of our drama. This is an arch-heresy here, where some of my young critical friends consider him as "sentimental." Is it not strange how the academic, critical point of view shrinks nervously away from the sympathetic? I have never read a play of Barrie's that didn't give me this curious "mixed" feeling. He is not trying to "prove" anything (thank Heaven) but, like Shakespeare and other old fogies, is more interested in the stories of human beings than in the labor problem. That's why I believe his plays will outlast those of his contemporaries, because people at all times can understand and appreciate the emotion of other people. Sceptics are referred to "The Trojan Women." This is the universal, eternal element in drama. After all, the conditions of which John Galsworthy wrote in "Strife" are becoming changed already; in twenty years we will still have a labor problem no doubt, but it will be one altogether different from the one "Strife" sets forth.

During the most inventive and mature years of his genius, G.B.S. expended his great powers of satire on the one thing he thought worthy of drama—the thesis. Then a war comes along that kills twenty million people and destroys nations, and suddenly we can't convince ourselves that "Mrs Warren's Profession" or "Widowers' Houses" deal with the biggest things in the world after all. If I were Shaw now, I think I should feel as if I had been equipped with a mighty bludgeon but had spent my life braining gnats.

I agree with you about Eugene O'Neill. He's the beacon light in our own drama to-day: he's kept his ideals and now seems in a fair way to prosper by them. Two new plays of his are shortly to come to New York; "Anna Christie" is there now enjoying a popular success. I saw "Beyond the Horizon" not long ago. It is a fine play. O'Neill is still a young man, c. 35, I think. I don't believe he has reached his greatest development yet. When it comes! There's one thing that worries me: in a forecast of his new play, "The Hairy Ape," which is to be produced soon, I see the subject is to be a stoker on an ocean liner. During the successive stages we will see him go back steadily to the primitive man. I hope O'Neill won't let this tendency run away with him. You see, he was "looking backward" in "The Emperor Jones" and, to a degree, we find this in other plays. Tragedy if continued in this vein, will become sordid and brutal. Surely this does not represent his outlook on life. Great tragedy, I think, must look ahead. . . .

J. S. Mill, whose autobiography I was reading the other night, said the greatest lesson the Greeks taught him was to dissect an argument, as did Socrates, and find its weak spot. If men ever needed to use that method, now is the time. There is so much claptrap, so much nonsense veiled behind intricacies, that we need all our sanity and common sense to tear the arguments of these buffoons to pieces. Oh, for a Swift to flay the free versists . . .

Well, I really must be going. I hope Mr. Roberts is feeling well. Give him my kindest regards. . . .

Your criticism of the last scene in my play [1] was unerringly accurate. I've cut Mag's speech. I've written the first two acts of the play as a three act, (also a prologue).

To HORACE WILLIAMS

67 Hammond Street
Cambridge, Mass.
[February (?), 1922]

Dear Mr. Williams:

. . . I have worked hard this first term and feel that I have accomplished more in an unseen way than in a visible manifestation. I remember one incident plainly in connection with my summer's work at the Langley Flying Field in Virginia three or four years ago.[1] Crews of negroes were grading and levelling the field that the flying machines might land there.

---

[1] *The Mountains.*
[1] Wolfe had worked as a time checker at Langley Field in the early summer of 1918.

Trees had been blasted out of the ground, which was right at the water's edge and filled with water rapidly. It was the duty of the negroes to fill these holes. It was depressing work. I have seen an entire crew throw dirt into a hole for a day, and as night came, there was little progress to show for their labor, for the water had devoured the dirt as if it were sugar. The effort to fill one's mind is like that, only more so.

I have one thing in common with Henry Adams. I do not feel at home when I am there, and I never feel at home anywhere else. Quanta patimus pro amore virtutis! I have decided to devote my life to the drama, if I have any gift in that direction. Therefore to go home now is impossible. I must be where I can read plays, see plays, and study plays. I think this is absolutely necessary if I'm ever to become an artist. A man may be a philosopher in Chapel Hill but hardly a dramatist. Again the limitations of my art are driven in on me.

Philosophy is gnawing me again. I read the other day of a star riding free and far in the universe, so that a ray of light from that star, travelling 186,000 miles a second would be 40,000 years in reaching the earth. That makes the head swim, doesn't it? Philosophy seems determined to make man the centre of the universe and a pretty important figure, and I suppose it's best to look at it that way. The other way leads to madness. Still, who can say but that life may express itself in many ways; can we affirm that we are the chosen vessels of that experiment?

I would like to see an "undying fire" of human progress in history but I am mighty dubious. I confess I have difficulty in seeing a projection of the Greek philosophy in Christianity, or a perpetuation of the Hebrew theology of vengeance in the Christian doctrine of mercy. Do philosophy, religion, or art really grow eternally, or do they grow to a certain point and then decay? Why shouldn't Greece have waxed stronger and profounder after Pericles, and Socrates, and Plato? Why should men regard Christianity as historical rather than living: i.e. something that was finished two thousand years ago and interpreted (or misinterpreted) ever since.

Finally, when literature produces a Shakespeare, after a period of steady fulfillment, why shouldn't the one who comes later be greater than Shakespeare? After the Elizabethan drama, why the decadence of the Reformation drama? Is this progress? If it is, it is surely a progress that seems to contradict itself.

Most everyone seems to waste his life in false attempts: a show of fine energy foully misplaced. Time after time it has seemed as if mankind was about to come upon the Absolute: to plunge into and discover the ultimate, impenetrable mystery; and then they quit, or turn to something else, to baffle and foul themselves anew. I tell you, Mr. Williams, I have become almost fanatically convinced that if the good and the wise and the great men would all turn to solving one problem at a time, all working in unison, searching together, and letting the false, misleading things go hang, something might be done. It is an insane dream, but I would be willing to obliterate my personality to work with men in that attempt. First we would try Religion, then Art, or Philosophy and Science. One by one we would drive them to the corner, Argus-eyed would we watch them, to prevent ducking or dodging, and if God could then escape us, my belief in the miracle would be established and I would ask no more questions but eat, and sleep and die!

It was William James, I believe, who said men knew as much of the universe as cats and dogs in a library know of the contents of the volumes therein. Yet, by no rational conviction can I convince myself that such ignorance is inevitable, or that such a problem can not be solved. What virtue is there in such ignorance? We are taught that knowledge is a liberating force, to increase and enlarge ourselves spiritually. Is it then reasonable to suppose that a definite knowledge of the supreme end of life would have a baneful influence, or that our efforts are being mocked, our paths twisted by an unseen hand? Surely, such belief is malignant.

The very nature of a philosophy, to me, is speculative. It must ever be on the hunt. Show me a man who has evolved a philosophy which, he says, has solved the problem of his life, and I believe you'll find a man who has surrendered to it. I have no use for a system which says that, after all, some things defy knowledge, and the only thing to do is to look around at the facts of life, never going beyond your vision, and work out a plan from these. Many a man, after running up blind alleys all his life, cries: "I have found it," and then tells you the answer is to read good books, develop a sense of the beautiful, enjoy the few and fleeting years to the utmost. He might as well have saved his breath, for he could have come to the same conclusion in high school.

The thing that continually chafes me in this highly cultivated community is the continual emphasis that is put on what they call "culture" as a means for attaining that divine consummation, a sense of the beautiful. But if this is all "culture" can do for one, teach one to enjoy and discern beauty, then I am ready to call it off. We don't need a "sense of the beautiful" any more than we need a "sense of the ugly," for the world is full of ugly things, Mr. Williams, and we've got to face them with our heads up. I have no use for the kind of "culture" that could discern the hand of a great artist in a painting but would withdraw into itself and cringe from the dirty, ugly, sweating crowd; that could read Sappho's poems and enjoy them and be shocked and resentful at the harsh voice of the subway guard, bawling to mason and professor alike to "Step Lively there—wheredyathinky'are?"

This is one thing that makes the matter hard. It is comparatively easy to imagine a kinship with the perfect and divine essence if we are forever handling and seeing and reading beautiful things, but we're put to it to find this relation in that which outwardly, at least, is ugly. I can read one of Walt Whitman's poems about the nobility and dignity of labor and the universal brotherhood, where Walt affectionately claps each artisan on the back and calls him "camerado," but when I go out, filled with a great desire to clasp mankind in my arms, the subway guard, or the man behind the counter can, by a few ill-timed remarks, change my desire to call him "camerado" to a desire to punch him on the jaw. So much for the universal brotherhood!

I hope the book[2] is going well. Count me in for an advance copy. I hope they're giving you the time you need so badly and that the class is not keeping the trail hot to your house at night. Please let me have some news when you are conveniently able.

To EDWIN GREENLAW

[67 Hammond Street]
[Cambridge, Mass]
[March (?), 1922]

Dear Professor Greenlaw:

I write you without the impertinence of expecting a reply for I know the times and you are busy. I am sorry you're not coming here this Spring term after all. Someone told me you were going to the University of Chicago.

I will get my M.A. now as soon as I remove the accursed French requirement. I'm putting in an application to teach but I don't expect to return South for a time. I feel the necessity of being where I can watch the theatre, of seeing what is going on, and you know the conditions at home. We must do something to remedy it. More and more, it seems to me, our Southern people are so much better adapted to an appreciation of fine things than these shy, clumsy Yankees, but it seems to be a case of the hare and the tortoise over again.

There are good plays being written. I've seen "Liliom" three times, remembering M. Arnold's injunction about "the good things two or three times." So I'm epicurean.

It won't be long now until America has a drama. If we have three or four men of the caliber of Eugene O'Neill, each with a capacity for a different form, our drama has arrived. I don't feel as if I'm walking toward

[2] *The Evolution of Logic* by Horace Williams.

the sun but as if I could almost touch it. The thing will surely happen soon.

The English are getting brittle. Their little social plays, and comedies of manners are hard and brilliant. They leave an unpleasant taste. . . .

The war seems to have torn away the foundations of our old beliefs. And we haven't much to tie to yet. We've got to build something new, something we can see and almost handle. If I'm ever to be a dramatist I must believe in struggle. I've got to believe in dualism, in a definite spirit of evil, and in a Satan who is tired from walking up and down upon the earth. These are things I can visualize. When we erase the struggle, our power of visualization seems to fade. I have the utmost difficulty in bringing into my mind the picture of Professor Williams absorbing a negation. (Confidential.)

You remember the story or legend of how the medieval monks, by the very intensity of their reflection, could bring out upon their foreheads and hands the sign of the cross, the nail-wounds of the Crucifixion. I feel deeply the necessity of symbols like these to tie to. This is no mere windy talk with me. I'm beginning to know the kind of thing I want to do now. And it calls for a grasp on the facts of life. When I attended philosophy lectures (and I rate these lectures very highly) I was told that there was no reality in a wheelbarrow, that reality rested in the *concept* or plan of that wheelbarrow. But the wheelbarrow is the thing you show on the stage and, so far am I from denying the reality of the fact that it must be admitted when we kick a stone it bruises our toes.

Professor Lowes' book on Coleridge [1] (not published yet, I believe) which he read to the class last year, had a great effect on me. In that book he shows conclusively how retentive of all it reads is the mind and how, at almost any moment, that mass of material may be fused and resurrected in new and magic forms. That is wonderful, I think. So I'm reading, not so analytically as voraciously.

[THE LETTER BREAKS OFF HERE]

The following letter to Professor Baker announcing Wolfe's intention of withdrawing from the 47 Workshop may never have been sent, since it was found in Wolfe's own files and is not to be found in Baker's files. Wolfe made out his application for a teaching position with the Harvard Appointment Bureau on March 24, 1922, but his heart was still set on writing for the theatre and he completed the three-act version of The Mountains *and submitted it to Baker in April or May.*

[1] *The Road to Xanadu* by John Livingstone Lowes. Wolfe had taken Professor Lowes' course, Studies in the Poets of the Romantic Period, in 1920–21, and was taking his Comparative Literature 7 in 1921–22.

To GEORGE PIERCE BAKER

[Cambridge, Mass]

[March (?) 1922]

Dear Professor Baker:

I am writing you to notify you of my withdrawal from your course. Having received some assurance from the university of teaching employment somewhere next year, and gaining my family's permission to continue the year here and get my masters degree, I shall finish up the term.

The conviction has grown on me that I shall never express myself dramatically. I am therefore ending the agony by the shortest way; I would not be a foolish drifter promising myself big things.

I can not find words to express the gratitude I bear toward you, not only for your kindness and encouragement but for the inestimable benefits I know I have derived from your course. I shall never forget nor cease to be grateful to you.

The letter which appears below was evidently sent to Professor Baker with the new three-act version of The Mountains.

To GEORGE PIERCE BAKER

[Cambridge, Mass.]

[April or May, 1922]

Professor Baker:

When one writes a play one feels there are a thousand ways of saying a thing and that one usually selects the worst. But when one rewrites the play it is found that a very definite mould has been formed which it is difficult to break. I believe I have broken the mould in the last act— whether for good or ill I dare not say. Not once in the rewriting have I referred to the original one-act.

The introduction of the romance element will not cheapen the thing, I hope. I did it not to popularize the piece but to make a more living figure of the girl, Laura, who was somewhat wooden before. It will be said, I know, that a love affair with a member of the opposing clan is a somewhat conventional device, but all plotting is somewhat conventional and I can not see why the device is not a good one if I have made a true and honest lover of Will Gudger and a more human figure of the girl Laura, "torn between" (as the saying goes) love for her beaten father and the blunt young apple grower. Thus, also, it seems to me I am able to deal at the end what you would call a "swingeing blow." . . .

[THE FRAGMENT BREAKS OFF HERE]

Through the Harvard University Appointment Office, Wolfe had been offered an instructorship in the English Department at Northwestern University, but in evident reluctance, had postponed accepting it. He was waiting for Commencement, at which he was to receive his Master's degree, when he was suddenly summoned home to his father's deathbed. The following postcard to Miss McCrady, head of the Appointment Office, was mailed by him in New York en route to Asheville.

To LOUISE McCRADY

[PENNY POSTCARD]

[New York City]

[June 20, 1922]

Dear Miss McCrady: A telegram announcing the expected death of my father has forced me to go home. I left on two hours' notice and was unable to see you—I will send the Northwestern people my photograph as soon as I get home. Would you send them a note explaining the circumstances? I will write you a letter as quickly as possible.

To LOUISE McCRADY

48 Spruce Street
Ashville, N.C.

Saturday, Aug. 26, 1922

Dear Miss McCrady:

I was informed, in a letter from your office, that you had gone to Europe for the summer. I trust you had a very pleasant holiday. . . . I regret nothing more than my delay in giving you and the authorities at Northwestern University an answer to their offer of an instructorship in the English department. However, when I have explained the circumstances which occasioned this delay, I am sure you will understand and pardon it. Matters at home were in an extremely unsettled condition following the death of my father, and it was not until very recently that I knew definitely whether I should stay at home with my mother, accept the offer from

Northwestern, or return to Harvard for another year with Professor Baker. My finances are now in such a condition as will permit me to return for another year to Harvard.[1] Professor Baker has been so unfailingly kind and encouraging that I believe this extra year which is now made possible will be of the utmost importance to me.

The only thing that could disturb my happiness at the prospect of returning would be to think that my delayed answer had caused any serious inconvenience to my friends at the Harvard Bureau, and to those at Northwestern who, by their extraordinary kindness and sympathy, have made me long to know them.

It is a pleasure to think I will renew my acquaintance with you in a short time.

To MARGARET ROBERTS

[Asheville, N.C.?]

[September, 1922?]

. . . Coming home this last time I have gathered enough additional material to write a new play [1]—the second fusillade of the battle. This thing that I had thought naive and simple is as old and as evil as hell; there is a spirit of world-old evil that broods about us, with all the subtle sophistication of Satan. Greed, greed, greed—deliberate, crafty, motivated— masking under the guise of civic associations for municipal betterment. The disgusting spectacle of thousands of industrious and accomplished liars, engaged in the mutual and systematic pursuit of their profession, salting their editorials and sermons and advertisements with the religious and philosophic platitudes of Dr. Frank Crane, Edgar A. Guest, and *The American Magazine*. The standards of national greatness are Henry Ford, who made automobiles cheap enough for us all, and money, money, money!! And Thomas A. Edison, who gave us body-ease and comfort. The

---

[1] Wolfe had evidently secured his mother's consent to enrolling in the 47 Workshop for a third year. The financing of his three years at Harvard was a complicated matter which is best explained in his letter to Fred Wolfe of January 22, 1938. He had originally persuaded his mother to let him go to Harvard for one year by suggesting that the expense be deducted from the legacy of $5000 which was left him in his father's will. Later, when he stayed at Harvard for two additional years, no mention had been made of deducting these additional expenses from his legacy. However, when Mr. Wolfe's will was settled, his estate was found to have shrunk so much that the bequests of $5000 to each of his children could not be paid. Wolfe accordingly signed a paper waiving any claim to his $5000, in return for the money which he had received during his three years at Harvard.

[1] *Niggertown,* which finally became *Welcome to Our City.*

knave, the toady, and the hog-rich flourish. There are three ways, and only three, to gain distinction: (1) Money, (2) more money, (3) a great deal of money. And the manner of getting it is immaterial.

Among the young people here there is one who spends two-thirds of his time in the drug store, and who announces boldly, and as a kind of boast, that he is going to "marry money." This boy's father is . . . an honest, industrious, straightforward sort of man who walks to his work every morning with a tin dinner-pail swinging from his hand. Meanwhile the boy rides through the streets of the town, in pursuit of his ambition, in a spick-and-span speedster which he has enveigled from these hard-working people . . . Another boy, of good but common stock, who had all his advances repelled to within a few months back, with contempt or indifference, has unlimited money and with a part of it has purchased an expensive roadster, like a foolish fellow. Now they cluster about him like flies, and feed upon his bounty.

These are but mean and petty things, which I could multiply indefinitely. But what of the darker, fouler things? What of old lust and aged decay, which mantles itself in respectability, and creeps cat-footed by the stained portals of its own sin? What of the things we know, and that all know, and that we wink at, making the morality we prate of consist in discretion? I assure you I am not barren in illustrations of this sort. The emotion I experience is disgust, not indignation. Moral turpitude on the physical basis does not offend me deeply—perhaps I should be sorry to confess it—but my attitude toward life has become, somehow or other, one of alertness, one which sustains and never loses interest, but which is very rarely shocked or surprised by what people do. Human nature is capable of an infinite variety of things. Let us recognize this early and save ourselves trouble and childish stupefaction later. I desire too much to be the artist to start "playing at" life now, and seeing through a rosy or vinous haze. Really I am un-moral enough not to care greatly how the animal behaves, so long as it checks its behavior within its meadow. The great men of the Renaissance, both in Italy and England, seem to me an amazing mixture of God and Beast. But "there were giants in the world in those days," and they are soon forgiven. What do their vices matter now? They have left us Mona Lisa. But what of this dull dross that leaves us only bitterness and mediocrity? Let pigs . . .

[A PORTION OF THE LETTER IS MISSING HERE]

I suppose the alarmist means that the time will come when the strength of our national life will wither and decay, just as all preceding national lives have served their times, and have withered and decayed, and passed on. But what is there in this either to surprise or alarm us? Surely a nation has no greater reason to expect imperishability than has an individual. And it is by no means certain that a long life, whether for man or nation, is the best one. Perhaps our claim to glory, when our page is written in the world's history, will rest on some such achievement as this: "The Americans were powerful organizers and had a great talent for practical scientific achievement. They made tremendous advances in the field of public health, and increased the average scope of human life twelve years. Their cities, although extremely ugly, were models of sanitation; their nation at length was submerged and destroyed beneath the pernicious and sentimental political theory of human equality."

I do not say that this is utterly base or mean or worthless. It will be a very great achievement, but it has left no room for the poets. And when the poets die, the death of the nation is assured.

Well, I have returned to all this at midnight. The fires of the hearth have burned to warm, grey cones of powder. There is a roaring in the wind to-night, the streets are driven bare, and my "autumn leaves" are falling already upon the roof in a dry, uncertain rain. The annual taint of death is in the air. . . .

[THE REMAINDER OF THIS LETTER HAS BEEN LOST]

According to the recollection of William E. Harris, who was a member of the 47 Workshop at this time, Wolfe submitted the first acts of six different plays to Professor Baker in the early fall of 1922, before he settled down to work on Niggertown *(which finally became* Welcome to Our City.) *The play discussed in the following letter is probably one of these six. Fragments of it found among Wolfe's papers concern a hero named Eugene Ramsay whose thirst for knowledge is very similar to Wolfe's own, and a Professor called Wilson or Weldon who somewhat resembles Horace Williams.*

To GEORGE PIERCE BAKER

[Cambridge, Mass.]

[September or October, 1922?]

Dear Professor Baker:

I am leaving herewith the first act of a three act play with a synopsis of the rest. I am on so unsure a footing, so troubled with doubt and misgiving that I feel the necessity of waiting your opinion before going on.

This is my first attempt at what is called the "problem play." But the play, as I conceive it, deals with a spiritual and a human problem, rather

than with a social or economic problem for which I have small use. I will
state it, as I see it, and it is unfortunate if the language seems involved and
complicated. In a system where things are forever changing, where is the
fixed, immutable, unchanging principle to be found? That is—where is
the Absolute? Moreover, by the very exigencies of this vast, mechanical
civilization we have built, life becomes bewildering and overpowering in
its complexity. In the last chapter of that remarkable book, "The Education of Henry Adams," Adams voices this sentiment when he returns to
New York after a long absence and looks at that terrific and chaotic sky-
line. Civilization has exploded. In this chaos of force and disorder, where
is to be found that principle of unity, order, which his spirit seeking
"education" (which is but knowledge of unity) is on the hunt for. He goes
to Washington and finds his friend, John Hay, a man of splendid ability,
already drained and sapped of his vitalities by the demands of this monstrous new world. Now, as I interpret it, Hay represents the finest we have
to offer to combat the demands of our present life. But he is not adequate.
A new type of man must be created. And so he leaves it up in the air.

But how, how? In the first act of my play I try to present the problem.
When the young man, Ramsay, tells Professor Wilson, the philosopher,
that he feels at times he is on the earth seven centuries too late, he is
giving expression to a sincere conviction. Adams mentions the mighty gap
that yawns between the unity of 1200 and the multiplicity of 1900. Consider the case of the young man Ramsay. He too is on the go for "education"—that is the quality of understanding and grasping present life in its
entirety. He knows the limitations of the Middle Ages, their comparative
ignorance and superstition, but he also knows the promise of fulfillment
they held open to the student. Ramsay could picture himself taking orders
and going into a monastery in the 13th century. There he could have spent
the years in his cell going through the monastery's precious collection of
manuscripts—not too many, however, for a life time. He would have
known Plato and Aristotle almost by heart, he would have been well-read
in the scholastic philosophy, and perhaps sub rosa (safe from the prying
eyes of a fat abbot) would have refreshed himself, in moments of relaxation, with Homer and the dramatists.

I do not expect people to be greatly interested in Ramsay's account of
his trials in the world of books. For this reason, I mention this problem only
in passing, believing that, for dramatic purposes, his trials in the world of
action will be more appreciated. Yet when Ramsay tells of wandering past
the countless, loaded shelves of the library like some damned spirit in
search of the unattainable, he is voicing that which has caused him acute
pain. How infinitely little of the contents of those pages can be made his
own: he, with a passionate thirst for knowledge, cannot become master

even here. It goads him to fury to think that some idle woman gorged to
the gills with the latest output of fiction, can speak knowingly of this, that
or the other book, which he has not come to. Ramsay feels passionately
that instead of there being too little science . . .

[A PORTION OF THE LETTER IS MISSING HERE]

. . . knows that once he loses this, he too is lost. Then we find him being
swept into the current. The bewildering cross currents of this life to which
he makes a frenzied effort to apply his philosophy, and for which he finds
his philosophy incomplete and inadequate, begin to sweep him about. He
realizes that he has so adapted his philosophy to each occurrence that
denies it, that it has lost its original quality and has become a mere agent
of expediency, through which he is trying to find—what?

Ramsay, as I should have stated, wants to interpret life through the
medium of literature. In the city he works for a newspaper (however I
have no newspaper scenes in the play). Time and again he writes, but
tears up what he has written, with a terrible sense of its incompleteness.
A cross-section of life will not content him; he wants to show in each type
the universal, in the one the many. At first he says "I will write nothing
now. But in five years I will know enough. Then I will be able to give a
broadside view of things." But the conviction grows that in five years this
knowledge of imperfection will be more oppressive than ever. It disgusts
Ramsay to hear the perfection of universal understanding of humanity
ascribed to such a writer as Dickens, for instance. He admires Dickens but
he sees plainly that Dickens, as so many other writers, had a very limited
point of view. He knew one particular side of life and he knew it well.

It would perhaps be much better for Ramsay if he could limit himself
thus. His own common-sense tells him that a sure limitation is the only
solution in the present frame of things. But the daemon goads him on.

As you have doubtless surmised, there is much that is personal in this
statement. But let there be no confusion between Ramsay and myself. I
am trying to portray a figure bound by his own strength, not by his limitations. In this, it seems to me, there is a tremendous irony. Consider the
cases of Coleridge and Wordsworth. Coleridge was a man of far deeper
and more varied genius. But this was his undoing. The brilliant promise of
his youth, which produced "Christabel" and "The Ancient Mariner," was
baffled and checked in his later years by the expeditions of that devising
mind which tried now poetry, now science, now philosophy—ever beginning and never ending anything. Wordsworth, possessed of less profound
but more single-minded genius, devoted his life to the production of the
one kind of poetry he could write well. And I will not deny that (on paper)
he's the greater poet.

Or there is Leonardo, who painted so little because of his other activities and researches as engineer, canal builder, geologist, speculator upon flight of birds and flight of men, astronomer, physicist, etc.

[THE LETTER BREAKS OFF HERE]

The play discussed in the following letter was probably another of the six which Wolfe considered writing in the early Fall of 1922.

To GEORGE PIERCE BAKER

[Cambridge, Mass.]

[Autumn, 1922?]

Sir:

The figure around whom this play revolves will suggest strongly to those who know him Jonathan Swift. But I wish to make it clear that this is not a biographical play. Swift is responsible for [it]—it is true, but out of his character I have drawn my own play. On reading Leslie Stephen's "Swift" recently, I was powerfully impressed by the tremendous humanity of the man. Here we have a really savage misanthropist. He regards mankind with none of the noble or patient scorn of Alceste, but with a terrible hate: he rakes them with the withering fire of an unequalled satiric talent. But —when I say he hated men, I mean that hard cold accretion that makes up the world.

The tremendous antithesis appears when we consider Swift's remarkable love and loyalty toward his friends; his extreme personal parsimony which he practices in order to be more generous to friends and dependents. Consider the pathetic contrast in this grim, bitter old man who yet, with almost womanish fear and trembling, keeps a letter from a sick friend unopened for five days because he fears bad news: or the grief he hides under harshness, at the death of a friend, when he tells us never to choose a sick or feeble person for a friend, because the danger and worry at losing them is so great.

[THE LETTER BREAKS OFF HERE]

The following brief fragment is evidently part of a letter which Wolfe submitted to Professor Baker with a play entitled The People. *This was probably one of the six which he began in the Fall of 1922.*

To GEORGE PIERCE BAKER

[Cambridge, Mass.]

[Autumn, 1922]

Dear Professor Baker:

In this play I hope to incorporate certain ideas that have been stirring about in my mind concerning the eternal warfare that is waged between the Individual and Society. The fiction I have invented to dramatize these ideas is fairly evident, I think, in the first scene. I will hastily sketch out the rest of the play, as follows: in Scene II we see the Fair and the People, who are a sort of chorus in the play. In the various tent shows and booths, under the guise of "bally-hoo men" and spielers, I propose to show in turn . . .

[THE LETTER BREAKS OFF HERE]

The following letter from Wolfe to his cousin, Elaine Westall Gould, the daughter of Henry A. Westall, was evidently called forth by a criticism of Welcome to Our City *which she had made at Wolfe's request.*

To ELAINE WESTALL GOULD

[21 Trowbridge St]

[Cambridge, Mass.]

[January 14 (?) 1923]

My dear Elaine:

Your letter was read with great interest and I return my thanks for the many valuable contributions you have made. I do not think, as you suggest, that there is any fundamental difference between us as to what constitutes a play; there is rather, I think, a misunderstanding as to the *kind* of play I have written, and as to what that play was primarily about. I have no doubt, when I come to the criticisms, that I shall run into the same difficulty with other people and I know that it is a difficulty to be reckoned with, since I can not hope to reach a general audience of any such intelligence.

First of all, I want to impress the fact that the play is not about any problem—least of all about the negro problem. I try to settle nothing, I want to prove nothing—I have no use for solutions.

My play is concerned with giving a picture about a certain section of life, a certain civilization, a certain society. I am content with nothing but the whole picture, I am concerned with nothing else. The racial aspect of the picture is deliberately diffused with the other elements at first, it gradually comes to the surface until it overshadows the whole picture at the end. There is no need of assuring you, who have lived in the South, that the part that element plays is not disproportionate. It is not.

So here, I think, you struck your snag, and you thought I had written two plays instead of one. It is sometimes difficult, of course, for people who have been trained in the theatre of the last twenty years to adapt themselves readily to the looser and more expressive structure of such a play as I have written. The mind is accustomed to the old forms, to the three, four, and five act forms, and adapts itself hardly.

[THE LETTER BREAKS OFF HERE]

Welcome to Our City *was chosen for production by the 47 Workshop, and was actually put on on May 11 and 12, 1923. Wolfe evidently wrote the following letter to Professor Baker when the selection of the play was first announced.*

To GEORGE PIERCE BAKER

[Cambridge, Mass.]
Sunday night.

[January or February, 1923]

I am submitting herewith a list of people and of sets required for my play. As I say, I think it can be done with two dozen people, perhaps with fewer.

I am letting you have the play in my fearful scrawl and with no revision whatever. I feel that many of the scenes may be strengthened by the introduction of more satirical material, most of which I have written.

Anyone, I think, is a little dubious about the matter of revision. Often it is nothing but a hit or miss sort of thing. I know of only one rule and think it covers the whole business. Revise with the sole purpose of writing a better play. This means, if possible, the making of each scene better, briefer, more direct, and more economical in the use of people. That I can do this *in time* I have not the slightest doubt: of doing it in twenty-four hours, or two days, or half a week, I am not so sure.

I think this states my position with this possible addition: I would be sorry to think that a close eye on the relevancy, the direct bearing of each scene and incident on the main problem, that of the negro, would conceal from you the fact that I knew what I wanted to do from the beginning to the end. With what success I did it, I can not even venture a guess. But will you please remember this: a play about the negro, a play in which each scene bore directly upon the negro, a play in which the negro was kept ever before you, might be a better play: it would not be the play I started to write. I wish you would bear this in mind when you read the mooted scene (VIII)—the cubistical, post-impressionist politician scene. It needs revision, but I'd hate to lose it. It's part of the picture; part of the total.

I have written this play with thirty-odd *named* characters because it required it, not because I didn't know how to save paint. Some day I'm going to write a play with fifty, eighty, a hundred people—a whole town, a whole race, a whole epoch—for my soul's ease and comfort. No one may want to produce it but it will make an interesting play.

And the next I do will have eight, ten, certainly no more than a dozen.

If you need a translator for my manuscript—I suspect you will—call me. I will be at your service when you want me.

To MABEL WOLFE WHEATON

[Cambridge, Mass]

[April or May, 1923?]

Dear Sister Mabel:

I am deeply sorry I have neglected writing you for so long, and in especial, to thank you for your beautiful gift Christmas. It's a pretty time to acknowledge it I know, but better late than never and I want you to know I've worn it daily and got great service. I know you're tired and I can appreciate your position. I don't think we'll ever forget what you have done [1]—I'm sure I won't, and if there's any poor consolation in this, perhaps I shall write a play someday about my family [2] in which it will be seen we're not all of us heroes nor all of us villains, but that we're all pretty human people, with more virtues than imperfections, and capable (you, in particular) of actions that make the heart beat a little faster.

Families are strange and wonderful things and one never sees the mystery and the beauty in them until one is absent from them. When one is present, the larger values are obscured sometimes by the little friction of daily events. I sometimes wonder for instance, if two people constituted as differently as are Fred and I could ever live together in perfect harmony?

[1] In her devotion to her father until his death.

[2] There are fragments of such a play among Wolfe's papers, using some of the material which finally appeared in *Look Homeward, Angel*.

Fred's generosity and his many acts of kindness to his younger brother are often remembered with deep emotion, but if ever we've lived together so much as a week without friction, I can't remember it. I would do anything in my power for him; he would do that and more for me but the plain truth is—when we get together we're apt to irritate one another. Once or twice —God help us—we were on the verge of fighting. It would have been a calamity. . . .

Mabel: don't think I overrate myself or have any false idea of my ability. I have no illusions about that and you may be sure if I ever do anything worthy [of] the name of Genius, I will not be too modest to admit it. Two or three times in my short life, I have had flashes that caused me to think for a moment that I had a spark—a very small one—of Promethean fire in me, but at present you can cover it all and more, if you say: I believe I have some *talent*. The one big hope I have now is that Professor Baker has more confidence in my abilities than I have. That sentence is badly stated. I mean, the fact that he does believe in me gives me hope. But if ever you thought I was given to puffed-up conceit, I entreat you to revise that opinion now, for I know that if you could have been with me at times this year, out of the very kindness of your heart you could not have forborne telling me I was not quite as bad as I thought.

[THE LETTER BREAKS OFF HERE]

It would seem impossible to date the following letter correctly, or to guess to whom it was addressed. However, the decomposed state of the paper on which it is written, the general flamboyant style, and the reference to "every drunken Sophomore, to every paunchy pickle salesman" seem to indicate that it was written while Wolfe was at Harvard, probably in 1923.

To AN UNKNOWN GIRL

[Cambridge, Mass?]
[1923?]

My Dear:

When I saw you first, and heard you speak, I loved your voice. It was low and husky, and strangely tender. It had little notes, and shades in it. There was something steadfast and fine about your carriage; I noticed your breasts when you walked—they were firm, and sprang forward.

I heard you speak a second time, and I asked the other girl—Margaret —to get you for me. I thought of Cordelia, King Lear's daughter. I think I have always loved her. When she died the old mad king [leaned] over her, and said:—"Her voice was ever soft and low—an excellent thing in woman."

That, my dear, is great poetry—simple, sensuous, passionate, poignant and beautiful. And your voice was like that, I thought. Or, rather, that queer false romantic part of me thought so—the part that is always lying to me. The other—the real, hard, practical part—said "Cigarettes and booze."

But—no matter what, I met you. You came to my room and said, "Well, where's the liquor? You're the first Southerner I've ever seen"—and so forth. I grew sick with horror, and fear, and shame. I'd heard that so often before and, somehow, I felt that I had lost you. To complete it, you need only have said: "My companionship for your booze. Is it a bargain?"

It was a blow, an insult to my intelligence—but I didn't mind that. I knew you had said it to every drunken Sophomore, to every paunchy pickle salesman you had known—but I didn't mind the classification. It was the fact that I had lost something; and I couldn't call it back.

So I got the booze, and you sat there on the bed with your hard, wise, knowing little manner, displaying all the shameful and degrading symbols with which this brute-blind world has marked you—what silly and vicious people call "worldly wisdom." That was when I began to love you, my dear. That surprises you, doesn't it? You have lovely eyes—and they looked at me now and then—it seemed with a frightened question in them. I thought I saw a child whom the world had bewildered: all the common hardness and pertness and flippancy of the "digger" was a protective covering.

Meanwhile, you were fulfilling your function as "the life of the party." With a sudden revulsion, I wondered how many times you had been "the life of the party." You told your filthy stories, I told mine. Only, you told yours beautifully. And I didn't mind. I wanted to kiss you. It was really amazing. I have never cared for a woman with a dirty mouth, even if she were a street prostitute—but I didn't mind it in you. Foulness dropped from your mouth like honey.

Strangely, I have no shame, because, I think, you will be tender, and sad, and will not boast of your conquest. I offer myself for a day, a week, or a month. I shall grow tired and forget you; you will be another beautiful phantom—and I shall ask of you not even so much as a picture, a garter, a handkerchief, a bit of perfumed lace to remember you by. I never do.

I shall kiss your lips—your beautiful mouth, your fine, soiled prettiness, tainted with so many foul and drunken kisses. I shall pour golden song— what my maddened heart has wrought and made lovely—into those ears which have heard every bawdy ballad in the country from countless drunken Sophomores. Only, my dear, when the time comes, you shall forget my poetry, and remember the ribald ballads.

Life has left his dirty thumb marks on you; you have been pawed over —yet, somehow the pity and the beauty. . . .

[A PORTION OF THE LETTER IS MISSING HERE]

. . . love you, and—at the end—I shall give you back into the vicious slimy sea from which you came.

Love me for a time, my dear. Hold me in your arms, and say to me: "You are fine, you are good, you are great, you are beautiful. You are my god—and I love you"—and, by God, I will be.

This

X

is a Kiss, my dear.

(If you don't destroy this letter you

will be shot at sunrise)

The letter below was found in Wolfe's own files and was evidently addressed to Merlin McF. Taylor, who was a graduate student at Harvard from 1921 to 1923, and a member of English 47 in 1921–1922. The last two paragraphs of the letter were written on a separate sheet of paper, and may be part of the letter to Taylor, or part of one to someone else.

Probably to MERLIN McF. TAYLOR

[Cambridge, Mass.]

[July, 1923?]

My dear Merlin:

Your letter came this morning to revive my fainting spirits from over the red Hell of a beautiful Cambridge day. I drew sustenance from the tidings of your fruitful industry. Know, then, that I, too, have not been inactive. I have written a prodigious amount which is piled here about me, on the floor—but nothing as yet which looks like a play. That is not to say the thing [1] won't dramatize—I think it will—I have merely attacked most of the juicy spots and left out the conjunctive ifs, ands, buts.

Summer School arrived in a swirl of petticoats and lilac-coloured drawers. Some of the arrivals are passably fair—the remainder teach school. There are a number of old women, of both sexes. . . .

I read prodigiously. The Widener Library has crumpled under my

[1] *The House* (later *Mannerhouse*).

savage attack. Ten, twelve, fifteen books a day are nothing. And, now and then, I write. With you away, I see few people that I know. Raisbeck [2] is here with his dog—or vice versa—but I rarely see him. Prof. Baker is reading manuscripts in the wilds of New Hampshire: the rest of the crew is missing. . . .

. . . I think my play "The House" will "pack a punch" for it is founded on a sincere belief in the essential inequality of things and people, in a sincere belief in men and masters, rather than in men and men, in a sincere belief in the necessity of some form of human slavery—yes, I mean this— and it deals, moreover, with the one period in our history that believed these things and fought for them and was destroyed because of its belief in them. This I am working out in my new play. I find it very interesting.

I have been reading the *Amores* of Ovid this morning. It is beautiful Latin and beautiful poetry—although it is altogether concerned with two topics: How am I going to get it and How fine it was when you let me have it. If our modern romanticists could be as honest, I'd make no kick. Ovid would never have written a verse to the Virgin Mary as an indirect address to . . .

[THE FRAGMENT BREAKS OFF HERE]

To KENNETH RAISBECK

[Cambridge, Mass]

[Early August, 1923]

My dear Kenneth:

I hung around your doorway yesterday like a second Laddie Boy. I have done everything but bay the moon. From your letter I infer that you left Thursday about midnight. I went by your lodgings at one o'clock, and concluded that you were in bed. Your letter was a shock,—a shock which has spurred me into feverish activity. I am packing! This is the last and heaviest calamity—for the present. I'm going up to Carlton's [1] for three or four days—though God knows why. Perhaps it is to see the kingdoms of my world from an exceeding high mountain,—if I only could! Misfortune has fallen like rain since you left. Last night I was caught in the Harvard Yard with a girl . . . doing the worst I could. The yard-cop was fat, and portentous.

[2] Kenneth Raisbeck was Professor Baker's assistant in the 47 Workshop, and a close friend of Wolfe's.

[1] Henry Fisk Carlton was a member of the 47 Workshop from 1920 to 1922, and had invited Wolfe to visit him in Madison, New Hampshire.

"Mister," says he, breathing heavily through his mouth, "this has got to stop."

I scrambled to my feet, and asked him what he meant, because I couldn't think of anything better to say.

"You were spooning with the young lady, she was sitting on your lap. The university doesn't allow that."

"You will please confine your remarks to me and to Harvard University," says I, as lofty as you please.

"I'm sorry," says he. "Them's my orders. I am only doing my duty." Here he threw back the lapel of his coat and displayed a badge as large as a small saucepan. "That's my authority," he says. When I saw it was official I made my exit.

Well, I came back to all this at midnight Sunday. I leave here to-morrow at six—vespers—on the Portland, Me. boat—that is if I can tear myself away from the —— girl. Again, I am in the toils, and fast nearing the breakers, physically and mentally. What shall I ever do? . . . How can I stick with anyone in the present state of my affairs? It is mad, mad, mad. I tell you there is no escape! And I, who fear and live in utter horror of this thing, am most in need of someone to supply the sheer physical wants—to provide me with decencies, mended sox, bleached linen, clean sheets, pressed trousers, and all the other trivialities by whose want I may sink!

There is a mighty conspiracy everywhere abroad—the more terrible because silent, and veiled in holy words—which crushes us slowly and relentlessly into the [souls] of the domestics and the Pure Young Men. Any suggestion that a male may hold physical communion with a female without first propitiating the priest and the Holy Ghost is met with invective, hatred, and relentless opposition.

By the way I saw Fritz Day and his wife in the Georgian last night. They are still living happily and Cathi (?) has apparently heard the play, because she told me it was 'awfully good'—probably because my eyes looked queer when I got the news. No! It is not about her! Fritz spoke of Art while I, in recent vein, spoke of Commerce. But Fritz has dwelt too long with his ear tuned to the rustling of the angel's wings: I could see he thought the conversation sordid.

They are going up to the Bakers' to play with the proteins for a few days. No doubt I will see them and hear the play,[2] which is now cut to eighty pages. I am going to send my play [3] in from New Hampshire. We can only hope for the best. Perhaps if I can get up there in the woods for a few days, with a little peace of mind, I can do considerable revision. I

[2] A play of Day's, *The Sea*.
[3] *Welcome to Our City.*

should never have met that girl! And who do you think introduced me? Brewster.[4]

The following fragments to Professor Baker were found scattered among Wolfe's papers, and were evidently written during his period of final disillusionment with the 47 Workshop which began with the failure of Welcome to Our City in May, 1923, and culminated in his acceptance of an instructorship at New York University in January, 1924. Since many of them were obviously written in the Summer or early Fall of 1923, they are included all together as of that date, although some may have been written a little earlier or later.

To GEORGE PIERCE BAKER

I feel that the time has come for me to speak to you, as becomes our friendship—freely, frankly and earnestly. You have something more than a play to deal with, sir. You have the fate and destiny of 190 pounds of blood, bone, marrow, passion, feeling—that is, your humble servant, in your keeping. I hope that's not an undue responsibility—but it's true and you must know it.

I admit the virtue of being able to stand criticism. Unfortunately it is a virtue I do not happen to possess. Last year my unfortunate play returned to let my blood; the springs of creative action froze and in the blackness of my despair, I doubted if they would ever return. They returned because my father died, because I was subjected to deeper tragedies of love, hatred, and contempt. These things dwindled and lessened the others. But according to the system . . .

The ability to take such criticism you said not long ago might make the difference between a second-rate artist and a great artist. I do not believe this. Being a great artist depends no more on such callousness than does his ability to swallow castor-oil, or blue-point oysters, or fried pork chops. It has nothing to do with it. You, or no man else, can make me a great artist, or a second-rate artist, or any kind of artist. That is a matter which was settled in my mother's womb—she, whose blood fed me, whose heart and whose brain lighted me and gave me being. That part of our destiny, believe me, is fixed, and nothing save death or madness can check or change it. And worldly wisdom on life, from the experienced traveller, is of no

[4] W. R. Brewster, who was a member of the 47 Workshop Company at this time.

avail. If there is genius, the thing is a marvellous intuition, little dependent on observation. If there is no genius, I'd as soon draw wages from one form of hackery as another.

I have no doubt that if I set myself to it and worked long and earnestly, I could ultimately be successful in writing plays which only the dramatic critic for the *Boston Transcript* could understand. Unfortunately for those who like myself are indolently inclined, the way out is not so easy. [Inch-brow (?)] drama deserves, and will get, a speedy, damnatory death. High-brow drama about low-brow people deserves an even quicker and more painful decease: I refer to plays like *The Hairy Ape*.

Dear Professor Baker:
I settled the affair with the typist as soon as the news of your award reached me.[1] I thank you very much for acting. You were made referee, I must tell you, at no instigation of mine. Indeed I was informed only after you were named.

In frankness, I do not consider the woman's services worth $88.00. I consider the original $75.00 as not only ample but generous. But, even so, I have beaten this unpleasant person from bonnet to bootstrap and when she gets through paying her attorneys she will be fortunate indeed to realize $50.00. I would be ashamed of my vindictiveness if I had not been forced to suffer from her false and perjurous tongue. . . .

It is a shameful commentary on our civilization that I, after seven university years, and the consumption of thousands of books, may earn barely $2000 a year—if I am fortunate—by teaching, while this creature is paid at the rate of $22.00 a day for incompetent, slipshod work. But when I speak of incompetence, let me, in shame, draw a veil over my own. Everyone is earning, procuring, achieving a measure of independence, it seems, except myself. A pretty little girl I picked up in the Yard the other night . . . earns $2200 as a school-marm—and $35 weekly for extra instructions. Can I hold my head up longer?

[1] Wolfe had engaged a stenographer to type one of his plays, and had been horrified to find that her bill was more than he could pay. He had done nothing about it and the matter had dragged on, until she finally brought suit against him. According to a letter written by his uncle, Henry A. Westall, who acted as his attorney in the matter, they let the typist get judgment against Wolfe, and then informed the court that he was still a minor when he had ordered the work done, that Mr. Westall as his "guardian pro tem" had not authorized it, and that the claim was therefore invalid. Professor Baker was then asked to referee the case, and a settlement was made.

There is a chagrin in my [youth?] threatening my happiness, making me bitter, morose. The brute is Money. With money I'll throttle the beast-blind world between my fingers. Without it I am strapped; weakened: my life is a curse and a care. If God had only made me with the soul of a villager! Then might I like Cowley—a gentle poet—see life in a thimble and be content. But I have the heart of a far-wanderer and a farer-forth into unknown places. And so begins my vagabondage.

By God—no one knows me—no one knows my capacity. Those who liked my play looked on it as a fortuitous accident—as something which might not happen again. But already I have a bigger play under construction—I do not say it will be better because my heart and my mind is bitter-sick—but the concept was bigger, truer, nobler.

I am leaving here as soon as I pack my junk to send it home. Where I am going I do not know, but I hope the journey will be far and long. I am an observant, fairly intelligent person, with an insatiable desire for this thing called life—and I will learn.

[The] world is a large, large oyster—but I do not think I will choke when I swallow it.

Good-bye, and may God bless you, and bring prosperity and fine accomplishment to your work.

Dear Professor Baker:

I am leaving here to-morrow—journey, as yet, unknown. I have hopes, however, that it will take me far and keep me going. I am destroying all my manuscripts. My apprenticeship has drawn to an end.

I am going to add to my manifold indebtedness to you by asking you to write, at your leisure, a short letter to my mother, in Asheville, North Carolina. She is a shrewd woman, of great discernment and penetration: she will understand and appreciate what you write in honesty and sincerity. If you can tell her with some measure of conviction that you do not think my time here has been wasted, that you believe, in time, there is some promise of fulfillment, you will render me (and her) a service of inestimable value. I ask you to do this because, I fear, she will be subjected to unpleasant criticism from people who look on my career here as a failure, and on the money which has been spent as wasted.

I could earn my living by teaching, I believe. Indeed I was offered an instructorship at Northwestern University last year, and I suppose I could go somewhere else even yet. But I have forsworn this course: I believe it is a false compromise. I do not know how I am suited to vagabondage, but I know myself for an observant and fairly intelligent person who ought to learn several things by the experience.

Life does not come to me evenly or gently. Do not deceive yourself. You can teach me no balance, equipoise, or moderation. Nothing will be gained by putting a fence around me: I will but burst forth the more intemperately at the end. My life is a rude, rash gamble—a curse and a care. I shall see presently if something useful may not be done with it. My affections were all too strong, my aversions too fierce—odi et amo— tells the whole of it.

Be of good cheer when you think of me. If the ship goes down it will be far enough out, I promise you, not to sadden the watchers by the shore. And we may, I hope and believe, swim through bravely at the end.

The world, by Bacchus, is a large, large oyster, but since I'm bent on opening it, there's nothing to be done but wait and see if it defies gustation. I am fairly strong, and of boundless energy. If anything, I have the odds and a dreadful fear of the mute, inglorious, to whip me on.

I think you are really a fine, good man, and when I consider the excellence of the fibre which has caused you to persist here in the face of disheartening conditions, resisting the lures of more seductive offers and greater personal opportunities, it seems to me you are an individual who has maintained himself on an impressive level of character—the most impressive level of character that I have ever known. Now, this is what I understand by the term *morality:* it seems to me that on the moral level you deserve to be called a great man.

If this is true, I want you to give me credit for actually seizing upon the fundamental and essential thing about you—something, I venture to think, which few people have discovered about you. Because we must fight against a whole background of tradition and convention when we consider your personality on the moral level. In the first place, morality at once associates itself with physical stability. That is, it is much easier to associate morality with Immanuel Kant who never travelled 100 miles from the place of his birth, who ate the same breakfast for 30 years, and whose morning walk was so minutely punctual that his neighbors set their watches on his appearance—this is much easier than when we have to consider the individual who is here this week, in New York. . . .

But I think I also feel this: a man on your level of conduct is apt to give the appearance of being more devoted to the abstract than to the concrete, to the ideal more than to the individual, and, if that ideal is expressing itself through an organization, to the organization more than to the individual who is a part of that organization.

One of your students recently said to me: "He's like us all—he's looking out for himself. You can't blame him—Jesus Christ, that man can't spend much time thinking of us—he's got too many things in his mind to think of."

It is difficult for me to escape the reflection that while you have been able to provide some tangible opportunity for everyone who has needed it—from Carlton to Brink to Raisbeck to Daly [1]—you have been generous to me only in words. I do not say that I would have accepted such aid:— I do not think I would at any time, certainly not now—but I would have felt considerably better about the whole thing. I have even heard you speak with deep emotion of the sacrifice Fritz Day [2] is making "for his art" —on $15,000 a year. Really, how does he do it?

I think that my complaint against you, and very nearly everyone else who has proffered advice during the past year concerning the manage-ment of my life—and, God knows, that advice has been copious enough —is that all of it has been beautifully indefinite, amazingly lacking in substance. If I meet you again soon, and breakfast or dine with you, I think I can foretell, from invariable experience, the result: There will be [an] other verbal outpouring on my part: I [will] talk freely and openly, and at the [end you] will say, as you have said each [time in] the past two years: "Now, you know [that you can] come to me at any time, don't [you?." And when] I assure you that I do know that I can, you [will nod] as if satisfied, and say: "Good, I want it that way." Really I despair of ever knowing you any better. You get so far with an individual and then you come up against a wall, and you can't get over it. You impress me at times as a man who is trying hard to get over his own wall, but who has never succeeded. Well, then, to get back to the point, you have told me the things I ought not to do, but you have left me adrift in the void as to the method of doing those things that I ought to do. No Europe, you say, at this time; no New York, no North Carolina; no [teaching] school; no outside work, as it [would take] too much time and energy. But [what, then?] You must write. You would be [unhappy] doing anything else. Quite so. [But you are a wise] and travelled citizen of this small [world, and it has] surely not escaped your observation that a young man of my age and growth [must eat.]

[1] Henry Carlton, Roscoe Brink, Kenneth Raisbeck and James Daly were all members of the 47 Workshop.

[2] Frederic L. Day was another member of the 47 Workshop.

If anyone in the future, should manifest enough interest in my life to ask you what I am doing, I hope you will not lift your shoulders and with a twisted little smile, impart the information that I am selling pickles, or laundry soap, or real-estate as the case may be, nor that you will add: "I did my best, but it was no use. He would see things that way." Rather, I hope you will say something like this: "Tom Wolfe, who was a poet and a dramatist, has begun to face life boldly and with courage. He was faced with the necessity of earning his own living, and he is doing well, representing the famous Katzenjammer Pickle People. Everybody had free and copious advice for Tom Wolfe except advice on the very simple matter of how he was to sustain the breath of life in his body. As we failed there, where the Katzenjammer Pickle Company has so splendidly succeeded, Tom Wolfe has quite properly rejected all our former exhortations as pretentious and windy bunkum. We may draw some sustenance from the fact that a few of us—a very few—believed he could write, and told him so, but this, too, is of very little importance since he knew the scope and depth of his talent so much better than we."

My energy—at one time vast, sustained, seemingly inexhaustible—is waning fast into its Indian Summer. It has proved no match for the mongrel sneer, the apathetic attention, or the misguided efforts of my friends who, honestly desirous to preserve and enhance the worth in me, tried to discipline, to subdue, to tame those things which were not consistent with their notions of balance and respectability! What, I take it, you were after was a thoroughly respectable, thoroughly balanced, thoroughly canny person, with artistic proclivities, who, upon demand would turn on the spirit and let the energy run out and express itself in three acts and a prologue. Drop a penny in the slot and I would turn out a golden sunset; for a five or ten cent piece, romantic love, or a tragedy of the soil; for a quarter (my top price) a bit of lashing satire.

Wolfe did not re-enroll in the 47 Workshop in the Fall of 1923. Instead, he went to New York at the end of August, to submit Welcome to Our City *to the Theatre Guild, who had asked to see it on the recommendation of Professor Baker. While waiting for the Guild's decision, he went to Asheville, then returned to New York where for six weeks he had a job soliciting donations from University of North Carolina alumni for the Graham Memorial Building. The following letter to George Wallace, a former member of the Workshop, was written when Wolfe first reached New York and was visiting a friend of Wallace's, Harold Duble of the Holland Advertising Agency.*

To GEORGE WALLACE

[Pleasantville, N. Y.]

[August, 1923]

My dear George:

I am writing you at greater length, as I promised. You see I occasionally keep my word. I am spending the night at the Dubles. I called them up and Mrs. D. invited me out. I came. That is how I treat your friends. Mrs. Duble asked me to stay longer, but I refused for a variety of reasons. The chief one is that I feel the impropriety of accepting the invitation of these kind and hospitable people who have come to know me solely and simply through you, and casually, at that. Lesser reasons are the typing of my play which is being done at the Remington Typewriter office on lower Broadway and which demands my daily attention now. I expect to give it to the Guild by the end of the week but when I shall hear from them only God, in his infinite wisdom, knows. My dear old friend, add a few lines to your prayers for me and my play. And burn the candles, boy, burn the candles.

Another consideration against my staying here is that it would cost two dollars a day going in and out, plus the time. I was out to Taylor's [1] at Mountain Lakes until this morning, but last night it was murmured that relatives were due to-day. So you see I've been kept moving. I shall try to make my own time now for such time as I shall be here, but where, I can't say. If you still think enough of me to write, address your letter to the Holland Advertising Agency. Hal will look after it.

George, if you come down before I leave, please let me see something of you. I feel like Horatio Alger's boy hero: alone in the cit-ee—which has no pit-ee—and that kind of thing, you know. I am flippant but, my dear old George, I represent the boy-hero in more than one way. God knows I'm poor enough, and my fortune at the present is tied up in my handkerchief, in the shape of a play in ten scenes—very badly typed. Unfortunately I have not the money-making penchant which all of Horatio's boy-heroes seemed to have. George, if anyone should ever tell you that "money doesn't matter," apply a length of lead pipe above his right ear with my kindest regards. Poverty is an awful, eventually a degrading, thing, and it is rare that anything good comes from it. We rise, old friend, in spite of adversity, not because of it. The unheated garret is *not* as favorable a place for the artist as the well-warmed study, cheese and crackers is *not* the fare on which great poetry is fed—and those who say it is so are fools and senti-mentalists. War! War! War to the death on twaddle! Of course great poets

[1] Merlin Taylor's.

have lived in garrets; great poetry *has* been written on cheese and crackers, but to advocate this as the true artistic environment is as much as to say that Mordecai Brown, having only three fingers, was a great base-ball pitcher, and that all base-ball pitchers should immediately therefore, have two of their fingers cut off.

But enough of this worldliness for the present. I have one monster at the present—that is money. I have one idol—commerce—and whoever prates big to me of "Art" and "Sacrifice" (words continually in the mouths of wretched little people who know the meaning of neither)— when they speak thus, I say, I shall fall upon them, and smite them hip and thigh. I will never respect my brains until I pick a few gold coins from them. That may be a shameful confession, but it represents the true state of my feeling. . . .

Goodbye, then, for the present. I shall hope to see you but if I don't, you will continue to find me . . .

To ALBERT COATES

[New York City]

[Early September, 1923]

My Dear Albert:

Just a few lines to tell you I'm on my way home and hope to see you on the Hill [1] before many more weeks have elapsed. I will not stop by on way down, but expect to go by as I return. I was in Cambridge until mid-August, working on my new play [2]—two acts of which are completed. I went to New Hampshire then for a week with Prof. Baker or other friends and have been in New York for three weeks now, part of the time with Lacey Meredith and Bill Folger,[3] who have an apartment on 123 St. I am now staying there. I have spent my time here getting my play [4] revised and retyped and will submit it to the Theatre Guild tomorrow or next day. Then—home.

Remember me—or rather that play—in your prayers, Albert. It's about all I have now, except my mother's confidence and Prof. Baker's belief in me. He wrote her a corking letter in my behalf, and then wrote me if she didn't "place the entire family fortune at my disposal and beg me never again to mention any career save that of dramatist, he missed his guess."

[1] Chapel Hill.

[2] *The House* (which became *Mannerhouse*).

[3] Two graduates from the University of North Carolina with whom Wolfe shared an apartment at 439 West 123rd Street that autumn.

[4] *Welcome to Our City.*

So, you see, I'm one of these people poor in money, but with some other things of value, one of which, of course, is your friendship.

I will be glad to get back home, if only for a little, glad to see my folks, Asheville, the Hill, you! You know, if you were writing plays, Albert, I think I would be jealous of you—they'd be such damned good plays. As it is, I take almost as much pride in your achievements as if they were my own, which is going pretty far. I see such certain success for you, whether as teacher [5] or practising attorney, that the prospect must at times seem monotonous to you. I hope you will try, every now and then, to fail at something, in order to give a little spice and variety to existence if it palls. I wonder if, in some respects, I'll ever cease being a child. I want to see the Hill unutterably, but the thing that has held me back has been the desire to go back with some definite achievement behind—namely, the *selling* of a play. Please God I get my wish before another year—another month!

Write me a line or so in Asheville. The address is 48 Spruce St. Should I close wishing you success? I might as well say farewell to Hercules and wish him health.

[5] Coates had returned to the University of North Carolina as Assistant Professor of Law, and is now Professor of Law and Founder and Director of the Institute of Government there.

III

NEW YORK UNIVERSITY AND EUROPE

1924–1926

In December, the Theatre Guild declined Welcome to Our City, *although they offered to reconsider it if Wolfe would shorten and tighten it. In despair, he returned to Cambridge for the Christmas holidays. He made no serious attempt to revise and resubmit the play, but finally faced the fact that he must become a teacher to support himself. The following letter to Professor Homer A. Watt, Chairman of the English Department at the Washington Square College of New York University, is his application for the instructorship which he was to hold for the next six years.*

To HOMER A. WATT

> 10 Trowbridge Street
> Cambridge, Mass.
> January 10, 1924

Dear Professor Watt:

I am informed that there will be several vacancies in the English department at New York University on the opening of the new term, in February. I have requested the Harvard Appointment Bureau to forward my papers, including letters and scholastic grades, to you. Mr. Dow,[1] formerly of Harvard, and now an instructor at the uptown branch of the university, may also be consulted.

I was graduated, as you will note, from the University of North Carolina, in 1920, and received my master's degree in English from Harvard in 1922. The appointment office secured me an offer from Northwestern University

---

[1] Robert Bruce Dow had known Wolfe at Harvard in 1922–23, and had then become an instructor in English at the University College of New York University. Dow is now Associate Professor of English at the Washington Square College, and Assistant Director of Admissions.

in 1922, which I ultimately refused, in order to return for another year under Professor Baker at the 47 Workshop. Thus, I have been a student in the Graduate School for three years.

I have had no experience as a teacher. It is only fair to tell you that my interests are centred in the drama, and that someday I hope to write successfully for the theatre and to do nothing but that. My play is at present in the hands of a producer in New York but, even in the fortunate event of its acceptance, I feel the necessity of finding immediate employment.

I am twenty-three years old and a native of Asheville, North Carolina. I do not know what impression of maturity my appearance may convey but it is hardly in excess of my age. In addition, my height is four or five inches over six feet, producing an effect on a stranger that is sometimes startling. I think you should know so much in advance, as the consideration may justly enter into any estimate of my qualifications.

If New York University feels justified in offering me employment as an instructor in English, and if I am satisfied with the offer, I promise to give the most faithful and efficient service of which I am capable.

I hope you will find it convenient to reply to this letter at some early date.

To HOMER A. WATT
[Telegram]

Boston, Mass.

January 21, 1924.

Accept instructorship. Will report Feb. first. Will you acknowledge wire.

To MARGARET ROBERTS

Hotel Albert, Room 2220
Eleventh St. & University Place
New York City

Sunday, Feb. 10, 1924

Dear Mrs. Roberts:

I am writing at length to answer your last heartening letter, which was written after I left home, and which has grown old, but more precious. I have seen a great many people, witnessed a number of events, and, like Satan, have grown, for the moment, weary of my goings to and fro and up and down the earth. It seems now that I will be fastened for several

months in this great madhouse of a city—for good or ill, who can say?—
but I think I have chosen wisely.

Briefly—since I saw you, I have been in New York for six weeks, when
I was busy with the Graham Memorial Fund at the University; later I went
to Boston and Cambridge for the holidays and remained a little more
than a month. The Guild held my play [1] for three or four months, as you
perhaps know,—held it until I was on the verge of madness and collapse
—and finally returned it, after wining and dining me, telling me I was "a
coming figure," and so on, and trying to extract a promise that all my
future work would be submitted to the Guild for consideration before any
other producer got hold of it. Of course, I made no such promise.

Before I left the city, however, one of the Guild directors,—a Jew by
the name of Langner,[2] and, I believe, a very wealthy, patent lawyer, had
me in to his apartment. He wanted me to cut the play thirty minutes—a
reduction I concede it needs. He wanted me, also, to cut the list of characters (this means cheaper production) and to revise—he insisted it
needed no rewriting—with a view to "tightening"; that is, to develop a
central plot which will run through each scene, and which would revolve
around a small group of central figures: Rutledge, the Negro, the girl, etc.
Of course this would mean a more conventional type of play. I told him I
had deliberately tried to avoid writing such a play; that I had written
a play with a plot which centered about the life and destiny of an entire
civilization, not about a few people. If I consented to this revision, Langner
promised his support and added that he was fairly certain he could place
the play. He observed, cheerfully, that he had really asked for very little;
that I could make all necessary changes in a week. This was a bit of
optimism in which I did not share. However, I promised to make the
effort, and departed for Cambridge.

Professor Baker was properly horrified when I communicated the evil
tidings. Not only, he said, would the proposed revision greatly cheapen the
play, but it was also impossible, since my play had been hailed and praised
as a new departure in American drama; its fate was on the rails. Thereupon, he read to me from a book on the American Theatre just published,
by Oliver Sayler,[3] in which my play is described at some length as "the
most radical and successful experiment ever made in the American Theatre." The Workshop comes in for its share of praise for doing my play.

This is, of course, sweet music to my ears, but my heart is assuming
a flinty cast, and the sound of the shekel is not unpleasing. I told Professor
Baker as much, as gently as I could, and he accused me of having allowed
New York to "commercialize" me in my six weeks' stay. This opened the

[1] *Welcome to Our City.*
[2] Lawrence Langner.
[3] *Our American Theatre.*

floodgates; I had heard enough of such talk. All the old and cruel sentimentality of the world, in its relation to the artistic, struck me with a bitter
blow. It was not a question of desiring cake and wine, I told him; it was a
question of naked need: Bread! Bread! Bread! Was this commercialism?
Then, indeed, was Christ a materialist when he multiplied the loaves?
Christ, by the way, unlike many of his present followers, was base enough
to recognize that men and women must be fed.

I broached the question of my future again. What must I do? The answer
came, as always: Write! Write! Do nothing else. Yes, but how? I had been
told this for three years: it was all, no doubt, very true, but not very helpful. I suggested teaching. At the suggestion, he looked as if he were being
rent limb from limb. Of all possible suggestions, this was the worst—and
he seemed to think that all of mine were incredibly bad. Finally—suprem-
est irony of all!—he confided that, after mature consideration, it seemed
to him that a year abroad was the very thing I needed most. The full
humor of this is apparent when I tell you that no later than August he had
descended on me in his wrath when I suggested this very thing, and he
had told me this would be colossal stupidity at the time. Now, plainly, he
has forgotten he ever made such a statement; the wind, for unknown
reasons, has veered from another corner, and he has tacked.

At any rate I began to understand—a bitter draught it was—that Professor Baker was an excellent friend, a true critic, but a bad counsellor. I
knew that, from this time on, the disposition of my life was mainly in my
own hands; that one profits, no matter how good the intention, not by the
experience of others, but only by such experience as touches him. At that
time I heard that New York University needed several new instructors for
the February term, and I directed the Harvard Appointment Bureau to
forward my letters, grades, and papers. I applied; I had friends in New
York speak for me. In two days I had their answer. An instructorship was
mine if I wanted it. I came to New York on a flying trip. I liked the men.
The offer was more than reasonable: $1800 for seven months over an
eight-hour-a-week teaching schedule; my work was to be concerned entirely with English composition. The men here at the University assure
me that I should easily complete my work, in and out of class, with three
hours a day. If this is true, I should have time to write.

There is one other advantage—a decided one. The college—this branch
of it—is but eight years old, and has no traditions. I am given great liberty;
personal idiosyncrasy is recognized and allowed. The students, moreover,
mainly Jewish and Italian, have come up from the East Side; many are
making sacrifices of a very considerable nature in order to get an education. They are, accordingly, not at all the conventional type of college
student. I expect to establish contacts here, to get material in my seven
months' stay that may prove invaluable. I am here until September; I must

teach through the summer. I am here where the theatre is—the theatre I love—and if I can't write plays, at least I can see 'em. What Professor Baker will say, or has said, I don't know. I never told him my decision.

But I have taught for two days now, and I am living; and nothing about me, so far as I know, has "suffered a sea change."

And this is all that I have to tell you for the time—over that which you know already: that you wax immensely in my affections and that, as ever, I am

Faithfully yours,

P.S. And—glory of glories—I'm free. The world is mine, and I, at present, own a very small but satisfying portion of it—Room 2220, at the Hotel Albert, where I hope presently to have the joy of reading one of your letters.

The new play [4] comes; I read it to a friend [5] in New Hampshire, who also writes 'em. He said I would sell it in spite of "hell and high water." The words are mine. And, by the way, I was in New Hampshire for four days and fished through the ice of the lake. This is the history.

The following letter to Frederic L. Day was found among Wolfe's own papers and is evidently a rough draft of a letter which was rewritten and mailed. Words in brackets denote those made illegible by the decomposition of the paper: double spaces denote separate fragments which may or may not follow in the order given them.

To FREDERIC L. DAY

Hotel Albert
New York

[April, 1924]

[With an arrow pointing to the picture of the Hotel Albert on the Letterhead]
Aint it perty, Fritz?

My dear Fritz:

Your letter is about the pleasantest thing that could have happened; if my pen trembles a little, remember it comes from eagerness. I've just finished reading yours. I noted, with a pained start, that you "hardly expect a reply"—and here one is off on the first mail. If this doesn't destroy

[4] *The House* (later *Mannerhouse*).
[5] Probably Henry Fisk Carlton.

for a time your faith in yourself as a character judge, you are safe [in] your own conceit. But you have little of [that], Fritz.

I don't know how long this letter will be but when I begin to sling ink, there's no stopping me. So, do your Daily Dozen now, take five deep breaths, and begin.

I have no intention of discussing here the wisdom or the folly of my decision to come to New York. I am more at peace than in four years, and during the moments when I have time to write, I write like a fiend. . . . I have over one hundred people in [my] classes here—boys and girls—mixed [in] race, but ninety per cent Jewish. Many of them come from New York's East Side. I believe I am making a contact which shall prove itself to be of the greatest value to me. I came without racial sentimentality—indeed with strong racial prejudice concerning the Jew, which I still retain. I shall learn—I am learning—a great deal.

Of one thing, of course, I am convinced. I am no school teacher. This, I think, will not occasion surprise in Cambridge. But *this* may surprise you —my little devils like me: I am "popular." And—keep this under the rose, Fritz—I am told that the girls—some of them are very pretty, you know— have a "crush" on me. The language is another's, I quote. A girl came to the English office late the other day—for what is technically known as "a conference." Nothing was wrong. She was passing her work. She was very pretty. On a sudden, however, she began to sob convulsively, ended by covering her face by her pretty little [hands]. Before I knew what was what, she was over on my shoulder. I looked around and saw that the head of the department was nowhere in sight. We continued the conference. Now, this is an amazing thing. Nothing was wrong: but it is April and something is stirring in their blood. And "in mine, in mine, so I sware [by] the rose." . . .

I am, I fear, an incurable romanticist cursed with a sense of humor. No true romantic should be able to see comedy, Fritz. You are forever "kidding" your own emotions, you know. And, certainly, it is not . . .

Perhaps you wonder, Fritz, what I have done with my ten-scene play— whether I have rewritten, revised, recast, cut, added, changed. No—I have done none of these things. As a matter of fact, I was hectored, badgered, driven, [harried?], to such a degree before, during, and after the play by commendation and criticism—none of which agreed—that I am wholeheartedly and completely tired of my first huge opus. I leave it to all the glory of its imperfections. My world has moved; I am writing a better play—I'll have nothing to do with the old.

Now, all this, I know, violates the Workshop standard of proper conduct for an "artist." If I were an "artist"—Thank God I'm not!—I should work unceasingly for five years until I had my play in that mythical state of perfection toward which every true 47-er is tending. But, unfortunately, I can not operate with such restrained decorum. I have a crude lusty young talent which is kicking up its coltish heels, and I have all I can do in keeping it within the pasture as it is. I have new ideas—I tire of a thing almost as soon as it's written. No man, I believe, writes solely to express himself— the idea of some kind of audience is always there—but, I suppose, I come as close to writing for pure expression—simply, that is, to get it out of me —as anyone you know.

Of course I realize that this is not likely to fill my wallet.

New York has been a stimulus, it has increased my enthusiasm for some things, my contempt for others. My love of the theatre has grown: my dislike of most of the people I have met who are concerned with the theatre has grown, also. If a play of mine is done, I think I should prefer Belasco or Geo. M. Cohan to do it rather than the Guild or that abominable little clique at the Provincetown. The latter, by the way, have had my play over four months now. I have gone to them repeatedly, pushing my way through the crowd of short-haired women and long-haired men who fill their rooms, in order to get news, news. Each time an evil-looking [hag?] with red hair has gone into a little room, shuffled some papers, and returned with the information that the playreader had the play, that "you shall certainly hear next week." Each time I have been asked for my address, and it has been noted piously. A month ago I went back for the last time. Escaping the red-headed harpy and a few of the degenerates, I got into the little room and asked the typist. She opened a cabinet and found my play—under an inch of dust. Ah God! It had been returned. I was honestly glad: I wanted it back. Besides, what would one of their productions, in their lousy little theatre, net me? Nothing.

But no. It had not been returned. It had not even been read. But,—she was sure that "in another week"— Groping blindly for the door, I staggered out. Of course I have heard nothing since. But I have almost finished a long and vitriolic letter which I end with three words: *Go to Hell* and which I conclude "with renewed assurances of my warm personal detestation." Of course, I tell them that I am young, I am unknown and that, therefore, they have been insolent. Such people know only two moods— insolence and servility. After all, as I tell them again, the problem is simple:—

it is one of fundamental honesty.

Perhaps this will shock you. It is not a good beginning when one is obscure and needs patronage. Unfortunately, Fritz, I have not the spirit to bow before such insults as these. In adversity I grow more stubborn. But— I am beginning to see that a mere course in play-writing is not enough. There should be a sister course in peddling, auctioneering, servility, fawning, licking, and whining—a kind of sales-course, you know.

They tell me constantly that one must have the friendship of such people. It is not true! It may be harder but, by God, this inner *daemon* of mine is not at the mercy of their knavery; this flame, once fired, may not be taken lightly, and, so help me God, the day will come when, unaided, I shall hammer them down upon their creaking knees.

This is big boasting, but men grow modest on prosperity—

it's a dishonest virtue. And I have sense to understand there's something schoolboyish in my ravings.

It amounts to this: they withhold the trumpet, but poetry remains: they cannot take it from me.

And that brings me to the proposal of Miss Helburn that I look her up. What for? I am not good at self-introduction. What is she going to say to me? Will a look of wonder greet me when I tell her that I have come at her suggestion? Will it be supplanted by vague recollection when I tell her she spoke of me to you—that it was through you. Will a perfunctory conversation ensue, in which she remembers vaguely that my play showed "promise"? By God, Fritz, I won't stand for it. A talky woman is bad enough; a woman organized artistically is to me—who am a feudalist— intolerable. Lemon and Langner were nice to me; I remember them with affection.

But the Gods in Olympus spoke by messenger through the clouds. Therefore, for all of me, they may go to Hell. They had my play four months; they drove me frantic by their inaction. Finally, they returned it with wretched evasiveness: "good—but doesn't fit in with our program now"— "perhaps you were a little prejudiced in Scene IX—but, then, perhaps you weren't."

And then, this charming Miss Helburn, whose lily-white hand has this far never clasped mine, asked G.P.—on a train somewhere—if I was making any of the changes suggested. Why do they pry around so? It goads me to fury. They could have talked to me if they had had any genuine interest. And now, damn them, they'll come to me—or not at all.

$150 every month, Fritz, gives one a tremendous sense of confidence in his [profanity?].

And by the way—I am being paid in twelve monthly instalments rather than in seven or eight. That means that in September when I finish, I shall have $750 due me. I'm going to England in October—[——] steerage. My plan is to go to Cornwall, to some little village where it's cheap—and stay a month or two—writing, writing, writing. I'm going to Heaven, that is, in October.

I am charmed, delighted to know that my disappearance has been completely successful—that the frantic efforts of the 47-ers to discover me have been foiled. Pray don't give me away, Fritz. It's die, dog, or eat the hatchet for me now. Alone or nothing. I want to do it unbeholden to anyone or anything. I feel like the Count of Monte Cristo who already has [——] "The world is mine," and who is to return twenty years later with fortune and a noble name.

As for 47, I don't think it will experience great difficulty in forgetting me. Its mind functions from day to day; to-day's masterpiece is forgotten to-morrow; yesterday's lion is not remembered to-day—last week's culture is outmoded and supplanted by a new already. There's good, kindly, foolish, futile Miss Loveman. Last year she pursued me. If I didn't go to her terrible teas on Sunday I was reprimanded Monday. I was Milton, Shakespeare, Keats—and more. At Christmas this year I saw her at the Opera House. A look of vague recognition lighted [up her face]. Somewhere she had met [me] before. I started to speak. She held up one finger admonishingly. "Don't speak! I know you! I have your name on the tip of my tongue. It will all come back in a moment."

And there, dear Fritz, spoke 47. Esau's skin, you know, but Jacob's voice.

I shall cut myself away entirely—from G. P. and all the others. However, he seems to have severed the cord already. For me the wine dark seas send coiling enticements; my bark puts out and as Columbus I shall find a green new world, where my spirit shall quicken, [and like] Odysseus, I shall come upon the enchanted isles—perhaps to eat the Lotus and sink Lethewards into a drowsy obliviousness of this present actual existence [————].

I must decide for myself. Everything for myself—and the wonder and the glory of that has not yet faded. For it was but recently that I put utter dependence in the power of older men to decide for me. A few quick words, an authoritative setting to rights and the wounding business of my life would be adjusted. And yet, in over two years, I never suggested a plan for my future to G. P. that was not condemned; nor did I get one from him which was practicable or which would devolve on him [————]. Lately for my future. I suggested *home, New York, teaching, Europe* —all, particularly *Europe,* were condemned. And now, at Christmas, when the thing is impossible, and as if the idea had never been suggested,

Professor Baker said: "You know, I think it would be a good thing for you if you took a year abroad now."

[THE LETTER BREAKS OFF UNFINISHED HERE]

To GEORGE WALLACE

Hotel Albert, New York

Friday, April 11, 1924.

My dear George:

I am sending you a pome—writ by me. It has the full flavor of the romantic ironist, you see. If you will give it to the girl from New Orleans [1] with my compliments, and wait until she reads it, noting her comments and reactions, I promise to buy you a horse's-neck at Steve Bozzanetti's.

And, believe me, George, with renewed assurances of reverence and respect, and all that sort of thing, I am

A.D.—2024

The great drums of the world may beat,
And the trumpets of earth may blare.
But, beneath the thunder of the feet,
Silent, I shall not care
Or stir, unless you come, my sweet,
With lilac or rose in your hair
And twice in pain, and thrice again,
The earth may be cloven through,
And my statue may get down and walk
From its place in the avenue.
I shall not know, I shall not care!
But I *shall* know if you
Should stir the grasses over me
　　With feathery, airy tread,
Should pass with the rustle of scented silk
　　Above my earthy bed;
And one of my bones would stand erect,
　　To show you I am not dead.

(Cetera Desunt) Know what that means, son?

[1] Efforts to identify "the girl from New Orleans" have met with no success.

To MARGARET ROBERTS

Hotel Albert
New York

May 5, 1924

Dear Mrs. Roberts:

This, briefly, to thank you for your fine letter, and to render my poor judgment on the subject nearest to your heart— ——'s future. I think I understand his position. Did you know I fell in love when I was sixteen with a girl who was twenty-one? [1] Yes, honestly—desperately in love. And I've never quite got over it. The girl married, you know: she died of influenza a year or two later. I've forgotten what she looked like, except that her hair was corn-colored. A woman five years older can make putty of a boy of eighteen. In one way, she is as old as she will ever be, and a great deal depends upon her own quality. . . . It seems that at this period man comes to grips with something elemental—beyond him. I'm beginning to question the wisdom of mixing education with adolescence, Greek with Seventeen, literature with love. Perhaps the academics should come later when we have leavened our madness with a grain of method. I'm not sure, and I suppose there's not time enough. . . .

You speak of Harvard. That's most difficult. I don't know what to say. But I'm sure of this:—if I had gone to Cambridge instead of to Chapel Hill—when I was sixteen—the result would have been catastrophic. Of course, —— is a big, fine, strapping fellow, well-grown, mature in appearance, with associations with wealthy boys which may have given him a kind of balance. But this, I think, is *now* true of Harvard: no boy should go there now until he is ready to mine his own ore. If he is still in need of dependence on someone or something—a *very* real and honest need, by the way—Harvard is not the place, I think. A sensitive young Southerner, fond of companionship and warmth, will find the sledding rough, I'm afraid. Of course, with a student of one of the great academies—Andover or Exeter—the situation is different, I believe. He is graduated with his class and accompanies them to Cambridge. This occurs as naturally as the transition, say, from Asheville High to Chapel Hill. But I have seen hundreds of boys submerged in the student life of Harvard. Unknown they enter—are swiftly appalled by the vastness of the system and its impersonality—and unknown they leave, at the end of four years, with a feeling of disenchantment and futility.

The quality of Harvard instruction is very high—the highest, I believe— but, again, many succeed in evading all attempts at education on the part

[1] Clara Paul.

of the University faculty. It is not difficult to slide through; and, in addition, you must prepare to calculate the probable effects of a metropolitan community of over one million people upon a fascinated young stranger thrust suddenly in from the provinces. A change of climate and geography might be intensely valuable . . . now. Remember, there are a number of first-rate small colleges in New England, beautifully located, with admirable scholastic standards. There is Amherst, for example, which still demands Greek, I'm told. And Williams, a lovely place, walled in by mountains not unlike our own. And Bowdoin—and, of course, Dartmouth, one of the best. In all these places a young fellow might assert himself, and grow. . . .

As for me, I work and am fairly happy. Really, I'm having a wonderful experience. This place—particularly the University—swarms with life, Jewish, Italian, Polish. My little devils like me. I tell them every week that I'm no teacher. I suppose they can see that for themselves; and perhaps that is why they like me. The head of the department [1] has asked me to come back next year, but I have given him no answer. The desire to write—to create—has, for the first time, become almost a crude animal appetite. And this is because of the obstacles thrown in the path of creation. During the few hours left to me, I write like a fiend on one of the finest plays [2] you ever saw. My first term is almost over—two weeks more, in fact—gone like a flash!

And did you know that I'm going to Heaven in September. That is, to England. From September 1, six months pay will be due me—September through February. This is $900. With economy I can stay over five or six months. I'm going down to Cornwall first—it's very beautiful, I'm told —and bury myself in a country village for two months. There I shall write my heart out. Then over the country, into London for a few days, Scotland, and France.

This is all for the present. I've snatched Time to write this. But, during the examination period, you shall have greater detail. The Provincetown Theatre has had my play [3] five months. I can hear nothing. One of the editors of D. Appleton left a note at the hotel this morning. He wants my play [4]—the Theatre Guild suggested it—to read for publication. I shall let him read it; I doubt that I shall let him publish—even if he wants to. Certainly, not as long as someone may produce it.

The new play is an epic. I believe in it with all my heart. Dear God! If I but had the time to write.

[1] Professor Watt.
[2] *The House* (*Mannerhouse*).
[3] *Welcome to Our City.*
[4] *Welcome to Our City.*

Professor Koch of Chapel Hill bounded into town a week or so ago, and looked me up. He wants to put one of my juvenile one-acts—the *Buck Gavin* thing—into his new book [5] which Holt is bringing out soon. He is insistent, and has just sent me a copy of the thing. I'm not ashamed of the play, but I wrote it on a rainy night, when I was seventeen, in three hours. Something tells me I should hate to see my name attached now. Of course I couldn't tell Koch that. Besides, he had his chance two or three years ago, when he brought his first book out. Please don't *publish*—but I'll give you my honest opinion: I believe his eagerness to publish the little play now comes from a suspicion that I'm going to get famous in a hurry now—God knows why!—and he wants to *ticket* me, so to speak. This is a rotten thing to say, but it's my honest opinion. I sent Koch an act or two of my new play [6]—you heard the prologue—and he did everything but break down and weep. It was the greatest thing ever; I was the American Bernard Shaw, etc.

Everyone, you see, is enthusiastic, but I notice that *I* earn my own living. The Theatre Guild is cordial. When am I going to bring my new play in? Their officials want to know me. Will I have lunch? Their play reader Lemon,[7] trumpets my name abroad. He told me recently he had spoken of me at the banquet of some dramatic association. I am grateful, but how I wish someone would *produce* one of my plays. . . .

But—I learn. I am acquiring patience. And I'm quite willing to wait a year or two for the unveiling exercises. Do you know, all that really matters right now is the knowledge that I am twenty-three, and a golden May is here. The feeling of immortality in youth is upon me. I am young, and I can never die. Don't tell me that I can. Wait until I'm thirty. Then I'll believe you.

I never hear from you but my respect for your intelligence waxes. You are a lovely, beautiful woman. Other women I have known—young and old—who wanted to mother me, to ruffle my hair when it's curly, or to feed me. But you mother the minds and spirits of young men until they grow incandescent. That is a nobler, finer thing.

So, it seems, you are a great woman.

To you all, as ever, my deepest love,

[5] *Carolina Folk Plays, Second Series.*

[6] *The House* (*Mannerhouse*). Probably Wolfe had read the prologue to her when he was in Asheville in October, 1923.

[7] Courtenay Lemon.

To GEORGE WALLACE

Hotel Albert, New York

Monday, Sept 8 [1924]

Et tu Brute:—One would think, from the insolent silence that has greeted my letters to hypothetical friends, that a man of my kidney has no higher purpose than to submit in silence. But 'ware the tiger! If I don't get some answers I shall turn and rend the world. Now, I charge thee, George, do thou as I desirest, and show thyself a good lad, a tall fellow.

Some days agone I writ to Mistress Ann Macdonald,[1] pleading pressure of time, and the exigencies of an impending voyage, and desiring her to get for me both copies of my play. Mistress Ann hath not suffered to answer yet, and I commission thee to go to her, lay siege, and take the play by frontal attack.

The point is, I must make haste, my dear boy, for time presses; and I infer by their silence, and the one letter, which I showed you, that they have no profitable intentions toward my play, but would cheer me with sounding praise and apparent consideration. (T'Hell wit dat stuff, George.) I must send the play out before I go: there *really* is a producer who wants to see it, and you might hasten its return if you hinted as much.

I wrote Miss M. about a week since, urging the necessity of speed: but in this hustling, go-ahead, up-and-coming theatrical business, speed means anything within six months. My letter, I fear, was full of proud and vaunting speech, courteous enough, however, as regards Miss M. Among many other things, I remember saying I was tired tossing gold nuggets at folks' heads, and that when Caesar returned to Rome again, (God help me—I said that, too) the people would come to him at the gates. If she is disposed to look askance, or do some other angry thing, you might say that I have been drunk these six weeks past, and have added hysteria to irrationality. That should protect you, my boy.

All this, of course, is written on the supposition that you have not drowned in a New Hampshire lake, and are again working your garden in Pleasantville.

Really, my dear George, if you would see me you'd best come in soon. I've had my last class, and was the recipient (that's the word, eh?) of a Dunhill pipe from one of my adoring classes; I give the final examinations Friday, and hope to *leave* somewhere around the twentieth, possibly a bit la-tah. . . .

Cordially, though in view of your perverse, unfriendly, and revolting silence, you deserve no such greeting,

[1] Miss MacDonald was a reader and translator with The Neighborhood Playhouse, to which Wolfe had submitted *Welcome to Our City*.

The following letter was evidently never presented to Professor Baker, since there is no trace of it in his own files.

To GEORGE PIERCE BAKER

On board the Cunard R.M.S. *Lancastria.*

Wednesday, October 29, [1924]

Dear Professor Baker:

On shipboard I have had the pleasure of the acquaintance of Mr. ——. ——. . . . His interests, he tells me, have always been creative—in short, he has wanted to write. He was faced in his thirties by that very blunt and very terrible economic necessity which most of us must face, and now that he has overcome it, he has the great good sense to abandon the profession which has always been hostile to his genuine interests. . . . I have given you so much of Mr. ——'s more intimate history because I know such material interests you, and may influence your decision toward a prospective applicant; and further, it is because Mr. —— feels he may apply for admission to 47 that I write this letter, hoping it may be of some small service to him should he ever care to present it.

As I write you, we are limping comfortably along through the North Atlantic at 300 miles a day, with an injury to the starboard engine that may delay us a day or two. I am taking with me the prologue and three acts of my new play, "The House." (Perhaps not my potential best, but better than anyone else's). At any rate, everything looks good when you do it. I am going, after my year in New York (in the "Latin Quarter" at the University) like a discoverer: the world is opening before me like an oyster, and valiant deeds are in me. . . . Ideas are simply boiling in my pan; the next one is a most tremendous thing. Also, I started my new birthday on 1500 words a day: and I shall continue.

I don't know where this will find you, since this is your sabbatical year, but I have heard that you are going abroad, and if you are near me, I shall ferret you out; and you may caution me on my lack of discipline, and on my heart affairs, and I shall promise faithfully to heed your warnings— haven't I always *promised?* At any rate, I may send the new play—if you'll stand for it—and prove all my boastings.

I have been silent a period of months—perhaps you've wondered why. I was in the furnace there in Jerusalem—I sponged up a million impressions; I admired, loathed, loved a million things; and in between the damnable corrections on Freshman papers, I wrote like a fiend—quite honestly the best work I've ever done. I cut myself away from all of which I had been a part; I went like a nameless ghost at night along the streets of the City—but I [got her?]

It was simply hell at times, but I'm older and wiser, and that counts.

I think you know how I really feel toward you. You are just about the best friend I ever had, and no year passes that does not compel renewed and increased affection for your character and courage.

P.S. Some of the most amusing people in the world are on this ship. There's an English cockney who has confessed to an interest in the theatre, and who asked me if I had ever seen "The Eyesiest Wye."

Wolfe's letter of November 8, 1924, to George W. McCoy of The Asheville Citizen *was written in an attempt to sell material describing his European trip to that newspaper. His journal of the voyage over, "A Passage to England," was never published, but a short piece entitled "London Tower" appeared in the Sunday, July 19, 1925, issue of the* Citizen.

McCoy had attended The North State School in Asheville, but did not actually meet Wolfe until he entered the University of North Carolina in Wolfe's senior year there. Later, when he was working on the Citizen, *he became a good friend of Wolfe's, who liked to drop in at the news room late at night to see him. He is now Managing Editor of the* Citizen, *and Secretary of The Thomas Wolfe Memorial Association.*

To GEORGE W. McCOY

The Imperial Hotel
Russell Square
London

Saturday, November 8, 1924

Dear George:

I am writing you this in the most extreme haste, in the hope that it shall bring us both to better fortune. I arrived in London on Wednesday after an amazing voyage, and I am now lost in the beauty and mystery and fascination of this ancient and magnificent city. I came over on the *Lancastria*, a 17,000 ton Cunarder. . . . The cabin list was small—ninety-six—but in that number were knaves, fools, aristocrats, tradesmen, fat Americans . . ., English traders and gentlemen who had traversed the seven seas many times, and who thought nothing of a two weeks' voyage to Chicago and back.

George—I put it all on paper from day to day; I let nothing escape me, and even when the sea made me feel a bit sorry for myself I put it down. Now that voyage—the poignant emotion of it all, and the astonishing differences in habit and custom and opinion of different races, English and American—is recorded hastily, it is true; sometimes clumsily. But it is there. I don't know what to do with it. I might send it to some American magazine, but it is a conglomerate of so many things—drama, comment, incident, opinion—that I scarcely know what to call it. I have given it a title: "A Passage to England." It is written, George, in my own hand on sheets of white and yellow paper. And my penmanship is poor.

Now to the point. Some of the *Citizen* people suggested that I send them a weekly letter. No pay was suggested, and perhaps none was intended. At any rate, I give and bequeath outright to you this letter with certain conditions. If it is suitable for publication in the *Citizen*—I don't know that it is—take it to Mrs. Roberts at once, read it to her, and ask her to censor it, if necessary. Much of it is so personal, written so rapidly, and I am so *close* to it—not enough detachment—that I don't know whether I work myself an injury (in the eyes of the burghers, you know) at times. Let her word go: if she gives the word to print it as it is, and the paper wants it, print it.

Now to brass tacks again. If this letter gets published and is of sufficient interest to call for others, see if you can get me some money for them. What I am doing from day to day now, primarily for my own use later when I shall create from these sources, is to watch people—their manners of eating, drinking, sleeping, acting. For these are the things that count. I have learned more of England on that boat by watching a Cockney at mortal sword-play with an English aristocrat—we were all at the table —than I ever did in reading the articles on political opinion and elections of all the Philip Gibbses and David Lawrences in the world. And people everywhere—their drama, their emotion, their humor—are interested in people everywhere else. Perhaps if I can do the thing plainly and clearly and honestly, without fear or favor, people at home may be interested.

I need the money—I want to stay a year, if possible. I have the utmost faith in your integrity and character—that is why I write you this foolish but very *earnest* letter, leaving the whole matter at your disposition. . . .

I am sending along the manuscript of the voyage over to-morrow.[1] Answer me as soon as you are able to let me know what you can do with it. Perhaps it might be Sunday feature stuff. If you sell my letters to one or many papers, you get your own cut-in, of course. If the paper doesn't want the stuff, give it to Mrs. Roberts to keep for me.

Since coming to London I have walked the queer, blind, narrow, incredible, crooked streets of the city, looking at the people, hearing them

[1] Wolfe did not actually send the manuscript at this time. In March, 1925, he sent the Prologue of it to Mrs. Roberts, but it was never published.

talk, getting them. Late at night, early in the morning, when the streets are deserted, I traverse great sections of the city, going down narrow alleys, stopping at small refreshment wagons, at pubs, taxi stands, anywhere, listening to them talk. And all the time I am making notes—London and New York, England and America.

I was twenty four a month ago, George. I would to God I might be twenty four forever. This is a magnificent adventure and the world is opening like an oyster.

Answer P.D.Q.
American Express Co.,
Haymarket St.,
London.
Sending mss. to-morrow.

To HOMER A. WATT

[Paris]

Jan. 15, 1925

Dear Professor Watt:

I am conscious that the letter I promised to write you has been long delayed; I shall tell you the extraordinary reasons for the delay.

I have had an astonishing voyage—I spent 1 month in England, went down almost every back alley in London, and into most of the disreputable pubs; about six weeks ago I came to Paris and settled in a small hotel in the Latin Quarter. I went to this place with my bags very late at night—one o'clock—the concierge who admitted me had been wounded in the war, and gave a great groan when he saw the baggage, and when I told him my room was five flights up. He pointed to his crippled leg, and hobbled around painfully; I suggested that he keep one of the bags until morning; I would take the other two myself; he agreed to this gladly. The story is that during the night a man entered, asked for a woman formerly resident of the hotel, and on the way out, stole my bag.

The bag was old and battered, the articles in it were not of great value; what it did contain that could not be replaced was the prologue and two acts in manuscript of the play [1] I had lived with for more than a year. I know it sounds silly, but nothing has hit me like this since the death of my brother Ben six years ago. I moved to another hotel the next day: I bought paper and swore that I should rewrite the play in two weeks—by

[1] *The House* which finally became *Mannerhouse*.

New Year's—and on January third I had not only recreated what was lost, but completed an entire first draft. Since then I have been re-writing. For three weeks I saw or spoke practically to no one; then I met friends, and have passed the time very pleasantly since. Good or bad, what I have done in these past five weeks is the best I have ever done. I am rather glad the thing was stolen: it has helped me.

The hotel people, after a very nasty scene, paid me 500 francs for the loss of the valise: they suggested it was a conspiracy (which they knew to be false), and I told them they were dishonest scoundrels—after I got my fingers on the 500.

Since very charming friends—including two attractive ladies—have purchased a car, and want me to go South with them for two or three months, I think I shall do this.

You spoke to me early about the February term; later you suggested that the matter was uncertain, because of larger enrollment, and so on. At any rate, although my own money is nearly gone, I feel that everything that is happening to me now is too important to be checked violently. I shall stay over, if possible, some months longer: my mother, I believe, will help me.

In five weeks time I have acquired enough French to read very easily —and to speak very badly, but comprehensibly, without the necessity of beginning all over. I am entering a new world of art and letters; during the past two weeks I have been to some incredible places—working men's dance halls; all night lodgings where the wretches are huddled in sleep, a hundred to a room, over long tables, drugged by their own weariness, and by the over-powering stench of the bodies, breathing as one like a great terrible organ.

If I didn't make it sufficiently plain before I left, let me emphasize now the gratitude and affection I bear toward you for your kindliness, patience, and forbearance last year—for me, just hatching out, a genuine anno mirabilis. When I come back I shall certainly be in to see you. If you only have time, meanwhile, to write me a line or two, you would give me a great deal of delight and pleasure.

If this seems to you to be hastily scribbled by a man coming out of a dream, I think your intuitions will be correct. But I'm all right now, and beginning to live.

The following letter was written by Wolfe in reply to one from his brother Fred which informed him that Mabel Wolfe Wheaton had undergone an operation, reproached him for having lost a check sent him by his mother,

*and suggested that it was about time he came home. In a comment made
later on this letter, Fred Wolfe says: "I condemned Tom then, for I truly
did not understand what he was about . . . I plead guilty that I and also
perhaps other members of the family (certainly not Mama) misunderstood
him then and 'bore down' too hard on him. I think Tom and I understood
each other fully later."*

To FRED W. WOLFE

Paris

January 27, 1925

Dear Fred:

I have just received your letter which contained the news of Mabel's
operation; I am writing her at the same time I send you this. I appreciate
the motives which kept you from writing me at the time. I am deeply
thankful that everything has turned out so well, and that she is recovering.

Also, let me thank you very much for your contribution to the check. I
have thanked Mama in a letter which should be home at this time. That
letter also contains explanations of the loss of the first check and that I
stopped payment here, and that it is absolutely safe.[1] It also gives an
account of my activities here and in England. I think you may understand
when you read it that there has been no foolishness on my part, and that I
have been hard at work.

You speak of my three months in Europe, and conclude that I will be
ready to come home about this time. I do not think you quite understand
the circumstances: I am going to try to explain them to you now.

I think you understand, Fred, that I have the greatest respect and admiration for you—I do not believe you have always understood my motives,
or a certain purpose in my life towards which I am striving. I want you
to know that I am ready and willing at all times to earn my living, and
that I am able to do this by teaching as instructor in some university. I
want you to know that I have worked faithfully and hard upon this trip,
and that until I received the check so generously sent by you and Mama, I
was using my own money. That it should be necessary for me to ask for
any help to anyone is a matter of the deepest regret to me. It is not my

[1] In a letter to his mother dated January 20, 1925 (see page 98 of *Thomas Wolfe's
Letters to His Mother*) Wolfe wrote: "What happened was this: I got your check
in January. It was made payable to you and drawn on the American Express, Paris.
. . . Your name was *not* on the back. I went to the American Express Co. here to
cash it. They explained that it could be cashed by no one but Julia E. Wolfe, and
not until her endorsement was on the back. . . . Somewhere, somehow—where,
when I don't know—I lost your check . . . but I am quite sure no one can cash it."

intention to ask anyone, particularly members of my family, for any considerable help on this trip. As I believe I told you, it will be possible, in May or June, for me to procure assistance, if I need it, from a friend who will inherit money at that time.

You must try to understand that I am working very hard, practically alone as to friends, because I believe in myself and in my eventual capacity to succeed. You must try to understand, furthermore, that the road I have chosen is not an easy one, and that the purpose of this trip abroad is to prevent the necessity, if possible of my return to teaching—teaching which is critical work, and which sometimes kills, or injures badly, a creative talent. It was my purpose when I came over here to stay as long as I could—eight or ten months, if possible, and in that time to finish my play, and to try to write some short stories for the commercial market. This was the last chance I gave myself before my return to teaching. As you know I had about $400. I mentioned this to Mama; the understanding was that I should go as far as I could upon it. I have been for three months in France and England: England is expensive. I have done as much travelling as I could. I have spent about $150 a month, travel and all, including the journey from London here.

Now it is my purpose to go to the South of France where I shall settle down in a small place and do my work. I expect to do this on less than $100 a month. When I return to America I shall come third class on the *Leviathan;* the fare is only $90.

If I return to America now, I return without a job—instructors at New York University have already been appointed for February, and it is the only place I know of where instructors are employed in the middle of the year. Furthermore, I know I can live a great deal more cheaply here than in New York.

I know that I have no right to ask anything from any of you, but I do feel that I set out with a certain understanding as to my plans and the length of my stay; I think I am entitled to this final chance to come through, without enslaving my time and what talent I may have as a writer, for years to come, or for all time, as a teacher.

If I can secure $500, I shall be able, I think, to complete my time, and to do my work. I am sorry my trip should cost anyone anything, but I do not believe it is costing a great deal.

I want you to remember, Fred, that I have believed in something in myself enough to put all the money I had, all that was given me, all that came to me from Papa's will, in my education and in my development. All I have to-day are two ragged suits of clothes, a few articles of apparel, and the manuscript of two plays. I submit that it has taken some courage to do this; a great deal of belief. It would be rather easy to be hard now;

I am not in a position to defend myself. But from you I expect no such treatment.

Somehow or other, the health of my family permitting, I intend to stay over here four or five months longer. If I do not succeed by that time in making my way alone, none of you will have cause to complain thereafter that I had not supported myself wholly and alone.

I trust that this will find you all in good health, with Mabel fully recovered from her sickness. With much love to all,

I am sorry the cable cost so much—it came to about $5.00; but at that time I thought I was going South with friends in an automobile. Your letter changes a good deal of that; I think I shall continue to stay here in Paris until I hear again from home. Good luck.

The following letter to Mabel Wolfe Wheaton was evidently never mailed, but was found among Wolfe's own papers.

To MABEL WOLFE WHEATON

[Paris]

[January 28, 1925]

Dear Mabel:

Fred's letter came to-day which informed me of your illness. I am terribly distressed and shocked to hear of it, but I pray God your trouble is now over; that you are on your way to perpetual health and happiness. God knows you deserve it.

You rarely—hardly ever—write me, Mabel, but I ask of you earnestly that you do it now. You may think it strange that I turn to you now, but it is quite honest and instinctive with me. I believe in you as one of the few women I have ever known to whom one could turn when one was in trouble: that, I believe, is why Papa loved you so.

And for God's sake, say nothing of what I am going to tell you either to Fred or Mama. Don't be worried. I haven't disgraced myself. I have worked hard and written, I believe, my best play—the unfinished play which was stolen with my old valise.[1] That doesn't matter: it was a good thing, for it made me work. And it is true also that I have run out of my own money and have had to appeal to the family for help; but I shall not be travelling hereafter, or living in big cities, and if I can get as much as $500 these next five months, I shall be able to live, travel in Italy and work.

[1] *Mannerhouse.*

And although I have no right to ask it, I hope from the bottom of my heart that Mama can spare it; because I am taking this last desperate chance to save myself from teaching. It is not my own money now—nothing is my own, except my belief and courage—but I believe it is the chance that will put me through.

And, my dear, I want you to know that I would not willingly take a cent that belongs to you or Fred—if the hope of repaying you were also taken. I am a mad fool who loves a vision, who has pursued a dream; it is harder than real estate or cash registers, I believe, but I know in my heart it will one day—very soon, I hope—come true.

But I come to you for another reason. This letter is so different from others I have written you that you may think me drunk or crazy—I am certainly not drunk—I want to say "my dear" to you for the first time, because I am badly hurt, and I believe in that thing in you which comes to the aid of people who have been hurt. And for God's sake, Mabel, don't laugh at me when you read this, because I'm a man now, and this thing is quite real. I'm hopelessly, madly, desperately in love with a woman who doesn't care a tinker's damn about me. She's in love with someone who doesn't care a tinker's damn about her. To make it harder, I know him: he's one of my best friends. Don't think I'm wasting my time mooning about it: there is only one impulse in me now—to work like a fiend, to cut her out of my heart, to forget. She has gone now—out of Paris. I shall not see her again—never; for there is something in me that won't break.

I wish to God there were something in me that would break, that would break down completely; but all I can feel now is that I should like for my heart to burst, but there's too much granite in it—it will never burst.

And if there's anything great in me I believe it's coming out now. I believe love is making a man of me. I hope you won't laugh at that, either. I took the thing without a whine; I told her good-bye; I told her not to worry—that I was the kind of person to whom these things mean very little; that I should be over it in a few days. Then I went away and left her.

Well, I shall get over it in the same way proud passionate fools of my sort get over these things. . . . You must not think anything of this woman that is not true: I tell you now, and I will always be ready to affirm it, that she is a great, good, and beautiful person. Also, because I suppose you always tie up love and marriage, I tell you that I never had the faintest intention of marrying her, or anyone. She is five years older than I am; as regards the world, she is a child. She's from a rich old Boston family who have kept her under lock and key all her life.

[THE LETTER BREAKS OFF HERE]

The following unfinished letter to Kenneth Raisbeck was probably never sent.

To KENNETH RAISBECK

[Paris]

[January 30 (?) 1925]

Dear Kenneth:

I was very sorry not to see you before I left. You told me you would see me before I went. I'm getting out of Paris as quick as I may, because the exchequer holds only about enough to take me where I'm going.

My dear old boy, as I get poorer, I get more grimly-gay. Perhaps I shall not be thoroughly happy until my last shirt has gone. Then I have visions of a tall ship along the docks of Marseilles, and a roaring life across the wine dark sea; to Quinquireme, or Nineveh, or Ophir, or wherever a fabled sea breaks on a fabled shore with perfumed waves. You've got to wrench the rhythm if you read that last one right.

I have had a terrible letter from home, and have spent these last few days quite pleasantly in hell. When I want gaiety, I refer to our little comic opera for a background. So much for contrast!

For God's sake, see that you get some work done on this trip. And don't moon—not until the time comes. It is quite surprising, you know, how much steel one's heart can hold; a good twelve inches is driven in, you break off six of them that stick out, the rest is grown over, and you go on quite nicely, thank you. I think if I were ever thrown into the pot, like the unfortunate gentleman in Jim Daly's "Crucible," [1] I should realize quite a tidy sum in pig iron.

[THE LETTER BREAKS OFF HERE]

The following unrelated and undated fragments were found in Wolfe's own files and were evidently never mailed, or recopied into final drafts and mailed. Since there are many variations on the same general theme, a selection has been made from the great mass of them to give the gist of the material. They were all evidently written between January and April, 1925, and are all undated. Therefore, they are arranged according to general tone and subject matter rather than in any definite chronology.

[1] One of the 47 Workshop plays.

[Paris]

[January 29 (?) 1925]

My dear ———:

I am on my way South with more money than I had hoped to have. I had 300 francs left and had to pay my hotel bill with part of that sum. Third class passage to the South is 135 francs. I went in and talked with the woman next door—the same one who had invited me to lunch. She loaned me 500 francs. It was an action of a very high order: I shall not forget it even when the debt is paid.

These past two days your humble servant has passed very pleasantly in Hell. A letter came from a brother at home: my youngest married sister had an operation January 12—a very serious and painful operation. She is getting over it now. I want to tell you something about her: she is ten years older than I am. Since she was ten years old she was the only person who could manage my father; he was bigger than I am, and quick as a cat; occasionally he drank terrifically. During the last eight years of his life, he was dying palpably—a huge, magnificent machine going to pieces: she gave her strength to him. She has lived in a constant state of nervous irritation and excitability: she is fierce, tender, angry, biting, caressing, by turns. Her voice breaks in sheer desperation. She is 5 feet 11 tall, and thin as a rail. She blazes with restless energy. Strong commonplace people drink her vitality like wine: they never forget her, and they return to her. I have never known her to be "brave" about anything. I have seen her weep, fret, and despair; I have seen her face death two or three times. She would die if she had nothing to spend herself on: nothing to weep, fret, despair about. She wants to be told she is generous, good, thoughtful. She likes adulation. But when one suffers a hurt, her voice is low and gentle: she has large wonderful hands, and all the pain goes out under their touch.

The simple and terrific fact is that with all her fuming, fretting, weeping, her love of adulation, I have never seen her do a selfish thing. I mean it is simply not a part of her. I say it is a *terrific* fact: it is. There's nothing beyond it. She has more human greatness in her than any woman I've ever known. I suppose, honestly, that's why I sometimes get tired of the women I meet—particularly women who are carefully calculated. You're not: that's why I liked you.

My brother also suggested in his letter that I come home: three months of Europe, he thought, was enough. . . . Beside this pleasant little communication the events of the past three weeks provide a rosy, pinky background. So much for contrast. God forgive me for ever playing golf with my emotions: yet, God knows, we must take our comic opera seriously, or how the hell do we face the other? I wrote a painful and humiliating letter home, in which I pled for $500, a few months time, and a final chance to save myself from the deep damnation of Freshman composition.

I am engaged at the present time in the composition of a story with the magnificent title of "Pigtail Alley":[1] try as I may, parts of it look good.

I owe you money and I've got to write you. I take pleasure in it, too; in this one, at least. Don't be a fool and not answer. You'd cheat yourself of some good letters, perhaps some damned good letters, at another time. Besides, I may run into some interesting things—it often happens with me. I'm really terribly upset by the news from home, and you're one of the few people near enough to listen. It's a rotten confession, but you've no idea how soothing it is to let things run out on paper.

On second thought, I shall stay here in Paris until I hear from home. If the wheat arrives, it's to the road again. I don't know where, but I've had an eagle eye fastened on Munich and beer, and robust blondes for some time. I want the South, too—honestly not so much, except that South that knows only two colors—the sea and the sun—the sky and the temple— the eyes of the Argive men above their robes—blue and white, blue and white, blue and white. And, for God's sake, an end to your curled moustaches, and your rapid hands, and your black hair, and your gleaming dark eyes. Blue and white, blue and white.

[Early February (?) 1925]

Dear ——

Thanks very much for your pleasant letter. I am still, as you see, in Paris waiting for funds to arrive from home, which may be ten days or two weeks longer. My friends in the South[1] have wired me several times, and written once, asking me to go to Italy and Spain with them, after that, if I can, to Austria and Czecho-Slovakia—but I will set out under my own steam. They are waiting a week longer, but I'm afraid it's useless.

Paris has not very many "distracting influences," as you put it, for me; but I am beginning to enjoy it thoroughly for the first time, and to get my teeth in it. I am buying books once more, thank God—Voltaire, Gérard De Nerval, Flaubert, Edmond Goncourt—and beginning to speak badly, and with some fluency.

You know, I am a very suspicious person *when I get started,* and you may remember you did nothing to allay my suspicions: I believe you poured

---

[1] Perhaps some of this material appears on pages 97–98 of *Look Homeward, Angel.*
[1] Professor D. D. Carroll of the University of North Carolina and his family, who were staying at St. Raphael and had invited Wolfe to join them there.

oil on them. It began to dawn on me that I was being asked to go along as a kind of stimulant and travelling companion to Kenneth. I pressed you on this the last day or so. I saw you, and you agreed, adding, as I recall, that I was "merely a happy fourth." Now my dear girl, that was really too much. I got in quite a rage about it. I felt dishonored and insulted. In a series of prolonged conversations with myself, I asked myself what kind of donkeys and fatheads would ask a battleship to convoy a fleet of Gloucester fishing smacks; Sir Launcelot to go a-jousting for the inmates of a Baptist school for girls; Caruso to act as Court Minstrel to the Governor of South Dakota. I assured myself that there were only three people to whom I would doff my colours and act as interlocutor, and that they were all dead. They are Sophocles, Samuel Taylor Coleridge, and Jesus Christ. I think I will do as much for my friends as almost anyone you can find, but I won't wipe their little nosies, take them to the little room where one goes all alone, or kiss them lovingly before [they go to bed(?)]

You were all having important things done to you. Your life, in this great new world of pulsing freedom and unrestraint, was opening like a flower—let us be big and say a sunflower. Kenneth's bleeding soul was being nurtured for the gestation of the opus, Marjorie was displaying her usual magnificent courage, with an occasional brave tear for baby, and a day or two in the wilderness to "think things out" alone. That sounds rather bitter—and I don't feel at all bitter. I am simply sorry, regretful. I had hoped for so much. When I met Kenneth, I had no idea he was with anyone here. This was New Year's Eve, I had an idea he was terribly alone and was cracking under the pressure. As we drank more and more, before setting out on our expedition, he began to hint darkly of some dark secret thing in his life—something of burning horror which had happened, no doubt, at Cannes. Next day we went to the studio, slept, and you returned with Marjorie. When I came downstairs I saw a woman whom I took for his Cambridge aunt or cousin—I don't know why, but for a good week I persisted in this error. When we went to Montmartre that night I saw in Marjorie an older person being nice to the boys, tolerantly amused at our pleasures.

Well, it's no good dishing it up again; in the days that followed I heard much talk of honesty by people who have had to think about being honest; much talk of unconventionality by people who have had to think of it—and who can never do anything but flutter around the safe edges, with a rather kittenish feeling that they are getting very *near* at times. It's simply no use. All the emotion was too carefully calculated; too carefully staged. All genuine contact with the world and with acquaintance is arid and stale because the genuine perception is missing, and people fall victim to the malignant evil of listening to the tickings of their own pangs and quivers, feeding their emotions with their beliefs about things, spinning, re-spinning; seeing, understanding, feeling very little of the most important reality—which is objective—beyond and without us.

In a word, my respect for the dignity and value and goodness of most people is such that I will not truckle to the device of planting in them qualities which they do not possess. I believe enough in most people to accept, without bitterness or despair, those things which are in them— those alone. Any other attitude has always seemed to me the deepest and most dishonorable insult to our fierce and secret honor.

I am going on Thursday night, in company with a man I met in a café at the side of the Opera, to a place where, so he assures me, the criminals of Paris are wont to come: they will be augmented that night by one rogue more. This, since you left, is my sole concession to E. Phillips Oppenheim.

I want you to understand that I hold nothing lightly; that I do not underestimate the importance of having met you all when I did. Someone has said that every man should see Paris before he is twenty-five. I came at twenty-four, the stage was set, not only by the magical place, but by the fortuitous and satanic theft of the manuscript. You were all given magnificent background to set yourselves in my life: there are terrific reasons why no man may forget his first Paris; and his last twenty-four. Very well. You may rest assured that you filled three weeks of that Paris, and may not thereby be forgotten. It is a grievous thought that there was a blazing inner life during that time which none of you quite reached, the sword was in your hands, the sword that pierceth very deep, and you did not plunge it to the hilt. And thereby, God help us all, I may say at 40, if I say aught:—"When I was in Paris for the first time, I met some friends— Americans."

My dear ——, when the fire blazes, the wood must burn: but only the fire remains. I have made cinders, ashes, dust of forests: only the flame is eternal, only the flame is enduring, only the flame is absolute among the Change. Oh God, for something outside of me to last.

I haven't the slightest intention of remembering any of you with anything but affection and regard. It is because of you that I am in Paris now— and that, which seemed at first a penance, has turned into a happy event.

[Later in February?]

My dear ——:

Your letter dishonors us both. I am returning it to you in no bitterness, but merely in order to let you read again, in a more generous and representative moment, what you have written apparently in pique and resentment. Out of that sad and weary meeting in Paris, so long ago that it is now, happily, only a dim horror, I think nothing more grievous has come than this little letter.

I am going to talk gently and painstakingly with you to-night, ——, because the old fires have burnt out—whatever fires you may have known —and I can speak to you, I think, with a calm weariness and horror. For that is what I feel. And I have been reading to-night great pages written by a great man, "La Rotisserie de la Reine Pedauque" of M. Anatole France; and I think something of the old tired gentle balance of spirit, which men call philosophy, and which flows through these gracious lines, has been inherited by me, who have read philosophy, but who am too young to be a philosopher.

But what I am going to say to you now will bring you no joy; and each word of it will become more hateful to me as I go on. And yet I feel an awful necessity in what I write, a necessity which may not be stopped.

You do me the honor to suggest, if I read your intent properly, that you feel some hurt at my proposed suspension of correspondence. And I thank you for this evidence of your interest. But this has caused in you a petulance of spirit, which seems to be a deliberate failure to understand and accept, and a corresponding desire to wound which I observed in you once or twice in Paris, and which I know is no true part of you: it is part of your evil inheritance from God knows what culmination of degrading experience.

You quote me as saying that I shall write you no more love letters, and you say you have never asked for such letters; but you know exactly and definitely, ——, that I have never written such a letter since I saw you: you know perfectly well that these letters of mine, foolish and mad, perhaps, but such letters as you will never receive again—were filled with a deep and earnest affection for you, and with nothing but that. When I think now to what purpose I have spoken, I am filled with a humiliation that knows no limit or no depth.—My God, I tell you truly, I am filled with repulsion as from a leporous blotch, with a visible shrinking away of the flesh.

In Paris toward the end the thing became comic and terrible. In Paris, ——, a long time ago, a young man—lonely, desperate, for he had been recently robbed of something he had distilled his blood in,[1] in a strange country and ignorant of customs and language—met a friend whom he had known well formerly, but not as well or as intimately as he had known other people, but a friend for whom he would have done a great deal. And this friend had told him he had come to Paris alone: he spoke of some

[1] His play, *The House* (*Mannerhouse*).

shadowy horror in his recent life, and he said that he had but 700 francs for the entire next month, but that he did not care. And he was willing to aid this friend under any circumstances, to any extent. It was in this way that he met you next day. He felt a terrible isolation; he lacked the comfort and the solicitude and the affection that might have been his elsewhere, and he turned to you. And he spoke to you without reserve of his affection for you; he explained to you exactly what this meant to him— that he found in you a primitive source of shelter and strength—and you, fastened in every wretched dogma of your kind, had the essential uncleanliness of mind that shows again in your letter. You could not think of an avowal of affection except as an exhibition of carnality, of physical contact—and you began at once to say: "You have not known me long enough to talk like this," etc. Finally, you began to talk of "friendship"— and rather wearily your young man agreed. It was a word you thought you understood. But you were not content: even when he had said "Very well, we shall be friends," you kept recurring to the other motif, harking back to it eternally, dragging it in by the horns, saying: "I'm sorry, but it is impossible"—long after, if you can remember, he had ceased to mention the possibility. And indeed, if you will be fair, he did not [really mention it at all(?)]

It is degrading to be led to these revelations, but you must know that you exerted very little physical attraction for me—you must know my affection for you was of quite a different order. Physically, I was repelled as I am repelled by most Boston women. On the one occasion that I remember touching you with any affection, I had the terrible internal shame, that feeling of wanting to cover my face with my hands and turn away that I have had only once before—when, as a child, I saw two very cold reserved people, a man and his wife, break down under emotional stress one day, and go into each other's arms. It is a terrible horror of the flesh. And you are not cold; I know that you must be physically attractive—it was my revulsion of the kind, and not of the person, that mattered. And that thing is deep in me—when I touched you, I felt your own shame and your own terrible awkwardness—and I couldn't stand it. That generous warmth of spirit that lies in you I felt like a definite flame, and that is what drew me to you. This is all so simple and honest that you cannot help seeing the truth of it. I shall tell you again what I mean, and I know that at my illustration you will not show the loathsome delicacy of the well-bred vulgarian, for you are not common.

Formerly in my life, ——, I knew a man of great courage and character, for whom, in spite of all the repellent coldness, and in spite of too much of the woman under a fairly masculine exterior, I had a deep affection. In fact, I think I loved this man. He was . . . a native of New England. One day, after I had known him for two years, we had had a talk of a most intimate and poignant nature—he saw in me, I think, a certain warmth and fire and spontaneity, and I saw his fire under the ice. On this day, I say, as I left him, in a terrible effort to get over his fences, he slapped me on the back, and when I got back to my room I writhed in such shame and torture as I have rarely known. I felt that there had been an indecent revelation. Later, one evening, I was dining at his home, and one of his sons was present. His wife came in and talked. I had tried to imagine them as man and wife before, and I had failed. Now for the first time, I saw them in family, with a son he had begotten on her; and as I looked at these two fine people, each walled eternally behind ice, the old horror of that dead cold Northern flesh came on me again. For the first time, I dared to think of this man in bed with his wife; and unutterable shame for him came on me again.

I render it to you as my solemn, and doubtless worthless, judgment of the New England temperament—about which I may know quite a great deal, because it represents the antithesis of nearly every *feeling* process I own myself—that there is generally something great about it: always something blasted, twisted, limited. When you consider it in its relation to our civilization—I know this sounds a bit pompous—you are forced to salute it for going so far: you are forced to regret its not being able to go far enough. You take its greatest representation, perhaps, in the world of spirit and thought—Emerson—and at one moment you are convinced you have someone you may place beside Plato and Kant and Hegel: the next moment, you see you have someone who lived near Boston.

There is very little in beauty and creation that escapes its eye—there is very little that is able to reach its heart. Thus you have the Boston ladies and the Browning Societies of a past generation—the sharp keen Northern head and eye sees, a little before most of the others, that another great original is writing poetry: and they begin to interpret what they can never fully apprehend. A little before New York and Chicago, there are articles in *The Transcript* on the German Expressionist plays, and pretty good plates of the scenes [when] the Dramatic Club does a play with experimental settings.

Likewise, a little before the rest of the people, your women understand that there is a great impulse astir in the world—an impulse toward the liberation of women in the social relation. So they go in for it. But their tragedy is that having torn down fences, they can not do without walls; they can never go beyond a half thaw; the fire never burns completely through the ice.

I feel about your people in a million different ways, that they know so much and understand so little. For example, I have eaten with them excellent food—splendid thick tender steaks, splendidly cooked, and I have been forced to agree with their unerring rational judgment that the food was good. But in my heart I have known what they could never understand—that the food was disappointing, somehow. Submit it to analysis, and you must admit it is an excellent steak—good as New York, Paris, anywhere—but the soul is out of it.

I wish there were more passion in what I am putting down here: if there were passion, there would be prejudice, and the likelihood of my being wrong. Unfortunately—for me—there is no such likelihood. I am too far away in spirit from something which I have comprehended too completely, with *almost an absolute objectivity,* for me to be wrong. What I feel, with appalling certainty, is the utter uselessness of my trying to *find* truth—as the saying goes—by some inward crucifixion of spirit. The truth is not for me either to discover or miss or define—it is there, outside me, a solid, unchangeable block of granite. There you all are; there you all stand—utterly damned because there is nothing in you that can possess utter damnation; you can not quite go mad; you can not quite grow satanic; you can not quite grow great.

It is quite useless to talk about vulgarity when one is trying to communicate a straightforward but yet a finely tapered state of mind. To illustrate: I could not hear of a liberated Boston lady going to bed with an unconventional Boston gentleman, without thinking: "Oh, hell! They've thought it all out!" I could not imagine bed with a liberated Boston lady anyway. I know that the steak would be excellent—but disappointing.

It strikes me now as comically illustrative of the whole weary business that I should again be making patient explanations about a thing so simple that only honesty and intelligence can grasp it. And I wonder—because my mind is so infinitely tired of it all—why I should explain anything. I am in somewhat the same position as God, called on to explain his gifts to his dunderpated subjects. And like God, with whom I am on very good terms at this writing, I could blast you with lightning or wither you like a blade of grass in my wrath. But I am not enraged; I am only weary—and I understand now why Zeus, Theos, Jahveh, Jupiter, Adonai, and Allah—calling Him by certain of His titles—does not exercise His royal prerogative of destruction oftener. He is bored, bored as I am bored—vanquished by His mightiest enemy, Supreme and Invincible Dullness. My dear girl, you win; to you are the bays and laurels; to you are the golden apples; yours is the jewelled coronet of all of the former Empresses of Night, who are small beside thee. The owls grow blind before thee; and the ground hogs belie their prophetic souls at thy approach, for thou puttest out the sun. On you falls the mantle of the lamented McFlecknoe who never had a lucid interval; to you as well goes Hooligan's Hat, the justly celebrated Wooden Derby, the Fur Lined Robe de Nuit, and the Cut Glass Frying Pan.

Huntress, on suppliant knees I sue for peace. Make an end to this uneven warfare—you are impregnable; you were dipped in the waters of oblivion long ago but, unlike Achilles, you have not even a vulnerable heel which may be assaulted by the Arrows of Comprehension.

Well, I really get some pleasure from this kind of thing, for it eases my weariness, and makes me grin a little as I write it, for I do see vaguely a large, grim body clutching this paper with murderous hands. That pleases me and makes me like you yet. And it is better than weariness.

I think that even in my most serious moments you have always inspired me a bit to bear-baiting; I observed a certain large and dogged determination, nay, more, an elephantine resolve, to do life thoroughly, taking an occasional note. Your pious reflection, in your horrid little letter, that after your forthcoming voyage to Alsace Lorraine you will know your France, touches in me pleasant springs of indulgent laughter.

I write you letters which ought to convince you that you drew at your birth the first prize in the Olympian Lottery, and you remark that you have enjoyed them very much. I know, of course, that you know only a few words, but it is as if Homer had read the Iliad to a young lady at the Misses Pringle's School, and had been told it was very pretty.

Your defense of a friend is worthy of you: but it is also thoughtless and unworthy treatment of a more or less innocent person. It is good to defend those you care for, even when they have acted badly, but a secret honor toward everyone in the world, known or unknown to us, should forbid our defending friends who have acted badly at the expense of other people who have acted well. You must do me the kindness of remembering that all I asked was to get away: I made no accusation against him, I make none now. That is past, and between us. I believe a time will come when that part of him which is fibre, and in which I believe, will supplant completely that other part of him which is jelly. But these things take time.

That terrible and degrading friendship which defends another for the flattery and unction of one's own soul—which says: "I will, I simply will believe in him," for the sake of appearing forthright and loyal against the world; which says: "Ah, but you have not known him as I," for the sake of a soothing overplus of pride for a greedy but incompetent ego; and which always takes that which it has degraded and humiliated as an object of defense, as the means of diverting the necessity for defense of oneself. My God, how have I suffered from this thing, first from my own blood brother, whose terrible selfish soul went wrapped in flattery for years; who converted each of his ignoble acts into a means for tribute, and who met my savage passionate accusals either in a great but wounded silence, or with a smile mixed with pity and pain.

You want, you say, my friendship; yet when you have it, you use it as a means to wound and degrade me. Somehow I do not hate you for it. I see you as you are, good and beautiful, disturbed by a hundred complicating things, groping desperately through the jungle of your will, inarticulately, desperately, inchoately, and ending finally by stabbing. Formerly I asked you not to try to understand—for I saw then how cruelly contorted things would get for us—and you saw in that only a foolish and vain desire to remain in mystery. I do not want nor do I desire mystery; but my instinct then was a right one, for all your efforts at comprehension have brought you to conclusions about me which do no honor to either of us. And I suspect, too, that once or twice you were kind enough to talk about me with our friends.

For the first time in my life I resent being talked about by acquaintances, even when, as you suggested, your talk with Kenneth about me was of a friendly nature. For the first time in my life I have a sense of shame for my honesty. Outside of certain bits of false emotionalism and of false romanticism, the result, no doubt, of a previous creative effort in real romance, I was terribly honest.

May I not suggest, if you want my friendship, that you seek it honorably upon your own account, and not on account of anyone else. That is the only basis on which any enduring or worthy affection may be established.

I knew you at a time and under circumstances which I do not care to recall. That I should care to see you again at all is a tribute to you. And I do care to see you again. But if you honestly do me the honor of wanting my friendship, you must come to it squarely on your own feet: you must not come to it bringing arguments, defenses, reasons for things that died a bloody death with me long since. In other words, I choose to know you without intrusions.

I think this is the last time I shall ever write you—I have forgotten the sound of your voice; your smile; the colour of your eyes—all except your generous largeness.

I offered you my affection—you gave me shame, humiliation, and dishonor. You have in you great qualities: you have in you also the qualities of a peasant woman. . . . I remember these last and I do not want to see you again. I do not like you now.

> Paris, Tuesday night at
> Ten of the Clock—

[February 23 (?), 1925]

Really a short one now to greet your last. Oh God, but this is the very ecstacy of joy—after a foul confinement I am free; I have dropped from the monastery window in the moonlight: and I hear laughter by the distant fountains. I am not mad: I am not talking in the moon. But I am free—the wind has lodged in my wings (I am an angel) as in a sail—and I am bellied up. . . .

A week ago I cabled. No answer. A slow spine-putrefying conviction came to me that the infernal chessmen were strangling me with tiny cords in the hands of petty people: I wanted to go like a tree in a high wind—I was being slain by the thousand tiny arrows, Sebastian-like, which pierce but do not kill. I was doomed to stay, to rot, to flow off in corruption here before a vast [chorus?] of high, evil sniggers.

To-day, God reft the sky in two in his great hands: Christ looked down on me and wept joyously, tears of golden blood; the bushes burst into lilac bloom; the great bells struck all through the town and bronze by bronze; the swallows and the larks flew from the towers with a gentle thunder—

In short, $125 came from home and I am drunk. Oh Gentle Jesus, there's a moon in Paris and the clouds make patterns round it.

Of all the worlds that I have known, this is the best. I rushed to pay the people of the hotel—the old man, his wife, the girls. I have given them nothing in almost a month—to-day they didn't want it, thinking I needed it. . . . They said it didn't matter when I paid: that I was a good boy—they thought I was much younger—bien gentil, who had fallen among thieves. The girl is lovely, peasant stock: I dined with her to-night, convent bred in Ireland.

You can purchase madness for ten francs: and a titled head of a goddess for forty.

To-night the drawn blinds and the coverlet of red, and Thursday to the world again.

[Early March, 1925]

. . . the peasants. And, all I knew now was "What does it matter—Orleans or Nowhere—I am going." I did not care. At times I rubbed the frost from the window and looked at the flat land, and at the sky. The girl kept looking at me under her shaded hat, and shivering, and smiling in a strange drowsy fashion: I could stand it no longer, and I put my arm around her—we said nothing—and came to Orléans. The peasants seemed not to mind it, or to be over-curious: they kept shouting and laughing among themselves.

At Orléans she got out: I said, "Pardon, Mademoiselle," when she almost fell over my suitcase. She waited outside for me, as I walked across the street to a hotel with a porter, but I did not speak to her.

Three minutes later at this hotel I had met the Countess Constance Hillyer de Caen, and I am at present engaged in collecting materials for a great and compassionate satire. She had been in my town, she had been everywhere in America making speeches to Rotary Clubs, Lion Clubs, Gold Star Mothers—she had been called "Little Mother" by thousands of Americans over here, and she puts flowers on their graves. She had expended all her fortune, her money—the French government did nothing.

She saw me, and pounced upon me as I entered the hotel; in two minutes she had given me the history of her entire war experience, had spoken of her 17 trips to America, and had given the names of everybody of prominence in my home town.

"I will show you the clippings," she [said]

Blois.
Monday night.
[Early March, 1925]

Dear ——:

Another enchanted week in my Mens Mirabilis. You are become a blurred sweet dream of which the lines, the notes, the shades are forgotten: it is a pleasant thing—I can be faithful only to the shades. I write you with no thought of your actual presence, somewhere on some dot of land—it is as if a woman in the moon is waiting on my letter. . . .

I have written you two or three times: I can't remember exactly what I said, but much of it, no doubt, was nonsense: some of it was golden numbers, golden numbers—and too good. But the deepest purest ray it is which sometimes finds the depth of the darkest mine. (Je ris, I jest—O beati pauperes spiritu, quoniam ipsorum est regnum coelorum. Pardon. C'est Chartreuse!)

But a wonderful week—a week of wonders. I have come to Blois in my journey of blunders. I hope you fathom my smooth profondeurs.

But to our tale—

The night was long, the way was cold: the minstrel young was over-bold: he carried in his great valise, two pairs of socks and one chemise; and in his hand, to stay the curse, the Oxford Book of English Verse. Under a sky of leaden grey, he went from Chartres unto Potay, and from that point he journeyed on, until he came to Orléans.

I am infinitely touched and moved by your honest letter, ——, if at any time in my letter I seem to be *writing*—God knows I'll try to avoid it— never doubt the sincerity and earnestness of what I say. Simply attribute anything that seems a bit too fine to an instinct to handle words, and never make the mistake of thinking that is not as much a part of me as my right hand.

At any rate, I can't be dishonest. Honesty with me is not a virtue, but a fact. This was true in Paris, when I was *asked* to be honest. I have a sort of shame in insisting to you now that I am honest, for I know that none of you are worth it; and yet I'm so fond of you that I keep on explaining.

I'm afraid that I'm a bit mad—I mean actually off. I think I have been since the first week after I came to France, when the play [1] was stolen. But I'm not afraid of it. I know that a week in England later with people I know will bring me back. Lately the fear of my madness has lost what terror it possessed, and has been tinged with a beautiful quality. Every-thing makes me dream. People look at me with a friendly interest, al-though few of them, save some of the women, speak to me.

[Middle of March, 1925]

You can understand, of course, that this life has become a great deal more tolerable to me than it was at first. For a number of years I have drawn a great deal of my strength from my ability to absorb innumerable

[1] *The House* (*Mannerhouse*).

experiences in books, in the streets, with women. Wildly, recklessly, and dangerously I burst suddenly into a new country, a new speech of which I knew nothing, a new life. I was oppressed with loneliness which had lost the power to be confident: I was crushed with a feeling of futility and despair. Well, in three and a half months, I have learned enough of their speech to read it rapidly, to understand it when it is spoken to me, to mangle it conveniently enough for all purposes, and to absorb a good part of that which goes on around me. And I have become a good Frenchman in a great many of their delightful habits of life. I shall never become a good Frenchman in other respects—shall we say a good American-Frenchman, who seems to me to be a very detestable and third rate person.

The Frenchman is lacking in true wisdom: he is tragically poisoned in his art, his life, his education by provincialism. He wastes himself in useless hatred and dislike of other nations: despite his great reputation for hard reasoning power, he is able to reason clearly not so well as he is able to reason sharply and shrewdly.

[Probably after March 16, 1925] [1]

I am enclosing a small sum of money—all I can afford to send at the time—and you must understand that there is nothing at all insulting in my action. I simply want to conclude an episode which fills me now with weariness and horror. I was told that I was expected to pay a certain sum, and I believe you vouched for it—but I am unable to determine whether it was $80 or $90. However, as it may be—as it no doubt will be—some months before I am able to settle the full obligation, there is no haste in knowing.

It would give me great pleasure to be able to pay you out of the receipts from my work for *Snappy Stories,* which you specify as the future receptacle of what I write. I should welcome the royalties a great deal more than I welcome your remark, for I can not smile at a jest—if such it was—when I no longer believe in the goodness of heart of its author. You, who will never know the dignity and secret courage of the work I have been doing, will never be able to realize the affront you have offered. But if you believe in gods and demons, I beg of you to go down before the mightiest of them and ask remission of your offense—you who have so terribly and stupidly mocked the poor song that was written for your glory and honor, you who have come to secret poetry with unclean ac-

---

[1] In a letter to his mother, dated March 16, 1925 (see page 108 of *Thomas Wolfe's Letters to His Mother*), Wolfe wrote "Both your checks came by way of the Nat. City Bank." He therefore probably began paying back his debt.

cusations, you who made a sty of Arcady and who have poured vitriol in what was all of honey and a song for sirens. I write this finely, not simply, in order that you may smile at it—for then you will know that you have really died.

Probably to KENNETH RAISBECK

[March (?) 1925]

The wind and the rain has come and gone a great many times since. I have not room enough here to examine these reasons: but I could explain them now, I believe, with fullness and clearness. That is not at all important. It is enough if I have understood the intent of your letter—I believe you ask if a renewal of our friendship is possible. It is not only possible, I believe, but desirable. Again, I understand you to intend friendship between us—not communal friendship. Life is too short and too disastrous for any love-me-love-my-dog obstinacy. Believe me when I say that I have only respect and good will for any of your friends. But I know of no way out of this except by a sword cut. As I told you, there is no room here to go into the web: it is only manifest that we did very well together until I was brought in with your two ladies in Paris. Then things went wrong. My dear boy, for me that is finished. Your own relations with either of these women will not be affected in the slightest: your only need is to keep us separate in your mind. I am a good butcher because I know . . .

[THE FRAGMENT BREAKS OFF HERE]

To MARGARET ROBERTS

Avignon, France,
March 21, 1925

Dear Mrs. Roberts:

My only plea for my tardiness is that my own life has had a little private Hell and Heaven of its own and I have been involved in my own wonder, my own emotion, my first bewilderment at a new civilization, at a new tongue, which is now beginning to unfold magically as I take hold. I am wandering across France like a ghost, alone and glorious in loneliness, knowing not at all my next step, save vaguely; trusting to miraculous accident to find the enchanted harbor for me—and at times it does. . . .

I have an enormous manuscript of my voyage—enormous notes.[1] I do

---

[1] Perhaps "London Tower," which was published in the July 17, 1925, issue of the *Asheville Citizen*, was originally part of this manuscript, or perhaps it was written separately by Wolfe when he returned to London in June.

not know where to peddle it—my one impulse is to write—and to send it to you. If you care to—you, mind, are my only literary executor and censor—you may give it to George McCoy for the *Citizen,* with this one condition which I make absolute: my name is not to be mentioned or published under anything I write. This is the one binding restriction, and I insist on it.

A few days ago, from Paris, the day I departed for Lyon, I entrusted the prologue of the *Passage to England* to a lady, a friend, giving her your address and requesting that she send it at once. In that prologue, about 10,000 words I judge, I said nothing of my actual voyage; I indulged, under a rather fantastic plot-work, [in] certain speculations of mine on voyages—the true voyages. The idea came to me when, on going over the notes of the actual voyage, it occurred to me that the account I gave of events and people, if ever published, might get the author and the publisher into trouble. I had honestly made these notes while at sea, and while feeling none too gay; but I wanted even then to do what, to my knowledge, had never been done: to isolate a transatlantic voyage, beginning and ending abruptly the moment the ship docks or sails, acting upon the belief that the sea and a ship disorganize the whole social scheme for a few days, and that the social scheme reorganizes a new pattern before the voyage is over. I did this absolutely without malice; you may accept the whole when you get it as a mélange of fact and fiction, with fiction emphasizing the truth of the business as I saw it.

That explains the subtitle: "Log of a Voyage That Was Never Made." This occurred to me at first purely as a device to escape libel; I changed the name of the ship and the characters. Then I remembered that I had not sailed on the day I had originally planned—that I had remained in Asheville [2] a week longer, and that during that time I had had a queer feeling that I was or should be on the Atlantic. This led to the fantastic prologue, and my own growing conviction in the spiritual need of true voyages.

The whole, when you get it, will amount I believe to 40,000 or 50,000 words—a short novel. It is queer journalism, I know, but since I *give* it, I feel that I am able to do and speak as I please. You may tell George that I have amusing and interesting notes on England (I believe they are), and a story of Orléans, France—a true one—about the town and a genuine countess who drinks horse's blood for anaemia, and an old villain of a Marquise, which, if I told it well, would make my future. I think, also, I may say things about people, about politics, about social differences, which may be superior to the banalities of the greater part of foreign

[2] Wolfe had gone to Asheville for a short visit in October, 1924, before sailing for Europe.

correspondence, which, nevertheless, earns its authors a good living. The reason for all this is simply that I am tired of writing for the four winds; I realize the desperate lack and hypocrisy of pure expression. We are children—we must have an audience; and if my audience may be the people of a little North Carolina town, well and good. That is my whole desire for the present—perhaps there is a tiny feeling that if any of it is at all good it may reach the ears of the gods.

I shall send you lots of manuscripts. I want to write—nothing else—and I have neither the patience nor the time nor the inclination to pull wires with literary agents, and so on. And honestly, I know of no one who would publish my account now; because, as I said, I shall write this once as I please. Let him put it all in print, if he wants, but my name must be absent. Some of it may be fiction; most of it may be fact seen imaginatively—it should have the same relation to reality as most autobiographical novels, as "Childe Harold" if you like. I appoint you censor: I have not been careful of myself in what I have said or am going to say—careful, that is, of what the townsfolk may think. That would be too petty, too dishonest. You must not be careful of that either in going over the manuscripts—it is not at all important. I think the sole thing—the *principal* thing—is the relation any of it may have to my family, to their position in the community. I shall never be too "advanced" to respect that.

It may be before I am done that I shall say something important—that in the mad rush to get it down, something of high worth may come out.

A letter has come, a very flattering and friendly letter, which asks me to return to N.Y.U. in September at $2000—Composition and Soph. Lit. I shall accept, hoping that the heavens may rain manna before, or that a syndicate of county newspapers will appoint me representative at the councils of the League of Nations. For God's sake, say a word to my people, and get them to extend sustenance as long as my period of sufferance lasts.

I am reading French like mad. I came here alone, ignorant of the language, and for two months wretchedly unhappy. Now I am jabbering villainously but adequately, and the world is brightening again. . . .

The duty I impose on you is arduous and long—but I turn to you in trust and hope in this, as in all things. Do not hesitate to deny the responsibility if it's too heavy. I'll understand that, and if the paper doesn't care for the stuff, keep it for me. After all, I'm *embalming* the moments for future exhumation.

To you all my deepest love. Forgive me again if I send no cards, no letters. I'll give them to you on my return. Meanwhile, read and accept my chroniclings as for yourself. It has been mad, bold, unhappy, lonely, glorious!

To HOMER A. WATT

St. Raphaël

[April, 1925]

Dear Professor Watt:

I am sending you a hasty scrawl here in answer to your letter of several weeks ago, but I shall follow with another of a more explanatory nature. I want to get this off on the day's mail. I am on the Riviera, in a little town possessed mainly by the English, and I am writing as if pursued by devils. This will perhaps show in my writing.

Let me say here that if I were methodical enough to keep a scrap book, your last letter would occupy a position of honor in it. I am very proud of it: proud and pleased to know that I am wanted for something and that I am worth as much as $2000 to anyone.[1]

I was in Tours when your letter came to Paris—my mail was being held for me, and I did not get your letter for several weeks. I departed almost at once for the South of France.

First of all, I am terribly shocked at the confusion that resulted when I did not return. I did *not* get your earlier letter offering me a place in February: you say that you sent it to my "American address," and I have wondered whether you meant the Albert, or Asheville, N.C. If you sent it to Asheville, it should have been forwarded by my brother, although my mother closed her house and departed for Miami early in the Fall.

Today I heard from home, and my family is evidently desirous that I return in August. I am therefore writing you to tell you that I accept with the deepest gratitude your offer of a post in September.

You have always shown the utmost patience with me, Professor Watt, even in circumstances where my greenness must have been excessively trying to your patience and good nature. But I have had one instinct towards you that has been a happy and a right one: I have never had the slightest hesitation in speaking to you in absolute honesty, without concealment. That is why I am going to give you certain information now about my domestic background and my present circumstances which I feel it is necessary you should have, in order to understand my present state of mind.

My mother is a very extraordinary woman in her middle sixties, small, strong, intensely vigorous, and uncannily canny in business affairs: she is part Scotch. Since my father's death a few years ago she has, by shrewd investment at home and in Florida, more than trebled her estate. For

---

[1] Professor Watt had asked him to return to New York University in September as a member of the regular September-to-June teaching staff at a salary of $2000.

every cent I spend I am, at the present time, absolutely dependent on my mother.

I spent the few thousand dollars that came to me following my father's death at Harvard. My other brothers and sisters, following my mother's advice, have profited hugely. And everyone, you understand, has been beautifully loyal to me. They seem to have a touching belief in me without knowing very well what I am doing. And what I am doing is to write, write, write—it may be the most frightful muck, but I can't help putting it down. At times I grow slightly bitter at the idea of having to stop writing, even temporarily, to do something of a more profitable character. I feel at such a time that my own destiny has been matched against that of a piece of black earth in Carolina, and a piece of sand in Florida, and that the land always wins.

At the same time there is another impulse in me which makes me rather fiercely independent: I have a horror of becoming like those wretched little rats at Harvard who are at the mercy of their pangs and quivers, who whine about their "art," who whine that the world has not given them a living. I'll be damned if I'll become a "chronic unemployable." It was this that Professor Baker could not understand; he protested that I was making a serious blunder in coming to the university,[2] he seemed absolutely unable to comprehend my reasons, he said "You must keep on writing," and he kept on saying this with a sublime disregard for circumstances. I settled the business for myself—the only possible settlement, as I found—and I lost, I fear, the friendship of a man who had stood by me for two years: at any rate, I have never heard from him.

That is why, even now, I doubt; and that is why I seem to hesitate. I observe a rather widespread tendency among older people to condemn the conduct of young people as headstrong and obstinate, but I do not observe a widespread tendency to give a plain answer to some of the questions young people ask.

I should like to think, frankly, that something I have written or am writing might in these next few months relieve me of the necessity of doing anything else. I keep hoping for a little more time, but I know that you need time as well. You may be assured, however, that, my word being given, I will come through to the scratch, death or disease excepted.

And I want to repeat what I believe you already know: for innumerable reasons I prefer to be at N.Y.U. to any other place North or South. There is, at the present time, one possible means for me to keep on with my work. If it is not too late, will you drop me a line, and let me know how much time for further meditation you can allow me? I beg of you not to be too impatient at what seems to be my indecision:—I am in a

[2] New York University.

web of tangled and troubling events, only the barest outlines of which I have been able to indicate to you. I hope you have not been bored with the recital. . . .

I am living here in a land of opulent Springtime, of incredible color. I should like to tell you more about it, but I'm not sure it's really true. My address continues at the American Express Co., Paris. Mail will be forwarded. I go from here to Italy, then to England.

To HOMER A. WATT

> Brasserie Vetzel
> 1 Rue Auber
> Place De L'Opéra—Paris
>
> June 22, 1925

Dear Professor Watt:

I went to Italy almost immediately after receiving your last letter; and I have been travelling and living with one valise since, returning to Paris only a day or two ago. I shall go back to America in August, and want to spend a few weeks at home before returning to the University. I believe the date of the term's opening is around September 20, and that you want, generally, the instructors to return a little in advance. If the request is not extravagant will you absolve me from this preliminary work of registration? I desire this solely because of the exigencies of time.

You asked me my preferences concerning hours. I have none, save a prejudice against nine o'clocks. I am incurably and unfortunately night-owlish, doing a good part of my work when most of the world, even in New York, is silent; getting Satanic inspirations from the dark.

I think you will understand that I express something stronger than a perfunctory regret when I tell you that I am profoundly sorry to hear that you will be absent next year.[1] My decision to return was not utterly contingent on your own presence, but it was considerably strengthened by the expectation of again working with you.

I await with great pleasure my association with Professor Munn.

Italy was for me the core of the world's loveliness; and this I take to be a miraculous thing, because that great current which draws some men toward the Latins does not draw me, who have fog in my soul, and think grey the best of colours, and London the most unfathomable of cities.

I stayed there until my money was gone; and I ended at last in Venice,

---

[1] Professor Watt was to teach as a visiting Professor at the University of Southern California during 1925–26, on leave of absence from New York University. In his absence, Professor James B. Munn was to be chairman of the Department of English.

which I shall remember not as a place which may always be reached by train, but as one of those cities that never were, formed in magic by the sweep of a wizard's arm.

I am going to England in a day or so, and I shall remain there for the remainder of my time. If you have any further communications, I suggest that you send them to the American Express Co., London. I wrote you before in pencil because I had no ink; I write you now upon the only paper provided by Vetzel's: it is used, generally, I believe, by young men and women naming a time and place. This is no reason why it should not Serve a Worthier Purpose.

I am thoroughly disreputable in appearance. I have no clothes, and I shall have none until more money comes from home. At the present moment I am drinking nothing stronger than beer; there is, five feet away, a Frenchman, all whiskers, with a glowing cigarette tip blooming dangerously in the midst of the foliage, an old man and his young mistress just beyond, two Americans drinking cognac across, and an amorous couple at the back, kissing each other with solid smacks between draughts of beer.

I've done my best to give you a picture of Parisian life.

The letter below to Mrs. Mildred Weldon Hughes, whom Wolfe had known in Paris, was found in his own files and may never have been mailed. Exactly what the "serious and disquieting news" about his health was is not known. In a letter to his mother dated July 27, 1925 (See page 119, Thomas Wolfe's Letters to His Mother) Wolfe wrote: "I took cold shortly after my arrival, and for the better part of three weeks I was a great deal more dead than alive." Probably he had consulted a doctor and been frightened by his diagnosis, but it is doubtful that the tubercular lesion on his lung was discovered at this time.

To MILDRED WELDON HUGHES

[London]

[Early July, 1925]

Dear Mrs. Weldon,—

Your black rimmed stationery is fairly familiar to me now; but if you use it with any expectation of putting *me* in mourning, your intent is frustrated.

Merry England has not been merry for me these past four days: I have come down with a most damnable cold—not this time blameable on the

English climate, which has been dry and warm, but on my restless toes which filched the cover from my bosom at dead o' night—and only by means of copious draughts of John Walker am I now able to wash it into Hell.

London is little better off than Paris, I judge, for tourists—the American Express here twangs with their squeaky voices; but London is bigger and one may lose them, or get lost.

Today I spent in very melancholy fashion at Wembley, which bored me infinitely. It was too big, too crass; and it repeated itself mechanically: nowhere was there gaiety.

I have lived quietly enough here, seeing only a few acquaintances. The night I came, on going into the Hotel Imperial for a drink, I was accosted by my friend K,[1] who used to stumble up and down the stairs in Paris. I let him pump me up to a point; but I asked him no questions concerning himself or his friends—I have lost the interest.

I am going down to the English country shortly. I have received serious and disquieting news about myself here this past week. Health—heart, all else quite sound. I have youth enough yet, I hope, for anything. . . .

Remember, my most cordial remembrances cross the Atlantic with me. Please write me again.

The following fragment is evidently a rough draft portion of the first letter which Wolfe wrote to Aline Bernstein, whom he had met on the ship coming back to the United States, and who was to have the greatest influence on him for the next five years, during which time Look Homeward, Angel *was written and published.*

To ALINE BERNSTEIN

Hotel Albert
New York
[September 1925?]

. . . me now with a profound sense of wonder and unreality. Through you, I slid back into America again; since then, my spirits have bounded, and my sense of the greatness and capacity for madness of this people has quickened beyond all measure.

I am just back from Boom Town, where everyone is full of Progress and Prosperity and Enterprise, and 100,000 by 1930, and Bigger and Greater

[1] Kenneth Raisbeck.

Asheville. Everyone is growing wealthy on real estate, and there is a general tendency to slap everyone on the back and call everyone by the first name. I did not know what it was all about, nor do I know yet, except that it is all perfectly useless along with everything else; but it made me glad to see them all so happy, and the enormous vitality of that town and of this country charmed and fascinated me.

For three weeks I went wherever they went, and made their ways my own: I drank their corn whiskey, and joined their parties, and was involved in their generous falsehoods which are so full of hope and good will for all things. They love success, these people, or what they conceive success to be; they put in their papers announcements that I was a professor and that I held the "chair of English" at N.Y.U.

I am no longer so arrogant, cruel, and so contemptuous of all this as I was a year ago: I think I like people a great deal better than ever before. . . .

[THE FRAGMENT BREAKS OFF HERE]

To FREDERICK H. KOCH

[Hotel Albert]
[New York]

Sunday night.
[January ?, 1926]

Dear Prof:

Your Playmaker pamphlets and folders came to-night, including your note suggesting that I go around to see Sheldon Cheney.[1]

The Guild has my new play,[2] and has had it for two months:—a letter a day or so back from Lemon, the play reader, in reply to a rather sharp one of my own in which I asked the return of the play, informs me that he read the play, passed it on to members of the board, and that it is now in the hands of Lawrence Langner. The board, he says, is going to vote on it finally. In view of this, I have consented to let them keep the play until a final decision is reached. Although I have several other copies of the play, I promised Mr. Lemon that I would not send it out until the Guild had seen it. I really have only the most trifling hopes of the play's production by the Guild, but when it is returned, I shall take a copy to Mr. Cheney and several other people who have asked for it.

Let me thank you very sincerely for the interest you show and have

[1] Cheney was with Equity Players (The Actors' Theatre), which, however, was discontinued around this time.

[2] *Mannerhouse.*

shown for years in the fortunes of my life. For two years now I have worked and travelled alone, ordering the events of my life as courageously and honestly as I could, compromising for my existence by teaching in order to escape the more odious restraints incurred by demands on my family. In that time, some people who disapproved of the compromise, and others—the honey flies who found me lacking in the promise of instant victory—have turned away and forgotten me. But a few people have never forgotten: they have given unbounded loyalty to a mad fellow who made loneliness his mistress, and among them I am happy to believe I may include yourself.

It would give me infinite pleasure to witness the success of my new play, because it was written in the silences, and because it would give me the chance, if necessary, to repel obligation where no obligation is due; but whether it is produced or not, or whether I succeed or not, I have the most unwavering confidence in the integrity of your friendship for me. For that, believe me, you will not find me lacking in affection or gratitude. . . .

My communication is infrequent, but my interest in you and in your work unwavering.

The following is the letter of submission sent with Mannerhouse *to* The Neighborhood Playhouse. *It was written on the stationery of the Hotel Gralyn in Boston, where Wolfe had gone for the third week in January to visit friends, and may have been intended for either Alice or Irene Lewisohn, since they were both directors of the Playhouse. Judging from Wolfe's letter of June, 1927, to Mrs. Roberts, it was probably addressed to Alice Lewisohn.*

To MISS LEWISOHN

The Gralyn
20 Charlesgate West
Boston, Mass.

[January, 1926]

Miss Lewisohn, this play belongs to no world that ever existed by land or sea. For it, I have created a medium as special as the one Coleridge used for "The Ancient Mariner."

This is what the play means to me:—one, three or four years ago, when I was twenty-one or twenty-two, and wanted to prove things in plays, I wanted to write a play that should describe a cycle in our native history—

I should show by it the rise and fall of a powerful Southern family. I was going to call it "The Wasters." I made a draught of it and destroyed it. Later, still significant, I called it "The House"—my house was to be the symbol of the family's fortunes—you saw it put up and torn down.

Finally in Paris, after that script had been stolen, and I was alone, I knew that I cared little for that, and beginning anew, I created this play—which has no relation to problem, none to history—save that any one may guess when it is supposed to occur, but no one, I think, will confuse it with realism. It became the mould for an expression of my secret life, of my own dark faith, chiefly through the young man Eugene.[1] If you would know what that faith is, distilled, my play tries to express my passionate belief in all myth, in the necessity of defending and living not for truth—but for divine falsehood.

That, simply, is what I mean; that has come as truly from me as anything I ever wrote; and I am a young man who read the Greeks at 15, and who read Kant and Hegel at 17, and who, like every other fool, thought himself wise when he saw God as a sea, himself as a drop of water on the way; but who knows now, at 25, that he had merely substituted an ugly superstition for a beautiful one.

I have no more time. You complained of a certain *diffusion* in my first play:[2] I do not believe you can complain of it here. There is certainly the focal power of one idea, developed with enormous concentration—I do not believe any speech is vague, but the whole is packed.

I have not tried to be smart or wise, nor have I adopted a cheap easy obscurity. I tell you again, this thing came out of me—even in its fierce burlesquing of old romanticism, it defends the thing it attacks.

Finally, of course, it contains the first complete expression of that thing that has fascinated and terrified me since I was a child. Are we alive or dead? Who shall tell us? Which of the people in this play are ghosts, and which are living?

Read it carefully, Miss Lewisohn. Certainly men must have felt like this, but I have never seen it expressed.

In the following note to Olin Dows, Wolfe speaks quite optimistically about the possible production of one of his plays. Probably he wrote this when he had high hopes that the Neighborhood Playhouse might do Man-nerhouse, or perhaps he was simply whistling to keep his courage up.

[1] The Eugene of *Mannerhouse* is not the autobiographical Eugene of Wolfe's novels, although Wolfe sometimes uses him as a mouthpiece for his own ideas.
[2] *Welcome to Our City.*

Dows had first met Wolfe at Harvard in the spring of 1923, after having seen and admired Welcome to Our City. *He painted Wolfe's portrait there soon afterwards; then left Harvard to go to the Yale School of Fine Arts. From 1924 to 1928, Wolfe often visited him at his family's house in Rhinebeck, New York, and in June 1927, he lived in a small cottage on their estate.*

To OLIN DOWS

[New York City]

[Spring 1926?]

My dear Olin:

I was very glad to get your note. It gave me what I had lacked—a New Haven address by which I could reach you; and it served to deny what I was beginning to fear—that I had become too scandalous a fellow for a decent, respectable lad. . . .

There's little about me to tell you—little that *can* be told. Make the most of that. It seems a theatre here may do one of my plays next season. Meanwhile, I seethe with the finest ideas I've ever had, and little time for writing. It's England in June, and the Continent for the next year or two.

Let me see you more often, Olin. I very honestly would like to have you as my friend; and very honestly I tell you that I have never been wholly sure I had your friendship. This is because you are fundamentally decent and courteous to everyone, and because you have a great deal of gusto for people. It cheers me to think that you may have ever found me interesting or strange or stimulating, but one sometimes grows a bit tired of existing as the Man-Mountain, the Wild-Haired-Wonder, and the like. Beneath the homespun shirt, and so on, as some one has said so beautifully, beats the heart of a man. At any rate, no matter how you feel, I get a great deal of pleasure from seeing you, and I will willingly perform my stunts for you, including thirty-seven hair-raising, awe-inspiring, and reason-defying novelties, exhibited to all the Crowned Heads of Europe (both of them) but never before upon this Continent.

Words in brackets in the following letter are only guessed at, since they have been eradicated by the tearing of the paper at one edge.

To MABEL WOLFE WHEATON

[Hotel Albert]
[New York]
Saturday [May, 1926]

Dear Mabel:

I have your letter; today is my best opportunity to answer it. I finished my work at the university yesterday, save for examinations. I give all my Freshmen examinations Monday and Tuesday, but I must wait around until Thursday, May 27, to give my [final] examination to the school teachers. During [the interval] I shall go up to [Boston], talk to Elaine who is going to Europe and wants information, and see old Henry,[1] in order to get my books from him. I suppose [Mama] has returned from Florida. After May 27, I should like to come [home] for a few days, if you are able to put me up. I am going abroad early in June. I think I shall leave my books here in New York, stored in the house of a friend who lives here.

I have heard from Mama, and I wrote her, and telegraphed her, too, the other day. Things seem to have gone badly with her—apparently she has [lost] money in Florida [real] estate. I know you are all . . . upset by the whole wretched business, but let us try to keep down [bitterness] and recrimination as far as we can.

I am sorry for her, if she has lost money, because she cares [for] money a great deal, and was happy in the belief that she was making money. But if she has lost part of it, it may be a good thing for the happiness of us all; for I have observed that people who make an end rather than a means of money, and even lower their own standard of living in order to have more of it, sometimes do a right-about-face when they find how insecure a foundation their life is built on: in other words, when they lose part of their coin, they become more liberal with what is left, and get more comfort from a little than formerly they got from much.

It seems a little pathetic to me now as I think of you all, and of Asheville people I saw Christmas—you were all hypnotized by the talk of Florida and Asheville, you were all full of convincing facts and figures, you were all secretly proud of "business ability," although everyone elsewhere knew you would have to wake up sooner or later—the sad history of these affairs has always been pretty much the same, I believe: everyone makes a million on paper and in pipe-dreams, until one day somebody calls for a dollar in cold cash, and things blow up.

I know things are not so bad as this at Asheville—the town probably

---

[1] Henry A. Westall, Wolfe's uncle.

has a certain assured growth, and if you never get $5000 an inch for property, you may in time get an honest price. If your boom returns this summer in full blast, the town will eventually get done in the eye—it always happens. The people who gain apparently are the near-swindlers and the near-thieves who stay within the letter of the law—the ——s and ——s who, at the top of the dope-dream, are reputed by the admiring boobs to be worth at least $200,000,000, or some such figure, but who usually get away with two or three million. And, of course, it is the Boob, the eternal cocksure Boob, who loses his (or her) shirt. Inasmuch as the last census listed some 97,500,000 specimens of the American Boob, the pickings for the ——s and ——s should continue to be soft and easy. For the Boob never learns, he never changes. Steal his shirt this year by [a] scheme for manufacturing gasoline from Florida grapefruit, he will cheerfully give next year his socks, trousers, and B.V.D.'s to a project which proposes to capture the American clothing trade by importing Bulgarian wool grown on cactus bushes. They never learn and they always lose. Quote a few figures to them and they will believe anything. If you told one of them that the population of Asheville would be a half million by 1930, you would not be believed; but tell him that the town has grown fifteen thousand during the last year, and that therefore it is bound to grow thirty thousand next, sixty thousand next, and so on, and he will give you the gold out of his teeth. The Boob believes anything he hears or sees, as long as he is given a few meaningless statistics. Print a picture in the newspaper of Washington Crossing the Delaware, and sub-title it "President Coolidge on his way yesterday to greet the Pope at Ellis Island," and he will swallow the bait, hook, line, and sinker. There is no limit to his ignorance, stupidity, and gullibility, but since he sometimes has good intentions, I side with him rather than with the crooks who rob him.

I hope the effect of the present slump in Asheville will be a corresponding slump in wise-acre real estate chatter during the time I am at home, but it will probably be my luck to get there just as the thing starts again, and just after —— has persuaded the surrounding boobery that Asheville is the logical place for the National Capital, and that a majority in the House of Representatives has already decided to start excavations on Battery Park hill for the Treasury, the Department of State, and the Congressional Library.

That everyone will be rich in his own mind I have no doubt, for all that is needed to persuade the suckers that they are rolling in wealth is to take $250 of their money in exchange for a piece of paper telling them they are the owners of Lot 693 on Haywood Heights, said lot being worth $3000 (on paper); to buy it back at the end of six weeks for $300, paper value now $4500; and congratulate them on having made $1500 without turning over a hand. And the sucker not only believes he has made it, but he begins to flatter himself on his cleverness, business foresight, and all round shrewdness. All that is needed after this is to walk up to him, take the greenbacks from his pocket, cut the buttons off his coat, and steal the chewing gum out of his mouth, leaving him a nickel for carfare home. He is ripe for plucking. . . .

Perhaps we dead may awaken someday and manage to get ten times the comfort from one tenth the money we thought we had. I assure you I am not disgruntled in writing this. I have no very selfish designs upon the family treasure, in spite of any dissenting opinion: money has always been to me only a necessary convenience, and fortunately I am going to be able to make it now without home help. But I really like you all too much to want to see you made unhappy by this mad folly. . . .

I am not being bitter, Mabel. Let us admit, before I close, that I have had more out of it than the rest of you; let us admit, too, that I will never be ungrateful for it. At any rate, what I was told was mine, I spent myself as I damned pleased, on the thing I wanted to do. For what was given beyond, my fervent thanks—but now that I speak as a free agent, asking no more, let us try, you and Fred and I, to forget about it, so far as we may, and to step upon the rotten poisonous thing that has never been anything but a source of bitterness, accusation, and suspicion. In other words, since few people we know will ever care for us more than we ought to care for one another, let us try to change the system by which huge sums for dirt are kept in secrecy, but a donation of a few dollars to feed hungry children is brandished about as if it were the war debt.

This may be cheek, since I can give nothing; but it also happens to be the truth—which ought to make it worth something. At bottom, I believe, we are all fairly decent and honorable people—somewhat given, perhaps, to parading our virtues—but with enough kindliness and loyalty for anyone. Mama is old; she has had a hard bitter life, and her sense of values has become distorted. But she, too, I have always believed, has our welfare at heart. In short, I believe she would do almost anything for any one of us, if she realized the necessity; but, as you know, it has been her tragic fate to realize that necessity sometimes too late—sometimes to the tune of clods of frozen earth upon a wooden board—the last venture in real estate, I might add, any of us will ever make. There's nothing to be done about that. She's too old; but she too is fundamentally a decent person.

I want very much to see you all. If you have room for me, drop me a line.

And, in spite of all I have said, which you will treat, of course, with discretion, I sincerely hope that none of you have been hard hit by this depression.

You'd better let me know right away.

To MARGARET ROBERTS

Hotel Albert
New York

June 1, 1926

Dear Mrs. Roberts:

I was away in Boston when your letter came, during a vacant interval in the examination period at N.Y.U. I came back Thursday for a final examination. . . . I shall see you perhaps in a few days. I may come home, although invitations have not been marked by their warmth or frequency, nor am I driven by my own inclination. . . .

Two years ago I was forced into work for which I had no affection, at the penalty of what talent I had. It may be said that I was not "forced," but I insist that money has been held over me like a bludgeon. Recently what little help I have secured from home to eke out my salary (and, I confess, my own lack of economy) has been withdrawn. Meanwhile, I get insane attempts at falsification—dark hints at "the poor house" and "old age" and the insistence that everything has been done "for the children" or in order to secure "a few dollars for old age." My uncle,[1] sniggering, told me he supposed my mother had not told me (she was too cautious) that she is building a $100,000 hotel at Brevard. This a week after a letter telling of pinch and poverty. These are the facts, and are prefatory to your letter. You are certainly wrong in supposing I took your letter badly. I honor the motive, and I trust in your friendship too much to wear a chip around you. But I will be forgiven, I know, and understood, I believe, if I say that a brief, but very intense and varied life has told me that all advice is bad—even that of so wise and understanding a person as you are.

Further, if, in this affair, you see only consequences of future unhappiness for me [2]—what, pray, should unhappiness mean to me who called for wine, and was given the sponge, and whose bread as a child was soaked in his grief. Am I so rich, then, that I can strike love in the face, drive away the only comfort, security, and repose I have ever known, and destroy myself just as my mind and heart, aflame with hope and maturity, as they have never been before, promise me at length release.

[1] Henry A. Westall, whom Wolfe had seen in Boston.
[2] This probably refers to Wolfe's having fallen in love with Mrs. Bernstein.

Well, I'm in no debater's mood. Thank God, I have escaped, at any rate, from *odious* bondage, and I shall come home and depart thence, free, because that ugly monster, money, which breaks the will and kills courage, has been banished for me. I expect nothing from my family—now or hereafter. I have given my life to the high things of this earth—I am free to say that I consider any debt that has been made has been repaid by the effort and example of my life; and I assure you that from now on, I shall strike a blow in the face of insolence, confessing no obligation where none is due, and repelling any hostility toward my life and my creation with all the energy and violence I command.

Of this you may be sure: I believe you have been my constant friend, that you have never stooped to the common daily treachery of the village, that in your heart you have believed in me and trusted in me. Be assured, then, that *you* at least I shall want to see when I come home.

I am sailing on the *Berengaria* June 23. Until we meet, then,

With great affection,

IV

EUROPE AND THE WRITING OF
LOOK HOMEWARD, ANGEL
1926–1928

To MARGARET ROBERTS

Bath, England

July 19, 1926

Dear Mrs. Roberts:

Here are just a few lines—a short record of my doings since I left you. I was in Paris ten days, in Chartres two days, in London a week, and here two days. I am on my way to the North of England—to Lincoln and York for a few days, and finally to the Lake District, where I settle down to work. My trip has been fuller, richer, more fruitful than I had dared hope. I looked, and looked so fiercely the first time that I return now to something which seems to be opening itself for me.

I have begun work on a book, a novel, to which I may give the title of "The Building of a Wall" [1]—perhaps not; but because I am a tall man, you know perhaps my fidelity to walls and to secret places. All the passion of my heart and of my life I am pouring into this book—it will swarm with life, be peopled by a city, and if ever read, may seem in places terrible, brutal, Rabelaisian, bawdy. Its unity is simply this: I am telling the story of a powerful creative element trying to work its way toward an essential isolation; a creative solitude; a secret life—its fierce struggles to wall this part of its life away from birth, first against the public and savage glare of an unbalanced, nervous brawling family group; later against school, society, all the barbarous invasions of the world. In a way, the book marks a progression toward freedom; in a way toward bondage—but this does not matter: to me one is as beautiful as the other.

[1] This was an early title for *Look Homeward, Angel*.

Just subordinate and leading up to this main theme is as desperate and bitter a story of a contest between two people as you ever knew—a man and his wife—the one with an inbred, and also an instinctive, terror and hatred of property; the other with a growing mounting lust for ownership that finally is tinged with mania—a struggle that ends in decay, death, desolation.

This is all I've time for now. I wish I could tell you more of this magnificent old town, held in a cup of green steep hills, climbing one of them, made on one plan from one material—the finest place really I've ever seen.

Write me, American Express Co., London. God bless you all.

Henry Fisk Carlton, to whom the following letter was written, was a member of the 47 Workshop in 1920–1922, and a fellow instructor of English with Wolfe at New York University from 1925–1928. Since then, he has been a free-lance writer for radio.

To HENRY FISK CARLTON

[32 Wellington Square]
[London]

[September 3, 1926]

Dear Henry:

I enjoyed everything in your letter except its brevity. I put *that* down to New York heat. While you were sweltering at Washington Square, I suppose I was being fanned by the chill breezes of the English Lakes, and Scotland.

I am living now in London's Chelsea, a so-called Bohemia, though why it should be, I don't know. Certainly none of the gay artists hereabouts are afflicted with any form of Exhibitionism. I have two rooms, a bedroom and an ample sitting room at Number 32 Wellington Square, in a house that looks exactly like all the other houses in Wellington Square, save that one of them, just opposite, is painted yellow. Thus far, I am sure you believe me—the rest, so help me God, is also true.

I am brought a cup of tea and a newspaper at 8:30 every morning by an old man who was formerly a butler—now with his huge, fat, one-eyed wife, proprietor of this establishment. I arise, dress, shave, and have a simple breakfast of tea, toast, marmalade, one fried egg and two slices of bacon. Later I read the paper again; depart at ten o'clock for my morning walk along the Thames, during which time my rooms are cleaned;

return; go to work until lunch, when I take a bus for the American Express where I hope to find mail. Then lunch near Piccadilly and Soho, a stroll about London, and back to work. I am in bed by midnight.

I have finished a very full and complete outline of my book [1]—the outline itself the length almost of a novel—and at present I am writing about 3,000 words a day, which I hope to increase to 4,000. The novel will be Dickensian or Meredithian in length, but the work of cutting—which means, of course, adding an additional 50,000 words—must come later. . . .

The best friend,[2] I believe, that I ever had went home almost two weeks ago. We came here from Glasgow two weeks ago yesterday. . . . She is a very exceptional person—the grit, determination, and executive capacity that men are mistakenly supposed to have, but good-humored and kindly always. "She knew what she wanted."—I saw the opus, by the way, the other night in London, as it finished its run here: it gives me additional proof of my error in trying to write plays. What is, is not; the Good is Bad; the Stupid Brilliant; the Shallow Profound; the Mediocre Significant. . . .

I am completing this several days later. England has had an unprecedented summer, warm and sunny, the dryest August in almost thirty years; but starting punctually on September 1, as if scheduled, leaden, misty, drizzly days have set in. It is now September 3: in just one month, Henry, I will have marked off another year of my life. I have hoped for much: the lurid phantasies of my young twenties of fame, wealth, and honor have become, if not less modest, more mature; but I believe I can tell you honestly my desire for excellence in my work has grown more intense—where once the Golden Apple was going to drop into my lap in some more or less miraculous way, I am now, for perhaps the first time in my life, engaged seriously in trying to pick the fruit. I am writing from five to six hours a day. . . .

If in any way possible, I will stay over here until I have written my book—perhaps, although I hope not, until I have been forgotten. But I believe the thing is as hard for me as for anyone. I have had for a year now companionship, affection, and the inestimable comfort of human belief. I am here now without resources of friends, without the pleasure of having my work either known or recognized, and with no establishment save what I fashion myself. I would not attempt to conceal from you the genuine hole this makes in my life. I have had, and given up, what I never had before: but I am not at all despondent, and I am doing my work. . . .

[THE LETTER BREAKS OFF UNFINISHED]

[1] *The Building of a Wall*, later called *O Lost*, and finally *Look Homeward, Angel*.
[2] Aline Bernstein.

To ALINE BERNSTEIN

Brussels

Wednesday, Sept 22, [1926]

My Dear:

. . . I have been in this very gay city for ten days now; in over a week I have not spoken in my own language, or talked with one of my own nation. My talk with nearly everyone has been impersonal—a matter of buying and paying. It's not bad, save at night. I get rather lonely, then.

I have done a great deal of writing—my book is going to enormous length, and I can't get done as quickly as I thought. To-day is the only day I haven't written—I am writing you this at dinner (8 o'clock) and shall try to get my day's work done to-night.

I took the day off and went to Waterloo in a bus—the first trip I've made. There were seven or eight of us only—two or three English, two or three French, and your old friend, James Joyce.[1] He was with a woman about forty, and a young man, and a girl. I noticed him after we had descended at Waterloo—I had seen his picture only a day or two ago in a French publisher's announcements: he was wearing a blind over one eye. He was very simply—even shabbily—dressed. We went into a little café where the bus stopped to look at the battle souvenirs and buy post-cards: then we walked up what was once the Sunken Road to a huge circular building that had a panorama of the battle painted around the sides; then we ascended the several hundred steps up the great mound which supports the lion and looks out over the field. The young man, who wore horn-rim spectacles, and a light sporty looking overcoat, looked very much like an American college boy: he began to talk to me going up the steps— I asked him if he knew the man with the eye blind. He said he did, and that it was Joyce. I commented briefly that I had seen Joyce's picture and read his book; after this the young fellow joined me at every point. Walking back down the road to the café, I asked him if Joyce's eyesight was better—he said it had greatly improved. He said Joyce was working on a new book, but thought it impossible to say when it was finished. We went back to the café—they sat down at a table and had tea—the young man seemed about to ask me to join them, and I took a seat quickly at another table, calling for two beers. They all spoke French together—he told them

---

[1] Mrs. Bernstein had known Joyce when his play, *Exiles*, was put on in 1925 by the Neighborhood Players, of which she was a director and stage-designer. She says that in 1926 she called on Joyce in London, to pay him his royalties from the play in American dollars. As she remembers it, Wolfe called for her there and was introduced to Joyce hastily in the dark hallway where he could not clearly see his face.

all about it, and they peeked furtively at me from time to time—the great man himself taking an occasional crafty shot at me with his good eye. As they had tea, they all wrote postcards. As they got up to go into the bus, the young man bowed somewhat grandly to me—I don't blame him; I'd be pleased too. I judge the people are Joyce's family—he is a man in the middle forties—old enough to have a son and a daughter like these. The woman had the appearance of a thousand middle class French women I've known—a vulgar, rather loose mouth; not very intelligent looking. The young man spoke English well, but with a foreign accent. It was tragic to see Joyce—one of the gods of the moment—speaking not one word of the language his fame is based on. The girl was rather pretty—I thought at first she was a little American flapper.

Joyce was very simple, very nice. He walked next to the old guide who showed us around, listening with apparent interest to his harangue delivered in broken English, and asking him questions. We came home to Brussels through a magnificent forest, miles in extent—Joyce sat with the driver on the front seat, asked a great many questions. I sat alone on the back seat—it was a huge coach; the woman sat in front of me, the girl in front of her, the young man to one side. Queer arrangement, eh?

Joyce got a bit stagey on the way home, draping his overcoat poetically around his shoulders. But I liked Joyce's looks—not extraordinary at first sight, but growing. His face was highly colored, slightly concave—his mouth thin, not delicate, but extraordinarily humorous. He had a large powerful straight nose—redder than his face, somewhat pitted with scars and boils.

When we got back to Brussels, and stopped in front of the bus office, the young man and two women made a little group, while Joyce went inside. The young fellow was looking at me, and I was swimming in beer. I made a dive for the nearest place, which was under a monument: they are more respectable here than in Paris.

Anyway it was too good to spoil: the idea of Joyce and me being at Waterloo at the same time, and aboard a sight-seeing bus, struck me as insanely funny: I sat on the back seat making idiot noises in my throat, and crooning all the way back through the forest.

I think really they might have been a little grand about it if they had known they were discovered. But they were just like common people out sight-seeing.

I'm going on to Antwerp to-morrow, Bruges the day after, London Sunday or Monday. . . . My life is utterly austere, utterly remote. I have eaten well here—some of the restaurants are excellent. But I have not sat at table or anywhere else with anyone, save a little English merchant who came over on the boat with me: he was a funny little man, . . . who conducted me, with many a sly wink to a table at a most respectable dinner hall: we drank orangeade, the little man looked at the girls, and winked at me, going off into fits of silent laughter.

You get nothing to drink in Brussels but beer and wine unless you buy *bottles* of the stronger stuff at stores. I drink beer mainly: there are places here where you get iced sparkling champagne for twelve cents a goblet.

Last night about midnight—I had gone out from my room after working, for a walk—a woman stopped me, and began to wheedle me. She was a large strapping blonde prostitute. I gave her money for a beer and sent her on. A few minutes later, I noticed a fearful commotion across the street. Prostitutes, with their eager delight in a brawl, came in magical hordes. My lady had cut a sizable hunk out of a drunken gentleman's neck with a razor, and was fiercely mauling a small man all over the pavement. There were several minor brawls going on between the whores and their pimps. Finally, someone yelled "Police," and the army disappeared up four separate alleys. The police came up and arrested magnificently the man who had been cut. . . .

I am going back to England to try to finish the book—it is a far vaster thing than I had thought, but it grows in clarity and structure every day. This letter is stupid—all my energy . . . has gone into the book. I may go to Oxford next month. Meanwhile I shall try to get back my old apartment in London. . . .

Good-bye—God bless you, my dear.

I'm tired after Joyce and Waterloo. Forgive a stupid letter. I just thought that I shall probably be 26 years old when you get this. At 23, hundreds of people thought I'd do something. Now, no one does—not even myself. I really don't care very much. . . .

To OLIN DOWS

Harvard Club
New York.
Thursday night.
[January, 1927]

Dear Olin:

I've just had your note—I've twenty minutes to answer it but I'm quite willing to take the rest of the night if my reply will fetch you to see me, or me to see you.

I came back from Europe January first: I am living in a huge garret at

13 East 8th Street (not the *village*) over a tailoring shop. I am writing a huge book, on which I started while in England. I write from eleven o'clock at night till six in the morning, and get up at one or two o'clock. For the first time in my life, I'm seriously at work. It is mad, drunken, wild— but it makes good reading.

Let me get this in—breathlessly. I have thought of you, my fine fellow, several thousand times, and I have wondered why I have lost you. I wondered if I had written something in a letter that offended you, or whether you were disgusted at my manner of life. Because, somehow or other, I imagine I may suggest to the thoughtful person the worst excesses of Nero, Caligula, or the most evil devotee of Gomorrhaean lechery. Let me reassure you: you will find me respectable, hard-working, poverty-stricken, dirty—and, I'm afraid, somewhat dull. A few friends from the old sunken world climb the steps to see me—beyond them, I see no one, go nowhere.

I may be forced back to teaching next September [1]—they want me back, God knows why (no modesty)—and I may go abroad this summer if I can get Moby Dick launched.

If you were waiting for me to write you, you would have had (as Sam Johnson said) the victory long ago. But I did not know where to find you. I thought of Yale, but didn't know the address, and I didn't think of Rhinebeck. The master mind again.

[THE REMAINDER OF THIS LETTER HAS BEEN LOST]

To MABEL WOLFE WHEATON

> Harvard Club
> New York.
>
> Monday, Jan. 24, [1927]

Dear Mabel:

I got your letter to-night, and I saw Ralph off last night.[1] Your letter to him came an hour or two before the boat sailed, and it was so full of love and kisses that he was unable to speak for five or ten minutes. Then he began a long oration celebrating your goodness, greatness, beauty, and so on, which ended when he ran out of breath and the boat sailed. Also, he was fairly sober at the time. But more of this later. . . .

I wouldn't have missed Ralph and his playmates for anything. It was

[1] Wolfe did not teach at New York University during the spring, 1927 term, but went back in September.

[1] Ralph Wheaton had gone on a cruise to Cuba conducted by the National Cash Register Company for their salesmen.

the first time I had ever seen several hundred up-and-coming go-getters together. I went down to the dock at five o'clock. Sleety icy nasty weather! Beautiful little boat, kept beautifully clean by the Dutch who run it. But it won't last. Ralph had a berth on B deck with an agent from Memphis, and Mr. ——, the —— Knockout. I found Ralph in his room, S—— doing a wild Charleston at the piano on the landing, and everyone else looking as if he had just come from Cuba.

I was touched by the manner in which the boys greeted each other after a year's absence. As they came aboard and spied their friends, their mouths would drop open in an expression of astonishment, they would drop their bags, let out a loud whoop, and rush forward roaring with laughter, shouting such pleasantries as:

"Joe, you old bastard, how the hell are you!"
    or
"Well I'm Goddammed if it ain't Pete—you lousy bum!"

And so on. The Company had presented each of them with a new walking stick, the hat of an Admiral of The Fleet, with a star for each trip—Ralph had nine—and $85, I believe, in cash. I went off the boat about six o'clock with Ralph, S——, the Miami agent, and the man from Hagerstown who thought he knew where we could get it. Only he didn't, and I took them to one of my places, an Italian restaurant, where we could. All of us ate the enormous dollar dinner, and put away a good amount of America's fine old table wine—synthetic booze—in the shape of rye, rum, beer, ale, and cocktails, of which last I, four, your husband two or three.

Poor devils, they were pleased as children because it was what they called "good stuff," but I've been worried over the state of their health all day. —— bought a bottle of Baccardi Rum which we took back to the boat and pretty well killed with the aid of the aforementioned Brother ——, who took a long pull, belched loudly, and remarked that it was damned good Scotch. He had apparently been in training for the last two or three days, and I saw no particular reason why he should go to Cuba at all since he seemed to be doing so well in New York. He was in love with all the world: his way of showing it was to pull an eight inch pocket knife from his trousers, open it, go off in a fit of insane laughter, and announce that he was going to cut your goddammed heart out. But there was no harm in the boy—he took a great fancy to me, informed me that I looked like a damned pirate, and was worse than my brother Fred— which was all he could say for anyone. By this time the effects of New York hooch had worn off a little from other members of the passenger list, and they stood about thirstily waiting for the ship to sail and the bar to open. I informed them that a ship's bar does not usually open until the next morning, if she sails at night, at which 437 voices yelled that she had better open (By God!) or they'd break the damned door down. So I suppose she opened. . . .

[THE REMAINDER OF THIS LETTER HAS BEEN LOST]

To HOMER A. WATT

Hotel Hemenway
Boston

Monday Night, March 7, 1927

Dear Professor Watt:

I have come to Boston for a few days to see some friends and to get several dozen volumes of divine poetry, relics of my youth, which . . . I left with my uncle, three years ago. . . . I had your letter several weeks ago: I have thought it over many times. Later, Carlton [1] told me that he had talked with you, and that you suggested that I accept the appointment to teach next September, with the understanding that I might withdraw my acceptance provided I informed you within reasonable time.

I know you will be glad to hear that I have worked hard and steadily in my garret, and that I hope to have my huge book on paper by May, and in the hands of a publisher (I hope!) by summer. I think you understand that what I want to do with my life is to live by and for my writing. That independence—I had better say that slavery—is the highest desire I have ever known. To hope for it at present is precarious. I thank you again, fervently, for your patience, your kindness, and your encouragement. May I assume that if the miracle (of publication and royalty) does not happen, I can have employment in the September division, and if it does, and I am able to go on under my own steam, that I may decently (before the term's beginning) withdraw?

I am returning to New York day after tomorrow. My mail address is still the Harvard Club. I shall come in to see you during the month.

Life is many days. But I'm at a time when it seems very short. My twenty-six years weigh on me and, rather desperately, I feel my lack of achievement. I surrender myself again, therefore, to your extraordinary indulgence, which has been unfailing.

This is a bad, groping, fumbling letter. I've said what I wanted to say, but badly. I've been roaming over Concord all day and climbing the tower in Hawthorne's house. I'm tired.

[1] Henry Fisk Carlton.

To MABEL WOLFE WHEATON

Harvard Club
New York
Sat. night, March 26, 1927

Dear Mabel:

. . . Your apples came while I was away in Boston. They were splendid apples, but they had been en route for some time, I believe, and a great many of them were getting soft. Mrs. B's [1] chef, therefore, converted the sick men into apple sauce—there were some for me too, when I got home. Don't feel badly about them—if I didn't cram them all down my own gullet, you can have the satisfaction of knowing they gave pleasure to a very great lady, the best friend I may ever have. . . .

I am working like a horse. I go nowhere—not even to the theatre. I am in my garret all day, and come here sometimes at night for mail, and to do a little reading. I hope to get my book written, revised, and typed this Spring. It has been suggested to me that I go abroad this summer, but I shall not budge from my present residence until the book is done and in the hands of a publisher.

My health is good, although I've lost weight since I came back, and no longer have my jolly red English complexion—a combined effect of rain and John Haig. Also, I am no better than an idiot usually by midnight, because I drink some dozen or eighteen cups of coffee during the day of my own brewing. It gets me simply crazy with nerves, but it keeps me alive and cursing. Like many of my more famous associates I work best at night, and I am not often in bed before three thirty or four o'clock in the morning. But I'm getting my work done, which is all that matters.

Thanks for your words of good cheer. I shall probably do something someday—soon, I hope. My greatest deficiency is a total lack of salesmanship—a quality that is quite as important in profitable writing as anywhere else. I never sent my plays to more than two or three managers and if I got no answer within a month I wrote insulting letters demanding their return. I have never known where to go, where to turn, or what to do. This time, certain friends will probably attend to that part of it for me.

The University job is open for me in September, and I have also been offered work with the radio,[2] and with an advertising company that's

---

[1] Mrs. Bernstein's.

[2] At this time, Henry Fisk Carlton was doing several free lance radio programs for WJZ and WEBF, and had suggested that Wolfe try doing some shows for his programs, also on a free lance basis. Carlton says Wolfe had similar offers from other people but never did any actual writing for the radio.

lousy with money.[3] I could probably make a great deal more from the advertising than from teaching, but it would take more time.

This is a bad, stupid letter. It's midnight, I've been at work all day. I'm fagged out. I'll write you again when I'm in better fettle. I'm glad to hear of your improved health. We may all live yet to die of old age. Give my love to Mama, Fred, and Ralph. Tell me what's happening as soon as you can.

I've been out once to parties of the great and near-great in New York— writers, poets, actresses—another effort of my friends to help me. Went to one terrible studio party where I met a man named Van Vechten, novelist, a . . . woman named Elinor Wylie, who is all the go now—she writes novels and poetry—and her husband, Will Benét—I hated them so that I managed to insult them all before the evening was over. So, if I get there, I shall probably have to depend on my own steam. . . .

To MARGARET ROBERTS

> Harvard Club
> New York
>
> [Early June, 1927]

Dear Mrs. Roberts:

Forgive my long silence and the shortness of this letter. I have poured my life, my strength, and almost all my time for almost a year into my book, which is now nearing its end. I think it is the best thing I've ever done: certainly it is the only thing I have ever really worked on. I have learned that writing is hard work, desperate work, and that (as Ben Jonson said) "Who casts to write a living line must sweat." I have lived since I came back to New York in a deserted ramshackle building that trembles when a car passes; I have lived in its huge dirty garret, without heat, without plumbing—without anything but light. My mother wrote me several weeks ago—I hear from at least one member of my family every two or three months—congratulating me on the possession of "rich friends." Well, I suppose I have rich friends—a few of all kinds, rich and poor, have shown me amazing devotion—but I have taken only what was necessary for the barest existence. I have lived closer to poverty this year than ever in my life. And I do not regret it. I have had all I needed. The world for me was ghost when I wrote.

I don't know what the outcome will be. I have no power to peddle my wares, and I strike patronage a blow in the face. The other day word reached me that a rich woman who has supported a famous little theatre

---

[3] The J. Walter Thompson Company.

here for years (Miss Alice Lewisohn of the Neighborhood Playhouse) had told one of the directors last year that she would have done my play ("Welcome") but that I was the most arrogant young man she had ever known. The news gave me pleasure: my proud foolish words to her of disdain and contempt came back to me and I felt that I had acted well— I who will never be dandled into reputation by wealth. I have forsaken all groups; I live, save for the affection of a few friends, as much alone as anyone can live. And I know I am right! I believe—they believe—I shall come through. . . .

I wish I could tell you more of my book. I meant alone this: I think I shall call it "Alone, Alone," [1] for the idea that broods over it, and in it, and behind it is that we are all strangers upon this earth we walk on—that naked and alone do we come into life, and alone, a stranger, each to each, we live upon it. The title, as you know, I have taken from the poem I love best: "The Rime of the Ancient Mariner":—

> Alone, alone, all, all alone,
> Alone on a wide, wide sea!
> And never a saint took pity on
> My soul in agony.

My state is not bad—in spite of the fact that I am considered arrogant and proud (the protective coloration of one who was born without his proper allowance of hide). I am told, by someone who loves me, that I could have what I wanted of people—"the city at my feet," and so on—if I let myself out on them. Perhaps not—but, what's better, my friends like me.

I'm very tired; my health has stood the pounding beautifully. I don't know what I shall do when I finish. I may go abroad for a short trip. . . . Good-bye for the present. Write to me soon. You are one of the few people that will never become a phantom to me. God bless you all.

To MARGARET ROBERTS

Harvard Club
New York

Monday—May 30, 1927

Dear Mrs. Roberts:

. . . You say that no one *outside* my family loves me more than Margaret Roberts. Let me rather say the exact truth:—that no one *inside* my family loves me as much, and only one other person, I think, in all the world

[1] Another early title for *Look Homeward, Angel.*

loves me as much. My book is full of ugliness and terrible pain—and I think moments of a great and soaring beauty. In it (will you forgive me?) I have told the story of one of the most beautiful people I have ever known as it touched on my own life. I am calling that person Margaret Leonard. I was without a home—a vagabond since I was seven—with two roofs [1] and no home. I moved inward on that house of death and tumult from room to little room, as the boarders came with their dollar a day, and their constant rocking on the porch. My overloaded heart was bursting with its packed weight of loneliness and terror; I was strangling, without speech, without articulation, in my own secretions—groping like a blind sea-thing with no eyes and a thousand feelers toward light, toward life, toward beauty and order, out of that hell of chaos, greed, and cheap ugliness—and then I found you, when else I should have died, you mother of my spirit who fed me with light. Do you think that I have forgotten? Do you think I ever will? You are entombed in my flesh, you are in the pulses of my blood, the thought of you makes a great music in me— and before I come to death, I shall use the last thrust of my talent—whatever it is—to put your beauty into words.

Good-bye for the present. This is Decoration Day. I am decorated with weariness, but I am going to try to get it all down on paper in the next few weeks and then I may go abroad for a short time. My attic is getting hot—my friend, Olin Dows (almost as great a saint as you are) came down from his 80 rooms and 2000 acres on the Hudson Saturday and asked me to finish the book in the country. But I'm afraid of the big house and all the swells. He's had it alone all winter—but now his mother's coming from Washington (with all the legations) and his sister from Sweden; they're in for a big summer. But there's a lovely little cottage of two rooms, with a bath, deep in the woods, by the bathing pool, and he's offered this to me, together with as many acres of land as I need, forever, if I should ever care to stay there near him. He paints, lives like a Spartan on vegetables, and is a Bertrand Russell Socialist (much to his father's sorrow).

Write as soon as you get this. When I pluck up more strength, I'll write a good one. Excuse the gibberings. Good-bye. God bless you all.

The following letter to Mrs. Roberts was never finished and never mailed. Instead, Wolfe sent a brief letter dated July 11, which is omitted here since it only duplicates this in much briefer fashion.

[1] His father's house at 92 Woodfin Street, Asheville, and the Old Kentucky Home at 48 Spruce Street.

To MARGARET ROBERTS

Harvard Club
New York
[July 8 (?) 1927]

Dear Mrs. Roberts:

I read your letter this afternoon a few minutes after I had purchased second class passage on the *George Washington,* sailing Tuesday. Thus, I will not be here to greet you if you come in August: I am returning in September. All this I decided at once on Sunday, after mulling the business hopelessly for months. I had thought before that I would finish the book here and go abroad in the autumn to stay for a year in Italy. Several considerations prevented me. First, I have exhausted my wits on a gigantic piece of work—and I shall not want to write more, I think, for several months. Second, I should be here in New York next winter to try to launch the thing and some of my plays. Third, my going away for a long period of time would cause the deepest pain to the one person on earth who has the greatest claim to my love.[1] There is nothing in my life as important as this: I was a lonely out-cast, and suddenly I became richer, in the one true wealth, than Maecenas.

I am going to Paris for a short time—then on to Prague, Budapest, and Vienna, all lovely and unvisited. I shall be back in Paris for a few days in September. . . .

I have been in the country several weeks with my friend Olin Dows. I'm much restored physically, but my brain is falling apart like over-scrambled eggs. Hence this stupid letter. I refused to live in the big house with the swells: he gave me the gate-keeper's lodge—a little bit of heaven with a little river, a wooded glade, and the sound of water falling over the dam all through the night. Beyond, the stream widened into the mighty Hudson—the noblest river I know of.

I had to dress up in my dinner jacket almost every night, which was good for me because I'm somewhat afraid of people, and sometimes conceal my fear by being arrogant and sneering magnificently. On the Fourth of July, in the evening, I went with Olin to a neighboring estate of one of his rich friends, a young man named Vincent Astor, who is one of the richest young men in the world—his chief claim, I believe, to distinction. The young man likes to play with every kind of steam engine (he has a miniature railroad on the place) and to set off fireworks. He set off several thousand dollars worth for our delight—they were the loveliest things I've ever seen and did incredible things, whistling like

---

[1] Mrs. Bernstein.

birds, bursting in cascades of color, changing their lights, and so on. The simple villagers—some hundreds or thousands—sat on the lawns, and all the swells upon the verandahs. How they stared at me! I looked very well in my clothes, but they knew I was an alien of some sort. I have a kind of notoriety among them, I believe, as Olin's wild Bohemian friend: whenever they met me, they asked if it were really true that I stayed up all night and was writing a book—and what was it all about! But they were all very lovely—I'm afraid if I had to do it I'd find them dull.

Astor's grounds were huge and beautiful (thousands of acres magnificently kept), his house was huge and ugly—a stone Victorian thing that belonged to his father—the rooms were also huge and ugly, stuffed with ugly red plush furniture. After the fireworks we went inside to the dining room and ate ice cream and chicken salad and punch with the assistance of eight or ten flunkies. I'm sure I'd go murderously insane and kill a few of them if I had them around long. Astor's wife is a tall, blonde, slender young woman—very elegant and beautiful, and cold. Olin told me it was the first social position in America: the big rooms, the people around her really gave one the sense of a court. (But I've heard them talk—opinions that would disgrace an English Tory.)

But I lived very simply at the lodge house—by myself—going to the big house once a day, or having one good meal brought to me, and poisoning myself on my own cooking the rest of the time. As for Olin, he is in many respects the finest young man I've ever known—a very great person. . . .

To MABEL WOLFE WHEATON

> Harvard Club
> New York
> July 10, 1927

Dear Mabel:—

. . . Mama and Mrs. Roberts have both written me that you have not been well. I am sorry to hear this; I hope you are better now and will write me how you feel. I think of you all with loyalty and affection; I wish you all health and the good life with all my heart. If I have been different from the rest of you, and you thought me "queer" and a "freak," please remember that my fundamental nature is something I could neither help nor change, and that I have never lifted a finger to injure or molest any of you. I am older now, and perhaps not so unpleasant as you thought me when I was a child. The hostility and bitterness that was shown when I was in college and at Harvard ought to be dead now; I want nothing that belongs to any of you except your good will. I want to know very much that you are well and happy and at peace with life. . . .

I have been up in the country with the swells for three weeks or more. . . . I found a card from Donald MacRae [1] when I got back: I looked him up last night at the maternity hospital where he's in training, and stayed until four o'clock in the morning watching a baby get born. The doctors dressed me up in a long surgeon's dress (they laughed like hell!) and took me in to the operating room. I saw everything; they explained everything. It was one of the most terrible and beautiful things I have ever seen. I shall never forget it. The result of everything was a fine eight pound boy with a very healthy set of lungs. The mother was a big husky Irishwoman. She screamed like a maniac, and every time she did, I screwed my face into a knot and clenched my teeth—which the young doctors thought very funny. But she did not really suffer as much as it seemed; she wouldn't help them, she fought them, things weren't getting along; so Donald finally put the lady to sleep and they took the kid with forceps. Wonderful! Wonderful! Wonderful! I was bothered at first by the rough-and-ready talk of the doctors and nurses—it seemed brutal; but I saw later they are really very good and kind people, doing a humane service to poor and common people. If their talk was rough, their hands were gentle—everything was beautifully clean, and the poor woman's baby came into this world with more care and skill and comfort than you and I had.

I wish I could tell you more—it's more thrilling than any story: the chief doctor kept coaxing her along by saying: "Come on, momma! Do your stuff now! Give us some help, momma! Push! Push! Do you want to have this baby, momma, or not? It's your kid, momma, not mine! Be a sport." and so on. Finally—ether, forceps, baby. It was ugly, bloody, messy, horrible—but somehow beautiful: when I saw the little skull begin to come, and then the little body, and the doctor held him up by the heels and spanked him, and he screwed his face up and let out his first yell (a good loud one), I could restrain myself no longer: I gave a yell of my own and said "Come on, baby! Come on!" That made them laugh: they did not understand why anyone should get so excited. The ugliness, the horror, the pain is gone now: all that remains is that little perfect child, and all the mystery and tragic beauty of life, which now seems greater to me than ever. I have been so excited and stirred all day that I cannot eat for thinking of it—I could hardly get to sleep when I got home this morning. You

[1] J. Donald MacRae had been a fraternity brother of Wolfe's in Pi Kappa Phi at the University of North Carolina, and was at this time an intern at Manhattan Maternity and Dispensary in New York. He is now radiologist at Highsmith Hospital, Fayetteville, N.C.

will understand me when I tell you that this thing has made a great music in me: something gathers in my throat and my eyes are wet when I think of all the pain and wonder that little life must come to know; and I hope to God those feet will never walk as lonely a road as mine have walked, and I hope its heart will never beat as mine has at times under a smothering weight of weariness, grief, and horror; nor its brain be damned and haunted by the thousand furies and nightmare shapes that walk through mine. This is no sentiment—but the stark truth, from a very deep place in me.

This is all I can write—I'm terribly tired. Write me at Paris, if you can. Keep yourself well, lift up your heart, be happy.

P.S. I think Donald is going to be a good doctor. He has much kindliness and gentleness. When it was over last night I went downstairs with the doctors and nurses. We sat down and told one another dirty stories. It sounds bad—but it is their escape, healthy and harmless: I was more convinced than ever that they are fine people. If I get sick let me have such people around me—expert and calm-tempered roughnecks. No weeping bunglers. This is a bad letter: too tired to write well.

To HOMER A. WATT

Vienna

Aug. 11, 1927

Dear Professor Watt:

This is just a line of greeting and a reminder of our conversation several weeks ago about my schedule. I hope you have finally managed (from the distressing network of schedules you have had to arrange) to give me the hours you thought possible. By this arrangement, I would have night classes M. T. W. Thurs: my free time would be lumped together—highly desirable to me.

I have been in this charming town of Vienna for two days: I came on from Munich and the Bavarian mountains. There was a revolution here three weeks ago in which four hundred people lost their lives, but you could not tell it now from the gaiety of the city's life. These people seem to belong to an entirely different civilization from the Germans. There is a lightness, a delicacy, and a charm in the life here which is as un-Teutonic as anything can be. The whole town is much more French in its appearance—a smaller Paris, but I believe the gaiety of the people is more spontaneous than that of the Parisian—there is a much more honest cordiality here: they lack the very bad Gallic hardness.

I am going from here to Prague, and from there back to Paris. I expect to sail for New York about September 10. This has been a quiet and very rich little voyage. I am devouring the German language in gluttonous gobs and buying books with both hands. Do you know that I talk German to these people—very bad, clumsy, halting German, it's true, but they understand me. I have very little facility for speaking a language well, but I have a real talent for understanding it and soaking it up. I can now speak French with a bad fluency and read and understand it as well as English. Before another year has gone by I'm going to do the same for German. Then I'm going to get Italian. It's simply fascinating to be sunk in a new language and to have the names of all the things you want—tobacco, soap, matches, veal cutlets, and so on—printed and spoken around you in a new tongue. In this way it soaks in through the pores of your skin.

The papers are terribly excited here (and all over Europe) about the Sacco-Vanzetti case. The entire front page is given to it. There seems to be a universal demand for the pardon of the men. I do not know enough about the case: I think it is likely the men *may* be guilty, but I think also the trial was long, fumbling, and prejudiced. The great pity is that a thing like this suddenly coalesces and *symbolizes*, so to speak, the terribly bitter feeling that is felt for America throughout the world today. I am finishing this letter, by the way, several days after I began it: I have been in Vienna almost a week, and the enormous charm of the place has invaded me. When I come again, I'm coming here for several months to get the language. Munich was a magnificent town, with some of the greatest things in it I've ever seen, but there's simply no denying it: there *is* a sort of German—young gentlemen with dueling scars on their face, and older ones with shaven bullet heads, small porky eyes, and three ridges of neck over the back of their collars—that I do not, I do not like! I gave over carefully and quietly on the pavements until I found that these gentlemen had an unhappy (and I believe unconscious) habit of taking not only the four yards which was theirs, but the eight inches which was mine. All that I had ever felt about the sacredness of liberty and the rights of men boiled over, I kept grimly on my way, increased my stride just as I got upon the startled Hun, before he could retreat. God forgive me for this meanness of spirit: let me assure you that my prejudice, if I had any, was in their favor, because of the war's vicious propaganda. They are a very powerful and energetic people, quite ignorant, I believe, of their unpleasant qualities; they have tremendous creative and intellectual power: huge, profound, murky, and earth-shaking (like Kant and Wagner), but they are lacking in the fine delicacy and urbanity of these Viennese.

I've got to end abruptly. I hope you've had a pleasant summer. Please get me the schedule, if you can.

The following letter was submitted to various publishers with the manu-script of O, Lost (Look Homeward, Angel).

NOTE FOR THE PUBLISHER'S READER.

[Late March, 1928]

This book, by my estimate, is from 250,000 to 280,000 words long. A book of this length from an unknown writer no doubt is rashly experimental, and shows his ignorance of the mechanics of publishing. This is true: this is my first book.

But I believe it would be unfair to assume that because this is a very long book it is too long a book. A revision would, I think, shorten it somewhat. But I do not believe any amount of revision would make it a short book. It could be shortened by scenes, by pages, by thousands of words. But it could not be shortened by half, or a third, or a quarter.

There are some pages here which were compelled by a need for fullness of expression, and which had importance when the book was written not because they made part of its essential substance, but because, by setting them forth, the mind was released for its basic work of creation. These pages have done their work of catharsis, and may now be excised. But their excision would not make a short book.

It does not seem to me that the book is overwritten. Whatever comes out of it must come out block by block and not sentence by sentence. Generally, I do not believe the writing to be wordy, prolix, or redundant. And separate scenes are told with as much brevity and economy as possible. But the book covers the life of a large family intensively for a period of twenty years, and in rapid summary for fifty years. And the book tries to describe not only the visible outer lives of all these people, but even more their buried lives.

The book may be lacking in plot but it is not lacking in plan. The plan is rigid and densely woven. There are two essential movements—one outward and one downward. The outward movement describes the effort of a child, a boy, and a youth for release, freedom, and loneliness in new lands. The movement of experience is duplicated by a series of widening concentric circles, three of which are represented by the three parts of the book. The downward movement is represented by a constant excavation into the buried life of a group of people, and describes the cyclic curve of a family's life—genesis, union, decay, and dissolution.

To me, who was joined so passionately with the people in this book, it seemed that they were the greatest people I had ever known and the texture of their lives the richest and strangest; and discounting the distortion of judgment that my nearness to them would cause, I think they would seem extraordinary to anyone. If I could get my magnificent people on paper as they were, if I could get down something of their strangeness and richness in my book, I believed that no one would object to my 250,000 words; or, that if my pages swarmed with this rich life, few would damn an inept manner and accuse me of not knowing the technique for making a book, as practiced by Balzac, or Flaubert, or Hardy, or Gide. If I have failed to get any of this opulence into my book, the fault lies not in my people —who could make an epic—but in me.

But that is what I wanted to do and tried to do. This book was written in simpleness and nakedness of soul. When I began to write the book twenty months ago I got back something of a child's innocency and wonder. You may question this later when you come to the dirty words. But the dirty words can come out quickly—if the book has any chance of publication, they will come out without conscience or compunction. For the rest, I wrote it innocently and passionately. It has in it much that to me is painful and ugly, but, without sentimentality or dishonesty, it seems to me, because I am a romantic, that pain has an inevitable fruition in beauty. And the book has in it sin and terror and darkness—ugly dry lusts, cruelty, a strong sexual hunger of a child—the dark, the evil, the forbidden. But I believe it has many other things as well, and I wrote it with strong joy, without counting the costs, for I was sure at the time that the whole of my intention—which was to come simply and unsparingly to naked life, and to tell all of my story without affection or lewdness—would be apparent. At that time I believed it was possible to write of all things, so long as it was honestly done. So far as I know there is not a nasty scene in the book—but there are the dirty words, and always a casual and unimpeded vision of everything.

When I wrote the book I seized with delight everything that would give it color and richness. All the variety and madness of my people—the leper taint, the cruel waste, the dark flowering evil of life I wrote about with as much exultancy as health, sanity, joy.

It is, of course, obvious that the book is "autobiographical." But in a literal sense, it is probably no more autobiographical than "Gulliver's Travels." There is scarcely a scene that has its base in literal fact. The book is a fiction—it is loaded with invention: story, fantasy, vision. But it is a fiction that is, I believe, more true than fact—a fiction that grew out of a life completely digested in my spirit, a fiction which telescopes, condenses, and objectifies all the random or incompleted gestures of life —which tries to comprehend people, in short, not by telling what people did, but what they should have done. The most literal and autobiographical part of the book, therefore, is its picture of the buried life. The most exact thing in it is the fantasy—its picture of a child's soul.

I have never called this book a novel. To me it is a book such as all men may have in them. It is a book made out of my life, and it represents my vision of life to my twentieth year.

What merit it has I do not know. It sometimes seems to me that it presents a strange and deep picture of American life—one that I have never seen elsewhere; and that I may have some hope of publication. I do not know; I am very close to it. I want to find out about it, and to be told by someone else about it.

I am assured that this book will have a good reading by an intelligent person in a publishing house. I have written all this, not to propitiate you, for I have no peddling instinct, but entreat you, if you spend the many hours necessary for a careful reading, to spend a little more time in giving me an opinion. If it is not a good book, why? If parts are good and parts bad, what are they? If it is not publishable, could it be made so? Out of the great welter of manuscripts that you must read, does this one seem distinguished by any excellence, interest, superior merit?

I need a little honest help. If you are interested enough to finish the book, won't you give it to me?

The following letter was sent to Professor James B. Munn with the manuscript of O, Lost (Look Homeward, Angel) *which Wolfe had asked him to read. Dr. Munn was Professor of English and Dean at Washington Square College, New York University, from 1928–1932, and had been Assistant Professor and Assistant Dean during Wolfe's earlier years as an instructor there. He is now Professor of English at Harvard University.*

To JAMES B. MUNN

[New York City]

Tuesday, March 27, [1928]

Dear Doctor Munn:

I give you my book with a feeling of strong fear. When you read my play [1] two or three years ago, you spoke about it in a way I shall not forget. The one criticism I remember concerned a page or two of dialogue which was tainted by coarseness. You spoke mildly and gently of that, but I felt you were sorry it had been written in. Now I give you a book on which I have wrought out my brain and my heart for twenty months. There are places in it which are foul, obscene, and repulsive. Most of those will come out on revision. But please, Dr. Munn, believe that this book

---

[1] *Mannerhouse.*

was honestly and innocently written. Forgive me the bad parts, and remember me for the beauty and passion I have *tried* to put in it. It is not *immoral*, it is not *dirty*—it simply represents an enormous excavation in my spirit. Saying that, I feel better. My energy is completely exhausted—I felt as if I should drop dead when I came to the last comma. I feel as if my life were beginning again, and what I shall do for a year or two, or where I shall be, I don't know.

But remember that I give you this for no other reason than for the tremendous regard I have for you. The thought that I may have written anything that will cause you to change any good opinion you may ever have had of me makes me pause.

But I can't go on explaining forever. Please read the "Note to The Publisher" [2] before you begin.

Here it is—my heart is in it.

To HOMER A. WATT

Harvard Club
New York
April 1, 1928

CONFIDENTIAL

Dear Professor Watt:

I am writing you this letter before I speak to you, because I feel you may want a formal record for your files.

After long consideration I have decided not to accept a teaching appointment at the university for next year.[1] I think the time has come when I must make a bold venture with my life: in some way—not, I am afraid, very clearly defined yet—I want to get the energy of my life directed towards the thing it desires most. In short, I am going to try to support myself by writing—if necessary, by hack writing of any sort, stories, advertising, articles—but *writing* of a sort. If my book should be accepted I should, of course, immediately start work on a new one. I know that this is a gamble, but it occurs to me that we can afford to gamble once or twice in an effort to get at the heart of our desire. The most reckless people, I believe, are those who never gamble at all.

During the last few days, in the tragic misfortune of Mr. Powell,[2] I have

---

[2] The "Note for the Publisher's Reader."

[1] Wolfe did not teach the Fall 1928 term at New York University, and only taught half-time in the Spring 1929 term. He accepted appointment for the academic year 1929–1930 and taught the Fall term, but resigned in January to devote himself entirely to writing.

[2] Desmond Powell had been an instructor in the English Department at New

seen again the splendid generosity which shows that New York University is not simply a group of buildings with elevators. And since an action of this sort must come from men, and not from brick and stone, I am inclined to place the credit for it where I have myself the deepest cause for gratefulness—with you and with Dr. Munn.

I have been more tired this Spring than at any other time of my life—I have felt, along with the finishing of my book, such damnable weariness of my brain and heart as I did not know existed. And often, I am afraid, I have been surly, ill-tempered, unable to join happily with other people. For this, if I cannot plead justification, I can at least ask pardon. But there is one assurance I must give you: once or twice, when I was in a chafed and bitter temper, I have heard some of the young men say that I occupied the position of a privileged character—that I was the departmental "wild oat," and any laxity or extravagance would be permitted me. Now this, I am sure, was harmless joking, but it touched rawly on me at the time. I think no one knows better than I do my deficiencies as a teacher —among which I would name a lack of orderly arrangement, an extravagant and useless expenditure of energy on all things, and a constant belief in miracles—but please believe that within my limits I have given you honest and faithful service.

It is perhaps childish for me to mention this, but I am childishly proud of this—that being notorious for a lack of discipline and regularity when I came here, I have, in my three years, missed only one class. That happened my first year, and was caused by the lateness of a boat returning from Boston. And I think I have never put a grade on a student's paper without trying to add a few lines of sensible and honest criticism. If you have ever had cause to doubt that, I think a very simple investigation would bear me out.

Will you please understand, Professor Watt, that I am not crying myself up vainly and boastfully? Most earnestly I want you to know, now that I'm leaving, that I have not tried to pose as a Bohemian or a temperamental fellow in order to get out of work—within the trap of my nature I have done all things I could to fulfill my obligation to you. It would cause me very real distress to think you doubted that. I have been at times a very difficult, a very moody and extravagant person, but I do not believe I have been a cheap or common person.

I think one of the chief reasons for my leaving now is not that I dislike teaching, and find it dull, but that I may like it too well. I find that it takes from me the same energy that I put into Creation: if this is true,

York University, and had been obliged by ill health to go to Colorado in March, 1928. Professor Watt had told him that the University would continue to pay his salary for the rest of the academic year and would also pay his travelling expenses.

and there is anything in me worth saving or having, I draw comfort from the belief that my classes must have got some of the best of me during my three years.

This is a bad and clumsy letter from a tired man. But none the less it comes from a very deep place in me. Three years of my life have been spent here. I know that they have carved a mark and left a deposit. Let me assure you that I will never forget your kindness, and your generous comprehension, and that if any *good* distinction ever attaches to my name, I shall be proud to acknowledge my connection with this place—if any *bad* one, I shall keep silent.

P.S. Will you please treat this as a *personal* communication?

To MARGARET ROBERTS

Harvard Club
New York

April 6, 1928

Dear Mrs. Roberts:

Forgive this long silence—I finished my book and sent it to a publisher [1] for reading ten days ago. This means nothing more than that it will get read, and that I will get an answer in another three weeks. I am completely, utterly exhausted—the last twenty pages were agony—but I have a feeling of enormous relief to know that it's done. I have done a rashly experimental thing—the publishing firm said it's the longest manuscript they've had since "An American Tragedy"—but like Martin Luther, I couldn't do otherwise. Hereafter I'll keep more within prescribed limits.

The dean of Washington Square College [2] (N.Y.U.), who is a young man, a millionaire, an idealist, and a sensitive, romantic person, has just finished reading it. He wrote me a magnificently honest letter about it: he was terribly shocked at the pain, the terror, the ugliness, and the waste of human life in the book—he thought the people rose to nobility and beauty only at the end (in this he is terribly wrong!). But he said the book was unique in English and American literature, that if it is published it must be published without changing a word, and that he felt he had lived with the people in it for years.

Whether any publisher can be found who is willing to take the chance, I don't know. But, for good or bad, I'm going the whole distance now. I shall not be back at N.Y.U. next fall. They have been splendid and offered

[1] Boni and Liveright.
[2] Dean Munn.

me a raise, and finally told me the latch string was out at any time—that I could come back any time I needed the job. . . .

After the sap has risen in me a little more, I'll write you a longer and better letter. This is just a filler-in. Let me hear from you when you have time. Give my love to all the family. And tell me something about mine. I write, but I don't always get answers.

How is Asheville? Still, I hope, repentant.

To JAMES B. MUNN

[New York City]
Monday, May 21 [1928].

Please read this at your leisure.

Dear Dr. Munn:

I have tried to reach you several times during the last two or three days, but your very capable office force has fended me off. I'm going to Europe next month, and I'm trying to get all the money I can together. I believe your sanction will carry a long way with the Bursar—I don't know if he'll give me *all* the remainder of my salary in one lump or not, but will you say a word for me?

I've got a *new* book in mind.[1] I thought I should not write again for several centuries, but there's no cure for my own kind of lunacy. I don't see how this one can fail—it has everything: rich people, swank, a poor but beautiful girl, romance, adventure, Vienna, New York, a big country house, and so on. Also, after a careful examination of 4,362 modern novels, I have decided to make it exactly 79,427 words long. Will you please order your copy now? But honestly, I'm excited about it. In spite of my summary, I've got stuff for a good and moving book—also, perhaps, stuff for a bad and trashy, but possibly successful book. Now what's a poor young guy to do, Dean Munn? I've got to do it one way or the other—straddling the fence is no good.

About the Monster—"O, Lost." I had bad news of it, and then a bit of good news. The good news came last. I sent it to Boni and Liveright first. After five weeks they rejected it. I had a polite but very firm note from Mr. T. R. Smith, the manager. It had been given three readings, he said—much of it had quality and originality. He had to admit, he said, he enjoyed reading much of it. But it was "so long—so terribly long." Besides, it was autobiographical. They had lost money on four books "of this type"

---

[1] *The River People,* which was never published, but of which a portion appears on pages 500–596 of *Of Time and the River.*

last year. Others would no doubt be published, and might even sell, but for the present, as far as B. and L. is concerned, etc.

Meanwhile Ernest Boyd, the critic, was giving it a private reading. I heard from him—rather, from his wife [2]—the other day. Boyd said he thought the book could not be published in its present form because of "crudities." I don't know what that means—I'll have to see him. Perhaps his sensitive soul recoiled at some of the *langwidge*. He grew up in Dublin, you know, with James Joyce. But Mrs. B.—who is a big fat Frenchwoman (I hear)—did not agree with her gifted spouse. She translates French novels, and is a literary agent, and knows everyone. She seems to think there's a chance for it. As for me—I think nothing. I'm still in a stupor when I try to think of it. I'm going to see her to-morrow.

Harcourt Brace is reading it now. I've heard nothing from them. Could you talk to me for a few minutes before I go? The irony of it is that the book—which may get me kicked out of doors by every highbrow publisher in America—has landed me a good job with an advertising company [3]—if I want to take it. God knows what I shall do! I want to write the other book.

To GEORGE WALLACE

> Harvard Club
> New York
> Monday June 25, 1928

Dear George:

I am going to Europe Saturday on whatever boat I can get on—but I hope a German one, so that I can get the beer. I want you to write me, if you can, before July 15, and send the letter to the American Express Co., Paris. I am asking this of a half dozen other people also, because I know that one of the ugliest feelings in the world is to come away from a foreign mail window empty handed. I do not know where I shall be—I shall be in Paris only a few days—but that mailing address is most convenient. Was going to Vienna, but I heard the other day that a great music festival is on, the town is full of our fellow countrymen, and prices, of course, have hit the ceiling. So I must look elsewhere. If I can get second

---

[2] Madeleine Boyd, who became Wolfe's literary agent at this time, and who sold *Look Homeward, Angel* to Scribners.

[3] In a letter to his mother dated June 7, 1928 (see *Thomas Wolfe's Letters to His Mother*, page 159), Wolfe wrote: "The J. Walter Thompson Company . . . has offered me a job writing advertisements for them. . . . They want me to begin in October—but they also want me to promise to stay for three years. . . . I don't like the three year business."

class passage on *Ile de France,* I'll get off at Havre, and go up the pleasant Seine to Rouen. And Brussels—that's a good place, too. Pretty girls and cheap champagne. Or München again. Or Buda-Pest—I have a typed list of all the good things to eat and drink there, given to me by Mr. Beer, the writer's brother.[1] And if it weren't so hot I should like to try Florence. I get no thrill from Spain, although everyone is doing it. I'm usually three or four years behind the moderns.

I haven't answered J. Walter Thompson yet. They gave me more time to think it over. But what I want to do is to write a new book. I've got one outlined that stinks with swank and money and romance.[2] It'll be just the length and everything. But honestly I think I can get a very good and moving story out of it.

About the first one—the *monster:* Mrs. Ernest Boyd has appointed herself my agent—at 10%. She says it's a good book, miles too long, but thinks she can find publisher. Says I must cut. Also, Mr. Melville Cane, attorney for Harcourt, Brace and member of the firm, says it's a *good* book—a fine, moving, and distinguished piece of writing. He says it's miles too long—he opened a copy of "Elmer Gantry," which his firm printed, and set that as *my* maximum length.[3] If I cut, he thinks it will get published. Mrs. Boyd gave the book to a young firm of publishers just out.[4] When she heard about Harcourt Brace, she called up and said I would do much better to stick with new firm. She said they wanted first option on my second book and would publish if writing is as good as the first, and the book *of a reasonable length.* Does this at last sound like anything to you? I don't see why they should kid me. . . .

This is all for the present. Went home for a week, and found everyone with lots of real estate and no money. Was going to Europe Saturday but dentist made fascinating operation on tooth and jaw. Hurt like hell, but good job.

Please write me a good letter to Paris, and I'll try to answer in kind. Love to the family.

[1] Richard Beer, who had been an American Vice Consul in Budapest in 1922 and 1923.

[2] *The River People.*

[3] Mr. Cane was not a "member of the firm." He did serve as a director of the corporation. He did not prescribe "Elmer Gantry" as the maximum length but simply offered it as an example of a good-size novel.

[4] Covici-Friede.

To ALINE BERNSTEIN

Savoy Hotel, Frankfurt A.M.
Begun last Saturday and
finished today, Friday Sept 7 (?),
[1928]

Dear Aline:

Here I am at another stage of my travels—a very short one, for I came on
here from Wiesbaden, which is only thirty miles away, to-day. . . . I
got here as it was growing dark to-night—the ride was not interesting:
the beautiful Rhine country ends about Wiesbaden, and the trip was
through a flat fat-looking country full of crops and grapes. I love to
come to a strange city along towards darkness—you get an impression, a
suggestion of things which is half magic: sometimes it fades completely
next day—you see how wrong you were. Again I have walked up and
down new streets—great broad avenues, filled with great broad solid
buildings, and rich shops. Have you ever noticed how all Germany seems
to be built in just *two* styles of architecture? There is the lovely Albert
Durer and Nurnberg style—great delicate gables, cross timbers, and lean-
over upper stories, and then there is the Kaiser Wilhelm Deutschland uber
Alles style—great rings, and avenues and boulevards filled with these
solid ugly masses—all bulging in front with bays and balconies and round
turrets. It is impressively rich and powerful and ugly—it seems to have
been done (most of it) between 1880 and 1900, about the time, perhaps, it
was becoming evident to them that the rest of the world ought to be
colonized and given the advantages of a *real* civilization. That sounds
like a malevolent speech full of the spirit that we ought now to put away
—but I did not mean it against Germany alone. The way she felt about her
excellence and her duty to enforce it on others is only the way England
has felt, and the way a great many of us in America are feeling now. . . .

I get very tired taking it in, and I really believe I am taking a great deal
in. But I feel like a great blundering child—I am feeling my way along by
myself, and what I get is good and lasting, but it does not come in that
brilliant and triumphant way I like to think it should. My life has been
full of bitter strife and spiritual labor—a great deal of it, you very correctly say, unnecessary—but then, things come to me in that way. . . .

Now I'm going to tell you a Great Big One—you won't believe it, but it
happens to be true. I made the Rundfahrt of the city to-day in a big bus:
when I got in at the Bahnhof Platz at 3:30, it was crowded with large
solid Germans—there was one vacant seat, and another opposite in which
a gentleman was sitting. He looked up quickly as I came down the aisle,

smiling in a nervous sort of way, and said very rapidly in English, "Sit down here." I sat down beside him: he pulled up his knees and crowded over against the side of the bus as if he was afraid of me. The man was James Joyce. I think he may have recognized me from the time we went out to Waterloo from Brussels just two years ago this September. He looked much older, he was quite bent, but very elegantly dressed—that is, better than he was last time, and instead of the single eyeshade, he wore black glasses in the sunlight; and he had another pair of plain ones for indoors.

We went into the Rathaus and Goethe's House: both were fine. In the Rathaus, which is called the Römer, everyone had to stick his feet into huge felt slippers before going into the Main Show, which is the huge Kaisersaal. He wandered around by himself peering at things while a German woman gave a long-winded lecture to the sightseers; then he got interested in the beautiful polished floors, and went skating up and down in his slippers in a very absent-minded way. We had not said a word to each other; but we kept smiling nervously and insisting by gestures that the other go in first through doors. We left the bus at Goethe's house, and after we came out again into the street he said to me that it was "a fine old house." I said I thought it was one of the finest houses I had ever seen—as it is—and that they were not able to do it any more. I said I was going back to the Old Town, which is right near the House, and which is as close to Elfland as we'll ever come. He said he thought he'd go "and get lost there for a while." Like a fool, I was too awkward and too shy to ask to go along—I am sure he would have let me: he wanted to be kind and friendly, and it would have been a grand thing for me to have gone with him. But I didn't, and I must wait now for the third time we meet—The Magic Third!—which will be in Dresden or in Heaven. Then I can speak. Joyce carried his right hand in a sling of black ribbon when he sat beside me in the bus, but he took it out when we got out of the bus.

After I left him I walked down one side of the street and he the other, both towards the Old Town. I peered into windows and looked at him from the corner of my eye; finally I went back to the Market Place, where the Rathaus is, and sat in an old house out of Grimm's fairy tales, where they sell the best Apfelwein and Frankfurters in the world. I had two orders of both. But all the time I kept thinking of James Joyce and the chance I had missed. I am not as certain as I was two years ago, when his son was with him and told me it was he; but the only reason I doubt it now is because *twice* seems so incredible. You won't believe it was if I tell you one item of his costume—he wore an old French beret, which he pulled off and left on the bus seat when we got out anywhere,—but it did not seem out of place. Besides, his "Portrait of the Artist"—"Jugendbildnis" here—is in a great many of the book windows; and the face of the author, I am sure, is the face of the man I was with to-day.

Wednesday Evening. My heart and soul have been at war with this German City, and now a kind of peace and certitude has come out of it. Last night when I came in, I saw scrawled on a slate in the hotel's lobby a notice in English which said that "Members of Tour 105 should be ready by nine o'clock to-morrow morning for the tour of the city, after which lunch will be served. The departure for Cologne will be at 12:30." Thus in a day and night these people traverse the country I have spent a month in . . . I talked to two old ladies from Ohio who were on this tour—they were very sweet, and told me all the things they had seen in their ride around town during the morning. One of them kept talking of "Goaty's House," and I wondered what in God's name it was until it occurred to me she meant Goethe's House. I wonder what Goaty would say if he could hear them—he has one of the handsomest and noblest heads I've ever seen, but there doesn't seem to be much humor in it. . . .

Thursday Evening. This has been a dull letter: I have wanted to tell you too much, and there is no room for it. The deeper, inner things I put in my little book: [1] I have filled one and begun another. . . . The world is very strange to me during these days—I have only been alone for two months among strange people, but the kind of *aloneness* I go in for makes that seem very long, and everything very far away. . . .

I lay down and slept for three hours—from eight to eleven—here; because I was up most of last night investigating the Old Town by moonlight. It was magical. This town has not the magnificent unity of Nurnberg; nor the grand quality that Nurnberg has. The Old Town here is a labyrinth of elfin houses, quainter and more like Grimm's than anything you will find elsewhere. I sat in the square before the Römer last night; the moon was blazing down. I was on the terrace of one of these houses, drinking a glass of Rhein wine. When you are tired, you can go to one of these faery tenements and drink apple wine—cold and heady—and eat hot frankfurters.

What else is here? A Volker museum, that has a magnificent collection of Asian, and Chinese, and African and Malaysian things. . . . Also a magnificent old church here—the *Dom,* with one of the richest interiors I've ever seen; and Goaty's house and museum; and the picture and sculpture galleries; and the Kunstgewerbe, which I have not seen—and Lord knows what else.

Their night life is heavy and brutal—I took it in last night—went to a couple of cabarets and bars and spent $1.25. A very poor and very heavy imitation of Paris—if anything can imitate an imitation. There is an im-

---

[1] The little notebook which he always carried in his pocket and in which he wrote down his random thoughts.

pression of variety everywhere: their life, however, is much more stand-
ardized than ours, no matter what they say. All over Germany they are
drinking beer and eating great slabs of pork and veal covered with heavy
sauces. The markets are filled with the most beautiful green vegetables
and fruits—enormous cucumbers, great clusters of grapes, peaches, plums
and so on—but you never get them on the menu. I am tired of the
heaviness and monotony of the food—to-night I had a beautiful inspiration and ate two soft-boiled eggs. I almost wept with joy, recovering one
of those simple and magnificent things I had almost forgotten. Then I
went to an enormous Bier Keller nearby in the Balonhof Platz, and watched
them. This is their *real* night life—Beer. There was an orchestra that
made a terrible noise, dressed up in the Bavarian costume: the leader
grimaced and went through antics and the crowd roared with laughter.
Someone would buy him a great mug of beer, and his band would play and
sing "Ein Prosit! Ein Prosit!" and the crowd would all join in, holding up
its glasses. Most of the people were large and heavy, they swilled down
quarts of beer, the air was heavy and thick, the band banged and
shouted, the crowd sang, now a sentimental song, now a smashing beer
song—the great tune of "Trink, Trink, Trink, Bruderlein, Trink." This is
the real Germany—it is impressive and powerful, and yet, after a time, I
dislike it. Nevertheless, I think this country interests me more than any in
Europe—can you explain this enigma? Here is this brutal, beer-swilling
people, and yet I doubt if there is as much that is spiritually grand in any
other people in Europe as in this one. This beer-swilling people produced
Beethoven and Goethe, the greatest spirits of modern times. And it produced long ago those faery and enchanted houses in Nurnberg and here.
And at the present time it has such men as Wassermann and Thomas
Mann writing for it. Also in its books—particularly in its thousands of
art books, magnificent books on Gothic, and the painters, and on everything—it far surpasses in delicacy and understanding any other nation.
Can you understand it? When I get up from a meal now, I feel that I have
eaten something brought dripping to me from the slaughter house. The
quantity of meat they consume is enormous—it has almost made a vege-
tarian of me: I did not know there was room enough in all Germany to
support so many cows and pigs; the air is filled with the death-squeals of
butchered swine.

Friday evening. Well, I've done it: I've devoured the city—almost—
enough for this once, and I'm on my way to Munich to-morrow morning.
I will not be sorry to leave here—it is a big, flat, dirty place, full of noise
and bustle, but intensely interesting. . . . Now I am thinking of Munich—
my heart begins to pound when I think of the letters I hope are there.
To-morrow is Saturday; I shall therefore not get my mail until Monday—
it will then be *seven* weeks since I've heard from anyone. . . . What has

happened in my world since I dropped out of it, I do not know. It has been only a short time, but I believe it has been a time of spiritual recuperation. I look wild and crazy and ragged, but I believe I am almost as sane as I can hope to be. I get a great draught of strength from looking at Goethe's lovely and tranquil head, and at Beethoven's fierce and all-sufficient one . . . I get, you see, a good part of my courage from better and greater people, but that is as it should be.

I still have moments of insanity when I rush into a big book shop and call for the name of some book in English which I know they haven't got, or which I invent, insisting that it is in the Tauschnitz edition. Then while they look, I stagger around like a drunk man from one shelf to the other, thumbing over countless volumes, leaping from one place to another, until they all begin to follow me around, to keep me from doing damage. And I have other charming little fancies—such as buying out all the sausage shops in Frankfurt, together with all the preserved fruits and plum-cakes in Rumpelmayer's here, and bringing it all back to America with me. Sometimes in the old market place here and in Mainz, or at the fruit stalls, I have grown mad to buy up all the wonderful fruits and vegetables. I have rushed from one stall to another, buying a peach at one, a bunch of grapes at another, and at Mainz, even a huge cucumber which I began to devour before all the yelling peasant women. But these fits are rare—I am calmer and more secure, and trying somehow to get at my picture of life. . . . I shall write again from Munich—but not a history next time.

P.S. . . . I've had nothing to eat to-day but two soft-boiled eggs and coffee which I had at Wiener Sacher's branch here. Now I'm going out to the pig-pens again. I think I shall have a dainty Vorspeisen—say, a Schwedish Gobelbissen—this is only a little cavair, a couple of Eggs à la Russe, some sardines, a piece of Bismarck herring, a slice of liverwurst, one of ham, and some tomatoes and—Kartoffel Salat. After this, I should have a good appetite for three or four slices of roast pork with mahogany sauce, and side dishes of Rotkohl and Bratkartoffel. In spite of their culinary skill, I know stage designers who cook better than the Germans do!

To ALINE BERNSTEIN

Munich
Thursday, Oct 4, 1928

Dear Aline:

. . . To-day is the first time I have been for mail since Saturday. I went to the hospital Monday and got out this afternoon. I had a mild concussion of the brain, four scalp wounds, and a broken nose. My head has healed up beautifully, and my nose is mending rapidly. . . . I am shaven as bald as a priest—in fact, with my scarred head, and the little stubble of black hair that has already begun to come up, I look like a dissolute priest.

What happened I am too giddy to tell you about to-night. I shall begin the story and try to finish it to-morrow. I had been in Munich three weeks —during that time I had led a sober and industrious life—as I have since coming abroad. It is now the season here of the Oktoberfest. What the Oktoberfest is I did not know until a week or two ago when it began. I had heard of it from everyone. I thought of it as a place where all the Bavarian peasant people come and dance old ritualistic dances, and sell their wares, and so on. But when I went for the first time, I found to my disappointment only a kind of Coney Island— merry-go-rounds, gimcracks of all sorts, innumerable sausage shops, places where whole oxen were roasting on the spot, and enormous beer halls. But why in Munich—where there are a thousand beer-drinking places—should there be a special fair for beer? I soon found out. The Oktober beer is twice as strong as the ordinary beer— it is thirteen percent—the peasants come in and go to it for two weeks.

The Fair takes place in the Theresien Fields which are on the outskirts of the town, just before the Ausstellungs Park. . . . I went out to see the show two or three times—these beer halls are immense and appalling— four or five thousand people can be seated in one of them at a time— there is hardly room to breathe, to wiggle. A Bavarian band of forty pieces blares out horrible noise, and all the time hundreds of people who cannot find a seat go shuffling endlessly up and down and around the place. The noise is terrific, you can cut the air with a knife—and in these places you come to the heart of Germany, not the heart of its poets and scholars, but to its real heart. It is one enormous belly. They eat and drink and breathe themselves into a state of bestial stupefaction—the place becomes one howling, roaring beast, and when the band plays one of their drinking songs, they get up by tables all over the place, and stand on chairs, swaying back and forth with arms linked, in living rings. The effect of these heavy living circles in this great smoky hell of beer is uncanny—there is something supernatural about it. You feel that within these circles is somehow the magic, the essence of the race—the nature of the beast that makes him so different from the other beasts a few miles over the borders. . . .

This is what happened . . . There is an American Church in Munich. It is not really a church—it is two or three big rooms rented in a big building in the Salvator Platz—a place hard to find, but just off the Promenadeplatz. They have six or eight thousand books there—most of it junk contributed by tourists. But you can go there in the afternoon for tea—if you are lonely you can find other Americans there . . . There was a young American there with his wife and another woman, his wife's friend. . . . I was delighted to talk to these people; they asked about rooms, life in Munich, galleries, and so on. . . . I told them about the Oktoberfest, and suggested that they go there with me during the afternoon, as the good museums were closed. So we went out together: the weather was bad, it began to rain. There was a great mass of people at the Fair—peasant people in their wonderful costumes, staring at all the machines and gimcracks. I took them through several beer halls, but we could find no seats. Finally, after the rain had stopped, we managed to get in at a table some people were leaving. We ordered beer and Schweirswurstt . . . and I was beginning to desire only to get rid of these people, who were full of quotations from the *American Mercury*. . . . I was nauseated by them, I wanted to be alone. I think they saw this; they suggested we all go home and eat together; I refused and said I would stay there at the Fair. So they paid their share, and went away out of all the roar and savagery of the place.

When they had gone, I drank two more liters of the dark Oktober beer, singing and swaying with the people at the table. Then I got up and went to still another place, where I drank another, and just before closing time—they close at 10:30 there at the Fair, because the beer is too strong, and the peasants get drunk and would stay forever—just before closing time I went to another great hall and had a final beer. The place was closing for the night—all over the parties were breaking up—there were vacant tables here and there, the Bavarian band was packing up its instruments and leaving. I talked to the people at my table, drank my beer, and got up to go. I had had seven or eight liters—this would mean almost a quart of alcohol. I was quite drunk from the beer. I started down one of the aisles toward a side entrance. There I met several men—and perhaps a woman, although I did not see her until later. They were standing up by their table in the aisle, singing perhaps one of their beer songs before going away. They spoke to me—I was too drunk to understand what they said, but I am sure it was friendly enough. What happened from now on I will describe as clearly as I can remember, although there are lapses and gaps in my remembrance. One of them, it seems to me, grasped me by the arm—I moved away, he held on, and although I was not angry, but rather in an excess of exuberance, I knocked him over a table. Then I rushed out of the place exultantly, feeling like a child who has thrown a stone through a window.

Unhappily I could not run fast—I had drunk too much and was wearing my coat. Outside it was raining hard; I found myself in an enclosure be-

hind some of the fair buildings—I had come out of a side entrance. I heard
shouts and cries behind me, and turning, I saw several men running down
upon me. One of them was carrying one of the fold-up chairs of the beer
hall—it is made of iron and wood. I saw that he intended to hit me with
this, and I remember that this angered me. I stopped and turned and in
that horrible slippery mudhole, I had a bloody fight with these people. I
remember the thing now with horror as a kind of hell of slippery mud,
and blood, and darkness, with the rain falling upon us several maniacs who
were trying to kill. At that time I was too wild, too insane, to be afraid,
but I seemed to be drowning in mud—it was really the blood that came
pouring from my head into my eyes. . . . I was drowning in oceans of
mud, choking, smothering. I felt the heavy bodies on top of me, snarling,
grunting, smashing at my face and back. I rose up under them as if coming
out of some horrible quicksand—then my feet slipped again in the mud,
and I went down again into the bottomless mud. I felt the mud beneath
me, but what was really blinding and choking me was the torrent of
blood that streamed from gashes in my head. I did not know I bled.

Somehow—I do not know how it came about—I was on my feet again,
and moving towards the dark forms that swept in towards me. When I was
beneath them in the mud, it seemed as if all the roaring mob of that hall
had piled upon me, but there were probably not more than three. From
this time on I can remember fighting with only two men, and later
there was a woman who clawed my face. The smaller figure—the smaller
man—rushed towards me, and I struck it with my fist. It went diving away
into the slime. I was choking in blood and cared for nothing now but to
end it finally—to kill this other thing or be killed. So with all my
strength I threw it to the earth: I could not see, but I fastened my fingers
and hand in its eyes and face—it was choking me, but presently it stopped.
I was going to hold on until I felt no life there in the mud below me. The
woman was now on my back, screaming, beating me over the head, goug-
ing at my face and eyes. She was screaming out "Leave my man alone!"
("Lassen mir den Mann stehen"—as I remember). Some people came and
pulled me from him—the man and woman screamed and jabbered at me,
but I could not make out what they said, except her cry of "Leave my man
alone," which I remember touched me deeply. . . .

These people went away—where or how I don't know—but I saw them
later in the police station, so I judge they had gone there. And now—
very foolishly perhaps—I went searching around in the mud for my hat—
my old rag of a hat which had been lost, and which I was determined to
find before leaving. Some German people gathered around me yelling and
gesticulating, and one man kept crying "Ein Arzt! Ein Arzt!" ("A Doctor!
A Doctor!") I felt my head all wet, but thought it was the rain, until I

put my hand there and brought it away all bloody. At this moment, three or four policemen rushed up, seized me, and hustled me off to the station. First they took me to the police surgeons—I was taken into a room with a white, hard light. The woman was lying on a table with wheels below it. The light fell upon her face—her eyes were closed. I think this is the most horrible moment of my life . . . I thought she was dead, and that I would never be able to remember how it happened. The surgeons made me sit down in a chair while they dressed my head wounds. Then one of them looked at my nose, and said it was broken, and that I must go the next day to a doctor. When I got up and looked around, the woman and the wheeled table was gone. I am writing this Saturday (six days later): if she were dead, surely by this time I would know. . . .

Sunday morning. I do not think I have told you what happened to me after the police doctors had looked at my wounds and dressed them that night at the Oktoberfest—or how I found doctors to look after me, and so on. From the doctors I was taken before the police next door where they asked me many questions which I did not answer. They also had two of the other men there, looking very bloody, also—and perhaps others I did not see. Then they let me go, when they could get nothing out of me. I had lost my hat, and was one mass of mud and blood: it was raining hard and wet: a young man I did not know went along with me, and when I asked him what he wanted, he said he "had no role to play." We got a street car and came back to the center of town where I got off and shook him— at the Odeonsplatz.

That day at lunch with the three people who had gone to the Fair with me, I had met a young American doctor who had come here for special study. Now I was going back to their place to get his address. I found the married pair in bed, and the other woman out with the doctor. They stood around and gasped and looked scared—the woman made me a cup of tea —and in a few minutes the woman and the doctor came back. He gave me the address of another American doctor who was working in a famous clinic here, and told me to see him the first thing the next morning.

I got a taxi and drove through town to the clinic. My appearance almost caused an earthquake in the pension, and people in the streets stared at me. I had been directed to Dr. Von Muller's clinic—and Dr. Von Muller is one of the greatest doctors in the world. His picture was in all the papers the other day—on his seventieth birthday. . . . I found the great man in the office, and when I asked for his American assistant—Dr. Du Bois,[1] whose name I had been given—I was told he was at home, and that

---

[1] Dr. Eugene F. Du Bois who at that time was working as a volunteer in the clinic of Dr. Friedrich von Muller. He is now Professor of Physiology, Emeritus, at Cornell University Medical College.

I should go there. I felt low-spirited and was on the point of asking old Von Muller himself to look at my head (which would have been a great breach), when in came this man Du Bois. The name is French, but you never saw anyone more prim and professorily American. He was very tidy and dull-looking, with winking eyeglasses, and a dry prim careful voice. I felt done for. I told him what had happened and where I was hurt, and he listened carefully, and then said in his precise careful way that we ought perhaps—ah—to see what can be—ah—done for you. By this time, I thought I was dead.

But here let me tell you the truth about this man, Dr. Du Bois, who is, I found later, a professor in the Cornell Medical School (hence the professorly manner). He is one of the grandest and kindest people I have ever met. In this dry prim way he showed me for days the most amazing kindness—and then refused to accept anything for his services, although he had come to my pension with me in a taxi, to help me pack, when the German doctor said I had to come to the hospital, and had gone back with me, and had visited me once or twice a day, and brought me books during the time I was there in the hospital. At any rate, he asked the great Von Muller first of all where we should go, and the great Von Muller had said that we should go across the street to the Surgical Building and see the great Lexer, who is the best head surgeon in Germany.

Monday night

Midnight—Salzburg

My dear, I held my breath until I got over the blessed border to-day—I have escaped. To-night—in spite of a desperate cold that is making me blind—I feel that life from now on is going to be freer and happier and wiser—and although I've had this silly feeling before, I believe somehow it's going to be true. Munich almost killed me. It scarred my head and broke my nose, and last of all smote me in ten wretched seconds with a deadly cold which burned like fire along the membranes of my nostrils, and then made a sour lump in my throat. Munich almost killed me—but in five weeks, it gave me more of human experience than most people get in five years. . . .

The Herr Geheimrat, I believe, has made a bad job of the nose. It looks to me hopelessly crooked, although people in Munich insisted it looked all right. My hair is out in a wolly nigger fuzz, and my scars shine through the brush. . . .

P.S. The accursed weather of Munich cannot be described. Snow fell there the other day—mid-October! And God! how I came to hate the leaden sky, the wet thin sunshine. But the magic that is around Salzburg—all white—and lovely!

To ALINE BERNSTEIN

Vienna

[November 1, 1928]

Dear Aline:

About the only thing I want to write during these days is a letter to you—and I want to write that all the time now. It is my only way at the moment of talking to the only person I care about talking to—my being-alone-ness has become a kind of terrible joke—I have somehow lost all power of breaking my own silence. . . . I live in a strange world—I will brood for an hour over a map of Vienna that I carry in my pocket, studying the vast cobweb of streets. Then suddenly I will rush into the Ring, seize a taxi, and yell out some address on the outer rim of the city that the driver has never heard of. He has to study my map—we go out and out, across the great outer girdle—to-day it was a great bare spot marked Sport-platz; when we got there, it was a huge field with a fence around it and turfed banks, which is used as a football field. All around the place were shabby looking buildings with small shops downstairs and people leaning out of windows above. The man was surprised and looked back at me to see if a mistake had been made. But I jumped out and paid him, and ran around the corner of the fence till he had gone. Then I walked on and on, straight up the long sloping street that seemed to reach to the Magic Mountains—the soft hills of the Wiener Wald looming against the horizon. It was All Saints Day: most of the shops were closed and the people were out in force. They were almost all walking in the same direction as I was —towards the Magic Mountains. The shutters were down on most of the little shops, and everything had a strange quietness, it seemed to me.

It was amazingly like a dream I used to have of a dark street, and dark shuttered houses. There was only one bit of light and sound in the street that came from a carnival. I was in this carnival riding the merry-go-round, surrounded by noise and lights and many people. Then it seemed that I was looking through the bars of a bright wooden gate into the dark street (from the carnival). In this street, there was no sound, no vehicles, no traffic except a great crowd of people all walking silently and steadily in the same direction. They did not speak with one another, they turned their faces neither to right nor left—not even as they tramped past the gate of the carnival and the white light fell over them. I know that in that white light the faces of these people looked thin and ghastly-sallow and damned;

and what their march meant, and all that silence I could not say, but I felt that death and doom and the end of all things was there in that place; but whether it was I who was dead in that carnival, or these strange phantom shapes from whom I was cut off, I could not say either.

This dream came back to me to-day as I walked up that long street with the people all tramping steadily towards the country. And strangely enough, when I got into the outskirts of the city, and the buildings were uneven and scattered about with much open ground, ugly and messy as the outskirts of great cities are, I began to come on shabby little carnivals—only a little merry-go-round and a few swings, grinding out old Schubert and Strauss tunes incessantly. Then I went on and on; the hills were very close and beautiful now; I was on their fringes; and I could see the edges of Vienna right and left, vast and smoky and roughly circular.

I came to a place where there was a whole colony of stucco houses, all alike, all ugly, with gardens behind, and trying to look like the Austrian equivalent for an American suburban stucco "English" cottage. I sometimes think that the enormous difference we think we see between Europe and America is not as deep as we believe—when you see these cottages all alike, it is not hard to imagine an Austrian Arnold Bennett or Sinclair Lewis writing a book about the people in them. The things you and I have liked best in Europe—the grand pictures, the buildings, and so on—belong mostly to an order of things that has gone: the world—the world that has to eat and drink and labor—is probably being "Americanized." At least, they groan about it, and deprecate it, but I think they earnestly want it for themselves. To be "Americanized" is simply to be industrialized in the most complete and serviceable fashion. America is the apex of the present industrial civilization, but that is the only civilization the modern world has got. The European who carries a really good load of hate against America, nearly always hates because America is rich and Europe is poor; because America is strong and Europe is weak. But the European does not always put it so honestly: he salves his pride by picturing himself as a lover of the good and beautiful, a defender and patron of the arts, and a despiser of filthy money, while the American cares for nothing else but money, and so on. A great fat boy in one of the big beer houses in the Neuhauser Street in Munich one night poured all this into my ear while he swilled down liters of beer and gorged himself with the fourteen different meats and sausages of a delicatessen aufschnitt. There is not a picture or a book in the world for which he would have foregone a liter of his beer.

Budapest

Thursday, November 8

Dear Aline: I have been here since last Friday night, and I have already heard of Hoover's election. The news seems to be authentic, and his election to be overwhelming. This only makes me sorrier than ever that Smith didn't get it. Why is it that the good people, the right people are so often the underdogs? From this great distance it looked as if the whole nation had gone mad in an effort to strangle the man. Now, what are they going to do with him? His intelligence for government will be wasted while small incompetent people thrive in great jobs. And now that it's over, the people who voted against him because he is a Catholic will insist that this had nothing to do with it. The only American paper I get to read over here is the *Paris New York Herald,* and this filthy little sheet, together with all the filthy little people who write letters to it, has nearly convinced me that most of the good Americans have stayed at home. We are a people who ought not to live out of our country too long—the attempt to make Europeans of ourselves succeeds in producing loose and abortionate idiots. But America is also a very difficult country for many people to live in, unless one can with a great hurrah join in the rush to elect the Hoovers and Coolidges. And think where you find yourself in this rush? With the Ku Klux Klan, and the Anti-Saloon League, and Senator Heflin, and John Roach Straton, and the Methodist Church, and the Rockefellers. My part of America is not with this. It is somewhere perhaps with the part that voted for Smith—and he got beaten four to one.

But I am coming home. I am an American and I must try to take hold somewhere. I am not burning with indignation or revolt, or anything. I am tired of struggle and should like to fall in step if only I knew how. But how? . . . I am a citizen of the most powerful and interesting nation of modern times—and I wish to God I knew how to make something of it. . . .

Monday Evening. My Dear: If all the rest of my journey has been waste and if I have done very little for myself with it, I think what I have seen these last two days might almost make up for it, not for what I may get from it, but for the news that I can now pass on to you. . . . Yesterday morning at six o'clock I got up here—with the aid of the hotel staff— and went to the East Station. At seven o'clock I left the station on an express train bound for the village of Mezö-Kövesd, about 100 miles away. Away *where* I do not yet know, for I had failed to look the place up on the map before I started, and have been so charmed by my fancies that I have not dared to do so since. . . . My belief now is that I was on the Bucharest express—for a ticket man in the station asked me if I was going there—and that Mezö-Kövesd is eastward or southwestward from Budapest. It was a grey, wet, foggy day of the sort that seems to afflict all Europe from England to Hungary—and farther perhaps—at this time of year. And the landscape was wearily depressing. For a while after leaving Budapest there were low hills and rolling dismal looking country—possibly everything looks dismal now. Then, for the greater part of the journey there was a vast muddy plain, stretching away infinitely until it was lost in the steam and haze of the horizon. This great plain is one vast farm: the land is striped with bands of plowed field and bands of green unploughed field, and these long bands stretch straight away as far as the eye can travel. This also adds to the impression of hopelessness. . . .

I got there a little before ten o'clock—the train stopped at a dreary station surrounded by the vast muddy fields. At first I did not know where the village was—there seemed to be scattered houses away in the distance—I walked away from the station around a huge field of mud. A great many of the young men of the village were assembled on this field: there were bugle calls and they were lining up in military formations—from little boys to young fellows of 18 or 20. The rain had collected in pools all over the place and the big fat ducks and geese were everywhere: in the muddy streets, the fields and yards of all the houses. I was terribly depressed. I wondered what I had come for—the place seemed so barren, so lost, that I thought Russia must be like this. But I heard a churchbell ringing away in the distance; and women, dressed up in these amazing costumes, began to hurry along, coming from the little white houses that bordered the road. Finally I came up to what seemed a main street—it was another mudhole, but it seemed originally to have been paved. I turned off to the left in the wrong direction, away from the main part of the town, and I walked straight along this street for a good distance until suddenly the last white houses of the village ended, and the great wet fields began, with the muddy road running straight into eternity. I realized that most of the people I had seen were going in the opposite direction. I turned and went back as fast as I could. All the people stared and whispered and frowned and snickered; little children, in their strange costumes, giggled at me—any one of these people would have stopped the traffic in New York. The children found me strange and comic, yet the men with their embroidered aprons and their ridiculous derby hats stuck straight off of their heads, and the women in their bewildering costumes, did not seem at all strange to the children.

Presently I saw the church ahead of me, and began to pass the little shops of the village. It is a very sinful place—everything was open and doing business—I suppose the people work during the week and that Sunday is their best day for selling and trading. The street opened into a kind of square before the church: it was obvious that this was the center of the town. There was a brisk business going on in the market place among the fruit and vegetable peddlers, and dozens of men hung around in groups, loafing and gossiping as they do in our small towns. I made straight for the church, after having provided the whole market place with a new subject for gossip. I went into the church and found it crowded. In the cold little vestibule outside the doors several old women were crowded muttering responses to the service, or kneeling on the dirty concrete near the doors. I went into the church and stood near the doors. A priest in gorgeous robes was making his sermon. The church was crowded: all of the aisles and bare space, as well as the seats, were filled with people. In one solid section of the pews sat all the married women, with black conical shaped bonnets, and sober costumes. The old men, the chief men of the place, I suppose, sat in another part wearing those wonderful robes which are among the beautiful things I have seen in Hungary—for what I have seen here seems to me to be wild and strange, for the most part, rather than beautiful. I have pictures of this wonderful robe in the great book I have bought for you—it is a garment in which every man looks an emperor. It is a great block of thick stiff white wool or felt with short sleeves, although most of the old men wear it as a cape. It sits upon the shoulders of a peasant in the most regal and splendid way. It can be embroidered along the edges and the arms and shoulders in any way that suits their barbaric fancy—and some of the decorations were magnificent. Most of the old fellows wear a kind of turban—very handsome—of fuzzy black wool, with this robe, and of course the stiff high boots that nearly all the men wear. And God, but they're dirty! After church I looked at some of the old fellows—some with the faces, moustaches, slant eyes, of the East—and their hides were stiff and caked with dirt.

The young unmarried women were together in all their splendor in another part of the church, and I suppose the young men elsewhere—although most of the young bucks were loafing around in the market place outside. The priest finished his sermon and left his cage in the wall; then the long Catholic ritual before the altars began. The people knew the order perfectly: they listened faithfully, made all the responses, began to sing from time to time, then listened again while the priest sang out Latin in a high, false, annoying voice—what he said was indistinguishable, and seemed calculated only to make a weird reverberation in the church. Old women remained on their knees on the hard cold floor during the whole service; there were wretches there in filthy rags; over the whole place there was a close warm odor of hay and manure—the place had an unmistakable smell of a stable. Nowhere have I ever seen the simple animal nature of men so plainly as in this church—I kept thinking of this as they all stood there with their smell of the stable, hearing of their kinship to God.

When it was over they all streamed out slowly—and immediately two men in blue uniforms outside the church began to beat rapidly upon small drums. The crowd split in two and gathered in two great circles around the drummers. Then when all was quiet, the drummer put aside his drum, pulled a slip of paper from his jacket, and began to read rapidly. The old fellows in the woolen robes stood around, looking wise and puffing thoughtfully at their funny pipes. The announcement, I learned later and guessed then, is a kind of weekly official journal—probably with decrees, laws, tax announcements, and so on.

When the reading of this was over, the two crowds broke away and streamed rapidly down the street, probably to gossip or to eat, or to their homes. But I began to look for a restaurant. I had been warned that it was hopeless—that I had better take a few sandwiches along, because I could not eat the food I might find there—but so much preparation is not in me. There was a place on the square marked Etterem—that means Restaurant—and I went in. I am sure it is the Swell Place of the town, for none of the gorgeous peasants were there; but a fat dirty waiter with a dirty stiff white shirt and greasy black hair, also several of the town Dandies (they must be all over Europe, just as Maupassant put them in his French country towns): a man with spats, and a Hungarian-English tailor, and a sensual barbered face with pointed moustaches, and a luscious smile showing his old-pearl teeth: I am sure he went to Budapest often and was a great Rounder. There were several of this kind there—one came in with a bald knobby head, a golf suit of loud checks, stockings to match, spats, and elegant brown shoes you could see your face in. He was the damndest looking monkey I've seen. A young fellow was drawing their caricatures at a pengo—17 or 18 cents—apiece. They all gathered around, looked knowing, said it was very good, ordered their own portrait, and roared with laughter when they saw the result. Then they took the drawing all over the place, showing it to their friends. I had him draw me—I recognize myself, but it is as if I have been in hell for several years. . . . I thought I would eat something, but an unfortunate visit to the urinal destroyed my hunger. I ordered a bottle of beer, knowing they could not do anything to this.

Then I left the place and began to explore the village. I walked out by the church along the muddy main street or road in a direction opposite the one I had first taken. I went straight on past the cemetery, past the little white houses, until I came again, abruptly as before, to the open country. Nothing but the land—the vast muddy land stretching away to nowhere. There were hills over to my left. But I was terribly depressed—the barrenness, the greyness and monotony of this life frightened me. It seems to me that the life of people in a middle western village must be gay compared to the life here, and I still think it may be. And the road stretched straight away until it, too, was lost in the fog and steam of the horizon.

I turned around and walked back towards the church. But instead of going the whole way, I turned off the main road, and went down a muddy road to the right. Here was the main body of the village which I had not before suspected, spread out behind the church. It is one of the strangest places I was ever in. All of the streets that I had seen heretofore running off the main one had been straight muddy alleys with the little white houses punctually spaced along the road. This straightness, and the feeling of open space, with the awful unending land all around had depressed me. Back in this part, however, I immediately became more cheerful. The muddy little roads that serve as streets wound and twisted about and met each other in a labyrinthine pattern. The little white houses were covered with roofs of dry reeds bound together, and of the thickness of a foot. On these reeds, patches of green moss were growing. The houses were one-story, with perhaps a half-story attic above—this upper part was often of wood with carved designs on it. The end of the house faced the street; the doorway, with a very narrow wooden porch that ran the whole length of the house, faced the side yard. This mudhole was full of quacking geese, and at the back there was always what seemed at first to be several stacks of beautifully rich hay, mellow and odorous. Then I discovered that these were not haystacks at all, but that they cover their pig pens and barns with hay—the pigs were rooting and grunting in the slime.

In the middle of the muddy street, people were drawing water from a well. These wells are as familiar in Hungary as that strange device in the pictures of Peter Breughel—I mean the wheel on top of a pole. The well is a bucket attached to a long pole which swings up and down, by weights and balances, I suppose. Back in this part, as I say, I lost a great deal of my depression, although the streets were mud-holes and the geese and swine were quacking and grunting everywhere. The little white houses with their thick walls and small windows, on which moisture was gathered, showing warmth therein, and the reed roofs, and above all, I believe, the mellow sweet hay covering over the barn and sty, shut out the awful emptiness of the plain all around, and gave a close warm look to things. They were huddled together here with their pigs and geese, but I felt that they must get a great satisfaction out of the elaborate ritual and convention of their lives. How elaborate it is I did not then know, nor do I yet know fully.

My train back to Budapest—the only one before night—passed at 2:30.
It was now 1:30. I found the Turkish spire of the church above the houses
and made my way towards it, knowing the public square was there. When
I came into the square again, I saw one of the most extraordinary spectacles I have ever seen—it is as bright and strange and wonderful to me
now as it was the moment I saw it. When I had left the restaurant an hour
or so before, the square had been almost deserted. Now it was crowded
with hundreds of people, some standing, others walking back and forth.
But what caught you immediately was that these people were not mixed
into the great shuttle of a crowd. They were divided into groups and
companies with military formality—the blazing color and pageantry, all
regimented, made me think of one of the old pictures of a battle, in which
you see the companies all drawn up in blocks upon a plain outside a city.
The young men in groups of twenty or thirty were stationed at various
places around the square; the married women elsewhere; the older men
still elsewhere; and the young girls, likewise in groups of twenty of thirty,
marched back and forth and around and up and down. Of course this explosion of color that simply turned that grey day into a pageant came
mostly from the girls. I can't go on to describe the costumes, for they were
infinitely varied—the one uniform detail came in the wonderful shawls
they wore over all the rest of the bewildering business. These shawls were
of some delicate material—silk, probably—with a great variety of patterns around the neck. Then they were fringed with a great thick border
of woolen thread—this was a solid color and was either a brilliant yellow,
or crimson, or red. Curiously enough, those groups with yellow, and
those with red, and so on, seemed to keep together. As to the rest of it, you
can see it better than I can—the long plaited skirts, covered with strange
designs—the skirts are one thick mass of ruffles, and when the girls walk,
the skirts billow and undulate and show inches of thickness where they are
kicked up by the feet. Over this they wear the apron—similar if not exactly the same as that worn by the young men—and I am told the apron
on the young man is a sign of bachelorhood. It is black or blue, this apron,
but it has across it a strip of embroidered flower and leaf work, which is
sometimes over half its length. As the girls go up and down in groups,
the young men stand together, or march off in columns of twos—they all
grin and snicker among themselves, but they act otherwise as if the other
is not there. I did not find this funny. I did not find it naive and delightfully childlike. I had a feeling of terrible disgust and revulsion against this
elaborate and evil ritual. The great swathings of pleats and ruffles and
shawls which concealed the bodily lines of the girls were only foils to the
evil, searching curiosity of the young men, whose talk—I will bet my nose,
because I was born a villager myself—was mainly of breasts and fornica-
tion. The huge sexual rituals of society are weakened and dispersed in

great cities because they exist mainly through close public observation. And they are all-powerful in the village for this reason—if you try to break a custom you will very likely break your heart as well. It is for this reason that I believe in cities more than in villages: I think there is greater good in them, and higher life, and a greater spiritual freedom. I am simple enough to understand the city and urbane life: I have never been complex enough to understand the village. That is what I felt at Mezö-Kövesd the other day—there was an evil and barbaric complexity about this that I loathed. But I recognized it as one of the most remarkable things I have ever seen. The thing that brings *wonder* is not the *strange* thing alone—it is the touch of the familiar with the strange thing: that is what makes it strange. And all the time I was feeling the strangeness of this parade the other day, I was simply being pounded all the time by its fundamental likeness to *all* village life.

When I was a college boy in the South, the young men used to go to a neighboring town on Sundays, a town where there were two or three girls' schools. The young men would line up in groups outside the churches where the girls attended, and wait for them to come out. Then they would snicker and talk among themselves, as would the girls. But they would not speak. Later in the day, or in the evening perhaps, they would go courting. And in Asheville, and in all American small towns, the young bucks line up before the drug store, or the post office, and watch the girls go by.

I looked at this parade in Mezö-Kövesd as long as I dared. I will never forget those blocks and company formations, with the Virgins marching up and down with rhythmically billowing skirts. Of course, I harmonized with this scene about as well as would a Chinaman at a meeting of the Ku Klux Klan, and I got many unfriendly glances; but my curiosity was stronger than modesty or good manners—I took it all in gaping. Then I had to run for my train and just got in, sleeping as well as I could most of the way back across that dreary misty plain upon the hard bench of a third class carriage. . . .

I have written these last pages on Wednesday night. About a thousand and one other things: the theatre, gypsy music, Hungarian literature (O yes, O yes, they have a literature), Hungarian food (which is very good as well as full of all kinds of colors)—I must tell you later. The people here have been very kind to me. They want to do all they can to interest the world in their cause, and of course they have been murderously treated. They had 20,000,000 people before the war, now they have 7,000,000. Over two-thirds of their country has been given to the Czechs, the Rumanians, and the Jugo-Slavians. How they can continue to exist they do not know. They despise the people who now have most of their wealth and land—the Rumanians, Czechs, and so on. They call them peasants and barbarians and speak of themselves proudly as "a highly cultivated people." And the Austrians speak of the Hungarians as barbarians! So it goes! What do we know? We say the world is a small place —but the fact is, it is much too large a place. What does the man in Nebraska know, or care, about this people or their troubles? Yet they have an extensive literature, a great capital, a history thousands of years old, and the honor of saving Europe twice against the Turks who came storming up out of the East. They were themselves a nomad Eastern people who settled upon these plains many hundreds of years ago—and now their young village men wear embroidered aprons, and the old men great coats of white wool, and the young girls are swaddled in elaborate costumes, every stitch, every pattern, every design of which has some meaning.

And here in Budapest, the Singer Sewing Machine has agencies, and Cadillac and Chrysler; and the people read Jókai and Herczeg Ferencz and Bibó Lajos and Molnar Ferenc and Lewis Sinclair, and Wallace Edgar and Bennett Arnold and Takáts Sándor, and a whole raft of other Hungarian writers. But what do they know about this in Newark; or what do they know about Newark here? What's it all mean? I think I have found a little meaning, a base of culture and understanding that is universal. Someday I shall tell you what it is.

I am going back to Vienna to-morrow. Then I want to get to the sea and a ship again. I seem so far away from it now that I can hardly believe I shall ever find it. . . .

When Wolfe returned to Vienna from Budapest in November, 1928, he found a letter waiting for him from Maxwell E. Perkins, the head editor at Charles Scribner's Sons, who was to become the greatest influence upon him and his work. This letter dated October 22, 1928, said in part: [1] *"Mrs. Ernest Boyd left with us, some weeks ago, the manuscript of your novel, O, Lost. I do not know whether it would be possible to work out a plan by which it might be worked into a form publishable by us, but I do know that . . . it is a very remarkable thing, and that no editor could read it without being excited by it . . . What we should like to know is whether you will be in New York in a fairly near future, when we can see you and discuss the manuscript. We should certainly look forward to such an interview with very great interest." The following letter is Wolfe's reply.*

[1] For the full text of the letter, see page 61, *Editor to Author, the Letters of Maxwell E. Perkins, Selected and Edited, with Commentary and an Introduction,* by John Hall Wheelock. Charles Scribner's Sons, 1950.

To MAXWELL E. PERKINS

Vienna,

Saturday, Nov 17, 1928

Dear Mr Perkins:

Your letter of October 22 which was addressed to Munich, was sent on to me here. I have been in Budapest for several weeks and came back last night. I got your letter at Cook's this morning.

Mrs Ernest Boyd wrote me a few weeks ago that she was coming abroad, and said that you had my book. I wrote her to Paris but have not heard from her yet.

I can't tell you how good your letter has made me feel. Your words of praise have filled me with hope, and are worth more than their weight in diamonds to me. Sometimes, I suppose, praise does more harm than good, but this time it was badly needed, whether deserved or not. I came abroad over four months ago, determined to put the other book out of my mind, and to get to work on a new one. Instead, I have filled one notebook after another, my head is swarming with ideas—but I have written nothing that looks like a book yet. In Munich I did write thirty or forty thousand words, then I got my head and my nose broken, and began to have things happen thick and fast with a great many people, including the police. I have learned to read German fairly well, and have learned something of their multitudinous books. But I had indigestion from seeing and trying to take in too much, and I was depressed at my failure to settle down to work. Now I feel better. I have decided to come back to New York in December, and I shall come to see you very soon after my arrival.

I have not looked at my book since I gave a copy to Mrs. Boyd. At the time I realized the justice of all people said—particularly the impossibility of printing it in its present form and length. But at that time I was "written out" on it—I could not go back and revise. Now I believe I can come back to it with a much fresher and more critical feeling. I have no right to expect others to do for me what I should do for myself, but, although I am able to criticize wordiness and over-abundance in others, I am not able practically to criticize it in myself. The business of selection and of revision is simply hell for me—my efforts to cut out 50,000 words may sometimes result in my adding 75,000.

As for the obscene passages and the dirty words, I know perfectly well that no publisher could print them. Yet, I swear to you, it all seemed to me very easy and practical when I wrote them. But already I have begun to write a long letter to you, when all I should do is to thank you for your letter and say when I am coming back. Then the other things can come out when I see you.

But your letter has given me new hope for the book—I have honestly always felt that there are parts of it of which I need not be ashamed, and which might justify some more abiding form. I want you to know that you have no very stiff-necked person to deal with as regards the book—I shall probably agree with most of the criticisms, although I hope that my own eagerness and hopefulness will not lead me into a weak acquiescence to everything.

I want the direct criticism and advice of an older and more critical person. I wonder if at Scribners I can find someone who is interested enough to talk over the whole huge Monster with me—part by part. Most people will say "it's too long," "its got to be cut," "parts have to come out," and so on—but obviously this is no great help to the poor wretch who has done the deed, and who knows all this, without always knowing how he's going to remedy it.

I am sorry that Mrs Boyd sent you the letter that I wrote for the reader. She said it was a very foolish letter, but added cheerfully that I would learn as I grew older. I wish I had so much faith. I told her to tear the letter out of the binding; but if it indicated to you that I did realize some of the difficulties, perhaps it was of some use. And I realize the difficulties more than ever now.

I am looking forward to meeting you, and I am still youthful enough to hope that something may come of it. It will be a strange thing indeed to me if at last I shall manage to make a connection with such a firm as Scribners which, in my profound ignorance of all publishing matters, I had always thought vaguely was a solid and somewhat conservative house. But it may be that I am a conservative and at bottom very correct person. If this is true, I assure you I will have no very great heartache over it, although once it might have caused me trouble. At any rate, I believe I am through with firing off pistols just for the fun of seeing people jump— my new book has gone along for 40,000 words without improprieties of language—and I have not tried for this result.

Please forgive my use of the pencil—in Vienna papers and pen and ink, as well as many other things that abound in our own fortunate country, are doled out bit by bit under guard. I hope you are able to make out my scrawl—which is more than many people do—and that you will not forget about me before I come back.

My address in New York is the Harvard Club—I get my mail there. Here in Vienna, at Thomas Cook's, but as I'm going to Italy in a week, I shall probably have no more mail before I get home.

V

THE ACCEPTANCE AND PUBLICATION OF
LOOK HOMEWARD, ANGEL

1929

To MADELEINE BOYD

Harvard Club
New York
Jan 8, 1929

Dear Mrs. Boyd:

I got your letter from Paris tonight—it had been sent from the Harvard Club to Paris, Munich, and Vienna, and back again. I was ready to write you anyway—I got back here New Year's Eve, and I am sure I have telephoned you at least ten times since. On two occasions I talked with your maid, left my name and told her to tell you.

Mrs. Boyd, I am terribly excited about the book. I have seen Mr. Perkins twice, and unless I am quite out of my head they have decided to take the book. I saw him first the day after New Year's—at that time it seemed to me there was little doubt about it, but yesterday he confirmed it. I told him I should like some definite news—that there was one friend I should like to speak to. He told me that I might go ahead; he said their minds were "practically made up." I told him I needed money and he said they would give me an advance. Now, don't be mad at me—I did *not* talk money; I asked him to get as much as he could for me, and he said he did not think he could get over $500, and that that was unusual for a first novel.

It is perfectly understood at Scribners that you are my agent and that I shall do nothing, sign nothing, until I have seen you. I also want to see Mr. Melville Cane the lawyer.[1] As you request, I am sending you a written

[1] For approval of the contract before signing it.

statement authorizing you as my agent. All that was said at Scribners I can not put into a short letter—I must see you and talk to you—but they have been amazingly generous, it seems to me, in what they are willing to print. Of course I must set to work, and work hard, but I have a very clear idea of what is wanted—they had made very full notes, and we talked the thing over in considerable detail.

Mr. Perkins told me to set to work at once and I have promised to deliver the first instalment of the revision in ten days. He said that I would get a letter from Scribners in a few days—I suppose business must be done in this way. It seems to me, Mrs. Boyd, there is no doubt of it.

Of course, I realize exactly how great a part you have played in this, and if I get rich nothing will please me more than to see you get prosperous. (This is a kind of joke, but I wish it would come true.) I am full of energy and hope—I know I have a big job ahead, but with this encouragement I can do anything. Although this is a business matter I can't help having a warm place in my heart for you, and I hope to God we both prosper.

This is all for tonight—it is past midnight and I haven't eaten. On another piece of paper I am writing out a statement authorizing you as my agent. When and where can I see you? I've almost given up hope of finding you at home.

I've taken a place at 27 West 15th Street (2nd Floor Rear—no telephone yet). You can phone or write here to Harvard Club, and leave a message. I'll do nothing until I see you.

To MAXWELL E. PERKINS

Harvard Club
New York
Jan 9, 1929

Dear Mr. Perkins:

I got your letter this morning and I have just come from a talk with Mrs. Madeleine Boyd, my literary agent.

I am very happy to accept the terms you offer me for the publication of my book, *O Lost*.[1] Mrs. Boyd is also entirely satisfied.

I am already at work on the changes and revisions proposed in the book, and I shall deliver to you the new beginning some time next week.

Although this should be only a business letter I want to tell you that I look forward with joy and hope to my connection with Scribners. To-day

---

[1] The terms for *O, Lost* (*Look Homeward, Angel*) offered in Mr. Perkins' letter of January 8, 1929, were an advance of $500 against royalties of 10% on the first two thousand copies sold, and 15% on all copies sold thereafter.

—the day of your letter—is a very grand day in my life. I think of my relation to Scribners thus far with affection and loyalty, and I hope this marks the beginning of a long association that they will not have cause to regret. I have a tremendous lot to learn, but I believe I shall go ahead with it, and I know that there is far better work in me than I have yet done.

If you have any communication for me before I see you next, you can reach me at 27 West 15th Street (2nd Floor Rear).

To MARGARET ROBERTS

This is a horribly long letter. I'm as limp as a rag. I pity the people who have to read it and I pity the poor devil who wrote it.

> Harvard Club
> New York
>
> Saturday, January 12, 1929

Dear Mrs. Roberts:

Everything you write has power to touch and move me and excite me. My heart beats faster when I see your writing on a piece of paper, and I read what you write me over and over again, exultant and happy over every word of praise you heap upon me. Nothing you have ever written me has so stirred me as your letter which I got today. I have mounted from one happiness to another during this past week since I came back from Europe, and the knowledge that you are now so generously sharing with me my joy and hope just about sends the thermometer up to the boiling point. For several days now I have felt like that man in one of Leacock's novels who "sprang upon his horse and rode madly off in all directions." I have literally been like that—at times I have not known what to do with myself. I would sit in the club here stupidly, staring at the publishers' glorious letter of acceptance; I would rush out and walk eighty blocks up Fifth Avenue through all the brisk elegant crowd of late afternoon. I am gradually beginning to feel ground again, and it is occurring to me that the only thing to do is to get to work again.

I have the contract in my inner breast pocket, ready to be signed, and a check for $450 pinned to it, $50 having already been paid to my literary agent, Mrs. Ernest Boyd, as her 10 per cent share. There is literally no reason why I should walk around New York with these documents on my person, but in a busy crowd I will sometimes take them out, gaze tenderly at them, and kiss them passionately. Scribners have already signed the contract. I am to sign it Monday, but, with their customary fairness, they have advised me to show it to a lawyer before I sign it. I am therefore going with Mrs. Boyd on Monday to see Mr. Melville Cane, a lawyer, a poet, a member of Harcourt, Brace and Co., and the finest attorney on theatrical and publishing contracts in America. I have met him once, he read part of my book, and he has since been my friend and well-wisher. He told the person who sent me to him sometime ago [1] that I represented what he had wanted to be in his own life, that I was one of the most remarkable people he had ever met. And when he was told yesterday that I had sold my book he was delighted.

I am filled at the moment with so much tenderness towards the whole world that my agent, Mrs. Boyd, is worried—she is a Frenchwoman, hard and practical, and she does not want me to get too soft and trusting in my business relations. I wrote Scribners a letter of acceptance in which I could not hold myself in. I spoke of my joy and hope, and my affection and loyalty towards the publishers who had treated me so well, and my hope that this would mark the beginning of a long and happy association which they would have no cause to regret. In reply I got a charming letter in which they told me I would never have to complain of the interest and respect they have for my work. Mrs. Boyd herself was almost as happy as I was—although she is agent for almost every important French author in America, and publishing and acceptances are the usual thing for her— she said the thing was a great triumph for her as well, as Scribners consider me "a find" and are giving her credit for it.

It is all very funny and moving. Seven months ago when she got the book and read parts of it, she got interested—it was too long (she said), but there were fine things in it, she thought someone might be interested, and so on. Now I am a "genius"—she is already sorry for poor fellows like Dreiser and Anderson; she told the publishers that "this boy has everything they have in addition to education, background, (etc, etc,). Of course, poor fellows," she said, "it's not their fault—they never had the opportunity"—and so on and so on. Also, she pictures the other publishers as tearing their hair, gnashing their teeth, and wailing because they are not publishing the book. She gave it to one or two to read—they all said it had fine things in it, but was too long, they must think about it, etc.— and meanwhile (says she) Scribners got it. She said she was talking to one of them (Jonathan Cape, his name is) a week ago. He said at once: "Where is your genius, and when can I see him?" She told him Scribners had it and (groaning with grief, no doubt) he begged her to let him have first chance at the next one. We must salt all this down—her Gallic impetuosity, I mean—and I've got to come to earth and begin work.

I've had to tell several people, and everyone is almost as glad as I am. The University people are throwing a job at my head. I can stop in June if I want, they say. This is absurd. Of what earthly use would I be to them

[1] Mrs. Bernstein.

for only a half year—but they will give me more money, I think, than last year, fewer hours, (eight or ten) and almost no paper work. Now that this thing has happened, I feel kinder toward teaching than ever. Of course, my $450 will not last forever, and even if the book goes well I must wait until six months after its publication (so reads a *regular* clause in my contract) for my first statement, and every four months thereafter. The University people are genuinely friends and well wishers—the dean,[2] a wealthy and fine young man (of thirty-eight or forty) would give me a job at any time—but I think this rather increases my value to them: it is a big swarming place, fond of advertising.

The people at Scribners want me to set to work on revision at once, but they told me they thought I would have to find work later. No one knows how many copies the book will sell, of course, and besides, I must wait eight or ten months after publication for my first money (if there is any, but perish *that* thought.) Mrs. Boyd says the contract is fair, regular, and generous—giving an advance of $500 on a first book is unusual—of course that $500 *comes out* later from my first royalties. The contract offers me 10% of the *retail* price of the book up to the first 2,000 copies: after that 15%. As the book is a very long one, it will have to sell, I think, for $2.50 or $3.00. You can estimate from this what it is possible to make—but for the Lord's sake, don't. This is a fascinating weakness I have succumbed to, and everything is too uncertain. There are also clauses covering foreign translation and publication, and publication in any other than book form. That means serial and movies, I suppose, but *that* won't happen to me on *this* book—but if it does, the publisher and author split the profits.

Mrs. Ernest Boyd is also recognized as my agent and business representative and all checks are payable to her. This may make my thrifty friends squirm—she also gets 10% of all my profits (I hope, naturally, her share is at least $100,000)—but it's the best arrangement. How hard she worked to bring this about I don't know. Nevertheless she did it and I'll pay the 10% cheerfully—that's the regular agents' rate. Also, I think it is just as well that I am managed by a practical person who knows a little business. Although it is a business matter and I ought not to get sentimental, I can't help having a warm spot in my heart for the old girl who brought it about. I might have done it by myself sooner or later, but she certainly helped enormously at the present.

Finally, I want to start and continue my life by being decent and loyal to those people who have stood by me—whether for business or personal reasons. If we muddy and cheapen the quality of our actual everyday life, the taint, I believe, is bound to show, sooner or later, in what we create. Mrs. Boyd is so happy that Scribners took it. She said I should be very

2 Dean Munn.

proud of that; she said they were the most careful and exacting publishers in America—others publish fifty or a hundred novels a year, but Scribners only ten or twelve, although they bring out many other books. They are also trying to get the younger writers—they now have Ring Lardner, Scott Fitzgerald, and Ernest Hemingway (to say nothing of Wolfe). They were reading sections of my book, they told me, to Lardner and Hemingway a week before I got home—I'm afraid somewhat coarse and vulgar sections.

Finally, I must tell you that the ten days since I got home on the Italian boat have been the most glorious I have ever known. They are like all the fantasies I had as a child of recognition and success—only more wonderful. That is why my vision of life is becoming stranger and more beautiful than I thought possible a few years ago—it is the fantasy, the miracle that really happens. For *me* at any rate. My life, with its beginnings, has been a strange and miraculous thing. I was a boy from the mountains; I came from a strange wild family; I went beyond the mountains and knew the state; I went beyond the state and knew the nation, and its greatest university, only a magic name to my childhood; I went to the greatest city and met strange and beautiful people, good, bad, and ugly ones; I went beyond the seas alone and walked down the million streets of life. When I was hungry [and] penniless, anemic countesses, widows . . . —all manner of strange folk—came to my aid. In a thousand places the miracle has happened to me. Because I was penniless and took one ship instead of another, I met the great and beautiful friend who has stood by me through all the torture, struggle, and madness of my nature for over three years, and who has been here to share my happiness these past ten days.[3] That another person, to whom success and greater success is constant and habitual, should get such happiness and joy from my own modest beginning is only another of the miracles of life.

Ten days ago I came home penniless, exhausted by my terrible and wonderful adventures in Europe, by all I had seen and learned, and with only the hated teaching—now become strangely pleasant—or the advertising, before me. The day after New Year's—truly a *New* Year for me—it began: the publisher's demand over the telephone that I come immediately to his office; that first long conference, as I sat there wild, excited, and trembling as it finally dawned on me that someone was at last definitely interested; the instructions to go away and think over what had been said two or three days; the second conference, when I was told definitely they had decided to take it; the formal letter of acceptance, with the terms of the contract, and finally the contract itself, and the sight of the blessed check. Is not this too a miracle?—to have happened to a penniless unhappy

[3] Mrs. Bernstein.

fellow in ten days? Are a child's dreams better than this? Mrs. Boyd, trying to hold me down a bit, said that the time would soon come when all this would bore me, when even notices and press clippings would mean so little to me that I would not glance at them. So, she says, does her husband, a well-known critic and writer, feel and act. But isn't it glorious that this should have happened to me when I was still young and rapturous enough to be thrilled by it? It may never come again, but I've had the magic— what Euripides calls "the apple tree, the singing, and the gold."

Of my voyage in Europe this time, of all that happened to me this time, and of how all this began, I can do no more here than to give you a summary: of my adventures on the ship, of my wanderings in France and Belgium and Germany, of all the books and pictures I saw and bought, of my new book,[4] now one third written, of my stay in Munich and the strange and terrible adventure at The Oktoberfest (with all its strange and beautiful aftermath). . . .

Then, of how, still battered and blue, with a dueling student's skullcap covering my bald head I went to Oberammergau; how one of my wounds broke open there, and I was nursed by the man who played Pilate (a doctor) and by Judas, and by a little old woman there, almost eighty, whom I had known in Munich—almost as mad as I was, no husband any more, children dead, even the name of her village in America only a name she couldn't always remember; a vagabond at seventy-eight around the world, hating the Germans she once loved, and loving only the Oberammergauers who had known her for forty years. She had written one book about them and was at work on another, but she was afraid she was going to die and wanted me to promise to write it for her. When I refused to do this we had fallen out and she had left Munich in a temper at me.

Now, all battered up, I was coming to see her again. She was the daughter of a Methodist minister, and despite her long life in Europe and the Orient she had never lost the stamp of it—she read insanely all the statistics concerning illegitimate children in Munich and Oberammergau, going almost insane when she discovered the guilt of her adored Passion Players. Her treatment of me now was a mixture of old Methodist intolerance and "it serves you right" combined with love and tender mercy.

Of how I left Oberammergau; of how she followed me up to Munich in a few days; of how the police almost drove me mad with their visits, questions, and inspections; of how the poor old thing became my accomplice, almost driving me mad with her advice and suspicions, seeing a policeman looking for me behind every bush, and rushing over to warn me at my pension at all hours of day and night. Of how finally she saw

4 *The River People.*

the great Zeppelin over Munich early one morning and came to pull me out of bed twittering with excitement; of how from this time on she lived only for the Zeppelin, staying in her cold pension nearly all day long with the radio phones clamped to her ears, her old eyes bright and mad as she listened to news of the flight to America. Of how a night or two later the pension people had tried to get me when I was at the theatre, and of how the old woman had died that night with the phones to her ears still.[5]

Of how they got me next morning and [I] went over and saw her there, and old Judas and his daughter Mary Magdalene who had known her for thirty years—they had come up that morning from Oberammergau —they were weeping gently and softly, they were taking her back, according to her wish, to bury her there (she had said it to me a hundred times). Of how I had asked if I should go with them, and they had looked into my wild and bloody eyes, at my swollen nose, seamed head, and gouged face, and shook their heads slowly. Then of how I knew I must leave this place which had given me so much—as much as I could hold at the time—and taken so much. My lungs were already raw with cold, I was coughing and full of fever—I felt a strange fatality in the place, as if I too must die if I stayed longer.

So that afternoon I took the train for Salzburg, drawing my breath in peace again only when I got over the Austrian border. Then four days in bed in Salzburg and on to Vienna. The first days in Vienna, still in a sort of stupor from all I had seen or felt—full of weariness and horror. Then slowly I began to read, study, and observe again. Then, just before I went to Budapest, Mrs. Boyd's first warning letter about the book I had forgotten—Scribners was interested; I should write at once. Forgot about it— believed in promises and the book no more—went to Hungary, went out among the wild and savage people of the plains, Asiatics now as they were when they came twelve hundred years ago under Attila. Then back to Vienna again and there a letter from Scribners—at last, it seemed, something really hopeful. This whole story—strange, wild, ugly and beautiful, I don't know what it means—but the drama and the struggle within me at this time was much more interesting than the purely physical things outside. What it means, I don't know, but to me it is strange and wonderful, and my next book, a short one, will probably be made from it.[6] I have never written home or to you about this before—telling the bare facts—because it takes too long and tires me out to tell it. You must say

---

[5] In an unpublished letter to Mrs. Bernstein, Wolfe says that his story about the death of the old lady was invented.

[6] Wolfe planned to use the story of his wanderings in Europe as part of *The River People*.

nothing of this to anyone. I will put it all down some day in a book, together with much more strange and marvelous, so that who can read may see.

Getting to present matters, the letter in Vienna six or seven weeks ago was the first indication I had of what has happened. . . . The Scribners letter was signed by one Maxwell Perkins, whom I have since come to know as a fine and gentle person, full of wisdom. Mrs. Boyd tells me to listen to him carefully—he is one of those quiet and powerful persons in the background, the sole and only excuse, she says, for Scott Fitzgerald having been successful as he is. In his letter he said he had read my book, and while interested he did not know whether any publisher could risk it as it is; he did know it was a very remarkable thing and no editor could fail to be excited by it (I didn't tell him one or two had failed). What he wanted to know, he said, was when Scribners could talk with me. I was excited and eager, and as usual too enthusiastic. I wrote him at once, saying briefly my nose was broken and my head scarred (which was beginning early with a stranger, of course) but that his words of praise filled me with hope and eagerness. Said I'd be home Christmas or New Year's. Followed two more weeks in Vienna, three in Italy, then home from Naples. Called him up morning after New Year's. He asked me if I had the letter sent to the Harvard Club [7] and I said no—it had probably been sent abroad. He asked me to come to Scribners at once. I went up—in a few minutes I was taken to his office, where I found Mr. Charles Scribner (simply there, I think, to take a look at me, for he withdrew immediately, saying he would leave us alone).

Mr. Perkins is not at all "Perkinsy"—name sounds Midwestern, but he is a Harvard man, probably New England family, early forties, but looks younger, very elegant and gentle in dress and manner. He saw I was nervous and excited, spoke to me quietly, told me to take my coat off and sit down. He began by asking certain general questions about the book and people (these weren't important—he was simply feeling his way around, sizing me up, I suppose). Then he mentioned a certain short scene in the book,[8] and in my eagerness and excitement I burst out, "I know you can't print that! I'll take it out at once, Mr. Perkins." "Take it out?" he said. "It's one of the greatest short stories I have ever read." He said he had been reading it to Hemingway week before. Then he asked me

[7] A letter from Perkins dated December 7, 1928, saying merely: "Thanks very much indeed for your letter of November nineteenth. I look forward impatiently to seeing you, and I hope you will call up as soon as you conveniently can after reading this. Then we can have a talk."

[8] "An Angel on the Porch" which was published in the August, 1929, issue of *Scribner's Magazine,* and which appears on pages 99–100 and 262–269 of *Look Homeward, Angel.*

if I could write a short introduction for it to explain the people—he was sure Scribner's Magazine would take it; if they didn't someone else would. I said I would. I was at once elated and depressed—I thought now that this little bit was all they wanted of it.

Then he began cautiously on the book. Of course, he said, he didn't know about its present form—somewhat incoherent and very long. When I saw now that he was really interested, I burst out wildly saying that I would throw out this, that, and the other—at every point he stopped me quickly saying, "No, no—you must let that stay word for word—that scene's simply magnificent." It became apparent at once that these people were willing to go far farther than I had dared hope—that, in fact, they were afraid I would injure the book by doing too much to it. I saw now that Perkins had a great batch of notes in his hand and that on the desk was a great stack of handwritten paper—a complete summary of my whole enormous book. I was so moved and touched to think that some-one at length had thought enough of my work to sweat over it in this way that I almost wept. When I spoke to him of this, he smiled and said everyone in the place had read it. Then he went over the book scene by scene—I found he was more familiar with the scenes and the names of characters than I was—I had not looked at the thing in over six months. For the first time in my life I was getting criticism I could really use. The scenes he wanted cut or changed were invariably the least essential and the least interesting; all the scenes that I had thought too coarse, vulgar, profane, or obscene for publication he forbade me to touch save for a word or two. There was one as rough as anything in Elizabethan drama—when I spoke of this he said it was a masterpiece, and that he had been reading it to Hemingway. He told me I must change a few words. He said the book was new and original, and because of its form could have no formal and orthodox unity, but that what unity it did have came from the strange wild people—the family—it wrote about, as seen through the eyes of a strange wild boy. These people, with relatives, friends, towns-people, he said were "magnificent"—as real as any people he had ever read of. He wanted me to keep these people and the boy at all times foremost—other business, such as courses at state university, etc., to be shortened and subordinated. Said finally if I was hard up he thought Scribners would advance money.

By this time I was wild with excitement—this really seemed something at last—in spite of his caution and restrained manner, I saw now that Perkins really was excited about my book, and had said some tremendous things about it. He saw how wild I was—I told him I had to go out and think—he told me to take two or three days—but before I left he went out and brought in another member of the firm, John Hall Wheelock, who spoke gently and quietly—he is a poet—and said my book was one of the most interesting he had read for years. I then went out and tried to pull myself together. A few days later, the second meeting—I brought notes along as to how I proposed to set to work, and so on. I agreed to deliver one hundred pages of corrected manuscript, if possible, every week. He listened, and then when I asked him if I could say something definite to a dear friend, smiled and said he thought so; that their minds were practically made up; that I should get to work immediately; and that I should have a letter from him in a few days. As I went prancing out I met Mr. Wheelock, who took me by the hand and said: "I hope you have a good place to work in—you have a big job ahead." I knew then that it was all magnificently true. I rushed out drunk with glory. In two days came the formal letter (I wired home then), and yesterday Mrs. Boyd got the check and contract which I am now carrying in my pocket. God knows this letter has been long enough—but I can't tell you half or a tenth of it, or of what they said.

Mr. Perkins said cautiously he did not know how the book would sell— he said it was something unknown and original to the readers, that he thought it would be a sensation with the critics, but that the rest is a gamble. But Mrs. Boyd says that to print such a gigantic manuscript from a young unknown person is so unusual that Scribners would not do it unless they thought they had a good chance of getting their money back. . . . I should love it, of course, if the book were a howling success, but my idea of happiness would be to retire to my apartment and gloat . . . and to let no more than a dozen people witness my gloating. But I think if I ever see man or woman in subway, elevated, or taxicab reading it, I will track that person home to see who he is or what he does, even if it leads me to Yonkers. And Mr. Perkins and Mr. Wheelock warned me not to go too much with "that Algonquin Crowd"—the Hotel Algonquin here is where most of the celebrities waste their time and admire one another's cleverness. This also makes me laugh. I am several million miles away from these mighty people, and at the present time want to get no closer. All the Theatre Guild people, whom I know through my dear friend,[9] have called her up and sent congratulations.

But now is the time for sanity. My debauch of happiness is over. I have made promises: I must get to work. I am only one of the thousands of people who write books every year. No one knows how this one will turn out. You must therefore say nothing to the Asheville people about it yet. In course of time, I suppose, Scribners will announce it in their advertisements. As for the Civic Cup business,[10] I am afraid that's out of

---

[9] Mrs. Bernstein.
[10] In her letter to him, Mrs. Roberts had asked if he would consent to being

the question. For one thing, no one knows anything about my book at home—whether it's good, bad, or indifferent. If anything is said about it, it must be later, after its publication. For another thing—and this troubles me now that my joy is wearing down—this book dredges up from the inwards of people pain, terror, cruelty, lust, ugliness, as well, I think, as beauty, tenderness, mercy. There are places in it which make me wiithe when I read them; there are others that seem to me to be fine and moving. I wrote this book in a white heat, simply and passionately, with no idea of being either ugly, obscene, tender, cruel, beautiful, or anything else—only of saying what I had to say because I had to. The only morality I had was in me; the only master I had was in me and stronger than me. I went into myself more mercilessly than into anyone else—but I am afraid there is much in this book which will wound and anger people deeply, particularly those at home. Yet terrible as parts are, there is little bitterness in it. Scribners told me people would cry out against this, because people are unable to realize that that spirit which is sensitive to beauty is also sensitive to pain and ugliness. Yet all of this goes into the making of the book, and because of this Scribners have believed in it and are publishing it. I will soften all I can but I cannot take out all the sting—without lying to myself and destroying the book. For this reason we must wait and see. If the people of Asheville some day want to heap coals of fire on my head by giving me a cup, perhaps I shall fill it with my tears of penitence—but I doubt that this will come for a long time. The people of Asheville, I fear, may not understand me after this book and may speak of me only with a curse—but some day, if I write other books, they will. And my God! What books I feel within me and what despair, since my hand and strength cannot keep up with all my heart has felt, my brain dreamed and thought!

I have spent an entire afternoon writing this to you—it is a volume, but now I have worked off my wild buoyancy and must get to work. Please keep silence about the cup business. You understand why, don't you?

God bless you for your letter, and forgive the great length of this one, so filled with my own affairs that I have not yet sent my love to Mr. Roberts. Give it to him with all my heart and tell him I want no better news from home than that he is up and hale again. I have told you about my own business at such length because I believed you really wanted to hear it all, and because I am so happy to share it with you. But God bless you all and bring you all health and happiness. If you see Scribners' advertisement you can speak, of course, but please use your excellent discretion.

---

nominated for the civic award cup which was being presented by the *Asheville Times* to the citizen who had rendered the finest service to Asheville in the past year.

I shall write you a short letter when I am calmer, telling you about N.Y.U. plans, and how my work on the book is coming. Love to all.

P.S. Whatever of this you think may interest my family pass on, but tell them also, for God's sake, to be discreet. It made me so happy to be able to wire them good news the other day. Now, let's all hope something comes of it. Again, God bless you all.

Note: I can hardly read parts of this myself, but you have had to puzzle my hen-scratching out before, and perhaps you can do it again. I wrote it in a great hurry and I was very excited—but I hope you make it out.

It's not a letter—it's a pamphlet. Maybe I'll ask you to give it back some day in order to see how foolish I felt.

To MABEL WOLFE WHEATON

[27 West 15th Street]
[New York City]
Wednesday, Feb 13 [1929]

Dear Mabel:

Thanks for your letter—and thanks again for the box of cake and candy. Everything arrived in good shape, including the jar of peaches which I have not yet eaten. I had a letter from Mrs. Roberts a day or two after I got yours: you are certainly right in saying they are "walking on air" about my book. She is soaring so high, in fact, that she has me worried—to read it you would think that I had already "arrived," that my book is already a crashing success, and so on. To think, she says, that it should come to you so soon, when you are only a kid (a 28 year old kid is getting about ready to put on long pants, don't you think?)—I had not expected you to get it (she says) for another ten years. And so on.

Now, of course, the effect of all this is to make me very nervous. That is why I wanted to be as quiet as possible about the book until it is published. I am still happy about it, I am still very hopeful about it, but, let me repeat, no one knows what kind of success it will have, or whether it will have any. And no one will know this until it is published. Of course, I was terribly stirred up about it myself when I wrote her that long letter, but I warned her again and again not to take it for granted that success and glory, and all the rest of it, is already gained. We *hope*—both publishers and myself—that the book will go well; but I ought to be satisfied if it goes just well enough to pay me enough money to live on while I write another, to pay Scribners for their expense and trouble, and to make them willing to publish my next one. You know that I hope, naturally, that it will do much better than this, but remember, there is always the chance that it will do much worse. I am a young unknown writer, this is my first book, it may perish in oblivion. So the best policy is to work, wait, and pray for the best.

I have found that your good friends—your best friends—have a bad habit of announcing your election before you have even begun to run. I certainly am grateful for their good wishes, but I shall also probably be the scapegoat later if things do not pan out as well as they want them to. For the rest of the world is not so friendly and generous—if it is talked about now that my book is a tremendous success, and then if my book turns out a failure—I shall get credit for having done a lot of premature boasting. That, unhappily, is the way things are (as you probably have found out.)

I have already had a letter of congratulation from my friend, ————— ———— of ————, —. ———— ———— opens with a rush of enthusiasm and congratulates me on the "tremendous royalties" which the publishers are already paying me. His mother, he says, has written him all about it. Now of course, I am very fond of Mrs. ——, but I know very well that she is not burdened by silence, and I am wondering just how many hundred thousand people she has told it to thus far, and how much each of them has added to her fairy tale. Since I wanted the thing—for the reasons I have mentioned—kept reasonably quiet, and since ———— is only about 1200 miles from Asheville, I am wondering just how long it will take for my little secret to reach Siberia. If Mrs. —— is in good form, the news ought to get there about Good Friday. So, if you see the lady, please try very tactfully to muzzle her.

I know you understand that I am not ungrateful for the generous good wishes of all these people. I value their friendship highly, and I have been touched and moved by all they have said. Only, I really think that too much talk at present may do more harm than good.

Scribners have also bought a story from me to print in their magazine.[1] They asked me if $150 would be satisfactory and I almost fell off the chair —it is a very short scene which they are taking from the book, and I had not expected over fifty or seventy-five dollars. N.Y.U.—that is, my good friend, Dean Munn—dug up a couple of courses to help me buy bacon and beans—they take only about half the regular teaching time, and will pay me $150 or $200 a month between now and June. So I shall manage very well at present. If I need money in the summer I can get work in the summer school, and they have already offered me a job for next September, if I need it.

[1] "An Angel on the Porch."

But I really do not need much money. My tastes seem to get simpler instead of more expensive, outside of food and books. When I was a child I dreamed of at least a million: now my imagination can not go beyond six or seven thousand a year. I hope that some day I shall have that much, but honestly I would not know how to do my work and spend much more. Yet such a sum would hardly be cigarette money for most of the people I know in New York, and I know there are dozens of people in Asheville who have more than this, although money goes twice as far there. I am simply bewildered at the amount of money in America. I have just come back from poverty-stricken Europe—from Vienna, where many a man thinks himself lucky to work for $20 a month. I have never seen anything like the wealth here, and I am sure there has never been anything like it in the world's history. . . . There are literally thousands of apartments along Park Avenue which rent . . . for twenty-five and fifty thousand. I find it very interesting to see all this wealth and power, but I certainly do not envy it. Most of these people have made it recently—they are ignorant and dull and unhappy: they don't know what to do with it. Only a few of them—(*none* that I know of)—have either the intelligence or talent of Mrs. B.[2] who saw long ago that there's no joy in life unless we can find work we love and are fitted for. She therefore works like a Trojan in the theatre, and has made a fine reputation for herself, solely through her own ability.

Another interesting thing is that money has come to mean so little that it can no longer buy people into cultivated society. On Sunday night I was lucky enough to be invited to the Dress Rehearsal of "Dynamo," O'Neill's new play, at the Theatre Guild. I was invited by Miss Helburn,[3] the head of the Guild, and I sat in the first row between Mrs. B. and a very beautiful and celebrated woman named Lynn Fontanne, who is now the Guild's star actress. Otto Kahn was three rows behind, and the place was filled with celebrities and beauties, all dazzling in evening clothes. The funny part is that people simply fight to get invited to the Guild Dress Rehearsal—but I am sure many of the people there that night were almost as poor as I am. Nevertheless, *they* are invited, while millionaire pork packers and their wives tear their hair in an effort to get in. (Of course, I got invited not through any merit of my own, but because the Guild will lay themselves out for Mrs. B. But they have certainly been friendly and kind to me and they all seemed glad my book was being published.)

I don't think I have any more news for you at present. I have done some work on the book, but not enough—must work much harder. The pub-

[2] Mrs. Bernstein.
[3] Theresa Helburn.

lisher wants the manuscript by first of May—I think they intend to publish about August. . . . Sorry to hear real estate is so dead. I think the business here—all the buying, selling, and making of fortunes—is a kind of boom, and that the bottom will drop out on a lot of people just as it did in Florida and Asheville. I'll try to write other members of family as soon as I get time.

The following letter to Madeleine Boyd was written in reply to a note from her enclosing a check for the sale of "An Angel on the Porch" to Scribner's Magazine, also a letter from H. L. Mencken. Mrs. Boyd had submitted several short sections from Look Homeward, Angel *to Mencken in hopes that he would publish some of them as short stories in* The American Mercury. *He had declined them, and she had suggested trying them with* The Bookman *and* The Dial. *They were never accepted by any magazine.*

To MADELEINE BOYD

Harvard Club
New York

Friday, Feb. 15 [1929]

Dear Mrs. Boyd:

Thanks for the note from Mr. Mencken, and for the short story cheque and receipt from Scribners. I am very much pleased by Mr. Mencken's note—his praise was moderate, but I take it at its literal value: I do not believe he writes such notes as a matter of form. And of course his belief in one's work would be of tremendous value to a writer.

I should certainly be glad to have you send the scenes from the book to *The Bookman* and *The Dial*—although *The Dial* terrifies me. I deliberately chose for Mr. Mencken scenes that are simply and clearly written, because I thought he would like these better, but they may seem too elementary to the subtle moderns who edit *The Dial*. If so, I could produce other scenes that would be practically unintelligible, even to the author. Seriously, what do you think of this?

I am at work on the book, but it is a stiff perplexing job. I stare for hours at the manuscript before cutting out a few sentences: sometimes I want to rip in blindly and slash, but unless I know *where* the result would be disastrous. Also my new book [1] fills my mind—I keep making

---

[1] *The Fast Express* which finally became the first part of *Of Time and the River.* Wolfe had stopped working on *The River People* when he returned to New York in January, 1929.

notes for it. But I shall finish this one first. I keep digging out old manuscripts [2] as I unpack and I shall probably give you a too-long short story
for reading. Wrote it several years ago. Took Mr. Perkins another 100
pages Monday. Thanks for the check again. If you want more manuscript,
let me know. Good luck to us both.

*The following letter was found in various versions in Wolfe's pocket note-
books and on the back of pages of his manuscripts, and was evidently never
mailed. That it was written long before publication of* Look Homeward,
Angel *is indicated by its chronological position in his notebooks; also by the
fact that the title,* O, Lost, *which he uses in it for* Look Homeward, Angel
*was discarded five or six months before publication of the book. Evidently,
in his anxiety about the reception that his book would have in Asheville,
Wolfe imagined that he might be asked to write a defense of it for the*
Citizen, *and began composing the various versions of this letter for the sake
of his own peace of mind.*

To THE EDITOR OF THE ASHEVILLE *CITIZEN*

[*April* (?) 1929]

Thank you very much for your friendly and courteous invitation to contribute an article to your columns answering critics of my book, "O, Lost."
I must decline to do so for several reasons, the most important of which are
as follows: at the beginning of my career as a novelist I have determined,
so far as possible, to let my books speak for me. The artist is neither a
debater nor a propagandist—certainly I have no skill as either—any defense of his works should be undertaken not by himself but by critics who
are competent for such work. If the Asheville critics of my work infer from
this that I am anxious to avoid controversy, they are certainly right. But if,
as I gather from several letters in your columns, they believe that my book
is a "bitter attack" against the town, the state, the South, they are certainly wrong. One does not attack life any more than he curses the wind;
shakes his fist at the storm; spits angrily at the ocean.

That there is bitterness in my book as well as pain and ugliness, I can
not deny. But I believe there is beauty in it as well, and I leave its defense
to those of my readers who found it there.

As to the implied criticisms of my personal life, I again have nothing to
say. I honestly do not care very much what these people think. None of

[2] Probably some of the sketches he had written in 1924–25, such as the story of
Eugene and the Countess in Orléans, which were later rewritten and published in
Of Time and the River.

them knows me, a few have seen me and talked to me: their efforts to pry and intrude into a life they can never know are ugly and revolting. But they are not surprising. One who has lived in New York a few years, hears too much of the sewage of a million mean lives—people who, unable to touch the sacred garments of the celebrities, feast on the familiarity of smut, contrive spurious nastiness, transfer the glittering vices they have themselves desired and have not had courage for, to the figures they honor with their venom and malice.

If the indignant Methodist ladies and gentlemen suspect me of fleshy carnalities, let them suspect no more. I am enthusiastically guilty. I have eaten and drunk with sensual ecstacy in ten countries. I have performed the male function with the assistance of several attractive females, a few of whom were devout members of the Methodist Church.

[THE LETTER BREAKS OFF HERE]

To MABEL WOLFE WHEATON

[27 West 15th Street]
[New York]
May, 1929.

Dear Mabel:

Thanks for your letter which I got to-day. I don't suppose I have written much lately—I have very little sense of time when I am working. I am working every day with the editor of Scribners, Mr. Perkins, on the revision of my book. We are cutting out big chunks, and my heart bleeds to see it go, but it's die dog or eat the hatchet. Although we both hate to take so much out, we will have a shorter book and one easier to read when we finish. So, although we are losing some good stuff, we are gaining unity. This man Perkins is a fine fellow and perhaps the best publishing editor in America. I have great confidence in him and I usually yield to his judgment. The whole Scribner outfit think the book a remarkable thing—and Perkins told me the other day when I was in the dumps that they would all be very much surprised if the book wasn't a success. When I said that I hoped they would take another chance on me, he told me not to worry— that they expected to do my next book and the one after that, and so on indefinitely. That means a great deal to me. It means at any rate, that I no longer have to hunt for a publisher.

I've already seen the title page and a few specimen sheets of the type. They call this the "dummy." Of course, I'm excited about it. I can't say enough for the way Scribners have acted. They are fine people. They sent me to one of the most expensive photographers in town a few weeks ago, a woman who "does" the writers.[1] What it cost I can't say, but she charges $150–$200 a dozen, I understand, and she kept me half a day. What in heaven's name they're going to do with them all I don't know—they say it's for advertising. They are going to begin advertising, I believe, this month or next, and they have asked me to write something about myself. Of course, that's always an agreeable job, isn't it? When the story and the book are coming out, I don't know, but everyone has become very busy this last month—I now have to go up to see the editor every day. I think the story will be held back until just before the book is published. Scribners are good salesmen, good business people, good advertisers. They are doing a grand job for me, and they believe in me.

That's enough about the book for the present. I am very sorry to hear of Mr. Jeanneret's [2] trouble. Your letter brought back to me the memory of my childhood, and of Papa leaning on the rail talking politics, and everything else with the old man. When my short story comes out read it—you will see them again as you have seen them many times—but *don't* mention this to anyone. Jeanneret was a true friend to Papa and admired and respected him. He belongs to a world that is gone, a life and a time that is gone—the only Asheville I can remember, as it was in my childhood and boyhood. Perhaps I see the change even more clearly than you do because I have been away from it. I think the Asheville I knew died for me when Ben died. I have never forgotten him and I never shall. I think that his death affected me more than any other event in my life. I was reading some poems the other day by a woman who died very suddenly and tragically last December.[3] I met the woman once. She was very beautiful, but I suppose by most of our standards we would have to say that she was a bad person. She ruined the lives of almost everyone who loved her— and several people did. Yet this woman wrote some very fine poetry, and is spoken of everywhere now. I thought of Ben—he was one of those fine people who want the best and highest out of life, and who get nothing—who die unknown and unsuccessful.

I can certainly understand your desire to be alone. With me it's a necessity. Yet in my heart I like people and must have them. Sometimes, as you know, I have gone away for months without letting people know where I was. But I always got homesick for the familiar faces and had to come back. I think I live alone more than any person I have ever known. I know many fine people in New York—some of them I see very often, but I must spend a large part of my day alone. I hate crowds and public meet-

---

[1] Doris Ulmann. She did not charge Scribners as much as Wolfe says here.

[2] Louis William Jeanneret, the Swiss watchmaker who rented space in W. O. Wolfe's marble shop.

[3] Probably Wolfe meant Elinor Wylie. See his letter to his sister Mabel dated March 26, 1927.

ings. You could not live the way I do: you must be with people, talk to them, join with them. But this is the only life I can lead. Sometimes I love to go out and join in with the crowd, and have a good time. But not often. The truth of the matter is that most people I meet bore me until I could cry out. This ought not to be but it is. And I am not often bored with myself or with my reading or writing. I have tried a great many of the things I dreamed of when I was a child—travelling about, Paris, Vienna, theatres, ships, and so on—but about the only real satisfaction I have had has been in work, the kind of work I like to do. And I have not worked hard enough. Most people are not happy when working, simply because very few people have ever found the work they want to do. It's pretty hard to think of a cotton mill worker or a ditch-digger getting much joy out of it, isn't it? And that goes as well for most business men: "realtors," pants makers, shoe dealers.

I may take your advice and come home for a few days when school is over. I could not come for long, because of my work here at Scribners, but I should like to stay a few days or a week. . . .

I suppose you are right about most of the money being in New York: there is certainly a lot of it here, although I have seen very little of it myself. Our "Prosperity" is a very uneven thing. There are a great many rich and well-to-do people, but there are millions who just make enough to skin through on. Most of the people in New York are like this—scraping by, with nothing left over. What's your politics? I suppose you are a Democrat or Republican, since the South is the most conservative place left. I believe a Socialist is regarded down there as being the same as an Anarchist. But wait until the poor people have to endure an empty belly and you'll see a change. I think if I had any politics, I'd be a socialist—it's the only sensible thing to be (if you're not a capitalist, and I'm *not*). But you think that's "wild talk," don't you?

I don't blame you for letting some of the club work go. I buy an Asheville paper once in a while, and there seems to be a club for everything under the sun, including hog raising. Apparently the women are getting all the "culture"—what do the men do? It is probably a farce—this club business—because most of these women don't give a damn if Shakespeare wrote "Hamlet" or "The Face on the Barroom Floor": it gives them a chance to sit around on their rumps and look "literary." I am sorry Mrs. Roberts is in so much of it. She runs the business down when she talks to me and winks over my head at J. M. Of course, I see everything, but the poor woman thinks I'm fooled. She's very ambitious for Margaret, and I think has just a little bit of the snob in her. But then we all have. She's a fine woman—one of the few who have stood the test of time with me. I shall always like her.

I'm glad to know all are reasonably well—sorry to hear of Fred's automobile accident, and to know it has upset him. It upsets me just to look at them here in New York: the average taxi driver is a dangerous criminal with no respect for life. If I am ever in a taxi that runs down a child—and I have feared this a dozen times—I think I shall be tempted to kill the driver. I no longer think it's smart or daring to drive fast. I am the one remaining American who knows nothing about driving a car and who has no desire to own one. Is this another sign of my "queerness"?

Well, I sometimes feel like the only sane person on a stroll through a madhouse: all the maniacs are nudging one another, and saying: "See that guy? He's crazy."

I have written the last several pages today (Tuesday)—the weather was fine: about the first real sign of Spring. All the people were out and God knows there are plenty of them. The buildings are so big and high, and the people swarming up and down look like insects. Most of them are. I think I know pretty well what I want to do with my life—but a lot depends now on what success my book has. Pray for me.

As I say, I hate crowds and parties, but I'm being dragged out to dinner with some swells on Saturday. I hate it, but my agent has arranged the thing, and says it will be good for me. I don't believe it, but maybe they'll give me a drink.

I've written too much and said too little. Give my love to everyone and ask them to write when able. Don't be afraid of going crazy—I've been there several times and it's not at all bad. If people get too much for you take a long ride on the train.

Henry T. Volkening, to whom the following letter was written, was an instructor in the English Department at New York University from 1926 to 1928, and is now an associate of Diarmuid Russell, in the literary agency of Russell and Volkening, Inc. Excerpts from the letters he received from Wolfe were first published in his article "Thomas Wolfe: Penance No More" in the Spring, 1939, issue of The Virginia Quarterly Review.

To HENRY T. VOLKENING

Harvard Club
New York

July 4 [1929]

Dear Henry:

This is Independence Day—I just passed one of Nedick's Peerless Orange Juice Stands, and when I did I thought of you, far away in Germany and England where you are completely cut off from this and many other blessings.

Your letters and postals have given me the greatest pleasure—I cried out for joy at your rapturous letter from Vienna: I had a great personal pride in it, as if I had discovered the place. Did you go to Budapest? Long, long ago I wrote you, when I got your letter—wrote page after page, but never finished it. This can only be a little note—I'm going up the Hudson to my friend's, Olin Dows, to-morrow—he lives in a little shack of seventy rooms, and no one else is there at present. Perhaps I'll write you a nice long one from there, filled with elegant quotations from good books—they have four or five thousand beauties, Lamb, and Browning and Arnold and everything. I'm going to Maine last two weeks in July—I'll look right across the Atlantic at you. And perhaps to Canada for a few days. (But why *Canada?*)

Everything turned out beautifully for you—there was nothing here but rain, rain through April and much of June. I'm so glad you and Nat [1] love Vienna—you are like Vienna people, I think—in spite of your good Deutsch name, you are *Wiener* Deutsch. Did you go to Nurnberg? It's a grand place. And are you going to *Ambleside* and the Lake district? I hope my advice has not yet played you false—bring back an earful of adventure for me.

My other letter was filled with news—which I've forgotten! Year at N.Y.U. is over and gone (with my prayers) to oblivion. When I saw the boys last many had turned slightly green, yellow, and purple from stored-up poison and malice. It's too bad. Many of them went abroad—to Paris and everything. Gottlieb I believe went to Germany, Troy got a scholarship and is going to live—where do you suppose?—in Dear Old Paree, and Dollard's [2] epoch making and universe-quaking quarrel with Herr Geheimrat Watt finally burst out in open battle late this Spring—he resigned, and when I said goodbye was talking of vagabonding, joining the Navy, going to Cambridge, etc. . . .

I feel splendid, and am fresh and fat. My proofs are coming in, my story [3] appears in the magazine next month (get it in England if you can—*Scribner's* for August), book's out in the Fall, and Scribners thinks it a grand thing and that it will go. I hope it makes a splash—not a flop!—but that it splashes me with a few dollars. Also writing some short stories [4] that they have asked me to write—without promises—and loaded to the decks with my new book.[5] Thank God I'm thirty pounds overweight, it's going to kill me writing it.

[1] Mrs. Volkening.

[2] Hans J. Gottlieb, William A. S. Dollard and William Troy were instructors in the English Department at New York University.

[3] "An Angel on the Porch."

[4] Nothing ever came of these. Wolfe had little or no idea of what constituted a saleable short story.

[5] At this time, Wolfe had only a rough idea of what his next book would

I am dining—or bootleg-beering—with some friends of yours next Wednesday: with Dashiell of *Scribners;* Mrs. D.; a young man named Meyer, who read my book for S. first; and your friend, the deaf young man, who is also a friend of Meyer's.[6]

This is all for the present—the free Americans have been shooting off firecrackers all day: it's about all they can do. The weather good and bad—today cool, bright, and lovely. But Hell to come. I'm naturally excited and hope something good happens to book.

I rejoice in all the joy your trip is giving you. You seem to be fortunate the whole way. Go to the Royal Oak to *drink* in Ambleside. Stay a day or two at Rosy Lewis' Cavendish Hotel in Jermyn Street—go to Bath, Lincoln, York, Fountain Abbey, Edinburgh, Trossachs—eat in Soho—Restaurant des Gourmets—Olde Cocke Tavern (Fleet St)—Simpsons: go to Trocadero bar for cocktails—Walk in old London City by moonlight (if there is a moon)—go to the bookshops, especially Foyles in Charing Cross Road. This is all for the present. Good luck and God bless you both.

The next four letters to John Hall Wheelock of Scribners were written from Boothbay Harbor, Maine, where Wolfe had gone to rest and read the galley proofs of Look Homeward, Angel. *Wheelock was the editor in charge of the final editing and proofs of all Wolfe's books published by Scribners. He is now a senior editor, occupying the office of Maxwell Perkins, who died in 1947.*

To JOHN HALL WHEELOCK

Ocean Point, Maine.

July 19, 1929.

Dear Mr. Wheelock:

Don't mind if I call you "mister" at present, but you must please not do it to me. I no longer have the slightest feeling of stiffness or diffidence

---

be. He had first thought of it as *The Fast Express,* which finally became the early part of *Of Time and the River.* Then, gradually, he began thinking of expanding *The Fast Express* and calling it *The October Fair.* He kept expanding *The October Fair* until it became so huge that it finally was cut in half, and the first half published as *Of Time and the River.*

[6] Alfred S. Dashiell, who was Managing Editor of *Scribner's Magazine* and is now Managing Editor of *The Reader's Digest;* Wallace Meyer, an editor in the book department at Scribners; and Byron Dexter, who is now Managing Editor of *Foreign Affairs.*

toward you, I have on the contrary the warmest and gratefulest feeling toward you and Mr. Perkins, but I could no more call you Wheelock than I could call him Perkins. Alone in my mind I know that I am now a man in years, and as I face my work alone I come pretty close at times to naked terror, naked nothing, I know that no one can help me or guide me or put me right—that's my job. Perhaps that is why in my personal relations with people I cling to the old child's belief—that there are older people who are wiser and stronger, and who can help me. I am far from being melancholy—I am more full of strength and power and hope than I have been in years—I have in me at the present time several books, all of which are full of life and variety, and rich detail. If I can only put down finally the great disease and distress of my spirit, which is to take in more of life than one man can hold, I can go on to do good work—because all men are certainly bound by this limit and I believe my chance to learn and experience, and my power of absorption, are as good as those of most men.

I feel packed to the lips with rich ore. In this wild and lovely place, all America stretches below me like a vast plain: the million forms that spend themselves in the city, and torture us so by their confusion and number, have been fused into a calmer temper—I am filled with a kind of tragic joy. I want to tear myself open and show my friends all that I think I have. I am so anxious to lay all my wares out on the table—when one thing that I have done is praised, to say: "You have not seen one tenth or one twentieth of what is in me. Just wait." Then I am tortured when I have talked to people that I have seemed too exuberant, too full of wild energy—I go away thinking they have this simple picture in two or three colors of me, when there are a thousand sombre and obscure shadings that have not been shown. I am full of affection and love for this first book, but when you and Mr. Perkins have praised it I have been stirred with the desire to do something far better—I will, I must show these men what is in me! Hence, again, we come to those reasons that make me say "mister" to some people—the spirit of the young man is thirsty for real praise, for admiration of his works: the creative impulse, which has such complex associations, may have roots as simple and powerful as this one.

It would be inexact to say that I feel that whatever I do is by its doing right. In my own life I am trying for greater balance, serenity, kindness to other people, but when I write at present I want to wrench the most remote and terrible things in myself and others: whatever scruples and restraints from the traditional morality I have—and I have many—vanish under the one surpassing urge to make everything blaze with light, to get intensity and denseness into everything. Thus when I write, my own lusts, fears, hatreds, jealousies—all that is base or mean—I drag up with strong joy, as well perhaps as better qualities, feeling not how bad these things may be, but what magnificent life this is, how little all else is by comparison. This is of course the most colossal egotism—but how else do people create? Not surely, by telling themselves they are dull, and their affairs petty or mean? What profit is in that, or where's the improvement? In short there are moments when I work when I feel that no one else has a quarter my power and richness—my baseness is better than their nobility, my sores more interesting than their health etc.—that, one way or another, I am a fine young fellow and a great man. I know you will not despise me for this confession. There are people all around, especially the critics, who would rail and sneer at this, but under their silly little pretenses of modesty and cynical urbanity they are nasty little mountains of egotism. I merely work in this way, by feeling when things are going well that I am something tremendous like a God; but as a person I am no longer insolent or proud at heart; I feel on the contrary a constant sense of inferiority, often to people I am in nowise inferior to. Professor Babbitt [1] at Harvard could figure all this out in 40 seconds by his patented . . . system, and have all my various romantic diseases headed with a half dozen tickets of his own manufacture—but his brand of "classicism" is so much more romantic than my wildest romanticism, that by comparison Plato might have begot me out of Lesbia.

I cannot tell you how moved I was by your letter—by its length, its patience and care: it is a symbol of my entire relation with you and Mr. Perkins. I could not a year ago have thought it possible that such good luck was in store for me—a connection with such men, and such a house, and editing and criticism as painstaking and intelligent as I have had. I should have once said that it was like a child's fantasy come true, but I know this is not exact—a child's dream is swollen with so much false magnificence that much in life seems stale and disappointing to the young man. But a slow and powerful joy is awaking in me as I come to see that life has real wonder that is more strange and marrowy than our fictions. Consider this: I was a little boy born among great mountains from obscure people, I saw strange and beautiful things when I was a child, I dreamed constantly of wonderful far off things and cities—and when I grew up I went away and saw them. I was a poor boy who grew up in anarchy, I said that one day I should go to Harvard, and I went. People who make jokes about Harvard would make a joke about this, but it was not a joke to that boy—it was magic—and the journey must first be viewed from its beginning. I read and dreamed about strange foreign cities, I grew up and went to see them, I met people in them, I wandered from place to place by myself, I had wonderful adventures in them. When I was 16 or 18 I

[1] Irving Babbitt.

hoped, I dreamed, I did not dare to speak the hope, that someday I would write a book that men would read. Now I have written a book, and a great publishing house is printing it, and men who have seen it have been moved by it and praised it. Seven months ago I came to Vienna from Budapest after months of wandering about in Europe: I had a scar on my head and a broken nose: I found there a letter from Scribners. Now I am writing this from a little cottage on the wild coast of Maine—the sky is grey and full of creaking gulls, the Atlantic sweeps in in a long grey surge. I have eaten delicious foods and drunk glorious wines in many countries: I have read thousands of noble books in several languages. I have known and enjoyed beautiful women, have loved and been loved by one or two.

Fools will sneer "How romantic!" I tell you merely what you will easily agree to—this is not romantic, this is only a bald statement of a few facts in a single ordinary life. No man can say that there is a single garnishment or distortion of fact here—whoever chooses to believe there is no wonder and no richness here is only stupidly and stubbornly hugging phantoms of sterility. No—what one comes to realize is that there is a reasonable hope that one may cherish in life, that makes it well worth living—and that the childish pessimist who denies this is as lying and dishonest a rogue as the cheap ready-made optimist—and that, indeed, of the two brands of rascals, the merchant who deals in Pollyanna optimism is a better man than he whose stock-in-trade is snivelling drivelling Pollyanna pessimism. The spirit that feels from its mother's womb the tragic under-weft of life, and never sees the End as different from what it is, is all the more certain that sunlight is not made of fog, wine of vinegar, good meat of sawdust, and a woman's lovely body of nitrogen, decaying excrement, and muddy water. To hell with such lying drivel—why do we put up with it?

I know that it is good to eat, to drink, to sleep, to fish, to swim, to run, to travel to strange cities, to ride on land, sea, and in the air upon great machines, to love a woman, to try to make a beautiful thing—all such as consider such occupations "futile," let them go bury themselves in the earth and get eaten by worms to see if that is less futile. However, these despisers of life who are so indifferent to living, are the first ones to cry out and hunt the doctor when they have bellyache.

There is an island in this lovely little harbor—I can look out on it from the porch of my cottage. It is covered by a magnificent forest of spruce trees, and a little cottage is tucked away in a clearing under the mighty trees at one end. One end of the island (where this house is) looks in on the bay and on the little cottages along the shore; the other end fronts the open Atlantic. Now I fantasy about buying this island (which has 15 or 20 acres), and so strange is possibility that one day perhaps I shall. Several weeks ago when I knew I was coming to Maine, I began to think about islands. Presently I saw myself owning one, living on one, putting off from the mainland (a decrepit old wharf) with my servant in a little motor boat stocked with provisions—to the minutest detail I saw this place even to the spring house where butter and milk and rounds of beef should be stored. This scene became a part of my dream. However blurred the actual details have become I cannot say, the picture remains vivid, only the island I dreamed about has become this one here—I am unable to distinguish one from the other, so imperceptibly have the two fused (even to the rotten old wharf from which I fish).

In a child's dream the essential thing happens—it is this that makes wonder—the long vacancies between the flare of reality are left out. He is, for example, on a great ship going to a strange country, the voyage ends, and the very next moment the ship is sailing into a harbor, he sets foot not on land, but on Paris, London, Venice. I am living in such a place—there is the harbor, with wooded islands in it, a little shore road that winds around by the water's edge, and all the little cottages, with tidy yards, bright flowers. Then immediately there is the ocean. I had ceased until recent years to believe there could be such scenes, and even now it does not seem real. I thought there would be preludes to the sea. But there are not. The other night I walked along the road. The little farm-houses slept below the moon, the gnarled apple trees full of apples getting ripe leaned over the hedges, and on the walls the wild wood lilies grew. You would not say along that road the sea was there behind the houses, behind the fir trees and the hedge, and the apples getting ripe—and yet you round a bend, and the sea is there. I thought there would be vast lengthenings into the sea, slow stoppages of land and rock, drear marshy vacancies, slow lapse and waste relinquishment of earth, but when you round the bend of the road the sea is there—he has entered at one stride into the land. This union of the vast and lonely with the little houses, the land, the little harbor, made a great music in me. I could not tell you all it meant but it was like Milton standing by a little door. And I thought that if one came into this place on a ship from open sea it would be with the suddenness of a dream.

To unspin all the meanings in these things would take too long—and my letter is much too long already.

I got the proof sent with your letter—through galley 100. I am sending off to you this afternoon the few galleys I had before—through 78 (including foul galleys for 71, 72). I am sorry the printer was upset by my one long insertion. I do not think it will happen again. I did it here to round out one detail in Leonard's life—much that showed the man in a favorable light had previously been cut, and I thought it proper to add a little here. But I shall not do this again. I note carefully all you say—I shall study the boys-going-away-from-school scene and cut where I can. I am sorry to know it is still too long. Mr. Perkins suggested a very large cut out of it, which was made. I have a much fresher mind for it now, and will perhaps find more. I shall certainly send all the proofs I now have (through 100) back to you by Tuesday of next week—they should reach you Thursday. I still have ten or eleven days in this lovely place—that is, until a good week from next Tuesday—you would therefore have time to send me more. I propose to go to Canada when I leave here, for a week, and return to New York before August 10. It would be good if I had proof to take with me.

You gave me a great start when you said 75 pages of manuscript had been lost, but on re-reading, as I understand your letter, it seems that we already have galley proofs for these pages. Even if we haven't, there is at Scribners a complete copy of the original manuscript besides the one Mr. Perkins and I cut. Of course what revisions were made in those 75 pages I don't know. It is a thrilling shock to know that you have already page proof for 70 galleys—of course I am excited and anxious to see them. I await eagerly the copies of the magazine with my story and the piece about my work [2]—what's the use of acting coy and modestly restrained when you don't feel that way!

This is another day—a glorious, blue-white, cold, sparkling day. Forgive the long letter, the personal rhapsodies—I have victimized you by making you the angel. My next letter will come with the proof and be strictly concerned with business. I fish, read, and write here.

To JOHN HALL WHEELOCK

[Ocean Point, Maine]

Monday, July 22 [1929]

Dear Mr. Wheelock:

I am sending you galleys 79–90. It was for this section (79–100) that the manuscript, you say, has been lost. Will you please urge the printer again to try to recover it? There are several places here that cause me difficulty. Naturally, without the manuscript I cannot remember word for word the original, but it seems to me that there are omissions in several places that are not covered by the cuts Mr. Perkins and I made. The most important of these is at the beginning of the boys-going-from-school scene which you say should be cut still more. Mr. Perkins and I took out a big

[2] The August issue of *Scribner's Magazine* in which "An Angel on the Porch" appeared, together with a short biographical sketch about Wolfe.

chunk, but there is now a confusing jump that nullifies the meaning of several speeches (you have pointed out one of these). I have tried to patch it up as well as I could. . . .

I do not remember what Mr. Perkins and I did on *galley 80*—where you have made a cut. It does not seem to me that what happens here is more likely to give offense than many other things that remain—as an alternative I have cut out parts of it, and I submit the result to your decision. If it still seems best to cut it all, please do so. (Cut).

Will you look over the titles of the German books on Galley 85 and correct mistakes in grammar—i.e. is it *Der* or *Die* Zerbrochene Krug? etc.

As I read over the proofs again, I become more worried. There is a reference, for example, by one of the boys in the coming-from-school scene to *Mrs. Van Zeck* the wife of a lung specialist—but the whole section describing her as she leaves a store has been omitted. I cannot recall making this cut with Mr. P. As to further cuts in this scene, I will do what I can—but it seems to me that conversation between the two boys, which you say is too long, has been cut down to very little—what you *do* have is the undertakers' scene, the W. J. Bryan scene, the Old Man Avery scene, the Village Idiot scene, the Old Colonel Pettingrew scene, the Men Discussing the War Scene—all of which it seems to me are good. But I'll do what I can.

In view of the gaps I have discovered, I think I shall send you by this mail only 79–90. I shall send the rest on as soon as I can do something to fill up the holes. I do hope people will not look on this section as a mere stunt—I really don't know what to do about cutting it—it is not a stunt, a great deal of the town is presented in short order. I'm going to send you galleys to 90 without further delay—I want you to go over the going-from-school scene and if you see cuts, make them. I shall cut where I can in the last part of the scene.

This is all for the present, I'm sorry to cause you all this trouble—but, as I think you know, deeply grateful. At times, getting this book in shape seems to me like putting corsets on an elephant. The next one will be no bigger than a camel at the most. I'll send more tomorrow.

To JOHN HALL WHEELOCK

(Ocean Point, Maine)

Tuesday Afternoon, July 23, 1929

Dear Mr Wheelock:

I am sending you herewith the proofs from Galley 91–100, which I have now gone over carefully. In spite of your advice to shorten this section (that part dealing with boys coming from school) I am afraid I have lengthened it a little. This was necessary because of certain omissions and gaps which it seemed to me either the printer had caused, or Mr. Perkins and I had failed to consider when we made cuts. I have written in the omitted segment on Mrs. Van Zeck somewhat shorter, I think, than it first was—I have had to pin this to the proof for want of space, and indicate the place where it is to be inserted. I have also written in various themes from poetry at places where it seemed to me there was a vacancy. This was the mood and temper with which the scene started—the inwoven poetry—and it seemed to me it should be continued.

Now Mr. Wheelock, I have not willingly run counter to your advice on this section—I am simply not able intelligently to select between what I have left. I should be troubled to think this is too long. Please consider it again as carefully as you can and, if it seems best, make cuts where you think they are needed.

Although the Van Zeck bit means extra work for the printer, I think it might take precedence over some other things in the scene for several reasons: first, it is war time, a discussion of the war, the allies, the "ancestral voices prophesying war" comes right after—the woman's German name, her position, wealth, etc. opens vistas and implication that may be interesting. Second, the boys mention her in their speeches—the whole may suggest how varied (not how uniform) may be the pattern of race, culture, background, etc. even in a small town. Please verify, if you can, my quotations. The "Nur wer *die* (?) Sehnsucht kennt" etc. is Goethe. "Drink to me only with *thine* (?) eyes," and the Keats "O for a draught of vintage" (I think its "Ode to Autumn"—not sure).[1] On Galley 93, I restored a sentence you had struck out and changed the words I thought objectionable. If you still find it too strong, cut it out. (Cut nozzles for end tips, for example.)

On galley 94, I added a sentence "Having arranged to meet her," (Mrs Pert) etc. for a scene between Ben and Mrs Pert which I cannot remember having been cut.

There was originally a burlesque of the English war books on galley 94 —was this omitted in the cuts? I have added a line here to sum up what remains.

This is all for the present. I now have left eight galleys, which I shall try to get off to you to-morrow. I am leaving here, I think, Saturday or Sunday. Do not send any more proofs after Thursday. If I get more before then, I shall return them all corrected to you before I leave. My present plan is to go to Portland and to take train or ship for Canada. I'll let you

---

[1] It is from "Ode to a Nightingale."

know. If I go there, I shall stay a week. I'll give you my address and also tell you when I am coming back to New York. Naturally I want to finish with the proofs now as quickly as possible.

Thanks again for your great care and patience.

To JOHN HALL WHEELOCK

[Ocean Point, Maine]
[July 25, 1929]

Dear Mr. Wheelock:

I am sending you herewith galleys 109–115. Galleys 116–125, with manuscript, and with a letter from you arrived this morning. Most of the corrections in today's batch have already been indicated by you—I think all corrections are plain. Usually when you suggest words or phrases for others that you consider of dubious meaning, I accept your revision, but once or twice I have stuck to my own. For example the other day for my "The world (or the earth) shook to the *stamp* of marching men" you suggested *to the tread*. On thinking it over I decided that *to the stamp* more nearly got my meaning. You have done glorious work on the *adverbs*—I get red in the face when I see them coming, and when they come, they come in schools and shoals. I hope my versions here are satisfactory.

Thanks for your splendid letter—the news about Mrs. Boyd is very exciting: [1] she is a shrewd and energetic woman, and knows many people. I am glad you are letting her have proofs. I wish it were possible to give her proofs for the whole book since some of the best of it, I think, comes in the closing chapters—Ben's death, etc. It would be a grand thing if a good English publisher did it.

I am very happy at the way the proofs are coming in. I shall get today's batch off to you to-morrow, and shall return all that I get hereafter in this place before I leave. I, too, am very anxious to get the galleys corrected and see it in page-proof. If I get to Canada I shall try to wire you my address. Perhaps under these circumstances I will not go, but if I do, I will not be out of touch with the book more than a week. . . . I am glad you liked my letter—it was written on impulse and I did not think until later how busy you are, and how little time you must have now for correspondence of this sort. Your own letters lift me tremendously—I hope in some way my book will deserve the labor you have put upon it.

[1] Wheelock had written Wolfe on July 24: "Mrs. Ernest Boyd sails for Ireland to-morrow on the *Westphalia,* and I am sending her all the proof we have of your book. She plans to be in London for some time, . . . and it is our hope that she may be able to find a suitable English publisher for *Look Homeward, Angel.*

I do hope there is time for the dedication. I have one that I want very much to use.[2] If you need it now let me know. I think perhaps I may have to use one of Scribners' old envelopes for to-day's proofs.

Benjamin Cone, to whom the following letter was written, was a classmate and friend of Wolfe's at the University of North Carolina, and had written to congratulate him on his "An Angel on the Porch" in the August issue of Scribner's Magazine: *also to call his attention to the biographical note written by the editors which said that Wolfe had been educated at "a small southern college." Cone is now a director of Cone Mills Corporation, cotton textile manufacturers, in Greensboro, N.C.*

To BENJAMIN CONE

Ocean Point, Maine
Saturday, July 27, 1929

Dear Ben:

I can't tell you how happy and excited I was to get your letter. It is the first (perhaps the last) I have had about the story. I read it in front of the post office here, with the Atlantic Ocean rolling in fifty feet away. I have been staying and correcting proofs at this lonely but beautiful little place on the Maine coast for a few weeks. I am going to Canada for a week Tuesday, and I shall be back in New York the rest of August, and, I suppose, for the winter too. N.Y.U. has given me another job—and, of course, I want to see what happens to my book. . . .

Now about the editor's note and the "small southern college": if you see anyone who has also read the note, for God's sake make plain what I think you understand already—that I had nothing to do with it and didn't see it until it was published. I do not deny that I may be capable of several small offenses, such as murder, arson, highway robbery, and so on— but I do deny that I have *that* sort of snob-ism in me. Whoever wrote the note probably put in "small southern college" because he did not remember where I did go, or because, for certain reasons connected with the book, he thought it advisable not to be too explicit. And after all, Ben, back in the days when you and I were beardless striplings—"forty or fifty years ago," as Eddie Greenlaw used to say—the Hill was (praise God!) "a small southern college." I think we had almost 1000 students our

2 The dedication of *Look Homeward, Angel* to Aline Bernstein reads: "To A. B." and is followed by the fifth stanza from John Donne's "A Valediction: Of His Name in the Window."

Freshman year, and were beginning to groan about our size. So far from forgetting the blessed place, I think my picture of it grows clearer every year: it was as close to magic as I've ever been, and now I'm afraid to go back and see how it is changed. I haven't been back since our class graduated. Great God! how time has flown, but I *am* going back within a year (if they'll let me).

Your letter is the sort of kindly, spontaneous action I really associate your name with. I have the warmest and most vivid memory of you, not only at Chapel Hill, but also several years ago in Paris. Tonight, when I got your letter, I thought of our trip to Chateau Thierry, our chartered automobile, and how we rode through the battlefields clutching a six foot loaf of French bread, a four pound Camembert cheese, and six or eight bottles of good red wine which we bought at a village *epicerie*. Frank Graham [1] of course, remained steadfast and true to the ideals of Mr. Volstead, but you and I and Mark Noble,[2] I believe, did our duty like men. I remember also a magnificent meal (catch me forgetting food!) that you and your kinsman set me up to at Prunier's, the great fish place. But most of all I remember how glad I was to see you and talk to you at that time. My play and baggage had been stolen from me (you mention this) and I was not only unhappy about this; I was a great deal more miserable than you suspected because I thought I was very much in love (one of the few times the noble passion has seized me). On second thought, I believe my romance started the day after I saw you last. I left you, I believe, New Year's Eve at the Café de la Paix, but the whole thing is all mixed together in my mind now. At any rate, I pursued a respectable Boston lady, six years my senior, around Paris for several weeks, fell sobbing on my knees before her in cafés, and did various other things that no doubt upset her. I was told at the time by friends (?) that it was not the real thing—that it was my first time in Paris, I was only a young fellow, I merely *thought* I was in love, but that did very little good. It was like being told by a Christian Scientist that you only *think* you have a bellyache, or being assured by your lawyer, after you have been put in jail, that "they can't do this to you." I wandered around Europe for about a year after this, and what mistakes I failed to make in Paris, I managed to make

[1] Frank P. Graham had been Dean of Students and Assistant Professor of History when Wolfe was at the University of North Carolina, and was in Europe on an Amherst Memorial Fellowship in 1925. He was President of the University of North Carolina from 1930 to 1949, when he was appointed to the United States Senate, filling the office made vacant by the death of Senator J. M. Broughton.

[2] Marcus C. S. Noble graduated from the University of North Carolina in 1921, and attended Harvard in 1922 to 1924 where he received his Ed. M. and Ed. D. degrees. He is now assistant professor of Education and Psychology at the University of Rhode Island.

in various other parts of the continent before I was through. I seem to have been born a Freshman—and in many ways I'm afraid I'll continue to be one. I don't suppose you remember me very well my first year at Chapel Hill, but I made history. It was I who made the speech of acceptance when elected to the Literary Society, I took the catalogue exam, went to Chapel Saturday and let a Sophomore lead me in prayer at noon. I made half the places on the Booloo Club [3] that year, and those I didn't make, I made during that first trip abroad. Even as recently as last October I got into difficulty with some nice German people in Munich which ended in a broken nose, a head laid open by a beer stein, several days in hospital and convalescence in Oberammergau, where the fellow who plays Pilate in the Passion Play bound up my wounds. It's a long story, but a good one. I'll tell you about it some time. . . .

Hope you read the book when it comes out, Ben. Even after cutting, it is still very long—it will make 600 or 700 pages—but I hope you manage to stick it to the end. I think you will like parts of it—I hope you will like it all, but some parts, I believe, will amuse and interest you. Perhaps you will regret that I have written some things in it—there may be parts of it that seem to you to be painful and ugly—but the whole effect, I hope, will not be ugly but will (excuse my solemn air!) have beauty in it. You will understand what I mean when you read it. . . . Certainly it would distress me very much to think what I had written would cause pain to any one I have known. Of course, this doesn't apply to you. You simply may not like certain things in the book. I don't know whether it will seem to be "Victorian" or "modern" to the reader: possibly it will seem "modern" to some people, and such people are very suspicious of the word. But remember I did not try to be either one or the other. I simply made a work of fiction as all fiction must be made, not out of thin air but out of the materials of human experience. Everything that could be done to make the outlines less harsh has been done—i.e. Scribners has carefully deleted all my good Anglo-Saxon words for the sexual act, urine, and human manure. I do not see how it can shock anyone, but it may.

I have written you a very long and, I'm afraid, a very dull letter, Ben but I have done it in order to explain a very simple thing which could be explained in one short sentence if I could find the words, but I can't, the simple things being the hardest. And now I'm afraid I haven't made myself clear at all. But this is perhaps the longest letter I shall write to anyone concerning my book, and I do it for this reason: you stand as a symbol of that happy and wonderful life I knew during 1916–1920 (don't think

[3] *The Carolina Magazine* satirically describes the Booloo Club as "a group of freshmen whose wit and sharply defined personalities had singled them out for special honor by the sophomores."

from this that my present life is wretched: on the contrary, now that I am really beginning to do the work I love, it is fuller and richer than it's ever been, but I shall never forget the great days at Chapel Hill and my friends there.) Such a time will come no more. I have kept silence for years. I have lived apart from most of those friends; probably most of them have forgotten me; but I think you will believe me when I tell you most earnestly that I value the respect and friendship of some of those people as much as I value anything, with two exceptions, one of which is my work. So, no matter what you think of my book, continue to remember the person who wrote it as you always have. In writing *you* this letter I somehow feel that I am speaking to all of them, although this is, of course, a personal letter, and I trust you to treat its contents with discretion.

Now please forgive me, Ben, for this long-winded letter. Excuse its solemn tone in places, and let me hear from you when you can. It is such good news to hear that you are still single, with no hope of a change. I get so depressed when I hear that another one of the boys has been folded away with the moth-balls. Look me up when you come to New York. I am thinking of wearing false whiskers and smoked glasses after the book comes out, but if I know you are coming, I will wear a red carnation in my buttonhole.

P.S. Wouldn't it be lovely if I made some money out of the book! Are you a praying man?

To HENRY T. VOLKENING

> Harvard Club
> New York
> Aug. 9, 1929

Dear Henry:

Please forgive me for not having written you more and oftener. I've been in Maine and Canada for several weeks. When I came back the other day I found a postcard from you, written in Switzerland. . . . I am so happy to know you have had a good trip—so anxious to see you and talk to and find what things and places we know in common (but not—dear me no!—too common). . . . Maine was lovely and cool—I was at a wild little place on the coast. I fished, corrected proofs, and read John Donne and Proust all day long. . . . I also went to Canada. Montreal is four-fifths imitation American, and one-fifth imitation English—but the beer and ale were splendidly real. Quebec was more interesting: it is entirely French-Canadian, and the people speak little or no English, and no French, either, so far as I am concerned. But this place too I found disappointing—it is like Dr. Johnson's dog walking on hind legs: "the wonder is not that he walks well, but that he walks at all." People are interested in Quebec only because it is a French town in America, and that means little to me.

I envy you everything in your trip except the hordes of tourists who are, you say, beginning to swarm around you. I note you are going to Paris; when you get this I suppose you will have been. I have heard recently that prices there are terrific—they were bad last summer—but I hear they are even worse now. Whenever I think of the French since the so-called "Great" war, I control myself and mutter "Voltaire! Voltaire!" And, after all, that is how a civilization should be judged, by its best, not by its worst—but its worst is pretty damned horrible, and unfortunately it requires superhuman fortitude and vision to see through to Ronsard when one is struggling to escape the snares of ten thousand petty rascals. Nevertheless, I have thought of France recently more than of any other country: it is physically the most comfortable and civilized of nations, and its highest and best spiritually is magnificent. The greatest evil in the national temper, I think, is "glory"—what they call "la gloire" —it accounts for the flag waving, "France has been betrayed," speechmaking, singing the *Marseillaise*, going to war, etc.—it represents what is cheap and melodramatic in them. I could go on like this indefinitely, but you can hear the other side from any of the 14,000 American epic poets, novelists, dramatists, composers, and painters now in Paris—they all "understand" France, and will point out my treason. We will talk of this and many other matters when I see you.

I hope you have good weather in England—it *is* possible, and there's nothing lovelier. Are you going to the Lakes? Also, did you go to old Rosie Lewis' Cavendish Hotel on Jermyn Street? . . . she—and it—are worth seeing.

My story came out in the August *Scribner's*—also a picture of the author in the back and a brief write-up of his romantic life—how he has "a trunkful of manuscript," "writes prodigiously," "forgets all about time when writing," and "goes out at 3 a.m. for his first meal of the day." I was more madly in love with myself than ever when I read it. I had expected convulsions of the earth, falling meteors, suspension of traffic, and a general strike when the story appeared—but nothing happened. I was in Maine. Nevertheless I am still excited about it. Proofs of the book will be finished in a day or two—most of the book already in page proof. Here's a final bit of news—I can send it to you because you're so far away—the Book of the Month Club heard of the book, came to Scribners and got the proofs just when S. was going to let Literary Guild have it. All I know is that the book has been read by the first group of readers (the mechanism of this escapes me) given the Freshman Camp grade of A, and passed on to the judges. No decision will be made for a week or two, but Scribners are excited, and so am I, of course. I think there's not much hope of its being their selection—they have pure and high-minded judges like William Allen White and Christopher Morley—and they may find some of the stuff too strong. Besides, I am an unknown writer and they have hundreds of manuscripts—but if! but if! but if! *Then,* of course, I should immediately accept the Abe Shalemonitch Chair in Anglo-Saxon Philology at N.Y.U. and devote myself to the noble profession of teaching. But I mustn't dream on this nebulous insanity. For heaven's sake say nothing—not even to Lady Asquith—about this. I'll tell you what happened when you come back.[1]

Scribners have been magnificent—their best people have worked like dogs on the thing—they believe in me and the book. To have found a firm and association with men like this is a miracle of good luck. . . . As for myself, I tremble now that the thing's done—I loathe the idea of giving pain; it never occurred to me as I wrote; it is a complete piece of fiction but made, as all fiction must be, from the stuff of human experience. . . . This too is a complicated thing about which I shall talk to you.

I am aching with a new one [2]—it's got to come out of me. I loathe the idea of not writing it, and I loathe the idea of writing it—I am lazy, and doing a book is agony—60 cigarettes a day, 20 cups of coffee, miles of walking and flinging about, nightmares, nerves, madness—there are better ways, but this, God help me, is mine.

This is a long stupid letter—forgive me. I have talked only about myself: I think of you and Natalie often, there are so many places I want to tell you to go to—it is hot, past midnight, and I am worn out. Naturally I'm absorbed in my own affair at present—say a spell for my fortune and good luck and God bless you both. Go to the lakes, look up the folks at the Royal Oak in Ambleside, tell me about it. Please let me know when you get back. How I wish I could be with you just for a morning walk and a bottle of ale.

Find an Englishman and make him *walk* you through the old *City* of London. If he has sense—and *some* have!—he'll know where to go and what to do. It is in many ways the grandest city in the world.

---

[1] Neither the Book of the Month Club nor the Literary Guild adopted *Look Homeward, Angel* or any of Wolfe's books.

[2] *The October Fair* of which the first half was published as *Of Time and the River.*

The publication of "An Angel on the Porch" in the August issue of Scribner's Magazine *had given Asheville people their first inkling of what* Look Homeward, Angel *was to be about. Wolfe's letter of August 11, 1929, to Mrs. Roberts was written in reply to one from her which is now lost but which evidently expressed grave concern about what Wolfe had written and the effect it would have upon his family.*

To MARGARET ROBERTS

Harvard Club
New York

Sunday, August 11, 1929

Dear Mrs. Roberts:

I have been away in Maine and Canada on a vacation and I came back to New York only two or three days ago. . . . I found your letter here when I came back. As usual, everything you say touches and moves me deeply. I wish my work deserved half of the good things you say about it: I hope that some day it will. The knowledge that you have always believed in me is one of the grandest possessions of my life. I hope it may be some slight return for your affection and faith to know that I have always believed in you; first, as a child, with an utterly implicit faith and hope, and later, as a man, with a no less steadfast trust. Life does not offer many friendships of which one can say this. I know how few there are, and yet my own life has been full of love and loyalty for whoever understood or valued it.

In your letter you say that many facts in my life you never knew about when I was a child—that much about me you did not understand until later. This does not come from lack of understanding: it comes because you are one of the high people of the earth, with as little of the earth in you as anyone I have ever known—your understanding is for the flame, the spirit, the glory—and in this faith you are profoundly right. It is a grand quality to see only with that vision which sees the highest and rarest. All that you did not see caused me great unrest of spirit as a child when I thought of you, and perhaps more now.

I hope you may be wrong in thinking what I have written may distress members of my family, or anyone else. Certainly, I would do anything to avoid causing anyone pain—except to destroy the fundamental substance of my book. I am afraid, however, that if anyone is distressed by what seemed to me a very simple and unoffending story,[1] their feeling when the book comes out will be much stronger. And the thought of that distresses *me* more than I can tell you. Nothing, however, may now be done

[1] "An Angel on the Porch."

about this. Everything that could reasonably be done to soften impressions that might needlessly wound any reader has been done by my publishers and me. Now, the only apology I have to make for my book is that it is not better—and by "better" I mean that it does not represent by any means the best that is in me. But I hope I shall feel this way about my work for many years to come, although there is much in this first book about which I hope I shall continue to feel affection and pride.

A thousand words leap to my tongue—words of explanation, persuasion, and faith—but they had better rest unsaid. Silence is best. More and more I know that the grievous and complex web of human relationship may not be solved by words. However our motives or our acts may be judged or misjudged, our works must speak for us, and we can ultimately only trust to the belief of other men that we are of good will. I can not explain the creative act here. That has been done much better than I could hope to do it, by other people. I can only assure you that my book is a work of fiction, and that no person, act, or event has been deliberately and consciously described. The creative spirit hates pain more, perhaps, than it does anything else on earth, and it is not likely it should try to inflict on other people what it loathes itself. Certainly the artist is not a traducer or libeler of mankind—his main concern when he creates is to give his creation life, form, beauty. This dominates him, and it is doubtful if he thinks very much of the effect his work will have on given persons, although he may think of its effect on a general public. But I think you know that fiction is not spun out of the air; it is made from the solid stuff of human experience—any other way is unthinkable.

Dr. Johnson said a man would turn over half a library to make a single book; so may a novelist turn over half a town to make a single figure in his novel. This is not the only method but it illustrates, I believe, the whole method. The world a writer creates is his own world—but it is molded out of the fabric of life, what he has known and felt—in short, out of himself.[2] How in God's name can it be otherwise? This is all I can say—I think you will understand it. Having said this, I can but add that at the last ditch, the writer must say this: "I have tried only to do a good piece of work. I have not wished nor intended to hurt anyone. Now I can go no farther. I will not destroy nor mutilate my work, it represents what is best and deepest in me, and I shall stand by it and defend it even if the whole world would turn against me." That, it seems to me, is the only answer he can make. Perhaps there are two sides to this question but this, at any rate, is my side, and the one I believe in with all my heart.

And now forgive me, please, for so long and dull a letter. It is late at

[2] This passage has a marked similarity to Wolfe's note "To the Reader" at the beginning of Look Homeward, Angel.

night, the weather is hot and enervating, and I am tired. But I hope I have been able to make clear what I feel about the book. . . . I hope this finds you all well and happy. Give my love to all, and forgive me for having again written about only my own affairs.

To GEORGE W. McCOY

Harvard Club
New York
Saturday, Aug. 17, 1929

Dear George:

Thanks very much for your note, and for your fine story about me which you enclosed.[1] I like to think that the story was of some news-interest to people in Asheville, but the warm and friendly temper that runs through it was not, I know, wholly professional. For that I must thank the spontaneous and unselfish good will that I always join with your name, and I thank you not only for writing me up, but also because you have been a generous friend.

What you said about my Asheville friends being "numbered by the score" touched me most of all. I think you will believe me when I tell you I value the respect and friendship of no group of people more than that of the people in the town where I was born, and where a large part of my life has been passed. I earnestly hope I may always keep it. It would only be stupid to deny that a young man is indifferent to the commendation of people he likes: he is, on the contrary, eager for it, and one of the great impulses of the creative act may come from a source as simple as this one.

I wish I could imitate your admirable brevity. I intended to write you a short note, but this will probably go to five or six pages. A newspaper would give me the sack in twenty-four hours—the murderer would be in Canada before I finished describing where the body was found. But you are getting off much easier than the folks at Scribners—my manuscript when first submitted was a dainty trifle of 330,000 words (not 250,000 as the blurb in the magazine had it). When they accepted the book the publishers told me to get busy with my little hatchet and carve off some 100,000 words. I had just come back from Italy with twenty-seven cents, but with Scribners advance money in my pocket I was naturally full of life and hope. I did get busy, and in a month or two had cut out twenty or thirty

[1] A piece by McCoy in the July 26, 1929 *Asheville Citizen* captioned "Asheville Man Is New Author," and beginning: "Thomas Wolfe's Asheville friends, and they are numbered by the score, will be much interested to learn that the August fiction number of *Scribner's Magazine* carries his first published short story entitled 'An Angel on the Porch.'"

thousand words, and added fifty thousand more. The editors then felt it was time to intervene: they restrained me, and helped me in every way with criticism, editing, and a vast amount of patient, careful work. They have been magnificent—I have not time or space to tell you how fine they have been—and now we have a book which can be read without demanding a six months' leave of absence.

A year ago, when I finished with the book and looked at the truck-load of typed pages, I never thought it possible that I should have such good fortune; an association with such a house and such men. But miracles *do* happen: in fact, I am coming to believe they *always* happen: no matter what success (or failure) this book has, my publishers will print the next one. I am already at work on it,² and hope, of course, to do a better one than the first. The publishers believe in me and in my book. I am profoundly grateful for all they have done, and hope, not only for my sake but for theirs, that we shall have some success.

Please forgive me for writing you at such length: my book is only one out of the vast number that are being printed all the time, but I can't help being happy and excited—it has happened to others, but it's the first time it has happened to me.

I finished the last set of galley proof to-day: it has been a long and tedious job, but my work on this book is practically done. All I can do now is remember all the prayers I ever heard. There are still several mechanical stages—page proofs, foundry proofs, and so on (no one who has not seen it would ever believe the amount of work that goes into printing a book)—but the people at Scribners will do most of the work now.

I think it is scheduled for release in September or October, but I can't be sure yet. I suppose the publishers send copies to reviewers (I'm still pretty green about this business): I shall ask them Monday, and have them send you one for reviewing, if this is the system. If not, I suppose they give the author a few copies, and I'll send you one of mine. I am very grateful for all the interest you have taken in my work: one of the pleasantest things I have found in the world, among a number of unpleasant ones, is that there is almost no limit to the loyal belief of old friends. The hardest thing is trying to live up to half the things they say about you, but that's a job we can work at with all our heart. So I hope you will not be disappointed in my book or in me. Of course, George, it may be a terrible flop (many or most books are) but if we can have only a modest success, that will perhaps be enough for a fellow who tries to fill a five foot shelf with his first one.

² *The October Fair,* of which the first half was published as *Of Time and the River.*

Thanks also for the splendid write-up of Billy Cocke.[3] I am delighted to hear of his success, but, of course, not surprised. I saw him a few years ago when I was staying at Oxford for several weeks: I knew then he would get along there and everywhere else. It is good to know he has made a connection with such a distinguished firm, and that he will be near me here in New York. There is perhaps a selfish motive in my interest —if I get put in jail for writing one of my books, I shall probably need at least an Oxford lawyer to get me out, and there is no one to whom I would trust my defense with greater confidence than Billy.

I hope to get home for a few days early in September. If I do, I want to talk to you about your plans, and mine. Thanks again for your story. Write me a few lines if you have time. My best wishes for your health and success go with this letter.

If there is any news about the book that I think you will be interested in, I'll send it on to you. Do you still work until half past three in the morning? If you do, we'll probably talk until the milk wagons come by—it's the time of day I like best for work or conversation. I used to carry *Citizens*, you know, and probably got the habit then. I've chewed many a doughnut at the Greasy Spoon at four A.M.

The following letter was written to John Hall Wheelock upon his presentation to Wolfe of a copy of his book of poems, The Bright Doom, with the inscription: "For Thomas Wolfe—in friendship and admiration."

To JOHN HALL WHEELOCK

[27 West 15th Street]
[New York City]
[Late August, 1929]

Dear Mr. Wheelock:

I like to write, rather than to speak, the things I feel and believe most deeply: I think I can say them more clearly that way, and keep them better.

In the last few months, when I have come to know you, I have observed again and again the seriousness with which you would deliberate even the

---

[3] William Cocke, a childhood friend of Wolfe's from Asheville, had joined the law firm of Messrs. Root, Clark, Buckner and Ballantine in New York City. He was an associate in that firm for a little more than a year before establishing his own practice in Asheville.

smallest changes in my book. As time went on, I saw that this slow and patient care came from the grand integrity of your soul. Consequently, when you presented me with a book of your poems on the day when we had finished our work together on my novel, this simple act was invested with an importance and emotion which I can not describe to you now— every one of the subtle and rich associations of your character went with that book of poems; I was profoundly moved, profoundly grateful, and I knew that I would treasure this book as long as I live.

When I got out on the street, I opened it and read your inscription to me and the magnificent lines that follow it. In this inscription you speak of me as your friend. I am filled with pride and joy that you should say so. I am honored in knowing you, I am honored in having you call me friend, I am exalted and lifted up by every word of trust and commendation you have ever spoken to me.

You are a true poet: you have looked upon the terrible face of patience, and the quality of enduring and waiting shines in every line you have written. The poets who are dead have given me life; when I have faltered I have seized upon their strength. Now I have by me living poetry and a living poet, and in his patience and in his strong soul I shall often abide.

I have now read all the poems in your book—I think I have read them all several times. But true poetry is a rich and difficult thing—we invade it slowly, and slowly it becomes a part of us. I have read few books as often as three or four times, but there are poems I have read three or four hundred times. I do not presume therefore to offer you a glib criticism of poems I shall read many times more, and I do not presume to think you would be seriously interested in my feeling. But there are some of your poems that are already communicated to me—I dare to say entirely—and that have become a part of the rich deposit of my life.

I wish to say that "Meditation" seems to me one of the finest modern poems I have ever read—*modern* only in being written by a man now living. When I read this poem, I had that moment of discovery which tells us plainly that we have gained something precious—it has now become a part of me, it is mixed with me, and some day, in some unconscious but not wholly unworthy plagiary, it will come from me again woven into my own fabric.

[THE LETTER BREAKS OFF HERE]

The following postcard was written to Maxwell Perkins from Asheville where Wolfe had gone for a two weeks' visit before the opening of the fall term at New York University.

To MAXWELL E. PERKINS
[Penny Postcard]

Asheville, N.C.
Sept 14, 1929

Dear Mr Perkins: I have had a very remarkable visit down here—the town is full of kindness and good will and rooting and boosting for the book. My family knows what it's all about, and I think is pleased about it—and also a little apprehensive. We get one another crazy—I've been here a week and I'm about ready for a padded cell. But no one's to blame. It's a strange situation, and God knows what will happen. I'll be glad when its over. Hope to see you next week in New York.

To GEORGE W. McCOY

Harvard Club
New York
Wednesday, Oct. 16, 1929.

Dear George:
Thanks for your fine letter. I am sincerely grateful for all that you have said and done. I know you understand my deep sense of obligation to you all. It is splendid to know that you and Lola will review my book,[1] and that Rodney Crowther[2] will talk about it over the radio. I can add nothing to what I have already told you, except to repeat that you have all been fine and generous, and that I know you understand and believe in the author, no matter what effect the book may have.

I have a bit of news which must not, however, be made public: they told me at Scribners yesterday that the advance sale of the book, not counting New York, is over 1600 copies, and one of the salesmen at Doubleday Doran told the advertising man that the book would be "the Fall sensation," whatever that may mean. All this is too marvelous—miraculous—the *last* I mean—to be probable. Thomas Beer, the writer, phoned Scribners last week that I was the best young writer who had emerged since Glenway Wescott wrote "The Grandmothers" (although why Wescott I don't know). Finally, my agent, Mrs. Boyd, who is abroad,

---

[1] The original plan for McCoy and his fiancée Lola Love to review *Look Homeward, Angel* together was later changed, and Miss Love reviewed it alone in the Sunday, October 20, 1929, *Asheville Citizen.*

[2] Rodney Crowther reviewed *Look Homeward, Angel* over Radio Station WWNC on October 21.

cabled Scribners that two English publishers, Cape and Heinemann, want the book for England. But for God's sake say nothing of all this!

It comes out day after to-morrow, and my nerves are ragged. Scribners are magnificent and want me to get busy at once on a new one. This I've already done, but much too excited to work at present. The new one will be better—I've many more books in me.

If I could, I should like nothing more than seeing your wedding. As it is, I shall think of you, and send you both my deepest affection. . . . Give my warmest regards to Lola. You know how I feel about you both. Thank Rodney Crowther for me and tell him I'll write him next week. Excuse this idiotic letter—I think you know how I feel at present.

To MARGARET ROBERTS

Harvard Club
New York

October 17, 1929

Dear Mrs. Roberts:

I sent you a copy of my book the other day. I hope it arrived safely. In it I wrote a few words which I ask you to accept as a sincere expression of the writer's feeling toward you.[1]

My book is published to-morrow. Nobody knows whether it will survive the avalanche of books that are being published at this season, or not: but we all hope for the best luck. Naturally I am tremendously excited about it.

I can not add anything here to what I told you when I was at home: I have tried to do a good and honest piece of work, and I hope that my friends like it. I shall be sorry if they do not like it, but I shall go on in the hope of writing something someday that may be worthy of their praise. I think I can not say more than this.

I send to you all my warmest and most affectionate regards. I shall write you a letter later, after I know more about the fate of my book.

With hope, and with love,

To GEORGE WALLACE

New York

October 25 (?), 1929.

Dear George:

Thanks for your fine letter, for your generous efforts, and simply for

[1] "To Margaret Roberts, who was the Mother of my Spirit, I present this copy of my first book, with hope and with devotion."

writing. I don't know whether I told you in my last that the book had been sold in England—Heinemann is publishing there and is sending me 100 pounds advance. The book is having a good sale in New York, although there have been no reviews yet—several booksellers, including the famous Holliday,[1] are recommending it. There will be a review in the *New York Times* on Sunday, I believe. Whether it's good or bad I can't say, but if it's good and you can do a little telling work with it, so much the better.[2] Also, there will be a review in the *Scribner's Magazine* for December, I believe, (out in November). People have told me about it—reviewer says I must be put with Whitman and Melville.[3] Hot stuff, eh? And Scribners, the publishers, insist they have nothing to do with it—that it's all straight shooting—and they've never lied yet.

Only reviews I've had are from North Carolina and, Boy! they are blowing off steam. All of them panegyrical about the writing, say it's thrilling novel, etc., but two or three say it's an insult to the state and the people, that "the worst side of people" is exposed, etc. Josephus Daniels' *Raleigh News and Observer* says the South and North Carolina "have been spat upon." [4] I am really distressed about it! In the first place, I never mentioned North Carolina, and it has never occurred to anyone up here that I was writing about either N.C. or the South—least of all to the author. Everyone thought the book was about *people*—who might have lived anywhere—and so far as their "worst side" is concerned, Scribners think them rich, magnificent and grand folks. What am I to do! I shall do nothing, say nothing. The book has many many different things and people in it, but we think its total effect is one of beauty. (Please forgive the personal bouquet!)

[1] Terence Holliday of The Holliday Book Shop.

[2] Wallace was a friend of one of the editors of the *Boston Evening Transcript*. Perhaps this was what Wolfe had in mind, or perhaps he simply thought that because Wallace was "an advertising man" he could "spread the news around" about the book.

[3] Robert Raynolds's review of *Look Homeward, Angel* in the December *Scribner's* said: "If we were to label Wolfe, we would put him with Melville and Whitman, although he has not the dramatic intensity and the perfection of epithet we find in *Moby Dick*, nor the grave purity incandescent in *Leaves of Grass*. But *Look Homeward, Angel* is a first book."

[4] *Look Homeward, Angel* was reviewed in the October 20, 1929, issue of the *Raleigh News and Observer* by Jonathan Daniels, who had known Wolfe at the University of North Carolina. The review was headlined "Wolfe's First Is Novel of Revolt. Former Asheville Writer Turns in Fury Upon North Carolina and the South," and said: "Against the Victorian morality and the Bourbon aristocracy of the South, he has turned in all his fury, and the result is not a book that will please the South in general and North Carolina in particular. Here is a young man, hurt by something that he loved, turning in his sensitive fury and spitting on that thing. In *Look Homeward, Angel*, North Carolina and the South are spat upon."

At any rate, as soon as I see what's what and get these nerves screwed down again, I'm going on with the new one.

Scribners do not want to have my book "Banned in Boston"—they are a very fine and dignified firm, and did not like the Hemingway ban,[5] although it helped the sale of the book. But—this is between *us*—if it does get banned, I hope it makes a loud noise—for God's sake try to get some publicity out of it for me.

During all this palpitating time I've got to teach school as usual and grade Freshman papers. God! the torture of it!

Give my love to Mrs. W. and the boys. Let me hear soon. Thanks for your noble efforts. In spite of my incoherence, they are deeply appreciated.

Scribners think it's a *swell* book, George—I can't tell you how much. And Thomas Beer has given it (and me) a blast that lifted my hair! Write to me—tell me how to be *calm*.

The brief note below was written in reply to a letter from Mark Schorer praising Look Homeward, Angel *in the highest terms. Schorer is now Professor of English at the University of California, and the author of* A House Too Old, The Hermit Place, The State of Mind, William Blake: The Politics of Vision, The Wars of Love, *etc.*

To MARK SCHORER

27 West 15th Street
New York City
October 25, 1929

Dear Mr. Schorer:

Your letter about my book is the first I have had from a stranger, although I have had several from friends.

I am moved and honored by what you say about the book. It is quite a grand thing to know that what one has written has leaped across the dark, and made a light, a friend. I hope, naturally, that I shall have other letters from people who like the book, but I shall always place a particular value on yours because it was the first.

[5] The June and July, 1929, issues of *Scribner's Magazine* had been banned in Boston because of the portions of Hemingway's *Farewell to Arms* published in them.

Margaret Wallace's review of Look Homeward, Angel *in the Sunday October 27* New York Times *was the first major review to be published, and one of the most favorable. Upon reading it, Wolfe immediately wrote her the following note of thanks.*

To MARGARET WALLACE

27 West 15th Street
New York City

October 27, 1929.

Dear Miss Wallace:

I want to thank you for your splendid review of my book in to-day's *Times*. I am moved and honored by what you say—it is my first book, and it is a grand thing to know it has been valued so patiently and so highly. The people at Scribners were very happy about your review: they feel now that the book has a good chance of commercial success—which would also mean a great deal to me. If this is true, I know that you have contributed a great deal to it.

But even if the book should never sell another copy, I shall never forget what you wrote about it. I shall always feel that something I wrote made its way out into the great jungle of the world, and found a friend there. A thing like this pays for all the pain and despair of writing.

The following night letter was sent by Wolfe to his sister Mabel upon receiving a letter from her describing the furor which publication of Look Homeward, Angel *had caused in Asheville.*

To MABEL WOLFE WHEATON
[Night Letter]

New York City

October 28, 1929

Thanks for wonderful letter. Great figures in novel are Eliza, Helen, Gant and Ben. Everyone here thinks they are grand people. No book should be read as gossip nor judged in isolated passages. When the book and leading characters are judged as a whole they are seen to be fine people. Read *New York Times* review for last Sunday, also *Herald Tribune* for next Sunday or week after.[1] No matter what Asheville thinks now, they will

---

[1] *Look Homeward, Angel* was very favorably reviewed by Margery Latimer in the Sunday, November 3, 1929, *New York Herald Tribune*.

understand in time that I tried to write moving, honest book about great people. That is the way the world outside Asheville is taking it. Tell Mama this and say I am writing in day or so. If you doubt what I say, read over chapter on Ben's death and burial scenes that follow. Then ask if anyone dares say these are not great people. Book selling fast. Looks like success but say nothing. You are a great person. Love,

Robert Norwood, to whom the following note was written, was pastor of St. Bartholomew's Church in New York, and the author of Issa, The Steep Ascent, The Man Who Dared to be God, *etc. On October 26, 1929, he had written to John Hall Wheelock: "I am reading* Look Homeward, Angel. *It is a remarkable book, not far from* The Brothers Karamazov. *It is an epic rather than a novel, and poetry more than prose. Thus far I have the feeling of an archangel with broken wings trying to regain the heights he has lost— the anguished cry of a disappointed idealist." Wheelock had introduced Wolfe to Norwood soon afterwards.*

To ROBERT NORWOOD

27 West 15th Street
New York City
November 15, 1929

Dear Dr. Norwood:

I want to thank you for the very wonderful two or three hours I spent with you the other day. And I want also to thank you for what you said about my book. It is quite a grand thing to know that something one has written has gone out into the world and made such a friend and been so generously valued.

I am honored and moved by all you said about it. Even if the book had no further sale, it would be a great deal to know that you feel about it as you do.

I look forward to seeing you again.

To ALBERT COATES

27 West 15th St
New York City
Nov 19, 1929.

Dear Albert:

Your name on a letter gave me a tremendous thrill. Neither of us, I'm afraid, is a very steady correspondent, but if I had written to you every time I thought about you these last 6 years, you would have a trunk full of my letters now.

You will certainly not pay $3.00 for any book I write (or $2.50 either) if I can be on hand to prevent it. . . . You should receive in a few days a copy of my book from Charles Scribner's Sons, handsomely inscribed with a touching sentiment (which I have not thought out yet). If you do not get it let me know. . . .

I was glad and happy to hear from you, Albert. I think you will believe me when I tell you that you are one of my old friends that I think of very often, and whose friendship I value very highly. I am very anxious to have you read my book and to hear from you about it. The book has caused me a great deal of joy and pain—pain because some people in the South and in my home town have read it as an almanac of personal gossip, and have construed it as a cruel and merciless attack on actual persons, some now living. I have had several bitter letters and one or two pretty ugly anonymous ones (one of them beginning in a proud dignified manner as follows: "Sir: You are a son-of-a-bitch, etc.") On the other hand, I have had magnificent letters, not only from strangers, but also from old friends. And the reviewers in New York and other cities have said some very magnificent things about it and I understand that literary folks in New York are quite excited about it. . . .

For God's sake, Albert, read the book as it was meant to be read—as a book, the writer's vision of life: you will find some things in it very naked, very direct, and perhaps very terrible—but the book was written in innocence and honesty of spirit,[1] and the people here do not feel that it is terrible or ugly, but that it is perhaps grand and beautiful. Excuse me for saying all this—it sounds like boasting—but I want my old friends to understand what I have done. But I know that I can depend on your fairness and intelligence. . . .

I can not write any more now, but I will later. I still work at N.Y.U. but I hope the book may sell enough to release me from grading Freshman papers. I want to finish a new book.

This is written in great haste, but I hope you can make it out. Let me hear from you soon. With warmest regards,

The following "My Record as a Writer" and "Plans for Work" were submitted with Wolfe's application for a Guggenheim Fellowship. If there was a covering letter making definite application for the fellowship, it has been lost.

[1] Here again Wolfe is repeating almost verbatim what he said in his note "To the Reader" at the beginning of *Look Homeward, Angel*.

To THE JOHN SIMON GUGGENHEIM MEMORIAL FOUNDATION

[27 West 15th Street]
[New York]
[December 16(?), 1929]

My Record as a Writer

I have written since I was twelve or fourteen years old. In preparatory school I wrote essays, poems and stories. During my Freshman year in college I began to write more formally. I wrote for the college paper and magazine and humorous publications: [1] later I became editor of the college newspaper, *The Tar Heel,* and associate editor of the other publications. In my junior year, I met Professor Frederick H. Koch, who had come to North Carolina that year, and who was organizing the Carolina Playmakers. I wrote little one-act plays for him and had two or three of them produced by the Playmakers.[2] One of these was later published in a volume of Playmaker plays published by Henry Holt.[3] It was called "The Return of Buck Gavin." It was written when I was seventeen years old. I mention this play because it was my first work to be published in book form, although many things had been published in college publications. I was at this time young and lazy; I scribbled constantly and at random; I had not learned to work, and what I wrote did not represent the best in me.

After my graduation from North Carolina in 1920, I went to Harvard with the intention of staying one year. I stayed three years; I took courses; I read a great deal and I wrote some plays for Professor Baker and his "47 Workshop," of which I was a member. Two of these plays, a short one and a long one, were produced by the Workshop. The long one, "Welcome to Our City," caused a good deal of excitement and many people thought I had a future as a dramatist. I came to New York with these plays, believing they might be produced here. "Welcome to Our City" was seriously considered by two theatres [4]—one asked me to "cut" it since it was an hour too long. This I tried to do, but made it longer.

Two or three years had passed since I came to New York and the conviction was growing on me that I would never write plays. I had begun quite by accident at North Carolina, and continued by chance at Harvard.

[1] *The Tar Heel, The Carolina Magazine* and *The Tar Baby.*

[2] The two that were actually produced were *The Return of Buck Gavin* and *The Third Night,* but Wolfe wrote others, such as *Deferred Payment* and *Concerning Honest Bob* which were published in *The Carolina Magazine.*

[3] *Carolina Folk Plays: Second Series.*

[4] The Theatre Guild and The Neighborhood Playhouse.

I loved the theatre, but I began to see I had to find a medium where I could satisfy my desire for fullness, intensity and completeness. I could never do this in the theatre, and my creative sense was troubled further by knowing what I did would be touched and reshaped by a hundred different people—directors, actors, designers, carpenters, electricians. What I did had to be my own.

During these four or five years I had been teaching at New York University. When I had a vacation, I took what money remained from my teaching, borrowed more, if possible, and went to Europe. Once I stayed a year, and other times six or eight months. I was quite unhappy about my writing—nothing I did ever saw the light of day. I wrote at random, but all the time. When I had finished something, a powerful inertia settled upon me—I would not show what I had written to anyone; I would not send it out for publication; I did not know what to do or how to go about it. Meanwhile I was teaching in America and wandering alone, from place to place, in Europe. Three years ago I began to write my book in London. I went down to the Chelsea district, rented two rooms in a lodging house and began to work. I was alone, and my writing came as a culmination of years of wandering back and forth in Europe and America. My first book dealt with experiences observed during the first twenty years of my life, but its theme was that all men are alone and strangers and never come to know one another. I worked hard on the book in London and Oxford during the Autumn: the first of the year I came back to New York. I rented a garret in an old deserted building on Eighth Street. It had been used as a sweatshop; there was no heat and no plumbing. I worked there for seven months and did the largest part of my book there. For the first time I put all my effort and time into writing. I worked between twelve and six in the morning, and slept in the daytime. I mention these facts not to give a romantic flavor to this statement, but because they are a true and honest account of what happened, and because I am proud to know I had such devotion and loyalty to my work.

After seven months of work in this place, I was very tired. I went to Europe that summer. When I came back, I went to work at the University again. That year I finished my book, working at night. When I had finished it, all the doubt, disbelief and hopelessness that I had not been able to feel for long while working, welled up: the manuscript was over 1200 typed pages—about five times the length of an average novel. I did not believe it would ever find a publisher.

It was the end of the teaching year: I was worn out and had no further hopes for my writing. I took what money was left from teaching and went to Europe again. I wandered about for four or five months. Meanwhile a friend had given the manuscript of my book to Ernest Boyd, the critic.

Ernest Boyd turned it over to his wife, Madeleine, who now acts as my literary agent. When I was in Vienna last year, in November, I got a letter from Mrs. Boyd, and shortly thereafter one from Mr. Maxwell Perkins of Scribners. It was a very wonderful letter: when I got back from Italy the first of the year, I went to see him. He said the book was too long, but that Scribners would publish it if it was cut to a more suitable length. In the next few months we cut out over 100,000 words, and the book was published in its present form in October, 1929, under the title "Look Homeward, Angel."

The book has had, I understand, an unusual success for a first novel. People have told me it has had the best reviews of any first novel in several years. But what sale it will have, no one can at present say. I am teaching again this year at New York University. I find it increasingly difficult to grade papers and get on with my new book. I need money desperately. My publishers have been fine, courageous and generous: they believe in me and are willing to help all they can, but I have no right to impose further on their generosity. It must in honesty be said that the commercial success of my first book is still in doubt. At present, it has not earned enough to keep me going while I finish my new one. For this reason I am appealing to the Guggenheim Foundation.

Plans for Work

My new novel will be ready in the Spring or Autumn of 1931. Its title is "The October Fair." I cannot outline its plan and purpose so exactly as a scientist could his course of study: the book has a great many things in it but its dominant theme is again related to the theme of the first: it tries to find out why Americans are a nomad race (as this writer believes); why they are touched with a powerful and obscure homesickness wherever they go, both at home and abroad; why thousands of the young men, like this writer, have prowled over Europe, looking for a door, a happy land, a home, seeking for something they have lost, perhaps racial and forgotten; and why they return here; or if they do not, carry on them the mark of exile and obscure longing. This is a hasty statement, but I hope it indicates a theme, or an emotion and experience, which this writer believes in passionately, because he has felt and experienced it with all his heart. It seems to him, further, to be a very living and a very national theme.

The writer did not receive the application blanks for the Guggenheim Fellowship until the last few days: this statement has therefore been very hastily written. The writer hopes, however, he has been able to justify his application for a Fellowship.

To MAXWELL E. PERKINS

Harvard Club
New York
Dec 24, 1929

Dear Mr. Perkins:

One year ago I had little hope for my work, and I did not know you. What has happened since may seem to be only a modest success to many people; but to me it is touched with strangeness and wonder. It is a miracle.

You are now mixed with my book in such a way that I can never separate the two of you. I can no longer think clearly of the time I wrote it, but rather of the time when you first talked to me about it, and when you worked upon it. My mind has always seen people more clearly than events or things—the name "Scribners" naturally makes a warm glow in my heart, but you are chiefly "Scribners" to me: you have done what I had ceased to believe one person could do for another—you have created liberty and hope for me.

Young men sometimes believe in the existence of heroic figures, stronger and wiser than themselves, to whom they can turn for an answer to all their vexation and grief. Later, they must discover that such answers have to come out of their own hearts; but the powerful desire to believe in such figures persists. You are for me such a figure: you are one of the rocks to which my life is anchored.

I have taken the publication of my first book very hard—all the happy and successful part of it as well as the unhappy part: a great deal of the glory and joy and glamour with which in my fantasy I surrounded such an event has vanished. But, as usual, life and reality supplant the imaginary thing with another glory that is finer and more substantial than the visionary one.

I should have counted this past year a great one, if it had allowed me only to know about you. I am honored to think I may call you my friend, and I wish to send to you on Christmas Day this statement of my loyal affection.

VI

FRANCE, SWITZERLAND, AND THE BEGINNING OF OF TIME AND THE RIVER AND THE OCTOBER FAIR

1930

To MABEL WOLFE WHEATON

Harvard Club

New York

Jan. 5, 1930

Dear Mabel:

The long letter I have promised to write you never gets done. If you knew what the last two or three months have been like you'd know why. People have almost driven me mad—the telephone rings twenty times a day, and it's someone I don't know, or don't want to know, or met once, or who knows someone who knows me. In addition, I get dozens of letters— invitations to speak, dine, write. I have all my papers to grade with examinations coming on, and Scribners keep phoning me every day for a story for the magazine. The only relief is that Scribners is now going to pay me a modest sum of money each month to live on,[1] and I am stopping

---

[1] On December 18, 1929, Perkins had written Wolfe a letter saying: "We are deeply interested in your writing and have confidence in your future, and we wish to cooperate with you so far as possible toward the production of a new novel. . . . We should be glad to undertake to pay you, as an advance on the earnings of the next novel, forty-five hundred dollars in installments, at the rate of two hundred and fifty dollars a month, beginning with February 1st." Scribners accordingly made these payments for the months of February through May, 1930. By then, Wolfe had received his Guggenheim Fellowship, and *Look Homeward, Angel* had earned royalties amounting to $3,500 in excess of the $500 advance already paid on it. Therefore, the monthly payments against the new novel were discontinued until June 21, 1933, when Wolfe began drawing irregular amounts against that book.

teaching in February. I must get to work immediately on my new book, but if people don't leave me alone, I'll have to go away somewhere. All I want is a little peace and freedom to work—if they will all buy my book, well and good, but let them leave me alone. I don't want to leave America, but some people are urging me to go to Europe to live where I can at least not be disturbed. The English publisher [2] is here, and has me at work making certain cuts in the book. The English are enthusiastic—say the people are wonderful and real Anglo-Saxons that the English understand—and that the book will go well in England. It's coming out there in March. [3]

I have had two or three hundred letters from all over the country. How in God's name I'll answer them I can't say. The whole business had me so stirred up that I caved in with cold and flu a week or two ago, and am just pulling out.

I get letters and cards and phone calls from Asheville people from time to time. I want to tell you that no one has been more surprised by the effect my book has had on some people than I have. I live in my own world: I go about looking, seeing, studying, observing, but the world I create is my own. I understand that several hundred copies of the book were sold in Asheville. That is far too many. Please understand that I am not trying to be "snooty" or "highbrow"—I have the greatest respect and liking for many, many people at home—but my book is not a book that every realtor, attorney, druggist, or grocer should read. They should stick to *Collier's* and *The American* and *The S.E.P.* There are perhaps two dozen people at home who might read my book and know what it's about. And please understand this is not to say a word of criticism of many other people whom I like, but who read perhaps one or two books a year, and who try to make my book a piece of local history. If they think my book is obscene, bitter, sensational etc., let them stick to Warwick Deeping and Zane Grey.

You, at least, know what I have in my heart: to create before I die something that is as honest, grand and beautiful as I can make it. If anyone thinks my first book is ugly and filthy, and can see no beauty or good in it, I am sorry; but I shall go on with my next as well as I can, and try to make it as good as I can. One man in Asheville wrote in to Scribners saying that the rumor was Wolfe had said he had wanted to cut certain parts of the book, but that Scribners had insisted they be left in so that the book would make a lot of money. To think that any damned fool couldn't

---

[2] A. S. Frere-Reeves, the editor of William Heinemann Ltd. who was most closely concerned with Wolfe's books. He is now Chairman of the Board of Directors of that house, and known simply as A. S. Frere.

[3] It actually did not come out until July 14.

see that this book was not written for money—that if I'd wanted money I'd have written something one third as long, full of the soothing syrup most of them want. We are all pleased here with the success the book has had—with the wonderful reviews, and also with the sale—but nobody is going to get rich off the book: there are hundreds of hack writers who make far more than I will make, and if money is my object, I could make far more out of advertising or something else than I can ever make out of writing.

Doesn't it mean anything to people at home to know that honest and intelligent critics all over the country have thought my book a fine and moving one? Surely there are people there who are fair and generous enough to see that I am trying to be an artist, and that I am not a sensational hack. Does anyone seriously think that a man is going to sweat blood, lose flesh, go cold and dirty, work all night, and live in a sweatshop garret for almost two years as I did, if his sole purpose is to say something mean about Smith and Jones and Brown? Listen, Mabel: what my book says in the first paragraph and what it continues to say on every page to the end is that men are strangers, that they are lonely and forsaken, that they are in exile on this earth, that they are born, live, and die alone. I began to write that book in London: it is as true of people in London and Idaho as of people in Asheville. You say that women in clubs have called you up and lectured you or sympathized with you. Very well, let them. You are bigger than any of them and they cannot hurt you. I suppose the sympathy was because you had a brother like me. Very well. That's all right, too. Apparently you can rob banks, be a crooked lawyer, swill corn whiskey, commit adultery with your neighbor's wife—and be considered a fine, lovable, misunderstood fellow; but if you try to make something true and beautiful you are "viciously insane" and your "big overgrown body" ought to be dragged through the streets by a lynching mob. These phrases are from one of the letters sent to me.

Well, they can not hurt us. I do not believe one fine person, worthy of being a friend, would ever turn either on you or me because I have written a book—and anyone who would is probably not worth knowing.

I am a young man, just beginning his life's work. The sad thing about this whole thing is not that people have misunderstood my first book, but that they do not know at all what I am like or what my vision of life is. A great deal of water has gone under the bridge since I left Asheville ten years ago, but I had always hoped that when I brought my first work before the world, I would find sympathy and understanding among my old friends there. Now I feel as if I had been exiled: that they no longer know the person I have become, and that they will not recognize me in the work I shall do in the future. I say this is the sad thing about it all. It is

like death. I know now that people do not die once but many times, and
that life of which they were once a part, and which they thought they
could never lose, dies too, becomes a ghost, is lost forever. There is nothing
to be done about this. We can only love those who are lost, and grieve for
their spirits. If, then, I am dead to people who once knew me and cared
for me, there is nothing more to say or do—I must go on into a new
world and a new life, with love and sorrow for what I have lost. If you
like, remember the kid in the cherry tree, or the long-legged schoolboy, or
the kid at college—I shall always remember you all with love and
loyalty. . . .

Wolfe had met James Boyd, author of Drums, Marching On, Long Hunt,
and Roll River, *through Perkins, and had asked Boyd to recommend him for
a Guggenheim Fellowship. The following note was written in reply to one
from Boyd saying he had done so, and adding: "Look Homeward, Angel
has become one of our permanent possessions and though it contains things
for which I denounce you before the throne of Form and Design (no doubt
a mere certified public accountant's stool) it has the simple and undebatable
merit of containing elements of greatness, and all of the formidable vigor of
life."*

To JAMES BOYD

[27 West 15th Street]
[New York City]
[January 12(?), 1930]

Dear Jim:
    You are a swell guy even if you do have decided theories of form. It
will be a proud day in my life when you wring my hand and say "Son,
the style and structure of your last book makes Flaubert look like an
anarchist. I have done you a great wrong."
    If I buy a set of false whiskers and revisit my native state, will you
introduce me as your Irish cousin, Ernest? [1]

*The following letter to Marjorie N. Pearson was written in reply to one
from her praising* Look Homeward, Angel. *Miss Pearson is the daughter
of Mr. Richmond Pearson, whose house Wolfe describes here, and came to
know Wolfe personally when he went back to Asheville in the summer of
1937.*

[1] James and Ernest Boyd were actually no relation.

To MARJORIE N. PEARSON

27 West 15th Street
New York City

Jan. 19, 1930

Dear Miss Pearson:

I want to thank you most warmly for your letter. I am moved and honored by what you say about my book, and the fact that you are a native of Asheville gives your letter additional value.

When I was a child, my father used to take me to the little amusement park at Riverside, across the river from Bingham Heights. At night, after the movies and fireworks on the little lake, we stood by the river and watched the great trains thunder past on the other side, with the firebox glowing and throwing light. There would be a few lights on the hill above. I remember a big, rambling, magnificent Victorian house up there with spacious grounds, and I knew that Mr. Richmond Pearson and his family lived there, and I often wondered what people who lived in so great a place would look like, and talk like and *be* like. Now I think I know what they would *be* like—spacious and grand, like the old house—for I believe you belong to that family.

If I am right, what I feel more and more about the strangeness and mystery of living, which weaves our destinies out of chaos back and forth across the world, becomes deeper and stranger—for after so much water has flowed under the French Broad bridge since the child and his father stood there, and after I have put so many days and months and years and thousands of miles of wandering between that time and this, I come to know one of the people in that house through my book.

If I am wrong—that is, if you are *not* a member of that Pearson family but of another one—I still feel the deepest gratefulness to you for writing your fine letter, and I know that no matter how many Asheville people may not like my book, it has not failed in its purpose and weaving as long as it has one such friend as you.

P.S. Please forgive the solemn air of all this—but I tried to say just what I really felt, and if I have said it badly, I think you will see what I was trying to say.

The following letter was in reply to one written by Mrs. Roberts immediately upon finishing Look Homeward, Angel, *in which she protested against Wolfe's portrayal of the Gant family and of John Dorsey Leonard and the Altamont Fitting School. The result of this misunderstanding was a breach between her and Wolfe which lasted for six years.*

To MARGARET ROBERTS

Harvard Club
New York
February 2, 1930

Dear Mrs. Roberts:

. . . Two or three months ago I wrote you a very long letter in reply to your own,[1] but that letter still remains, folded and unfinished, in my note-book. It has been almost impossible for me to write letters, or anything else, during the last three months . . . —Now I am finishing my work at the University. Scribners have very generously made it possible for me to live modestly until my next book is done—I have already begun it, and it is to be called "The October Fair." It deals with different scenes, with different characters, and with a different theme from the first. I hope, naturally, that it will be a better book than the first, and with all my heart I hope that people who thought my first book ugly and painful, will find beauty and wisdom in the second. That is a wish I shall always keep for my work, and I hope in some measure it comes true.

I am very happy to know that most of the reviewers have found beauty and wisdom in my first book, and many of them have found the people in the book magnificent and heroic. I have just finished reading a review by Carl Van Doren in which he says just that. The review is published in the February issue of a little magazine called *Wings:* it is the journal of The Literary Guild of America, of which Mr. Van Doren is the head. If you can get the magazine, I hope you will read the review.[2]

I shall have time to write you the letter I want to write after next week. Meanwhile, will you let me say again one thing in reference to your own fine letter: I think you are mistaken in the estimate you put on some of the characters in my book and I know you are wholly mistaken in your inter-pretation of one of the scenes.[3] You are certainly right in saying I would not do such a book twenty years from now—I hope I will do one that is

[1] The letter is still among Wolfe's papers, but has been omitted here since he rewrote the major part of it into this letter of February 2.

[2] Van Doren said: "Mr. Wolfe, with much that is heroic in his constitution, has had the courage of his heroism. He has dared to lift his characters up above the average meanness of mankind, to let them live by their profounder impulses, and to tell about them the things which smooth, urbane novelists insist on leaving untold about men and women."

[3] Probably the material on pages 232–235 in *Look Homeward, Angel,* to which Mrs. Roberts specifically refers in one of her letters.

much better and much more beautiful, but such growth as that must come with time, and with maturity and wisdom.

But I do believe sincerely, Mrs. Roberts, that any bitterness in my book —and I would not deny that there is bitterness in it—is directed not against people or against living, but against the fundamental structure of life, which seems to me, or at least seemed to me when I wrote the book, cruel and wastefully tragic. I may be wrong in that feeling, but at any rate, it was deep-seated and real.

The other thing I want to say is longer and more difficult, and I must write you about it later at length, but here it is indicated in outline: that all creation is to me fabulous, that the world of my creation is a fabulous world, that experience comes into me from all points, is digested and absorbed into me until it becomes a part of me, and that the world I create is *always inside* me, and never *outside* me, and that what reality I can give to what I create comes only from *within*. Its relation to actual experience I have never denied, but every thinking person knows that such a relation is inevitable, and could not be avoided unless men lived in a vacuum. . . .

You said in one place of your letter that you knew I was sincere, no matter what anyone said. I thank you with all my heart; but how could you ever doubt it? Have you ever known me to be lacking in sincerity, to be evasive, dishonest, or to have my eye glued on the main chance? . . .

Finally, Mrs. Roberts, will you please believe me when I tell you sincerely and earnestly that when I began this book in London, and finished it in New York, I shaped and created its reality from within: my *own* world, my *own* figures, my *own* events shaped themselves into my *own* fable there on the page before me, and that I spent no time in thinking of actual Smiths, Jones, or Browns; nor do I see yet how such a thing is possible? If anyone thinks it is, let him take notes at street corners, and see if the result is a book.

I have written you more than I intended at present; let me, in concluding, entreat you to remember that I have written only *one* chapter of my *whole* book, and that if you do not think the first is worthy of me, I shall try to do something that will deserve your faith and affection in those that follow. Let me also say now that the saddest thing about all of this to me is not that some people have misunderstood the intention and meaning of my first book, but that some people I still love and honor have misunderstood me. I will not say a word against them—the really sad thing is that we lead a dozen lives rather than one, and that two or three of mine have gone by since I was a kid in Asheville. If people now draw back when they see the man, and say: "I do not know him. This is not the boy I knew"—I can only hope they will not think the man a bad one, and that they will be patient and wait until the boy comes back. And I think he will, after the man has made a long journey.

Good-bye for the present. I send you again my warmest, my deepest affection, and my most devoted wishes for your health and happiness. I think you are one of the grandest people I have ever known.

P.S. I hope you have seen some of the reviews of my book. They have been on the whole very wonderful—the best reviews, I understand, a first book has had in several years. I hope you have read some of the most important ones—those in the New York *Times, World, Herald Tribune, New Republic, The Bookman, Plain Talk,* and others; as well as the statements made by Hugh Walpole, Thomas Beer, F.P.A., the columnist, and many other people. I hate to speak of all this, but all of these people have found beauty and heroism in my book, both in the events and in the people; and I hope you will be interested in what they say, in what they think and feel.

If I am to be honest I must create my vision of life as I see it; but I hope that in my future work everyone I respect and like will find beauty and wonder in everything I do.

Forgive me for talking so much about the book—it is my first, and naturally close to my heart.

Again, I send you my warmest and most devoted remembrance.

In "The Conning Tower" in The New York World *for February 6, 1930, F.P.A. had published a letter from an anonymous correspondent in Asheville, saying that the townspeople were "raucous in their condemnation" of* Look Homeward, Angel *and of Wolfe, and ending with the remark which Wolfe quotes in this fragmentary letter, found in one of his notebooks, and undoubtedly never mailed. Adams himself ended the column with the remark that "all good novels—and most poor ones—the psychos [at this time the word as used here meant psychologists or psychiatrists, rather than, as at the present time, their patients] tell us, are closely related to the author's emotional life."*

To F. P. A.

[New York City]

[February 7, 1930]

Dear Mr. Adams:

I am twenty-nine years old. I have lived 10,765 days and nights. When your correspondent says "I shall be interested in a novel by Mr. Wolfe not so closely related to his own emotional life," the writer will not have it. I have only these 11,000 days to go by. "Mr. Wolfe," if he writes further, has at present eight or a dozen novels which come from his

11,000 days and nights. . . . Since your correspondent is un-interested to the extent of writing 350 words and a quarter column about my book, . . .

[THE LETTER BREAKS OFF UNFINISHED]

In an interview on January 7, 1930, with H. Allen Smith of the United Press, Hugh Walpole, who was in New York at the time, was quoted as praising Wolfe in the following words: "His novel is as nearly perfect as a novel can be. I feel it a duty as a literary man to say something in his favor. Let America awake to him, for he has the making of greatness." On January 9, Wolfe was taken by Frere-Reeves to meet Walpole and have lunch with him. In the Herald Tribune *for Sunday, March 16, an article by Walpole appeared under the title "A Londoner in New York," and said, "A few weeks ago I was interviewed by a charming young lady who asked my opinion of Mr. Wolfe's book,* Look Homeward, Angel. *I gave my opinion. I liked the book very much. I thought it a work of fine promise. In the newspaper a few days later my words were as follows: 'Awake, America! A new genius is upon you!' Well, I never begged America to awake. She seems to me awake enough as it is." Upon reading this, Wolfe wrote Walpole the following note.*

To HUGH WALPOLE

27 West 15th Street
New York City
March 16, 1930

Dear Mr. Walpole:

Almost every week I see some new evidence of your generosity toward my book: in to-day's *Herald Tribune* there was another. Please accept again my most grateful thanks. It is very fine for a man of your reputation to take such friendly interest in a young writer.

I hope you got my book. I sent it to the address you gave me, with an inscription—probably a very dull one, but at all events one that I meant. I am worn out by New York; I am going to France next month, and to England a little later.

To-day's *Tribune* said this is your last month in America. I don't know if that means you've already sailed, or not. But if you are still here, and ever have a free hour for lunch, I wonder if you could let me know? It would give me great joy to see you again. If you *have* sailed, I hope someday in England to have the pleasure of having you to dinner —a wonderful dinner with glorious food and drink.

Arthur Davison Ficke, a well known American poet, author of Sonnets of
a Portrait Painter *and other books of poems, had written to congratulate
Wolfe upon* Look Homeward, Angel, *saying: "You depict, with a high nobility and generosity, the mean disorder of the world we live in; and you at
the same time give an equally vivid picture of the Lost Atlantis of the heart.
You have unquestionably written a memorable book . . . and I can see
no very good reason why you should not go on to more and more impressive novels. There has never been a great novelist in America. Are you that
long-awaited white-haired boy?" The following is Wolfe's reply.*

To ARTHUR DAVISON FICKE

27 West 15th Street
New York City

March 25, 1930

Dear Mr. Ficke:

Thanks very much for your fine letter. I have known and admired
your poetry for a long time, and what you say about my book fills me
with pride. I agree with you entirely in your criticism, and if I were
writing the book now I should cut out most of the college stuff.

Thanks also for believing I will do better work in the future. I think
so, too, although the comments of some critics that "he has probably
not shot the whole wad yet," "we shall see what he can do in another
book" etc., do not have the effect of calming me or making me feel
better. It had never occurred to me that I had made more than a beginning until I read such reviews. I am twenty-nine years old, the book
was mostly written when I was twenty-six to twenty-eight; it seems to
me they might allow me two or three years more before senile decay
destroys me.

I hope you will read my next book, and write me about it, as you did
about this. I think it's going to be a fine book, and I know it will if my
vitality comes back. The last four or five months have worn me out—
having a book published has happened to millions of other people, but
it's the first time it ever happened to me and, thank God, I took it hard
—letters, excitement, reviews good or bad, sales, invitations, telephone
calls, everything.

Now I'm done with it, I'm going away to France next month, and
spend several weeks looking at a cow and a hill, and drinking lots of
wine. After that I'm going to write a good book. I've made this letter
too long. I eat, talk, write and do everything too much, but your letter
was the letter of a friend, and of a man whose work I respect. Please
accept again my grateful thanks.

To MABEL WOLFE WHEATON

Harvard Club
New York.

March 29, 1930

Dear Mabel:

Thanks for your very nice letter. I have not written you in some time because the excitement and confusion of the last few months have pretty well worn me out. . . . I think I'm pretty well physically, but my mind feels like a piece of worn-out rubber. But I'll be all right with a little peace and rest.

I was very happy about getting the Guggenheim Fellowship.[1] It amounts to $2500 a year, and is given for one year, but it will be extended if the work one is doing demands more time. About the only string tied to it is that one go abroad—I do not want to go for a whole year, but I think they will let me go for six months now and six months next year or the year after. I can use this money now and keep the money Scribners might pay me as royalties or as an advance on the next book as a reserve fund for the future.

I have a new book under way—I think it will be a very beautiful book—but I need a rest and the old vitality in order to work on it hard day after day. I have done a great deal on it, but mainly scenes, notes, scraps, fragments. People know about me now, and are waiting for the next book; so I must try to do a good piece of work. I have plenty of "stuff" yet: the only thing that worries me is that I'm so damned tired at present. But getting away will fix that. New York eats up your vitality; I have been out a good deal, but I have spent even more time avoiding going out, making excuses, etc.—and all that takes it out of you. I have had enough of personal fame—modest as mine has been: now I want my books to be famous, but to be left alone myself. I want a few friends, and time to work.

By the way, the first edition of the book is now worth money. I won't get any of it, but I understand collectors are advertising for it and are already paying $7.50. It strikes me as funny as hell, but if you've got one, hold on to it.

I wish I could tell you about the last few months—but it's too long, too wild a story, and I'm too tired. . . . I wish I could see you and talk to you: I'm trying to get a story done for Scribner's before I sail,[2]

---

[1] Wolfe had recently been appointed a Fellow of the Guggenheim Foundation.

[2] This was evidently not completed or not accepted by *Scribner's Magazine*. No stories by Wolfe were bought by them between "An Angel on the Porch" accepted on February 4, 1929, and "A Portrait of Bascom Hawke," accepted on January 28, 1932.

and I'm having my teeth worked on. It's damned hard about your losing money on the property—I'm sure you've seen the worst of it now—that you're in the trough of the wave—and that, no matter what happens, things will get better later.

We are all going to be all right. You are still young and the best of life is before you. I think our youth is the hardest time of our lives: after that I am sure we get more wisdom and greater peace. Please have faith in me. I am still young; I have written, I hope, only the first chapter or two of my own life; and I believe I shall do some beautiful books yet, and make you all proud of me. . . .

With love,

Lenore Powell [3] called me up a few weeks ago when she was here and I went to see her. She is a fine girl, and one of my old friends. And of course my feeling for old friends is what it has always been. But there are other people who have called me up, who never knew me at home and who have never spoken or written a word to me since. When I have sidestepped their invitations, or refused to let them come to my place, some of them have been quite bitter and sarcastic—they have accused me of "forgetting my old friends," being "high hat," etc. My feeling toward such people as this is that they can go to hell. Don't you think I'm right? I am happy to think that the people who know me and care anything for me know what my value is, and that I have always been a real person.

To JAMES BOYD

27 West 15th Street
New York

April 17, 1930

Dear Jim:

I think "Long Hunt" [1] is a beautiful book, and aside from personal feeling I am proud to know the author. There was not a poor line or a shoddy page in it. The book has soaked into me and is a part of me and the other night I began a scene in my new book as follows: "In red-oak wilderness at break of day, long hunters lay for bear." [2] That was a great scene—I mean the bear fight. The book has a great deal

[3] Lenore Powell, now Mrs. Robert Whitfield, had known Wolfe for many years in Asheville.

[1] Boyd's *Long Hunt* had just been published by Scribners.

[2] This passage occurs in "The Names of the Nation" which was first published in the December, 1934, issue of *The Modern Monthly*, and appears in *Of Time and the River* on pages 861–870.

of the magnificence, the savagery, the power and the beauty that the early history of this country has. It has in it the vision of mighty rivers and of the enormous wilderness, and of the richness and glory that this country has had, and still has, and that only ignorant fools deny. I want to get that in my book. Some hundreds of my kinsmen and forefathers are buried in the earth of this country: many of them, I know, were long hunters and pioneers with Crockett's [3] blood in them. The other day I went down for the first time to the Pennsylvania Dutch country— my father came from there. One half of me is enormous red barns, immense fertile fields, and all the meaty spermy groaning plenty of nature; and one half of me is the great hills of North Carolina, the wilderness and the pioneers. I am beginning to brag like your hero did in the rum joint, but your book has done it to me: I'm a Long Hunter from Bear Creek, and a rootin', tootin', shootin' son-of-a-gun from North Carolina.

I may not get away now until after May 1, and I hope I get to see you if you come to New York by then. You have written a grand book, Jim: it has in it the sense of glory. I have been going to Atlantic City and riding in the engine cab of the fastest train in America—83 miles an hour on a steel cyclone—and I have soaked up the power and the glory until it's oozing out—and I'm going to try to get some of it in my new book. I don't think all the pioneers are dead yet. . . .

The following letter to Henry and Natalie Volkening was never mailed. Instead, Wolfe wrote and mailed a very brief note three days later.

To HENRY AND NATALIE VOLKENING

S.S. *Volendam*

Wednesday, May 14, 1930

Dear Henry and Natalie:

. . . I have had a good voyage so far—I am writing this the fifth day out which means, on this placid Dutch boat, that we are about mid-Atlantic. Most of the people, thank God, are elderly and stolid, and there are very few of those bastards who want to "get a crowd together and have a big time." The food is good and the beer is splendid. That dreadful apprehensiveness, that awful jumpy nervousness has al-

[3] Elizabeth Patton, the sister of Wolfe's great-great-grandfather, George Patton, and a cousin of his great-great-grandmother, Nancy Patton, was the second wife of David Crockett.

most left me—although I can't yet quite realize in the morning that the G.D. Telephone won't ring. My skin is bright and fresh again, and my eyes are clear as a child's. It sounds foolish but it's true.

It's all over at last—the bad part I hope forever: the ballyhoo, the gush, the trickery, the intrigue, the envy, the hatred, the horrible weariness. I remember the enormous beauty, vitality, and the horrible impermanence of New York. The sounds of the streets and subways are more real in my ears than a dream. I am haunted by our brief days: at sunset the moon comes up opposite the setting sun like a balance, and at night it makes great pools of light upon the water.

Our effort is to wreak out of chaos and the impermanent hours some lasting beauty: the effort usually fails, but it is a thing for the strong and faithful to try for. There is a Jewish family aboard who are going to visit Max Beerbohm: the wife's sister is Beerbohm's wife. They have been telling me about him. He lives quietly at Rapallo, one of the most beautiful places in the world. He sees few people; he sits on the terrace and paints a little, reads a little, walks about a little, occasionally he writes a little. He is lazy and never forces himself. Yet he has done fine work, and a considerable amount of it, too. It is a good life for an artist —but it is not my kind of life.

I like the Dutch: they are hearty, clean, calm and innocent as children—they have bright blue brittle eyes. I have a good table—a middle-aged French couple, an old Viennese and his wife, and a young German girl with straw hair. They are nice people: we all drink wine together, laugh a lot, talk about different things in Europe and America and have a big time: the various representatives of the Keokuk and Chillicothe smart sets who dress up every night for God knows what, look at us with wellbred University of Kansas snobsfaces. We have had and still have magnificent people in America, but these country club and women's club horsesbristles will ruin the place. They are all potential neo-Humanists—"genteel," the probable successors to Mencken.

Meanwhile what will the real "humanists" do—I mean myself and a few others? For God's sake, don't tell yourself lies, or let others tell them to you: if you are distressed by the savagery, the beauty, the horror and the incessant vitality of living, become a genteel fellow, but don't dress it up with fine words and reasons, or think you have found truth, or that there is any possible connection between Professor Norman Foerster and Sophocles. Anyway, I have found out that although there are millions of people who swear they are willing to live and die for what is good and beautiful, I have never known a half dozen who were willing to be out of fashion. And this is more true of the critics, the reviewers, the writers, than anyone else—most of them have the spirits of rats: they are humanists now, romantics next season, something else again. They call Dreiser a great writer in 1927 and a son of a bitch in 1930.

Enough for the present. I shall think of you often, and I want you to write me, but I shall not write anyone for some time. I am working on my book every day—I have decided that I have no one to please but myself, and I am going ahead in that way. I have decided that anyone who is either grateful or impressed by the kind of notoriety that may come to him in New York, and tries to serve it and justify it, deserves the fate that will certainly come to him. There are perhaps six people in the world whose good opinion I would like to have—I shall write the book for them and for myself, and I hope the public has good sense enough to like it.

I hope this finds you well and flourishing. I send you my best and kindest wishes for happiness.

To MAXWELL E. PERKINS

S S *Volendam*

Saturday May 17, 1930

Dear Mr. Perkins:

The ship is stopping at Plymouth tomorrow—I wanted to write you a line or two so that it would get off on an early boat. The voyage has been very quiet and uneventful—I have done little except eat and sleep and prowl all over the boat. I have had a good rest, and am now ready to get off. I am going to Paris Monday morning directly from Boulogne. I shall write you from there and let you know future plans. . . .

I feel like a man faced with a great test, who is confident of his power to meet it, and yet thinks of it with a pounding heart and with some speculation. I am impatient to get at my book: I know it will be good if I have power to put it on paper as I have thought it out. One thing is certain—I have not used up my nervous vitality: I am prowling around the decks like an animal. I am restless to get off. I have talked to all the passengers, and already I have violent likes and prejudices.

I miss Scribners and seeing you all very much—I think of you all with the warmest and most affectionate feeling. During the last year the place has become a part of my life and habit.

I wish I could tell you how magnificent a great ship at sea is, or of the glory and beauty of the sea and the sky, which are always different. We are nearing the coast of England, the days are much longer, and we have begun to pass tramps and steamers outward bound for America. All day the gulls have been sweeping over the water: I look forward with the greatest excitement to seeing land to-morrow: it has never failed to touch me very deeply.

I can't write a good letter on ship—the movement, the tremble of the engines, and the creaking of the wood destroy concentration. I'll write later from Paris. Good-bye for the present. . . .

With my best and warmest wishes,

To A. S. FRERE-REEVES

Paris

May 23, 1930

Dear Frere:

Thanks very much for your letter. I expect to come to England in June and shall look you up right away. It is very good to be away from all the jangle and noise of New York: I have seen absolutely no one I know in Paris and have not tried to find them. But it is not good to be too much alone, and you have no idea how much comfort I get from knowing you are so near at hand, and that I can go to see you. I am full of a new book and have brought some of it with me. My experience has been that Americans who come to France to work get very little done—they sit in cafés and talk about it. Perhaps one should be able to work anywhere, but England is better for me. I have about fifty pounds a month—do you know of some little village near you where I might go? My idea is as grand as renting a cottage and finding a woman to cook—do you think that is too grand for fifty pounds a month? It seems that the simple things are sometimes hardest to get, but I like to be alone when I work, and I do not like to feel I am disturbing anyone. I have a horror of those little hotels and lodging houses full of embalmed old men and women, and ugly furniture. My habits are not so bad, but I love to stay up all night if necessary, and I do a lot of walking up and down.

Perhaps you can help me with a few suggestions when I see you. I want with all my heart to do a good piece of work and I am a little terrified at the idea of complete isolation. I used to be able to do it when I came abroad, but I want someone to talk to once in a while now. Thanks again, dear Frere, for your letter: I am looking forward to seeing you next month.

To FRED W. WOLFE

Rouen

June 2, 1930.

Dear Fred:

Thanks very much for your letter and the enclosed clippings from the *Asheville Times*. I read them very carefully—I do not think that the man who interviewed me, Lee Cooper,[1] did badly. Of course he did not write the headlines, and cannot be held responsible for such flights of the poetic fancy as "Wolfe Denies Betraying Asheville." I confess that I am tired of the whole business and care very little whether the *Times* or Asheville or anyone else thinks I "betrayed" them or "portrayed" them, or whatever one pleases. But I do not think you will find, if you go back over the files of the local papers, that any of them has ever accused any of the gentlemen who had charge of the city's government several years ago and who, I am told, plunged the city several million dollars in debt—or of the gentlemen who told them that property was worth $9000 the front foot in a town of 40,000 people— or any of the other gentry who have stolen, robbed, murdered, thieved, or raped. I say I do not think you will find a single one accused of being the local Judas, or of "betraying" the town.

In all this I have no bitterness against Asheville or its people. I think some of them have acted very unintelligently, very ungenerously, and very meanly about my book, but one has to expect that from people everywhere. The dark threats that I had "better not come back to Asheville again," or that I can "never come back to this town" etc. affect me very little—apparently people who make such threats have not considered that I have lived away from the town for ten years now and may not have any overpowering desire to return. For many people in the town I feel the greatest affection and respect, but if I ever grow the least bit homesick it is not for the town of Asheville, but for the great and marvellous hills of North Carolina in which I was fortunate enough to be born, and in which Asheville had the good sense to get built. My feeling is for the land, my blood kin, and a few people— beyond that, I care very little.

What does distress me is to think that anyone I care anything about may have been caused any pain or any embarrassment because of any-

---

[1] Lee Cooper, who had been City Editor of *The Asheville Times* and was at this time a reporter on *The New York Times,* had interviewed Wolfe in New York shortly before he sailed for Europe. The interview was published in *The Asheville Times* on May 4, 1930.

thing I have ever written. I have not the least apology to make for the honest use of whatever talent I have, but I do not want nor intend to cause pain to any person. In the end those people who are capable of understanding will understand, and those who are not capable will not understand—and that will be all there is to it: those who understand and like my books will buy them and read them just as if I came from Spokane, or Topeka, or Paris, or Rouen—and those who don't understand or like them will say that "that guy Wolfe is a nut and a highbrow," and they will not buy my books but will go on very happily reading *Western Stories* and *True Confessions*. So much for that.

To talk of other things. I have been in France two weeks, and came to Rouen from Paris yesterday. This town is about 70 miles from Paris on the Seine: there are about 130,000 people here, a very old Cathedral, some old churches and wonderful old houses, and the market square where they burned Joan of Arc. She is now a saint of the church, and they had the cathedral all decorated because of her when I went there to-day.

I have seen nothing of Europe this time except France, but France is in mighty good shape: there is no unemployment at all, everyone is at work, and everyone seems to have enough to eat and drink and wear. The French are a hard-working and thrifty people: they always put by a little either in the bank or under the kitchen floor, and when it comes to haggling over a penny, the Scotch are a race of two-fisted spendthrifts by comparison. The French live for themselves, their families, and their country: they do not like foreigners and regard them with a cold and fishy eye: they endure them because they pay, but there are many other countries where I had rather go broke and trust to luck. They are in many ways a very wonderful people: they are industrious and intelligent, they have great vitality and have a great history and a great literature—but there are many people I like better. I like the country much more than the people—it is one of the most comfortable and beautiful countries in the world. . . .

I am terribly sorry to hear of the trouble Mabel and Ralph Wheaton have had with their property. You are wrong in supposing I was ever "laughing at you" for investing your money in real estate: the subject was one for tears rather than laughter. I have nothing but the deepest and sincerest regret now, and the hope that matters may turn out better than they look, and that things will come right, at least in part. Asheville is one of the saddest little cities in the country to-day—the whole place got drunk, and is now paying for it. But the place and the people will get back on their feet, I know. . . .

With my very best wishes for prosperity and health,

If the newspaper people and the newspaper readers want to believe that the angel in the photograph [2] is the angel in the book, or on the porch, or in the title, or anywhere else, let them go to it: you can't keep them from believing what they want to believe. There is not a scene or a page in the book that is not completely invention, but of course as time goes on these "old inhabitants" I read about who "remember every character" will also remember every scene, and will even remember having been present when it occurred. Such is life.

To A. S. FRERE-REEVES

Paris

June 23, 1930

Dear Frere:

Your letter came this morning. Although it probably embarrasses you to have me say so every time I write, I am so damned glad because you write me—it does me so much good, and I'm grateful beyond words for it, and for everything else you've done. You know, I'm getting soft-hearted in my senility, but I'm afraid I believe in human goodness—and in badness, too.

Frere, by God, I'm so excited I can hardly keep still, but I'm also a little *scared* it may not be true; so I go softly. I am *working* from six to ten hours a day; Paris has no more interest for me than Sauk Center. I sleep till noon, go for a walk, buy an aperitif, lunch, go to a book store and buy a book, read for an hour, then back to my room and work from four or five o'clock until ten at night. Then out to eat and walk, back at midnight or one o'clock, and at work till three or four. And by God, Frere, I mustn't talk about it, but I believe it's the real stuff this time —it's going to be a tremendous piece of work, but I hope I can do it as I plan. Perhaps when I see you I can talk to you a little about it—you and Perkins are the only people I would talk to about it—but I promise not to show you or read you the manuscript.

I have literally seen no one I know in almost two weeks—if ever anyone was a hermit, or marooned on a desert isle, I fit the bill—suppose

---

[2] *The Asheville Times* had published a photograph of a stone angel in Riverside Cemetery there, saying that it was the "angel on the porch" about which Wolfe had written. This was not true. As Wolfe says of this incident in *The Story of a Novel,* "The unfortunate part of this proceeding was that I had never seen or heard of this angel before, and that this angel was, in fact, erected over the grave of a well known Methodist lady who had died a few years before and that her indignant family had immediately written the paper to demand a retraction of its story, saying that their mother had been in no way connected with the infamous book or the infamous angel which had given the infamous book its name."

it's a good thing since it makes you think about your work a great deal. The French have always been to me the most *foreign* men in the world: I constantly get the sensation that they are creatures from another planet: I have never felt this with the English, Germans, or Austrians. I *do* want to get out of Paris, and think I'll go before another week. If I come to England I'll probably come like a shot—if you are not in London but at the sea, I'll wait on you.

Mr. Arlen [1] spoke to me when I was in Smith's Book Shop the other day—he pointed out one of his books just out in the Tauschnitz and I immediately bought it. I'm reading "War and Peace"—a modest affair of about 1500 closely packed pages, but a tremendous, magnificent book. There is also a grain of biography. It seems to me that all good writers draw heavily on their own experience, but I suppose most bad ones do also: not so much, though—the bad ones grind out "fiction." All good writing, I am sure, is in some measure autobiographical, but it is the right use of this with the imagination which makes a good book: there is more imaginative power in one page of *Ulysses* than in all the novels of Oppenheim together. Don't you think so?

Also, it is right to howl about living, about the scheme of existing— every good man does howl about it—but it is wrong to hate individual people in your work: I mean it is wrong to make Jones and Green out rascals, if that is your only purpose in doing it. It seems to me that *that* will cheapen a man's work as quickly as anything—a desire to "get back": but if a man is a good enough artist he rises far above that—I mean Proust and Joyce, although I suppose Joyce does pay off a few old scores.

Well, this is too much serious thinking for a sticky day. I first wrote you a long letter telling you all about my new book, but my nobler nature triumphed and I tore it (the letter) up.[2] If you go to the seaside before I see you, please soak and bask in it, but behave yourself with the mermaids: don't pinch their little tails or scales, or whatever they have. Now and then I think of London, and how great and magnificent it is, and the beer and ale, and what a good piece of meat you can get in certain places, and I kick myself for not coming. Dear Frere, I am the world's champion dawdler and proscrastinator but eventually I arrive. I think at the present time I feel that solitude and hermitage is good for my soul, because it's such bitter medicine—does that make me an old Yankee Puritan? God bless you, and please write me when you can.

[1] Michael Arlen. Frere-Reeves had come to Paris for a few days and had introduced Wolfe to him.

[2] Fragments of this letter still remain among Wolfe's papers, but are not included here since they closely resemble Wolfe's letters of June 24 to Wheelock and July 1 to Perkins.

To JOHN HALL WHEELOCK

Guaranty Trust Company
Paris

June 24, 1930

Dear Jack:

Thanks very much for your fine letter—I can't tell you how touched and grateful I was. I'm not going to write you a long one now—I'll do that later when things have settled a little more. Briefly, this has happened: I have been in Paris almost all the time since I landed, with the exception of a few days in Rouen. This not because I love Paris, but because after two weeks of casting around, moving from one hotel to the other, I suddenly decided that we spend too much of our lives looking for ideal conditions to work in, and that what we are after is an ideal condition of the soul which almost never comes. So I got tired and disgusted with myself, went to a little hotel—not very French, I'm afraid, but very touristy—and set to work. I've been doing five or six hours a day for almost two weeks now—the weather is hot and sticky, but I sweat and work—it's the only cure I've found for the bloody hurting inside me.

Dear Jack, it's been so bad I can't tell you about it: I feel all bloody inside me—but have faith in me, everything's going to be all right. What do you know about it? I am writing a book so filled with the most unspeakable desire, longing, and love for my own country and ten thousand things in it, that I have to laugh at times to think what the Mencken crowd and all the other crowds are going to say about it. But I can't help it—if I have ever written anything with utter conviction it is this. Dear Jack, I *know* that I know what some of our great woe and sickness as a people is now, because that woe is in me—it is rooted in myself; but by God, Jack, I have not written a word directly about myself yet. God knows what Maxwell Perkins will say when he sees it, but I've just finished the first section of the first part—it is called *Antæus*, and it is as if I had become a voice for the experience of a race. It begins "Of wandering forever and the earth again"—and by God, Jack, I believe I've got it—the two things that haunt and hurt us: the eternal wandering, moving, questing, loneliness, homesickness, and the desire of the soul for a home, peace, fixity, repose. In *Antæus*, in a dozen short scenes, told in their own language, we see people of all sorts *constantly in movement*, going somewhere, haunted by it—and by God, Jack, it's the *truth* about them—I saw it as a child, I've seen it ever since, I see it here in their poor damned haunted eyes.

Well there are these scenes: [1] a woman talking of the river, the ever-moving river, coming through the levee at night, and of the crippled girl clinging to the limb of the oak, and of how she feels the house break loose and go with the tide, then of living on the roof-top with Furman and the children, and of other houses and people—tragedy, pity, humor, bravery, and the great wild savagery of American nature. Then the pioneer telling of "the perty little gal" he liked, but moving on because the wilderness was getting too crowded; then the hoboes waiting quietly at evening by the water tower for the coming of the fast express; then a rich American girl moving on from husband to husband, from drink to dope to opium, from white lovers to black ones, from New York to Paris to California; then the engineer at the throttle of the fast train. Then a modest poor little couple from 123rd St—the woman earning living by painting lampshades, the man an impractical good-for-nothing temporarily employed in a filling station—cruising in their cheap little car through Virginia and Kentucky in autumn—all filled with details of motor camps, where you can get a shack for $1.00 a night, and of "lovely meals" out of cans—whole cost $0.36—etc. Then a school teacher from Ohio taking University Art Pilgrimage No. 36, writing back home "—didn't get your letter till we got to Florence . . . stayed in Prague 3 days but rained whole time we were there, so didn't get to see much, etc." Then Lee coming through Virginia in the night on his great white horse; then the skull of a pioneer in the desert, a rusted gun stock and a horse's skull; then a Harry's New York Bar American saying, "Jesus! What a country! I been back one time in seven years. That was enough. . . . Me, I'm a Frenchman. See?" But talking, talking, cursing, until he drinks himself into a stupor. Then a bum, a natural wanderer who has been everywhere; then a Boston woman and her husband who have come to France to live—"Francis always felt he wanted to do a little writing . . . we felt the atmosphere is so much better here for that kind of thing"; then a Jew named Greenberg, who made his pile in New York and who now lives in France having changed his name to Montvert, and of course feels no homesickness at all, save what is natural to 4000 years of wandering. And more, and more, and more!

Then amid all this you get the thing that does not change, the fixed principle, *the female principle*—the *earth again*—and, by God, Jack, I know *this is true* also. They want love, the earth, a home, fixity—you get the mother and the lover—as the book goes on, and you see this incessant change, movement, unrest, and the great train with the wanderers rush-

[1] This material, greatly cut, appears on pages 861–869 of *Of Time and the River*, in the section called "Kronos and Rhea: The Dream of Time," rather than in the preceding one called "Antæus: Earth Again."

ing through the night. Outside you get the eternal silent waiting earth that does not change, and the two women, going to bed upon it, working in their gardens upon it, dreaming, longing, calling for men to return upon it. And down below in the mighty earth, you get the bones of the pioneers, all of the dust now trembling to the great train's wheel, the dust that loved, suffered, died, and is now buried, pointing 80 ways across 3000 miles of earth, and deeper than all, eternal and enduring, "the elm trees thread the bones of buried lovers."

Through it all is poetry—the enormous rivers of the nation drinking the earth away at night, the vast rich stammer of night time in America, the lights, the smells, the thunder of the train—the savage summers, the fierce winters, the floods, the blizzards—all, all! And finally the great soft galloping of the horses of sleep!

Mr. Perkins may say that the first part is too much like a poem—but Jack, I've got it loaded with these stories of the wanderings of real people in their own talk, and by God, Jack, a *real unified* single story opens up almost at once and gathers and grows from then on. The chapter after "Antaeus" is called at present "Early October," [2] and begins "October is the richest of the seasons"—it tells about the great barns loaded with harvest, the mown fields, the burning leaves, a dog barking at sunset, the smell of supper cooking in the kitchen—"October is full of richness," a thousand things. Then a section begins "October is the time for all re-turning"—(which is true, Jack). It tells how exiles and wanderers think of home again, of how the last tourists come back on great ships, of how the old bums shiver in their ragged collars as the newspaper behind the Public Library is blown around their feet, and of how they think of going South. It tells of the summer girls who have gone back home from the resorts; of the deserted beaches; of people lying in their beds at night thinking, "Summer has come and gone—has come and gone." Then in the frosty dark and silver, they hear the thunder of the great train. Then the October of a person's life—the core, the richness, the harvest, and the richness of the end of youth.

By God, Jack, I'm just a poor bloody homesick critter, but when I think of my book sometimes I have the pride of a poet and a master of man's fate. Don't sigh and shake your head and think this is a welter of drivel— I've slapped these things down wildly in my haste, but I tell you, Jack, this book is *not* incoherent—it has a beautiful plan and a poetic logic if I am only true to it. *I have not* told you the thousandth part of it, but I hope you can see and believe in the truth and worth of it—and then if you do, please pray for me, dear Jack, to do my best and utmost, and to write the kind of book I want to write. In case you should doubt my

[2] A version of this appears in *Of Time and the River* on pages 329–332.

condition, I am perfectly sober as I write this, it is a hot day, and I am now going back to my little room to work like hell. I have really not told you *about* my book—all this has been coming in the sweat and heat of the last few days, and this letter, however crazy, has made things clearer for me.

I shall not leave Paris until I finish that first section—then I'm going like a shot to Switzerland, I think. I won't waste time moving about—I have a horror of moving now at all. Reeves,[3] the English publisher was here, took me around to see Aldington,[4] Michael Arlen, and other literary lights—I was so unhappy at the time I have not been back since, although they were very nice. Reeves wants me to come to England and stay with him, the book is coming out there next month, but I've a horror of reading more reviews—I don't want to do anything more about it. Hope and pray for me, dear Jack. Write me soon and talk to me. I've said nothing about you, forgive me, I'll write you a regular letter later.

Dear Jack—I'm sending this on a day or two later. I guess I'm really started—six hours a day, kid. . . .

To MAXWELL E. PERKINS

> Guaranty Trust Co,
> Paris.
>
> July 1, 1930

Dear Mr. Perkins:

I have a long letter under way to you, but I shall probably not send it until I have left Paris. The main news is that I have been at work for several weeks, and have worked every day except last Sunday, when I met Scott Fitzgerald for the first time. He called me up at my hotel and I went out to his apartment for lunch: we spent the rest of the afternoon together talking and drinking—a good deal of both—and I finally left him at the Ritz Bar. He was getting ready to go back to Switzerland where he has been for several weeks, and had come up to close up his apartment and take his little girl back with him. He told me that Mrs. Fitzgerald has been very sick—a bad nervous breakdown—and he has her in a sanitarium at Geneva. He spoke of his new book and said he was working on it: he was very friendly and generous, and I liked him, and think he has a great deal of talent, and I hope he gets that book done soon. I think we got along very well—we had quite an argument about America: I said we were a

---

[3] A. S. Frere-Reeves of Heinemann's.
[4] Richard Aldington.

homesick people, and belonged to the earth and land we came from as much or more as any country I knew about—he said we were not, that we were not a country, that he had no feeling for the land he came from. "Nevertheless," as Galileo said, "it moves." We do, and they are all homesick or past having any feeling about anything.

I have missed America more this time than ever: maybe it's because all my conviction, the tone and conviction of my new book is filled with this feeling, which once I would have been ashamed to admit. I notice that the Americans who live here live with one another for the most part, and the French exist for them as waiters, taxi drivers, etc.—yet most of them will tell you all about the French, and their minute characteristics. I have been absolutely alone for several weeks—Fitzgerald was the first American I had talked to for some time, but yesterday I was here in the bank, and in walked Jim Boyd: I was so surprised and happy I could not speak for a moment—we went out to lunch together and spent the rest of the day together. He has been quite sick with the sinus trouble, as you know. We went to see a doctor, and I waited below: this doctor made no examination and gave no verdict, but is sending him to a specialist. I hope they do something for him—he is a fine fellow, and I like him enormously. We went to a nice café and drank beer and talked over the American soil and what we were going to do for literature, while Mrs. Boyd shopped around town. Later we all drove out to the Bois and through it to a nice little restaurant out of town on the banks of the Seine—we had a good quiet dinner there and came back. I think Jim enjoyed it, and I am going to meet them again to-night. It has done me a great deal of good to see them . . .

I am going to Switzerland—I have several places in mind but must go and see them—I would have gone long ago, but I did not want to move fast when I had started. I do not know how long I shall stay over here, but I shall stay until I have done the first part of my book, and can bring it back with me. It is going to be a very long book, I am afraid, but there is no way out of it. You can't write the book I want to write in 200 pages. It has four parts, its whole title is "The October Fair," and the names of the four parts are (1) "Antaeus"; (2) "The Fast Express"; (3) "Faust and Helen"; (4) "The October Fair." [1] I am working on the part called "Antaeus" now, which is like a symphony of many voices run through with the beginning thread of story that continues through the book. I propose to bring back to America with me the parts called "Antaeus" and "The

---

[1] *Of Time and the River,* which was only the first half of what Wolfe calls *The October Fair* here, finally had eight parts: "Orestes: Flight Before Fury"; "Young Faustus"; "Telemachus"; "Proteus: The City"; "Jason's Voyage"; "Antæus: Earth Again"; "Kronos and Rhea: The Dream of Time"; and "Faust and Helen."

Fast Express" (all these names are tentative and if you don't like them we'll get others). The book is a grand book if I have character and talent enough to do it as I have conceived it. The book has to do with what seem to me two of the profoundest impulses in man—Wordsworth, in one of his poems "To a Skylark," I think, calls it "heaven and home" and I called it in the first line of my book, "Of wandering forever and the earth again."

By "the earth again" I mean simply the everlasting earth, a home, a place for the heart to come to, and earthly mortal love, the love of a woman, who, it seems to me belongs to the earth and is a force opposed to that other great force that makes men wander, that makes them search, that makes them lonely, and that makes them both hate and love their loneliness. You may ask what all this has to do with America—it is true it has to do with the whole universe—but it is as true of the enormous and lonely land that we inhabit as any land I know of, and more so, it seems to me.

I hope this does not seem wild and idiotic to you, I have been unable to tell you much about it here, but I will in greater detail later. I ask you to remember that in the first part—"Antaeus"—the part of many voices—everything moves, everything moves across the enormous earth, except the earth itself, and except for the voices of the women crying out "Don't go! Stay! Return, return!"—the woman floating down the river in flood on her housetop with her husband and family (I finished that scene the other day and I think it is a good one). The whole scene, told in the woman's homely speech, moves to the rhythm of the great river; yet the scene has pungent and humorous talk in it, and I think does not ring false. You understand that the river is in her brain, in her thought, in her speech; and at the very end, lying in her tent at night while a new house is being built where the old one was (for *he* refuses to go up on high ground back beyond the river where nothing moves) she hears him waken beside her— he thinks she is asleep—she knows he is listening to the river, to the whistles of the boats upon the river, that he wants to be out there upon the river, that he could go floating on forever down the river. And she hates the river, but all of its sounds are in her brain, she cannot escape it . . . "All of my life is flowing like the river, all of my life is passing like the river, I think and dream and talk just like the river as it goes by me, by me, by me, to the sea." [2]

Does it sound idiotic? I don't think so if you could see the whole; it is

[2] This scene became very long and was finally omitted from *Of Time and the River*. However, the words "goes by me, by me, by me, to the sea" were changed to "flows by us, by us, by us, to the sea" and used as a refrain throughout the book, as on pages 333, 510, 860, etc.

full of rich detail, sounds and talk. I will not tell you any more now—this letter is too long and I have had no lunch. The river woman is only one thing . . . I'll tell you all about it later. Everything moves except the earth and the voices of the women crying out against wandering!

I miss seeing you and Scribners more than I can say. I hope I can do a good book for you and for myself and for the whole damn family. Please hope and pull for me and write me when you can. Excuse this long scrawl. I hope this finds you well and enjoying the summer, and also that you get a good vacation. Jim Boyd and I will think of you every time we drink a glass of beer and wish that you were here just for an hour or so to share it. I send everyone my best and warmest wishes.

Don't tell anyone where I am or where I'm going unless you think they have some business to find out. Tell them you don't know where I am (if anyone asks) but that mail will get to me if sent to The Guaranty Trust Co., Paris.

To MAXWELL E. PERKINS

Hotel Lorius
Montreux, Switzerland
July 17, 1930

Dear Mr. Perkins:

Your letter was sent on here from Paris, and I got it this morning. I suppose by now you have the letter I sent you from Paris several weeks ago. I have been here five or six days. . . . The other night at the Casino here I was sitting on the terrace when I saw Scott Fitzgerald and a friend of his, a young man I met in Paris. I called to them, they came over and sat with me: later we gambled at roulette and I won 15 francs, then Scott took us to a night club here. This sounds much gayer than it is: there is very little to do here, and I think I saw all the night life there is on that occasion. Later Scott and his friend drove back to Vevey, a village a mile or two from here on the lake: they are staying there. They asked me to come over to dine with them, but I am not going: I do not think I am very good company to people at present. It would be very easy for me to start swilling liquor at present but I am *not* going to do it. I am here to get work done, and in the next three months, I am going to see whether I am a bum or a man. I shall not try to conceal from you the fact that at times now I have hard sledding: my life is divided between just two things:—thought of my book, and thought of an event in my life which is now, *objectivally,*

[sic] finished. I do not write any more to anyone concerned in that event— I received several letters, but since none have come for some time I assume no more will come. I have been entirely alone since I left New York, save for these casual meetings I have told you about. Something in me hates being alone like death, and something in me cherishes it: I have always felt that somehow, out of this bitter solitude, some fruit must come. I lose faith in myself with people. When I am with someone like Scott I feel that I am morose and sullen—and violent in my speech and movement part of the time. Later, I feel that I have repelled them.

Physically my life is very good. My nerves are very steady. I drink beer and wine, mostly beer, I do not think to excess; and I have come to what is, I am sure, one of the most beautiful spots in the world. I am staying at a quiet and excellent hotel here; have a very comfortable room with a writing desk and a stone balcony that looks out on the lake of Geneva, and on a garden below filled with rich trees and grass and brilliant flowers. On all sides of the lake the mountains soar up: everything begins to climb immediately, this little town is built in three or four shelving terraces, and runs along the lake shore. Something in me wants to get up and see places, the country is full of incredibly beautiful places, but also something says "stay here and work."

That, in a way, is what my book is about. I hope in these hasty scrawls I have been able to communicate the idea of my book, and that it seems clear and good to you. I told you that the book begins with "of wandering forever, and the earth again," and that these two opposing elements seem to me to be fundamental in people. I have learned this in my own life, and I believe I am at last beginning to have a proper use of a writer's material: for it seems to me he ought to see in what has happened to him the elements of the universal experience. In my own life, my desire has fought between a hunger for isolation, for getting away, for seeking new lands—and a desire for home, for permanence, for a piece of this earth fenced in and lived on and private to oneself, and for a person or persons to love and possess. This is badly put, but I think it expresses a desire that all people have. I think the desire for wandering is more common to men, and for fixity and a piece of the earth to women, but I know these things are rooted in most people. I think you have sometimes been puzzled when I have talked to you about parts of this book—about the train as it thunders through the dark, and about the love for another person—to see how they could be reconciled or fit into the general scheme of a story; but I think you can get some idea of it now: the great train pounding at the rails is rushing across the everlasting and silent earth— here the two ideas of wandering and eternal repose—and the characters, on the train, and on the land, again illustrate this. Also, the love theme, the male and female love, represent this again: please do not think I am hammering this in in the book, I let it speak for itself—I am giving you a kind of key.

There is no doubt at all what the book is about, what course it will take, and I think the seething process, the final set of combinations, has been reached. I regret to report to you that the book will be very long, probably longer than the first one, but I think that each of its four parts makes a story in itself and, if good enough, might be printed as such. I have been reading your favorite book, "War and Peace"—it is a magnificent and gigantic work—if we are going to worship anything, let it be something like this: I notice in this book that the personal story is interwoven with the universal—you get the stories of private individuals, particularly of members of Tolstoy's own family, and you get the whole tremendous panorama of nations, and of Russia. This is the way a great writer uses his material, this is the way in which every good work is "autobiographical"— and I am not ashamed to follow this in my book.

The four parts of the book as they now stand are:

(1) "Antaeus" or "Immortal Earth" (Title to be chosen from one of these)

(2) "Antaeus" or "The Fast Express"

(3) "Faust and Helen"

(4) "The October Fair."

I do not think "Immortal Earth" or "The Immortal Earth" is a bad title; and if you are not keen upon "The Fast Express"—we might call Part I "Immortal Earth"—and Part II "Antaeus"—since in Part I the idea of eternal movement, of wandering and the earth, of flight and repose is more manifest, and in Part II, even though we have the fast train, the idea of redoubling and renewing our strength by contact with the earth (Antaeus) is more evident.

Now, the general movement of the book is from the universal to the individual: in Part I "The Immortal Earth" (?), we have a symphony of many voices (I described this briefly in my other letter) through which the thread of the particular story begins to run. I think this can be done with entire clearness and unity: we have a character called David [1] (Chapter II is called "The Song of David") but this character appears at first only as a window, an eye, a wandering seer: he performs at first exactly the same function as the epic minstrel in some old popular epic like "Beowulf," who makes us very briefly conscious of his presence from time to time by saying, "I have heard," or "it has been told me." Thus in Part I, in the chapter called "The River," the woman telling the story of the river in flood refers to him once by name. In the chapter "Pioneers, O

[1] At this time, Wolfe called his hero David Hawke instead of Eugene Gant.

Pioneers," we understand that David is a member of an American family, two or three hundred of whose members are buried in different parts of the American earth, and we get the stories and wanderings of some of these people. In the letter of the tourist from Prague he is referred to by name, in the chapter "On the Rails," we know that he is on the train, although the story is that of the engineer; in the chapter "The Bums at Sunset," we know he has seen them waiting for the train at the water-tower; in the chapter called "The Congo," the wandering negro who goes crazy and kills people and is finally killed by the posse as he crosses a creek, is known to David, the boy—etc.[2]

So much for some of the general movement: now among the twenty chapters of this first part are interspersed the first elements of the particular story—the figure of David remains almost entirely a window, but begins to emerge as an individual from what is told about him by other people, and by the way all these episodes, even the general ones—"Pioneers, O Pioneers," "The Congo," etc., give flashes of his life—but in this first part, not to tell about him, but to tell about his country, the seed that produced him, etc. It will be seen in the particular story that the desire and longing of David, is also the desire and longing of the race—"wandering forever and the earth again." These half dozen chapters, moreover, are concerned with the *female* thing: the idea of the earth, fructification, and repose—these half dozen chapters interspersed among the twenty are almost entirely about women and told in the language of women: the mother, the mistress, and the child—sometimes all included in one person, sometimes found separately in different women.

Now, if you will follow me a little farther in this, here is another development. I have said that wandering seems to me to be more of a male thing, and the fructification of the earth more a female thing—I don't think there can be much argument about this, immediately we think of the pioneers, the explorers, the Crusaders, the Elizabethan mariners, etc. I am making an extensive use of old myths in my book, although I never tell the reader this: you know already that I am using the Heracles (in my book the City is Heracles) and Antaeus myth; and you know that

---

[2] Most of this material was omitted from *Of Time and the River*, but parts of it were published as short stories in various magazines. The letter from the tourist in Prague became "One of the Girls in Our Party" in the January, 1935, issue of *Scribner's Magazine;* part of "On the Rails" probably became "Cottage by the Tracks" in the July, 1935, issue of *Cosmopolitan;* "The Bums at Sunset" appeared in the October, 1935, issue of *Vanity Fair;* and "The Congo" was entirely rewritten in the spring of 1937 and published as "The Child by Tiger" in the September 11, 1937, issue of *The Saturday Evening Post*. All of these stories were included in *From Death to Morning*, with the exception of "The Child by Tiger" which appears on pages 132–156 of *The Web and the Rock*.

the lords of fructification and the earth are almost always women: Maya in the Eastern legends; Demeter in the Greek; Ceres in Latin, etc.

Now I hope you don't get dizzy in all this, or think I am carrying the thing to absurdity: all intense conviction has elements of the fanatic and the absurd in it, but they are saved by our beliefs and our passion. Contained in the book like a kernel from the beginning, but unrevealed until much later, is the idea of a man's quest for his father. The idea becomes very early apparent that when a man returns he returns always to the *female* principle—he returns, (I hope this is not disgusting) to the womb of earthly creation, to the earth itself, to a woman, to fixity. But I dare go so far as to believe that the other pole—the pole of wandering—is not only a masculine thing, but that in some way it represents the quest of a man for his father. I dare mention to you the wandering of Christ upon this earth, the wanderings of Paul, the quests of the Crusaders, the wanderings of the Ancient Mariner who makes his confession to the Wedding Guest—please don't laugh:

"The moment that his face I see
I know the *man* that must hear me.
To *him* my tale I teach."

I could mention also a dozen myths, legends, or historical examples, but you can supply them quite as well for yourself. Suffice it to say that this last theme—the quest of a man for his father—does not become fully revealed until the very end of the book: under the present plan I have called the final chapter of the fourth and last part ("The October Fair"), "Telemachus."

Now, briefly, in the first part on which I am now at work (to be called "Antaeus" or "The Immortal Earth"), I want to construct my story on the model of the old folk epic: "Beowulf," for example. I want the character of David to be the epic minstrel who sings of the experience of his race, and I want to do this with eloquence, with passion and with simplicity. I want my book to be poetry—that is, I want it to be drenched in a poetic vision of life. I believe at this moment in the truth and the passion of what I have to say, and I hope, in spite of this fast scrawl, I have been able to make parts of it clear to you, and to show you it has a coherent plan and purpose.

In the first chapter of the first part (after the prelude)—the first chapter is called "The Ship"—I think I have done a good piece of writing: I tell about the sea and the earth; I tell why they are different; of the sea's eternal movement, and the earth's eternal repose. I tell why men go to sea, and why they have made harbours at the end; I tell why a ship is always called "she"; I tell of the look in the eyes of men when the last land fades out of sight, and when land comes first in view again; I tell of the earth; I describe the great ship, and the people on it—and, so help me, when I am through, I am proud of that ship and of man, who built her, who is so strong because he is so weak, who is so great because he is so small, who is so brave because he is so full of fear, who can face the horror of the ocean and see there in that unending purposeless waste the answer to his existence. I *insist*, by the way, in my book that men are wise, and that we all know we are lost, that we are damned together—and that man's greatness comes in knowing this and then making myths; like soldiers going into battle who will whore and carouse to the last minute, nor have any talk of death and slaughter.

Well, I have almost written you a book, and I hope you have stayed awake thus far. I don't know if it makes sense or not, but I think it does. Remember, although this letter is very heavy, that my book as I plan it will be full of richness, talk and humor. Please write me and tell me if all this has meant anything to you, and what you think of it. Please don't talk about it to other people. Write me as often as you can, if only a note. We like to get letters when we are in a strange land.

Please forgive me for talking so much about myself and my book. I hope I can do a good piece of work, and that any little personal distress does not get the best of me—I do not think it will.

One final thing: please understand—I think you do—that my new book will make use of experience, things I have known and felt, as the first one did—but that now I have created fables and legends and that there will be no question of identification (certainly not in the first two parts) as there was in the first. The David I have referred to is part of me, as indeed are several other characters, but nothing like, in appearance or anything else, what people think me. This is very naive and foolish, and for God's sake keep it to yourself: in making the character of David, I have made him out of the *inside* of me, of what I have always believed the inside was like: he is about five feet nine, with the long arms and the prowl of an ape,[3] and a little angel in his face. He is part beast, part spirit —a mixture of the ape and the angel. There is a touch of the monster in him. But no matter about this—at first he is the bard and, I pray God, that is what I can be. Please write me soon. I'll tell you how things come.

P.S. My book came out in England last Monday, July 14. I hope it goes well and gets good notices, but I have instructed them not to send any reviews—I can't be bothered by it now. Some *kind* friend probably will send reviews, but I hope for the best. . . .

[3] It is interesting to note that Wolfe thought of changing his hero's appearance as early as this date, although he did not actually resort to this device until *The Web and the Rock* and *You Can't Go Home Again*.

To MAXWELL E. PERKINS

Hotel Lorius
Montreux
July 31, 1930

Dear Mr. Perkins:

Please forgive me for flooding you with letters, but I think the news I send will interest you. I told you before that my book came out in England July 14. I wrote Frere-Reeves and told him not to send me any reviews as I am working on a new one, but this morning he sent me a great batch of clippings (twenty or more) and a long letter in which he was quite enthusiastic. He said that the book, in spite of its high price on account of its length (10/6d instead of the usual 7/6d), was selling at the rate of a thousand copies every *four* days: if this is true, it is selling faster in England than in America. He also sent one of their advertisements from *The Observer* (I am sending it to you along with one or two clippings of which I have duplicates: I'll send you the rest a little later). I've read all the clippings over briefly, and they seem to me mighty good. Four or five got in some nasty cracks about formlessness and filth, but all were favorable and some of them said things that made my head swim—as good, it seems to me, as the best we had in America. I hope he didn't handpick them to spare my feelings, but he seems to have most of the big ones: *The Times, The Sunday Times, The Times Literary Supplement, The Sunday Referee, The Morning Post, The Evening Standard, The Evening Telegraph, The Daily Mail,* etc. I want to send you Richard Aldington's review in *The Sunday Referee* [1] later (it made me dizzy), but I am sending you to-day *The Times Literary Supplement,* which Frere-Reeves says is the most important in England—it sounds pretty swell to me: please read it and tell me what you think.[2]

I suppose the book has stopped selling in America: do you think it would be a good idea to print some of these English things (in an ad, under some such heading as "What The English Are Saying")—do you think it would make some of the snobs buy the book?

I am sending you one of the Heinemann ads, together with *The Times Supplement:* later I'll send the others. Do what you think best about it, and write me. I suppose I'm jumping too fast at conclusions, but if this *thousand* every *four* days business keeps up a few weeks, I'll have nothing to complain of. I think Frere-Reeves and Heinemann have done a mighty

[1] Aldington's very favorable review of *Look Homeward, Angel* was published in the July 6, 1930, *Sunday Referee.*

[2] The very favorable unsigned review of *Look Homeward, Angel* in the *Times Literary Supplement* appeared on July 24, 1930.

fine job. I am an American but I have more English blood in me than the English royal family. They were my heroes, my mighty poets when I was a child. I was so hurt and bitter about them when I saw them after the war—but I cannot deny to you that it would make me happy if the people who invented the language I use like my work. I do not think there is one God-damned ounce of snobbishness in this!

I am very lonely here, but I work: there's nothing else to do. I think if I see it through, it will be very good—I am all alone and sometimes I doubt: do you think I'll ever amount to anything? I read Shakespeare, Racine, The English Poets—and the Bible. I have not read the Bible since I was a child—it is the most magnificent book that was ever written: when Walter Scott was dying, he called for "The Book," and they asked "What book?" and he said "There is only one"—and it is true. It is richer and grander than Shakespeare even, and everything else looks sick beside it. In the last three days I have read "Ecclesiastes" and "The Song of Solomon" several times: they belong to the mightiest poetry that was ever written—and the narrative passages in the old testament, stories like the life of King David, Ruth and Boaz, Esther and Ahasueras, etc., make the narrative style of any modern novelist look puny. I am soaking in it, and for the first part of "The October Fair," which I am calling "The Immortal Earth," I have chosen this verse from the great book of "Ecclesiastes" as a title page legend: "One generation passeth away, and another generation cometh: but the earth abideth forever." I am sorry to say that this verse comes immediately before the verse Hemingway used, "The sun also ariseth" etc., and people will say I have imitated him, but it can't be helped, it is chance, and this is the verse I want.

I am now at work on a section of "The Immortal Earth" which has the curious title of "The Good Child's River." [3] I like the title and hope you will too when you see the story: it is complete in itself, and very long—a short book—and I will send it to you when it's finished.

I'm excited about Frere-Reeves' clippings and letter, and I'm going to take a little trip this afternoon: I'm going to catch a train in a few minutes and go to the neighboring town of Lausanne and see if there are any pretty girls or women. I am very lusty: the air, the mountains, the quiet, and the very dull, very healthy food have filled me with a vitality I was afraid I'd lost.

I wish you were here and we could take a walk together—please write

---

[3] *The Good Child's River*, which told the story of the early life of Esther Jack, was finally omitted from *Of Time and the River*. One section of it was later published as "In the Park" in the June, 1935, issue of *Harper's Bazaar* and included in *From Death to Morning*. Other portions of it appear in *The Web and the Rock* on pages 406–433.

me when you can. I am very lonely, but I really think we must have some of it now: . . . I hope to God I can do a good piece—in "Ecclesiastes" a great passage says: "The Fool foldeth his hands and eateth his flesh," and that is what the little sneering Futility People the world over are doing—I think the Bible has very probably said everything. With their bitter, sterile thirst for failure in New York, people—some people—are waiting with bitter smiles for my ruin and wreck. I will tell you honestly I do not know if they are right or wrong. I myself am in the process of seeing, but I think the bastards are wrong, and we shall see. . . .

Write me when you can. I am glad you got a good manuscript, but I hope you won't forget me or cease to be my friend. I hope this finds you well and enjoying your vacation. I wish we could drink a big bottle of wine together.

P.S. About these people, both in England and America, who say: "This is not a great book" or "great art" or "a work of genius"—I have never said it was: but why should they be so hard and exacting on a young man's book, when they are willing to slobber over any amount of dirty trash? Even Van Doren [4] told me how lucky I was to get so much reputation out of one book, as if the vilest rubbish doesn't get ten times more, everywhere you turn. Why have things got to be made so unfair and hard for me? In addition to my personal troubles, I have to listen to eight thousand Jeremiahs yelling: "Wait and see. . . . We will be pleasantly surprised, of course, if he amounts to anything, but . . ." etc. It makes me vomit! Sometimes I think everyone in the world is that way: their idea of helping you is to kick you in the face: if you succeed, it's because you have been trampled by adversity and they've really done you a good turn. Why shouldn't people in America buy more copies of my book than they have bought? Why should I be so damned humble before them, when they will rush out and buy trash by Wilder or someone else by the million? Please write to me soon.

To A. S. FRERE-REEVES

Hotel Lorius
Montreux
Aug. 2, 1930

Dear Frere:

Thanks for your long letter and the big batch of clippings. When they came, I took them to a café, ordered a big beer, took a long breath and

[4] Carl Van Doren.

began! I am still alive, I am not cast down, I do not want to curse God and die. I don't know whether you had to hand-pick these notices carefully to spare my feelings—I hope not!—but it seems to me those you sent were pretty good, and three or four of them were pretty damned splendid. Of course, Richard Aldington is a peach—I think this is one of the most generous things I ever heard of, and I am writing him to-day to tell him so: if the rest of them had rotten-egged me, I could never forget what he's done. I thought the *Times Literary Supplement* was mighty good, too, as well as all the other *Times* notices. As for the thousand copies every four days—that sounds stupendous: I think of The Thin Red Line, and the tenacity of the Bulldog Breed, and I hope this present generation of Britons will not prove degenerate: let them stick to their guns for at least forty days (Sundays included)—and if they want to keep it up longer, they won't hurt *my* feelings.

As for [you,] Frere, I think it was a lucky day when I met you, and you became my publisher. I can never know the history of all you've done, but please don't think I accept all this complacently: I know your value, and I am filled with profound and enormous gratitude. I hope you will always be my friend and that you will find no strangeness to me because I am from another country and speak a different accent. Remember that I am an American and that I will open my heart to you on any thing that may belong to my vision of life and not to yours; but never remember me as a foreigner and a stranger—the real republic of this earth stretches from here to China, and just as you are closer to me and nearer to the color of my hand and heart and spirit than most Americans, so, I hope and believe, do I come closer to your thought and language than most Englishmen. Sometime I want to tell you how I felt that day when you took me around to see Richard Aldington and you were all old friends and talked the same language: you and Mr. Aldington and Mrs. Patmore [1] and Tom McGreevy.[2] I felt so strange and foreign, and yet I felt so close to you, as if I had only to find the knob somewhere and open the door or poke my finger through the wall. We are all four in Exile, but sometimes there are flashes of lightning and we see a way we thought we had forgotten. . . .

I suppose, Frere, that you may have spared me some rough reviews, but your letters to me seemed really cheerful about the book: I hope this is true, and that you and Heinemann are really pleased about the way it's going. Please don't be polite to me about this: speak plainly. But if some of them said I am no good, don't believe it: I will write you other books that will put this one in the shade, and we will make the Forces of Darkness eat crow before we've done. . . .

[1] Mrs. Brigit Patmore, mother of Derek Patmore.
[2] Thomas McGreevy, the Irish poet.

. . . The weather is hot but very fine here, and my pastime is to eat that good lake fish you like so well. Scott Fitzgerald telegraphed me from Paris this morning that he had just finished my first book after twenty consecutive hours, and that he was "enormously moved and grateful." I hope he repents and leads a better life hereafter. I am working on my new book every day.

P.S. And please send the author a copy of that English first edition before it becomes so damned valuable he can't afford to buy it!

The following letter to Susan Hyde (now Mrs. Joseph Tonetti) was never mailed, but was found among Wolfe's papers. He had met Miss Hyde in New York shortly before he sailed on his Guggenheim trip, and had occasionally seen her and her brother, Robert McKee Hyde, and the other members of their party in Paris in June.

To SUSAN HYDE

Geneva, Switzerland

[August, 1930]

Dear Susan:

Thanks for your nice letter, and also for the hundred French francs. I won't call it a gift, since you say you owe it to me, and I'm not going to argue with such a nice girl about a little filthy lucre. I don't honestly remember the incident at all. Anyway, I've already changed it into twenty Swiss francs, and the drinks are on you: I'm sorry you can't be here to share them with me. I will take great care not to spend a cent of this windfall on Swiss food—it's all going into French wine. Swiss cooking has easily lived up to all that has been said about it: it is not bad; it is a great deal worse than that—it is so horribly dull that when you eat it, weariness and horror rushes over your soul, you chew meditatively and black despair overwhelms you; and when you have, as you almost always have, an accompaniment of grey, soggy sky and English spinsters, you want to curse God and die. God knows what they do to it, but unquestionably food takes on the colour of one's soul, and all the grey cloudy stuff these people have in their souls gets into their cooking. Things are brought to you in magnificent style, in great silver tureens, and the waiter bends reverently over you as he serves you: when this farce is enacted I burst into insane laughter and cry out: "What a travesty! God! God! God!" He pulls off the cover of a magnificent silver dish, and there lies a piece of boiled lake fish; with pride and exulting, he puts this dead white flabby corpse, still covered with its slimy skin, upon your plate; hot boiled fumes of dreary sudsiness come up from it, and meanwhile he tells you how good it is to-day: you taste it and your mouth is full of desolation and the delicious savor of old boiled flannel—and suddenly you know the man has. . . .

[A PAGE IS MISSING HERE]

Thanks again for your letter and the hundred francs: I did not need either to make me think of you (God! Wolfe! You're turning out to be a regular Frenchman!) but I thank you and send you my warmest and kindest greetings. Write me (old address) when you get time. I do not know how long I shall be over here: it depends on whether I get my work done.

The following cablegram was evidently sent by Wolfe in reply to a letter from Mrs. Bernstein in which she expressed great anxiety about his failure to write to her and threatened to sail immediately for Europe to find him unless he cabled that he was all right.

To ALINE BERNSTEIN

[Cablegram]

[Geneva]

[August 12 (?), 1930]

Let's help each other. Be fair. Remember I'm alone. Letter follows. Hotel Bellevue, Geneva, three days. Paris address thereafter.

The following letter to Mrs. Bernstein is evidently a fragmentary rough draft of the one Wolfe actually sent, since it was found among his own papers.

To ALINE BERNSTEIN

Grand Hotel Bellevue
Geneva

[August 12 (?), 1930]

Dear Aline:

I cabled you this afternoon and said that I would write, but I am unable to say very much to you. I have tried to write you, but the letter

I started had too much bitterness in it about our life together, and about your friends, so I destroyed it. I no longer want to say these things to you because they do no good, and most of them have been said before.

We have known each other for five years, I can never forget you, and I know that nothing else to equal my feeling for you in intensity and passion will ever happen to me. But we are now at the end of the rope. My life has been smashed by this thing, but I am going to see if I can get back on my feet again. There is just one thing ahead of me:—work. It remains to be seen if I still have it in me to do it. If I have not, then I am lost.

You have your work, you have your children, you have your friends and family. If you feel the agony about me that you say you feel in your letters and cables, I can only say that you should give yourself completely to those things that you have. A letter as short as this one is bound to seem harsh and brutal, but you know what I feel and that I gave everything in me to my love for you.

[THE LETTER BREAKS OFF UNFINISHED HERE, OR THE REMAINDER
OF IT HAS BEEN . LOST]

Wolfe sent the following letter to Frere-Reeves after reading two very unfavorable English reviews of Look Homeward, Angel: *one by Frank Swinnerton in* The London Evening News *for August 8, and one by Gerald Gould in* The London Observer *for August 17.*

To A. S. FRERE-REEVES

Geneva

August 18, 1930

Dear Frere:

Please accept my sympathy for the death of your dog: I think there is a kind of sorrow over the death of a fine animal that we do not feel for a person, although people would misunderstand this and think it bad. At any rate there's not much false about how a dog feels.

I left Montreux a week ago, but returned for baggage and mail a few days later and found a letter, a note, and some clippings. I read the Swinnerton review and also one in yesterday's *Observer*. There's not much I can say to you now: I'm pretty badly hit by these reviews, and also by some personal affairs, and I had rather write you later. I have stopped writing and want a little time to think things over. Please do not think I am belly-aching when I tell you that I had hoped for a better reception from the critics of these important English papers, and that I think some of them have been unfair and prejudiced.

As for you, please understand that my feeling will always be full of warmth and gratitude because of what you have done. You have been more than my publisher, you have been my friend, and I assure you that I think of your own disappointment over the book almost as much as of my own.

I have stopped all mail from Paris, but my address will continue to be The Guaranty Trust Co. Please write me there. I still intend to come to England to see you, but I am coming later when I've forgotten about this business, and the critics have stopped writing about it.

Meanwhile, dear Frere, I send you my kindest greetings, and I hope you are getting time for a holiday and for a rest.

The following fragment was found among Wolfe's own papers and was never mailed. It undoubtedly is part of the unfinished "Answer to Critics, Point by Point" which Wolfe mentions in his letter of September 9 to Frere-Reeves.

To A. S. FRERE-REEVES

Grand Hotel Bellevue
Geneva

[August, 1930]

. . . My whole position is simply this: I was a young fellow of twenty-six or twenty-seven and I wanted to write a book, and I wrote it. I realized the book had great imperfections, and I realize them more keenly now, but I thought then, and still do, that it had good things in it, and that it might find a kindly public who would value it, and believe in it, and hope I would go on. I had a fairly comprehensive idea of the writing being done in England and America, and without comparing myself in any way to any writer, I thought that if the work of these people was valued and respected I had a right to hope for some appreciation of mine: I thought then and I still think that I have something to say, but I am rapidly coming to the point where silence seems best. I have found out during the past year that a writer is an open target for anyone in the world who wants to throw a rotten egg—and he can do nothing about it. The most personal and insulting things may be said about his work and about him, and it must all be swallowed down as "unbiased criticism." Moreover, old ladies in Akron, Ohio, in Leeds, and in Georgia, or in New York and London, open up and call a man's book dull, clumsy, incoherent, of no interest whatever and not worth reading, but they will take two columns to say this which might be said in twenty words: what they really mean is that they think your book is foul, indecent, a menace to morals and established government, etc. This kind of hypocrisy makes you want to vomit. I have had every name in the library hurled at my head from Euripides to Ruby M. Ayres. It seems that I have "imitated" all of them—I shall some day be a circulating library on my own hook if I ever finish reading all the books I am supposed to have imitated. Joyce, Dreiser, and D. H. Lawrence are pitched at me most often, and very often together (the reason, of course, these three utterly different people are lumped together, particularly Joyce and Lawrence—could two writers be *more* unlike?—is that the reviewer feels that they are very "free"—that is to say "sex, you know"—that is to say, "bordering on the salacious"—that is to say "dirty.")

Any work therefore that uses the word *"shit"* is stolen from Rabelais, and any work in which a man goes to bed with a woman, or in which the sexual act is mentioned, is obviously inspired by the good old team of "Joyce and Lawrence." Now, as to my own book, I own up to the Joyce— I read the works of that talented gentleman very assiduously and if some flavour of them has crept into my book I can not deny it: but as to Lawrence, I had read nothing of his until I finished the book except "The Captain's Doll," a short piece, and not I think sufficient to make of me the devoted disciple the reviewers would have me be. As to "Moby Dick," I read that magnificent work for the first time about six months ago in America in order to understand something about this man Melville that I had been imitating. I'm afraid these simple facts would not convince the reviewers, they would smile in a superior way and say that all this didn't matter at all, that I had soaked up "influences" from the atmosphere without knowing it, etc. God! it makes you long for the desert, Swiss cooking, lake fish—anything to bring oblivion.

Now for Dr Swinnerton: his review starts out with a long preamble about "this generation." [1] It is true the quotation marks are his own—

---

[1] Swinnerton's review began: "A superior-minded reviewer said last year that a certain novel by an author of the 1884 vintage 'had no interest for this generation.' As the book subsequently sold largely, I assume that the reviewer was wrong, and that all he meant was that he did not like it himself. In the circumstances, I think it needs to be stated clearly that, although the youngest writers of to-day must often feel impatient with those of their elders who are better known and more successful than themselves, they have no right to feel as they do. . . . Those novelists who are to-day big enough to be shot at could not have survived if they had not possessed exceptional talent. To sneer at that talent is to be guilty of silliness. Silliness because 'this generation' will soon be attacked in turn."

he is quoting from "a superior-minded reviewer"—but by the time he gets ready to settle my hash, the reader feels that "this generation" is my own product, or the contribution of one of my co-conspirators. Now, in the first place, dear Frere, as I have told you in other letters, I am not very much concerned with "generations" at the present. I have lately had a very thorough soaking in "Ecclesiastes" and that remarkable man had the very strange idea that one generation is very like another: "One generation passeth away, and another generation cometh: but the earth abideth forever." This talk about "generations" seems to be most common among people of Swinnerton's "generation"—I don't know what his "generation" is—(you see, he's got me to doing it, too)—I had always felt he was still a fairly young man who had written a book called "Nocturne" that I read one time and thought very good—but now, since I have been put in my place and told where I belong, I suppose I shall have to imagine Mr. Swinnerton standing at the window of the Union Club, or whatever the English equivalent is, staring out with an apoplectic face and a quivering goatee at all the young fellows who are behaving indecently in the street just to shock him.

I have observed that the "this generation" business is prevalent both in America and England, but I think it is more prevalent in England. Perhaps it is the war, but these *older* people (they have themselves insisted on that age, remember) seem to think that the young people are banded together in some deliberate movement against their traditions. For example, Swinnerton says: "As for the work of the really young, how 'new' is it." (This 'new' business of course preys upon their mind.) "Is there new technique? Are there new ideas, new feelings about life? I shall be told 'yes,' but I do not agree."—He may be told "yes," but he will never be told "yes" by me—he will probably be told "yes" by this straw dummy he has created as a sparring partner in his article, and that he knocks down so frequently with such delightful ease. Wouldn't life be wonderful, Frere, if we could settle our opponents and justify our prejudices in this way—simply by creating a little dummy that we could flatten out on every occasion, crying: "You think you are pretty smart, don't you? (Bam!) You think you have something new to offer, don't you? (Biff!) Have you any new feelings about life? (Wham!) Do you think you can shock *us*? Do you think you're the only one who has ever been young? Do you think you can sneer at your elders? *I'll* show you! (Baff! Bam! Bing! Wham! Sock!)"

As far as I am concerned, I do not think I have any "new ideas" or "any new feelings about life." Perhaps this is a discreditable confession for a member of "the new generation" to make, but I have never understood that a man is compelled to create out of the fundamental and unchanging structure of life a reality that is not there. In "Ecclesiastes," in

"Job," and in "the Song of Solomon," I have this summer found magnificently expressed what I have myself been almost thirty years in finding:
I not only have nothing to add to what I found there, I even fall far short
of the wisdom in those poems, and I fall infinitely short of their beauty
and talent. Each man weaves out bloodily his own vision of life, in each
case the combination of experience may be somewhat different, but to
demand that it be "new," to call for some phantom and impossible
"originality," is insane. Swinnerton suggests that he is past forty—I suppose he was born along in the 80's. I was born in 1900, but I imagine
he came from his mother's womb in much the same way as I came from
mine, I suppose he has drawn his breath in much the same way as the rest
of us, and that the processes attending his decay, death, and dissolution
will be the same as it is for all men.

Swinnerton uses the words "glib," "superficial" and "pretentious" [2] in
his discussion of my book, but I think he might better have applied them
to his own review. I do not put much faith in the people who rely on the
word "pretentious"—it is simply a curse-word, a term of abuse, a word
wherewith we can ease ourselves of our prejudices; and I have noticed that
it is most often used by folk who pride themselves on "the quiet note,"
"urbanity," "restraint"—and all the things that have no part of your
magnificent literature. I have loved and honored your great poetry since I
was old enough to hold a book in my hands, but my dear Frere, I thank
God it was pretentious. At the present time you have Mr. Frank Swinnerton—you have better than that, I grant you—but you *had* Dickens, you had
Donne, you had Shakespeare, you had Coleridge, you had Pope, you had
Chaucer, you had Sterne and Fielding and Sam Johnson. A nice bloody
Goddamned lot of "quiet" "restrained" "urbane" bastards, weren't they?
In the name of Jesus, where has this horrible business of "quietness,"
"restraint"—the "steady, old man" school of literature come from? You had
Smollett and Defoe and "Moll Flanders," and now you have Squire Galsworthy with his quiet manly gulps. I don't say a word against *that* man
because Perkins tells me he's a fine fellow—but Good God! Frere, where
did this great English convention of *not having any emotions* come from?
No people in the world use the word "sentimental" so often as your people
do to-day, and no people in the world are so tainted with sentimentality.

[THE LETTER BREAKS OFF HERE]

[2] Swinnerton did not actually use the words "superficial" or "pretentious" in regard
to Wolfe. He did say: "Mr. Wolfe has a very dangerous fluency. He is almost glib,
particularly in his improvisations of bar-room scenes, domestic scenes in which a
ranting father performs mechanically, and scenes of coquetry; and to my mind he
is intolerable in his passages of ecstatic apostrophe. . . . The book is a great jumble
of good and bad. It is labored with adjectives and abverbs. . . . It is emotional
without feeling, crowded with violences and blasphemies, and to one reader appears
incoherent, not from strength or intensity, but from over-excited verbosity."

To JOHN HALL WHEELOCK

Grand Hotel Bellevue
Geneva

August 18, 1930

Dear Jack:

Thanks very much for your good letter. There is very little that I can say to you now except that (1) I have stopped writing and do not want ever to write again.

The place that I had found to stay—Montreux—did not remain private very long: (2) Fitzgerald told a woman in Paris where I was, and she cabled the news to America—I have had all kinds of letters and cables speaking of death and agony, from people who are perfectly well, and leading a comfortable and luxurious life among their friends at home. In addition, one of Mrs. Boyd's "young men" descended upon me, or upon Montreux, and began to pry around. This, of course, may be an accident, but too many accidents of this sort have happened.

(3) The English edition has been a catastrophe: some of the reviews were good, but some have said things that I shall never be able to forget—dirty, unfair, distorted, and full of mockery. I asked the publisher not to send any reviews but he did all the same—he even wrote a special letter to send a very bad one, from which he said he got no satisfaction. Nevertheless the book is selling fast and they continue to advertise. All I want now is money—enough to keep me until I get things straight again. It is amusing to see the flood of letters and telegrams I began to get from "old friends" who were "simply dying to see me" when the first good reviews came out in England—but it is even more amusing to see how the silence of death has settled upon these same people recently.—I want to vomit. I should like to vomit until the thought and memory of them is gone from me forever.

There is no life in this world worth living, there is no air worth breathing, there is nothing but agony and the drawing of the breath in nausea and labor, until I get the best of this tumult and sickness inside me. I have behaved all right since I came here: I have lived by myself for almost four months now and I have made no answers: people have charged me and my work with bombast, rant and noisiness—but save for this letter to you, I have lived alone, and held my tongue, and kept my peace: how many of them can say the same? What reward in the world can compensate the man who tries to create something? My book caused hate and rancor at home, venom and malice among literary tricksters in New York, and mockery and abuse over here. I hoped that that book, with all its imperfections, would mark a beginning: instead it has marked an ending.

Life is not worth the pounding I have taken both from public and private sources these last two years. But if there is some other life—and I am sure there is—I am going to find it. I am not thirty yet, and if these things have not devoured me, I shall find a way out yet. I have loved life and hated death, and I still do.

I have cut off all mail by wiring Paris, and I am going to stay alone for some time to come. I know that that is the only way. Write me if you can. The address is the Guaranty Trust Co., Paris. I hope this finds you well and that you get a good vacation.

To MAXWELL E. PERKINS

Geneva

August 18, 1930

Dear Mr. Perkins:

Will you please have Mr. Darrow [1] send me, at his convenience, a statement of whatever money is due me? I shall not write any more books, and since I must begin to make other plans for the future, I should like to know how much money I will have. I want to thank you and Scribners very sincerely for your kindness to me, and I shall hope someday to resume and continue a friendship which has meant a great deal to me.

I hope this finds you well, and entirely recovered from the trouble that took you to Baltimore. Please get a good vacation and a rest away from the heat and confusion of New York.

The following unfinished and unmailed letter to Maxwell Perkins was evidently written during Wolfe's period of depression in August, 1930— probably soon after his letter of August 18 from Geneva.

To MAXWELL E. PERKINS

Dear Mr. Perkins:

We create the figure of our father, and we create the figure of our enemy. The figure of my enemy I created years ago: he is a person, he has a name, he is an inferior thing, he has no talent, but I made of him my Opponent: it is this person who will always appear to cheat you of what you most desire: he is nothing; he has no life save that you gave him, but

---

[1] Whitney Darrow was at this time head of the Trade Department at Scribners and a Director of the firm. He was a Vice President of the firm from 1931–1953.

he is there to take all you want away from you. Thus, if you love a woman, and your Opponent is millions of people, thousands of miles away, he will come to trick her from you. He is there like a fate and a destiny. He is nothing, but he is all the horror and pain on earth. This has happened to me.

Where are you? Are you crawling out of it? Send me my money or send me my ticket home. Send me your friendship or send me your final disbelief. I will tell you this very plainly: I do not think I am a good venture for Chas. Scrib. Sons. I think I may be done for utterly. I think you may now get out of it profitably. If anything's left, send it to me, and break our pub. relations.

To A. S. FRERE-REEVES

Basel, Switzerland
September 9, 1930

Dear Frere:

I have been up in the air—literally: I have made my first flight by airplane and I think there's nothing like it to ease a distressed spirit. I left Geneva several weeks ago, flew to Lyons, stayed there or in that district for a week, then flew to Marseilles. From there I went to Arles and Provence. God! it was hot: the sweat made puddles in your ears when you tried to sleep. Then I flew back from Marseilles to Geneva where I found your telegram which made me feel better. Now I am here on my way to the Black Forest, and I shall write you a long letter there. I was unwinding an immensely long letter on you when I started my travels—an answer to critics, point by point, etc.[1]—but it will never get finished now, which is a good thing. While I was flying three thousand feet above the valley of the Rhone, I looked down and saw a little moving dot in one of the fields shovelling manure: it looked so much like a critic that I have not wanted to finish my letter since. Besides, the only thing a writer can do is to keep his mouth shut: I have discovered that once his book is published he is the target for what anyone in the world wants to say about him or his work, but I think he ought to hold his tongue and his peace.

At any rate, there's much to be thankful for—I no longer have to eat lake fish. I don't know whether I told you my new theory, but here it is. I no longer believe it is boiled flannel as you say. I think it is really lake fish—only they don't tell you what lake it is from. It is from the Lake of Galilee, and it is what was left over from that great catch 2000 years ago when our Lord Jesus Christ commanded his disciples to cast in their nets.

[1] The unmailed letter of August, 1930.

What do you think of this? Don't you think there is much to be said for it?

Basel is a very German town and there are some magnificent pictures here. I have written two or three shorter pieces and done a good deal on my book but I may finally come to England and try to finish it during the winter. I am a little tired of being alone, and I am sure that there are two or three people there who would let me see them from time to time. Your secretary wrote me (enclosing clippings) that you had gone to the South of France: I hope the trip did you good, and that this letter finds you well and happy. Thanks again for the telegram and all the other marks of kindness and good cheer. I am all right now, and hope to bring something to England with me that can be typed and shown to people.

The following notes were written on a page of Wolfe's small pocket notebook, and were never mailed. "Emily" was probably Emily MacRae, now Mrs. Benjamin C. West, who had known Wolfe in Asheville and New York. "Jack" was John Hall Wheelock. "Mr. Holzknecht" was probably Professor Karl J. Holzknecht of New York University who had written Wolfe some months earlier about the possibility of his talking to the English Club there, and who may have written further about this on August 3. The initials K.M.R.A.A. in the note to Ezra Pound are evidently an American version of the following passage from James Joyce's Ulysses:
                    " K. M. R. I. A.
    He can kiss my royal Irish arse, Myles
    Crawford cried loudly over his shoulder.
    Any time he likes tell him. "

NOTES WRITTEN IN THE BLACK FOREST

[Freiburg, Germany?]

[September, 1930]

Dear Mr. Perkins: I got your letter in Basel, Switzerland.
                    Yours,

Dear Emily: I got your note in Geneva, Switzerland.
                    Yours truly,

Dear Jack: I got your letter the other day. It is a fine letter. I wish I could answer it. I am all right now and will write you later.

Dear Mama: I died in Marseilles on Aug 22. I am buried in a good Christian Churchyard there and I hope you will come to see me.

Dear Mr. Holzknecht: Thanks for your letter of Aug 3.
                Y'rs Tr'ly

To Mr. Ezra P'd.
Dear Mr. P'd: I r'd a p'm of y'rs once. K.M.R.A.A.
                Y'rs Tr'ly

To MAXWELL E. PERKINS
[Radiogram]

Freiburg, Germany
September 13, 1930

Working again. Excuse letter. Writing you.

The following letter was never sent to Henry T. Volkening but was found among Wolfe's papers. Instead Wolfe wrote him a briefer and more restrained letter on September 22, which was less revealing and has therefore been omitted here.

To HENRY T. VOLKENING

Hotel Freiburger Hof
Freiburg, Germany
[September, 1930]

Dear Henry:

Please forgive me for having made you such a poor return for your fine letters. I haven't been too busy to write . . . I have two very long unfinished letters to you stuffed in among my junk: the reason I didn't send them was that I couldn't finish them—they would have each been ten million words long, and then I should not have been able to tell you about it. . . . The only way I'll ever be able to tell you about these last four months, Henry, is to talk to (not *with*) you, and I long to do this, although I do not know how long it will be before I have that happiness. You must prepare yourself for the ordeal in whatever far off future: clasp a bottle of your bootlegger's finest brew in your right hand and endure until the tidal wave shall have spent its force.

I am at length in the Black Forest. I arrived here a few days ago by a kind of intuition—the inside of me was like a Black Forest and I think the name kept having its unconscious effect on me. It is a very beautiful place —a landscape of rich, dark melancholy, a place with a Gothic soul, and I am glad that I have come here. These people, with all that is bestial, savage, supernatural, and also all that is rich, profound, kindly and simple, move me more deeply than I can tell you. France at the present time has completely ceased to give me anything. That is no doubt my fault, but their books, their art, their cities, their people, their conversation—nothing but their food at the present time means anything to me. The Americans in Paris would probably sneer at this—I mean these Americans who know all about it and are perfectly sure what French literature and French civilization stand for, although they read no French books, speak little of the language, and are never alone with French people.

I cannot tell you much at present about these last four months: I will tell you that I have had some of the worst moments of my life during them, and also some of the best. All told, it has been a pretty hard time, but I am going to be all right now. I don't know if you have ever stayed by yourself for so long a time (few people have and I do not recommend it) but if you are at all a thoughtful person, you are bound to come out of it with some of your basic ore—you'll sweat it out of your brain and heart and spirit. The thing I have done is one of the cruelest forms of surgery in the world, but I knew that for me it was right. I can give you some idea of the way I have cut myself off from people I knew when I tell you that only once in the past six weeks have I seen anyone I knew—that was Mr. F. Scott Fitzgerald, the master of the human heart, and I came upon him unavoidably in Geneva a week or two ago.

I can tell you briefly what my movements have been: I went to Paris from New York and, outside of a short trip to Rouen and a few places near Paris, I stayed there for almost two months. I think this was the worst time of all: I was in a kind of stupor and unfit to see anyone, but I ran into people I knew from time to time and went to dinner or the theatre with them. My publisher came over from England and was very kind—he is a very fine fellow—he took me out and I met some of the celebrities—Mr. Michael Arlen and some of the Left Bank People. This lasted little over a day: I was no good with people and I did not go back to see them. I began to work out of desperation in that noisy, sultry, uncomfortable city of Paris and I got a good deal done. Finally I got out of it and went to Switzerland. I found a very quiet, comfortable hotel in Montreux; I had a good room with a balcony over-looking the lake; and in the weeks that followed I got a great deal accomplished.

I knew no one here at all—the place was filled with itinerant English and American spinsters buying postcards of the Lake of Geneva—but one night I ran into the aforesaid Mr. Fitzgerald, your old time college pal and fellow-Princetonian.[1] I had written Mr. F. a note in Paris, because Perkins is very fond of him and told me for all his faults he's a fine fellow, and Mr. F. had had me to his sumptuous apartment near the Bois for lunch and three or four gallons of wine, cognac, whiskey, etc. I finally departed from his company at ten that night in the Ritz Bar where he was entirely surrounded by Princeton boys, all nineteen years old, all drunk, and all half-raw. He was carrying on a spirited conversation with them about why Joe Zinzendorff did not get taken into the Triple-Gazzaza Club: I heard one of the lads say "Joe's a good boy, Scotty, but you know he's a fellow that ain't got much background."—I thought it was time for Wolfe to depart, and I did.

I had not seen Mr. F. since that evening until I ran into him at the Casino at Montreux. That was the beginning of the end of my stay at that beautiful spot. I must explain to you that Mr. F. had discovered the day I saw him in Paris that I knew a very notorious young lady, now resident in Paris getting her second divorce, and by her first marriage connected with one of those famous American families who cheated drunken Indians out of their furs seventy years ago, and are thus at the top of the established aristocracy now. Mr. F. immediately broke out in a sweat on finding I knew the lady and damned near broke his neck getting around there: he insisted that I come ("Every writer," this great philosopher said, "is a social climber.") and when I told him very positively I would not go to see the lady, this poet of the passions at once began to see all the elements of a romance—the cruel and dissolute society beauty playing with the tortured heart of the sensitive young writer, etc.: he eagerly demanded my reasons for staying away. I told him the lady had cabled to America for my address, had written me a half dozen notes and sent her servants to my hotel when I first came to Paris, and that, having been told of her kind heart, I gratefully accepted her hospitality and went to her apartment for lunch, returned once or twice, and found that I was being paraded before a crowd of worthless people, palmed off as someone who was madly in love with her, and exhibited with a young French soda jerker with greased hair who was on her payroll, and who, she boasted to me, slept with her every night. ("I like his bod-dy," she hoarsely whispered, "I must have some bod-dy whose bod-dy I like to sleep with," etc.)

The end finally came when she began to call me at my hotel in the morning, saying she had had four pipes of opium the night before and was "all shot to pieces," and what in God's name would she do: she had not seen Raymond or Roland or Louis or whatever his name was for

---

[1] Volkening went to Princeton six years after Fitzgerald and did not know him, but says that Wolfe always persisted in lumping them together as Princeton men.

four hours; he had disappeared; she was sure something had happened to him; that I must do something at once; that I was such a comfort she was coming to the hotel at once; I must hold her hand, etc. It was too much. I didn't care whether Louis had been absent three or thirty hours, or whether she had smoked four or forty pipes, since nothing ever happens to these people anyhow—they make a show of recklessness but they take excellent care they don't get hurt in the end—and for a man trying very hard to save his own life, I did not think it wise to try to live for these other people and let them feed upon me.

So I told Mr. F., the great analyst of the soul, to tell the woman nothing about me, to give no information at all about me or what I was doing, or where I was. I told him this in Paris, I told him again in Switzerland, and on both occasions the man got to her as fast as he could. That ended Montreux for me. She immediately sent all the information back to America—and the heart-rending letters, cables, etc., with threats of coming to find me, going mad, dying, etc. began to come directly to my hotel. I wanted to batter the walls down. The hotel people, who had been very kind to me, charged me three francs extra because I had brought a bottle of wine from outside into the hotel. (They have a right in Switzerland to do this), but I took my rage out on them, told them I was leaving next day, went on a spree, broke windows, plumbing fixtures, etc. in the town, and came back to the hotel at 2 A.M., pounded on the door of the director and on the doors of two English spinsters, rushed howling with laughter up and down the halls, cursing and singing—and in short, *had* to leave.

I went to Geneva where I stayed a week or so. Meanwhile my book came out in England. I wrote beforehand and asked the publisher not to send reviews because I was working on the new one and did not want to be bothered: he wrote back a very jubilant letter and said the book was a big success and said "Read these reviews—you have nothing to be afraid of." I read them; they were very fine; I got in a state of great excitement. He sent me great batches of reviews then—most of them very good ones, some bad. I foolishly read them and got in a very excited condition about a book I should have left behind me months ago. On top of this, and the cables and letters from New York, I got in Geneva two very bad reviews —cruel, unfair, bitterly personal. I was fed up with everything: I wrote Perkins a brief note telling him good-bye, please send my money, I would never write again, etc; I wrote the English publisher another; I cut off all mail by telegraph to Paris; I packed up, rushed to the aviation field and took the first airplane, which happened to be going to Lyons. . . .

It was a grand trip, lasted three weeks, and did me an infinite amount of good. All the time I scrawled, wrote, scribbled. I have written a great deal—my book is one immense long book made up of four average-sized ones, each complete in itself, but each part of the whole. I stayed in Geneva one day and of course Mr. F. was on the job, although he had been at Vevey and then at Caux. His wife, he says, has been very near madness in a sanatorium at Geneva, but is now getting better. (It turned out that she was a good half hour by fast train from Geneva.) When I told him I was leaving Geneva and coming to the Black Forest, he immediately decided to return to Caux. I was with him the night before I left Geneva; he got very drunk and bitter; he wanted me to go and stay with his friends Dorothy Parker and some people named Murphy [2] in Switzerland nearby. When I made no answer to this invitation, he was quite annoyed; said that I got away from people because I was afraid of them, etc. (which is quite true, and which I think, in view of my experiences with Mr. F. et al, shows damned good sense. I wonder how long Mr. F. would last by himself, with no more Ritz Bar, no more Princeton boys, no more Mr. F.). At any rate, I came to Basel, and F. rode part way with me on his way back to Caux.

A final word about him: I am sorry I ever met him; he has caused me trouble and cost me time; but he has good stuff in him yet. His conduct to me was mixed with malice and generosity; he read my book and was very fine about it: then his bitterness began to qualify him: he is sterile and impotent and alcoholic now, and unable to finish his book, and I think he wanted to injure my own work. This is base, but the man has been up against it: he really loves his wife and I suppose helped get her into this terrible fix. I hold nothing against him now—of course he can't hurt me in the end—but I trusted him and I think he played a shabby trick by telling tales on me.

At any rate, I got over my dumps very quickly, sweated it out in Provence, and here I am, trying to finish up one section of the book before I leave here. I may go to England where Reeves, my publisher, assures me I can be quiet and work in peace: I like him immensely and there are also two or three other people there I can talk to. I have never been so full of writing in my life—if I can do the thing I want to, I believe it will be good.

I found a great batch of letters and telegrams when I got back from exile. Reeves was very upset by my letter and was wiring everywhere. He sent me a very wonderful letter: he said the book had had a magnificent reception and not to be a damned fool about a few reviews. And Perkins wrote me two wonderful letters—he is a grand man, and I believe in him with all my heart. All the others at Scribners have written me, and I am ashamed of my foolish letters and resolved not to let them down.

I know it's going to be all right now. I believe I'm out of the woods at last. Nobody is going to die on account of me; nobody is going to suffer any more than I have suffered: the force of these dire threats gets a little

[2] Mr. and Mrs. Gerald Murphy of New York.

weaker after a while, and I know now, no matter what anyone may ever say, that in one situation I have acted fairly and kept my head up. I am a little bitter at rich people at present: I am a little bitter at people who live in comfort and luxury, surrounded by friends and amusement, and yet are not willing to give an even chance to a young man living alone in a foreign country and trying to get work done. I did all that was asked of me; I came away here when I did not want to come; I have fought it out alone; and now I am done with it. I do not think it will be possible for me to live in New York for a year or two, and when I come back I may go elsewhere to live. As for the incredible passion that possessed me when I was twenty-five years old and that brought me to madness and, I think, almost to destruction—that is over: that fire can never be kindled again.

[THE LETTER BREAKS OFF HERE]

To HENRY T. VOLKENING

[POSTCARD: ST. JEAN ET LA SAINTE VIERGE: DETAIL FROM THE
CRUCIFIXION PANEL OF THE ISENTHEIMER ALTAR OF
MATHIAS GRUNEWALD]

Colmar, Alsace Lorraine

[September 23, 1930]

Dear Henry: This is one of the greatest men in the world. You've no idea how beautiful the whole thing is (it is immense—this is only a small part) until you see it.

VII

LONDON, AND WORK ON OF TIME AND THE RIVER
AND THE OCTOBER FAIR

1930–1931

To A. S. FRERE-REEVES

Paris

September 27, 1930

Dear Frere:

Thanks for your letter. I am coming to England the first part of next week (about Tuesday, I think). Of course I shall be delighted to go down to your place in the country for a day or two: it is most kind of you to ask me, and I am looking forward to it. I think I shall go to London for a day or two in order to get the feel of England once more (it has been over three years since I was there) and to get some much-needed repairs made upon my wardrobe. If I am going to visit an English gentleman on his country estate, I ought to get patched up in the places that show.

Please forgive me for being so skittish about the book. I am prepared to talk on almost any subject under the sun—the German elections, the weather, the cathedral at Strasbourg—but I hope to God I do not hear about the book at present. I am a burden and a care to you but be patient with me a little and I shall do better.

The weather here is most dismal—where in God's name did that superstition ever come from about the beautiful weather of Paris? The London climate is universally condemned, but of the two I think it is perhaps the better.

I think I shall go to a hotel in Russell Square, and I'll phone you or send you a telegram from there. Meanwhile, good luck and God bless you.

To MAXWELL E. PERKINS
[Cablegram]

London
October 14, 1930.

Established small flat here alone in house.[1] Old woman looking after me. Seeing no one. Believe book finally coming. Excited. Too early to say. Letter follows.

The next letter to Perkins was written from London in October, but was never finished and never mailed.

To MAXWELL E. PERKINS

[London]
[October, 1930]

Dear Mr. Perkins:

I did not know how long it had been since I had written you, or sent that cable from the Black Forest, until I got your cable [1] the other day. When you are alone for a long period, Time begins to make an unreal sound, and all the events of your life, past and present, are telescoped: you wake in the morning in a foreign land thinking of home, and at night in your sleep you hear voices of people you knew years ago, or sounds of the streets in America. The changes in time also help this feeling of unreality. I am writing you this at ten o'clock at night in London, for a moment I think of what you may be doing at the same time at ten o'clock, and then I realize it is only five o'clock in New York, and that you are probably at Scribners just before going home.

I think of you a dozen times a day, and I think all of you are in my mind like a [sack (?)] of living radium deposit, whether I am consciously thinking of you or not. My longing for America amounts to a constant ache: I can feel it inside me all the time like some terrible hunger that can not be appeased. It will always be the same: the other night, after listening to miles and miles of the silliest talk by English people about America —it was not a nation but a raw mass of different peoples; Americans were incapable of real feeling, only sentimentality; the country was a matriarchy, the women ruled it; the Americans were incapable of love, with all the rest of it, including the machine age, Puritanism, Rotarians, etc.—I

[1] Frere-Reeves had found Wolfe a flat at 15 Ebury Street.
[1] A cable sent on October 8 which said: "How are you. Please write."

could listen to no more of it and I told them, I think without passion and I know with utter conviction on my part, that to anyone who had ever known America as I have known it, no life in Europe, no life anywhere, can ever seem very interesting. It surprised and angered them, for they saw I meant it, and they had never expected to hear anything like this. People here, specially Mr. Reeves at Heinemann, have been very kind to me. I have not done much going out, but I get a good many invitations.

I am resuming here after several days—it has become for some reason terribly difficult for me to write letters: the more I am away from home, the more I miss seeing a few people, the harder it seems to write to them—it has always been this way. I think the reason is that I have really got started at length, I stay alone in my place here a great deal (I will tell you about it later), I go through periods of the most horrible depression, weariness of spirit, loneliness and despair, but then I think about the book for long stretches and work on it. Only, in God's name, is there not some way to find peace and kindliness in this world, to do one's work without paying so bitterly for human relations!

I have cut almost everything away from me, and if I do not get my work done now I do not know what I shall do: there is nothing else left for me—surely to God it does not have to be made so cruelly and needlessly difficult. I must now tell you plainly certain things—much more plainly than I have ever been able to tell them to you in person, but if I can not tell them to you, who in God's name am I to talk to? I shall try never to cause you any distress or embarrassment—my great fear now is that I will cause you disappointment by failure to do the work you expect me to do. I must tell you now very plainly that you occupy an immense place in my belief and affection:—please do not think I am exaggerating, and please do not be at all embarrassed by this statement—I think it is very unfair to you for me to feel this way, I have no right to place the burden of this feeling on any man, but I think you have become for me a symbol of that outer strength. . . .

[THE LETTER BREAKS OFF UNFINISHED HERE]

To MAXWELL E. PERKINS

The Guaranty Trust Co.
London

October 27, 1930

Dear Mr. Perkins:

I am writing you a separate letter telling you what there is to be told at present about myself: this concerns another matter. Two . . . New

York dentists are trying to extort $525 from me for two weeks unsatisfactory work. I left instructions with Mr. Darrow to pay them, but fortunately told him not to go beyond $200 which I thought would leave a big surplus. Now these dentists are threatening ominous things if I do not pay in full at once. I have written them courteously telling them I have not money enough to pay such a bill, and have never had. (One of them had just come back from his vacation when I left, business was bad, I think he intended me to pay for it.) In letters to Mr. Darrow they are *threatening* to "put the matter in the hands of their Paris representative"—why Paris, I don't know: I don't live there and have no connection there. I am assured here in London that they can touch nothing in Europe—letter of credit, personal belongings.

Now I have been worried enough. I am not trying to avoid payment of my just debt, but I tell you this thing is an abomination: one man has charged $285 for seeing me five times and doing an unsatisfactory piece of work. If I have any money in America—i.e. at Scribners—I want it to be protected against these people by any means possible. I do not know the law, but I know that I have the right to dispose of my money as I see fit and I am therefore sending you a separate statement in which I make over to you any money that is due me. These people are trying to get money from me that I cannot afford to lose. I left enough to pay them amply, the thing is a cheat. Let's don't let them do it: please get my money made over to you if that is necessary to protect it—you could let me have it as I need it, I would not bother you, but they would not be able to touch it. I wish to God I could have a little peace. I am writing you a long letter. I shall finish that book, so help me God, and if agony and loneliness can make a book, it will be good. You are the only person in the world that I can turn to—I am a solitary and an exile. People in comfortable homes surrounded by friends, may sneer, but it's the simple God's truth! The weather here is like a sodden blanket of wet grey; misery is on the faces of the poor; the King opened Parliament today; there is only one thrilling and interesting place in the world—and that is America: but I am not cast down, and I will do the book, only *now, now,* is the time they must not bother me. I am writing you a long letter—I cannot begin to tell you how I miss seeing you, it is unfair to make you the goat this way.

On October 23, 1930, Sinclair Lewis had written to Wolfe: "Dear Thomas Wolfe: I wish there hadn't been quite so many brisk blurb-writers these past twenty years, using up every once respectable phrase of literary criticism, so that I might have some fresh phrase with which to express my profound delight in Look Homeward, Angel! *There is, you needn't be told, authentic greatness in it. It and* Farewell to Arms *seem to me to have more spacious*

power in them than any books for years, American OR foreign. . . . God,
your book is good!"

While this letter was on its way to Wolfe in London, Lewis was awarded
the Nobel Prize for Literature for 1930, and in an interview in the New
York Times *on November 6, again expressed his admiration for* Look Homeward, Angel, *saying: "If Mr. Wolfe keeps up the standard which he has set
in this work, he may have a chance to be the greatest American writer. In
fact, I don't see why he should not be one of the greatest world writers. His
first book is so deep and spacious that it deals with the whole of life."*

*The following fragmentary letter, found among Wolfe's own papers, is
evidently a rough draft of the one which he wrote to thank Lewis.*

To SINCLAIR LEWIS

[London]

[November, 1930]

Dear Mr. Lewis:

Thanks for your letter. I am honored and deeply grateful for what you
said about my book—it is a most generous thing and I will never forget it.
I have read your books since I was twenty: I think you are a man of
genius with the most enormous talent for writing—I am sure very few
people of my age in America have escaped your influence, and certainly I
have not. In view of some of the books I may write, you may not care to
have this crime laid upon you, but there it is.

Your letter came just a few days after we got the news here of your
winning the Nobel Prize: I was happy to hear of it, and. . . .

[THE REMAINDER OF THIS PAGE IS MISSING]

I have got a little flat here and an old woman who looks after it and
cooks for me—the whole thing for three pounds ten a week. I am really at
work every day, and think it is coming now. Sometimes I get homesick as
hell for America—this is honest God's truth, although I have spent half
my time over here for several years. I want to live at home now but I
think New York is out of it. It will be good to get home again and get a
drink of real liquor—this bootleg stuff over here is not worth a damn. I
hope you like it there in Westport—I went there once and thought it was
a beautiful place: the air has a bite and sparkle to it, it is not this wet
wooly stuff they have here at this season.

When I get back to America, I hope

[THE REMAINDER OF THE LETTER IS MISSING]

To ALFRED S. DASHIELL

The Guaranty Trust Co.
50 Pall Mall
London

[November, 1930]

Dear Fritz:

Please forgive me for not having answered your fine long letter before. I have done very little letter writing of any sort to anyone for some time: at one time I wanted to take my pen in hand and "tell you all about it," but telling you all about it seems such a long and complicated business just now that I must wait until I see you, and then I hope they are still running that German place and that I can talk eloquently until I see signs of fatigue and care on your face.

I have been here in this great cit-ee for about two months. I have a bally little digs on Ebury Street (hyah, hyah!) and for over five weeks I have been working like the son-of-a-bitch many charming but misguided bastards consider me. November—lovely London November—soft, wet, woolly, steamy, screamy, shitty November—is here: if you have ever contemplated horror and weariness, if you have ever thought of such jolly subjects as misery, damnation, and death, if you have ever wanted to curse God and die, you have really known nothing but a spirit of rollicking comedy, a child's happy prattle—you have not known London in November. You draw your breath in agony and despair, you walk the leaden air as if you were forcing your way step by step through a ponderous, resisting, and soul-destroying mush: it soaks into your skin, your legs, your bowels, it gets into your heart, it is a grey mucousy substance in which you smother in ennui and dull horror as if you are slowly drawing in some ocean of obscene and unspeakable substance. If, in addition to this, you are invited to a Sunday afternoon tea in a detached "villa" belonging to a literary architect in St. John's Wood, a gent who has written a novel that was well spoken of, and who wears grey-looking glasses on his grey-looking face, if you meet there his wife who also has glasses and a grey face, and their little child, also with glasses, if you drink the weak tea and eat the cold Sunday night lamb, if you hear Mama telling the infant the quaintest, cunningest bedtime story all about a character named Oyjee-Boyjee—Mama invented him and each night he must do the *very dullest* thing you can think of ("It's really awfully hard," Mama said, "to think of a dull thing every night!"—to which I made no reply)—if, I say, you have gone through this, and talked about art and life by the cheerful fumes of the gas burner by which London warms itself, if you have sat in the parlour reeking with its gravedamp chill, if then you go out in the steaming air into a street of villas, catch your bus, and ride home through vast areas of drab brick, lightened by an occasional pub in which you see a few sodden wretches mournfully ruminant over a glass of bitter beer— if you have gone through this, then, my boy, you will smite your brow, and rend your flesh to see the blood come, and cry, "O woe is me! O misery!" and your guts will ache with passion for the Happy Land, the beautiful glorious country with the bright Sunday evening wink of the Chop Suey signs, the roar of the elevated, the sounds of the radio, the homelike jolly glow of the delicatessen stores, and the peaceful noise of millions of Jews in the Bronx slowly turning the 237 pages of the *New York Sunday Times*. Thank God you live in the beautiful and interesting place where all these things are accessible; and also thank God for the great sounds that roar across America, the howl and sighing at the eaves, the lash and din of it at the corners, the bite and sparkle of the air, the sharp color of October, the baying of the great boats in the harbor, the thunder of the great trains in the night, the exulting and joy that grips your guts and makes you cry out—and when you see some bastard who tells you lies about Europe, and worse lies about America, when you see some fool who wants to leave the most interesting and glorious place on earth to live here—remember what I have told you: spit in his face—no, piss on him instead, for the carcass of such a lying degenerate must not be dignified by spittle from the lips of an honest man.

I have been shy and silent before these liars and fools far too long. I have eaten crow and swallowed my pride for ten years before the waste-landers, the lost generationers, the bitter-bitters, the futility people, and all other cheap literary fakes sicklied o'er with a pale coat of steer-shit— but now I will hold my tongue no longer: I know what I know, and I have learned it with blood and sweat. I have lived alone in a foreign land until I could not sleep for thinking of the sights and sounds and colors, the whole intolerable memory of America, its violence, savagery, immensity, beauty, ugliness, and glory—and I tell you I know it as if it were my child, as if it had been distilled from my blood and marrow: I know it from the look and smell of the railway ties to the thousand sounds and odours of the wilderness—and I tell you I had rather have ten years more of life there than fifty years of Continental weak tea and smothering in this woolly and lethargic air, than a hundred years of shitty ex-patriotism. You have seen them in Paris sitting on their rumps around the café tables and pretending to know France and Europe: they know nothing, and as for the superior European "culture" some of them profess their love for, how many of them do you think give one good Goddamn for it? They do not know either Europe or France, their life is a vile cardboard affair, the French hate and despise them, and they know it—but they are like pimps who will endure slaps, insults, and mockery so long as they can have their whore. I tell you this "living abroad" business is bloody balls: I know something about Europe, I have gone alone and known some of the Europeans—at least I know more of their language, literature, and ways of living than most of our Paris friends—and I have heard all their stale jargon: that we are "not a country", that we are base and mean; that there is no glory, dignity, or beauty in our life; that we are Puritans, Babbitts, Rotarians, etc., etc.—but these people know nothing of anything, they have read it all in books, and they know less than nothing of America. I tell you we have got to live in our own country and be what we are, and that no one who has ever known and felt America can find living in Europe as interesting or beautiful.

I am certainly not bitter against Europe at the present time, and in spite of my violent attack on English dullness, I have an enormous liking and sympathy for them—they have been most kind and friendly this time. I do not go out often, but there are a few people I can go to see and talk to, which is a comfort after many months of being alone. There are also other blessings: I have the top two floors of a tiny little house on Ebury Street, it is nicely furnished, and I am completely alone in it at night; also I have a charwoman who cooks for me, brings her darling tea in his little beddy, coddles and coaxes him, and is in fact a perfect priceless damned Kohinoor—all, house, woman, etc. for £3.14s a week. I stay in from 6 o'clock on, read, eat the meal she has left for me, or cook one of my own, brew vast quantities of tea and coffee, and at midnight— the present hour—when all outside is quiet save for the massive footfalls of the bobby, and a few gay dogs reeling home from the American talkies—I set to work, and work, with time off for tea, coffee, or beer, until broad daybreak. Then I see life awaken in a London street, which is one of the nicest things I have seen: I see the light come on the yellow walls and the smoky brick: the milk wagon comes through with the milkman making a funny cry, and I hear the sound of a horse in the empty street— a sound that makes me think of a thousand mornings in American streets. Then the housemaids come out and scrub, the shops open, the noise begins. I light the "geyser," have a bottle, and go to bed, where my charwoman finds me, brings me tea and toast, all gossip to her pet about the movie she saw last night.

Farewell, dear Fritz. Someday, some far-off future day, Tommy is coming sailing home again, and then I will tell you all about it. There is no joy in the world comparable to the cessation of intolerable pain—sometimes I think that is what joy is, the way you feel, how beautiful and glorious life is, after the tooth stops aching—and that is what it will be like when I come home again. The most exultant, the most glorious, the most incredibly magnificent experience in the modern world is the voyage to America, and I pity the poor wretches who will never know it. If you speak of me to anyone, for God's sake do not communicate any of this letter to people who would use it to mock at and injure me: I mean the futility boys and girls, the stealthy lasses, the elegant mockers, the American T. S. Elioters. They are a low but vilely cunning lot of bastards and they will not see their cheap little stock in trade—I mean the what-is-the-use-we-are-a-doomed-generation, life-here-is-a-barren-desert, we-can-do-nothing—they will not see this little business cursed without a hissing and jeering retaliation. It is all they have, and even vermin will bare their teeth and bite if their stale cheese is menaced, even bawds and pimps will fight to protect the commerce of the drab who feeds them.

You know that I am no Pollyanna now, or that I think God's in his heaven. I don't, and I agree with Ecclesiastes that the saddest day of a man's life is the day of his birth—but after that, I think the next saddest day is the day of his death. I have had some bad times recently, but I think I shall always love life and hate death, and I believe that is an article of faith. The futility people hate life, and love death, and yet they will not die; and I loathe them for it. Observe carefully: you will find that the man who kills himself is almost always the man who loves life well. The futility people do not kill themselves; they wear rubbers and are afraid of colds. The waste-lander does not waste himself: it is the lover of life who wastes himself, who loves life so dearly that he will not hoard it, whose belief in life is so great that he will not save his own: I mean Christ and Coleridge and Socrates and Dostoievsky and Jeb Stuart and David Crockett. My! how the boys would snicker if they could hear that!

Goodbye for the present, Fritz. We'll drink beer again at Weber's some happy day, and we'll be a couple of damned tourists together, and we'll stand on the bridges of Paris at midnight again, and remember the voices of men in Virginia, and the smell of the tar in the streets. . . . Tell Max Perkins that I will really write him—if I could only say in a letter all I want to say to him!—and that I am really working, and sometimes I am full of joy and hope about it, and other times depression, but that I shall finish it (when, I don't know) and that it will have to have in it the things that are bursting in my heart and mind. Forgive this long and violent letter: I did not mean to write it myself when I started. Remember me to the folks at Scribners, and love again and good wishes to you and the family. I have Scotch blood in me, and often I see spooks: there is a happy land, there is a good life, and better times are coming for all men of good will.

To MAXWELL E. PERKINS

London

Tues., Dec. 9, 1930

Dear Mr. Perkins:

I am sure this is a bad year and that all the bad news is coming at once—there is only three weeks more of it, and then things, I know, will get better. For one thing, some time next year I hope to come home again and end this sometimes ghastly pain of homesickness. I am working like hell and I hope it will be worth something when I get it down.

Before I go on with the letter I want to get something off my mind: my family have suffered the most terrible calamities—they have simply been wiped out. Mabel and Ralph (that is my sister) have been sold out in Asheville, they have lost everything they had, every piece of property, every cent of money, and he has lost his job: they are at present living in Washington where he is trying to earn a $50 a week commission salary. My other sister's big family have been for the most part out of work, and my brother Fred has been struggling to keep them up. In addition, he has had to quit his job because there is no business. Things in the South are in a horrible hell of a shape, and the last calamity I read of was that the leading bank at Asheville, where I am afraid they had some money, has smashed. Now these people are too good and too proud to ask for anything—their letters have been full of courage and cheerfulness, but they are simply wiped out. Two or three months ago from Paris, when I thought my profits on the English publication were much greater than they turned out to be, I wrote Fred and told him for God's sake to let me know if he needed money and I would let him have what I could. He wrote me the other day and assured me none of them is in actual want for food or clothing—thank God for that! Then he asked me, if I really had the money, would I let him have $500 for a year. He sent along some damned document giving me security, 8% interest, etc.—of course, I won't have the damned thing, nor a penny's interest: I tore it up.

Mr. Perkins, I know it's a bad year for everyone, but *if I've got it there* at Scribners, or even if I haven't got it, for God's sake get that money for the boy, and I will work my fingers to the bone. If it comes to a question of these damned . . . dentists and my own people, *I want my people to have the money.* Please understand my people have not asked me for a damned penny, and my brother wrote me only when I had written him and assured him that I could spare the money and would not forgive him if they needed it and would not speak. At that time I thought I would have more—but no matter: if I am able to help these people now, it is a

Godsend for me, and if I don't do it, I shall regret it bitterly as long as I live. I think you understand how much joy it gives me to think I may be of a little help now in time of trouble—we have always stood together in trouble before, and I don't want to fail them now. There is no question about Fred paying me back someday—he would do that if he had to mortgage his right arm—but even if he never did, it would be all right and I don't want his damned notes or mortgages or interest. He has never asked me nor anyone else for anything before, and he has got everybody's burden on him now. I know he would not ask unless he were hard pressed. I wrote him the other day and told him not to worry, that I could afford it and it wouldn't pinch me, and that I would get you to send him $500.— *Please* do this for me, and I will make it up to you somehow: I'm a young man and I have never failed anyone yet to whom I was indebted. . . .

Now don't get worried and think I'm going to flop on you and be a sponge—I'll make this $500 up to you in extra work and sweat: I can't promise to write a good or a great book or even one that will sell, but if that fails, I'll make it up to you in some other way. There's money in me somewhere if I'm put to it—I've always believed I could make it if I had to. I want you to know this: I believe I have acted decently and honestly to everyone—certainly I have tried to—if you hear scurrilous and slanderous stories about me, about any action of mine, about anything to do with me, spread by any of the ten million envenomed and reptilian ——— ———s who walk the streets of this earth full of hate, malice, and poison, put them down as lies. I have been in a hell of a jam this last year or so, and during the last six or eight months I have sweated out blood and agony—but *I have behaved all right:* I have done what I thought I had to do, and what people asked me to do, I have never betrayed or deserted anyone—in the end, if anyone gets betrayed or deserted it will be me. I have done the best I could, I have done some things badly, but please understand that I have behaved all right: if anyone thinks I have not, let him come forward and say so to my face—otherwise let them hold their tongues in fairness, and someday they will know I have been square. You know me much better now than any of these people, you know what a nest of lies and venom New York is, for God's sake make any judgment or opinion on me for yourself, and out of our own relation. You are my friend, and one of the two or three people that I would not let anyone in the world say a word against, so until I get back at least, don't listen to opinions and judgments from people who don't know a God-damned thing about me, whether Scott Fitzgerald, ———, or anyone else. Please don't be alarmed at all this, or think I've gone suddenly mad—there's so much I want to say to you and so little I can say in a letter that part of it comes in convulsions and bursts.

I seem to have to spend a maddening amount of time talking about dentists, and making foolish answers. I should like to tell you about the book, but I'll have to write another letter. But here is the title, at any rate, and it seems to me to be a good and beautiful title and to say what I want it to say—if anything about it puzzles you, I'll try to interpret all of it for you next time. Here it is:

"THE OCTOBER FAIR"

or

"Time and The River : A Vision:"

The Son, The Lover, and The Wanderer;
The Child, The Mistress, and The Woman;
The Sea, The City, and The Earth.

"One generation passeth away, and
another generation cometh; but the earth
abideth for ever."

For title page:

Part One

"A N T A E U S"

"Who knowth the spirit of man that goeth upward, and
the spirit of the beast that goeth downward to the earth?"—

(If this *Argument* seems bad or inadvisable we won't use it. It gives a kind of key.)

Argument: of the Libyan giant, the brother of Polyphemus, the one-eyed, and the son of Gaea and Poseidon, whom he hath never seen, and through his father, the grandson of Cronos and Rhea, whom he remembereth. He contendeth with all who seek to pass him by, he searcheth alway for his father, he crieth out: "Art thou my father? Is it thou?" And he wrestleth with that man, and he riseth from each fall with strength redoubled, for his strength cometh up out of the earth, which is his mother. Then cometh against him Heracles, who contendeth with him, who discovereth the secret of his strength, who lifteth him from the earth whence his might ariseth, and subdueth him. But from afar now, in his agony, he heareth the sound of his father's foot: he will be saved for his father cometh!

Now, don't get alarmed at all this and think I'm writing a Greek myth. All of this is never mentioned once the story gets under way, but it is a magnificent fable, and I have soaked myself in it over a year now: it says what I want to say, and it gives the most magnificent plot and unity to my book. The only other way in which the Antaeus legend is mentioned directly is in the titles to the various parts which are tentatively, at present (1) "Antaeus," (2) "Heracles," (or "Faust and Helen"), (3) "Poseidon."

To give you the key to all these symbols and people:—Antaeus of course, is a real person; he is in me but he is *not* me as the fellow in the first book was supposed to be; he is to me what Hamlet or Faust may have been to their authors. Thank God, I have begun to create in the way I want to—it is more completely *autobiographic* than anything I have ever thought of, much *more* than the first one, but it is also completely *fictitious*. Nobody can identify me with Antaeus—whose real name is David Hawke, but who is called Monkey Hawke—except to say, "He has put himself into this character." It is a magnificent story, it makes use of all the things I have seen and known about, and it is like a fable.

The other symbols are: Heracles, who is the City; Poseidon, who is the Sea, eternal wandering, eternal change, eternal movement—but who is also a real person (*never* called Poseidon) of course, the father of Monkey Hawke, whom he has never seen, and whom, I have decided he shall never see, but who is near him at the end of the book, and who saves him (the idea that hangs over the book from first to last is that every man is searching for his father). It is immensely long, I am bringing the Antaeus (which has two parts) back home with me and parts of the second—the City scenes are already written.

The woman in various forms, at different times, is Gaea, Helen, or Demeter—but these things are never told you, and the story itself is direct and simple, given shape by this legend, and by the idea I told you. But it is also tremendously varied—it gives the histories of my people and it reconstructs old time. The idea of time, the lost and forgotten moments of people's lives, the strange brown light of old time (i.e.—America, say, in 1893: photographs of people coming across Brooklyn Bridge, the ships of the Hamburg American Packet Co, baseball players with moustaches, men coming home to lunch at noon in small towns, red barns, old circus posters and many other phases of time) is over all the book.

I'd like to tell you of a chapter I'm now writing in the Second part of "Antaeus"—the chapter is called "Cronos and Rhea" (or perhaps simply "Time and the River"—that means "Memory and Change"). My conviction is that a native has the whole consciousness of his people and nation in him; that he knows everything about it, every sight sound and memory of the people. Don't get worried: I think this is going to be all right. You see, I *know* now past any denial, that *that* is what being an American or being anything means: it is not a government, or the Revolutionary War, or the Monroe Doctrine—it is the ten million seconds and moments of your life, the shapes you see, the sounds you hear, the food you eat, the colour and texture of the earth you live on. I tell you *this* is what it is, and this is what homesickness is, and by God I'm the world's champion authority on the subject at present.

"Cronos and Rhea" occurs on board an Atlantic liner—all the Americans returning home—and the whole intolerable memory of exile and nostalgia comes with it. It begins like a chant—first the smashing enormous music of the American names: [1] first the names of the States: California, Texas, Oregon, Nebraska, Idaho, and the Two Dakotas; then the names of the Indian tribes: the Pawnees, the Cherokees, the Seminoles, the Penobscots, the Tuscaroras, etc.; then the names of railways: the Pennsylvania, the Baltimore and Ohio, the Great Northwestern, the Rock Island, the Santa Fe, etc.; then the names of the railway millionaires: the Vanderbilts, the Astors, the Harrimans; then the names of the great hoboes: Oakland Red, Fargo Pete, Dixie Joe, Iron Mike, Nigger Dick, the Jersey Dutchman etc. (the names of some of the great wanderers i.e.); then the great names of the rivers (the rivers and the sea standing for movement and wandering against the fixity of the earth):—the Monongahela, the Rappahannock, the Colorado, the Tennessee, the Rio Grande, the Missouri. When I get to the Mississippi, I start the first of the stories of wandering and return— the woman floating down the river with her husband in flood time tells it. It is good—the whole thing is this pattern of memory and [neuroticism?] —don't get alarmed. I think it's all right and fits in perfectly, I have plenty of straight story anyway.

I have told you too much and too little. I have had to scrawl this down and haven't time to explain dozens of things—but please don't be worried —it's not anarchy, it's a perfectly unified but enormous plan. I want to write again and tell you some more, expecially about the last scene in "Poseidon." It is the only fabulous scene in the book. He never sees his father but he hears the sound of his foot, the thunder of horses on a beach (Poseidon and his horses); the moon [dives] out of clouds; he sees a print of a foot that can belong only to his father since it is like his own; the sea surges across the beach and erases the print; he cries out "Father" and from the sea far out, and faint upon the wind, a great voice answers "My Son!" That is briefly the end as I see it—but can't tell you anything about it now. The rest of the story is natural and wrought out of human

---

[1] This is a portion of "The Names of the Nation" which was published in the December, 1934, issue of *The Modern Monthly*, and appears in *Of Time and the River* on pages 861–870.

experience. Polyphemus, by the way, the one-eyed brother of Antaeus, represents the principle of sterility that hates life—i.e. waste-landerism, futility-ism, one-eyed-ism (also a character in the book).

I don't know whether you can make anything out of this or not—it is 10:30 o'clock, I have worked all night—as I finish this on the morning of Tues Dec 9, there is a fog outside that you can cut, you can't see across the street, I am dog tired. I want to come home when I know I have this thing by the well known balls. Write me if you think it's a good idea, but say nothing to anyone.

I'm a week late with this letter. I don't want my brother to suffer—*please* Mr. Perkins send him $500 at once if you can—address *Fred W. Wolfe, 48 Spruce Street, Asheville, North Carolina*—get it to him before Christmas. I'm writing you about dentists—but don't pay them if my brother has to suffer.

I'm sending this out right away to be mailed. I hope this finds you well. I'd like to be able to see and talk to you.

Address again   Fred W. Wolfe
                48 Spruce St
                Asheville
                N. C.

Don't tell anyone about this letter. If I've talked foolishness I'd rather keep it between us—at ten in the morning after being up all night you're not sane.

Wolfe never completed or mailed the following letter to Mr. Perkins, but wrote and sent him a briefer version of it on January 9, 1931. Since this first unfinished letter is more revealing, it has been included here and the one of January 9th omitted.

To MAXWELL E. PERKINS

[London]
[December, 1930]

Dear Mr. Perkins:

I suppose you have by now an enormous letter I wrote you about two weeks ago—it was filled with work and woes: I want to write you this short one to tell you my plans and intentions. First, it is only three or four days before Christmas, I have the satisfaction of feeling completely exhausted with work for the moment: my mind is tired and I can not sleep very well. I am going to keep it up until Christmas, then I am going to Paris for four or five days, and I am going to do nothing but sleep, eat and drink the best food and wine I can get. Then I propose to come back here and work till I drop for about six weeks, until I know I can bring the first part in consecutive chapters or in draft back home. Then I propose taking third class on the fastest boat I can find—the *Bremen* or *Europa*—so that I'll be in New York in five or six days after sailing. Then I should like to proceed *immediately* (this is the hard part) to a place *where I can get to work again.*

I have told you that my new book is haunted throughout by the Idea of the river—of Time and Change. Well, so am I—and the thing that is eating at my entrails at present is when can I have this formidable work ready. You have been wonderful not saying anything about *time,* but I feel you would like to see something before next Fall. I don't make any promises but I'll try like hell: I am distressed at the time I spent over personal worries, excitement over the first one, and fiddling around, but it's no good crying about that now—I think this came as fast as it could: now I've got it all inside me, and much of it down on paper, but I must work like hell. The thing that is good for me is almost *total obscurity*— I love praise and flattery for my work, but there must be no more parties, no more going out. I must live in two rooms somewhere until I hate to leave them: I want to see you and one or two people, but I want to come back without seeing anyone in New York for several weeks *except you and one or two others:* don't think I'm talking through my hat, it's the only way I can do this piece of work and I must do it in this way.

Now about the place to work. This is a hell of a lot to ask you, but I don't want you to do it if you can get someone else to do it—try to help me if you can. I don't know whether it is good to live in New York now. My present obsession is that I am going within the next few years to get married and live somewhere in America in the country or in one of the smaller cities—in Baltimore, or in Virginia, or in the Pennsylvania farm country or in the West—but I have no time to go wandering all over America now.

(My book, by the way, is filled with this kind of exuberance, exultancy and joy—I *know* if I can make people feel it, they will eat it up: I hope to God the energy is still there, this homesickness abroad has made me feel it more than ever—I mean the richness, fabulousness, exultancy and wonderful life of America—the way you feel (I mean the young fellow, the college kid, going off on his own for the first time) [1] when he is rushing through the night in a dark pullman berth and he sees the dark mys-

[1] This is described on pages 74 and 75 of *Of Time and the River.*

terious American landscape rolling by (Virginia, say!) and the voluptuous good-looking woman in the berth below stirring her pretty legs between the sheets, the sound of the other people snoring, and the sound of voices on the little station platforms in the night—some man and woman seeing their daughter off, then you hear her rustle down the aisle behind the nigger porter and they knock against your green curtain—it is all so strange and familiar and full of joy, it is as if some woman you loved had laid her hand on your bowels.

Then the wonderful richness and size of the country, the feeling that you can be rich and famous, that you can make money easily—the wonderful soil, sometimes desolate and lonely-looking as you found the parts of North Carolina you visited, yet that same earth, Mr. Perkins, produces enough pungent and magnificent tobacco to smoke up the world, and from that same clay come the most luscious peaches, apples, melons, all manner of juicy and wonderful things. I was thinking of it in Switzerland this summer—how incredibly beautiful Switzerland is—the story-book lakes, the unbelievable mountains, the lush velvety mountain meadows— and how desolate and ugly North Carolina would seem to a European— and yet Switzerland is a kind of fake—horribly dull food, dull stunted little fruits and vegetables, dull grapes, dull wine, dull people, and horrible dead sea fish that comes from those lovely Alpine lakes. Switzerland, for all its rich grand beauty can not produce anything one-tenth as good or pungent as North Carolina tobacco, melons, peaches, apples, or the wonderful ducks, turkeys, and marvellous fish along the lonely desolate N.C. coast—and that is America, the only country where you feel this joy, this glory, this exuberance, the thing that makes the young fellows cry out and squeal in their throats. These poor dull tired bastards with their terribly soft woolly steamy, dreary skies—do you think *they* can ever feel this way? They may sneer at us, hate us, revile and mock us, say we are base and without beauty or culture, but no matter how much they call on their dead glories, their Shakespeares, Molières, Shelleys, you know there can be no lying, no hocus-pocus about their beastly, damnable dreary air—they can't argue about that, they have to breathe it, and it will rot and decay anyone after a time, just as bad food, bad housing, will do it. I feel pity and sorrow for them—the plain truth is that the lives of most of their people are dreary compared to ours—they have to go to American movies for amusement. No, they can't have the feeling we have in Autumn when the frost comes and all the wonderful colors come out, and you hear the great winds at night and the burrs plopping to the ground and the far-off frosty barking of a dog, and the wonderful sound of an American train on the rails and its whistle.

The people of North Carolina are like that wonderful earth—they are not little, dull, dreary Babbitts: I am going to *tell the truth* about these people and, by God, it is the truth about America. I don't care what any little worn-out waste-lander, European or American, or anyone else says: I *know what I know*. The people in North Carolina have these same wonderful qualities as the tobacco, the great juicy peaches, melons, apples, the wonderful shad and oysters of the coast, the rich red clay, the haunting brooding quality of the earth. They are rich, juicy, deliberate, full of pungent and sardonic humor and honesty, conservative and cautious on top, but at bottom wild, savage, and full of the murderous innocence of the earth and the wilderness. Do you think this is far-fetched? Scott F.G.[2] did and ridiculed the idea that the earth we lived on had anything to do with us—but don't you see that 300 years upon this earth, living alone minute by minute in the wilderness, eating its food, growing its tobacco, being buried and mixed with it, gets into the blood, bone, marrow, sinew of the people—just as breathing this dreary stuff here has got into these dull, depressed, splenetic and despondent wretches who have to breathe it: how in God's name can anyone be pig-headed and stubborn enough to deny it?

You are a New Englander and quieter about it, but every American has this exultant feeling at times—the way snow comes in New England and the way it spits against your window at night and the sounds of the world get numb, you are living like a spirit in wonderful dark isolation: my bowels used to stir with it and once I got off the Fall River boat after a night of storm and snow on the dark water of the Sound, and the wind and powdery snow were blowing and howling at dawn, everything was white and smokey wonderful grey, and there was the train for Boston in the middle of it, black, warm, fast, and all around the lonely and tragic beauty of New England. (Yes! and *another* good-looking woman in the stateroom next to me coming up on the boat.)

This is glory and wonder, and I shall not be ashamed to tell all of it—what else is homesickness, loyalty, love of country than this—each one of the million moments of your life, the intolerable memory of all the sounds and sights and feelings you knew there. I shall neither try to defend or condemn anything—it is in me, all of it, I shall tell of the cruelty and horror, murder and sudden death, the Irish cop, the smell of blood and brains upon the sidewalk, along with everything else—it is all part of my story, and I *know it is time* and so do you. It is also glorious and exultant and nowhere else in the world can they feel this way: if I tell about it as it is, in all its magnificence and joy, how can it fail to be good? I do not say that I can, but we shall see.)

All this was a parenthesis: to get back to the question of lodgings—

[2] Scott Fitzgerald.

once you mentioned in conversation, also in a letter, the possibility of finding a place out in your part of the country: in a talk, you spoke of boarding-houses and said there were some good ones, but I will never get along in a boarding-house—I must have two rooms where I can be absolutely free, tramp about and work all night, and sleep all day if I want to. You can't do this with peace of mind in a house with other people. An apartment house, or rooms in a business building that's deserted at night, is more in my line. Also I must have a gas stove where I can cook bacon and eggs and make all the coffee I want. If I can get this out in the country, it would be fine: I notice they are building apartment houses out in the country now—Bronxville, etc.—the idea is not bad. I should like to be either out your way, or else I have thought of Brooklyn—somewhere I can look at the wonderful *river*. I think of Brooklyn because people will not bother you or come to see you there so much.—All I need is two rooms, one to sleep in, one to work in, a little kitchen or kitchenette, and a gas-stove—also a showerbath or bath. Don't you think I could get this in some modest place for $60 or $70 a month? I want to be quiet, and I want to see either the earth (that is, out your way) or the river. Could something be done about it? Also, in view of the present hard times, couldn't I get something without signing a year's lease—say for three or six months, or month-by-month, with a privilege of staying on if I want to. Sinclair Lewis wrote me two nice letters—he said Vermont is the most beautiful and cheapest place in the country—maybe I could go there in the hot weather.

If you don't know of anything yourself, could you speak to someone who does? There's a boy named Kizenberger (or something like that) down with Miss DeVoy in the Art Department [3]—he seemed a fine, friendly competent fellow: do you think he could help us? It is a lot to ask but it would be a Godsend if I could have a place waiting for me when I came back and not lose time. I do not want to lose at the outside over *one* month of the *nine* months that elapse between Jan 1 and next October—whether on steamers, trains, hunting rooms, or anything else. I'll stand by any arrangement you can make—just see if it's quiet and they'll let me work, eat, and sleep as I please. Will you please write me about this and tell me if it can be done?

Paris, Dec. 29, 1930. I have come to Paris for two or three days before New Year's—and I am going to finish the letter here. I was damned tired

[3] Edward Kizenberger was in the Art and Manufacturing Department of Scribners at this time. Miss S. Elizabeth DeVoy was then Associate Art Editor, and was Art Editor from 1939 until her retirement in 1951.

and had brain fag but already I am nervous and restless and feel impatient to get back to the book. I have brought the big ledgers in which I write and I keep fooling with it here, although I ought not to, I think. I have got the desperate feeling about it and think I may come through to something.

Now here is the plan: I may be here another day or two until New Year's, then I go back to London, and write like hell until the flesh can do no more, for six or eight weeks. Then America again, and a quiet place of my own to work, and I will show you something complete (a complete book and story but *not* the whole of *The October Fair*—the part called *Antaeus*) sometime during the summer. It is *bound* to be good if I can be hopeful and exultant while I write it: when I am that way I can do anything—to-night I am afraid. I am afraid of no one person, no thing, I am afraid of fear, desolation, and the nauseous sickness and horror of the guts that comes from unknown fear. Paris gives me that feeling. I can hardly bear to go to the Left Bank for fear I shall see some of these God damned life-hating, death-living bastards: but I *did* go yesterday, because one of them had been phoning me in Paris [London?] last week and I had promised to look them up here.

I refer to Mrs —— ——, . . . and my prophetic soul told me it was a frame-up of some sort—one of *three* things. Well, it turned out to be all three: one was to pry into my supposed history with someone I knew in London, another into my supposed New York history, another, how much had I written on my book, what was it about, when would it be ready? When I got there, they had the gang lined up—on one side someone who knew a friend in New York, an another side, someone who knew a person in London—they volleyed and thundered—from the right: "I believe you knew so-and-so in London—she is my cousin"—from the left: "I believe you know so-and-so in New York—she is related to me." Then the sly looks and snickers—God, it makes me vomit! Then the prize bitch, Mrs. ——, spoke of your friend, Mrs. Colum,[4] who is here. I want to see her if I can see her away from these scandal-mongering apes and baboons. This is Paris and I loathe it! They are here to *work*—Jesus Christ! none of them has ever worked here: I am here to eat and drink and sleep, and I shall stay to myself and do it.

For God's sake, don't think I am mad with suspicion and distrust—I have never hated or *in the end* suspected a good person, but I know that my exultancy is right, that the sense of joy and glory is true and just, that the richness, glory, beauty, wonder and magnificence of America—the feel of the wind, the sound of snow, the smell of a great American [steak?]. By

[4] Mary M. Colum, author of *From These Roots, Life and the Dream*, etc.

God, these are real things and true things, and these people are liars and cheap swindlers. But if I am going to get this glory and faith and exultancy into my book, I must feel it myself: and I *do* feel it most of the time, only when I meet these people, my heart turns rotten, and my guts are sick and nauseous.

After the book is written, I will be afraid of nothing—but now I am afraid of anything that gets in the way. That is why I want to see you and one or two others and no one else when I come back. I should like to go with you to that 49th Street speakeasy and have a few drinks of American gin and one of those immense steaks—then I should like to talk to you as we used to: these seem to me to be mighty good times, and that speakeasy was a fine place—I have remembered it and put it in my book.

Mr. Perkins, no one has ever written a book about America—no one has ever put into it the things I know and the things everyone knows. It may be grandiose and pompous for me to think I can, but for God's sake let me try. Furthermore it will be a story, and I believe a damned good story. You know what you said to me over a year ago about the book that might be written about a man looking for his father and how everything could be put into it—well, you were right: don't think that I gave up what I wanted to do, only I had this vast amount of material and what you said began to give shape to it. I have gone through the most damnable torture not merely rewriting but in re-arranging, but now I've got it, if I can get it down on paper. The advantage of your story is not only that it is immensely and profoundly true—namely, all of us are wandering and groping through life for an image outside ourselves, for a superior and external wisdom we can appeal [to] and trust—but the story also gives shape to things. Coleridge said that Ben Jonson's play, *The Alchemist*, had one of the three finest plots in the world (the other two were *Oedipus* and *Tom Jones*) and Coleridge mentions as the wonderful virtue of *The Alchemist* the fact that the action could be brought to a close at any point by the return of the master (the play, as I remember, concerns the tricks of a rascal of a servant palming himself off as the master on a world of dupes and rogues). Well, so in this story, the action could be brought to a close by the son finding his father. I have thought over the Antaeus myth a lot, and it seems to me to a true and beautiful one: it says what I want about man's jointure to the earth whence comes his strength, but Antaeus is also faithful to the memory of his father (Poseidon) to whom he builds a temple from the skulls of those he vanquishes. Poseidon, of course, represents eternal movement and wandering, and in a book where a man is looking for his father, what could be more true than this?

About Sinclair Lewis: it was a wonderful thing for him to do [5] and I wrote and told him so. He also wrote me two letters and said he would try to see me over here. I hope it sells a few copies of the book—thanks for using it and advertising it—but I am a little worried by it also: the Great American Writer business is pretty tough stuff for a man who is on his second book, and I hope they won't be gunning for me. Also, I have begun to come to a way of life—I meant what I said about *obscurity:* it's the only thing for me, otherwise I'm done for: I want to write famous books, but I want to live quietly and modestly. Also, I am determined to resist in my own heart any attempt to make or be made the great "I Am" of anything. If I tell myself that I am not anybody's "I Am," but only a fellow who is going to stick relentlessly to the things he has seen and known, to say the things he has to say as honestly and beautifully as he can, to realize that is all he has, and that if it has any value it is because other people have felt these things or will feel their truth—why, then, if I stick to this and work like hell, I don't believe they can hurt me seriously either when they praise me or turn against me. Don't you think this is the only wise and honest way to work and live?

Now, finally, about the book again. If I have been incoherent and chaotic, it has been from haste and not from lack of certainty. As well as I can tell you quickly and in this small space, this is what my book is about: First, it is a story of a man who is looking for his father—this gives it plan and direction, and it also expresses a fundamental human desire. The story of a man's love for a woman is told with the utmost passion and sincerity and sensuousness in one part of it, together with all the phenomena of lust, hunger, jealousy, madness, cruelty and tenderness—but the idea that the two sexes are from different worlds, different universes, and can never know each other, is implicit; and the father idea—the need for wisdom, strength and confession, with the kinship and companionship of one's own kind and father, hangs over the story all the time. Under this story structure are the ideas of the fixity and eternity of the earth and the beauty of man's life.

[THE LETTER BREAKS OFF UNFINISHED HERE]

[5] After praising *Look Homeward, Angel* in his interview in the November 6 *New York Times,* Lewis had gone to Stockholm to receive the Nobel Prize for Literature, and in his official speech of acceptance before the Swedish Academy, had said: "There are young Americans to-day who are doing such passionate and authentic work that it makes me sick to see that I am a little too old to be one of them. There is . . . Thomas Wolfe, a child of, I believe, thirty or younger, whose one and only novel, *Look Homeward, Angel,* is worthy to be compared with the best in our literary production, a Gargantuan creature with great gusto of life."

To MABEL WOLFE WHEATON

[Written on a Christmas card]

[London]

[December, 1930]

Dear Mabel:

I'm writing as soon as I can—I know all about things at home and how bad conditions are. Don't worry—nobody's going to starve, I will be delighted to help in any way possible and I know I can get money if I have to. We must all stick together now, and you must let me help you if I can. I think you are well out of it in Asheville for the present—later on things are going to be better everywhere. This is the real test now, if everyone keeps cheerful and courageous at this time things are bound to come all right. We will not be beaten because *we can not be beaten.* In a pinch I believe I can come back home and begin to write articles and short stories, or get a job advertising, and get more money. I wish you all a happy and cheerful Christmas. People have been kind to me here, and I get invited out but I have been terribly lonely and homesick. It will all come out right yet. Write me—

To HENRY T. VOLKENING

The Guaranty Trust Co.
London

January 14, 1931

Dear Henry:

Thanks again for another letter. I can't tell you how happy your letters make me, and with what care I read and reread them. I know I have fallen far short of doing my share—whenever I take my pen in hand, like our old friend Lord Tennyson, I would that my heart could utter the thoughts that arise in me, but it's no use: for some reason I have developed the most damnable caution in writing letters, even to the three or four people I should like to write good ones to. . . .

I am rapidly becoming a great authority on the subject of *Work* because I, my boy, have done some—"and penance more will do." By the way, that would be a good title for almost any book—"Penance More"—for that, I think, is what it takes to write one. But hearken again, lad—I have not only worked, but I have worked with metaphysical and spiritual belly-ache, toothache, headache—as well as something like a virulent abscess just over my left lung,[1] and I think now that I shall probably work under almost any kind of conditions. Then, attend, and do these things at once: buy a book written by one Anthony Trollope, Esq. who wrote about ninety-seven other books in addition. It is called "An Autobiography"; it is quite short; you can . . . read it through at one sitting. The book was published after his death and, I understand, did his reputation a good deal of damage among the kind of readers who think a book gets written in two and one half hours of passionate delirium by an inspired maniac. Brother Trollope, with great good humor and some cynicism, describes his methods of work, and tells how he managed to write fifty or sixty novels while riding all over Ireland and England in the Civil Service, going hunting twice a week, entertaining many friends, and in general leading a hell of an active life. Brother Trollope was a rugged man and he let no day go by without writing for three hours—no more, no less. He worked five days a week, wrote 10,000 words, estimated the number of words and pages in a novel, wrote exactly up to that point, got it to the printer in time, and started a new one. Further, he learned to write his daily stint in railway compartments, on Channel steamers, on horseback, and in bed, and with great glee and gusto he attaches an itemized list of his books at the end, together with the exact number of pounds, shillings, and pence each one earned.

I shall never write fifty books or learn to write in railways or on boats, nor do I think it desirable, but it is certainly a damned good idea to get ideas of steady work, and I think this is a good book to read. I am able to do thirty or thirty-five hours a week—thirty-five hours is about the limit, and if I do that I am pretty tired. If a man will work—really work— for four or five hours every day, he is doing his full stint. Moreover, I find very little time for anything else—I practically spend twenty-four hours getting five hours work done: I go out very little. But it soon gets to be a habit. I wish sometimes I were less homesick, less lonely, and some-times less heartsick: I could certainly imagine better conditions for work, and I am firmly decided (between us!) that the "going abroad to write business" is the bunk. I went to Paris Christmas: it is one of the saddest messes in the world to see all these pathetic bastards who are beginning to get ready to commence to start. Why a man should leave his own coun-try to write—why he should write better in Spain, France, England or Czechoslovakia than at home is quite beyond me. . . . It seems to me that one of the most important things a writer can have is tenacity—without that I don't see how he'll get anything done. Someone told me a year or

[1] If Wolfe did have an abscess over his left lung, nothing is known about it now. The old tubercular lesion which was opened by pneumonia in 1938 and caused his death was in the right lung.

two ago that the pity about modern writers is that the people who have the greatest talent for writing never write, and an embittered and jealous Irishman told me that one of the people Joyce wrote about in "Ulysses" was a much better writer than Joyce if he wanted to write—only he didn't want to. All this, in the phrase of my innocent childhood, "makes my ass want buttermilk."

There can be no talent for writing whatever, unless a man has power to write: tenacity is one of the chief elements of talent—without it there is damned little talent, no matter what they say. Which I suppose is only another way of saying Arnold's dogma: Genius is energy. I think I would agree that the best writers are not always the people with the greatest natural ability to write. For example, I have never felt that Joyce was a man with a great natural ability: I don't believe he begins to have the natural ease, fluency, and interest of, say, H. G. Wells. But he had an integrity of spirit, a will and a power to work that far surpasses Wells. I don't mean mere manual and quantity work—Wells had plenty of that, he has written a hundred books—but I mean the thing that makes a man to do more than his best, to exhaust his ultimate resource. That is the power to work and that can not be learned—it is a talent and belongs to the spirit. At any rate, the only way out for us is work—work under all circumstances and conditions: I am sure of that! . . .

But now forgive me for being such a wiseacre: I am not nearly so easy and certain as I sound—but I am sure what I said about working is right. I do not know whether what I am doing now is good or bad—the impulse and idea are very good—but, as *always* between us, I think I have been on the verge of the deep dark pit for two years, and I am just beginning to get away from it. I am tired of madness and agony; I am willing to let the young generation have a fling of it—after all, I'm an old fellow of thirty and I deserve some peace and quiet. If work will do it, I'll come through: I'll work until my brain and the last remnant of energy go.

I suppose some people would say I have never spared others, but I should say that I never spared myself, and on the whole I think other people have done pretty well by me. I have given away what I would never sell if I had it again for diamond mines—years out of the best and most vital period of my life—and I find myself to-day where I was ten years ago, a wanderer on the face of the earth, an exile, and a stranger, and, by God, I wonder why! I can't help it if it sounds melodramatic—it is the simple truth. Frankly, I want to live in my own country. I am tired of this Europe business, I know it is all wrong—but where to live on that little strip of four thousand miles of earth is the question. I notice that people who have never been alone for five minutes in their lives cheerfully banish you to solitude, assure you there's no life like it, how they envy you, and it is all for the best, after all, etc. But I've had thirty years of it, and I confess now to a low craving for companionship, the love and affection of a few simple bastards, and evenings spent by the ingle nook with a bottle of bootleg port, a jug of imported English walnut, and a volume of the Olde Englisshe essays of —— —— on which I could wipe my arse from time to time and pretend I was back in the Olde Countrye. I have even begun fondly to meditate a loving wife (my own, this time), and a few little ones; but where to start searching for these simple joys is beyond me!

Most of the people I like, and a great many I dislike, are in New York, but I can't go back there: it would be like walking around with perpetual neuralgia at present: the place is one vast ache to me, and I've offered quite enough free entertainment to the millions of people who, having no capacity for feeling themselves, spend their lives on the rich banquet some poor buck from the sticks (like myself) has to offer. I've learned a few things and the next time the bastards want to see a good show they're going to pay up!

To-day is another *night!* and I . . . am going to see the Four Marx Brothers to-morrow with my English publishers. They are here in the flesh, and the swells have suddenly discovered they were funny, so I suppose I shall have to listen to the usual horrible gaff from the Moderns: "You know there's Something Very Grand about them—there really is, you know, I mean there's Something Sort of Epic about it, if you know what I mean, I mean that man who never says anything is really like Michael Angelo's Adam in the Sistine Chapel, He's a Very Grand Person, he really is, you know, they are really *Very* Great Clowns, they really are you know," etc. etc. etc. ad vomitatum. I took some people here to see the Marxes in a talkie, and I had to listen to it for two hours. I got so mad because the woman next to me kept saying that "There was something Very Sinister about" Harpo's face—when he began to play the harp she said: "Ah, there is something Lovely about him when he Does Things with His hands—He's doing Something he likes, you see." The dear moderns, you will find, are cut from the same cloth and pattern all over the world—unplatitudinously they utter platitudes, with complete unoriginality they are original, whenever they say something new you wonder where you heard it before, you believe you have not heard it before, you are sure you have heard it forever, you are tired of it before it is uttered, the stink of a horrible weariness is on it, it is like the smell of the subway after rush hours, the best answer to it is Groucho's famous remark: "Even if this was good I wouldn't like it," or alternatively, "The next number will be a piccolo solo which will be omitted." I am tired of these weary bastards: they hate life, but they won't die.

I had a damned good lunch at Simpson's to-day—usually I eat at home here—I had enormous portions of delicious roast beef, Yorkshire pudding, Cavendish sauce, Stilton cheese, biscuits and a bottle of Beaujolais. Simpson's is one of the best places in England: the food at most restaurants is incredibly dull and bad, and the misery and depression of millions of beaten people is constantly seeping into the dull and horrible weather —the whole thing makes a wet dreary thick compost which you breathe and eat and feel, but at Simpson's there is still joy! Do you still go to Luchows? That is a fine restaurant, Professor Wolfe the food expert speaking! Also, I remember some New York speakeasies with pleasure, one I went to just before coming here in particular: the food was most delicious. In the universal mockery and contempt of prohibish, these things and places don't always get their due—but I believe some speakeasies are very wonderful places!

In the last year I have looked at a half dozen countries and thirty or forty million people. But nowhere have I seen people walking on their hands, breathing through fins, or rolling like hoops along pavements. Today I went into a bookstore. There were millions of books. I did not find one that would teach me not to draw my breath in pain and labor, or how to cross a street, or how to find a moment's wisdom and repose. These things are in us! . . . The literary business in America has become so horrible that it is sometimes possible to write only between fits of vomiting. If you think that is extreme, I mention a few names. . . . I . . . say keep away from them: go with doctors, architects, bootleggers—but not with writers. This is not bitter advice: it is simply good advice. No one has ever written any books about America—I mean the real America. I think they bring out ten or twenty thousand books a year, but no one has ever written about America, and I do not think the "writers" will.

Good-bye for the present. I send you and Nat my love and warmest wishes for the New Year. Thanks again for all those fine letters, and for the fruit cake, and most of all for thinking of me and being my friend. Let me hear from you when you can. . . .

Just before leaving England, Wolfe wrote the following letter to Henry Allen Moe, Secretary of the John Simon Guggenheim Foundation.

To HENRY ALLEN MOE

London

February 25, 1931

Dear Mr. Moe:

This is a very belated letter, but since I hope to come in to see you very soon anyway, I shall be able to tell you myself what I have done here abroad: I am going back to New York in a day or two, and may be there as soon as this letter. I have spent about ten months here instead of the six I originally intended, and I am bringing back six enormous book-keeping ledgers with about 200,000 words of manuscript and a great many notes. I do not know if the words are good or bad ones, and a great deal remains to be done, but it is so firmly on the rails now that nothing can stop it. I am going into the woods at or about New York for about six months, and then I hope to emerge with the pelt. I have been horribly lonely and homesick at times—more, I think, than ever in my life—but for five months now, in my little flat in Ebury Street, and for months more elsewhere, I have thought and worked, and dreamed about America, and now I know what I know, which may be little or much, but it is my own. So, first of all, I want to thank you and the trustees for giving me the chance to come abroad and work, and then for the chance to achieve that meditation and solitude which, painful and difficult as both may be, are nevertheless precious things, and perhaps harder to get at home than in most places. People have been most kind and generous to me here. I have found out more about England and Europe this time than ever before— that is, I have entered doors, gone past barriers, that the stranger usually never passes, and found at least two or three friends: but I have also found out more about my own country, and I do not think I shall ever lose what I have gained.

It was most important, I think, that I went away when I did for these reasons, and for others about which I may tell you someday. I wish I could promise you, in return for your generosity, that I will write a good book or a grand book—but I can not make that promise: I hope that it will be, and I shall not let it go until I think it is worth publication, and if I work and do not falter, and say what I have to say with all the energy and ability I may have—then I think the book *will* be worth it. At any rate, I have gained something this year that I will never lose, and in the end I am a better and wiser person than when I went away.

I have just drawn the last of the letter of credit for steamer fare, clothes, some books and a little fund when I land in New York: thank you again for all of it, and for what it helped me to do. If you are interested in seeing it, I'll bring you some of the typed manuscript during the next two or three months in New York, but I hope to see you and talk to you and have lunch with you before that.

I send my best wishes for health and happiness. Please don't say any-thing to anyone about my coming back. Not many people would be in-terested anyway, and I have committed no indictable crimes, but I am coming to work, and won't be much in sight for several months. . . .

VIII

BROOKLYN AND WORK: A PORTRAIT OF BASCOM HAWKE *AND* THE WEB OF EARTH

1931–1932

The following letter to Henry Allen Moe may be somewhat confusing to the reader since Wolfe uses in it titles for large portions of his material which were later used for smaller portions. The "book . . . in four volumes" which he says "will have the name The October Fair" *was the entire series of novels he had planned:* The October Fair *(of which the first half became* Of Time and the River), The Hills Beyond Pentland, The Death of the Enemy *and* Pacific End. "*The first of these books which . . . I hope to have completed by January" was the entire novel of* The October Fair, *for which he was considering* Time and the River *or* Of Men and Rivers *or* The River *as alternate titles. The decision to divide this novel into halves and publish the first half as* Of Time and the River *was not reached until late December 1933, after Perkins had read the rough draft manuscript of the entire novel and pointed out to Wolfe that it described two separate cycles.*

To HENRY ALLEN MOE

> Harvard Club
> New York
>
> July 2, [1931]

Dear Mr. Moe:

I got your letter with its inquiry concerning the work I am doing, and I want to answer you before I go away—to Maine for a week or ten days. Since coming back from Europe in March, I have been living in Brooklyn and I rarely come over to Manhattan. I am working on the book I began in Europe when I was there on the Guggenheim Fellowship. The book, if I survive to complete it, will be in four volumes, and will have the name "The October Fair." Each of these four will be a complete novel—

the four are related more by a plan and a feeling than by a central group of characters which appear in each of the four. The first of these books, which is a very long one, I hope to have completed by January, and, if published, it will appear next year. I don't know what its name will be— I have thought of several: "Of Men and Rivers," "Time and the River"; "The River"; or simply "The October Fair," which I had thought of as a general name for all four. I am up to my neck in it and have worked like a nigger this summer. I have had it in my head for over two years, knew where I was going, but didn't get it straight until six or eight months ago. Now I think I've got it. While abroad on the Guggenheim I wrote two or three hundred thousand words, and went through hell in arranging, re-arranging, trying to get it into sequence.

I've wanted to come in to tell you about it, but I have come to New York so seldom, and I wanted to show you something more coherent than the big ledgers I had filled with writing. Anyway, when the book comes out, if it has any merit, I hope you will accept it as the work I did with the Guggenheim money, and even if coherence was long in coming, I think those first months abroad, while I stewed around in chaos plucking out separate nuts here and there, were the months I really wrote the thing, pulled it out of limbo, got it on the rails. I hope you'll like it when you see it—anyway, you'll be able to see I've worked. I will come in to see you when I come back. I'm living at 40 Verandah Place, Brooklyn—it's an alley in the Assyrian district, but it's cheap and quiet. . . . If you want to reach me, you can get me quicker there than through Scribners. . . .

Brooklyn is a fine town—a nice, big country town, a long way from New York. You couldn't find a better place to work.

Wolfe sent the following letter to a girl whom he knew, but later demanded that she return it to him, and kept it among his own papers.

To ———

[Summer, 1931]

Dear ——:

I just found your special delivery upstairs and my first impulse, on reading it, was to call you up right away. But your letter seemed so clear and fine to me that I thought I would try to answer you in the same way, before talking to you, and I wonder that I did not try it before—this is my usual means of expression—paper and pencil—and I believe I can be much more direct and less confused in this way than in conversation.

First of all, I want to say that anyone who can write such a letter as you sent me—which seemed so fine, so true, and so generous—can get anything she wants out of living: you can conquer everyone and everything by such means, and people will love you. Such a letter as that is so much more potent than the craftiest craft, the deepest and most subtle cunning that a person like myself, who is sometimes gnawed by a devil of suspiciousness and doubt, may wonder if there is not a skill and cleverness here too great for him to cope with. (Please don't think I feel this way—I am enormously touched and grateful for your letter, and so happy about getting it.) What I am trying to say is that men have been told so often, since their childhood, of the subtlety of women, and so often warned against vain-glorious assurance in their dealings with women, that even when we think we know what we know, we are checked by a fear that we are fooling ourselves—that even when we read vanity and pride into the conduct of others, however affectionately, we are really guilty of vanity and pride ourselves. Having said so much, as my only means of defense and qualification, I am now going to kick caution out of the window, and tell you exactly how I feel, and what I think went wrong.

Let us review our relation from the beginning, which was only about three months ago. That first time I met you, it seemed to me we were two young people, "alone in the world," although we had friends who were loyal and good to us, and our lives were at that time smooth enough, although both of us had had rough passages in the past. Perhaps I was still looking around for dry land. When I left you in the morning and walked toward the subway through deserted streets and among the enormous and inhuman masses of the buildings, I had a feeling of the most enormous exultancy and joy to think that there were young women like you in the world. As I have told you, I saw you in all this setting—by the great river with its bridges and its sliding lights, in the enormous city at daybreak—you were alone, strong, brave, and independent; you had been through a bad time and came through it without being warped; everything about you was sweet and lovely, and in addition to this you had a good position (which also seemed thrilling and fine to me); you were immensely capable, and probably one of the handsomest and most desirable young women on earth.

I mention the job, by the way, because I thought how much more desirable and seductive such women as you are than the Southern girls I knew as a boy: here, I thought, in New York, were wonderful girls with good jobs who had their own flats and would also stand a round of drinks. The Southern girl had become repulsive to me: her drawly voice, her coquettish airs, her apologies for working or boasts of never having worked —I thought of them now with such revulsion that I believed them to be foul, dull, stupid, nasty—with a litter of gummed combs and hair upon the dresser, and a rancid swimming chamber-pot below the bed. Everything about you was so clean, sweet, and desirable; you were as independent as I was, you asked no more of me than I of you, we were two free and decent people, and that morning as I walked home, New York seemed magnificent in the young light, and I thought discovering you was one of the best things that ever had happened to me.

I go into these particulars so fully because I want you to know something of the state of my feeling—I cannot hope to reproduce the whole state of joy that I felt, because it was touched by so many shades of things, but I think one element that was most important was this feeling of dignity and independence—I thought of us both being just and equal in our dealings, in giving and taking equally, in admitting an equal share and satisfaction. Later on, you began to say other things about our relation —how it could not be as fine or complete as it might be until there was a deeper or more fundamental relation between us. I asked you if you meant marriage, and you said that might be, but that you did not demand this— but you did want something that was complete and, however long it lasted, would be a primary experience while it did last. As I thought of this, it seemed to me that a frank and simple translation was this: you thought that the finest relation came when people loved each other with all their hearts, and lived faithfully and entirely in that love. I think so, too, and I have told you I think so; but for that very reason it is not a thing which can be planned, meditated, or determined upon deliberately. If it were, I would be a fool not to try to determine myself immediately in love with you, because you are a desirable and lovely woman. It does not come that way, however, and I told you at once what my feeling was: the joy and exultancy I had over meeting you, the deep and tender affection I had for you, the relief you brought me from the trouble I had been in, the great value I set upon you.

At one time, you accused me of using you as a stop-gap while I worked on my book and was adjusting myself after the insanity of love which obsessed me for several years and from which I was just fully emerging. What you said might be harshly and coldly true, but what seems to me more true is that I thought of you with delight and tenderness, and enormous relief, as . . . my friend, and the companion with whom I could find comfort and peace. I also hoped that you might have this same deep pleasure and comfort from me. I think I understood exactly what you hoped to get from life, and I never argued against it—I thought you were right in wanting it—but I never deceived you as to what I could give, or as to my feeling.

Now I think we come to a big difference in feeling here: I agree with you as to what is the best and most wonderful relation between people, but on that account I do not believe that all other relations are trivial or vile. There is a higher relation than the one we had, but I feel that the one we had was a good one, and I shall always be glad of it, and think I am better for having had it. I earnestly hoped you would feel the same way. I am no longer promiscuous, I do not wander from bed to bed, I have a great deal of fidelity in me: as you know, my life at the present time is very simple—I stay in Brooklyn and work, and when I went to New York I went with a feeling of delight and joy because I knew a beautiful and intelligent young woman there with whom I could talk, eat, and go to bed. As time went on you apparently got the idea that what was wrong with our relation was not the talking and eating but the going to bed. Now this is very blunt and plain, but I think it is a fair statement: you began to say a short time ago that what you valued in our relation was "friendship" and not "sexual relations." You know that the reason I have protested at this is that I do not see how you make this complete division between our friendship and our sexual relations. We began with sexual relations and our whole relation is integrated with this: I do not know how you can make a separation in your own mind, but I know that when I think of you I shall always remember that we went to bed together—you understand I am not saying this is the entire memory, but it is an integral and essential part of my picture of you. For my part, it is something I shall always remember with the deepest and most grateful tenderness.

During the last month I have not seen very much of you—it seemed to me I could no longer argue with you over what I believed was false: it seemed to me you wanted the sex relation as much as I did, but later you were always giving reasons and justifications for your action—it seemed to me everything but the real one. First you said you did it because you were trying to break the hold and memory of some former lover; then a few weeks ago, when we saw each other less frequently, you said you did it as a sort of bribe to me—you no longer cared for it with me, but it was the only way you had of holding my friendship—if you did not do it, I would not see you any more. This I felt to be intolerable and unjust. It put me in such a shabby and humiliating position. ——, I have known hundreds of women, but I have never forced myself on anyone, nor ever thought of this sort of coercion. Neither have they. I have had plenty of women as friends, and never thought of any other relation, but I have never had one tell me before that the only reason she went to bed with me was to hold my friendship. If a woman no longer wants to go to bed with you, that is her own business, but then, if that has been the relation, it is over and they can sometimes see you later and be your friend.

But I know the reason you went to bed with me was because you wanted to, and I thought it unfair and shabby for you to say later that it was because I wanted it and would not be your friend without it. You were certainly an equal partner in it all, no coercion was ever brought to bear on you, and that first night, it seemed to me you allowed it to be plainly understood that this was what you wanted. Had you not desired it, had you chosen not to, it would have showed plainly in your speech, the way you sat, in everything. . . . Now I think it is wrong for you to deny that you did it as freely and willingly as I did. If you no longer have this desire where I am concerned, I shall accept your decision, although sadly, but you ought not to say that what you did gladly and freely was done to bribe me. Also, if you now insist that this is finished, I will accept your decision, although I do not know why it has ceased to be desirable to you. and I will try to be your "friend" as you understand the term, but for me, at least, it will mean beginning anew with you and knowing you in another way. The other relation was the one in which I went to bed with you, and I will always remember it—the sound of the boats out on the river, the lights, the darkness, and you beneath me in the dark—I shall remember it with pride and delight as long as I live: I know your look, your size, your smell—the feel of your breast and belly, the swell of your hips, the taste of your mouth, the grip of your thighs. You were like the best butter and eggs and honey that was ever made, as lovely and desirable as any woman on the earth.

Finally, I think you were right in the way you felt and said you felt at first—about wanting the best and finest in human love and friendship, and I have always agreed with you. But I think what we had was, to me at least, very good and wonderful. In your letter you speak of your own "hurt and humiliation" as explaining the things you said to me:—I am giving you my own opinion without defense or explanation—I think you hoped or believed I would fall deeply and utterly in love with you and when I did not, you said you had had sexual relations with me to keep my friendship.

I want to say, ——, that no one can "hurt or humiliate" you except yourself. I have found that out in my own life. You are one of the finest and most desirable young women I have ever seen and your letter was an action of the highest order. You deserve nothing but the best and finest in life and you will get it. Do you understand from this letter of mine— this remarkable, honest, and *wholly serious* letter—that I know your value as a person, your great worth and beauty. Do you understand that I could never misprize or undervalue such a person as you—that if I could not offer you everything in me, it is because everything in me once went into something, someone, else, and if it ever returns like that, it will take time? As for myself, I think it will never come that way again but it will come in another way, and I am going to try to have a good life.

[A SECTION OF THE LETTER IS EVIDENTLY MISSING HERE]

. . . out of me as utterly as birth and death. It can never be lost now but it will never be regained. But I hope and have faith that someday I will be able to offer someone with some of your own quality something that is wise, true, and abiding, even if it is not the fiercest and most lyrical feeling we have had in us.

Meanwhile I hope this letter has made things clearer rather than obscurer, and gives us a place to start, to continue, or what you will—so long as it enables us to stand together again.

To FRED W. WOLFE

[40 Verandah Place]
[Brooklyn, N.Y.]
July 19, 1931

Dear Fred:

Thanks for your several letters. I owe you more than one answer, but will have to make this do for the present. I am plugging away at my book, and in this weather—what Papa would have called "this hellish, fearful, awful, damnable and bloodthirsty weather"—it is about all I can do to get four or five hours of writing done each day.

First of all, I got your check for $275 [1]—as you already know. Now I'm not going to talk any more about it—I believe you fully understand that I am delighted to help to the extent of my ability, and trust you to let me know if you need anything for yourself or for the family. Of one thing I am almost sure: I think I can always manage, no matter what hard times may be ahead of us yet, to get money enough to keep Mama going, and of course I think that is the first and most important consideration. There seems to be a hope and belief here that business is going to improve soon. People think Hoover's debt agreement with Europe will help. I have a feeling it's not going to be so quick or easy—the little speculators who lost their shirt last time are all ready to go again. . . . But the whole thing is wrong: how do people expect to create any real or solid prosperity by sitting on their tails in a broker's office all day long? The whole thing is cockeyed, and if they do give it a shot of dope this time, it will only bring it back temporarily. I think we may be up against

[1] In a letter to his mother dated June 8, 1931 (see page 206, *Thomas Wolfe's Letters to His Mother*), Wolfe wrote: "This morning I got a letter from Fred with a check for $275, returning almost all the money I sent to Effie."

a much more serious disaster than most of us yet realize—although how in God's name people in a town which has been wrecked and ruined as Asheville has can fail to recognize it, I don't see. I think, and other people think the same, that we may even be at the end of what is called an "era" —that the old system is shot to hell, and we will have to get busy and find a newer and better one. I went to town to see a show to-night—the weather has been hot and muggy with low-lying clouds, and when I came out and crossed Fifth Avenue, the top of the Empire State was completely hidden in mist. It's a rare sight but I've an idea it will be a hell of a time before they put up another to beat it: I understand Al Smith himself is legging it all over town in an effort to rent it, but they say he's not having much luck—it looks as if he's bitten off a mouthful this time. . . .

I note what you say about my new book. I cannot tell you much about it because I do not like to talk about anything I am writing, but I will put your mind at rest upon one score: it has nothing to do with the first book in any way—the scenes, characters, and story are all different: if the gossip-mongers in Asheville are licking their chops in anticipation of a feast, they're in for a surprise. My experience with the first book was so depressing, so far as Asheville is concerned, that I was almost sorry any-one there had ever read a line I had written. I assure you I have found out a great deal more about the world and Asheville, too, in the last year and a half than in the rest of my life put together. But if I ever return to the scenes of the first book, as someday I shall, it will be at least five years before I am ready for it. Meanwhile, I do not care, save from a business point of view, whether they read what I write or not, but if they are living in hope of scandal let them pursue their delusion to the end—I mean to the end of buying the book.

By the way, I may have made more money for them all than I ever made for myself—I don't know what ever became of all the books that were sold in Asheville, but there must have been hundreds of copies of the first edition there. I have been told that collectors will pay $10 or $15 for the first edition, and with a copy of the "dust wrapper"—that is the paper cover that came with it—and with my autograph, I have been told it brings as much as $25. At any rate I know a collector who buys them and pays this much for them, and will furnish his name on request. It's all the more a joke to me since I don't own a copy of the book myself, and have just about enough money to live on simply until I finish the new one.

Thanks for your invitation to come home. I'd like to see the family but, aside from that, I have no great interest in coming at this time. I think you understand the reason—just the thing we have been talking about. If I ever come back to Asheville I want to feel either that I can come quietly to see my family and a few friends, without having to talk to a lot of lying gossips, or that people in my own town have some respect for my work, and some understanding of me. I have heard so much slander, vituperation, gossip, and indirect and anonymous threats that I have grown weary of it, and want to forget it. Several times I have heard, indirectly as usual, that I am "afraid to come back to Asheville," and that "people there have threatened to kill me." Well, if I am afraid, it is not because of this, but for reasons they have never understood. I don't think anyone is "going to kill me": I have heard of these threats, but no one has ever made them to my face, and I assure you I lose no sleep on this account. Naturally, however, I have no great urge to go back to a place where such things are said—I might go back simply for the purpose of "showing them," but I have no desire to show them anything. Somehow a man can devote his life to the work he likes best, and, in his own way, create something that will satisfy him and hold in it his vision of life. Of this, most of them know nothing: they will never understand that I am interested neither in gossip or making money. I tried to explain this long ago, but found it useless—now I don't try. But if they do boast in Asheville that I am "afraid to come back," it seems to me a pitiful boast to make. I am not afraid of any man living, nor do I apologize for my life to anyone, but I will not walk knowingly and willingly into any place where the population has threatened to attack me, unless there was something there I had to do, something to be gained by going. That is not the case: if I ever come home I want to be treated with the consideration and respect of any ordinary citizen—I don't care either for bouquets or lynching bees.

This is all for the present . . . remember I will always help when you ask me, but I depend on you to holler when the time comes. Come up to see me if you get a chance—if you can pick up a ride, the rest of the trip will cost you nothing. Meanwhile, good luck and best wishes to every one.

To ALFRED S. DASHIELL

[Postcard: Monument Rock, Eagle Island, Me.]

Orrs Island, Maine
August 8, 1931

Dear Fritz:

I'm cooked with sunshine from head to foot—it hurts something awful. I'm taking my meals at a boarding-house and the crowd of boarders is the same as it always was—they sit on the porch and rock—they never change. . . .

On August 27, 1931, Perkins wrote Wolfe saying: "I think you ought to make every conceivable effort to have your manuscript completely finished by the end of September. I meant to speak of this when we were last together. I hope you will come in soon and tell me what you think you can do." The following was Wolfe's reply.

To MAXWELL E. PERKINS

[40 Verandah Place]
[Brooklyn]
Saturday, August 29, 1931

Dear Max:

Thanks for your note which came this morning. I am glad you wrote me, because I have some definite idea of when you expect to see my book, and I can say some things about it that I wanted to say. You say you think I ought to make every conceivable effort to have the manuscript completely finished by the end of September. I know you are not joking and that you mean *this* September, and not September four, five, or fifteen years from now. Well, there is no remote or possible chance that I will have a completed manuscript of anything that resembles a book this September, and whether I have anything that I would be willing to show anyone next September, or any succeeding one for the next 150 years, is at present a matter of the extremest and most painful doubt to me.

I realize that it has been almost two years since my first book was published and that you might reasonably hope that I have something ready by this time. But I haven't. I believe that you are my true friend and, aside from any possible business interest, are disappointed because what hope you had in me has been weakened or dispelled. I want you to know that I feel the deepest regret on this account, but I assure you the most bitter disappointment is what I feel at present in myself. I don't want you to misunderstand me, or think that, aside from you and a few other people whose friendship has meant a great deal for me, I care one good Goddamn of a drunken sailor's curse whether I have "disappointed" the world of bilge-and-hogwash-writers, . . . or any of the other literary rubbish of sniffers, whiffers and puny, poisonous apes. If what I am about to lose because of my failure to produce was, as I once believed, something beautiful and valuable—I mean a feeling of deep and fine respect in life for the talent of someone who can create a worthy thing—then my regret at the loss of something so precious would be great. But do you really think that after what I have seen during the past eighteen months, I would cling very desperately to this stinking remnant of a rotten fish, or any longer feel any sense of deference or responsibility to swine who make you sign books to their profit even while you break bread with them, who insolently command you to produce a book and "be sure you make it good or you are done for," who taunt and goad you by telling you to take care since "other writers are getting ahead of you," who try to degrade your life to a dirty, vulgar, grinning, servile, competitive little monkey's life—do you think I am losing anything so wonderful here that I can't bear the loss? You must know that I don't care a damn for all this now.

I want you to know, Max, that the only thing I do care for now is whether I have lost the faith I once had in myself, whether I have lost the power I once felt in me, whether I have anything at all left—who once had no doubt that I had a treasury—that would justify me in going on. Do you think anything else matters to me? I have been a fool and a jackass—cheapened myself by making talks at their filthy clubs and giving interviews, but my follies of that sort were done long ago. For the rest I haven't tried to do anything but live quietly by myself without fancy mysterious airs, and there is as decent stuff within me as in anyone. I have kept my head above this river of filth, some of the dirty rotten lies they have told about me have come back to me, but I have yet to find the person who uttered them to my face. I want you to know that I consider that my hands are clean and that I owe no one anything—save for the debt of friendship for a few people. I did not write the blurbs, the pieces in the paper, the foolish statements, nor did I tell lies: no one can take anything from me now that I value, they can have their cheap, nauseous, seven-day notoriety back to give to other fools, but I am perfectly content to return to the obscurity in which I passed almost thirty years of my life without great difficulty. If anyone wants to know when I will have a new book out, I can answer without apology "when I have finished writing one and found some one who wants to publish it." That is the only answer I owe to anyone (I don't mean you: you know the answer I have tried to make to you already) and please, Max, if you can tactfully and gently, without wounding anyone, suggest to whoever is responsible for these newspaper squibs about my having written 500,000 words, and more all the time, that he please for God's sake cut it out, I will be grateful. I am sure it was intended to help, but it does no good. I assure you I am not at all afraid or depressed at the thought of total obscurity again —I welcome it, and I resent any effort to present me as a cheap and sensational person. In spite of my size, appetite, appearance, staying up all night, 500,000 words, etc., I am not a cheap and sensational person: if there is going to be publicity, why can't it tell the truth—that I work hard and live decently and quietly; that no one in the world had a higher or more serious feeling about writing; that I made no boasts or promises;

that I do not know whether I will ever do the writing I want to do, or not, or whether I will be able to go on at all; that I am in doubt and distress about it, but that I work, ask nothing from anyone, and hope, for my own sake, that I have some talent and power in me. I say, I am not afraid of publicity like this, because it would be the truth, and it could not injure me save with fools.

I thank God I am in debt to no one: I have sent my family all I could, Mrs. Boyd has had her full whack, the dentists are almost paid. Now, if they will all leave me alone, they can have the rest—if anything is left. I can't find out. I wish you'd find out for me and have Darrow send it to me. I've tried for a year to find out but I can't. I appreciate this paternal attitude, but it may be wasted on me, and I want to clear the board now. Above all, I don't want to owe you money. As things stand, in my present frame of mind about my work, it is a blessing to me that I owe you no money and have no contract with you for a second book.[1] Max, won't you ask Darrow to send me whatever money is coming to me? As things stand now, it seems important to me that I should know where I stand financially, and what I am going to have to do. I have earned my living teaching and in other ways before, and I believe I can earn my living again. As I told you the only thing that matters now would be to feel that the book has value and beauty for me, and that I have the power to do it—if I felt that, I could do any work to support myself and feel good about it.

Max, I have tried to tell you how I feel about all this, and now I want to sum it up in this way: Two years ago I was full of hope and confidence: I had complete within me the plans and ideas of at least a half dozen long books. To-day I still have all this material, [but] I have not the same hope and confidence; I have, on the contrary, a feeling of strong self-doubt and mistrust—which is not to say that I feel despair. I do not. Why this has happened I do not know. I think one reason is that I cannot work in a glare; I was disturbed and lost self-confidence because of the notice I had; I think my success may have hurt me. . . . I don't know whether this means I am unable to meet the troubles of life without caving in—this may be true, and in my doubt I think of some of the old books I read: "The Damnation of Someone or Another," [2] "The Picture of Dorian

---

[1] The contract for *Of Time and the River* was not drawn until May, 1933. In his letter of December 18, 1929, in which he confirmed the agreement to pay Wolfe an advance of forty-five hundred dollars in installments, Perkins had written: "We should be glad to draw up a contract with regard to your next novel . . . which would embody this agreement. We only defer drawing this contract because it is unnecessary so far as we are concerned, since this letter is binding. . . . For the present . . . this letter may stand as a definite agreement."

[2] Probably *The Damnation of Theron Ware,* by Harold Frederic.

Grey"—in which spiritual decay, degeneration, and corruption destroys the person before he knows it. But I think that is literary nightmarishness: maybe these things happen, but I don't think they happened to me. I think I have kept my innocence, and that my feeling about living and working is better than it ever was. And I don't think I am unable to cope with the trial of life, but I think I may meet it clumsily and slowly, inexpertly, sweat blood and lose time. What I want to tell you is that I am in a state of *doubt* about all this.

Finally, the best life I can now dream of for myself, the highest hope I have is this: that I believe in my work and know it is good and that somehow, in my own way, secretly and obscurely, I have power in me to get the books inside me out of me. I dream of a quiet, modest life, but a life that is really high, secret, proud, and full of dignity for a writer in this country—I dream of a writer having work and power within him, living this fine life untouched and uncoarsened by this filth and rabble of the gossip-booster [set?]—I dream of something permanent and fine, of the highest quality, and if the power is in me to produce, this is the life I want and shall have.

Thus, at great length, I have told you what is in my mind better than I could by talking to you. Max, do you understand that this letter is not bitter and truculent, save for those things and persons I despise. I want to tell you finally that I am not in *despair* over the book I have worked on—I am in *doubt* about it—and I am not sure about anything: I think I will finish it, I think it may be valuable and fine—or it may be worthless. I would like to tell you about it, and of some of the trouble I had with it. I can only suggest it: I felt if my life and strength kept up, if my vitality moved in every page, if I followed it through to the end, it would be a wonderful book—but I doubted then that life was long enough, it seemed to me it would take ten books, that it would be the longest ever written. Then, instead of paucity, I had abundance—such abundance that my hand was palsied, my brain weary—and in addition, as I go on, I want to write about everything and say all that can be said about each particular. The vast freightage of my years of hunger, my prodigies of reading, my infinite store of memories, my hundreds of books of notes, return to drown me—sometimes I feel as if I shall compass and devour them, again be devoured by them. I had an immense book and I wanted to say it all at once: it can't be done. Now I am doing it part by part, and hope and believe the part I am doing will be a complete story, a unity, and part of the whole plan. This part itself has now become a big book: it is for the first time straight in my head to the smallest detail, and much of it is written —it is a part of my whole scheme of books as a smaller river flows into a big one.

As I understand it, I am not bound now to Scribners or to any publisher by any sort of contract: none was ever offered me—neither have I taken money that is not my own. The only bond I am conscious of is one of friendship and loyalty to your house, and in this I have been faithful—it has been a real and serious thing with me.

I know that you want to see what I have done—to see if I had it in me to do more work after the first book, or whether everything burnt out in that one candle. Well, that is what I want to see, too, and my state of doubt and uneasiness is probably at least as great as your own. It seems to me that that is the best way to leave it now: the coast is clear between us, there are no debts or entanglements—if I ever write anything else that I think worth printing, or that your house might be interested in, I will bring it to you, and you can read it, accept it or reject it with the same freedom as with the first book. I ask for no more from anyone. The life that I desire, and that I am going to try to win for myself, is going to exist in complete indifference and independence to such of the literary life as I have seen—I mean to all their threats either of glory or annihilation, to gin-party criticism or newspaper blurbs and gossip, and to all their hysterical seven-day fames. If a man sets a high value on these things he richly deserves the payment he will get. As for me, I tell you honestly it is a piece of stinking fish to me—their rewards and punishments. I see what it did to writers in what they now call "the twenties"—how foolishly and trivially they worshipped this thing, and what nasty, ginny, drunken, jealous, fake-Bohemian little lives they had, and I see now how they have kicked these men out, after tainting and corrupting them, and brought in another set which they call "the younger writers," among whom I have seen my own name mentioned. Well, I assure you I belong to neither group and I will not compete or produce in competition against any other person—no one will match me as you match a cock or a prizefighter, no one will goad me to show smartness or brilliance against another's—the only standard I will compete against now is in me: if I can't reach it, I'll quit.

It is words, words—I weary of the staleness of the words, the seas of print, the idiot repetition of trivial enthusiasms. I am weary of my own words but I have spoken the truth here. Is it possible that we are all tainted with cheapness and staleness: is this the taint that keeps us sterile, cheap, and stale in this country? When I talk to you as here and say what I know is in my heart, am I just another Brown—a cheap stale fellow who pollutes everything he talks about—justice, love, mercy—as he utters it? It isn't true—I am crammed to the lips with living. I am tired with what I've seen, I'm tired of their stale faces, the smell of concrete and taut steel, the thing that yellows, dries, or withers us—but did it mean nothing to you when I told you the beauty, exulting, joy, richness, and undying power that I had found in America, that I knew and believed to be the *real* truth, not the illusion, the thing we had never found the pattern for, the style for, the true words to express—or was it only words to you; did you just think I was trying to be Whitman again? I know what I know, it crushes the lies and staleness like a rotten shell, but whether I can ever utter what I know, whether staleness and weariness has not done for me, I don't know. Christ, I am tired of everything but what I know to be the truth, and do not utter—I have it inside me. I even know the words for it, but staleness and dullness has got into me, I look at it with grey dullness and will not say it—it's not enough to see it: you've got to feel the thick snake-wriggle in each sentence, the heavy living tug of the fish at the line.

I'm out of the game—and it is a game, a racket: what I do now must be for myself. I don't care who "gets ahead" of me—that game isn't worth a good goddam: I only care if I have disappointed you, but it's very much my own funeral, too. I don't ask you to "give me a chance," because I think you've given me one, but I don't want you to think this is a despairing letter, and that I've given up—I just say I don't know, I'm going to see: maybe it will come out right someday. By the way, I'm still working, I've been at it hard and will keep it up until I have to look for job: I may try to get work on Pacific Coast. I'll come in to see you later, Max. Please get Darrow to send me what money is coming to me.

When I was a kid we used to say of someone we thought the best and highest of that he was "a high class gentleman." That's the way I feel about you. I don't think I am one—not the way you are, by birth, by gentleness, by natural and delicate kindness. But if I have understood some of the things you have said to me, I believe you think the most living and beautiful thing on this earth is art, and that the finest and most valuable life is that of the artist. I think so, too: I don't know whether I have it in me to live that life, but if I have, then I think I would have something that would be worth your friendship. You know a good deal about me—the kind of people I came from (who seem to me, by the way, about as good as any people anywhere), and I think you know some of the things I have done, and that I was in love with a middle-aged Jewish woman old enough to be my mother—I hope you understand I am ashamed of none of these things—my family, the Jewish woman, my life —but it would be a hard thing for me to face if I thought you were repelled by these things, and did not know what I am like. I think my feeling about living and working and people is as good as you can find, and

I want you to know how I feel: it's so hard to know people and we think they feel inferior about things they really feel superior to, and the real thing that eats them we know nothing of.

I'm coming in to talk to you soon, but I can talk to you about some things better this way. Meanwhile, Max, good health and good luck and all my friendliest wishes.

P.S. I'm attaching a clipping [3] a friend sent me from a Boston paper. You see how quickly people can use an item like this injuriously. I think it has done harm, and I don't deserve it: please get them to cut it out and leave me alone.

To A. S. FRERE-REEVES

Harvard Club
New York

Saturday, September 19, 1931

Dear Frere:

I'm sorry I've been so long in answering you. I have plugged away as hard as I could during the summer—and the summer has been past all your dreams of hell. Maybe there's a law of distribution and compensation which gives England the horrible winters and America the horrible summers.

About the five shilling edition of L.H.A.—if you think it is a good move, both for Heinemann and me, go ahead and do it.[1] I'm almost stony broke—sent all I could to my family in the South and have nothing left. I'm living . . . in Brooklyn, which is a vast sprawl upon the face of the earth, which no man alive or dead has yet seen in its foul, dismal entirety. I don't know how it *looks* but I'm an authority on how it smells. . . . In the subway, where we are still using the air the subway people bountifully provided last April, all of these stinks have been mixed, melted, fused and wrought into one glamorous, nauseating whole—and *that* is the way Brooklyn smells.

Do what you think best about the five shilling edition. If it means a

---

[3] The clipping reads as follows: "Fiction is threatened with an epidemic of obesity. One of the latest symptoms in this country—the English situation is general and serious—is word from Thomas Wolfe who is working on a Maine coast island on a novel to be called *October Fair*. He confesses to a total of 500,000 words to date, and Charles Scribner's Sons are telegraphing their pleas for a process of selection, revision and condensation."

[1] This edition of *Look Homeward, Angel* was published by Heinemann in February, 1932.

little money for me, it will be most welcome. Whether and when I shall ever get another one finished is at present a matter of extreme and painful doubt. Whenever anyone asks me when it will be published, I tell them when I finish writing it and find a publisher who is willing to print it. Whether I find one is also a matter of doubt. For one thing, however, I am grateful—at last I am left alone—I may breathe the seventy-nine stinks of Brooklyn but I no longer breathe the unutterably fouler stink of *la vie litteraire,* as practiced in this noble city, and I suppose elsewhere. I am free, finished, deserted, left gloriously alone, by the last son of a bitch of an autograph collector and gossip writer, and the last stale whore of a literary party-giver. . . .

If you think I am talking through my hat—(I haven't got one anyway: the one I bought at Lodis is worn out)—when I say that this sweet cool gloom of obscurity again is balm and healing to my soul—then you know nothing about me; but maybe you wondered when I would find out what a piece of stinking fish the literary racket is. Well, I knew it all along, but there are some things you can't believe until they happen— the truth is so much more incredible than either *The Daily Mail* or *The Express.*

I understand Richard Aldington's book [2] has made a great stir in England, and is being denounced on the playing fields of Eton, etc., and is a big success, and I am heartily glad. It is being spoken of here a great deal, and I am going to read it as soon as possible. One doesn't have to go to war to understand bitterness. I think Renan said that the only thing which could adequately describe the idea of the infinite was the spectacle of human stupidity—and God knows he hit the nail on the head. I've just come from dear old Broadway—first visit in months—and as you look at them sweating along through this stale monotony of glare, noise and idiot illumination, you wonder at the quality of intelligence which has spent thousands of years in order to bring men to this—and yet the poor unhappy bastards try to tell themselves they are being amused!

I don't think I'd leave the country now, even if I could. I think some very interesting things may happen here, are happening, have already happened—although most of them still stand around with their mouths ajar and looking upward, as if they expected the gates of heaven to open up the next moment and piss milk and honey all over them. That really is just what they *do* expect—they think there is some law of matter or quantity which governs their crazy economic system: they talk profoundly about "the pendulum swinging backward" etc., when there's no reason to suppose it ever will, although it may. Meanwhile, Mr. Hoover ("The Great Engineer," you know) and the other noble politicians are

[2] *The Colonel's Daughter.*

giving a wonderful illustration of the blind man searching in a dark room for a black cat that isn't there. There are seven million out of work— and Mr. Hoover issues a call for $20,000,000 so that each of the unemployed will have $2.50 to squander away during the winter. It is masterly. The real Russian menace, so far as I can see, is simply that Russia does not seem to be governed by a set of Goddamned fools! Even an intelligent and purposeful lunatic would be a formidable menace against a school of feeble-minded jelly fish.

Enough, enough! Do what you can with the book and try to get me some money for it. The best I can tell you about myself is that I am well, bad-tempered, and full of work. Maybe I'll get something done some day—I don't know. . . .

The following letter was written to a mutual friend of Wolfe's and Kenneth Raisbeck's shortly after Raisbeck's body had been found in a graveyard in Connecticut. At first it was thought that he had been murdered, but an autopsy found that he had died of acute meningitis.

To ————

[40 Verandah Place]
[Brooklyn]

[October, 1931]

Dear ——:

I have seen and talked to —— ——, he called me up late Saturday afternoon, said he . . . would like to see me. I made an appointment with him at the Harvard Club, met him there at 7:30, went to a speakeasy for some drinks and then to a restaurant where we talked to 1:30. When I left him, he was on his way to see Emily Davies.

I think I have heard the whole story now. He showed me the remarkable letter Kenneth had written him a couple of years ago, naming a list of people whose friendship he valued—I am mentioned along with several others, including yourself. He also showed me another sensational story which he had clipped from one of the tabloid papers on Saturday. It was a mass of obscene rumours and suggestions—there was no tangible evidence, but hints of "nude cults," "fashionable artistic colonies," rendezvous with married women and vengeance by husband or lover, etc.

The cumulative horror of the story has weighed on me so heavily that at times it amounts almost to physical nausea. I understand your anxiety and desire to keep the names of innocent people whom Kenneth may

have known out of this mess. But I cannot for the life of me see why any
of us should cower before these slimy, scandal-mongering bastards of the
yellow press. If their crooked power is so complete that they can hurl
filth all over decent people whose only relation to the case is that they
knew the dead man—then I think we had better not concern ourselves
very much with fear of a public opinion that will swallow such muck,
hook, line and sinker.

Of one thing I feel reasonably convinced now—that Kenneth came to
his death by natural causes, that he was not murdered. Of these other facts
which you and —— have told me, I don't know what to say or think—
I have had at times a sickening sense of horror or doubt, but I think that
these things must now remain forever in mystery, buried in our memory
or obliterated by our faith. My final sense about the matter is this: I
remember him as he was when we were students together at Harvard,
as my friend—as the remarkable, fine and brilliant person I believed and
believe him to have been. I believe your sentiment is the same, and I
know of no reason why we should change it. . . .

> [THE LETTER BREAKS OFF UNFINISHED, AND WAS EVIDENTLY NEVER
> MAILED.]

To FRED W. WOLFE

Harvard Club
New York

October 4, 1931

Dear Fred:

. . . I have been away for a few days, but came back Thursday
night: was up in the Catskill Mountains on the estate of some friends.[1]
. . . When I got back I read some news in the paper which depressed me
greatly. A man I used to know at Harvard—in fact, we were the closest
friends there—has just died. His body was found in a graveyard in Connecticut, and the doctor's report was that he died suddenly of acute
meningitis, but the police believe he was murdered: they found bruises
on his neck, and the grass round about him was torn up—the doctor says
this might have happened from his own convulsions in his dying moments. He was a very brilliant young fellow who had many friends ready
to help him—every one believed he had a great future; but he did nothing with it. I had a falling out with him in Paris several years ago and we
have not seen each other since, although I had a chance to befriend him
a year or two ago, and did it—I took his play to someone who got it put

[1] Probably the L. Effingham de Forests at Onteora Park.

on for him. But the play failed.[2] I have felt very depressed about it: I forget about the falling out we had and I remember the time we were both young fellows at Harvard full of hope, and what good friends we were. It seems a terrible thing that his life should end as it did.

I have not made the trip to Pennsylvania yet, but may go down later. Thanks for sending me the very full and complete information [3]—it will be very useful when I make the trip. . . .

There's very little more to tell you at present, so I'll cut this short hoping it finds you and Mama well, and conditions a little improved at home. I am writing this from the Harvard Club which two years ago was full of life and bustle and laughter: to-night it's as dead as a tomb and you can cut the depression with a knife. They had their fling and they're in for a very long morning after.

Goodbye for the present and good luck and good health to everyone. . . .

If you need anything, holler: it may not do much good, but I'll always make an effort.

P.S. I think the depression's so bad they've begun to water the ink here at the club. . . .

To SINCLAIR LEWIS

[111 Columbia Heights]
[Brooklyn]

[January, 1932]

Dear Red:

I have thought of you often and I am sorry I have not written you before—anyway, I send you now my best and warmest wishes for health and happiness this New Year. I have been living in Brooklyn since I came back and working like hell—going to finish my new book this year or fall in my tracks.

Red, I want to thank you gratefully for getting your German publisher [1] to take my book and publish it—the reason I have never written you

---

[2] Wolfe had taken the manuscript of Raisbeck's play, *Rock Me, Julie,* to Madeleine Boyd who sold it to a Broadway producer. It opened at the Royale Theatre on February 3, 1931, but ran for only seven performances.

[3] Wolfe planned to go to York Springs, Pennsylvania, to look up the remaining members of his father's family there, and had written home for information about them.

[1] Rowohlt Verlag.

about it is because I never knew it was an accomplished fact until this morning. You told me in England last year that you had spoken to your German publishers and that they had accepted the book, but I heard no more about it until today. . . .

I hope you will accept this letter as a full and sufficient apology for my failure to write and thank you for your generous and kind interest in this matter: I know perfectly well that I owe the publication of my book not only in Sweden but also in Germany to your own efforts, and I want you to understand how deeply touched and grateful I am for all you have done, and how much I regret the trouble you have been put to. Whether I shall ever justify the wonderful things you said about my work I do not know, but I will try, and am trying at present with all my heart; and if I cannot do it now, maybe I will some day in the future. But I will never forget what you said or did—your praise and powerful commendation dropped on me like a bolt of beneficent lightning—it was one of the most generous and wonderful acts I ever knew or heard of, and I'll never forget it.

I'm living at 111 Columbia Heights, Brooklyn, and my phone number is Main 4–0189, and I'd like to see you and Mrs. Lewis some time. If you're too busy, it's all right, but I hope we can get together. I don't go out much: I'm working away: I've got magnificent material for a book—whether I am as good as the material is another thing. Good bye for the present, Red, and good luck and good health always, and many many thanks for what you have done. You said something to me about Max Perkins a year ago: I'd like to say to you that he has the most genuine and whole-hearted admiration for your genius and power as a novelist—he feels, as I do, that your talent is unique and permanent, that there is no one like you, and that if they read any of our books in the future they will have to take account of you. You may think I'm laying it on with a trowel, but I'm not: I'm hurling it at you with a bucket—and what's more, I mean every damned syllable and letter of it.

I hope this finds you all well and happy, and I send you my best and warmest wishes for the New Year.

The following brief note was left on Perkins' desk with a manuscript, probably that of "A Portrait of Bascom Hawke," which was accepted by Scribner's Magazine on January 28, 1932, and published in the April, 1932, issue. A somewhat different version of it appears in Of Time and the River *on pages 104–111, 116–130, 132, 136–141, 141–150, 177–184, 185–186, and 192.*

To MAXWELL E. PERKINS

[January, 1932?]

Dear Max:

Part of this was written some time ago, and part very recently—and some of it quite rapidly. I've simply tried to give you a man—as for plot, there's not any, but there's this idea which I believe is pretty plain—I've always wanted to say something about *old men* and *young men,* and that's what I've tried to do here.

I hope the man seems real and living to you and that it has the unity of this feeling I spoke about. I could do a lot more to it, but I'd like you to see it. Please read all of it, Max.

To HENRY A. WESTALL

[111 Columbia Heights]
[Brooklyn, N.Y.]

[January, 1932]

Dear Uncle Henry:

Thanks very much for your letter. I was relieved to know that Mama had arrived safely,[1] and sorry to hear she has not been feeling well: I trust she is now better. . . . I thank you very sincerely for your kind invitation to come to visit you: I am afraid it is not possible for me to make such a trip at present, but I assure you nothing would delight me more if I come to Boston again. . . .

I note what you say about the advantages of seclusion and quiet for a writer. I entirely agree—but whether that is to be obtained more easily in a small town than in a great city I do not know. It seems to me that a man might find comparative peace and isolation among the swarms of people in the city, and be hounded and worried out of every attempt at privacy by the women's literary clubs, chambers of commerce, and curiosity seekers of some small town—particularly if he had reached any degree of reputation and success. I am, unfortunately, of a temperament that is easily distressed and distracted by outer disturbances, and I am constantly making an effort to control this, but my feeling is that one will get his work done wherever he is if he wants to do it hard enough. I am reminded of the saying of the poet Horace which strikes me as one of the truest and wisest things I have ever heard: "You may change your skies but not your soul"—and accordingly, I feel that it would be unwise to

---

[1] Wolfe's mother had come to visit him in Brooklyn and then gone on to see her brother, Mr. Westall, in North Reading, Mass.

move from my present home until I finish the piece of work that I am now busy with. I feel that it would be unwise because my tendency has been to wander and roam in search of a peace and security which I must find inside me, and although I may some day adopt your suggestion and move to a quieter and smaller place I shall not do that, I think, until I have finished the job I have set myself at present.

My mother, of course, has lived a long life and seen a great many things, but I do not think she or any of my immediate family understand very clearly just what the difficulties of the artist are, or what pain and labor of the spirit a man goes through in order to create something good. My family, for example, were more concerned with the gossip and scandal of the people of Asheville about my book than with the book itself: they still tell me what one of the Asheville butchers or grocers or lawyers had to say about it, and I don't think they ever asked themselves whether the book had any literary merit or not—when they read the opinions of critics in various papers later that the book did have merit, and heard that it was also enjoying a fair sale, they decided then that it was a success. Now please understand, Uncle Henry, that I am saying not one word in criticism of any of my family for feeling this way about it, but I do say that they have never understood and will never understand what goes on inside me when I write, or why I write. My family, I think, would like to see me succeed, but I believe their idea of my success would be to have me write a book that would sell one hundred thousand copies and make a lot of money. Now this would be very nice, I admit, and I should be glad to have the money—but that is not the reason I write: I write because I want to do the best that's in me, to create my vision of life as I have seen and known it, and to leave something, someday, that may have, I hope, some enduring value—and whether my book sells one hundred or one hundred thousand copies is not of primary importance to me. Neither do I write, as many people in Asheville mistakenly thought, in order to rake up the private lives of Brown or Jones or Smith—I was not "writing a book about Asheville," as many of them thought—I was writing a book about people living on this earth as I had known them, and what I said was as true of Pittsburgh or Boston or Brooklyn, as of Asheville. In doing this, of course, I used the materials I had, I made use of life as I had seen it, of experience as I had known it, I made use of what was my own—and, of course, this is what all men must do. I know that you will understand this: an artist does not work in order either to praise, wound, insult, or glorify particular people—he works in order to create some kind of living truth which will be true for all men everywhere.

[THE LETTER BREAKS OFF HERE]

To MABEL WOLFE WHEATON

111 Columbia Heights
Brooklyn, N.Y.

Jan 27, 1932

Dear Mabel:

Your post card came this morning. I have heard nothing from Mama since she left here and I am also beginning to be a little worried. I know that she arrived safely in Boston because I wired Uncle Henry immediately after she left New York. . . . He wrote me a few days later saying that Mama had arrived and been met on time and that she had not been feeling so well since her arrival but was now better. I am sure if there were anything seriously amiss someone would have informed us. . . .

This letter is being typed for me through the kindness of a young lady friend of mine here in Brooklyn. I suffered a trifling accident last night but very fortunately, I think, escaped injuries which might have been more serious. There was some question among the doctors as to whether my left arm had been broken or not, but that was apparently all cleared up to-day when they took X-rays and assured me they were confident that there was no fracture whatever, although I must wait until tomorrow morning to get a definite decision. I also severed a vein in my arm but the doctor very neatly stitched this together and I think, I have no doubt, that I shall be perfectly all right in a few days. If you write Mama, please don't say anything to her about this. I didn't mention it in my letter, because there is no need to worry her.

The way it happened was this: I had been having dinner in town with my friend, Maxwell Perkins: he lives in New Canaan, Conn., and he made me promise to see that he made his train without fail. When he got to Grand Central Station I went into the train with him and was talking with him about a piece of manuscript I had just given him to read when the train started off. The train was gathering motion as I reached the platform and I was thrown to the concrete pavement. They took me to the Emergency Hospital in the Grand Central Station where a doctor examined my arm and stitched up the cut place. I am very fortunate indeed that the accident was no worse, and I thank God that it was my left arm rather than my right, since my whole chance of living at present depends more or less on my right hand.

I have really been awfully worried about getting my work done, but I know it is going to be all right now, if I only stick to it and let nothing come in the way until I finish. . . .

I am sending my best wishes for health and happiness. I suppose Mama will want to stay with me for a day or two when she comes back through New York, and I hope she does. I wish it were possible for me to do more for her at the present time, but if I can finish my book maybe we can all meet together for a real celebration.

Goodbye for the present, Mabel—good luck, of course, as always. Write me when you have the opportunity.

The following letter was written in answer to a list of questions asked by Julian Meade, author of I Live in Virginia, The Back Door, *etc., who was writing an article on Wolfe for publication in* The Bookman. *Evidently Wolfe's reluctance "to get any more publicity at the present time," which he expresses in the final paragraph of his letter, made him postpone mailing it. At any rate, he failed to do so until July 7, after Meade had written the rough draft of the article and sent it for him to read. The piece was then re-written and submitted to* The Bookman, *but declined by them. It finally appeared under the title "Thomas Wolfe on the Use of Fact in Fiction" in the April 14, 1935, issue of* The New York Herald Tribune Books.

To JULIAN MEADE

> 111 Columbia Heights
> Brooklyn, N.Y.
> February 1, 1932

Dear Meade:

Thanks for your latest letter. My accident fortunately did not turn out as badly as I thought it had and as I told you: it now appears it did not break my arm but that it is only strained and bruised.

I want to give you some sort of answer to the questions you asked me in your first letter but as it is still a little hard for me to sit at the table and write, I am going to have to try to answer through dictation. I should like to be a great deal more careful and detailed in considering and making these answers but what I give you at present is more or less off-hand, and I hope, therefore, you will help me by using your own discrimination and by not letting me say anything that would tend to incriminate me.

As to your first question: you ask what answer I have to those who say I did a faithful picture of one city and its people. I should like to avoid this question completely if I could, as well as the other one which asks what answer I have for those who speak of me as an autobiographical writer. I should like to avoid them, Meade, not because I am in any sense afraid of the consequences of answering them as directly as I can, but because these questions have been asked before and my answer, although it seemed perfectly clear to me, only led to fresh argument, misunderstanding, and dispute. I should like very much to say something of what I feel about the relation of the writer to what is sometimes called autobiographical material: I don't want you to misunderstand me here and I know that I could be completely coherent about this if I only had time and could make the effort of writing down a complete statement. But I will say this to you: I think the roots of all creation in writing are fastened in autobiography and that it is in no way possible to escape or deny this fact. I think that a writer must use what is his own, I know of no means by which he can use what is not his own—do you? —nor would I think it desirable that he should. I made once before what seemed to me a very clear and simple statement of this obvious fact—namely, in a short preface to the reader which I wrote at the beginning of "Look Homeward, Angel"—and I was accused by several critics, including one or two on the Asheville newspapers, of "evading the issue" and of trying to avoid a direct answer whether my book was about Asheville and its citizens by a clever twist of words. Well, I have been so exasperated by what I considered an unfair and trivial comment that I said I would never attempt to make any answer at all to such criticism, but if there are really people who still want to know whether my book is about Asheville, North Carolina, and is a faithful picture of its inhabitants, I will say here and now that it is not about Asheville, North Carolina, and that it is not a faithful picture of the inhabitants of Asheville, North Carolina, or of any other place on earth that I have ever known; and finally, that I do not believe any book ever got written in this way. Certainly I could never write anything in this way: that is not the way a writer works and feels and creates a thing—he does not write by calling Greenville Jonesville or by changing the name of Brown and Smith to Black and White: if it's that easy let's all start out for the nearest town with a trunk full of notebooks and pencils and start taking down the words and movements of the inhabitants from the most convenient corner. I could go on with this indefinitely but I get hot under the collar when the word autobiography is mentioned because the way most people use it seems to me to have no sense or meaning whatever.

And yet the whole question of a writer's use of his material and of his true and essential use of autobiography seems to me an important and a fascinating one and I really believe I could say something about it that would have value, if I only had time to set it before you here now, because it is a question I have thought about so long, so carefully and so earnestly.

But I want to repeat that nowhere can you escape autobiography whenever you come to anything that has any real or lasting value in letters. For example as I walk around my room in the act of dictating this letter the first book my eye falls on is called "The Road to Xanadu": it was written by my old teacher, Professor John Livingston Lowes at Harvard and in it he attempts to trace the genesis, the sunken and hidden sources, of two of the most remarkable poems in the language—"The Rime of the Ancient Mariner" and "Kubla Khan." Professor Lowes has managed to track down almost all of the obscure and bewilderingly manifold elements which had gone into the making of "The Ancient Mariner." He knew, of course, that Coleridge was an enormous reader, that he literally read almost everything, and Lowes, by plowing through ten thousand forgotten and obscure books, has managed to show where almost every line, every image, every sentence in "The Ancient Mariner" comes from. Coleridge, of course, was not even conscious of the extent to which his own reading had influenced him: he has made use of a thousand elements of apparently unrelated experience to create something that was his own and that was beautiful and real and in the highest sense of the word original. Lowes goes on to attempt to show that the thing that happened when Coleridge wrote this poem happens when the artist creates anything—in other words, that this use of experience which is sunken in the well of unconsciousness, or which is only half remembered, is a typical use of the creative faculty.

Now what is this, Meade, except the most direct and natural use of autobiography, and how could Coleridge have written differently from the way he did write, and how could Joyce have written differently from the way he wrote, and how could Proust have written differently from the way he wrote? Coleridge's experiences came mainly from the pages of books and Joseph Conrad's experiences came mainly from the decks of ships, but can anyone tell you that one form of experience is less real and less personal than another, or that Coleridge's books had less reality for him than Conrad's ships; and finally, could anyone tell you that Joyce and Proust are either more or less autobiographical than Coleridge or Swift, and if they do tell you so, would you think their words any longer had meaning or were worthy of serious consideration?

Well, as I told you, I could go on with this for a long time but I think I have said enough to show you anyway the trend of my thought, and I know that I can trust your understanding and intelligence not to make me seem to speak illogically or foolishly or evasively when I am really standing on very firm ground.

You ask again if I look upon writing as an escape from reality: in no sense of the word does it seem to me to be escape from reality; I should rather say that it is an attempt to approach and penetrate reality. This I think is certainly true of such a book as "Ulysses": the effort to apprehend and to make live again a moment in lost time is so tremendous that some of us feel that Joyce really did succeed, at least in places, in penetrating reality and in so doing, creating what is almost another dimension of reality. I certainly think that most writing represents a struggle with reality—that most good writing has been done because the writer was in conflict with the world about him and, of course, each writer has had his own way of expressing that conflict—Mr. Cabell has had his way which you say he calls an escape from reality, and Coleridge had his way. But I do not think "The Rime of the Ancient Mariner" was for Coleridge an escape from reality: I think it was reality, I think he was on the ship and made the voyage and felt and knew it all. Swift's terrible conflict with the world about him resulted in "Gulliver's Travels" and I should certainly not call that book an escape from reality, but one of the most savage and inspired attempts to make his comment on the real world through a fable that literature knows.

I wish I could answer your other questions as fully and clearly as I should like, but I am afraid there is not time here. You ask if I think my work will be influenced by travel or whether my most vivid impressions were formed some time ago. I can't answer this question I am afraid very satisfactorily, but I want to say this: during the last few years I have often heard from the lips of those brillant amateur psychologists who seem to be swarming all over the country now by the millions, extraordinary statements to this effect—that everything that is of any value to a man happens to him sometime before he reaches the ripe old age of three years; that all of his impressions, emotions and traits of character are defined and fixed by that time, and that, in short, everything which a writer has to write about has already happened to him by the time he quits crawling around on the floor of the nursery. To my mind this is just another of those imbecilic things people say which deserves no comment whatever. If you want to know whether the most important part of my experience was acquired during my boyhood in the South, I have no means of telling you, but I do know this: I left home for college when I was not quite sixteen years old and I have not been back for any great length of time since. Almost half my life, therefore, has been spent in wandering and in living in various places on the earth's surface. I was driven to these by an impulsion of hunger and desire about which I can say very little here, which I can never tell any one about by means of a dictated letter, and which I may never be able to tell anyone about anyway, but it represents for me as much pain, as much effort, as much loneliness, as great a struggle to find some kind of better life on earth, some sense of peace, certitude, and direction in my own life and some answer to the riddle of this whole vexed swarming and tormented world as any effort I have ever made. I gave to it all the strength and power and passion that I have in me and it represents to me as much reality as I know: perhaps I may never be able to make use of any of it in my writing, perhaps I shall have to return to the things I knew about in my childhood, but I see no reason whatever why this should be true and I certainly shall not accept without protest the silly statements of people who say that everything that is of any value to you happened before you were five years old.

As to your other questions, Meade: I will have to lump them together now and come to a hasty conclusion. You ask if I write easily or with difficulty. I think I write with the most extreme difficulty: the trouble is not so much a lack of material but an over abundance of it. Condensation and brevity are terribly difficult for me, my manuscripts are hundreds of thousands of words long and almost my whole effort at the present time is to get my book within some reasonable length. I have two lives, one which is intensely conscious of the world around me, and one which lives with an equal intensity in the past: my memory is a kind of hunger and as I go on, my memory seems to get better, or worse, depending on which way you look at it. I am haunted by a sense of time and a memory of things past and, of course, I know I have got to try somehow to get a harness on it.

You ask me if I am still interested in the stage: if you mean by this am I still interested in writing plays, or will I ever write another one, my answer is no. I haven't the slightest interest in ever making the attempt again, although I think a man who is able to write a fine play has done one of the best things in the world. I don't think I could write one and I don't believe there is any need in telling you why I lost interest in making the attempt, and why it no longer means anything to me. I suppose the real answer is that it probably never possessed as much reality for me as I thought it did. As to whether I like music: I do like it, I have always thought I liked it very much, but my interest in it cannot be of the highest kind because I really know very little about music and although I live here in New York where I could hear the best music if my desire were strong enough, I almost never attend a concert of a symphony. My real interest has been in poetry—I really know a great deal about poetry, it seems to have taken the place in my life that music takes in the lives of many people. I have known and loved it so well that I remember it and I read it constantly. I do not read a great deal of new poetry and for this I am sorry: I do not suppose I have read a dozen books as often as four times apiece, but I have read hundreds of poems hundreds of times,—that is the only kind of writing that I can return to again and again without weariness or satiety.

Finally, you ask me about my literary preferences among living and dead authors: I am afraid that's too large an order for me to deal with here. For a great many years during my childhood and later when I was at Harvard, I read everything I could lay my hands on: the amount of reading I did was incredible and I can't attempt to tell you about it here. Upon the top shelf of my bookcase, however, I have attempted to put some of the books which I use all the time and which I am able to read again and again. All I can do is to give you a few of the titles, at any rate it will tell you something of the books I like best. At the present time, reading from right to left, the books in my top shelf are as follows: my old college edition of "The Illiad" parts of which I sometimes read; the Bible which I really read a great deal—I mean a few books, "Ecclesiastes," "The Book of Job," "The Song of Solomon," "Revelations"; Webster's Collegiate Dictionary which has in it some of the best reading in the world; the plays of Shakespeare; the poems of Coleridge; the poems of John Donne; "The Anatomy of Melancholy"; "Ulysses"; "War and Peace"; "The Brothers Karamazov"; "Leaves of Grass"; "Moll Flanders"; the plays of Molière; the poems of Heinrich Heine and a book of German lyrics. I delight in all manner of anthologies: I believe some people laugh at them but I have some great fat thick ones, all of them good ones, and I go back to them again and again. I can read French and German but these are the only modern languages besides English that I know anything about. I am afraid that is all I can do for you at the present, and I hope it will be of some use to you.

If you write this piece, Meade, I wish you'd send it to me and let me see it before you show it to anyone else. If it means anything to you at all, I am, of course, glad to help as much as I can, and, of course, I am pleased and grateful to think that you should want to write a piece about me and that anyone is interested in publishing it. I don't know, however, if this is really a good time for such an article: I am quite sincere in not being very anxious to get any more publicity at the present time because I think this is the time when I should try to work and produce, and I believe your article might have greater value if you let it go until I got at least one more book finished and published. But anyway please let me know what you do about it, and if you write it, please let me see a copy in advance. . . .

The following letter was written in reply to one from Stringfellow Barr suggesting that Wolfe might have some stories suitable for publication in The Virginia Quarterly Review. *At this time, Barr was editor of the* Quarterly, *and Professor of Modern History at the University of Virginia. He is now President of The Foundation for World Government, and author of* Citizens of the World.

To STRINGFELLOW BARR

111 Columbia Heights
Brooklyn, N.Y.
February 24, 1932

Dear Mr. Barr:

Thanks for your letter and excuse this scribbled note. I've been getting the proofs ready for a piece which is coming out in *Scribner's Magazine* this spring [1]—it was 30,000 words long, and of course that meant cutting —which is agony and weariness of the soul to me. I've also finished another story which must be typed [2]—it's about 15,000 and I'm going to show it to Max Perkins at Scribners: if they can't use it, maybe you'd be interested in seeing it for the *Quarterly.* Of course, I know you probably can't afford to pay high prices and I don't expect it—I am hard up, but I don't live in a very expensive way: I must do something to earn some money now. I also had another piece of 15 or 20,000 words [3]—finished before Christmas—but knew it would not be suitable for *Scribner's.* I talk knowingly about what is "suitable" etc., but really I don't know what the magazines want—I just write and hope I can do my best once in a while— but it *does* occur to me that some pieces of writing might have merit and yet be somewhat too special even for such a liberal magazine as *Scribner's.* And of course I say this humbly—I'd like nothing better than to write something that was both very good and very popular: I should be enchanted if the editors of *Cosmopolitan* began to wave large fat checks under my nose, but I know of no way of going about this deliberately and I am sure I'd fail miserably if I tried. It seems to me all a man can do is to write what he has to write as well as he can and then hope for the best. But am I right in supposing that the *Quarterly* is even more free from these demands of popular fiction—whatever they are—than *Scribner's?* I wrote a piece about a train a year or so ago—it is called "K 19" (the name and number of a pullman car) and the action occurs while the train is crossing the state of Virginia at night. I thought it was a pretty good piece and so did Perkins—I'd always wanted to write about a train: the way it looks, smells, feels, the sounds it makes, the quiet voices on the little country

[1] "A Portrait of Bascom Hawke."

[2] Probably "The Web of Earth" which was accepted by *Scribner's Magazine* on May 16, 1932, published in the July, 1932, issue and later included in *From Death to Morning.* However, the final version of "The Web of Earth" was about 39,000 words long.

[3] Probably the first draft of "Death the Proud Brother." Wolfe had been working on this during the summer and fall of 1931 but temporarily abandoned it in November to write "A Portrait of Bascom Hawke."

platforms when it stops—as well as the story of the people on the train: what they say, do, and think about. It wasn't in the usual magazine sense of the word a story, although to my mind it was, and a unified story to boot. Now, one of these small private presses [4] has asked to see it and I've promised to show it to them—if they don't use it, would you like to see it? I've never been very enthusiastic about small, elegant, privately-printed books which are sold at a high price—I think a book ought to give honest value, and even though my railroad piece might be good, I don't like the idea of printing it in a book and charging four or five dollars for it: I hate the hocus-pocus of professional book collecting; there's something scavenging and stinking about it.

I've got to get back to my book. I really work hard and am able to finish things—then a kind of paralysis sets in, I won't get them typed, I won't send them out, and once a publisher gets anything I write into proofs, I become more and more reluctant, humble doubts assail me, I keep the proofs until they are taken from me—I've got to do something about this, and, no matter what happens, I'm glad I finished that piece for *Scribner's* —it's out of my hands now, I can do no more about it, and I'm going to try to forget it.

Yes, please send me the *Quarterly*. I'd be delighted to have it, and thank you gratefully for it. . . . and if you come to town, please call me: Main 4-0189. Meanwhile, with best wishes,

The following letter was evidently written in reply to letters from George McCoy and Robert McKee of The Asheville Citizen, asking Wolfe for news about himself to be used in a piece about him in that paper. However, efforts to find such a piece have met with no success. Probably Wolfe never mailed the letter, since it was found in his own files and McCoy could find no copy of it in his.

To GEORGE W. McCOY

111 Columbia Heights
Brooklyn, N.Y.
March 22, 1932

Dear George:

Thanks very much for your letter and please give my apologies to Mr. Robert McKee.[1] I did get a letter from him a good many months ago I

---

[4] This private press remains unidentified.

[1] McKee was at this time City Editor of the *Citizen,* and is now with *The Atlanta Journal.*

am afraid, and had all those good intentions about it which are said to be a very popular kind of paving brick. I am going to try to answer the questions you asked me in your letter, and I will try to give you the information you ask for. I don't know what kind of news is of the greatest interest to the readers, so I am just going to write you this letter, and while dictation is a new and rather awkward experience for me, I know I can trust you to weed out anything that may sound too foolish. Just use your own discretion about it, George: it will be all right.

I ought to tell you how much I appreciate any interest the people at home may have in me or what I am doing, and I have certainly not refrained from writing you because I did not value that interest. The last two years have been very busy and very exciting ones for me: at one time I was swamped under an avalanche of letters which came from everywhere: many of them were very fine ones and I was sincerely grateful for them, but I am afraid a great many of them went unanswered. I did the best I could but the job was too much for me and I had my own work which I had to get on with, but I would like to take this opportunity of thanking anyone who may have written such a letter and never got an answer. Some day I think I will write a book about what happens to a fellow who writes a book: that's one subject that I now feel like an authority about, and I think it might make strange and interesting reading. I think I was about the most surprised and excited person on earth when I saw some of the difficulties the book had and some of the meanings that were read into it.

I know I may be treading on shaky ground here—I know so well what I would like to say to you about my intention and purpose as a writer, but it is hard to do it on the spur of the moment and I don't want to say anything that might be misunderstood. I would be most grateful to you, George, if you could convey to your readers the fact that I am simply a very hard worker and, I think, a very honest man, who is trying to master a very difficult and painful art and who wants to do the best work that is in him.

I wish for your sake, and the sake of the readers who want interesting news, that I could describe to you a very gay and Bohemian life, but the plain truth of the matter is that I lead about as solitary and obscure an existence as anyone you know. I live in an old house in Brooklyn Heights. I have two big bare rooms here which at the present moment are inundated under piles of manuscript, books, and stray shirts, socks and neckties. I live on Columbia Heights, which is the last street over and commands the finest view of New York harbor that can be had: unfortunately I am on the wrong side of the street to get the harbor view, but I can hear the ships blowing out in the harbor at night, a sound which sometimes starts up in me again all of my desires to wander. Outside of this, there is really no noise over here: it is about as quiet as any street you will find in Asheville.

As to my daily schedule, I begin to work about midnight and keep at it until four or five o'clock in the morning, then I go to bed and sleep until about eleven, get up, make coffee, of which I drink a pot or two every day, and then work on my manuscript until about one or two o'clock in the afternoon when the young man who is typing my book comes. We work together until six or six-thirty when he goes, and then if I have any energy left in me, I take a bath, get shaved and dressed, and go out to eat. I have a few friends here in New York of whom I am very fond and who have been wonderfully kind and decent to me: occasionally I spend the evening with them but most often I spend it alone. Sometimes I go over to town—by town I mean Manhattan—and eat late and then go the Harvard Club and read for an hour or two before it closes at one o'clock; then I come home and, if I can, get to work again.

That is a pretty accurate picture, George, of my life at the present time. I am sorry it sounds no more exciting but it suits me a good deal better than a gayer and more social existence. I scarcely ever go to a party unless one of my friends is giving it, and I am not a success at party-going anyway. I tell you all this because it has taken me a long time and cost me a great deal of difficulty and distress to find the kind of life I am best suited to lead. I live alone a great deal of the time; I make friends slowly and I value the few I have as highly as anything on earth. It seems to me now that the only sensible and decent life for the artist is an obscure, modest and fairly solitary one. I assure you I value fame as highly as any young man and hope with all my heart that I can some day do work that will justify it, but if it comes, I want it for my work and not for myself. I assure you this is not hokum: I think you understand I am telling you the plain truth. When I was a child, of course, and I thought that some day I might write something that would be published, I had the most glittering dreams and visions of a romantic literary life in which I not only was able to do magnificent work but also to be surrounded by adoring throngs of brilliant people. This dream has long since vanished and I am really not sorry to lose it.

It seems to me the reality I have now achieved is really a far better and more satisfactory way of living. I have found out that the man who hopes to create anything in this world of any enduring value or beauty must be willing to wreak it out of his spirit at the cost of unbelievable pain and labor: I know of no other way in which it can be done; he must work in the solitude and loneliness of art; no one can do it for him, and all of his childish dreams of a various and golden life, in which he has time to do everything and to triumph in all of them, are out of the question. I have tried to tell you how I felt about this as plainly as possible because I want you to understand that the thing which happened to me two years ago when my first book was published caused me a great deal of confusion and bewilderment: I read every scrap of criticism, or near-criticism, or praise, or abuse, whether it appeared in a New York paper or in the *Podunk Daily Curse*, and I was excited, elated, depressed, confused, or full of exultant joy over all of it. I took it all with a most tremendous earnestness: I was going inside all the time like a dynamo. I don't think anyone will condemn me very much for making this confession. I was a young fellow who had got his first book published, and I would be a damn liar if I told you that I took the whole thing in a calm and matter-of-fact way, but I do want to emphasize the fact that the man who writes a book is sometimes more astonished and confused by the effect it produces than anyone else. The whole effect, not only in Asheville but also in New York, was different from anything I had ever imagined, and for several months I was like a man trying to find his way out of the labyrinth.

I was deeply distressed to know that the book had caused any misunderstanding or resentment at home, and I was grateful and happy for what success it had up here and elsewhere, for the letters I received, and for some of the reviews. Then I discovered what seemed to me to be a tendency here in New York either to leave a young man who comes here without friends or position painfully and severely alone, or if he achieves even a modest success and some public notice in the press, to overwhelm him with invitations and hospitable attention. Please understand that I am not condemning the people here in New York on this account: it simply fits in with the custom and habit of life to which they are accustomed. They like to have the latest news about everything and to see the new writer: they mean well enough by it, of course, but it does sometimes put an honest and decent person whose chief desire in life is to do the best work of which he is capable, to make his own friends in his own way and to live the kind of life he wants for himself—it sometimes puts this man, I say, in the position of a damned dressed-up monkey on a stick, and if he is young and has not had any experience before in meeting a situation of this sort, he may be swept off his feet for a time. Now please don't misunderstand me or read anything boastful into this statement—I did not get very much of this treatment, I was not being lionized all over the place and pursued and hunted by the great ones of the city, but I did have a little of it and the little was too much.

Fortunately about that time I got the Guggenheim Fellowship which enabled me to go abroad for a year. While I was over there I was able not only to do a great deal of work on my new book, but I was able to think the whole situation over and to decide what kind of life I was going to have for myself and to determine, by God, to have it. I have already described to you what that life is.

I have outlined at the present time the material and plan of eight books: [2] enough work to keep me busy for years—and all I want in addition is peace and quiet and a few friends and a very moderate income, two hundred or two hundred and fifty dollars a month. If I work hard, there is no reason why I should not achieve all of these. I assure you with complete sincerity that I do not care to make money and want no more than enough to support me modestly and with a little comfort, and, perhaps, to let me ease my hunger once in a while for making voyages. That is about as good a statement as I can make to you at the present time. . . .

When I came back from Europe about a year ago, I was really in a state of despair about my book, not because I could not write it but because I could do nothing else but write it. I had written until I had hundreds of thousands of words; it was reaching a staggering length and I did not know what I could do to cut it or get it within some reasonable reading compass. The plan and the material, every incident of it, had been clear in my mind for months and months; I saw the whole thing through to its end, down to the minutest detail, and the more I thought about it, the longer it got. Then, because I needed money and had a feeling of despair over the book, I stopped suddenly, worked furiously for a month on a short novel and completed it. *Scribner's* immediately accepted it and published a part of it, as much as they could, in the magazine: I think it came out in this April's issue.[3] I immediately got busy on another short piece which rapidly lengthened into another short novel and *Scribner's* also accepted this: it is coming out, I understand in a few months, I don't know when, and my friend, Maxwell Perkins, who is the director at Scribners and whose literary opinion means more to me than anyone's, tells me it is one of the best things I ever did.[4] Finally, I have just completed another short novel which is really a part of my long book, "The October Fair," and which Perkins has not seen as yet, but which I hope and think may be good.[5] I am getting my novel typed now at the rate of

[2] What eight books Wolfe had in mind here is difficult to tell. Perhaps he simply meant the eight "books," or sections, of *Of Time and the River,* or perhaps he meant that entire series of novels, although only six are listed for it in the Publisher's Note at the beginning of *Of Time and the River: Look Homeward, Angel, Of Time and the River, The October Fair, The Hills Beyond Pentland, The Death of the Enemy, Pacific End.*

[3] "A Portrait of Bascom Hawke." It did come out in the April issue of *Scribner's Magazine,* which was published late in March, at just about the date of this letter.

[4] "The Web of Earth."

[5] This short novel remains unidentified. According to one of Wolfe's notebooks, he wrote "The Train and the City," "Death the Proud Brother" and "No Door"

about 3,000 words a day, and I hope to have the manuscript ready within the next three months. . . .

You ask about my plans for coming back to Asheville and when I am coming back: I can't give you any definite date at present. I have got to work like hell and produce: I can think of no better or happier fate at the present moment than working myself to a frazzle in getting this book and one or two other things I have in mind completed. Then, if I can make a little money, I would like to take a short trip to Europe and then go West, where I have never been, and explore that district for a time; then I would like to find a place to settle down and live and work, and, of course, I have always had it in my heart that I would come back home some day. I think of you all a great deal, and I think you understand that it is impossible for a man ever to forget the place where he spent the first twenty years of his life and where most of his people have lived for a matter of one hundred and fifty years or so. I miss Asheville, but although I was born there and grew up there, I think that what I miss most is the country around there and the mountains.

Frankly, I don't want to come home until I have done more work and until people understand plainly, as I hope and believe they will, what it is I am trying to do and what my work is about. I know you understand, George, that I do not say this in any resentful or truculent spirit. I decided after "Look Homeward, Angel" was published that if, either through my own fault or the fault of certain readers, the intention of that book, which was simply to rig out a part of my vision of life as I had seen and known it, . . . and which certainly had in it no conscious and deliberate intention of saying a word to attack, wound or offend any living person—after the publication of that book, I say, and the experience I had with it, which I have tried to describe to you and which astounded and bewildered me more than anyone, I decided never to write a word if I could help it in answer to any criticism, whether in the form of a personal letter or in the press, which seemed to me to be unfair and unjust; and I have lived up to that decision ever since and hope that I will always be able to, although my first tendency two years ago was to take pen and paper at once and make some kind of a hot answer or impassioned defense. But I feel that a man's work itself must be his answer, and if he has not been able in his first book to reveal his intention and meaning, then I think if he is misunderstood himself, he must learn to possess his soul with patience, and stick to his job resolutely until he has revealed himself, and people know the kind of person he is.

That is what I propose to do and I want to make it very plain to you that in all that I have said, there is neither a word of truculent resentment

---

between March 9, 1932 and March 9, 1933. Probably he meant a version of "The Train and the City."

or of rancor toward anyone or anything in Asheville, or a word of apology and defense for myself. I have no apology and defense to make, and at the same time I want you to know, as I think you do know, that I am bound to my home and the people I knew there by the warmest and deepest ties. If I ever come home to live, I want to come neither in the role of the town villain nor as the conquering hero: I assure you I am not equipped to play either of these parts. I want to come to my own home decently and quietly and to see my old friends again, and, if necessary, to tell prying and curious people to go to hell. I think I have made my meaning clear and I don't believe that there is a word in this letter at which any sensible and decent person would take offense or disagree.

Now, George, I have tried to get it off my chest, and I hope I have been able to give you the information you asked for. I rely absolutely on your good sense and discretion not to put anything in the paper that would give people a wrong idea of how I stand. Use anything you like in this letter, whatever may be of use to you and that will not do any damage to me, but if it seems to you that it would be unwise to use part of it, or all of it, I would be grateful to you if you would chuck the whole thing. Also, if you do write a piece in the paper about me, I wish you would make it plain as gracefully as you can that I am not trying to rush into print and inform the folks at home of my doings, and say that I have written and given you this information in a personal letter in response to several requests which you and Mr. McKee made to me. I am not a publicity hound and I don't want any more of it than I can help until my new book is published. This is also the plain unvarnished truth, although it is hard to convince a good many people in this sometimes cynical world of the sincerity of such statements. I think this is all I can tell you at the present.

Thanks again for writing and for your friendly interest. I assure you once more that I am deeply grateful for any friendly interest the people at home may have in what I do. . . . With very best wishes to you and all my friends.

To A. S. FRERE-REEVES

Harvard Club
New York
April 15, 1932

Dear Frere:

Thanks very much for your letter which came a day or two ago. I have thought of you often. I wanted to write but for the past six months

I have been working harder . . . and faster than I ever did before. "The October Fair" will not be one novel, but a series of novels, and each, I hope, complete in itself but all related to a single thing. The section I am working on at present, and which I hope to have down on paper within three months, and which Scribners wants to publish in the autumn, is called "K 19," [1] which is the name of a Pullman car on an American train. I cannot tell you very much more about it now save that it will be a very long book and it will have the lives and stories of a great many people in it, and I hope it will be full of interest and movement. I am writing at the rate of three, four, and occasionally five thousand words a day, which is more work than I have ever done before. I work every day until I can literally do no more, and then I quit, get something to eat, if I still have appetite for it, take a walk across the Brooklyn Bridge and back, and then try to get some sleep if I can. This is the reason I have not had much time to write you. I get terribly tired, but I am also very happy to be getting something done at last, and I think everything is going to be all right now.

I did a terrific amount of preparation and preliminary work on that book, and I am sure my time and labor was not wasted but what I was really doing apparently was getting the cement mixed for the building. Anyway I have learned a great deal about working, and I think it will come easier in the future.

It has been a hell of a job. I think I was deluded by some fantastic notion that I could say the final and ultimate word about everyone and everything all at once in a single huge and monstrous tome. I learned bitterly that it could not be done and I will have to write my books as other men have written theirs, one at a time. At any rate, if you ever hear the sad news of my sudden and tragic extinction, which God forbid you won't, I want you to remember that I was not a man who starved to death but a man who died of gluttony, choking to death on an abundance of food, which surpassed everything but his hunger.

Spring is coming on here now. I think of you very often—also of April now that England's there, and maddening memories and visions return

---

[1] By this time, Wolfe and Perkins had decided that he could not possibly include all of his material in a single book. Wolfe accordingly went back to a variation of *The Fast Express*, which he had planned to use as part of *The October Fair* and which he now proposed to publish as a separate book under the title *K 19*. However, as he worked on it, he began writing long digressions on the lives of some of the passengers on the train, with the result that it became too long and too diffuse. Finally, in July, 1932, Perkins read the manuscript and broke the news to Wolfe that it was not good enough to be published as a separate book. Parts of it, such as many of the train scenes and the story "Boom Town," were later used in *Of Time and the River, The Web and the Rock,* and *You Can't Go Home Again.*

to me of Stone's Chop House and the ale you get there, and of Simpson's and the beef and mutton you get there, and at the present moment I could even do very nicely with an ordinary pub and half a dozen bottles of Bass Ale.

I live in Brooklyn Heights, on the last street above the harbor, and I can hear the ships blowing at night as they put out to sea for "Yurrup" and other fabulous coasts, and the desire to arise and go and fall upon your neck is very strong within me, but my purse is lean since I am only a poor American and not one of you bloated, blasted, foreign plutocrats.

I also have a publisher who has been angelic in his patience, but who is now beginning to call up from day to day and to say anxiously "when can you deliver the first 2,000,000?" So unless your employers decide suddenly and soon to hurl you across the ocean again on some mission of great and delicate trust, I must defer the pleasure of seeing you until I have freed myself of this octopus of a book with whom I am now engaged in deadly combat. Nevertheless, I am looking forward to the day when I shall reel and totter into your office, only a wisp and shell of my former self, or perhaps be borne in upon a litter, in the reclining posture which has been made so famous in recent years by all the leading British heavyweights. Anyway, Frere, if I finish that damned book and come to England will you go to Stone's with me? Will you go to Simpson's with me? If I rent an airplane, will you get in the pilot's seat and fly to Paris with me? These are only a few of the suggestions I have to make, but we might do these things right away and then settle down later to the more serious business of visiting the Scandinavian countries, Russia, Greece, India, Ireland and Japan. . . .

I think you said something about publishing "The Portrait of Bascom Hawke." I haven't thought very much about this. With the new story which *Scribner's Magazine* is going to publish and which is called "The Web of Earth" and which Perkins says is very good, and with another story which I have written, there would be enough to make a good-sized book, but I think it might be better to wait until the long book is published. I do need money and if you know of any publications in England which can print stories as long as the "Hawke" or "Web of Earth," which is also thirty or forty thousand words, and you think they might be interested in them, I should be glad if you would speak to them about it, but honestly the thing I would like most of all to do, Frere, is to get this job completed, come to England, and have a grand party with you—a barbaric and ghastly American orgy, beginning with ale, beer, port and sherry, and passing through successive nightmares of roast beef, mutton, champagne, brussels sprouts, hock and burgundy. Write and let me hear from you when you can. It will probably be some time before I am able to write to you again.

Meanwhile give my kindest and best wishes to Tom McGreevy, Richard Aldington, The Duke of York, The Prince of Wales, Mrs. Lavis, my charwoman, the Piccadilly Sirens, and any of my other friends you may happen to see. . . .

Good luck and good health, and all my best and warmest wishes, as always, Frere,

The following letter is the first in the correspondence between Wolfe and Robert Raynolds, author of Brothers in the West, *the Harper Prize Novel for 1931,* Saunders Oak, Fortune, May Bretton, Paquita, *and other novels and plays. Raynolds had reviewed* Look Homeward, Angel *very favorably in Scribner's Magazine (see the footnote to Wolfe's letter of October 27, 1929 to George Wallace for an excerpt from this review) but had had no personal contact with Wolfe until he had written him on March 31, 1932, to praise "A Portrait of Bascom Hawke."*

To ROBERT RAYNOLDS

111 Columbia Heights
Brooklyn, N.Y.
April 20, 1932

Dear Mr. Raynolds:

I got your letter some time ago and sat down and wrote you a very long reply which I did not finish and which stared accusingly at me for several weeks, and which has now been lost among the tottering piles of manuscript. I appreciated your letter and all you said in it tremendously, and I should be delighted and most grateful if you would send me a copy of "Brothers in the West" which I have not yet read. I have heard Fritz [1] speak of you a great deal and I knew of you as the author of "Brothers in the West" and Fritz told me something of your bold and courageous move in giving up everything and moving out into the country in order to write. Therefore, when I heard your book had won the "Harper Prize" I was genuinely delighted and felt there was justice left on earth after all, but I did not know until I got your letter that you were also the man who wrote the review of my book for *Scribner's Magazine.* I never made the connection nor completed the circuit until the

[1] Alfred Dashiell.

letter came. That review was the first I read about my book. Max Perkins called me up one day and read it to me over the phone, and then I went out and walked about the streets in a great many different directions. I hope that I have that feeling of jubilation and glory many times hereafter and that I shall always deserve as well and be treated as generously, but I know it will never again happen to me in just that way because that was the first time and it could not be brought back.

What you say about that circle of leering eyes which draws in about the poor wretch who is trying to write his second book, armed with tomahawks in one hand and a bouquet of roses in the other, and ready to hurl either— that also went right to the spot. It got on my nerves pretty badly for a while, but fortunately I had to forget about it the last few months out of sheer necessity. . . . The book on which I have been working for the last two or three years is not a volume but a library. I was never in the position of that fabulous creature we hear so much about who has nothing more to write about, but rather in the position of another unhappy monster who can do nothing else but write and can never come to the end of what he is writing. The book turned out to be not one volume but about four volumes, each complete in itself, and all belonging to a general thing. Goaded by desperation and necessity, I came to Brooklyn and have so far forgotten our friends of the leering eyes, but I hope to have the first folio completed in two or three months now.

I wish I could write you as good a letter as your own deserved but I cannot and I can only thank you for writing me and hope that we can get together some time when we have earned a holiday from this grievous agony of distilling out on paper your blood and marrow. . . . Meanwhile, I send you all my best and warmest wishes, for health and success in the work you are doing.

To JULIAN MEADE

> Brooklyn
> New York
> April 21, 1932

Dear Meade:

I have just received your last letter and I want to send you some sort of answer right away. Your various notes and letters have haunted my conscience for several weeks. I have literally been too damned busy with the work which I must now complete to attend to correspondence. I really wrote you a long and detailed answer to the questions you sent me and that letter is still around the place somewhere. I think I am going to get it out and send it on to you, perhaps with this one, but I want to read it over first to see if it still seems to me to be sensible and suitable to your purpose.[1] . . .

I am going to send you that letter anyway, because you seem to want to go ahead with the article and I know you will do a good job of it. I am still so much in an experimental stage myself, I have sweated so much blood the last two or three years in a sheer agonizing effort to find out how to use my material and how to work without such tremendous expenditure of labor and energy, that I feel it might not be the best time for an article such as you propose. Everything has started to come with a great rush during the last few months. . . . Suddenly a few months ago when I was at the very bottom of a deep black pit of depression and despair, I seemed to get hold of the free end of the knot and to yank it, and since then everything has begun to come. I work now every day as long and as hard as I can and I have very little time for anything else. I have forgotten that horrible sensation of being watched with critical eyes and I have got back the self-confidence which I had almost lost.

Go ahead and write the piece if you like. I wish somehow you could tell in it plainly and simply the real truth about me which is also the best thing about me and the thing I am not ashamed of—namely, that I was a young fellow, swarming with ideas and loaded with material for books he wanted to write, who went through a period of the greatest perplexity and distress, and who has tried with all his might to learn how to work and to learn how to live decently and obscurely and like an artist.

I wish I could tell people what happens to a man when he begins to write, and how the effect his first book has on him and on his readers is entirely different from anything he ever imagined, and how even in the very element of success which he dreamed of and wanted there is something terrifying and disquieting which fills his spirit with unrest and perplexity. Well, I can't tell you about it now, but some day I want to write a piece about it and tell the story.[2] I think it would make a good one. I think what I am trying to say to you is that a man in his desire to protect his talent and his spirit from a brutal public aggression, may get a bit of a chip on his shoulder: he feels mistrustful some times and disturbed even at the praise his work may get, however generous it may be and however much his soul may thirst for it, and he resolves therefore to put himself in a position to build up a power and strength within himself that will enable him to meet triumphantly not only the clamours and shouts of

[1] The letter dated February 1, which Wolfe did not send to Meade until July 7.

[2] This piece eventually became *The Story of a Novel,* which appeared serially in the December 14, 21, and 28, 1935, issues of *The Saturday Review of Literature* and was published in book form by Scribner's in April, 1936.

success but also the contempt and scorn and sudden isolation of failure. . . .

Finally I want to make it plain that I shall go on writing, that nothing can keep me from it, that I shall not allow myself to be pushed or goaded so that I feel that my whole life and chance of fulfillment or happiness is made to depend upon a single cast of the dice, a turn of mischance or good fortune. Please don't think that I am speaking ungratefully here of the generous and liberal support which is given so freely to-day to any-one who deserves it in any degree, but I have learned to hate with all the intensity of my spirit the Goddamn pushing literary racket. I'll have no part in it and I am not going to let it touch me if I can help it in any way whatever. I will not be driven into some obscene jargon of literary competition against any man or woman living. The only man I will compete with is myself, and the only conflict I will record is the conflict of the artist with the world about him and with the elements of confusion and chaos and dissonance in his own spirit. I assure you that's a big enough job to occupy all the time and energy a man has and that's the only one I am concerned with at present. I will not say any more about this now because it is a subject I could continue with almost indefinitely, but I hope I have managed to indicate something of what I feel about the way a man has to do his work and meet the world. . . .

I wish I had more time to help you in any way I could with the piece you propose to write but I am now pressed for time and the necessity of finishing my book. Anyway, if you write the piece, won't you please send it to me before you send it to the publisher, and if you should get to New York, of course I want you to call me up and spend an evening with me if you can. . . .

P.S.—Meade, I read the piece Laurence Stallings wrote about the Bascom Hawke [story] in his column in *The Sun* [3] and I can't tell you how moved and happy and bucked up I felt about the thing. He is a grand

---

[3] In his column, "The Book of the Day" in *The New York Sun*, March 31, 1932, Laurence Stallings reviewed *Kamongo* by Homer W. Smith and compared it unfavorably to Wolfe's "A Portrait of Bascom Hawke" as follows: "The Scientist" (the central figure in *Kamongo*) "speaks of the eddy of energy which makes for life and throws out some pretty serious thoughts about protoplasm. . . . Has anyone failed to admire a story in the *Scribner's Magazine* (for April) by Thomas Wolfe? There's an eddy of energy for you; and a lyrical paean to life. . . . It seems to me that Thomas Wolfe has shown in this story that his *October Fair*, announced for next fall, will be even finer than . . . *Look Homeward, Angel.* . . . He seems to have all the gifts, all the talents. . . . *Kamongo* is going to cause some hoity-toity thinking among Book of the Month Club habitués. . . . But we'd still think that Thomas Wolfe's 'A Portrait of Bascom Hawke' is the book of the month."

man and really it is for this kind of reward that men work and live, and the reason they go through that agony of distilling their blood and marrow out upon a printed page which is known as writing. I wanted to tell you a while ago that we really want fame and love it as in decency we ought, but it is not the fame which is given to you by a set of driving and pushing and contriving literary racketeers who will fall upon you and rend you with gleeful howls the moment they think you have stumbled and fallen, but it is for the respect and admiration of such people as Stallings and perhaps a dozen more that we sweat and labor. Good words from people like this are sweeter than honey and it seems to me one of the best and highest rewards on earth. As for the other thing, the racketing, gossiping, hoop-de-doodle thing, it is a piece of stinking fish and the man who lets himself be seduced by its putrid fragrance deserves everything that he can and undoubtedly will get. So much for that—I forgot to tell you that in this great burst of work I have been enjoying I have written another story of about forty thousand words which *Scribner's* have taken and which they are going to publish in July or August if I can take the time off to do the proofs and revision. It is called "The Web of Earth" and Max Perkins says it's grand. It is different from anything I have ever done; it's about an old woman, who sits down to tell a little story, but then her octopal memory weaves back and forth across the whole fabric of her life until everything has gone into it. It's all told in her own language. I had the whole spring and source and fountain-head within me. I really believe, although this is a terribly boastful thing to say, that I knew this old woman better than Joyce knew that woman at the end of "Ulysses" and furthermore that my old woman is a grander, richer and more tremendous figure than his was. If I haven't been able to make her seem so, the fault is in me and not in the material I had to work with. I wish to God Max Perkins would let me write a whole long book about her. I haven't used one-tenth of the material I had, but he wants me very properly to finish the book I am doing before going on to some of these other ones, and of course he is right about it, but that story about the old woman has got everything in it, murder and cruelty, and hate and love, and greed and enormous unconscious courage, yet the whole thing is told with the stark innocence of a child. I really think it is going to be a good story if they won't make me cut out some of the things in it. Of course I know a few of the scenes can't be printed in *Scribner's Magazine* but I think that they are wrong, or rather that the world is wrong, in this attitude because the only thing that can possibly make for what is revolting and obscene is the intention, and it ought to be apparent in the very first paragraph of a good thing that the intention has nothing to do with deliberate and calculating profaneness.

P.S. I have just this minute finished an 80,000 word mss., the complete story of a man's life, part of my new book.[4] I have written it in less than a month, it is the largest completed work I have done in a long time, and I am happy because I know I'll be all right now.

Stanley Olmsted, the author of At Top of Tobin *etc., had written Wolfe inviting him to visit him at one of the Dickey House Annexes outside Murphy, North Carolina, and saying that Mrs. Dickey, the proprietress, wanted him to be her honor guest and would "kill the fatted calf" for him. The following letter was Wolfe's reply.*

To STANLEY OLMSTED

New York

June 14, 1932

Dear Mr. Olmsted:

Thanks very much for your fine long letter. Mabel has spoken of you and your sister many times and although I have not yet had the pleasure of meeting any of you personally, I no longer feel any strangeness whatever when I think of you and I am really looking forward to that happy day when I can appear suddenly before you and Mrs. Dickey and try to do justice to her fabulous table of which I have heard so much.

I suppose you know that *Scribner's Magazine* published, several months ago, a piece by a travelling salesman in which he described one of his visits to Drummer's Rest [1]—I believe that is the name of Mrs. Dickey's place. My friend, Fritz Dashiell, who is the editor of Scribner's Magazine, told me he had had several letters from subscribers after this piece was published asking if it could be true and, if it was, how to get there in the quickest way. Fritz . . . gave the people who had written him the necessary information: he told me the other night that he has since then received further letters from three or four of them and that all of them say that if the travelling salesman erred at all, it was on the side of understatement. Anyway, I wish you would thank Mrs. Dickey for me for her gracious invitation, and I assure you that I am holding before me as a reward, at the end of this desperate conflict with a book in which I am now engaged and

[4] "The Man on the Wheel" which told the story of Robert Weaver and which was written as a part of *K 19*. The greater part of it was never published, but a few sections appear in *Of Time and the River*.

[1] "Drummer's Rest" by Edward Hilts in the August, 1931, issue of *Scribner's Magazine*.

from which there can be no escape for me until it is finished, such a journey as you suggest.

I keep thinking of that travelling salesman who wrote the piece in *Scribner's* and his honeyed words. I would like to arrive there just as he did with the winds howling and night coming on and the old nigger coming out with his maddening list of delicacies. I have seen the whole thing in my mind a thousand times: I only hope the man's article didn't start such a stampede that there will be no room for me when I get there.

I am so glad you stopped off to see my mother.[2] . . . She seems to be the most completely fearless and independent person I have ever known: although she is seventy-two years old and in her old age has lost every penny she had, there are many younger people I worry about more and about whom I feel greater misgiving. Her courage is of an absolutely spontaneous and natural kind which is not even conscious of itself. She has endured the most crushing blows in life with no suggestion of ever giving in to them and with no idea that there was anything else to do expect to endure them and live through them, and, of course, with a person of this kind there is never any question of defeat or failure. Even if they lose all of their material possessions, they lose nothing of themselves because they are unconquerable. I have written a short novel which is to appear in *Scribner's Magazine* in a few days. It is called "The Web of Earth," and my friend, Maxwell Perkins, who knows you, and whose word in a matter of this sort means as much to me as anyone's, tells me it is a grand thing and as good as anything I ever did. . . . I have never yet asked anyone to read a word I had written, but if you do get the time and see a copy of the July *Scribner's*, I wish you would look at it.

There is one more thing that occurs to me: I have written and told my mother about my story. . . . I know she will understand it and see that it is all right, and I think it is obvious, as does Max Perkins, that the story has been written to the glory of man and not to his defeat. As you may know, I went through some pretty bad times two years ago because of some of the things that were said and thought about my first book in Asheville. It does not seem possible to me now that there is anything in the present story which could cause a reoccurrence of that misunderstanding, but I do not want my mother to be troubled by the attentions of prying and curious people whose only interest in a book seems to be in trying to discover whether Jim Smith is really Oscar Brown or whether such and such a thing ever happened, etc. As I say, I don't think their folly could possibly carry them to such abysmal depths this time, but if you read the story and like it, I should be grateful to you if you would write my mother and tell her so, and that if the world holds no worse

[2] Olmsted had written that he had spent a night at the old Kentucky home.

people than these there is a pretty good hope that it may yet be saved.

Meanwhile, with thanks again for your letter and your invitation. . . .
I am,

To JULIAN MEADE

> 111 Columbia Heights
> Brooklyn, N.Y.
>
> July 7, 1932

Dear Meade:

I got your letter and enclosed article yesterday. I think you have done
a good job of it and I don't believe there is much I could suggest at
present by way of change. But since you say this is a first draft, I am doing what I always intended to do—I am sending you the long letter
which I wrote you several months ago in answer to the list of questions
you sent me and which I never mailed.[1] I have read the letter over and
I think it does attempt some more detailed answer to your questions than
any I have yet given you, and therefore I am sending it along in the
hope you may still find it of use.

In your own article I have taken the liberty of making one or two slight
changes in things you quote me as saying, although you got it perfectly
right and I did say them. On page 7 the phrase "racketing, gossiping,
hoop-de-doodle thing" occurs, and I am going to change this for various
reasons, chiefly because "hoop-de-doodle" does not belong to my own
way of speech and is probably Menckenian. Likewise I am changing the
phrase "stinking fish" and the sentence which follows because it also
sounds a little awkward to me, although it does represent what I mean.

The only other thing I can qualify at the present is a very pleasant one,
my protest is only a very feeble one and if you will take the responsibility
for the statement I will say nothing whatever about it. You refer to me
in one place as a very learned man and you speak of me as reading and
speaking fluently several languages and of being a Greek and Latin
scholar. Now I wish all of this were literally true but I am afraid it does
go a little beyond the actual facts. The only thing I feel really guilty
about is the Greek and Latin. I can still read my Homer after a fashion
and I do believe I could still put up some sort of battle with Xenophon
and I can still read Caesar; I can do fairly well with Catullus; but I regret
to say that whatever modest accomplishments I may have once had with
the ancient languages I have let slip away. I do read French and German
and am in fact fairly proficient, particularly in French which I can read

[1] The letter of February 1.

about as well as my own language. And I have done an enormous amount of reading. I can make that admission without qualification. Probably all this explanation is unnecessary but although I was tremendously pleased with your soft impeachment as regards my learning, I can't quite let it go by without mumbling a few words of half-hearted protest. Having said so much, the rest is up to you.

One possible change or increase in emphasis occurs to me. You mention the fact that I have worked hard in an effort to learn how to use my material in the most effective way. I think you might even somewhat emphasize the fact that a large part of my toil and trouble at present comes from having almost too much material to deal with and the consequent effort it has cost me to find out how to shape and release the units in separate volumes of a readable and publishable length. This has really been a tremendous problem and has cost me terrific labor. Thus, out of all the writing I have done in the past two and a half years—writing which would amount quite easily, I think, to a half-million words—it is doubtful if I will be able to use over a third or a fourth of it in my next book. And yet I think that in one way or another I shall eventually use almost all of it. I suppose what I am trying to say to you is that every man has his own special problem and his own conflict with his material and it seems to me that each man has got to learn it in his own way for himself, that no one can help him very much to do it and that, for good or worse, a man's work and the way he does it is more particularly than any thing else on earth a unique possession, and his entire relation to it is a process of constant and entirely personal discovery.

This is all I have time to say to you at present. I hope that the letter which I am enclosing will be of some service to you. I thank you for the interest you have taken and for treating me so fairly and honestly and I wish you luck with the article. One thing you say I do especially agree with, in hope and aspiration at any rate, if not in actual achievement. That is that I should like my work to be of one piece with all my life, and that to me the labor of writing does seem to be united to a man's whole vision of life, and that the writer can fully appreciate, I believe, more easily than another man the whole meaning and emotion of John Keats' sonnet: "When I have fears that I may cease to be." I do think it is one of the deepest desires of the artist, or of some artists, that he will be able to give his whole and final measure before he is done.

I should greatly appreciate it if you will let me know what further progress you make in this piece and where and when it will be published. I shall also be grateful for a carbon copy if you have one. . . .

To HENRY ALLEN MOE

111 Columbia Heights
Brooklyn, N.Y.

July 12, 1932

Dear Mr. Moe:

In response to your recent inquiry asking for copies of any recent work I have published, I am instructing *Scribner's Magazine* to send you their issues for April and July, which contain two short novels of mine: "A Portrait of Bascom Hawke" and "The Web of Earth." It may be of interest to you to know that I had a great and very unexpected piece of good fortune in connection with the first of these stories, the "Bascom Hawke." *Scribner's* was holding a five thousand dollar prize contest at the time when I submitted this story, although I knew nothing of the contest at that time. Consequently I was made very happy the other day when they telephoned me and informed me that the judges had selected my story and that of another man for first prize. I shall therefore share the prize with someone else.[1] An announcement to this effect will be made in the August number of *Scribner's Magazine,* but as the editors seem to be particularly anxious that no public mention be made of it until that time, will you please say nothing about it? But I wanted to tell you about it anyway, because it was a grand and unexpected windfall and because I thought you would like to hear about it.

As for my other activity at present, I am going ahead daily with my book, or one section of it, which, no matter what publishers' announcements and statements say, will be published when I am done writing it and when I think it is fit to be published.[2] That is all I can tell you at present because that is all I know myself, but I shall certainly send you an advance copy as soon as one is available.

I have been in to see you two or three times, but have always missed you. I live in Brooklyn now, and rarely get to New York in the day time. But I do hope to find you one of these days. . . .

The following letter was written in reply to one from Elaine Westall Gould about "A Portrait of Bascom Hawke," which she had deliberately refrained from reading, but which she suspected of being an unfair and ruthless portrayal of her parents, Mr. and Mrs. Henry A. Westall.

[1] "A Portrait of Bascom Hawke" and "The Big Short Trip" by John Herrmann tied for first place in the *Scribner's Magazine* Prize Short Novel Contest. Therefore Wolfe and Hermann divided the prize of $5000 equally between them.

[2] This was written soon after Perkins had persuaded Wolfe to give up publication of *K 19.*

To ELAINE WESTALL GOULD

111 Columbia Heights
Brooklyn, N.Y.

July 15, 1932

Dear Elaine:

Your letter from the Prince George came this morning. It was sent on to me from my old address and I am afraid I have now missed seeing you until your return here at any rate. I have constantly intended and constantly deferred answering your last two letters and I assure you the only reason and the only excuse I have to offer is procrastination and the pressure of a great deal of work. I have thought all along that I would get to Boston at least for a weekend during the summer and I still have hopes of doing that, but I should be delighted to see you here if you have time and the inclination when you get back. Anyway, if you don't call me when you return I shall undoubtedly telephone you one of these days in Boston and then, as always, hope you will be able to come into town and chew the rag and a little lunch with me. Because in your last letter, although you did speak to me in a very stern and straight-forward fashion, I gathered from the ending that you would not throw me out of the window if I came knocking at your door again, and I assure you it made me feel better than anything else could have.

I had never really intended to attempt an answer to your letter anyway, because it was too good a letter, and answering it would have been an act of solid creation in itself and I thought I would do better if I waited until I saw you, and then I thought I might do better if we talked as always and I said nothing more about it. I was just going to send you a note and to tell you I was glad you wanted to see me and that I would call you up when I came to Boston. The only thing I will now say to you about the letter you wrote me concerning my story which came out in April is this: I think it was a fine letter and I think the things you said in it about ruthlessness and the ruthless man, for example, are generally and forcibly true, but I do not think that these things are true about me nor about the story I wrote, nor does Maxwell Perkins at Scribners, who is as fine a man as I know and the greatest editor in the country. The story was not about ruthlessness nor about a ruthless man, nor was it written to idealize those qualities. Someday I will try to tell you what I wanted the story to be about. I should not be deeply disturbed if I thought your objection to the story was based on the fact that you thought I had made a heroic figure out of [the] man. . . . That, after all, is a matter of personal vision, and in that respect the writer must be true to his own—he can do nothing else but be true to his own, whether it coincides with that of his friends or not.

But I was seriously disturbed about another allegation in your letter. That was that in the act of making a heroic figure of your father I had made by contrast a weak and ridiculous figure of your mother, and that you and other members of your family felt so strongly about your mother's life and character that your feeling toward me could never hereafter be the same. You said your sister [1] was so furious about this that she had started to work on an "answer" to my story which would be in effect a vindication of her mother. . . . Now in reference to all this, I want to say that the business of answers and vindications or of getting revenge on anyone or "showing them up" has never yet been the motive behind anything I wrote, although I was savagely accused of doing this and threatened with anonymous letters and denounced from press and pulpit in Asheville, North Carolina, two years ago because of my first book—and now, by the way, the same people who accused me most bitterly, the same paper which attacked me in its columns, write me letters and ask for a summary of my plans and work for the future, and when am I coming home, and "your many friends here are eager to know what your plans are and what your new book is going to be about, et cetera."

I can tell you honestly that I was the most surprised and bitterly wounded person about the fate of that book in my native town. A dozen times I started to take pen in hand and write a furious answer to the local critics, but I thought the whole thing out alone and in my own mind, and I came to the conclusion then that I would never write a letter in answer to such an attack or to the public press if I could help it, and I have stuck to that ever since, and I hope I always will. The result of my conclusions is this: that the writer is creating a world of his own visioning and that in so doing he creates a new kind of reality and a new set of values, and that his work, in so far as it has living value, is not concerned in exalting or degrading a particular Jones, or Brown, or Smith, but rather in finding in any particular Jones, or Brown, or Smith the things that unite him to the whole family of the earth. I can go on and talk to you about this for a long, long time and furthermore I know that I would be standing on solid ground, but I will say nothing more about it here save that when you speak of your father and your mother, that awakens one set of memories in my mind, but when you speak of a man and a woman in one of my stories, that awakens an entirely different set of memories and a different kind of reality, and I assure you that in this statement, although I would improve it if I could and if I had the time, there is not one word of evasion or desire to deny responsibility. I also want to say this: that you may be right in saying that I have done an injustice to your mother

[1] Hilda Westall Bottomley.

in my brief picture of a woman in the story, but I hope you are not right, and I will say that if an injustice was done, it was not intended and that my fault consists not in my being too much concerned with the weaknesses and imperfections of the character but rather of being very little concerned with that particular character at all. Now in this I say an injustice may have been done, but if it was, it was not intentional and in the end you will see that it does no damage, that it can do no damage to any person, dead or living.

What I am here saying to you is that I concentrated in that story upon the portrait of a man: that I tried to show him as he looked, as he spoke, as he dressed, and as he walked along the street, and that whatever scenes or persons were introduced into the story were introduced for this purpose. The sole example of the ruthlessness of which you speak consisted in ruthlessly cutting away everything I did not find immediately useful to the purpose of this single portrait: if I had completed the story of the man's life in its connections with all the other lives about him, I should no longer have had a story, I should have had a novel of very considerable length. Now let me repeat again:—if I was unfair to your mother again, as you say I was, it came not because I was meditating her portrait, but because I was not meditating her portrait. And neither, let me say, was I meditating the portrait of your father, because that is not the way the writer works—at least that is not the way I work.

You may find this hard to believe but I do not consider the man in my story, for better or worse, to be even a close approximation of your father, although I would not deny that we both know where much of the clay that shaped that figure came from, and I could further tell you, if I had to, where a great deal of it did not come from: of sources, experiences, and actual moments of my own life and seeing of which you know nothing, but which went into the making of the story.

Finally, as an example of the confusion and perplexity that always attends this kind of argument when people try to identify by word and letter the scenes, characters, and rhythm of a piece of writing, you inform me that your sister is writing a piece in vindication of her mother; but my mother wrote me that your sister had written her about the story, expressing indignation that I should have held up to ridicule not her mother but her father, and saying that her father, for all his faults and eccentricities, was really a grand and lovable character, and so on. As I told you at the beginning, it is perhaps better not to get involved with these arguments or explanations at all because they lead to endless confusion, and in the end, a man's only explanation should be his work itself; and that explanation should cover the whole course of his life and appear in everything he does, and he should rest confident and certain in the conviction; and if his work is good or has any truth or living value in it, he has done thereby no real or lasting injury to any person, alive or dead; and this is a part of my faith and in this I shall try to live, although you say that it will leave me without friends, without love, without security, or support, in life. If that is true, then it must be true. But I hope it is not true: it seems to me that in a world which has so much affection, love, esteem, and offers so many rewards to the frauds, charlatans, thieves and criminals who betray it constantly—witness New York and its Mayor, Jimmy Walker, or Asheville and its beloved thieves and swindlers who have wrecked the town, or for that matter, the whole world for the writers who betray it constantly with lies and sugared slop—in such a liberal world, I say, there must still be a little mercy and charity left for an honest man who wants only to do the best work in him, who is out to rob, swindle, or betray no one.

You speak of me as ruthless, of being a young Freudian and a cynical intellectual who makes a virtue of ruthlessness and the gratification of what you refer to as ravening desires. I tell you that if you think these things of me, they are phantoms of your mind and have no relation to me or to my life whatever. Further, I tell you in all sincerity and with the deepest friendship that if your own life or the life of your friends or members of your family is as free from rancor and bitterness as mine is, then no one in this world can complain of any lack in charity and under-standing in any of you. As to the ravening desires, if it be a ravening desire to love life fiercely and to hate death and all the living forms of sterility in death like hell, then I am a victim of these ravening desires you mention.

Well, I've got part of it off my chest now, although I did not mean to say so much. I took the liberty, which I don't think you will mind, of showing your letter to my friend, Maxwell Perkins, and he said it was a fine letter and that the person who wrote it is all right and also mistaken in some of the things she said, and with this opinion I also agree. And finally, using some of your own unvarnished speech, I think you had a nerve to write me a letter accusing me of certain crimes and misdemean-ors in a story which you had not read.

I think it is grand that you and Harold are able to take this trip.[2] It sounds fascinating and also hot as hell. I wish you all kinds of happiness and good luck and good adventure on it: I hope this letter reaches you at your boat in Panama and that you will call me up and have lunch with me when you come back. But if you don't, I shall look forward to seeing you anyway in old New England later in the summer. I suppose it's too late now for the grackles—when you wrote me that letter I won-

2 Mr. and Mrs. Gould had gone on a southern cruise.

dered what the hell a grackle was, and whether you were getting literary on me, but after consulting an authority on grackles I was assured you had used the speech of the land and that animal does exist. With love to all and best wishes for a happy vacation.

IX

BROOKLYN AND CONTINUED WORK: THE COMPLETION OF THE FIRST ROUGH DRAFT OF OF TIME AND THE RIVER

1932–1933

The following letter was written in answer to one from DuBose Heyward, author of Porgy, Mamba's Daughters, Peter Ashley, *etc., in inviting Wolfe to join the Conference of Southern Writers to be held in Charleston in October, 1932. He finally decided not to go, and stayed in Brooklyn and worked. Wolfe had first met Heyward through his wife, Dorothy Kuhns Heyward, who had been in the 47 Workshop and who is the author of* Porgy *(in collaboration with her husband),* South Pacific *(with Howard Rigsby),* Set My People Free, *etc.*

To DuBOSE HEYWARD

> 101 Columbia Heights
> Brooklyn, N.Y.
>
> September 8, 1932

Dear DuBose,

I know I am guilty as hell about not answering your last two letters. Please forgive me. I have been involved with this stinking New York heat, with having to move in the middle of summer, . . . and with this nine-headed monster of a book. I have not been away from here all summer except for a three-day trip to Montreal from which I returned last night. I hope to be able to take a vacation later on, and if I can, I will try to make it come in October during the time you are having the meeting in Charleston. . . . I assure you nothing would delight me more at present, not only for the fun I would have, but also for the good I might get out of it. God knows, I need relief, succor, help and enlightenment of some sort, but I'm afraid I will have to try to dig it out of myself—I don't believe all the writers in the world could help me now, although I suppose a good many of them have suffered from the same ailment. With me, it is now a question of eat or be eaten; of subduing the monster or being devoured by it, and above all of learning how to make an end. I think I've gone through most of the other stages. I am now an exalted master in sweating blood, beating my head against the wall, stamping across the Brooklyn Bridge in the middle of the night. I have learned almost everything, in fact, except how not to write a book in eighteen volumes, and if I thought you and our friends in Charleston could help me settle this problem, I would be down there licking my chops with greedy anticipation a week before the rest of you got there.

DuBose, I will be there if I can. I want like hell to get away from here, if only for a few days, but I really have a feeling of inescapable necessity as regards this book and a feeling of deep responsibility and obligation towards Max Perkins and the other people at Scribners who have been so decent to me. Therefore, coming to Charleston depends on what progress I make between now and the opening of the meeting. I think you will understand from this how things are. . . . Meanwhile, I send you and Dorothy my best wishes for your health and happiness and I wish you all possible success in preparing for this meeting.

Owen Francis, to whom the following letter was written, is the author of "Hunky Wedding," etc., and had written Wolfe suggesting that he come to Hollywood and work for the motion pictures.

To OWEN FRANCIS

101 Columbia Heights
Brooklyn, N.Y.
September 8, 1932

Dear Owen,

. . . I was delighted to hear from you and jubilant about all the fine news your letter had in it. I have never known just what to say to a man when he tells me he has just been married. I suppose you know very well the feeling of the bachelor when he sees his friends slipping away from him one by one into the jaws of matrimony. He is happy about it for their sake but for his own he feels a little lonely and regretful. And the pressure on him to go and do likewise becomes a little greater all the time. Unfortunately for me, I have felt for some time that wild, growing impulse but I have neither the cash to gratify it nor a willing and attractive target at which I could direct it. Owen, I am very happy about your marriage and all the other success which seems to have come along with it and I want to wish you both as much happiness and good fortune as any two people can have. You say, also, that the Hollywood sultans are giving you 200 of what it takes each Wednesday. The first thing it takes for me is my breath. Such a figure is simply appalling. I know, however, that you are worth it and ten times more, if some of their other henchmen are paid the salaries they are said to get. I hope to God you get it and also, Owen, although I am the worst person on earth to urge you to moderation in anything and particularly in the streak of lavish generosity that runs through you, I hope you manage to put a little of it aside because this coming winter looks very cold and bleak to my jaundiced eye in spite of all the hopeful prophecies and predictions of Roosevelt and Hoover.

About your warm assurance that I could make much more than you if I came out, and fatten up my lean bankroll in a few weeks, I am not so sure. I do know that you are competent and a good enough craftsman to earn every penny they would pay you but I am afraid I would be completely useless to them. I am grateful to you for your confidence, but you really have no idea how stupid and blundering I am. I swelter around and sweat blood and struggle terribly in an effort to get my own work done and by my own work I mean the work I may possibly be able to do. I swarm with lavish and sensational and gaudy ideas and stories and visions which might possibly be of some use in a moving picture but then they are no use whatever to me until I can get them woven in, somehow, into the color and vision of my own life and even then I often have to cut them out. What I am trying to say to you is that I seem to be able to write only about the things I have seen and known or imagined and which, therefore, have become a part of my own life. I swear to you that if I thought I could do such work as you suggest and earn even a portion of these fabulous salaries you mention, I would come out there like a shot, but I have not one atom of confidence in my ability to do so. I think they would give me the gate in a week's time.

I am in a maddening position as regards the movies and everything else on which I might be able to realize a profit. For two or three years I have had, from time to time, personal or written inquiries and letters from high paying publications such as the *Cosmopolitan* and *Collier's* and here, recently, for what reason I can't say, I have had a whole burst of popularity with the movie people. Owen, my mouth waters and my tongue lolls out of my mouth in my greedy lust to do something about it, but there is nothing I can do. If I could have written a *Cosmopolitan* or *Saturday Evening Post* story, I should have done so long ago with howls of triumph, and if I could write anything that might be useful to the movies, I would fall over myself in my haste to do it. But when I have had these letters from them recently asking me about my new book and when would it be ready and would I please send them proofs as soon as possible, I have usually failed to answer—not from discourtesy—but simply to avoid useless complications and trouble for us both. If some moving picture company should want to buy the rights for my new book, if and when it is completed and after reading it, I should be the happiest fellow on earth. But I don't see how this can happen; I don't see any possible chance of their being able to use it, and the only wisdom I have concerning all this is in an instinctive feeling that I may do better in the long run if I stumble and sweat in my own way and try to do some work which I may be capable of rather than work for which I have no capacity whatever. But if any of them out there are interested, even mildly, in little Tommy's moving-picture possibilities, for God's sake don't give me away to them! Because some miracle might happen, some day, where something I did might be of value to them. . . .

Owen, your invitation to come out and stay with you is the most alluring prospect I have had for a long time and your generous proposal to buy my railroad ticket is as fine as anything could be. If your letter had come during the last stinking spell of heat around Labor Day, I think I might have got in a train and come on out. As it is, it has turned now cool and fresh and delightful here, my little trip to Canada set me up, and I have decided it is best for me to stick on grimly here and to finish the thing I am trying to do or be finished by. I am exactly in the position of Macbeth when he said, in words more beautiful than I can remember, that his soul is so steeped in gore that it was easier to go on to the end of it than to attempt to go back to the place where he began. I have a little money, not much, which came to me as a result of dividing the Scribner prize. That was a wonderful windfall and so far as I was concerned it was like picking gold up in the street. . . . Now thanks to this lucky break, I can go on here for a little longer. Then, if I am as broke as I will be unless some miracle happens, I may come on out and join you, provided you are still there and you think there is any prospect of my finding anything to do.

I wish you had been with me on that little trip to Montreal. Montreal is not so much, but the beer and the ale and the Bourbon and the Scotch are as glorious as they always were and the ride back in the train, yesterday, was one of the most beautiful and magnificent journeys I have ever made. I came down the Hudson River just at sunset, it was the first brisk autumn day we have had and I doubt if even California has anything that can surpass the richness, the mystery and the beauty of that landscape at sunset on such a day. . . .

This is all for the present, Owen, and the letter has gone on too long already. But I am tremendously grateful to you for what you say and for your generous offer and if I can't accept it now, I still want to think that there is a chance of my doing so in the future. Write me when you have a chance and give me the news about yourself. I hope that every letter you send me has as good news as this last one had, and for the present, I send you both my most affectionate wishes for your good health and happiness.

To ELAINE WESTALL GOULD

> 101 Columbia Heights
> Brooklyn, N.Y.
>
> January 24, 1933.

Dear Elaine:

I am awfully sorry not to have acknowledged your letters and Christmas card before. . . . I have wanted for months to come to Boston and will confess to you now that I was there, or rather in Andover, for a few days at the end of October. I landed there on a ship coming from Bermuda, a place which I detested thoroughly, although many people seem to love it. I went there to spend a vacation but I spent nothing but a lot of money, and got madder and madder all the time at the island, the inhabitants and everything else they have there. Andover seemed to me ten times more beautiful and desirable in every way. I am afraid I must be a Yankee at heart. I don't believe that I could ever live in the Tropics. I was so completely shot to pieces with exhaustion and a cold on the chest that I could do nothing but emit a few feeble and incoherent bull frog croaks when I got off the ship at Boston, and that is really the reason why I did not call up. I went out to a friend's house in Andover [1] and slept for three or four days, and that fixed me up. But I am looking forward to seeing you soon, and I promise that the next time I come I will try to be fit to see and talk to you. . . . It would really be useless for me to try to put in a letter all the things I would like to talk to you about, so I am going to stop now, and hope to see or hear from you before long.

[1] George Wallace's.

To ROBERT RAYNOLDS

101 Columbia Heights
Brooklyn, N.Y.

Jan 25, 1933

Dear Bob:

The book [1] you sent me arrived safely and in good condition. I read all the stories and was deeply impressed with "Karain." . . .

I took a little trip down to Baltimore and Washington last week which set me up and made me feel good, and I am now getting some of those stories typed that I told you about. I am going to take the one I am having typed [2] at present to *Scribner's* and see if they are willing to do anything with it. If they are not, perhaps I shall make use of the addresses you gave me and consult your friend, the agent,[3] or, take it around myself to *Harper's Magazine.*

I had lunch finally today with a very elegant, highly perfumed and fancy talking Hollywood lady, an agent out there. She has sent me telegrams, written me letters, and a friend of mine who works out there among the movie people, and who sometimes allows his enthusiasm to run away with him, had already assured me that all I needed to do was to meet the lady, sign the contract, and then start raking the thousand dollar bills into an open valise. However, all I got out of it was a good lunch and an invitation to come to Hollywood. When I asked her how I was going to get there, and who was going to pay the fare, etc., and what I was going to do when I got there, she had the gall to suggest that I hitchhike, and added that she was sure she could do something wonderful and mysterious and immensely prosperous for me if I did come out. Therefore, it looks as if I will still be trying to do business at the same old address in Brooklyn for some time to come. So if you come to town call me up. . . .

[1] *Tales of Unrest* by Joseph Conrad.

[2] "The Train and the City," which contained some of the train scenes from *K 19,* and which was accepted by *Scribner's Magazine* on February 9, 1933, and published in the May issue. Portions of it appear in *Of Time and the River* on pages 407–419, in *The Web and the Rock* on pages 91–94, 441 and 447–449, and in *You Can't Go Home Again* on pages 3–4.

[3] Paul Reynolds. Raynolds had spoken to him and to Lee Hartman, editor of *Harper's Magazine,* about Wolfe's work.

To A YOUNG MAN WHO HAD ASKED FOR
ADVICE ABOUT A CAREER

[Brooklyn, N.Y.]

February 1, 1933.

Dear Mr. ———:

I have your letter of January 26th which my mother sent to me from Asheville. . . . I am sorry to have to tell you that the question you ask me is too much for me to answer. I am afraid it is a question each of us has to try to settle for himself with his own life, and that there is little we can say or do for anyone else no matter how much we want to, which will help him to conquer the confusion and distress of his own life.

I can tell you, however, that the greatest satisfaction and happiness I have had in my own life was when I was able to work hard and be proud of the work I was doing and feel that I was doing something that had some value or merit. This may not seem to you to be much of an answer to your question but it is the best one I can give you, although I know it does not apply to everyone because many people, in fact most people in the world, work hard and yet are not happy because they do not like the work they are doing and their heart and interest is not in it. I do not know how old you are but I imagine you are younger than I am, and part of your trouble at the present time may be due to the fact that you have not found the kind of work you want to do. If this is true, I can assure you that most young fellows have this same trouble. I had it when I was about eighteen in college; I was miserable and unhappy because I could not discover what I wanted to do or what I was fitted for. This may be your trouble now. What I am trying to say to you is, that if I came from the country and liked it and wanted a farm I would become a farmer and not be ashamed of it. If I liked machinery I would try to find out about machinery and become a mechanic or an engineer. If I liked business I would try to get into a business and find out about it. But I would not try to be a business man because I thought it was a higher kind of occupation, if I really liked to farm better, or I would not try to be a farmer if the thing that interested me was machinery.

I have tried to give you some kind of an honest answer to your letter and something which might be of help to you, because I think a great deal of the trouble in the world comes from this thing I have been talking about. People who are misfit do not really care for the work they do.

As you say in your letter if you are a sailor there are a great many other things in life that you know as much about as I do, and no one needs to give you any advice about what to do with food, and liquor or with girls.

I have found all these things good and I think that I have enjoyed them as much as anyone, but I know that in themselves they are not enough to complete the life of a man with any intelligence, ambition and a desire to make life better.

This is all that I can write you but I thank you again for your letter and hope that I may have said something that will be of use to you.

With best wishes for your success in everything you do,

The following hasty and undated note could have been sent to Perkins with almost any section from Of Time and the River *which Wolfe hoped to sell to* Scribner's Magazine. *It probably was sent with "No Door," which was published in the July, 1933, issue of* Scribner's. *The first part of this story appears in* From Death to Morning: *the rest appears in* Of Time and the River *on pages 2, 90–93, 327–334, 601–608, 611–613, and in* You Can't Go Home Again *on pages 37–44.*

To MAXWELL E. PERKINS

[February 1933?]

Dear Max:

Here is the manuscript. It is out of my book. Max, there are a dozen things I'd like to do to this—I have a passage about Time that I want to put in, other things I want to take out—but I want you to read it now: I believe you can see what it is about. Max, it may be no good, or it may be good—I'm too tired to know at the moment—but of one thing I'm sure: it is made from the real stuff of life, it is made out of material I know to the bottom of my heart, and I have tried to put something of my vision of life in it. I ask you to remember that my book is about Time: I hope the Time theme is evident in this story. Well, here it is, Max—it's no good explaining any more—I hope it's good and you like it.

During all this time, Wolfe had written hundreds of thousands of words for his book, but still had failed to come to grips with it by beginning at the beginning and continuing with it until he reached the end. The following letter to his sister Mabel was written just after his return from a trip to Baltimore and Washington with Perkins, during which they constantly discussed Wolfe's difficulties and found the solution to them. From this time on, Wolfe got off to a new start, which resulted in the completion of the first rough draft of Of Time and the River *and* The October Fair *in December, 1933.*

To MABEL WOLFE WHEATON

[101 Columbia Heights]
[Brooklyn, N.Y.]
February 9, 1933.

Dear Mabel:

. . . I did not come over to Washington the day after I saw you as I should have liked because I knew Fred would be here the next day and I had no way of getting him to tell him to come to Washington. Also, I had no time to call you the next morning because we [1] decided to get a morning train to New York, and managed to pack and get to the station with just a minute or two to spare but I thought you would be able to guess what had happened. Fred came up on Sunday, of course, and spent the day and suggested that I meet him in Philadelphia or Harrisburg after Mama comes up and we can drive down to Washington. Of course I plan and shall somehow arrange to get down and see her some way but just at what time I will be able to do it I do not know, that is, I do not know whether I will be there for her birthday. I will take a chance on the Inauguration.[2] I confess I would not mind seeing the Inauguration if it weren't for sweating and jamming your way through those crowds. I am so sorry it does not come down your street and under your windows. That would be fine, wouldn't it? But then I suppose you could do a rushing business yourself in renting out window space.

I have finally and at last some good news, after so much that is depressing. When I came back from my trip with Mr. Perkins I knew that it was now or never with me. My money was all gone and I really got down to my last ten dollars, with the rent to pay. Anyway during the last two or three weeks I have worked as never before in my life, wrote over 60,000 words in that period and now have, so Perkins says, the novel in the hollow of my hand. Perkins told me last night that he had been almost desperate about me, trying to figure what was wrong and how to get me out of it, but, if he was desperate you can imagine what my own state was. Now something far better than even money has happened. I seem suddenly to have found a way of getting started, which Perkins thinks was the real trouble all along, and having made the start everything has been going with a rush. Of course I have tons of stuff piled up now which I want to get in but that is the trouble, as Perkins thinks I will do too much, but I have promised to hold to the plan we have agreed on and by early Spring I feel pretty sure now that I will have the first draft of the whole book complete. This means that it will come out next fall and it also means

[1] Wolfe and Perkins.
[2] The inauguration of Franklin Delano Roosevelt.

that I am living again with hope and confidence for the first time in almost a year.

It has been a tough time for me and the whole trouble seemed psychological rather than anything else. I think that I got afraid after the first book. I was afraid that I could never live up to the things they said about me and furthermore tried to listen to the advice of a hundred well-meaning people, all of whom could tell you how they would do it, which after all is not what you want; you want to find out how you can do it yourself, and the only way I have found it out I have now discovered is to go ahead and do it. I do not know whether it will be as good as the first book. Perkins thinks it will and maybe better but I think it will be good, and the main thing will be to do a big piece of work once more and to get my hope and confidence back and then to go ahead to all the work I have still got in me. I feel somehow that having gotten out of this awful time, this kind of hump in my life, I will never have this same trouble again. The whole thing is almost unbelievable, because my trouble never was wondering whether I would have enough but how in God's name I would ever manage to get one-tenth of what I did, and Perkins tells me that I ought not to try to say everything in one book, but to put some of it in the others.

Anyway, when I went up to see him last night—he stayed in to talk to me—I had just $7.00 left in all the world, but he told me right away that they were going to take one short story out of the book and use it for the magazine and would pay me $200 for it,[3] so I have this for the present. Also, another long story which I think they will take and for which, of course, I will get more money.[4]

This is all the news I have to send you at present but of course it is very big news to me and I suppose you understand how things are with me at present, and that I cannot afford either the time or the money to do much travelling or to make extended visits as I would like to. I think this is really the critical time in my life and that if I can get through this I will be all right.

Of course I do not know how many copies the book will sell when it is published or how much I will make because if times continue as they have been or get worse the sale will not be one-half as great as it would have been three or four years ago; but Perkins tells me I have a big reputation which of course I know nothing about, as I stay over here in Brooklyn all the time and have no way of finding out. Anyway if it will earn me a little money I shall be glad.

[3] Probably "No Door."

[4] Probably "Death—The Proud Brother" which was accepted as of March 13, 1933 and published in the June, 1933, issue of *Scribner's Magazine*. It was later included in *From Death to Morning*.

I hope this finds you and Ralph well, Mabel, and not worrying too much over the general state of affairs which cannot be helped. I shall get down to see you if for only a day or so while Mama is there and while I am very happy to have some good news to tell you, I do not think that I shall want to talk to you about the book when I come down, lest talking spoil the charm or hoodoo it, and also since I have it on my mind all the time, [I] would like to forget it for a little.

Good bye for the present and let me know what your additional plans are, if any. Meanwhile I send you all my love and best wishes for your health and success.

Wolfe's letter of February 20, 1933 to Lora French Simmons was in answer to the first he had received from her since 1920. She had heard of his success as a writer and had written to congratulate him.

To LORA FRENCH SIMMONS

Brooklyn, N. Y.

February 20, 1933

Dear Lora:

I was delighted to get your letter and of course I knew right away who it was because I looked at the signature first to see who it was in Los Angeles that would write me such a nice fat letter. . . . I do not understand how you could think that I would have any trouble remembering you, since I have thought of you hundreds of times and have often wondered what had happened to you during these years and if you have had from life the happiness and good fortune you deserve. . . . I see that you are married and I wonder if you have a family by this time, and I can tell by your letter that you are the same nice person that you always were, just as if you were talking to me. I think we wrote each other a few letters after you left Asheville and even after you went west, but I lost your address and was unable again to find it. Therefore to hear from you again is like getting back a friend that one thinks he has lost forever, and I hope now you will not forget me but write me a few lines every year or so and let me know how it goes with you. Yes, I remember almost everything that happened during those few weeks in Asheville, although I have forgotten about jumping across the hedge and tearing my trousers, but I remember that too, now that you mention it.[1]

[1] Mrs. French says that one evening in the summer of 1921, Wolfe had talked so long on the porch of the Asheville boarding-house where she was staying that the

I cannot tell you very much here about my life since then. I had much rather hear about yours. I can tell you that after I saw you I went to Harvard for three years, wandered about the country for a while, came here to New York and got a job teaching at New York University, went abroad and wandered around Europe, living in one country after another for three or four years, meanwhile coming back here to teach again when I had no money left, and finally after a great deal of confusion, unrest, lashing about and unhappiness, such as most young men know, I suppose, I began to find myself a few years ago and started to write. My first book was an enormously long book called "Look Homeward, Angel," which came out two or three years ago and was lucky enough to have a considerable success not only here but in Europe. . . . I do not think you had better read it because a great many people at home and in the South were shocked by it, although I had no idea anyone would be, and I had no intention of shocking or offending anyone.

Since then I have written several short novels, two of which came out in *Scribner's Magazine* last year. I was lucky enough to win the Scribner prize for the best short novel for one of these which came out in the April, 1932 issue. I have two or three more of these short things coming out in *Scribner's Magazine* this year . . . and at the present time I am working night and day as hard as I can getting another of these tremendous long books done. Scribners will bring it out in the fall and its present title is "Time and the River" [2] although, of course, that may be changed. This is all that I can tell you here. I work very hard and lead a very quiet life in Brooklyn and see almost nothing of the gay literary life that I hear so much about. I understand that my books have made a reputation, that I am considered a success, but I know almost nothing about this as I go around very little and work constantly. But when this next tremendous job is done I am going off on another big trip, probably to Europe first, but then if I make any money I am coming back to see some of the parts of this country which I have not explored. That means the West and when I do go West, I shall certainly look you up.

The Hollywood people have been after me the last year or so to go out and work for the movies and even offered me more money than I believed there was in the world. I suppose that is the reason that I did not take it. I could not believe it was true and besides I do not think that I could do anything for them that would be any good anyway, since I have always

---

landlady repeatedly came out and ordered him to leave. Finally at her command, he left precipitously, jumped a hedge, stumbled and tore the knee of his trousers, swore furiously, and was embarrassed about calling there again.

[2] Wolfe was still considering *Time and the River* as an alternate title for the whole of *The October Fair*.

had to write what I want to write and what I know about, and I would not know how to begin to write a movie.

I have spent all the money I have ever made but I do not worry much about money if I can only do a good piece of work, and perhaps if what I do is good, I will make some more money. This is all that I can write you for the present, and excuse me for talking so much about myself, but your letter was so kind and friendly and you seemed so glad to hear that I had had a little success that I wanted to tell you a little more about it. Just hope and pull for me to do a fine piece of work in this book because that means more to me than anything in the world right now, and I find that a man cannot be happy unless he can love and be proud of the work he does. And now, Lora, that I have gone and unloaded all this rather uninteresting information on you, I wish you would write and tell me about yourself, because, if you want to find out about me I hope some day you will find it in my books, if they are any good, but, if I want to find out about you and I do want to very much—you will have to write it to me or tell it to me yourself.

You know, of course, that I wish you all the happiness and good fortune it is possible for anyone to have. I was so happy to hear from you again and I now send to you my warmest regards and my best wishes for your health and success.

P.S. . . . Lora—you speak of me in your letter as being a tall and proud young man, when you knew me and when I was nineteen years old. Well, I am just as tall as ever, perhaps even a little taller. I do not think that I am so proud as I used to be, and in honesty I have got to add this note which just occurred to me as I closed the letter. I am afraid my appearance has changed a great deal since you saw me and probably not for the better, although I do not think I have changed much inside, and certainly not in the way I feel about an old friend. I have got very heavy, and people who meet me I find constantly speak of my gigantic and overwhelming size. Of course, I do not feel that way about it because I do not see myself the way others do but if I ever had even a very modest claim to good looks, and I do not think that I ever had, I am afraid that I have lost them all, and therefore, when I come knocking at your door in Los Angeles you must be prepared to see a great lumbering fellow about six feet five who weighs 235 pounds. I am sure that you are going to look just the same as you always did, except that I can tell by your letter that you have got better and better all the time. . . .

The following letter was written in reply to one from Donald V. Chacey, a naval aviator, praising Look Homeward, Angel.

To DONALD V. CHACEY

February 27, 1933.

Dear Mr. Chacey:

I do not suppose I answer one letter in a dozen, and I have always felt very bad about this because procrastination and good intentions I have not followed out are the reasons I do not answer them, but I am going to answer yours even if all I can do is to bang out a short note by way of thanks.

Your letter made me feel good because if my book was as you say, meat and drink to you and you read it seven times and further are not a literary fellow, and do not know anything more about me than what you found out in the book, or whether I got any success or reputation for it—then your kind of letter is also meat and drink to me, and would make anybody proud whoever wrote a book. Your letter also touched me up a bit and got me a little hot under the collar when you asked me if I was ever going to do it again, or if the old well had gone dry.

I will tell you the plain truth to start with which is—I will be damned if I know myself. The well certainly has not gone dry, in fact, I seem to have tapped a whole subterranean river and the water is spouting up in columns and geysers more than it ever did. But whether it will be that life-giving beverage which you liked so much in the first book I do not know, but I hope and believe it will be and my publisher also thinks so. At any rate, it will be out next autumn [1] if I can hold on long enough to finish it, and I hope when it comes out people like yourself who thought well of the first one will also like this one.

I realize that a flying officer writing such a letter as you did from his ship at sea does not do so because he belongs to one of the ten thousand literary gangs who live the cute, quaint, gossiping life of the literary gangster but for some better and more substantial reason, and that is the reason I am writing you this letter. You may wonder why anything in your letter should touch me up at all or get me a little hot under the collar, but let me put in to you this way. If at one time in your life you had gone up about 30,000 feet—that is a good height isn't it?—and your colleagues congratulated you and pounded you on the back when you came down, but at the same time asked you whether you would be able to get up to that height again, you might get a little hot too. But, at the same time you

[1] At this time, Wolfe and Perkins hoped that he could finish the book in time for publication in the fall of 1933.

might grind your teeth together and say: "I won't eh, well by God we'll see about that. I will show these birds, and just for that I am going to hit 35,000 feet next time."

Well Chacey, that is the way it is with a writer, except that with a writer much more I guess than with a flying man, he goes through periods of doubt, despair and confusion when he does not think he is worth a damn and never will be any good again, and this is particularly true of a young fellow who is just starting out and who has not tested his strength and resources far enough to understand fully what he can do or what his limits are. Also, 10,000 well-meaning people praise him, write him letters, call him on the telephone, etc., tell him what was wrong with his first book and what was right with it, and how to do it better the next time. Finally, after lashing and batting around like a mad man, tortured by all kinds of self-doubt and loss of confidence he may have sense enough to get away from all these clever minds and forget their good advice and lose himself somewhere out in the wilds of Brooklyn and work like hell twelve or fourteen hours a day doing his job as best he can in his way, which may not be a good way, but is the only way he knows and that is what I am doing now.

The book will be out next autumn. It will not be and never would have been called *K 19*, which was only the name of a section in it which an ambitious publicity man at Scribners picked up and sent out to the press.[2] The whole final and complete book, which I hope to live long enough to write will be called *October Fair*, but this present volume which we are trying to keep to 800 or 1000 pages long will be called, according to my present intention, *Time And The River*. . . .

This is all that I can write you, and I have written you at such length because I suppose it is for the respect and belief of such persons as yourself who have no literary ax to grind and no literary style to follow that a fellow like myself is writing. Also, I would like to say this. A flying man who hits 30,000 feet on one flight can probably hit 35,000 feet on his next big effort if he sets his mind and heart on it, but it does not always go so evenly as this with a writer. I hope and believe that I am going to hit that 35 the next time, but if I do not I hope I hit 25, and still believe there is a chance left for me to break the record some day. I have myself done considerable flying in my time and spent a good part of my life up in the air, but not in the way you have, although the way you do it is the way I have always wanted to do it.

Any way, as one flying man to another, I am writing you this letter and thank you for your own, and think that it did me good.

I send you my best wishes for your success in everything you do.

[2] In the margin opposite this sentence, Wolfe wrote in longhand: "I am sorry I put this in about *K 19* because it is not just the way it happened."

To GEORGE WALLACE

101 Columbia Heights
Brooklyn

March 9, 1933

Dear George:

I got your letter this morning and want to send this answer off right away. I will be delighted to see that the manuscript of your friend, . . . gets a good reading at Scribners. No, I don't think that this is a hell of a time to submit a book, but I do think that it would be a hell of a time to publish one. The faces around Scribners have looked pretty long and gloomy during the last month or two but, of course, that simply is part of the nation's history at present. The book business has been hit and hit hard, as has everything else, and I do believe that publishers have cut down their lists in a radical fashion, but of course they are just as anxious to get something good as they ever were. . . .

I just wanted to get this letter off to you before I get to work, so I won't write much more now. I was in a horrible, ugly and furious temper when you were down here, because after all my bloody sweating in the last two years I seemed to have gotten nowhere, and in fact, the whole game seemed to be lost. But just after you left in January I took a little trip to Baltimore and Washington, came back almost completely broke—in fact I was down to my last ten dollars and had no idea where any more was coming from—and in this mood I plunged into work and in the next month wrote over 100,000 words. I seemed suddenly to get what I have been trying to get for two years, the way to begin the book, and make it flow, and now it is all coming with a rush. Perkins says I have got it in the hollow of my hand: perhaps he said in the hollow of my head—I am not sure and beyond peradventure—that's a good word, isn't it, George. *Scribner's* have taken three very long sections out of the book which they propose to publish as stories beginning with the May issue,[1] for which they are paying me a very lousy price, unless I desert *Scribner's Magazine* and take them to an agent [2] who swears he can get two or three times as much for them. Anyway I am still hanging on by my toenails but a great deal happier and more hopeful than you have seen me in a long time, and I believe everything is going to be all right with us all and with the world.

I took three days off over the weekend and carted my weary bones to Washington where my mother, brother and sister were assembled to see Franklin D. inaugurated. I saw nothing but the back of my mother's

[1] "The Train and the City," "Death—the Proud Brother" and "No Door."

[2] Probably Ray Everett of Curtis Brown Ltd. Wolfe considered having them as his literary agents at this time but never did anything definite about it.

shoulders for three hours and forty minutes, but this was good enough, for I was determined that she should miss nothing and I worked her down into the damndest jammed crowd you ever saw, sent home to my sister's house for a chair, got Mama up in it and held her there. She saw the whole show and that was what we wanted.

Well, George, I do not know whether we will be using scrip or getting rations from the Government the next time we see each other, but if it comes to that, I hope we both fare well and get enough of both. . . . It was good to see you the last time, in spite of what justifiable doubts you may have on that score, but I assure you that what you saw was Mr. Hyde and that Dr. Jekyll has now broken the evil spell and is his affectionate and benevolent self again. . . .

Wolfe had always wanted to find out all he could about his paternal ancestors, and this interest had been intensified by his visit in October, 1932, to his father's birthplace, York Springs, Pennsylvania, where he had stayed with his uncle's widow, Mrs. Gilbert Wolf and his first cousin, Edgar E. Wolf. The following letter to Dr. Hiram Shenk of the Division of Archives and History at the Pennsylvania State Library in Harrisburg is the first of many inquiries which he wrote in an effort to trace the genealogy of his father's family.

To HIRAM H. SHENK

101 Columbia Heights
Brooklyn, N.Y.

April 3, 1933.

Dear Sir:

I write to inquire if you can give me certain information about members of my father's family who lived in Pennsylvania, or if you can tell me where to go to get such information.

My father, whose name was William Oliver Wolfe, was born about 1850 a few miles from the village of York Springs, Pa., and members of his family still live in that vicinity. It is concerning the origins of my father's mother and father that I am writing you.

My father's father was a farmer or a farm laborer, named Jacob Wolf (although the name apparently was spelled both Wolf and Wolfe by members of my father's family), and his mother was a woman named Eleanor Jane Heikes Wolf, and both of them are buried in the church-yard of the church at the little settlement of Lattimer or Lattimer's

Church, Pa., which is two or three miles from York Springs. I believe that the church belongs to the United Brethren or Brothers of Christ Sect, although I am not sure of this fact. The inscription on the grave of Jacob Wolf, my grandfather, reads that he died in 1860, aged about 54 years, but without giving the exact date or year of his birth. The information for my grandmother, Eleanor Jane Heikes Wolf is a little more exact for she lived to be 96 years old and died as recently as 1912 or 1913. I judge from these inscriptions my grandfather was born about 1806 and my grandmother some ten years later.

I visited York Springs last October and found some of my relatives living there and many people in the vicinity who remembered my grandmother very well. I found no one, however, who remembered my grandfather except one old man, who said he remembered my grandfather from his own childhood and remembered that my grandfather had sometimes worked on his father's farm as a laborer. He also said that my grandfather had several brothers and that they all came from the district around York Springs but he did not remember what had become of these other members of the family. I also learned that my grandmother had been born a few miles from York Springs. These were all the facts that I could find out.

I want very much to know more about these people, to find out if possible who their parents were and where they lived and how long this branch of my family has been in America. I should be very grateful to you if you could give me some information on these facts or tell me where I could find out about them. I am writing you because I understand your department has a very complete record of the histories of the people who settled in Pennsylvania and that if anyone had such information as I desire you would be most likely to have it.

With thanks for any assistance you may be able to give me

The letter below was written to Robert Raynolds about a poem of his entitled "In Memory of a Common Man," which he had sent to Wolfe in March.

To ROBERT RAYNOLDS

101 Columbia Heights
Brooklyn, N.Y.

April 3, 1933

Dear Bob:

. . . I have wanted to write you many times but I think the responsibility of writing you about your poem probably accounts for the delay.

I am glad to think you value anything I might say to you about a poem. It is true I have read and known a great deal of poetry but to speak of it critically and academically to scan its lines has always been too much even for my own audacity. Everything I know about poetry has come to me through a terribly long process of filtration and of living until the poem has become a part of what I have known and felt about life. I can never endure to hear a poem read, which seems a favorite occupation of young poetizers, nor did I ever feel competent to express honest judgement of any poem, particularly of any poem that was any good after a first reading. To me it is and always has been the most difficult kind of reading, just as it is the most difficult of writing, and the poems that I have liked the best and that have meant the most to me are those that meant nothing at all to me when I first read them. There is in the reading of every great poem a moment of discovery, which is just exactly as if you suddenly knocked a hole through a wall and suddenly found yourself inside of places you have never been before. I had this exact experience with a poem of John Keats when I was eighteen years old, and it was suddenly like being inside a country that I had never been in before, and the first time I understood and saw what the poem was about, although I must have read it a dozen times.

I liked your poem and the story that it told and the plainness and the sincerity with which you told it. This I can say to you honestly, without committing myself to dutiful criticism which I am not competent to make at the present time. As to whether its lines scan properly I did not notice or examine it for that purpose, neither does one I think examine the monologues of Robert Browning to see if they scan as he reads them, but I should think that many of them do not, and nevertheless are powerfully moving and beautiful, and are made of the stuff which is poetry.

I would rather talk to you about it when I see you. . . . Let me hear from you when you come to town, and if you can arrange to meet me for dinner at a fairly late hour, say nine o'clock, I should like to see you and talk to you. . . .

The following brief note was clipped to a few galleys of "Death—The Proud Brother."

To ALFRED DASHIELL

[March or April, 1933]

Dear Fritz:

I have done all that I can—and maybe more than I should. There is one short passage about Death which I have written in and which may be all right.

The other *long* passage which I have inserted in the Fifth Avenue scene I want you to look at very carefully. I think the idea and purpose of it is all right, but don't let me do anything here to hurt the story—my head is not good enough to-day to know whether I have or not.

I think these proofs ought to be read again.

The following note was clipped onto the first seven galleys of "No Door" and left on Dashiell's desk after the office had closed for the day.

To ALFRED DASHIELL

[May [?] 1933]

Dear Fritz:

I am leaving you the first seven galleys and will try to get the rest to you in the morning. I have gone stale on this thing and my head won't work for me—but this is the best that I can do at present—and here is what I have done and the way I feel about it:

(1) I have rewritten about 80 lines in galleys *four* and *five* and estimate that I have saved about 350 words. Get the girl [1] to type what I have written and then judge for yourself whether I have helped or harmed that section. You can cut the rewriting down all you can, but I feel the stuff on loneliness may set the mood for the scene that follows better than the present one.

(2) I think the prologue ought to stand *as is.*

(3) Of your minor cuts, I thought the most important one was the one about the drunken woman and the men who robbed her, and since I have already softened this I don't think it should be prettified any more and would like to see it included.

(4) Finally, if you can take my revision and cut it, if necessary, so that it would balance the needed cuts elsewhere, I would be grateful to you. —And if my revision will balance up your suggested cuts in these 7

[1] Elizabeth Nowell, who at that time was secretary to the editors of *Scribner's Magazine.*

galleys, I will take my chance on the rest and try to cut so as to include the little scene I showed you.

I have taken your own galleys beyond galley 7 to work on to-night.

To MABEL WOLFE WHEATON

[101 Columbia Heights]
[Brooklyn, N.Y.]
June 5, 1933

Dear Mabel:

Thanks for your letter. I am sorry you have been having so much trouble with your lodgers and suppose this is a difficult time for everyone, particularly people in your business.

I have managed to keep going so far but have been almost broke and have the money worry hanging over me all the time now. I never worried much before but now I do want to go ahead and do the kind of work for which I seem to be best fitted and which I want to do, and I do not see much prospect at the present time of getting much money out of it. Like you, I am very tired yet must go on somehow and try to finish this huge piece of work which has taken up all my life for two or three years. I dread this summer and have got to keep going. Maybe I shall get something from it some day. . . .

I agree with you when you say that bitterness is one of the things in life that kills and there is a grim justice in the fact that [it] kills most often those who let it feed upon them. There is another thing in life that is hard to bear that fortunately you do not know much about—that is loneliness. If you have time and are interested in knowing anything about my own life for the last ten or fifteen years, you might look at a piece I have written for the next number of *Scribner's*.[1] Some of them think that it is the best piece I have ever written. I do not know about that. But, a little of my life went into it.

I think I learned about being alone when I was a child about eight years old and I think that I have known about it ever since. People, I think, mean well by children but are often cruel because of something insensitive or cruel in their own natures which they cannot help. It is not a good thing, however, for older people to tell a little child that he is selfish, unnatural and inferior to the other members of his family in qualities of generosity and nobility, because a child is small and helpless and has no defence, and although he is no worse than other children, and

[1] "No Door" in the July issue of *Scribner's*.

in fact is as full of affection, love and good-will as anyone could be, he may in time come to believe the things which are told him about himself, and that is when he begins to live alone and wants to be alone and if possible to get far, far away from the people who have told him how much better they are than he is. I can truthfully and sincerely say that I have no bitterness and nothing but pity for anyone who ever did that, but I can also say that the habit of loneliness, once formed, grows on a man from year to year and he wanders across the face of the earth and has no home and is an exile, and he is never able to break out of the prison of his own loneliness again, no matter how much he wants to.

So with all your troubles and misfortunes of the last few years you can be thankful being alone has not been one of them. I wish for you and for us all some new and wonderful happiness and success which will compensate us for all we have lost and suffered, and somehow, I believe it will yet come to us. I have led about as solitary a life as anyone could, yet I have felt much closer to people in the last two or three years than I ever did in my life before, and the misfortune and suffering everywhere around me has touched me more than it ever did before. I really think, without knowing why I think so, that better days are ahead of us and that if we go on with faith and courage we will gain a little of the security and happiness we all need. . . .

I send you all my best wishes, as always, for your health and success in everything you do, and hope we will all get together before long and at a more fortunate and happy time.

To ROBERT RAYNOLDS

101 Columbia Heights
Brooklyn, N.Y.

June 5, 1933

Dear Bob:

Thanks for your letter and for what you say about "Death the Proud Brother." It made me feel good and compensates for all the bloody sweat of writing to know that someone likes something you have done. I have another coming out next month [1] which they think may be the best of the lot, and I hope they are right, for it caused me enough anguish and groans before I was done with it. I finally got it cut down from something over fifty thousand words to about eighteen or twenty thousand, but some of the things which were left out are now painful to think about.

These pieces are only a small fraction of all the work I have done in the

[1] "No Door."

last two or three years and I hope some day to get most of the rest of it published. I have put myself into them and tried to do the best I can, and although I want to get better and learn more all the time, I should like to have the kind of relief, the sense of having cleared something out of my mind, that publication gives me. Today we have been tying together great bundles of manuscript which I am going to give away to someone or send away to-morrow to Scribners, I think, simply because I cannot bear to look at it any more. I have, I think, a typed copy of everything I am sending away, which is written in my own hand and which is a formidable amount of writing, enough to fill to overflowing a box four feet long by two or three feet high, but I will be relieved to get it out of the house.

I am delighted to know that you have been getting so much work done and I think to complete and get ready for publishers a manuscript of ninety thousand words in two months time is a remarkable performance. I wish you all good luck with it, and hope to hear more about it the next time you come to town. . . .

To JOHN HALL WHEELOCK

[101 Columbia Heights]
[Brooklyn, N.Y.]

June 14, 1933

Dear Jack:

I want to thank you for your kind and generous letter about my story.[1] It did me so much good to know you feel that way about it because I had worried considerably the last day or two about sections which had to come out on account of space, and I was afraid so many cuts had been made that the completeness and substance of the story had been hurt by it. In that story I was really trying to say something which comes from a deep place in my life and which I think will color almost everything I do for years to come.

It makes me so happy that I succeeded with you and Max in saying what I wanted to say, because there are no other two people in the world whose judgment and good opinion mean as much to me as yours. So thanks again for writing me as you did. I value these fine letters of yours, and particularly this last one and your belief in what I do, more than I can put down here in words.

As I have told you before, I have read some of your poems so often

___
[1] "No Door."

in the last two or three years and have been so deeply impressed by some of them that I am sure they have passed into my own work, and if you come upon evidences of that theft I want you to believe that it was done unconsciously, and all I can hope is that it was sometimes done worthily.

I want to come in and talk to you the next time I go to the office. Meanwhile, with all my thanks again and best wishes to you,

Alfred Dashiell had sent Wolfe a letter written to Scribner's Magazine *by Donald V. Chacey in praise of the stories of Wolfe's which they were publishing. With it, Dashiell had sent a covering letter of his own, saying: "This is the way people feel about you. It is the expression of thousands who don't write. Why then should there ever come to you moments of doubt? . . . Or suspicions that people are likely to betray you? You are what you are. You can not be betrayed. . . . You have a triumph awaiting you and you should not be kept from your reward by a perturbed spirit." The following was Wolfe's reply.*

To ALFRED DASHIELL

June 28, 1933.

Dear Fritz:

Thanks for your letter and for the enclosed letter from Chacey which I am returning to you. It is certainly a heartening and splendid thing to know that anyone feels this way about one's work.

I won't say anything more about the letter now because I have just been talking to you over the telephone and said some of the things that I was going to write. Yes, I think that it would be an excellent idea to ask him, when you answer his letter, if he has ever written anything about flying or his own experiences and why he does not send it in to you. If a flying man could really put down the sensation and experience of flying in such a way as to make the rest of us feel it, I for one would be intensely interested in reading what he had to say. Of course we do not know whether he has the gift of putting such an experience into words, but it is a hunch and it could do no harm to follow it.

I cannot tell you how much good it does me to know that such a person, whose interests are so remote from a literary life and who leads, as he says, a life of action, should think so well of what I do. While I have never felt that a man could do his best work for the huge public and that all good writing is in a way limited to a special and almost indefinable public, my feeling nevertheless is very strong that the best writing is not a precious thing and not limited to a little group of adepts and professional critics. In other words, I think there is scattered throughout the world the kind of public which this man represents, which is that limited and yet hearteningly numerous group of people of fine feeling and intelligence and unprofessional appreciation. Somehow I really feel that the real mark of a writer's merit and the real measure of his success comes in the end far more from these people than from the professional literary critic, and that it is really for the respect and belief of this unseen and unknown audience that a man instinctively does his work, and that is the reason I put such a high value on a letter like this one. . . .

Last of all, Fritz, I want to thank you for your own letter which you sent along with Chacey's. I am not only deeply and sincerely grateful for what you say but I have also taken it to heart and recognize the truth of it. All I can say to you here is that the effort of writing or creating something seems to start up a strange and bewildering conflict in the man who does it, and this conflict at times almost takes on physical proportions so that he feels he is struggling not only with his own work but also with the whole world around him, and he is so beset with demons, nightmares, delusions and bewilderments that he lashes out at everyone and everything, not only people he dislikes and mistrusts, but sorrowfully enough, even against the people that he knows in his innermost heart are his true friends.

I cannot tell you how completely and deeply conscious I have been of this thing and how much bloody anguish I have sweat and suffered when I have exorcised these monstrous phantoms and seen clearly into what kind of folly and madness they have led me. But I really think that even at the worst and craziest time of conflict and delusion, we retain the saving grain of truth and judgment somewhere within us which keeps us from going completely out of our head. This is as near as I can come at present to telling you about it. But I live constantly in the hope, and I have never lost it, that a man can make his life better and cure himself of some of his grievous errors. In my good moments I do not believe any man on earth values the friendship and affection of his friends more than I, and desires more earnestly to be worthy of their belief and is more cruelly tormented when he thinks he has misused them.

At the present time, however, I have given up cursing the iniquities of mankind and am venting my curses on the weather, and even feel a great surge of brotherly love and sympathy when I think of my eight million fellow atoms who are forced to sweat, melt, and swelter their miserable way through the glutinous and interminable horror of a New

York summer. If it would only turn cool again I think I could love everyone, even Mrs. Ella Boole.[1]

I will come in to talk to you about the story in a day or two.[2]

*The following letter from Wolfe to his boyhood friend, Leroy Dock, was
evidently written during one of his intense fits of homesickness for the mountains of western North Carolina. He never did go back to stay at Balsam, but
finally rented a cabin at Oteen, N.C. in 1937.*

To LEROY DOCK

[Brooklyn, N.Y.]

June 29, 1933.

Dear Roy:

I want to write you before you go away to tell you how glad I was to
see you again and how much I enjoyed our talk and lunch together. . . .
I did not get to talk to you very much about Balsam and, as I said, it looks
at present as if I will have to be here most of the summer into the autumn,
but I am really thinking not only of a short vacation but also of a possible
future when I speak to you of Balsam. I suppose if I came for a week or
two I could put up somewhere without much difficulty, but I should also
be grateful, Roy, if you would write me after you get down there and tell
me if you know of any available shacks or cabins that would do for a
fellow who does not have much money and is not too particular about comfort and modern conveniences. Of course, I should like electric lights, if I
can have them, because I am used to working by them, and plumbing
and cooking arrangements—my cooking is confined largely to making
several pots of strong black coffee a day—would be desirable if I could
afford them. Finally, when I work I like three things very much: coolness,
quietness, and solitude.

I have been alone very much in my life that I am afraid loneliness has
become a habit with me now and it is certainly essential when I write. Yet,
I like the companionship of people as well as anyone and sometimes miss

[1] The late head of the W.C.T.U.

[2] Dashiell had written: "I'll talk to you about 'Exile' when I see you. I think something can be made of it." Perhaps this was an early title for "Dark in the Forest:
Strange as Time," or "Dark October." The latter was never actually published in any
magazine but appears, with changes and additions, on pages 353–404 of *Of Time and
the River.*

it desperately, and that is one reason I feel warmly about Balsam because I think my mountain blood has given me some of the same qualities as those mountain people there have—that is, we like to be alone part of the time and yet we like friendship too. I think you are that way yourself and I know you will understand it.

You spoke to me about a colony of cabins which some Daytona people had built there. I wonder if you could tell me what these cabins are like, how they are built and equipped, if any of them is for rent or sale and how much the rent or cost of such a place would be. I know that this is a hell of a lot to ask, but I am really seriously interested in this thing even if there is no immediate prospect of my doing it, but I think there is a very decided prospect of my doing it in the next year or two.

As I told you, after so many years of wandering about the world the pull towards some sort of established place and towards some sort of place where a man feels at home and among scenes and people who are familiar to him becomes very strong, and although I have seen many cities and many strange and beautiful places in the last ten years I have had that feeling of familiarity and home only in two places. One is the country where I was born, western North Carolina, and the other my father's country, among the farms and orchards of the Pennsylvania Dutch in southern Pennsylvania. I have an idea that some day I am going back to one of these two places. I have never forgotten my stay with you in Balsam, thirteen years ago,[1] and how kind and friendly the people were and what a grand and familiar place it seemed to be. It sometimes seems that it could not have been as good as I imagine it and I know I was only a kid then and full of a kid's dreams and visions about the world and maybe that is why Balsam seemed so wonderful a place. But I don't think I was mistaken about it and I am going back again to find out. Meanwhile, if you can give me any information about some of these things I have mentioned I will be sincerely grateful to you. . . .

The following letter was written in answer to one from Arthur Palmer Hudson, folklorist and Professor of English at the University of North Carolina, who was making a study of folksongs in the work of various contemporary Southern writers for his article, "The Singing South," which appeared in the July, 1936, issue of the Sewanee Review.

[1] Wolfe had visited Dock in Balsam in 1920, before he went north to enter Harvard.

To ARTHUR PALMER HUDSON

July 11, 1933.

Dear Mr. Hudson:

Thanks very much for your letter of July 8th. I have looked up your references to song-tags in *Look Homeward, Angel* and found all of them excepting the one you mention on page 288. I should be glad to help you in any way I can because your subject interests me and I recognize its value but I must admit that my knowledge of folk song, if by folk song you mean such songs as the southern mountain people have sung for generations, is very slight, or if anything I have written shows traces of such knowledge I was not conscious of it and simply absorbed it with a million other memories and sensuous impressions in childhood. I was born in Asheville and although my mother's family have lived in the hills of western North Carolina for a very long time, my own experience as a child was probably more the experience of a boy in a fair-sized American town than anything else.

The reason your subject interests me is that songs of all kinds more than almost anything else, except odors, can evoke the memory of some lost or forgotten moment of childhood with a literal and blazing intensity that makes the whole thing live again. But these songs, I am afraid are not folk songs but simply popular songs like, "Has Anybody Here seen Kelly," "Yip I addy I Aye," "Tammany," "Take Me Out To The Ball Game," "Love Me And The World Is Mine," "K-K-K-Katy," "Alexander's Rag Time Band," and so on. Many of them, I am afraid, are very trashy songs but able to make me live again some night in summer twenty or twenty-five years ago and hear the people talk on their porches, or my father's voice, and smell the earth, the honeysuckle vines, the geranium beds and live, hear, and see everything again, as nothing else on earth could do.

This is all that I can write you for the present. If I had time and it would be of any interest or value to you I should be glad to tell you about many of these songs and the memories they evoke and the meanings they have for me, not only the popular song hits of the time but also all those scraps and fragments and chants of songs that children use, such as

"I asked my mother for fifteen cents
To see the elephant jump the fence."

and that came from God knows where. But I am afraid that none of these were folk songs, unless my understanding of a folk song is amiss. I wish I had known more of the songs you write about. What I have heard in recent years of the songs that mountain people sang makes me sorry that I missed it as a child. . . .

I am afraid that I have not been able to help you very much but I thank you again for writing and wish you the best success with your study.

Percy Mackaye, author of The Canterbury Pilgrims, Jeanne d'Arc, The Scarecrow, My Lady Dear, Arise, The Mystery of Hamlet, King of Denmark, *etc., had written Wolfe, saying: "From a quiet niche in your own mountains —your incomparable, tumultuous, earth-drinking, star-brooding peaks of the spirit—I write you this word of true gratitude that at last, in unspoiled words which are their counterparts, you have made them articulate with their own grandeur and fecundity. You have done so in 'The Train and the City,' which is for all time one of their first inspired scriptures." He had also written to John Hall Wheelock of Scribners, saying: "The work of Thomas Wolfe . . . seems to me a colossal landmark in our poetic literature, for it is all quintessential poetry, both prodigious and delicate in power." The following is Wolfe's letter of thanks to Mackaye.*

To PERCY MACKAYE

July 19, 1933.

Dear Mr. Mackaye:

. . . I cannot tell you how happy your letters have made not only me but my friends Jack Wheelock and Maxwell Perkins at Scribners. Wheelock was so pleased about your letter to him that he wrote me quoting a long excerpt from it. He is one of the kindest and most gentle people I have ever known, a man of deep feeling and I think of high poetic gift and his respect for you and the value he puts upon your judgment are immense.

I don't know if you know Mr. Perkins but I think he has met you. At any rate he has seen you and remembers you and was delighted with your letter. He is a great editor and in a quiet, devious and unobtrusive fashion, most completely his own man, I think the most extraordinary individual I have ever known. He was more delighted with your letters than if there had been a big sale for a book, and made one of his characteristic comments which never seem to get at things in the usual way and seem simple and almost irrelevant and really go right to the heart of a thing. I think he said he knew you and had talked to you, but the thing he did say was that anyone who saw your face would not forget you and would know that they were looking at *somebody* when they saw you. Knowing how to translate his reticence in my own way now, I realize this is about as great a tribute as could be paid to anyone.

It is a very fine thing for me to know that a man of your position and maturity has kept his spirit as flexible, young, and generous as it ever was and is able and happy to give the work a young man does heartening and unstinted praise. I hope that my own spirit will always be young and generous in just that way, for that, it seems to me, is the sinew, the blood, the living integument of life and passion that flows from one generation to another and that can keep the world alive.

I wish I could make the trip to Marion, Virginia with you in August.[1] I should be delighted to see a thing like that which would be new to my experience and if by any chance I come home about that time I think I would ask you if I could go along with you, but if I don't see you this summer or go home in the autumn I hope you will let me know when you are coming to New York and I will look forward with hope to seeing you then.

Meanwhile all I can do is send you again thanks for your grand letters of friendship and generous enthusiasm. I cannot hope to equal those letters in any way except with the warmth and sincerity of my grateful thanks. That I can offer and give to you, and I send it now with all my heart.

Wolfe wrote the following letter to the editors of various quality magazines in an attempt to find a wider field than Scribner's for the sale of his short stories. However, several of the editors answered that pieces of ten to thirty thousand words were too long for short stories, although they might be publishable as novelettes or serials. This discouraged Wolfe: he did not submit any manuscripts himself but renewed his efforts to find a literary agent.

To THE EDITORS OF *HARPER'S MAGAZINE*, THE *FORUM*, THE *AMERICAN MERCURY* AND THE *ATLANTIC MONTHLY*

[101 Columbia Heights]
[Brooklyn, N.Y.]

[August, 1933]

Dear Sir:

I am writing to inquire if your magazine ever publishes stories that are from ten to thirty thousand words in length and if you would care to

[1] Mackaye had invited Wolfe to attend with him a folk festival of fiddlers and ballad singers to be held on White Top Mountain near Marion.

consider, with a view to publication, some stories of that length which I have written.

I have published a book and have had several of these stories published in *Scribner's Magazine* during the past year but I have never yet sent a manuscript to anyone save *Scribner's Magazine,* because I did not know whether any other publication would care to publish pieces of such length. The stories I would send you have never been shown or submitted to *Scribner's Magazine,* or anyone else, and I want to send them to other publications now not only because I need money but because I think it would be a good thing for me if I could get something published in some magazine other than *Scribner's.* If I can get them published I should like to have each of them published as a unit and not in separate installments.

I now have several of these long pieces on hand and I should be grateful to you if you would let me know whether you care to see them or whether the policy of your magazine is against the publication of pieces of such length.

To MAXWELL E. PERKINS

[101 Columbia Heights]
[Brooklyn]

August 8, 1933

Dear Max:

In last Sunday's book section of *The New York Times* there was a favorable notice about the reception of "Look Homeward, Angel" in one of the Scandinavian countries—Sweden, I think. I think some sort of publicity also should be given to the fact that the book got fine reviews in Germany.[1] Jack Wheelock read me the advertisements the German publishers sent me and the excerpts which they used from some of the leading papers of Germany, Austria and Switzerland, which are as good or better than anything I ever got in this country. Why should we conceal this fact? I notice that publishers of other writers use foreign reviews which cannot touch these notices, and make full use of any favorable foreign publicity they get. The publicity I kicked about was that which seemed to me to be personal and gossipy and irrelevant and not substantiated by fact,[2] but I see no reason at all to be ashamed of the fact that my book got fine reviews in Germany and Austria, and I do not see why that is not publicity which could be honorably and creditably used.

Therefore, since we both hope that I may again come through some

[1] *Look Homeward, Angel* had been published in Sweden by Albert Bonniers Forlag, and in Germany by Rowohlt Verlag.

[2] See Wolfe's letter to Perkins of August 29, 1931.

day with a solid achievement and that you may profit from your investment in me, why not make use now of what is honestly our own and
what we might use to our advantage?

I am completing another section of my book which will be called "The
Hills Beyond Pentland," [3] and which, I think, in some ways may be as
good as anything I have done.

I will come in to see you in a few days.

To PERCY MACKAYE

[Brooklyn, N.Y.]

August 17, 1933.

Dear Mr. Mackaye:

Thanks very much for your recent letter. By now I suppose you have
returned from the song festival in Virginia which I should so much have
liked to attend.

Of course I know about George Grey Barnard and his work, although
I have never met him. I think I shall follow your suggestion and go to
see him some day, although I may not be able to demand to see him in
the same superb way he demanded to see his old friend Michelangelo,[1]
and I may, therefore, mention your own name when I go.

It is a fine thing for a young man when he meets a great old man, because I think we never lose entirely the hope that we have in childhood
and that persists strongly in the first years of our youth that we will meet
someone of such invincible strength and wisdom and experience that all
the grief and error in our own lives will be resolved by him. Perhaps this
is a deplorable weakness, but if it is it is certainly one that all humanity
shares in to some extent, and although I now know that we must find the
remedy for our own error in ourselves and get out of our own lives the
power to live by, and that there is no one on earth who can speak a word

[3] Only a few portions of *The Hills Beyond Pentland* were ever written, and most of
these were used in Wolfe's other novels. This book was planned to tell the history of
Mrs. Wolfe's family who had lived in the mountains of North Carolina since the Revolution.

[1] Mackaye had suggested that Wolfe call on Barnard, saying: "If this were the
Florentine era, you might just as well keep from going to see Michel Angelo in his
workshop at Florence, as keep from going to see Barnard in *his*, at New York. . . .
So, at the first opportunity, I hope you will stick this letter in your pocket (by way of
an introduction—though really needless) and . . . walk in on him there. If anyone
should intervene, just say quietly: 'You don't understand; I've come to see my friend,
Barnard; I've known him for several hundred years.' For that's exactly what *he* said to
the doorkeeper of the Sistine Chapel (substituting Michel Angelo for Barnard) when
he first called there, to commune with his old friend."

so magical as to release us from the confusion, struggle and bewilderment in our own spirit, I still feel always a great awakening of power and hope and joy when I meet a man like this, whose whole life is an act of faith and who has lived and worked with such grand fortitude.

If I do not get to see him myself this summer perhaps when you come to town you would take me out to meet him. I am going away somewhere in October and may come home, and if you are still there [2] I will come to see you. If you come to New York before that time won't you let me know? Meanwhile, I send you again my wishes for your health and happiness in all you do.

To ROBERT RAYNOLDS

> 101 Columbia Heights
> Brooklyn, N.Y.
>
> August 29, 1933

Dear Bob:

I haven't had my typist here in a week—hence my lazy failure in writing you. It was so nice being out there at your place—I think the place is magnificent and have never seen a finer family and such affectionate children. Can I come again and stay *two* days—and when can I come? If I come can we have some more hot cakes?—they seemed about the best I'd ever eaten.

I am doing a very exciting piece of writing—at least it's exciting to me, so much so that I'm in a delirious mental state and a horrible physical condition—a sort of cross between delirium tremens and Olympian calm. Sometimes when I'm working at it I think it's going to be so good I almost cry about it but when I'm not working at it I curse God, men, and everything. I'm calling my piece, which like everything else is a section of the fury theme,—"The Image of Fury in the Artist's Youth"—is this a good or lousy title? I just slapped it down, so it can be changed, and thought of "In the Artist's Youth" as a subtitle and not really essential to it. Anyway it's about Fury, not especially artist's fury, but the kind of fury young men have, probably more in this country than anywhere on earth —the madness, exulting, desire to eat and drink the earth, getting into the wind on lonely roads, etc.—and it starts in just about the most furious way it can, on a train smashing northwards across the State of Virginia at night with three drunken youths, as drunk with the exultant fact and fury of going to the city for the first time, out to conquer the world, do everything, see all, etc., as with the corn liquor they keep passing from

[2] Mackaye was living in Arden, North Carolina, at this time.

hand to hand.[1] The thing starts out on the end platform of the pullman car, singing, roaring, bellowing with laughter, full of the illusion of power —a wild, mad, profane and bawdy scene all mixed up with the rhythms of the wheels, the thousand sounds the train makes, the immortal pulse and eternity of the earth outside against this projectile, of fury, youth, the brevity of man's days, illusions, thoughts of power, all the tones, moods, and haunting memories the motion of the train induces in him; and finally sleep and one of the sleepers, lying in his berth not asleep but in that strange coma mixed of dreams and visions with the dark mysterious earth floating past him, finally before he sleeps a vision of two horsemen riding abreast the train over the dark earth, keeping time now to the rhythmical pounding of the wheels, with a kind of hypnotic chant about

> Lean Death and Pale Pity
> Rode out for to take
> A City a City
> Pale Death Awoke and Lean Pity
> Rode out for a City
> Rode out for a City to take—etc.

Anyway, I know it's true, the way I have felt, the way we all have felt, and I hope they publish it and the damned fools don't put it down as wild ravings, freak eccentricity, etc., I am trying to do in my limited way what the great men have done—not reality as facts literally reproduced, but reality as facts absorbed, undeniable, fused into an image—here in image of train, youth filled with all the fury of its power and joy and faith— which may not be like any one train or any group to be met on trains, but more like the basic human experience than any average of facts could be. I know it's true because I've lived it, felt it, made it part of me. Now I hope it will be good as well. This is the first time I've told anyone about anything I'm writing in years. That in itself is a youthful thing to do— the longing to display your wares before [they're built?]. So don't tell on me. The train part is only one small part. I hope to see you soon. . . .

To FREDERICK H. KOCH

[5 Montague Terrace]
[Brooklyn, N.Y.]
October 9, 1933

Dear Professor Koch:

Thanks very much for your letter of September 22nd and for the attached check for four dollars as royalty on "The Return of Buck Gavin." [1]

---

[1] This episode appears in *Of Time and the River* on pages 69–76.
[1] In *Carolina Folk Plays, Second Series.*

. . . I want to say something to you now about this play for which you have sent me the royalty check. If I thought for a moment there was any danger of my being misunderstood, I would not say it, but I have known you for fifteen years and I feel that I know you pretty well by now, and I know you are my friend and will understand what I want to say. And what I want to say is this:

I am very proud to call myself one of the Playmakers and to remember that I belonged to the first group you ever taught at Chapel Hill, and had a part in writing and producing some of the first plays. I want to tell you also that no one is prouder than I of the great success the Playmakers have achieved and of the distinguished work which has been done by them. The fact that I was associated with that work at its very beginning, even in an obscure and unimportant fashion, is another fact I am proud of. I am also proud to remember that two little one-act plays [2] that I wrote were among the first plays put on by the Playmakers and that I acted in them and helped produce them. I was a boy of eighteen years when I wrote those plays, and I wrote each of them in a few hours because I did not then understand what heart-breaking and agonizing work writing is, and I think those plays show this and are fair samples of the work of a boy who did not know what hard work was and who wrote them in a few hours. But I do not think they are fair samples of the best which the Playmakers can do and have done, nor of the best in me. I therefore want to ask you, as my old friend who will not misunderstand my plain and sincere feeling in this matter, that you do not allow either of these plays to be used again for production. I should like to be remembered as a Playmaker and as one who had the honor to be a member of that pioneer first group, but I do not want to be remembered for the work which a careless boy did.

Will you believe me and understand my feeling in this matter, and believe me to be as well your friend, and one who is proud to know that he was once a member of a group which has done so many fine and memorable things since? And understanding this, will you do as I ask in this matter?

Meanwhile, dear Prof, I send you, as always, my best wishes for your health and success in everything you do. Please let me know when you are coming to New York.

Ever since the expiration of his Guggenheim Fellowship in 1931, Wolfe had been living on the royalties from Look Homeward, Angel *and the money*

[2] *The Return of Buck Gavin and The Third Night.*

he received for stories from Scribner's Magazine. *He worried constantly about his finances, and in the following letter he approached the Guggenheim Foundation through Henry Allen Moe, its Secretary, concerning a renewal of his fellowship. However, his application was finally turned down.*

To HENRY ALLEN MOE

5 Montague Terrace
Brooklyn, N.Y.
November 15, 1933

Dear Mr. Moe:

I am writing to inquire if there would be any hope of my obtaining further help of the Guggenheim Foundation, to tell you something of the work that I have been doing and to ask if you would be interested in having me come to see you and show it to you.

During the past three and one-half years since I received the Guggenheim award, I have published in *Scribner's Magazine* two short novels, "The Web of Earth" and "A Portrait of Bascom Hawke" which divided the prize at *Scribner's Magazine* offered for the best short novel in 1932. In addition to this, there have been published in *Scribner's Magazine* this year three long pieces, "The Train and the City," "Death the Proud Brother" and "No Door." Scribner's have just taken from me two more pieces, the first of which is to be published in *Scribner's Magazine* in February, and the other in the succeeding number.[1]

All of these pieces, except the two short novels, have been taken from the book, or rather series of books, on which I have been working for the last four years, which have the inclusive title, "Time and the River." During the past four years I have written over a million words, most of which I now have in typed manuscript, and can show to you. The book, when completed, will be one of the longest books I suppose anyone ever attempted, and of course I will then have to face the problem of revision and cutting with the publishers, but the only thing I can do now, the only thing I know how to do, is to go ahead in my own way until I reach the end.

Of course, I can not judge now the merit of the book, but I do believe, and Mr. Perkins, the editor at Scribners believes, that it contains the best work I have ever done, and all my time and life and energy for several years now have been given to doing it. The only source of income

[1] These were probably "The Four Lost Men" which was published in the February, 1934, issue of *Scribner's*, and "Dark in the Forest, Strange as Time" which was published in the November, 1934, issue. Both of these stories were later included in *From Death to Morning.*

I have at the present time comes from the sale of these pieces to *Scribner's Magazine*. I have no knowledge of any other publishers or magazines besides Scribners and I have no time to try to market any of my unpublished manuscript at the present time to other magazines, even if I knew where to take them. Moreover, I do not know of any other magazine which would print pieces of such length as my stories which have been published in *Scribner's*, all of which, with one exception, were from 20,000 to 35,000 words long. Scribners tell me they propose to bring out a limited edition of one of these pieces, "No Door," which appeared in *Scribner's Magazine* in abbreviated form, and which will be published in the limited edition in its original length of 30,000 to 40,000 words some time in the spring.[2] From this they tell me I may hope to get a little money, $400.00 or $500.00.

There are also the two pieces I mentioned to you which they have taken, and which will come out in the magazine in a month or two. This is all I have to live on at present, unless I can sell something else out of the manuscript I have on hand.

Meanwhile, I am going ahead at full speed on the first part of "Time and the River." The first part is a tremendously long and complete novel in itself, and has the title "The October Fair." If I keep going at my present speed, I will finish it this winter and I already have almost a complete draft of the second part, which has at present the tentative title of "Hills beyond Pentland."

I don't believe I ever did better work than I am doing at present. I think Mr. Perkins and other people who have seen the manuscript and read some of the stories in *Scribner's* will agree to this and I am also willing to show you what I have done if you would care to see it. My difficulty of course is one of enormous length and completeness. I suppose what I should like to do would be to write a book that filled a library, but anyway, this is the only way I can do it, and if I didn't believe it was worth doing, I wouldn't live and work as I do.

I have told you the plain truth about the situation so far as I can in a letter and although I hope and we all hope that I may some day get some sort of reward and security from all this work that I have done, I am really hard up and badly in need of money at the present time and have been, in fact, badly worried about the immediate future until the other day when I sold those stories.

I should appreciate it if you would write me and let me know if you would care to talk to me and see some of this work I have been doing, and if there is any hope of my getting additional help from the Fund.

[2] The proposed limited edition of "No Door" was never published.

The following letter to Belinda Jelliffe, the wife of the psychiatrist, Dr Smith Ely Jelliffe, was written in reply to one from her expressing admiration for Wolfe's work. With Wolfe's and Perkins' encouragement, Mrs. Jelliffe later wrote an autobiographical novel, For Dear Life, *which was published by Scribners in 1936.*

To BELINDA JELLIFFE

5 Montague Terrace
Brooklyn, N.Y.
November 21, 1933

Dear Mrs. Jelliffe:

Thanks very much for your kind letter. Anyone would be proud and happy to know that something he has done has meant so much to any reader. You say I may not care what you or the world thinks of me and my work, but you would be wrong in thinking so. I assure you I am by no means immune to what you and the world may think. In fact, I am about as far from such an impassive and negligent assurance as anyone could be, and have even been too much concerned about what people said and thought, or, what was worse, with what I thought they said and thought. But it is true that when I am at work I do not think much about anything else and I guess it is a good thing for me that this is so.

Perhaps some people who have been unwise, furious and bewildered, ruinously wasteful of their own and other people's lives, and tormented and pursued by all sorts of demons, phantoms, monsters and delusions of their own creation, may get out of the work they do the certitude and truth that has escaped them elsewhere. This may be true of me. At any rate, when I work I am happiest, and although I do not think of other things and people very much when I am working, I work because the strongest and highest wish I have ever known is to do the best work that is in me to do, and the reason I wish to do this is to communicate it to other people, and I want to communicate it to other people because I want to make my life prevail, to win the fame, the high esteem, the rare and fine success for which a young man hopes and works. If anyone says that this desire has nothing to do with his own work, I think he speaks falsely and with evident hypocrisy.

For these reasons, I am not indifferent to what you and the world may think or say about my work, but am proud and happy when I get such a letter as you wrote me, and thank you gratefully again for writing it.

Dr. Arthur C. Jacobson, to whom the following letter was written, was Wolfe's physician during the time he lived in Brooklyn, and also his personal friend. Wolfe had told him of his interest in the history of his father's people: also of his bewilderment and irritation at the rumor that they were of part-Jewish descent. Dr. Jacobson at that time was doing research in other Pennsylvania-German genealogies, and in the course of it found that a Hans Georg Wolff and Hans Bernhard Wolff had come to Philadelphia in 1727 on the ship William and Sarah. *He accordingly had written Wolfe this information and suggested that he consult the records of the Genealogical Society of Pennsylvania for further facts. However, Wolfe seems never to have got around to doing this.*

To ARTHUR C. JACOBSON

5 Montague Terrace,
Brooklyn, New York

November 25, 1933

Dear Dr. Jacobson:

Thanks very much for the references you sent me and the information contained in them. I think almost certainly you have given me the most accurate information that I have ever had about my father's people. I feel sure that with these references and other information which I have, I can now trace the origins of his family in America. Of course, the members of his family who are still living down in Adams County, Pennsylvania, have told me a good deal from what they remember and what their parents and grand-parents told them, but like most people out in the country, they have kept few records except a few letters and inscriptions in the bible, etc., and I could never go back before 1806–7, which was about the time of my grandfather's birth, although they told me where he was born, and that means there were other members of his family there before him.

Is it not a strange and wonderful thing to weave back through the past and find out where you come from? And it seems especially strange and wonderful here in America, which is such an immense and lonely country and still so like a wilderness. Most of our lives here have been so nameless and obscure and governed by blind chance. A boy grows up upon a little farm in Southern Pennsylvania. When he is fourteen or fifteen, after the Civil War, he goes to Baltimore, becomes apprenticed to a stonecutter there, and after five years, becomes a stone-cutter himself. Four of my father's brothers followed him in this stone-cutter's trade, and that also has seemed strange to me because all of them were farming people before that.

And, still by accident, chance and the opportunity of the moment, he drifts off and after several years, he got up into the Western part of North Carolina where my mother's people came from, although where they came from before that I don't know. They were mountain people and had lived there as long as anyone. And then you send me a letter and tell me that the first of my father's family may have come over here in a ship called the William and Sarah, sailing from Rotterdam and coming to Philadelphia in September, 1727.

All these things I suppose are simple and matter-of-fact enough, but all the strangeness and mystery of time and chance and of the human destiny is in them for me and they seem wonderful. I suppose according to your theory we are what we are and have been shaped so by the past and can do nothing about it if we would.

Anyway, thanks again for so kindly sending me this information and the references. I will look them up when I can and let you know the result of my findings.

Kyle Crichton, who at this time was Associate Editor of Scribner's Maga-*zine, had written Wolfe for biographical information to be published in the "Behind the Scenes" column of the February issue. The following was Wolfe's reply.*

To KYLE S. CRICHTON

5 Montague Terrace
Brooklyn, New York
December 11, 1933

Dear Kyle:

Thanks for your note. I'd just as soon have you make up something on your own hook for the "BEHIND THE SCENES" column, as I thought what you put in before was fine and better than I could do, but I will take a chance anyway to give you something that you can use, and if you can use any of it go ahead, but please put it in your way and not as if I said it.

I have written over a million words in manuscript the past four years, which makes a box five feet long by two and one-half feet wide piled to the top. Also, I have worn a wart on my second finger, almost as large and hard, but not as valuable, as a gambler's diamond. Maybe you can say that I have come through the great depression with over a million words of manuscript and a large, hard wart on my second finger, as my tangible accumulations (but I don't think Max would want you to print such a vulgar and mercenary bit of news). Or

You can say that of the last ten years I have lived about four in Manhattan, four more in various other countries of the world, and about two and one-half in Brooklyn—and that the largest and most unknown continent of all is Brooklyn. You can say that I have gone out into the wilderness five hundred times, armed with a trusty map, now worn to tatters, and have prowled about, exploring the place in the dark hours of the night as not even Stanley explored Africa in his search for Dr. Livingston, though maybe you can say I met another white man here one time and that we recognized each other instantly, lifted our hats at once and stepped forward courteously with extended hands, saying: "Dr. Livingston, I believe?"—"Mr. Stanley, I presume?"—but maybe you'd better not put that in either.

Or perhaps you can say that I live in Brooklyn instead of Manhattan because, as my favorite Brooklyn waiter put it: "Duh difference between dese guys oveh heah and dose guys oveh dere, is dat oveh heah we have all been trained to t'ink." The Brooklyn people boast that you can live here a lifetime and never get to know their town, and they are right about it, but if I ever tell even what I know up to the present time, they would lynch me for it. If I ever do tell about it, I will not be here in Brooklyn at the time, and I shall call it "The Locusts Have No King." But maybe if you have customers out there, you'd better not put that in either.

Or finally, you might say that I'd still rather see the New York Yankees win than any other team, and go to watch them play a dozen times a year, but that I always go to see the Brooklyn Dodgers at least twice a year because they are such quaint fellows and you never know which one is going to get hit in the head next with a fly ball.

Well, this is the best I can do at present and if you can use any of it, go ahead, but please don't get me in any more trouble than I am in already.

Meanwhile, with best wishes, I am,

The following letter, found among Wolfe's own papers, is evidently a first draft of the one he sent to Mrs. Bernstein upon the publication of her book, Three Blue Suits, *in which he is portrayed as "Eugene Lyons."* [1] *In the final section of this book, Eugene announces to the heroine that, acting on the*

[1] This fictional character has no reference in any way to the well-known writer and editor, Mr. Eugene Lyons.

advice of his editor, "Mr. Watkins," he has applied for a Guggenheim Fellowship and is planning to leave her and go abroad.

To ALINE BERNSTEIN

5 Montague Terrace
Brooklyn, New York
December 11, 1933

Thanks for your letter. I have read your book and want to write you about it and congratulate you on its publication. I am sorry you did not send me a copy yourself or let me know that it was being published. Some news about its publication apparently came to Perkins some time ago, but he did not tell me about it for some reason, apparently because he thought it would worry me. I wish you or he had told me. The first news I had of it was last Sunday when I looked at the book columns of the *New York Times* and saw it listed there. I was tremendously excited about it and went out the first thing next day and bought a copy in Scribner's book-store, so you don't need to send me one now.

I can understand your feeling of happiness and achievement in having published these stories and with all my heart I want to wish you the best and finest kind of success with them—the kind of success I believe you want yourself. As you know, I had the manuscript of two of your stories, the first and the last, which you sent to me a year and one-half ago, but I had never seen the second story, the one about Herbert Wilson, until I read the book.

I think that piece about Herbert Wilson is very fine. Of course, I know where the other two stories came from and whom you had in mind, but I will talk to you about them later. I don't know if Herbert Wilson has an actual counterpart in life as has Mr. Froehlich or Eugene, or whether you got him from intuition and your observation of life, but I cannot tell you how moved I was by that story and how proud I am to know you could have done it. I am not a critic but a reader, and I believe in the reality of the character and the feeling in the story from beginning to end.

I think it is a very wonderful thing that a person who has never tried to write before can do something so true and good and full of pity. You made me live through the whole day with the man and understand all of his hope and expectancy in the morning when he saw that new and wonderful life opening up before him and then you made me feel how weariness and disappointment crept up on him as the day in the department store wore on; and finally, the cruel pity of his realization when he gets home at night and knows that his wife is dead and that there is no brave new world for him.

I thought all the other things in the story were fine: the cathedral and the shabby, dingy lives of the department store people and all the smells of food and sounds of people on the different landings of the tenement when he comes home. I think you can be proud of having written this story. As I say I am not a critic, but I do know that to get into the life of a little pavement cipher and make the reader feel and hope with him and understand him and finally feel that running pity at the loneliness and loss of life, is a rare and wonderful accomplishment and not often to be found in a piece of writing, even the writing of people with great reputations.

As you know, I was already familiar with your stories about Mr. Froehlich and Eugene, because I read them over a year ago when you sent the manuscript to me. I didn't know then what you intended to do with this manuscript and thought you were sending it to me as a kind of letter to tell me something of yourself and the way you looked at life. The other night I took your book and compared the printed version of those two stories with the manuscript you had sent to me. I found that they were practically verbatim the same, with the exception of one or two minor changes. That also seems remarkable to me—that you could on your first attempt say what you wished to say so clearly and with so little revision. I wonder if you know what agony and heartbreak it costs many people when they write.

In your story about me, you picture me as a fellow who wants to look out the window dreamily, do a dozen things at once, and escape all the sweat and labor that goes into a piece of work—just to think his books out of his head, while he looks dreamily out of the window and have them magically appear on paper with no effort of his own. Is it not a strange and sorrowful fact in life that people can live together for years and love each other, and yet find out no more about each other than this? I wonder if you've ever understood what anguish writing costs me and how hard I have worked. Didn't you ever see any of that during all the years you knew me? Well, it has been five times worse since then.

During the past four years, I have written over a million words and none of them, to my recollection appeared magically on paper while I stared dreamily out of the window, swilling down a drink of gin. Do you know how much writing a million words is? Well, it is a crate full of manuscript, six feet long and three feet deep, piled to the top, and it is more writing than most people ever do in the course of a life-time. Of those million words not over 150,000 have so far been published. A great deal more, and I hope and believe the best of it, may some day see the light of print, and there will be still more—how much I don't dare to think—which will be cut out, thrown away or destroyed.

I do not say that it is good—I only say that I have worked like hell, lived the life of a galley slave and done more hard work than anyone you know. And yet you picture me as a dreaming loafer. It seems to me that what people think and say of one another and the estimate the world puts on you and your life is usually just about as wrong as it can be—so wrong that if you stated just the opposite, you would usually come closer to the truth. You always said that you were the worker and that I had the inspiration without your capacity for work. Wouldn't it be funny if just the opposite were true?

I have never in my life been able to do a piece of writing that was so free from revision and the necessity to change, cut and rewrite as your own pages are. I don't know if you have ever seen one of my pages when I get through with it, or after I get through with the proofs—but it looks like a map of No Man's Land in Flanders. So again, you have done an extraordinary thing and shown at the beginning a clearness and certainty of purpose for which many of us would give our right eye.

But maybe, with all this talent and cleverness with which you have been so richly endowed by nature, you can still learn something from me—the final necessity of sweat and grinding effort. I think you have done some very fine writing in your stories about Mr. Froehlich and Eugene, but I think you could have done better if you had worked harder. By work in an artist's life, I do not mean eight hours a day or fourteen hours a day, or all the different things you get accomplished, but I mean an integrity of purpose, a spiritual intensity, and a final expenditure of energy that most people in the world have no conception of.

I don't believe that you really think of your husband and me as you have portrayed us in these stories. I am sorry that you said some of the things you did, and that you have been willing to give out to the world these portraits as representing your own estimates of us. Perhaps it is false for the artist to picture people as being better than they are, but I think it is even more false to picture them as being worse, and I do think that in your stories about Mr. Froehlich and Eugene, you have sometimes been uncharitable and unjust, and that you could have shown them as better people than you make them, without injuring the truth or quality of your writing.

I never got to know your husband very well and I don't suppose there was much love lost between us, but you did tell me many times that he had many fine and generous qualities—a generous devotion to his family and children and great liberality and affection for friends of the family and some of your own friends who were down on their luck, which he demonstrated time and time again by helping them. Don't you think since this is true, you could have made this element in his character plain without injuring your story? You made him a leathery-hearted broker with hardly a spark of generous human affection left in him, and I think you were unfair in doing this.[2]

I think you were also unfair in your story about me, and I want you to believe the truth of this, that I am sorry about this for your sake more than for my own. I hope and believe that through what you have done I can myself learn a valuable lesson. As you know, I have sometimes written pretty directly from my own experience—as directly as you did in your story about me—and now I admit, I want to be very careful in the future to be as fair and comprehensive in my understanding of people as I can be. I don't think that I have ever wilfully and maliciously distorted what I believed and knew to be true about people, in order to satisfy a personal grudge. I think I have generally said what was true about people I put in books, and what everyone knew to be true, and have even under-stated facts about people which were discreditable to them, but even in doing this I am now conscious that I have sometimes been thoughtless of the distress and worry that something I have written may have caused certain people.

I don't believe that anything that is good and shows the integrity of the artist's spirit can do anyone any damage in the end, and of course, as I have found out in the last four years, the trouble and confusion comes from the difference between the artist's point of view, which is concerned with the general truth drawn from his personal experience, and the point of view of people which is, particularly if they are in your book, concerned with making personal identifications from something which is intended as a general truth.

What I am trying to tell you now I tell you not to criticize or condemn you for what you have done, but simply in the hope that it may help you when you next write something. I have learned things very slowly in my life, and I think you learn them very rapidly. But what I am going to tell you now I have learned in my whole life and know that it is true: It is right to have a passionate bias in everything you create. It is right to feel the indignation, the conviction, the certitude, the sense of conflict, with which it seems to me everyone who creates something must have, but I don't think you can stack the cards against someone in order to justify yourself without being yourself the loser for it. The temptation to do this

[2] In a reply to this letter, Mrs. Bernstein vehemently denied that the character of "Mr. Froehlich" in any way resembled that of her husband.

carries with it its own punishment, and if you try to set up dummy figures of your own instead of real people just for the satisfaction it gives you to knock the dummy figures down, your work will suffer for it in the end.

I think that what you did wrong in the story you wrote about me was to identify a living person so exactly, even to giving a kind of paraphrase for my name, describing habits of disorder and confusion in my life and giving other information about me which was so unmistakable that no one who knew me could fail to identify me, and then from this basis of fact, you proceeded to create a situation and a conflict which was false. You gave some of the facts, but the other facts which were vital to an understanding of the situation you suppressed, and in doing this, I think you have been the loser.

In your story, you make the man desert the woman and all the self-sacrificing love and devotion she has given him because someone suddenly suggested to him that he could get the Guggenheim fellowship and go away to Europe for a year. As you say in the story, he sells her out for $2500. What you did not say in your story, however, and what you know to be true, is that the Guggenheim fellowship and this sudden spur-of-the-moment decision had nothing to do with the real situation. It gives you a false and easy means of justifying yourself in putting another person in a discreditable position, but of the real trouble which had already happened long before this thing you speak of, you say nothing. You say nothing of the bitter and complicated struggle which has been going on between two people for two years. You do not even mention the fact that at the time you write about, the woman in the story is almost fifty years old and the man less than thirty. Perhaps you would say that this is a trifling and unimportant fact and has nothing to do with the truth of what you want to say, but I think few impartial and fair-minded people would agree with you on this score and I doubt very much if you yourself believe it in your own heart. You do not even mention the fact that the woman in the story is a woman of wealth and fashion, a married woman and the mother of grown children, and that she has never for a moment had any intention of leaving any of these things for the sake of this man who, she says, is now basely deserting her.

You do not mention the fact that the man has no money of his own, must live on what he can earn by teaching school and that such a thing as a Guggenheim fellowship, with the chance it would give him to do the work he wants to do, would be a God-send to him. Neither do you mention countless other vital and fundamental facts about the relations between these two people, and I think so long as you were going to write the story you should have done so—that would have been a vastly more difficult thing to do, both as an artist and as a human being. It might even have been more painful for both of us, but you would have done a better, a more powerful piece of work.

I showed that story to only one person, Mr. Wheelock at Scribner's. He spoke warmly of the many fine things in it, of the skill and talent with which the appearance of the room, the meeting between the two people, etc. were presented, but in the end, he doubted the sincerity of the emotion. The situation described, the picture of self-abnegating love which the woman draws of herself, the declarations of incurable grief and intolerable suffering and the vows of eternal faithfulness, did not seem convincing to him, and I think the reason they were not convincing to him was because you shirked your task and stacked the cards against one of your two people in favor of the other one.

I have told you all this, not in the way of condemnation, but because I honestly want to give you what help I can, if it is worth anything to you and if you will take it. In all your stories you show the remarkably sharp, accurate and cynical observation of your race—a quality which I must confess I never knew you had to such a degree, but which may be a most characteristic thing about you. I think, moreover, it is a quality which you can make use of with compelling and even cruel force in writing and that it will be a great asset to you if you use it in the right way. But you cannot use it upon other people and become a romantic sentimentalist when you think about yourself, so remember that all these fine gifts, valuable as they are, carry in them an explosive and destructive power against the person who uses them if he does not use them in the right way.

I agree with you that these stories are a triumph of self-mastery on your part and I assure you I am genuinely proud of you for some of the things you have done. I doubt if your own excitement about getting them published could have been any greater than my own. You say you hope I can share in your happiness about it. I assure you that I do with all my heart and in the best way, otherwise I could not have written you as I have. I want you to have from these stories and everything you do only the best and finest kind of success, the only kind worth having, the respect of fine people for fine work.

As for the other kind of success, the ugly, cheap and rotten kind, I hope and believe you have it in you to loathe and despise it with every atom of your life. What I am trying to tell you is that if these stories get pawed over and whispered about by wretched, verminous little people who want to poke around, pick out identities and gloat over whatever scandalous morsels they think they can pick out of them, I only hope for your sake that you won't allow yourself to be touched by it, and I can't believe you would be gratified at being the center of such attention, on account of the glamour you think it might give to you. If you would, I am sorry for you.

I don't know the names of all the people who have been associated with you in this enterprise, I only know the names of two of them which were told to me the other day for the first time at Scribner's; and I can only tell you plainly that I am sorry you achieved publication with the help of such people.

In your story, you call the people at Scribners and Mr. Perkins a set of snobs. I have not found them so. I have found them thus far to be true friends of mine and among the best people I ever knew, although there are some very shabby, small people who might agree with you in your estimate. But if that kind of injury is in your mind, I don't believe it can do any real harm to any of us.

I think you will find people who would be glad to hear of any discreditable or malicious thing concerning me or of my failure, but even that does not bother me very much any more, and I still cannot believe you really had it in your heart to do me injury, even though other people that you know might want it.

I have just written you all this to hope that you will get the best from your success and happiness and not what is cheap and dirty, and I hope I have made myself plain. I think you let resentment toward me get into your story and that it made you unfair, but I cannot and will not believe you were actively malicious. Finally, after saying all this, I do want to tell you again how genuinely proud I am for all the fine and real and extraordinary writing you were able to do in this, your first piece of work. No one will hope for your success more than I do, and no one will speak more warmly about it when I have the opportunity, although, because of its personal reference to me, with the chance of misunderstanding it, I will not speak about it as often and in the way I would like to, and I know that this is also right.

But I congratulate you again with all my heart and know you will believe me when I tell you I was as happy about your fine work as you are.

The following letter to Perkins was written by Wolfe immediately after delivering to him the rough-draft manuscript of the first part of The October Fair, *which was to be published as* Of Time and the River *fifteen months later. According to* The Story of a Novel, *he then continued sorting and arranging the last part of* The October Fair, *and delivered this to Perkins on December 23.*

*This completion of the rough draft of his book was one of the most impor-
tant milestones in Wolfe's life. As he says in* The Story of a Novel, *"It was
not finished in any way that was publishable or readable. It was really not a
book so much as it was the skeleton of a book, but for the first time in four
years the skeleton was all there. An enormous labor of revision, weaving together, shaping, and above all, cutting remained, but I had the book now
so that nothing, not even the despair of my own spirit, could take it from me.
He [Perkins] told me so, and suddenly I saw that he was right. I was like a
man who is drowning and who suddenly, at the last gasp of his dying effort,
feels earth beneath his feet again. My spirit was borne upward by the greatest
triumph it had ever known, and although my mind was tired, my body exhausted, from that moment on I felt equal to anything on earth."*

To MAXWELL E. PERKINS

5 Montague Terrace
Brooklyn, N.Y.

December 15, 1933

Dear Max:

I was pretty tired last night when I delivered that last batch of manuscript to you, and could not say very much to you about it. There is not
much to say except that to-day I feel conscious of a good many errors
both of omission and commission and wish I had had more time to arrange and sort out the material, but think it is just as well that I have
given it to you even in its present shape.

I don't envy you the job before you: I know what a tough thing it is
going to be to tackle, but I do think that even in the form in which the
material has been given to you, you ought to be able to make some kind
of estimate of its value or lack of value and tell me about it. If you do
feel on the whole I can now go ahead and complete it, I think I can go
much faster than you realize. Moreover, when all the scenes have been
completed and the narrative changed to a third person point of view,[1] I
think there will be a much greater sense of unity than now seems possible, in spite of the mutilated, hacked-up form in which you have the
manuscript; and I do feel decidedly hopeful, and hope your verdict
will be for me to go ahead and complete the first draft as soon as I
can; and in spite of all the rhythms, chants—what you call my dithyrambs
—which are all through the manuscript, I think you will find when I
get through that there is plenty of narrative—or should I say when *you*
get through, because I must shamefacedly confess that I need your help
now more than I ever did.

[1] *Of Time and the River* was originally written in the first person. Wolfe never did
get around to changing it to the third person, so Wheelock finally did this for him.

You have often said that if I ever gave you something that you could get your hands on and weigh in its entirety from beginning to end, you could pitch in and help me to get out of the woods. Well, now here is your chance. I think a very desperate piece of work is ahead for both of us, but if you think it is worth doing and tell me to go ahead, I think there is literally nothing that I cannot accomplish. But you must be honest and straightforward in your criticism when you talk about it, even though what you say may be hard for me to accept after all this work, because that is the only fair way and the only good way in the end.

I want to get back to work on it as soon as I can, and will probably go on anyway writing in the missing scenes and getting a complete manuscript as soon as I can. I wanted to write you this mainly to tell you that I am in a state of great trepidation and great hope also. Buried in that great pile of manuscript is some of the best writing I have ever done. Let's see to it that it does not go to waste.

Max, I think the total length of the manuscript I gave you is around 500,000 words.[2]

[2] Scribners' estimate of the length of the manuscript, as given in a letter written by Perkins to Frere-Reeves on January 18, 1934, was 344,000 words.

X

THE COMPLETION AND PUBLICATION OF
OF TIME AND THE RIVER

1934–1935

The following note was left on the desk of Alfred Dashiell with "Dark in the Forest, Strange as Time." This story was accepted by Scribner's Maga-zine *as of January, 1934, published in the November, 1934, issue, and in-cluded in* From Death to Morning.

To ALFRED DASHIELL

[New York City]

[January, 1934]

Dear Fritz:

Here's the story, with such corrections as I could now make. I think I've succeeded in changing it to *past* tense everywhere—and will you please look at the insertion which I have written in on page 9 to see if it is clear, and if I have succeeded in doing what you suggested there: namely, to leave the knowledge of whether the dying man saw or did not see his wife meeting with her lover in doubt. I've got to have an-other crack at this in proof, and know I can improve it.

As to the title, will you consider this one tentatively—"Dark in the Forest, Strange as Time" (or "Dark in the Forest, Dark as Time" as a variant). Don't ask me what the title means, I don't know, but think it may capture the feeling of the story, which is what I want to do.

This is all for the present—and please let me go over it again when you get proofs.

P.S. I did not make the *cuts* on pages 5 and 6 as you suggested, but rather omitted the reference to Uncle Walter's drawers to avoid arous-ing the natural repugnance of your readers, etc. If you think there's too much of this dialogue, go ahead and cut it out, but I wish you'd look it over again to make sure.

At Perkins' suggestion, Wolfe had given several pieces from his book to Elizabeth Nowell, who had left the editorial staff of Scribner's Magazine *to serve an apprenticeship in the literary agency of Maxim Lieber, with the understanding that she was to cut and edit them and try to sell them to magazines other than* Scribner's. *The first of these, "Boom Town," was purchased by the* American Mercury *soon after the date of the following letter, and was published in the May, 1934, issue of that magazine. It was finally omitted from* Of Time and the River, *but appears on pages 88–120 and 142–146 in* You Can't Go Home Again.

To ELIZABETH NOWELL

[5 Montague Terrace]
[Brooklyn, N.Y.]

February 2, 1934

Dear Miss Nowell:

Thanks for your letter and for the revised copy of "Boom Town." I have not been able to read your revision carefully yet, but I shall read it over the week-end. I am sorry you have had to work so hard on this and have had no better luck in placing it. Of course there's no use arguing with editors who know what they want or think they do, and I don't know of anything I can do to free them from their quaint superstitions concerning characters who stammer, etc. This was surprising news to me, and now I can no longer pretend even to guess at these prejudices or know what the next will be.

Frankly, I don't see that we can do very much more with this story, and it would seem to me to be the wiser course to let it drop. I have been very hard up and badly in need of money, but as much as I need and want it, it has never yet occurred to me that I could do honest work by carving, shaping, trimming, and finally by changing the entire structure and quality of a fundamental character. I think if I knew how to do it and understood more about the mysteries of magazine publishing, I would be tempted to go ahead and try to do it in order to get a little needed money, but I don't know how to do it, and I know nothing of these mysteries. It seems to me that it would be foolish for me to try to do something I do not understand.

One thing in your letter does surprise me, and that is that you now agree with the editors' complaint that the character of "Lee" comes as too much of a shock in the story, that he over-shadows the boom theme and takes away from the emphasis. My understanding at the beginning was that both you and Mr. Lieber liked the character of "Lee," felt definitely that he had a place in the story, and even thought that the character should be more fully developed and given a more important place which, as you remember, is exactly what we did in the revision.

I know you understand, Miss Nowell, that I am not quarreling with you about this, and that I do appreciate the pains you and Lieber have taken with this story. I am genuinely sorry not only for my sake but for yours that we are not likely now to get anything out of the work we've put into it. Moreover, I also believe that as a result of your comments and suggestions, I was able to make the piece more effective and interesting than it was in the beginning; and, of course, in the end that will always be a gain. But I do think that after we have talked and argued together about a piece we ought to come to some fairly definite agreement or conclusion about it, and that we can't go jumping around like a Jack-in-the-box changing our minds and opinions every time we come up against a new editor.

I am very grateful to you for all the extra work you've gone to on your own hook in making this new revision and shortening the piece and cutting out "Lee's" stammering; but it seems fairly evident to me now that the piece is not commercially saleable, and I doubt that we are going to have any success with it. But I will read your copy over carefully Sunday, and either call or write you about it next week.

Now about the *Esquire* proposition. I think something can be done about this, and if you can get $175 that will be swell.[1] I have been talking to Mr. Perkins about it, and he has suggested two or three short pieces which are either in the manuscript of the book or have been cut out of it. One is a piece about two boys going down to see a big circus come into town, unload, and put up the tents in the early morning. I think I will send you this piece today or tomorrow. It is out of the book and in its present form is only seven typed pages long, or about 2100 words. The thing needs an introduction which I will try to write today, but otherwise it is complete enough, although, again, I am afraid it is not what most people consider a story.[2]

I also have what Max calls one of my "dithyrambs." He and Dashiell are very kind about it, and Dashiell even suggested it might be used

---

[1] Arnold Gingrich, editor of *Esquire,* had asked to see some short pieces of Wolfe's and had agreed to pay $175 for any which he might accept.

[2] This was "Circus at Dawn" which finally appeared in the March, 1935, issue of *The Modern Monthly* and was included in *From Death to Morning.*

for the magazine, but I sold them another story the other day, which makes three they have taken recently, so I don't know whether they would care to use it. The thing is about the names of America—the names of rivers, the tramps, the railroads, the states, the Indian Tribes, etc. The only story element in it is that it begins with four episodes in dialogue of different people abroad who are thinking of home. Perkins thinks this piece goes beyond the 3,000 word limit, but I believe it could be brought within that limit without much trouble. It is to start the seventh section of my book.[3]

I also have a piece called "The Bums at Sunset" which we cut out of the book the other day, and which is about some hoboes waiting beside the track to pick up the train, but I don't know if this is any good or could be used.[4]

There are a great number of these pieces, and I think you might very probably find something among them that you could use, but I have lost confidence in my own powers of selection, and apparently have little idea which part of my writing is going to please people and what they're going to like. The piece about the names of America I wrote two or three years ago, and I'm almost positive I showed it to Mr. Perkins, but he says now he never saw it before and that it is one of the best things I ever wrote. . . . All I can do now and what I am doing in addition to revising and re-writing the book is to get all of these things typed so that he can read them. If I had time I think I'd ask you to go over my manuscript with me, but I haven't got the time because I am meeting Mr. Perkins every day now to work on the book, and all the rest of the time I spend in writing and in getting the manuscript typed. But I'll send the circus piece to you and you can see if there's any chance of doing anything with the *Esquire* people about it, and if you don't think there is, I'll send you something else.

If and when I get through with this enormous manuscript, I have a number of short pieces that I want to write, and maybe then I can really give you something that you can sell.

This is all for the present. Try to sell something to *Esquire* if you can. I do need the money badly.

[3] This was "The Names of the Nation" which was published in the December, 1934, issue of *The Modern Monthly* and appears on pages 861–870 of *Of Time and the River*.

[4] "The Bums at Sunset" was published in the October, 1935, issue of *Vanity Fair* and included in *From Death to Morning*.

To ROBERT RAYNOLDS

5 Montague Terrace
Brooklyn, New York
February 2, 1934

Dear Bob:

Thanks for your letter. Ever since I came back from New Year's at your place, I've wanted to write you and Marguerite and tell you how good it was to be with you New Year's and how it set me up. I am sorry that you have seen me so often just after I've been run through the sausage mill. I suppose one should want to see the people he likes best when he is sitting astride of his own world, but instinct in me seems to turn me toward the Raynolds family for succor everytime I begin to wander around in the valley of despair. I won't do it again, or not very often, anyway, and before I go away I swear I will reveal to you all the noble Jekyllesque side of my nature.

I feel fine outside of an awful crick in the back which may be cold or may be the result of my misguided efforts to shove a taxi, which I had hired the other night, out of the snow. But I really do feel grand now in every way that counts. I went into a slump of awful dejection for two or three weeks after leaving your place, was doing little work except cutting and going over the manuscript with Perkins every day. We really got a great deal accomplished, but I was not getting on with my own work at home. Then I had to hunt up typists again, and the Remington and Underwood agencies sent me several of these poor, dumb fumbling misbegotten creatures who, for the most part, inhabit the earth. One was lame and very good and willing of heart, and would come limping heavily in to my table every time she couldn't make out a word—which was every other word I wrote. I was about to go crazy with the thing, cursing her under my breath, and wanting to choke her, and feeling that awful pity and shame about it at the same time.

Now I have a young lady from Utah who has only been here ten days and doesn't know whether she's going to like New York or not, but I hope she will because she types even my most indecipherable Chinese without difficulty, and we're going like the wind, and I am very happy. It seems too good to be true that I am really out of the woods at last, but Perkins says such is really the case, and he may be right. There is a tremendous lot to be done this spring by way of cutting, revising, rewriting, and even getting new pieces typed out of my notes, but the big job, I believe, is done.

We still have to thresh out little matters such as how many of my several hundred thousand words can possibly get printed in a single volume, but these bagatelles do not disturb me after all I've suffered and endured these past four years.

I am glad you liked the last piece in *Scribner's*.[1] Perkins liked it, too, and says the time will come when every one will know what it's all about, which seems plain enough to me now, but I think some people may be puzzled by it.

I sold another story to *Scribner's*, and no longer have any confidence in my power of selection. Perkins has the most tender and paternal affection for the piece I ever saw in any editor, and swears he never saw it before, and why had I never shown it to him, which somewhat bewilders me since I wrote it seven or eight months ago as part of the manuscript that was printed as "No Door," and which we cut out of the magazine as being something which could go.[2] Now, it appears, it is a gem of purest ray serene with the same haunting strangeness as "La Belle Dame Sans Merci," but ye author goggles like an idiot now when he hears these words, grins stupidly and says, "Yes, sir." . . .

The only surprising thing about this is that I swear I showed it to him two or three years ago when I wrote it, and he swears just as positively that he never saw it until a few weeks ago. It's pretty bewildering, but, then, isn't it beautiful to think of all the buried masterpieces which I will be able to unearth out of these manuscripts and give to the world after my seventieth year.

Anyway, the young lady is going to type up everything that is untyped in my books now, and I'm going to let Max see the whole works so far as possible, since I no longer seem to be able to tell what's what myself. God knows what I would do without him. I told him the other day that when this book comes out, he could then assert it was the only book he had ever written. I think he has pulled me right out of the swamp just by main strength and serene determination. I am everlastingly grateful for what he has done. He is a grand man and a great editor, and from the bottom of my heart I know that he is hoping and praying far more for my own success and development than for any profit which may come to Scribners as a result of it—a profit which, I sometimes fear, may be very small indeed, although, of course, I hope for better luck for all of us.

If you are coming in next Wednesday, I should like to see you and have dinner with you. . . . Let me know sometime before four o'clock Wednesday because I am going into Scribner's these days at four-thirty and working with Perkins until six-thirty.

[1] "The Four Lost Men," which had appeared in the February, 1934, issue of *Scribner's*, and which was included in *From Death to Morning*.

[2] "The House of the Far and Lost" which was published in the August, 1934, issue and appears on pages 619–627 and 637–652 of *Of Time and the River*.

This is all for the present. Please give my love and best wishes to Marguerite and the children. . . .

To ROBERT RAYNOLDS

5 Montague Terrace
Brooklyn, New York

March 10, 1934

Dear Bob:

Thanks for your letter. I'm afraid we've begun to count those spring-time blossoms too soon. It's snowing again in Brooklyn now. But I may yet be able to visit your establishment before the daffodils arrive.

My literary agents, of whom I am now inclined to think very highly because they finally succeeded in getting a hundred and ninety-two dollars out of the *American Mercury* for a 20,000 word story which I rewrote three times, and of the same length that *Scribner's* have paid me four hundred for,[1] were out here last night ransacking the manuscript in search of new material. Most of it was dismissed with polite regrets as "not [a] story" whatever that means—I've never been able to find out myself. But they departed at length with a half dozen pieces and seem to think they can sell something else for me.

The reason that I tell you this is because I mentioned your name to the agent and told him you had written some stories. He told me that he would like to see if he could do anything with them. I am inclined to think well of these two agents whose names are Maxim Lieber and Miss Elizabeth Nowell. Miss Nowell, in particular, I believe is a person of good judgement and ability. She worked for several years in the *Scribner's* office, and the suggestions and comments she made to me for revising the story which the *Mercury* is publishing were very concrete and definite and, I think, improved the story, although they did yield to certain assinine superstitions of various editors such as taking out the stammer from a character who stammers, and whose whole character stammers, on the ground that stammering slows up the reading, and that editors have a great prejudice against it. Anyway, we had to write my good stammering character out straight. But in other ways I think the story is improved. . . .

This is all for the present. I am doing three or four thousand words a day and by the end of the week I get pretty tired, but I think we will get there now. Scribners sold the rights to "Look Homeward, Angel" to the *Modern Library* the other day and got an advance of five hundred, which

[1] "Boom Town."

of course, I must split fifty-fifty with the publisher. Of course, both the royalty and the price of the book will be much lower in this edition . . . but Perkins felt it was a wise move because the chance of a considerable sale is much better now in the *Modern Library* edition. He thinks also that the kind of audience that is reached with these *Modern Library* books will be useful to us in the future.

Let me know if you want to do anything about Lieber, and write to him yourself if you do. Meanwhile, good luck and good wishes to all of you.

To JAMES BOYD

5 Montague Terrace
Brooklyn

April 23, 1934

Dear Jim:

Thanks for your letter. It made me feel good, not only because of what you said about my story [1] but also because it was you who said it. I don't think that there is any other writing man whose good opinion would mean so much to me, and your letter gives me hope that I may finally be learning something about my job. I have sweated so much blood and done so much work and I seem to learn things so slowly that often I don't think I am very bright, and for that reason I felt like cheering when I got your letter.

It seems to me that you yourself do better work constantly. I thought *Long Hunt* was the best book you had written up to that time, and although I don't know what's to come in the new one, *Roll River*, it seemed to me the first installment was as moving and exciting as anything you've ever written. [2] It is a great gift to be able to bring the past to life again and it seems to me that about the most difficult job of all is to bring the past of fifty years ago to life again, more difficult, even, I should think, than to write about three hundred years ago, yet I had constantly a feeling of complete reality and intimacy with all the people in your story. The way you evoke Pennsylvania, or the feeling that it has always given me, is quite astonishing. I know the country around Harrisburg quite well for my father came from a country village about twenty miles from there on the road to Gettysburg. I don't know if Harrisburg is the town described in your story, but at any rate it was Harrisburg and the River Street there

---

[1] "The Sun and the Rain," which was published in the May, 1934, issue of *Scribner's Magazine*, and appears in *Of Time and the River* on pages 797–802. Boyd had written Wolfe that it was "near perfection."

[2] *Roll River* was being serialized in *Scribner's Magazine*.

that I saw and felt all the time as I read it. Wherever it is, it is wonderfully real and interesting.

It was good to see you again when you were here last, and fine to see you so well and husky looking. You said something about coming back again in a month or so and if you do I hope you'll let me know and that we can get together again in those Atlantean chairs at the Plaza. Meanwhile, with best wishes, and thanks again.

To ROBERT RAYNOLDS

5 Montague Terrace
Brooklyn, New York
May 1, 1934

Dear Bob:

Thanks for your letter. I should be delighted to come up May the 14th or 19th, and unless something unfortunate happens to prevent it. . . . This will make the third time this spring that I have started out to go on a trip. The other two times I wound up by going to Brooklyn instead, but I hope this third time will break the charm.

My agent has been working me daytime and night-time, and when I had any time off I slept. I finished up another piece which we hope *The American Mercury* will take. The editor [1] saw it in its first version and practically promised to take it if I did certain definite and specific things which he enumerated. I have done them and think I've done a good job. I hope he doesn't back out on me now. It is quite a funny piece, and if it gets published it will be different from anything else I have ever written. It is all about a little man who gives up a fat job on the Hearst syndicate in order to come to Cambridge and take somebody's celebrated course in playwriting. It tells how everything he writes is about food and how his plays keep getting hungrier and hungrier as he goes on, and also of other grotesque adventures. I called the piece "The Hungry Dutchman." [2] It made the agent laugh and I hope it will have the same effect on *The American Mercury*. . . .

This is almost a red letter month with me as regards magazine publication. I have two pieces—count them, two—appearing simultaneously in two different publications, *Scribner's* and the *Mercury*. If the time ever comes when I have as many as three at the same time, I think I'll feel practically like Dumas or Edgar Wallace or one of those hydra-headed writers.

[1] Charles Angoff.
[2] Wolfe finally changed the title of this story to "Miss Potter's Party." It failed to sell to any magazine, but appears in *Of Time and the River* on pages 282–301.

The *Mercury* piece [3] is quite a long one—long, that is, for the *Mercury* —but cut so severely from its earlier forms that it hurts to think about it.

I don't know if I told you that the *Mercury* got very enthusiastic a few weeks ago and began to make all kinds of glittering proposals, none of which, unfortunately, I could accept. They first wanted, so my agent tells me, to publish the whole manuscript of my new book in three issues of their magazine, printing nothing else at the time. I have never heard of such a proposal but I am told they made it. Of course the whole thing is impossible. I don't think they could get the present manuscript in twelve issues of their magazine even if they printed nothing else, and if they could, I think it would be grossly unfair to Perkins to do such a thing after he's worked as hard as he has. The next proposal was that they should publish a series of installments out of the book which should be consecutive and about 25,000 words each. This also was not practicable because they demanded to see all the installments at once and also that they should follow each other in a kind of narrative sequence, and it would be hard to give them this because *Scribner's* has already printed so many pieces from various parts of the manuscript. However, the *Mercury* still seems to be interested in seeing my stuff and we may be able to sell them a few pieces.

I am glad to know you are coming along so well with your book. It will be good to see you again. I am looking forward to being there just when spring is at its best. Meanwhile, with best wishes for health and success to you and all the family.

To FRED W. WOLFE

[5 Montague Terrace]
[Brooklyn, N.Y.]
May 12, 1934

Dear Fred:

. . . I am sorry that I was not here your last night in Philadelphia when you tried to get me. Perkins was in Baltimore that very day and I planned to go down and meet him and Scott Fitzgerald and try to get you to meet us in Gettysburg or some other place, but I did not go, chiefly because I was pretty tired at the time and was also working at night with my agent here. . . .

I hope this new job [1] turns out better for you and that you will be able to get enough out of it to feel a little easier and a little more comfortable.

---

[3] "Boom Town."

[1] Fred Wolfe had taken a new job with the Bluebird Ice Cream Company, in Spartanburg, S.C.

I know you have had a hard time and have often had to figure very close, and as this is probably not according to your nature, I hope things will get better for you from now on. If you are really taking this job partly for experience and want to find out about the business, I think it may be a very good move. People seem to continue to eat ice-cream in spite of hell and high water, and perhaps it is less affected by the depression than most other businesses have been. I suppose you have sometimes thought of being your own boss and having a business of your own, and if I ever make any money, as I may possibly do some day if I have some luck and the whole system does not go to smash, I will gladly help you to get started if I can. . . .

I went over to Pennsylvania Monday on the invitation of a very nice and intelligent young lady.[2] She drove me out and we came back again on Thursday, and while I was there I did little except sleep and eat and see some very beautiful country. I was over on the banks of the Delaware River straight across New Jersey from New York, thirty or forty miles above the Delaware water gap. Coming back Thursday, we drove down through the gap and saw some very beautiful country. Spring is later this year than it was last but is just beginning to reach its peak now.

I suppose you will laugh if I tell you the kind of place I was staying at, but it is not so funny when you see it with your own eyes. The young lady who invited me was the superintendent of a private school or home for defective children. I had a good room in a studio which has been built behind the house and therefore could be as private as I pleased. The place itself was beautiful with a mountain rising right behind the house and the Delaware down below, but the first time you see and talk to the children is pretty bad. It gives you a sick feeling. They call them children, of course, because in intelligence that's all they are and some of them aren't even that. The youngest is a boy of twelve or thirteen years, and the oldest is a woman past thirty who chatters away all the time and who has no more brains than a three-year-old. Of course they all get the very best of food and care and are treated with the utmost kindness by the teachers, but it is a sad thing to see. However, you do lose somewhat that first feeling of horror, and the young lady tells me you even become very fond of them and have no feeling of revulsion at all.

One of them is a boy of twelve, as fine and healthy and handsome a child as I ever saw until he comes close to you and you look in his eyes and see that he has no more intelligence than a baby. . . . It is terribly

[2] Catherine Brett, Director of the Brett School, at Dingman's Ferry. She is now Mrs. Miles Spencer.

sad for the parents of these children, too. Of course, it is something that could happen to anyone and often happens to people who are completely innocent of any wrong and who have other healthy and intelligent children. There is one girl at the place who is . . . considerably more intelligent than most of them and has a very friendly and affectionate nature, which makes it all the sadder because her mother is dying and has only about two weeks more to live. It is going to be very hard to tell her when it happens. She came in the other day laughing and excited and hugging the letter which her father had just written her, and talking about and looking forward to her next trip home when she could get to see her mother and her sister again. By the same mail, the father, who seems to be a very intelligent and high grade man, had written the young lady who is the superintendent, telling her that the mother could not live over two weeks longer and giving her instructions how to go about preparing the child for it.

I am glad that I got to see the place and had the experience. We have all been through hard times and known grief and suffering, but I think we sometimes forget how tragic and horrible life can be, and when we see a thing like this we realize that after all our own lot is fortunate. It is good to know that there are places like this in the world where these unfortunate children are treated kindly and are taken care of, but the bad part of it is that only a very few people can afford to keep their children in such a place and for the most part children like these must be sent to public institutions where they cannot receive the same care and attention and where the conditions, I understand, are sometimes very bad. The terrible thing is that there are over 2,000,000 [3] of these people in the country, which is about three times the number of people in colleges and universities.

Well, this is all on this depressing subject for the present. I thought you might be interested in hearing about it, and it has also been on my mind so since I saw it that I think about it a great deal.

If my health and energy hold up I should finish finally another big piece of work this summer, and then if I could forget about everything for two or three months I could go on and finish the next one and the next one after that. I sometimes feel that I am in the position of a tight rope walker for whom things may be very good or very bad. I have done enough work in the last four years to make three tremendous big books all of which belong to the same series. Now the first of these is almost finished. The second and third require a great deal of work, but everything

[3] This figure seems to be somewhat inaccurate. Wolfe was probably giving a rough estimate.

will be all right if I can hold out. All I can do is to keep on and see what happens.

This is all for the present. . . . Write me and give me the news when you can. Meanwhile, with all good wishes for your health and success,

To ROBERT RAYNOLDS

5 Montague Terrace
Brooklyn, New York

June 5, 1934

Dear Bob:

Thanks for your note. . . . I have written 75,000 words or more in the past three weeks, which ought to be some sort of record. Mr. Perkins and I are working at night from 8:30 to 10:30. It seems almost unbelievable that we've really got the first four chapters ready for the printer. I suffer agony over some of the cutting, but I realize it's got to be done. When something really good goes it's an awful wrench, but as you probably know, something really can be good and yet have no place in the scheme of a book. The hardest thing so far has been giving up an opening chapter which was one of the best things I ever wrote and Perkins himself said so.[1] I actually thought it had a place in the beginning of the book but we've taken it out. Mr. Perkins has done a wonderful job on the chapter that now opens the book. It was originally 25,000 or 30,000 words long and by drastic surgery we have cut it down to 10,000 words and the people he has showed it to seem to think it reads wonderfully. I have got to keep going now until we get done. I think he wants to start sending manuscript to the printer right away. . . .

I am glad to know that you have kept working on your book and that it is progressing. . . . I suppose now that you country squires are realizing dividends on the weather, you have no inclination to visit the greatest summer resort in the world—that is what one of our local patriots called New York the other day. But if you do, let me know when you are coming so that we can get together. Perkins and I, after finishing our work at night, have been going to our old haunt, the Chatham, except that we sit outdoors at their out-door café and it is really very nice, something like Paris walled in with forty-story skyscrapers on every side.

This is all for the present. Good luck and success to you in all you're doing and let me hear from you when you can.

[1] This was introductory historical material, "The Men of Old Catawba" which was published in *From Death to Morning*. One section of this appeared in the June, 1935, issue of *The North American Review* under the title "Polyphemus"; another appeared in the April, 1935, issue of *The Virginia Quarterly* under the title "Old Catawba."

To ROBERT RAYNOLDS

New York City, N.Y.

June 8, 1934

Dear Bob:

I was awfully tired when I saw you the other night and not able to talk much to you and for that I am very sorry. I know that on these rare occasions when you get into town you hope for something better than a conversation with a blank wall.

I want to tell you how much I am looking forward to getting through with this terrible job in order that I may see a few of my friends again and actually try to live among them for a while as a free man and not as a slave in a galley chained to an oar. Also I want to tell you how much faith and hope I have for you and for the book you are now doing. I think we both know what a lonely job writing is and how no one can help us very much except with their belief in what one does. That is all that I can offer you, but you have it with all my heart, and I wish for you nothing but the best and highest kind of success—the kind I know you want for yourself. . . .

P.S. The book is coming beautifully. Perkins and I did some fascinating work last night with a long pair of scissors, paste, typed manuscript and pages from *Scribner's Magazine*. The result was so good that he forgot his customary reticence so far as to say he didn't see how the book could fail. It made me feel good, and I'm in a strange mixed state of happiness and tormented doubt—sometimes regretting bitterly all that has come out and all that I can't get in, and delighted to see things falling into shape as well as they have. Someone said that writing a book is like sifting constantly with an enormous sieve, and certainly this one of mine has been done that way. I can only hope now that the customers will find the deposit to their liking.

To PERCY MACKAYE

5 Montague Terrace
Brooklyn, New York

July 1, 1934

Dear Mr. Mackaye:

Please excuse me for not having answered your letter sooner. I failed to get in touch with you when you were in New York at The Players' Club, because for several months I have been working all day at home on a manuscript and then meeting Mr. Perkins at Scribner's every night to revise and edit it. In this way time gets away from you and one loses count of the days, and I am afraid you had come and gone before I knew it. . . .

In just another month or two I expect to be finished with an enormous manuscript which has occupied most of my waking, and a good part of my sleeping time for more than four years. It is itself just one of four books, but three of them are already practically complete in manuscript; and this first one, after untold agonies of cutting, re-writing and re-weaving, is about ready for the printer. I can't tell you how long these four years seemed to me. They don't seem measurable in terms of years or days or months. They seem to stretch back over eons through fathomless depths of memory, and they also have gone by like a dream.

I have never felt or known this great dream of time in which we live as I have felt and known it during these last four years. It has been a dream of constant wakefulness, of unceasing struggle, of naked reality. I don't think I have ever lived with such energy and with such perception of the world around me as during these four years of desperate labor. Yet the time has got by me like a dream. It is almost unbelievable now that I am really approaching the end of another piece of work. There were times in which it seemed that I was caught in an enormous web from which I can never extricate myself. I lived for nothing but the work I was doing, and I thought of the work I had yet to do. But I was too tired to work. I could not rest or get any peace or repose for thought of the work which was yet to come, and the work even invaded my sleep so that night was turned into an unending processional of blazing and incredible visions, and I would sleep and yet know that I was sleeping, and dream and know that I was dreaming. There were times when I felt sunk, lost forever, buried at some horrible sea-depth of time and memory from which I can never escape.

I don't suppose many young men attempt a work of such proportions as the one which has occupied my time these last four years; and I don't know whether I could have faced it had I known what lay before me. The sheer physical labor has been enormous. I can't use the typewriter, and have to write every word with my hand, and during these last four years, as I estimate it, I have written about two million words. The manuscript is piled up in crates and boxes and fills them to overflowing. It inundates my room.

But now I feel like a prisoner who has been given his release and comes out of a dungeon and sees the light of day for the first time in years. Perhaps I ought not to tell you this long and tedious story of my work, but you are yourself a writing man and I know you understand the intolerable amount of anguish that goes into the work of writing and you will be able to forgive an escaped prisoner who babbles drunkenly about his release.

During these four years I have had the unfailing faith, the unshaken belief and friendship of one man, and as long as any man has that, I believe he always has a chance of coming through; but if I had not had it, it is hard for me to know what I could have done. Mr. Perkins has stuck to me all this time. He has never once faltered in his belief that everything would yet turn out well—even when I had almost given up hope myself. He has stood for all the rage and desperation and the crazy fits, and, with firm and gentle fortitude, has kept after me all the time—until now, at length, it seems to be my impossible good fortune to have come through. I have never heard of another writer who had such luck. No success that this book could possibly have could ever begin to repay that man for the prodigies of patience, labor, editing and care he has lavished on it. And now I can only hope that there will be something in the book that will in some measure justify it.

I have not known such happiness in many years as I have known these last few weeks when, for the first time, it became apparent that I would have the whole thing in hand and that we were coming to the end. Perkins never lost faith that this would be so, but there was a black and bitter period when all he had to go on was faith, because I was unable to show him the whole design, and when I had the whole thing in me but for the most part still unwritten. I would bring him fifty and eighty and a hundred thousand words at a time—sometimes even as much as two hundred thousand—and although these sections would sometimes be as long as a long book, they would still be only sections and parts of a whole, and there would follow a period of exhaustion when I could not write for days or even weeks and when I would wonder if I really had the thing inside me and would some day get it out of me or was only a deluded madman being devoured by his own obsession. I know you can understand now why I feel happy no matter what happens to this book or what they say about it. I know now, and Perkins knows that I was not a madman, but that I had the whole design in me all the time and had stuck to it. Therefore, I feel like a man who has swum upward from some horrible sea-depth where he thought he was lost and buried forever and come back into the friendly and glorious light of day again.

I still have a hard summer's work ahead of me, but I am looking forward to the Autumn and toward going somewhere on a train or ship again—if I have anything to go on—and also toward seeing some people I know and renewing friendship with them. I want to see you and talk to you, and I hope that our meeting will not be deferred much longer. This letter has been all about my work, and I should not have talked so much about it. I had not intended to say anything about it when I started to write you, but I just felt a sudden desire to get it off my chest and to tell somebody else about it who had been through the mill himself.

I hope this finds you in good health and enjoying your summer holiday. It is too bad that a cranky heart forced you to leave those mountain altitudes you like so well, but I hope even that trouble has been righted now and that you will have no further recurrence of it.

I continue to meet Mr. Perkins and to work with him from 8:30 to 10:30 every night except Sunday, but if you ever come into town and have time for dinner, I wish you would let me know, and where I can meet you.

Meanwhile, with best wishes to you and your family,

P.S.—I want also to thank you for "The Faith of Poetry," and for the inscription. I shall value and keep both. Meanwhile, I have put it on the shelf beside those books to which I shall be able to return as a man comes home—soon now, when that wonderful time again comes when I shall be able to read a book instead of trying always to write one.

To ROBERT RAYNOLDS

5 Montague Terrace
Brooklyn, New York

July 8, 1934

Dear Bob:

Thanks for your note. Yes, we have all stewed in our grease here, but I have kept busy and have not minded it so much this time.

It seems unbelievable, but Perkins and I finished getting the manuscript ready for the printer last night. There are still three full scenes to be written, and parts of a few other scenes to be completed, but he wants to start getting the stuff to the printer at once. As for myself, I am fighting against an overwhelming reluctance to let it go. There are so many things I want to go back over and fill in and revise, and all my beautiful notes I long to chink in somehow, and he is doing his best to restrain me in these designs.

I had lunch with Perkins and Scott Fitzgerald yesterday, and Scott tried to console me about the cutting by saying that "you never cut anything out of a book that you regret later." I wonder if this is true. Anyway, I shall do all I can in what time is left to me, and then I suppose I will have to leave the matter on the lap of the gods and Maxwell Perkins. After all these years of bitter labor, and sometimes of despairing hope, I have come to have a strange and deep affection for this great hacked and battered creature of a manuscript as if it were my son—and now I hate to see it go.

I am glad to know you are so near the end of your own. I judge that my own idea of being near the end and yours differ radically, and you will probably see the real end sooner than I do. I think Perkins' benevolently crafty design is to start giving this thing to the printer at once so that there will no longer be any possible drawing back on my part. He has already carefully impressed it upon my mind that the thing that costs is not so much the setting up into print but keeping the setters-up waiting once they have begun.

I had a chance to sell a story to the Redbook for $750. and to my unspeakable anguish was forced to turn it down. They wanted the story for their December issue and refused to publish it any earlier and said that if the story did appear in the book, even in a completely modified form, the publication of the book would have to be deferred until November 30th.[1] Perkins refused to agree to this, so we had to turn it down, although at the present time so much money looks mountainous to me.

Max also keeps discovering wonderful new stories in the manuscript that could have been used for the magazine, but it is now too late. Anyway, it is better now to finish and to go on with finishing the next two books to follow. If it were only possible to go back some day when all these books have been published and to rewrite and work on them again and do all to them that I have always hoped to do! Perkins says he thinks it will be, but the trouble, as I well know, is that there is a kind of strange fatality to print—not only for the reader but more especially for the writer—and once a book has been printed he is inclined to turn away from it and forget it and go on to something else.

Goodbye for the present and good luck to you. I hope to take a vacation somewhere on a ship or a train in autumn, and would like nothing better than to preface it with a few days in Vermont. If you are yourself free at that time, perhaps you would go along with me. Last year's trip up there was wonderful.[2] I shall never forget some of the places we saw that awoke all of those latent and virulent passions for ownership which have been the ruination of my family, and to which I thought I was immune! So I may yet live to become a landed proprietor with forty rocky but beautifully green acres and an old white house set snug and low against the shoulder of a hill! Things as strange have happened.

[1] At this time, Perkins was still hoping for publication of *Of Time and the River* in the late fall of 1934. The story was called "Dark October" and appears in *Of Time and the River* on pages 334–338 and 361–401.

[2] Wolfe had gone to Vermont with Raynolds in September, 1933.

Let me know if and when you come to town and we will get together for refreshment in one of the local brasseries. Meanwhile, best wishes,

To CATHERINE BRETT

5 Montague Terrace
Brooklyn, N.Y.
July 12, 1934

Dear Catherine:

Thanks for your letter, which has just arrived. I spent three hours to-day trying to get started to work, and I hope that writing you this note will work some sort of magic spell, or bring me luck, or get me started!

. . . It seems unbelievable after all these bitter years, but Mr. Perkins sent my huge manuscript to the press yesterday. It threw me into a kind of panic for a while. I suppose I have got attached to it, as one might get attached to some great, monstrous child, and I was a little terrified when I had to give it up. It means that the proof will start coming back within a few weeks now, and it also means that all I expect, or want, or hope to get done must be done within a little more than two months.[1] After that, the die is cast.

I think Mr. Perkins is right in feeling that I ought to submit to this necessity, and that with a book which is as long as this and which has taken as much time, it is possible to get a kind of obsession, so that one can perfectly well work on it forever in an effort to perfect it and to get in everything he wants to get in, but I believe it is more important to get this one done now and to go on to other work, particularly to the next two books [2] which follow this one, which I already have in manuscript, than to spend any more time with this. But I do intend to do my damndest in the two months that are left to me, and I know that Mr. Perkins himself has lavished more care and patience and hard work on this manuscript than any other editor I ever heard of would do. . . .

This is all for the present. . . . Later on, when this job is over, I really do want to get away for an extended vacation—although I don't know how extended it can be. Mr. Perkins has already got together the material for a long book of stories,[3] made up of stories which have been published and other things which have been cut out of my manuscript. He would like to follow the big book with the book of stories next Spring, and in that case I couldn't stay away from here very long. In addition, Part II,

[1] Actually, Wolfe kept on working on *Of Time and the River* until late December 1934 or early January 1935.

[2] *The October Fair* and *The Hills Beyond Pentland.*

[3] *From Death to Morning* which was published on November 14, 1935.

or the second book in this series of long books,[4] ought to come out next year also, and that probably means I will have to be here to work on it with him. He already has most of the manuscript in his desk, but it will be another huge book and I suppose there will be another siege of cutting and revision to go through.

I hope all goes well at Dingman's, and that you succeed in getting another governess to relieve you of some of your work; also that I shall see you soon.

Elizabeth Lemmon, to whom the following letter was written, is a close friend of the Perkins'. She had telephoned from Middleburg, Virginia and had Wolfe paged at Chatham Walk to invite him to visit her at her historic farm, "Welbourne," which Perkins was anxious for him to see. He finally spent a weekend at "Welbourne," in October, 1934.

To ELIZABETH LEMMON

5 Montague Terrace
Brooklyn, N.Y.

July 27, 1934

Dear Elizabeth:

I want to thank you for your kind invitation to come down and visit you for a day or two, and to tell you a little more coherently why I can't come. I don't know what was wrong with the telephone connection last night when you called me. I heard everything you said plainly, but although I was bawling at you, apparently you couldn't make out what I said. . . .

The trouble with a holiday, as I have found, is not just that one is away for a day or two, but one has such a good time seeing someone that he likes and meeting new people, that it is hard to get back into the grind of work when he returns. This is a mortal weakness and with me, a very dangerous one. I work very hard, I think about as hard as anyone I know, but I am also a very lazy person. I don't like work, and never shall. And like all big people, the force of inertia I have to fight against constantly is horrible. I have to fight to get out of bed in the morning, and to get myself started to work. And to get myself launched into action to go anywhere. So at the present time, during this hellish weather we've been having here, I am terribly afraid to stop working, because of all the sweat and agony it would take to get started up again. I am going to be through by October, and then I should like to go somewhere by a train or a ship—

---

[4] *The October Fair.*

if I can. Perhaps I'll go south for a short time before going anywhere else. Maybe you'll let me come to see you then. Would it be all right if I were borne in on a litter? I feel now that is the way I should like to travel. I should also like to sleep for about six weeks solid, without any of these dreams, waking-sleeping visions of the night and horrible nightmares which are like being stretched out on an operating table watching yourself dream—the kind of dream I have been having for two years.

It was awfully good to hear from you. It has been a long time since I had a long distance telephone call from anyone and to get one from Virginia at the Chatham, on a hot summer's night, was one of the nicest and most exciting things that has happened to me for a long time. I was sitting there with Max and Louise and a Miss Iredell [1] (who was, I believe, a former schoolmate of yours), and I thought there was some mistake when the waiter came and said I was wanted on the long distance telephone. Everybody wanted to go to Virginia right away, when I told them it was you.

I know that no sensible person would want to stay in New York at this time of the year, if he could get out into the country. But I wish you would be delivered here by telegraph or radio, just for an hour or two some night, to join us at the Chatham. They have a big outdoor café now where people sit at night and drink. Max and I have been working together every night until half past ten or eleven, and we go there later. It seems mighty pleasant for me, maybe because I spend the day in Brooklyn and sweat at manuscripts, and then ride over in the subway to New York and meet Max and work some more. After Brooklyn and the subway in July, one's tastes become very simple. And the Chatham seems wonderful to me this summer. Most of the men there look handsome, and all of the women beautiful. The outdoor café is really a nice place. . . .

So, as I said, I wish you could be shot or cabled up here some evening and meet us there. Louise and Max and I get together and pound the table and shake our fists and argue about Communism. After the second round of drinks I make Trotsky look like a republican. Max got so alarmed about my political tendencies that he subscribed to the "Christian Science Monitor" for me. They were running a series of articles by their Russian correspondent. The total effect of which was somewhat "agin" it, but maybe I got converted in spite of them.

I think Max went to Baltimore this morning, and will be there for the rest of the week. I wish you could take him down to Virginia for a day or two. I think he is very tired, and know that a vacation would do him a lot of good. He has sweated and labored and lavished untold care and patience upon this huge manuscript of mine. There is no adequate way

---

[1] Mr. and Mrs. Perkins and Miss Eleanor Iredell.

in which I can ever express my gratefulness, but I can only hope the book may have something in it which will in some measure justify his patience and care.

This is all for the present. Thanks again for your kind invitation, and please give me another chance some time when I am better able to take advantage of it.

Meanwhile, with best wishes for happiness and success in all you do,

The following letter to Helen Trafford Moore, an old friend of the Wolfe family in Asheville, was written in reply to one from her praising "The House of the Far and Lost."

To HELEN T. MOORE

5 Montague Terrace
Brooklyn, N.Y.
July 30, 1934.

Dear Helen:

Thanks for your letter. I was glad you liked the last story, and as usual, were kind enough to write and tell me so.

I was sorry to have missed you on your last visits to New York. I have been trying to wind up four years' of hard work by a last desperate effort. And I have been glued to my Ms. for several months. I stay at home all day and write, and every night this summer I have been working upon the Ms. with my friend, Mr. Perkins of Scribner's. This does not leave much time for seeing one's friends, as much as I should like to. I had hoped to get away this summer, but so far I have not been out of the city even for a week-end. The weather has been hellish, particularly this horrible sticky sweltering heat which was expressly invented in Hell for the inhabitants of New York City. Nevertheless, I have kept on working, and so great is the power of Necessity, I haven't noticed or minded the heat so much as usual. Is it not strange when one is a kid in a little town, all that you think and dream about is somehow getting to the great city. And when one reaches my present doddering age, he begins to dream fondly of the green pastures again—of finding a nice cool spot on top of some fairly convenient mountain in western North Carolina.

If I ever have a little luck and make a little money, perhaps I may realize some such dream as that. And I'll also be very simple. All that I want is a comfortable cabin with a front porch—and lots of shade. Then if I can find some good strong girl who is willing to share the hardships of my lot, that is to say, who can do the chores, haul up the water from the well, cook, wash and iron, tote provisions up the mountainside, lay in the wood and cut kindling, and tidy up the place generally, while I sit on the front porch and enjoy the magnificent panorama of the smoky mountains, I will be all set. Do you know any prospects? I am not in a position to make a definite offer of employment at the present time, but if I ever am, keep me in mind when you see a likely candidate. I can promise nice easy hours—not more than eighteen a day—, a roof to shelter her, that is if she is handy at carpentering and can keep it patched —and plenty of plain substantial food—if she can cook it.

This is all for the present. Maybe these idiocies will serve the purpose of getting me started off to work. So far I have done nothing today except drink coffee. I wish you would find out why one works so much better one day than another—and let me know.

I am glad you went to see my mother and sister and found them well. At one time I had hoped that I might see them this summer, and I am afraid now that will have to wait. I am looking forward to a grand vacation in October, and have considered various parts of Europe, Asia, Africa and the North American continent, but maybe I'll just wind up by getting on a train and going somewhere. Most of all I would like to go somewhere on a ship—anywhere, so long as it's a ship that will take a long time to make the voyage, and I could spend the whole time sleeping.

Let me hear from you when you next come to New York. Meanwhile, with best wishes for health and happiness and success in all you do.

To ROBERT RAYNOLDS

5 Montague Terrace
Brooklyn, New York

August 29, 1934

Dear Bob:

Thanks for your letter written on ship-board. . . . I should very much like to be in England with you—it's a fine country. One gets fed up with it sometimes while one is there, but it comes back to haunt you later. There are a thousand things I hope you get to see, and probably you will see many of them, but if this gets to you in London while you are there, I do wish you would go up to Stone's Chop House in Panton Street— it runs off Haymarket there—and try a pint of their old ale.

Also, Sir John Soane's house, which is, I believe, in Lincoln's Inn Fields —I think you can get in for the payment of a small fee. The house has all manner of collector's junk in it, but it has some of the greatest Hogarths in the world—one room in particular, which opens out in panels, has about all "The Rake's Progress." I have always thought the National Gallery was one of the finest and best arranged art galleries in the world, and it has in it more good things and less junk, and some of the pictures that I like best are there. There is another one by Hogarth— just a small one—a canvas on which he has painted the heads of six or eight of his servants, and I think it is one of the finest and truest paintings I ever saw. But you will see it all for yourself and tell me all about it when you come home. . . .

I have already been given more than a hundred galleys of the book, which is over 150,000 words. There is still an infinitude of things to be done, but I don't think that I will get to do them. They feel, in fact, that it is almost ready and they want to publish it as soon as they can. I suppose they are right about it. When one works so long on a manuscript as I have worked on this one, it becomes very hard to stop working or willingly yield to the persuasions of the publisher that you are now ready to publish. It does read wonderfully well; they all seem to believe in it. My tendency, of course, is to want to put into one volume the huge accumulation of all I have done in the last four or five years, but that is neither a possibility nor would it be advisable, and it is good now to have such careful and wise editing to help me and restrain me.

I hope by this time you have received good news about the manuscript of your new book, and that they are getting it ready for the press. Time goes so swiftly when you are working that it is hard to realize you have been gone three weeks already, and that soon you will be coming home again. . . . I long to get out in the great world and voyage around some more myself, but since that is still impossible, the next best thing will be to talk to someone who has done so. . . .

The brief note below was left on Wheelock's desk with galleys 7 through 11 of Of Time and the River. *Wolfe read and corrected these himself, although soon afterwards he got behind on correcting the galleys as they came back from the press and gave up any attempt to read them whatever.*

To JOHN HALL WHEELOCK

[New York City]

[August, 1934?]

Dear Jack:

I am leaving you five more galleys up through galley 11. I would have had more but had to correct proofs of the stories in addition. I found little to do here although I am not wholly satisfied with the way it *flows* —I put some question marks in margins of galleys 10 and 11 for this reason: the tense changes from past to present—present when describing the look of the little town from the train window.[1] Do you find this change of tense jumpy and confusing—and if you do will you change it all to past tense? I hope to give you some more galleys tomorrow and to get on now more rapidly.

The following letter was in reply to an invitation from the L. Effingham de Forests to spend a weekend at their summer house at Onteora Park, in the Catskills. The de Forests had first known Wolfe through Alfred Dashiell, and saw him frequently at one period.

To ANNE DE FOREST

[5 Montague Terrace]
[Brooklyn, N.Y.]

September 7, 1934

Dear Anne:

. . . I have done nothing but work this summer and in fact have not gone away for a single weekend. I am pretty tired at present, completely played out, and I think that I will go away for a day or two at the end of the week when I hope to finish another big section. The proofs of my book are now coming in and although a desperate struggle is being waged between the young author and his publisher, one to put in and the other to take out, I think the publisher may soon prevail. . . .

Although only a half million of my two million words will get displayed to the public in this first installment, that is something, and it will be wonderful to get to the end of it at last, if only for a month or so.

I don't know whether or not I can accept your kind invitation to come to Onteora September twentieth. From now on until they take the manuscript away from me finally and irrevocably, I have a tremendous job of work to do, because once the thing is gone out of my hands this time, it is gone for good. There is something final and terrifying about print, even about proof, and I want to pull myself together for this big effort to keep at it if need be until I drop. My instinct prompts me to go away right now for several days and try to get myself in shape for this final struggle. . . . If I see any chance of coming to Onteora on the

---

[1] This probably refers to the passage which appears on page 31 of *Of Time and the River.*

twentieth I will try to let you know in sufficient time—at any rate, I wanted to explain the present situation, and to thank you for so kindly inviting me. . . .

To ELIZABETH LEMMON

Brooklyn

Thurs., Nov. 8, 1934

Dear Elizabeth:

Max showed me your letter: the reason I haven't written you before this is that I'm just a bum and haven't done a thing—not written a line or done a lick of work for six weeks now. . . .

I shall never forget my visit to your beautiful home as long as I live. Your America is not my America and for that reason I have always loved it even more. There is an enormous age and sadness in Virginia—a grand kind of death—I always felt it even when all I did was ride across the state at night in a train—it's in the way the earth looks, the fields and the woods and in the great hush and fall of evening light. I've got to find my America somehow here in Brooklyn and Manhattan, in all the fog and the swelter of the city, in subways and railway stations, on trains and in the Chicago Stock Yards. I'm so glad you let me see your wonderful place and see a little of the country and the kind of life you have down there.

I haven't done a stroke of work since I came back and I hadn't worked for almost a month when I went down there—I just led an eating sleeping drinking kind of life. All I know how to do now is work and if I don't do that I'm a bum—and I'm not going to let my life go like that— I want to live a long time and get my work done and learn how to use my talent and make my life prevail and also get something out of life besides work. . . .

I've been trying to move back to Manhattan—am fed up with Brooklyn, have lived here long enough and finished a big job here, and now it's time to go—but find it hard to get a place in Manhattan that will fit my pocketbook, which is small, and my demands, which are pretty big— i.e. air, light, space and quiet, which in N.Y. have become capitalistic luxuries. Good-bye for the present—and all good wishes and thanks to you and Mrs. Morison [1] and all of you.

Please excuse pencil—all I've got to write with.

[1] Mrs. N. H. Morison, Miss Lemmon's eldest sister.

Lura Thomas McNair, to whom the following letter was addressed, had written Wolfe to ask if she could interview him for The State, *a weekly survey of North Carolina published in Raleigh. This interview was never written.*

To LURA THOMAS McNAIR

5 Montague Terrace
Brooklyn, N.Y.
November 18, 1934

Dear Miss McNair:

Thanks for your letter, and for what you say about my work. I sincerely appreciate your interest in what I am doing and your wish to make some mention of it in "The State." At the present time I am about as busy as I can be, working on proofs and making revisions in the manuscript, and I think it would be better for both of us if the piece you want to do could be deferred until after the first of the year, either before or after publication of the book which is now in press.

I confess that I have never had much experience with interviews or personal sketches, and the two or three times I did have, it seemed to me I was not very successful. When you are conscious that someone is talking to you with a view to publishing what you say, and that every word, so to speak, will be used "agin" you, a kind of panic seizes you and you are likely either to freeze up or to blurt out something in your confusion that sounds even more foolish than usual. So I think it might be a good idea if you asked me some definite questions which you think might be of interest to your readers, and I would try to answer them if I could.

I do want you to know that I appreciate your letter and the interest you have in what I do, and if I can be of any help to you, I shall be glad to do so.

Meanwhile, with kindest regards and best wishes for your success,

The following letter was written in reply to one from a Miss Elizabeth Cattelle who had sent Wolfe some of her own stories, asking him to tell her if he thought she could write or not.

To ELIZABETH CATTELLE

5 Montague Terrace
Brooklyn, N.Y.

November 18, 1934

Dear Miss Cattelle:

I am very sorry not to have answered your letter of October second before this. I was away on a vacation when you wrote and did not have the opportunity of reading your stories until quite recently.

I want to thank you for what you say about my work, and I sincerely appreciate the faith in my judgment that led you to send the stories to me; but what talents I have are perhaps creative; they are certainly not critical, and the last thing on earth for which I have any proficiency is giving people advice on any question so delicate and grave as the one you ask me. I think the best thing I can tell you is this: that no one has a right either to tell you to keep on writing or to stop writing, and that the answer to the question is one you will have to find out for yourself. My refusal to give you any advice on this matter may seem obstinate and unreasonable to you, but it is not. I think that I myself realize, as much as anyone, the anguish and the damage that may be done to a person whose heart is set on writing by incompetent or mistaken criticism, however well-meaning it may be. Since you have been kind enough to like some of the things I have written and to believe in them, perhaps you would be interested in the following little story, which may illustrate what I am trying to say.

When I was a student at Harvard University a little more than ten years ago, I was a member of a certain celebrated course in play writing which was being given there then. At that time in my life it seemed to me that the only thing worth living for was the writing of plays, and that if I could not do that, my life would never be of any value. The first play I wrote [1] was produced there at the University, and although the play read well in class, it was a complete and dismal failure when it was put on. No one thought it was any good, and most people took pains to tell me so. It was a very desperate occasion for me. It seemed to me that my whole life and future depended upon it, and in this state of mind I went to see a man on whose judgment, honesty and critical ability I relied to the utmost.[2] I asked him what he thought of my abilities as a writer, and if he thought I would ever succeed in doing the thing

[1] *The Mountains.*

[2] An older member of the 47 Workshop who, at Professor Baker's request, had befriended Wolfe. However, he insists that he never advised Wolfe to give up writing, and that such advice would have been unthinkable for him.

I most wanted to do; and although he tried at first, out of the kindness of his heart, to evade the issue, he finally told me pointblank that he did not think I would ever become a writer and that he thought my abilities were critical rather than creative and therefore advised me to devote my time to graduate study in the University, leading to a Ph.D. degree and a position in the teaching profession. I know now that the man spoke honestly and according to his sincere conviction. He may also have been right in what he said, but I am not yet ready to concede that he was. I will never forget the almost inconceivable anguish and despair that his words caused me. Therefore, since that time I have never been able to give a person advice on such a matter as this one, not only because of the infinite possibilities for error, but also because of the damage that may be done either by rousing false hopes or by causing useless and unnecessary distress.

The best thing I can tell you is this: that if writing means as much to you as you say it does, I should let nothing in the world stop it. And in the end I think that that will be not only the most logical course but also the one that is inevitably the most right. In other words, I think no one in the world except yourself can find out whether you can be a writer or have the power to write within you, and I also think that no one in the world except yourself can satisfactorily find out whether you lack that power. So it seems to me that the answer to your question must be discovered by yourself.

Please do not understand by this that I am taking this method of informing you that I think your stories are without merit. I am saying no such thing, and what I have said has no reference at all to your stories, but rather to my own reasons for not wanting to give advice on such a question as you ask.

I shall be willing, however, to talk to you about your stories, with the understanding that I am talking just as an individual reader, and not as a critical expert. If you are ever in New York you can reach me by calling Triangle 5-5683, and if I am able to see you I will let you know.

Meanwhile, with thanks again for your letter, and for letting me see your stories,

To ROBERT RAYNOLDS

5 Montague Terrace
Brooklyn, New York

January 14, 1935

Dear Bob:

Thanks for your card. . . . I certainly won't go away before the first of February and since I've done absolutely nothing about it so far, I imagine it will be somewhat later than that. Perkins is going to Florida this week to visit Hemingway and I shan't go away until he gets back.

For better or for worse, everything I can now do about my book has been done and ended. It has all now been taken out of my hands and put into pages and I cannot make a change or alteration now even if I would. Of course I continue to have regrets. I feel that I have been very lazy during the last two months and think of all the additional scenes I could have written. But Perkins and Wheelock both feel that these scenes would not contribute as much as I think they would and in fact might do more harm than good. I hope they are right. At any rate, it is over, done for, ended, and in this awful fatality of print I feel now, come what may, a kind of tremendous relief. I have just finished writing out the title and dedication pages the way I want them to go and am trying my luck at an introduction which, if it is any good, I should like to see included in the book but which anyway I may be able to sell to the magazine.[1]

Did you ever try dictation, that is, for anything which you hope to get published? I am trying it in this introduction for the first time in my life, simply because I had a feeling that I should like to have the introduction sound like talking rather than like writing. We made a good start the other day and got several pages done and although a good deal of it was very clumsy, a lot of it nonessential, I had better luck than I expected, so I am going on and try to say my little piece out to the end and then get busy at it with a pencil and see what happens. Of course I suppose the idea of dictation is one that at one time or another lures every writer. Most of us are so lazy that the sheer brute labor of putting words down on paper, especially as I have to do it—a million words of writing to get perhaps a hundred thousand words of print—is something we will get out of in any way we can. Maybe it is the best way of doing it in the end because it never allows us to forget the grim nature of our occupation.

This is all the news for the present. . . . I certainly do want to see you before I go away and I hope that all goes well with you and that you can manage it. Meanwhile, with all my best wishes for you and your mother and all the family,

LeGette Blythe, to whom the following letter was written, had known Wolfe at the University of North Carolina, and was Literary Editor of The Charlotte Observer *from 1930 to 1950. He is the author of* Marshal Ney: A Dual Life; Alexandriana; Shout Freedom; Bold Galilean; William Henry

[1] This was omitted from *Of Time and the River* and published later as *The Story of a Novel*. It first appeared in the December 14, 21, and 28, 1935 issues of *The Saturday Review of Literature,* and was then brought out in book form by Scribners in April, 1936.

Belk: Merchant of the South; A Tear for Judas; Miracle in the Hills *etc.*:
also of an article, "The Thomas Wolfe I Knew," which appeared in the Au-
gust 16, 1945, issue of The Saturday Review of Literature. *At the bottom*
of a letter written to Blythe by Scribners on January 4, 1935, Wolfe had
written the following brief note: "Hello, LeGette. I'm going to Denmark in
February—as part of the freight on a freighter. Better pack up your extra
shirt and come along. How are you?" To which Blythe had answered that he
was fine and had a wife and two small sons.

To LeGETTE BLYTHE

[5 Montague Terrace]
[Brooklyn, N.Y.]
January 18, 1935

Dear LeGette:

Thanks for your nice letter. It was good to hear from you and at such
length after so long a time. No, I agree with you, if you are involved
to the extent you say, you would need a good deal more than an extra
shirt to take that trip with me. Please accept my heartiest congratulations.
I had no idea you were the head of such a thriving family and my own
lack of accomplishment in that direction makes me a little envious when
you tell me of it.

It's awfully good of you to take an interest in what I do and I want you
to know how sincerely I appreciate it and how much it means to me. I
have worked like hell these past four or five years and although I am still
in the apprentice stage I hope and believe I have learned something and
will keep on learning. It took me a long time. My idea was all right but
my calculations were a little off. In other words, I thought I was going
to write one book, a mere paragraph of two hundred thousand words or
so, and I ended up by writing three, each of which is about a half million
words long. Furthermore, I started out by writing number three first,
then number two, and at last I got back to number one [1] which is now
finished and which Scribner's are publishing in a few weeks. The end is
not yet. There are still two more to follow before the awful deed is done
and the reading public, if it manages to survive, may refer to the author
of "Anthony Adverse" as a writer of short sketches. Anyway, the story
ought to sound pretty familiar to you and I suppose it proves that the
leopard never changes its spots.

No, I don't think I have changed very much since the Chapel Hill days,

[1] Wolfe probably meant *The Hills Beyond Pentland, The October Fair,* and *Of
Time and the River,* although *The Hills Beyond Pentland* was never completed nor
anywhere near a half million words long.

not inside at any rate. Outside I regret to say I have changed heavily. The gaunt Wolfe of the mountains is no more. I weigh around two hundred and forty pounds and I am afraid I'll never get back the old greyhound model. However, if I get to Norway perhaps I can bound gaily around from crag to crag and from fjord to fjord and shake a few pounds off around the middle.

I see Bill Weber [2] at Scribner's quite often and he always tells me when he has a letter from you. Of course, I am interested in the book you are working on and I wish you the best kind of success with it. When you find a publisher I hope naturally it will be Scribners. I have the greatest reason to be grateful to them. They have not only stood behind me and believed in me in every way but the whole outfit has sweated with me in an effort to get me to deliver the goods or produce the child. And I know that the reason they have done this has been far more because they wanted to see me come through and do a good piece of work than for any commercial motive. The amount of labor, patience, and devotion which the editors put in on my huge manuscript is something that can never be reckoned in terms of money and which can never be explained or paid for except in terms of friendship and belief. I think they are the finest and most honorable group of people I have ever known, this comes right out of my heart and I can wish you therefore no better luck than to hope you find such publishers for the books you write.

This is all for the present. I was mighty glad to get your letter and to hear your voice again after so many years. I hope to see you long before another such period of time has gone by, and at any rate I hope neither of us wait so long to write another letter. I appreciate your offer to help me in any way you can. [3] I should be grateful for anything you did but the best help is the knowledge of your interest in the work I do and your good wishes. With thanks again for your letter and with best wishes for your success and happiness.

P.S. I see John Terry [4] every week or so. He lives just a few blocks away from me here on Brooklyn Heights and we get together for dinner and then discuss the strange vexed state of man until the cold, grey dawn and the last milk wagon have gone by. So you see we haven't changed much from Chapel Hill days, after all.

[2] William Weber was head of the publicity department at Scribners at this time.
[3] With publicity in *The Charlotte Observer*.
[4] John S. Terry had graduated from the University of North Carolina in 1918 and become an Assistant Professor of English at New York University. He was the editor of *Thomas Wolfe's Letters to His Mother*, published by Scribners in 1943.

The following is probably a fragment of a letter written by Wolfe to Mrs. Bernstein from the Île de France, in answer to a letter from her congratulating him on having finished Of Time and the River. *The letter which he actually sent to her is lost. As a result of this correspondence, a reconciliation took place between them when Wolfe came back to America, but they saw each other only infrequently after that.*

Probably to ALINE BERNSTEIN

[On board the *S.S. Ile de France*]

(March 2 ? 1935.)

When I got your letter I wept with joy and pride. I have kept silence, have not spoken or written to you in over five years—but not with an ugly stubbornness, only with a stubbornness that made me want to show you something that was worthy of me—and of you. My heart is full of affection and loyalty for you—it has always been: I am devoted to the memory of everything you ever said to me, of every kind or generous thing you ever did for me. Your proud words of faith and glory make a great music in me—I know your value, know the princely ore of which you're made. You are the best, the highest

[THE FRAGMENT BREAKS OFF HERE]

To BELINDA JELLIFFE

Cie Gle Transatlantique
French Line
Wednesday, March 6, 1935

Dear Mrs. Jelliffe:

This has been a very wild and stormy day on the Atlantic, so I thought it would be appropriate to write a few lines to *you*. (I trust my delicate allusiveness is not lost on you!) The voyage has been uneventful—the ship rocked and lurched from side to side like a great cradle, until to-day when it began to heave up and down also—with the result that quite a few people seem to be feeling it. Fortunately, I have felt all right, and my appetite—I know you'll be sorry to hear this—has been too, too hearty! The food is excellent, and the accommodations about those of a good hotel—my only complaint is that the damned tremendous rocking and lurching of the boat has made sleep difficult at night—I've gone rattling about in my bunk from side to side like a pea in a pod—a delicate little 250 pound pea if you never saw one and want to know. I've done nothing yet with that beautiful little typewriter,[1] but then I can use the Atlantic Ocean as an excuse—the way tables, chairs, and other unfixed objects have gone flying across floors I'd have had to be another daring young man on the flying trapeze to use it. The ocean has been magnificently beautiful and to-day most of all—to-day a terrific, appalling smoky welter coming immediately out of ash-grey sky, waves mountain-high exploding all around, a whistling of wind, and a hissing of water like a tornado, and spume and spray blowing by like hell, the poor little 46,000 ton *Ile de France* bounced and tossed about in it like a rotten straw— and the appalled and stricken heart of man wondering if he had ever known earth or remembered home or would ever see such things again.

I want to thank you first of all for your radiogram because it wished for me the things we all want most and would carry with us everywhere if we could. But I have had little joy or peace or love yet—still tormented, still driven on by drink, goaded by useless requests, beset by wild and foolish apprehensions—wondering what the swine will have done to me or to my book by the time this reaches you,[2] if there will still be heart and power in me to go on with my work if they damn me up and down and say that I'm no good—and knowing all the time that I'll go on!

It's no use—I think there is joy and peace and love on earth for us, but we needn't go across the sea to find it—no truer words were ever written than those of Horace—"You can change your skies but not your soul." But I'm here now and I'm glad to be here and I'm going to see something strange and new before I return. Meanwhile, thanks for all your acts of loving kindness—I'll never forget them. I don't know if I'd have got off without your help or not but I'm damned sure of one thing —I wouldn't have been on the *Ile de France*.[3] So thanks, thanks again —and *please, please,* do your home work [4]—if you don't, you'll not only bitterly disappoint me, but another friend of yours who knows more than I'll ever know and who believes in you.[5]

The Cie. Gle. Transatlantique and the U.S. Post Office apparently order their pens from the same maker—so excuse it please!

[1] Mrs. Jelliffe had given Wolfe a typewriter, knowing that if he would learn to use one his work would be much easier for him. However, he never did learn, but continued to hire various typists who either copied his longhand writing or, during the last two years of his life, typed his work from dictation.

[2] *Of Time and the River* was to be published on March 8.

[3] Mrs. Jelliffe had helped Wolfe to move out of Brooklyn, to store his manuscripts at Scribners and his furniture at her house, and to catch the *Ile de France.*

[4] The writing of her book, *For Dear Life,* published by Scribners in 1936.

[5] Maxwell E. Perkins.

On March 8, the day of publication of Of Time and the River, *Perkins cabled Wolfe as follows: "Magnificent reviews, somewhat critical in ways expected, full of greatest praise." This did not reassure Wolfe sufficiently and he wandered around Paris, drinking heavily and feeling dizzy and nauseated and mentally upset. Finally he sent Perkins the following cablegram.*

To MAXWELL E. PERKINS

[Cablegram]

Paris

March 13, 1935

Dear Max: To-day if I mistake not is Wednesday March thirteenth. I can remember almost nothing of last six days. You are the best friend I have. I can face blunt fact better than damnable incertitude. Give me the straight plain truth.

To this, Perkins cabled on March 14: "Grand excited reception in reviews. Talked of everywhere as truly great book. All comparisons with greatest writers. Enjoy yourself with light heart."

To A. S. FRERE-REEVES

[Telegram]

Paris

[Tuesday, March 19, 1935]

Dear Frere: Is England cheaper than France? Money melting fast here. Would like to come over for week or two if possible. Address Amexco Paris.

To A. S. FRERE-REEVES

[Telegram]

Paris

[Thursday, March 21, 1935]

Taking 10:30 Sunday train. Visit entirely friendly and recreational. I never read a book nor heard of one and don't want to. Best wishes,

To ROBERT RAYNOLDS

St. George's Court
26 Hanover Square
London, W.1

Friday, March 29, 1935
This is the day of the Grand National
and the talk is all of horses!

Dear Bob:

I have a heavy charge of expiation and atonement towards you and Marguerite—for not having come to see you more often when you were in the hospital, for being rude to Marguerite over the phone, for not having written you sooner. It is perhaps too much for me to expiate alone —may I ask you again to help with more forgiveness than I deserve, but with some more of the understanding and loving kindness you both have shown me. I can't go into explanations over what cannot be explained— I can only say that I hope that time of anguish, frenzy, hopelessness and madness is gone forever—and that somehow I have won through and will return restored to do better work, and to grow in wisdom, power and humanity—all that you wish for me, and I for you. May I tell you both how much I value and cherish your friendship—how much your belief has meant to me—how deeply and genuinely I want to be for you the kind of friend you have been for me?

I can't write much more here—they're closing the American Express and I am finishing this there and must get out now. As for what I've done and seen I'll have to tell you later. . . . Have had no mail from America and read no papers—Max sent me two cables and a letter—and for his sake and Scribners, and for my own, I hope and pray to God that all goes well. Love to all,

The letter below was addressed to the mother of John Hall Wheelock.

To EMILY HALL WHEELOCK

St. George's Court
26 Hanover Square
London, W.1

Sunday, March 31, 1935

Dear Mrs. Wheelock:

Will you forgive me for not having written sooner to thank you for your fine and generous steamer letter? . . . I have written no letters until the last day or two. I don't know definitely how things have gone at home about the book—I have read no American newspapers and had no mail save a letter and two cables from Mr. Perkins. These were immensely heartening and full of hope, and not only for my own sake, but for his sake and that of another dear friend of mine at Scribners— your son, Jack—who have both put into the book an incalculable labor of devotion, I hope and pray to God that all has gone well with it, and that my book is having the fortunate and happy life we all want it to have.

Dear Mrs. Wheelock, I can never adequately tell you of the great debt of gratitude I owe to Jack and Mr. Perkins, but, believe me, I am profoundly conscious of it, and hope that I may go on to do work that will in some measure justify their faith and friendship. Your own belief and words of praise are also deeply treasured by me. Let me thank you again for your wonderful generous letter and wish you all good health and happiness. . . .

To MAXWELL E. PERKINS

St. George's Court,
26 Hanover Square,
London W1.

Sunday, March 31, 1935

* This is Section *one*—am sending letter in sections.

Dear Max:

I know I should have written you before this, but until the last two or three days I have written no one at all—save for one or two letters written on the ship—and of course have saved your letter to the last, because it was probably the one which should have been written first.

Thursday, April 4th. I am picking this letter up again after three or four days intermission—I seem to have a hell of a time getting on with it, which is strange, as it is the one I most especially want to write. Charlie Scribner is in town and called me up day before yesterday and I had lunch with him and his wife at their hotel yesterday and am meeting them again for dinner tomorrow night. It was good to see him, and in spite of Mrs. Scribner's instructions that we should not talk shop, I'm afraid we did talk shop. I have stuck to my resolution not to read reviews in the American papers, but I confess that I was unable to resist the temptation to buy N.Y. papers of recent dates to see what your advertising was like, and if any mention of the book in sales-lists was made. I saw a fine big page advertisement in the *Times* for Sunday, March 24th—and also ads in other papers. Charlie had several clippings that showed the book on best seller lists, and the latest one I saw—the *N.Y. Times* for Monday, March 25, showed it leading in New York, Philadelphia, Washington and San Francisco—my own South apparently has left me flat. Of course, Max, this is good and cheering news and I hope it will continue and mean that you will sell the book—the copies that you have printed—not only in order to pay off my money-debt to Scribners,[1] but so that both Scribners and myself may get a little profit—for me, also, a little feeling of security. How unreasonable and contradictory our natures are! It would be fantastic and comical to know that I had written a "best seller," it would be wonderful to get the money that would come from it, and yet I would be troubled by it too—to know I had written a best seller, was a best-seller kind of writer: I would worry then to know what was wrong with my book, whether you and I had done something to cheapen it and make it popular.

I was in a very bad state when I got over here, but think I am much better since coming to England a week or so ago. People have been very kind to me here—Frere-Reeves, his wife, Hugh Walpole, some people I know in Hampstead and in Bloomsbury, etc.—and the English have a way of putting you into an ordered and regular way of life, which I certainly needed badly. I am living in what is called a service flat in an old square right in the heart of fashionable London, Mayfair. It is much too grand for me and much too expensive—5 guineas ($25) a week—but it is so damned comfortable and well run that I hate to leave it. There is a valet like Ruggles of Red Gap, and neat maids, and in the living room a nice coal fire. They bring up breakfast and set a morning table every morning, come in and tell me it is ready and I come out and read the morning *Times* and eat ham and eggs, kippers, sausages, marmalade and tea.

Frere-Reeves was waiting for me at Folkestone when I crossed the channel, I was in a sorry shape, but it was good to see him, and the familiar look of England again, which makes me feel at home, and as if I've always known it. He drove me up to his weekend house which was only fifteen or twenty miles from Folkestone, overlooking a beautiful tract of green country known as The Romney Marshes. His wife was waiting for us, we had tea, and went for a walk across the fields and through a wood, and I began to feel better. We came back and had a fine dinner of English roast beef, tart, cheese, wine etc., and started to drive up to London about ten o'clock that night—I was dozing off to sleep whole way up, went to a hotel for the night and got my first good night's sleep in weeks.

[1] As of March 8, 1935, Scribners had advanced to Wolfe a total of $2,050 against royalties on *Of Time and the River.*

In Paris I couldn't sleep at all—I walked the streets from night to morning and was in the worst shape I have ever been in in my life. All the pent-up strain and tension of the last few months seemed to explode and I will confess to *you* that there were times there when I really was horribly afraid I was going mad—all the unity and control of personality seemed to have escaped from me—it was as if I were on the back of some immense rackety engine which was running wild and over which I had no more control than a fly. I came home to my hotel one night— or rather at daybreak one morning—tried to get off to sleep—and had the horrible experience of seeming to disintegrate into at least six people —I was in bed and suddenly it seemed these other shapes of myself were moving *out* of me—all around me—one of them touched me by the arm —another was talking in my ear—others walking around the room—and suddenly I would come to with a terrific jerk and all of them would rush back into me again. I can swear to you I was not asleep—it was one of the strangest and most horrible experiences I've ever had. There were about three days of which I could give no clear accounting—and loss of memory of that sort is to me one of the worst things that can happen. That was the reason I sent you that frenzied telegram—I had found your first cable when I got to Paris, but I wanted to know the worst. Your second cable cheered me up tremendously and at last when your letter with the excerpts from the reviews came I felt enormously relieved.

I hope to God it all really is true as you said—that we have had a genuine and great success and that when I come back I will find my position enormously enhanced. If that is true I feel I can come back and accomplish almost anything. If that is true—if it is true that we have successfully surmounted the terrible, soul-shaking, heart-rending barrier of the accursed "second book"—I believe I can come back to work with the calm, the concentration, the collected force of my full power which I was unable to achieve in these frenzied, tormented, and soul-doubting last five years. More than ever before, I have come to realize during this past month when I have had time to look back on that period and take stock of it—more than ever before I have come to realize how much the making of a book becomes an affair of honor to its maker. The honor of the artist—his whole life, all his character and personal integrity, all that he hopes and wants and dreams of, everything that gives his life any value to him—is at stake each time he produces any work—and that is really what the whole business of creation amounts to in the end. I hope to God that you and I have come through this ordeal honorably—I hope that we have won a true and worthy victory. You, I think, have done so in your great labors with me as an editor and a man. As for myself, the victory, if I have really won it, while a precious one, is not entire and whole as

I would make it. If I have made my stamp come through—if through the ordeal and the agony of that book, the main outline of my full intention is revealed—that is a victory. But I can not ease my heart with the thought that I came through unshaken—I was badly shaken, time and again I was driven to the verge of utter self-doubt and despair by the sense of pressure all around me—the questions asked, the doubts expressed about my ability to write another book, the criticisms of my style, my adjectives, verbs, nouns, pronouns, etc., my length and fullness, my lack of Marxian politics and my failure to expound a set position in my writings—by all this, and countless other evidences of this pressure, I allowed myself so seriously to be disturbed and shaken that once or twice I may have been upon the very brink of total failure and submission. And now although, thanks to your great and patient efforts, I may have won through to a victory—and pray to God this may be so!—that victory, as I say, is but a partial one, the full sum and import of my purpose has not been revealed. I feel I have by no means begun to make a full and most effective use of my talent, and I hope this book will give me a position of some security, and freedom at last

This is Section Two

from the kind of perturbations that have tormented me these past five years, so that I may be able to achieve the concentration and totality I desire.

Sunday, April 7. Well, here I go again and I'm *bound* to finish this time, because it's an English Sunday and as I look out on Hanover Square there is nothing except the fronts of houses—not a person in sight, not a sound except a bird in the park—just an enormous slab of petrified time —that's England on Sunday. I saw Charlie and his wife again on Friday night—wedging into a dress suit I haven't worn for years—it is horrible how fat and heavy I've become—I've got to remedy it somehow. I told Mrs. Scribner to have a barrel ready when I got there, for I didn't know what would happen if I drew a deep breath. We had dinner together and spent the rest of the evening talking in their rooms—most of the talk being about home again, Scribners in particular: why you wore your hat in the office—Mrs. S. was particularly anxious to know about that and I volunteered my own explanation—whether Jack has had a great mysterious love—she was sure he could not have written some of his poetry if he hadn't—and the various manifestations of Whitney [2] in all his forms.

I have had several long talks with Charlie and got to know him better than I ever did before—I think he is a very fine, a very generous and sensitive man, with an almost anguished sense of his responsibility, the most earnest desire to be fair and just and generous to all his people. He told me

[2] Whitney Darrow.

that he felt that Scribners now constituted a tradition and that he felt it was somehow his duty to preserve it and pass it on. I told him that I thought he was right in feeling this way, and speaking as an "outsider" who had had some experience with the house and a chance to observe and know its people for the past five years, I was certain that dozens of people there, even people in subordinate positions, felt the same way about the place as he did; and that I had never seen another place where the spirit and feeling of the people was on the whole as good.

Charlie seemed particularly anxious to do something for Scribners while he is here in England—he told me that since Galsworthy's death there has been no one to fill his place on the list. He thought Hugh Walpole might do this, and told me that Walpole is dissatisfied with Doubleday and had approached Scribners indirectly through an agent. At any rate, I took Charlie at once up to see Frere-Reeves who, although not Walpole's English publisher, is very intimate with him, and of course had former connections with Doubleday. Charlie put the matter to him, and told him that he had heard Walpole was dissatisfied with Doubleday and would like to come to Scribners. Reeves said he thought these facts were correct and agreed it would be proper to write or speak to him— Charlie wrote a letter, but Walpole has gone away on a three weeks cruise to Greece.

That is the way the matter stands: I offered to help in any way I can— if anything I can do *will* help—and since there seems to be nothing at all improper in the circumstances. But, although I did not tell Charlie so, and have myself no knowledge of publishing, I thought he had too high an idea of Walpole's value and of his ability to take Galsworthy's place. I have not read any of his books; in recent years, of course, his reputation has been in the decline, and he has been the subject of much criticism, including a cruel portrait by Somerset Maugham in one of his books—which by the way in many respects was amazingly accurate. Walpole for example has a little book filled with names and engagements and when asking you to lunch will consult it, etc. But Charlie told Frere-Reeves jokingly that Walpole was "a good selling plater"—in contrast to a fellow like me, for instance, who was a horse who might run like hell and put up a performance that Walpole couldn't touch, but on the other hand might fall down completely. —Walpole, you see, being the kind of animal who might not touch the heights, but would always perform creditably and "never do anything bad." Now, this certainly doesn't hurt my feelings, in fact, I think human vanity is such that we are inclined to be pleased at being considered the "eccentric genius," but in the end I think such reasoning is wrong—i.e. if it were true, just for the sake of illustration, that I am a man of great talent and Walpole a mediocre one,

I think it would be much more likely that my own performance would be consistently better than his, and that the house would profit by me. This has nothing at all to do with me but simply with that rubber-stamp judgment of people that seems to me so profoundly wrong—I am going to talk to you about it in a moment in connection with these excerpts from reviews you sent me, for I think we may do something about them that is important and needs to be done.

As to Walpole again, I think it very likely that you can have him if you want him. My impression of the man is this: a very amiable, genial, robust-appearing kind of man, with much real friendliness and generous feeling in him towards other people, particularly young writers starting out. But also a man completely sold out to success, comfort, "getting on"—so much so now that, no matter what the purpose and ideal (if any) of his youth may have been, he no longer could make the sacrifice, the effort, and the risk of attempting an important work. He was apparently a little ruffled at the criticisms made of his books in recent years, and he told me never to accept the opinion of unsuccessful people about anything—this seems to have some truth in it until you reflect that it is often dangerous to accept the opinion of successful people, too. Walpole, I think, is a man for whom the work of writing has become a necessary but rather tedious adjunct to the more pleasant occupation of being a successful popular novelist. He has a magnificent apartment overlooking the Green Park, three flunkies to wait on him, and an immense treasure in original manuscripts, autographed first editions, paintings, sculpture, jade and amber ornaments etc. For three hours every morning—from ten to one—his servants have orders that he "is not to be disturbed" by anyone—it is during this time, I suppose, that he writes his novels—one a year, he told me, for the last twenty-five years. The rest of the day is all mapped out in the little black book—lunch with so-and-so, the young first-novelist at one, address Golder's Green Woman's Club at three, tea at Atheneum with Sir So-and-So at five, dinner with Lord and Lady This-and-That at seven, theatre with somebody later, read the new books and write column for *Herald Tribune* book review before going to bed. There's your "selling plater" and of course I hope you get him and that his books are profitable for the house. He has diabetes, by the way, and takes a heavy injection of insulin twice a day, almost died of arthritis Christmas, but looks the picture of ruddy, robust, English-country squire-lord.

Another bit of news that may interest you: Frere-Reeves called up the other day and told me that the Book Society (leading English book club, anyway) of which Walpole is a member [3] are apparently interested in

[3] He was Chairman.

Of Time and the River, and had indicated they might choose it, if he deferred his proposed publishing plans—I think he intended to publish in June. He said it was not a definite promise but that it looked fairly sure, and of course I agreed that it would be right to defer publication to fit in with their plans if they agree to take it—it would help the sale enormously, Frere said.[4]

As for my other plans, it looks now as if I'm going to Berlin the end of this week or beginning of next, from there to Copenhagen, and then on to Russia in time for the May Day celebrations—this because I am now planning a monumental work in three volumes on The Success of Russian Communism, and following the example of some of my American colleagues, I figure I shall need at least a week in Russia to gather the necessary material. It looks as if I've got to go to Germany—it is apparently the only way of getting any money, if there is any—I understand it can not be taken out of the country, so I might as well go there and spend it. I wired the German publisher a week ago and asked him if he wanted the new book and what his intentions were, and said I was coming to Berlin. He wired back emphatically that he did want it, was "enchanted" to welcome me to Berlin, and when would I arrive? To which I wired back, on Frere-Reeves cold business advice, that I was delighted, but was also hard up, and what sort of offer would he make. To which he answered that he was "certain" I would be satisfied with his offer, and offered to pay the expenses of my trip. That's how the matter now stands, so I suppose I'm going.

My money has melted away like snow—Europe, particularly France, is now horribly expensive for the impoverished and devaluated Americans. Of course, I bought round trip steamship's passage which was around $250 before leaving—at any rate I've got my ticket home, although it's by the French line, and if I go to Germany, there's no way of using it unless I can turn it in (as they said I could) and exchange it for passage on a German or Swedish boat. In addition to that, there have been railway fares, visas, etc. I am buying clothes—an overcoat, a hat, having shirts made, and a suit of clothes by Prince of Wales trousers-maker, and will be the damndest dude in American literature when I come back— but still owe about $65 on clothes, etc., and counting up this morning found I had only $250 left. I hope to God you really *are* selling that book. Thank heaven, I don't have to see the look on Cross's [5] face when he hears the bitter news. Having been bitten by the bug of foppishness I would

---

[4] In spite of Walpole's efforts on behalf of *Of Time and the River,* the Book Society finally declined it, probably chiefly because of its length.

[5] Robert Cross, head of the Accounting Department at Scribners and one of the directors of the firm.

now go the whole hog and get another suit of clothes—they make 'em so good here—but perhaps had better not until I know more about the extent of my prosperity.

Max, I have done no writing—i.e. no formal work—since coming here, but I have kept a sort of notebook, or diary, in an enormous book I carry around in my pocket. The Paris parts, because of my state at that time, are somewhat distracted, incomplete, but the whole will be fairly complete by time I finish, and in spite of my state of mind over book, etc., I have seen and noted some very amusing and interesting things, persons, events—one, for example, in Paris late one night that tells more about the French and their character than whole volumes of speculation. It was in a *bistro*—i.e. a cheap bar with a few tables, a semi-circular bar of zinc, man behind bar, avaricious dark-visaged madame at cashier's desk counting up coins with holes in them, a couple of waiters, two young, apathetic, unsuccessful-looking prostitutes at tables with a beer before them—two o'clock in the morning, Place St Michel: at the bar only two customers, one a dingy looking little man, harmless, but very drunk, pounding on zinc bar, arguing in hoarse loud voice with bar man and other customer. Bar man young, hawk-visaged Frenchman, alert and able looking, blue apron, sleeves rolled up, keeping sharp eye on situation as barmen do the world over, finally calls on drunk to pay up and get out. Little dingy drunk refuses to pay—he owes *three* francs—gets very hoarse and obstreperous, pounds on bar, and finally offers to fight. "Very well! Good!" says bar man coolly, "But if you are going to fight, why don't you take off your coat?" The little drunk considers this with drunken solemnity for a moment, then wagging his head in drunken agreement says: "Good! All right! I *will* take off my coat!", and considers the idea such a good one that he not only takes off his overcoat, which he hands to one of the waiters, but peels off his *other* coat as well, and hands it to other waiter —at which dark-visaged madame, who has been murmuring tender cajoleries to a little dog and feeding him sugar which she cleverly conceals in her hand under her shoulder and various other places, making him hunt for it, saying "Ah,

This is Section Three

you are wicked, you! You're the naughty one!" etc. (one of the grotesque things in them is this sentimentality towards animals and their hard-boiled treatment of each other)—anyway she now turns from this tender dog-baby-talk and begins to screech out harsh instructions to the waiters who have both of the poor little drunk man's coats. The bar man speaks a few curt words of instructions to them, and the waiters, grinning from ear to ear with delight, rush off triumphantly towards the back of the place bearing the little man's two coats as security for his unpaid three francs. At this, of course, he is wildly indignant, bellows with rage, and takes a drunken swing at the barman. This is just what the barman has been waiting for—he vaults over the zinc bar like a flash, the waiters rush up, and they bounce the poor little man, minus both his coats, and in his shirtsleeves, right out on his ear—on the cold and frosty pavements of the Place St. Michel. Now I submit that this is a *French* story: the little man would very probably have been bounced out on his ear in England or America, but I think it is highly improbable that we would have thought of getting his two coats away from him first.

Anyway, I have kept this sort of diary, people, events, conversations of all sorts—the great boat race between Oxford and Cambridge Saturday, which I saw, a wonderful spectacle, and the look and talk of the English poor all around me, lining the banks of the Thames as the crews came by—what it is like being back in Europe for an American after the last four years in America—how Europe seems to me now after the first abashment and bewilderment of my first visits in the twenties has worn off—why I know I could not live here—many other things. I intend to make the same sort of notes for Germany and Russia if I go there—just what I see and feel and hear—and it occurred to me that the whole thing, starting the moment I left New York on ship until I return, very much pruned and condensed, of course, might make interesting and entertaining reading under some such title as "The Busman's Holiday." What do you think?

Now, as to those excerpts from the reviews you sent me—They were splendid, wonderfully heartening, and I hope they were not too *hand-picked.*—i.e. I hope that, as you said, they were taken more or less at random, and if the reviews on the whole were, as you say, better than these excerpts would indicate, that would be wonderful. But even from these excerpts, good as they are, and from one or two indications in advance notices before I left New York, I think I can spot the trend of some of the enthusiasm. Max, Max, perhaps you think I hate all forms of criticism, but the sad truth is, how much more critical am I, who am generally supposed to be utterly lacking in the critical faculty, than most of these critics are. God knows, I could profit by a wise and penetrating criticism as much as any man alive, but as I grow older I am beginning to see how rare—how much rarer even than *Lear, Hamlet,* the greatest productions of art—such criticism is—and how wrong-headed, false, and useless almost everything that passes as criticism is. I know for example that the great length of the book will be criticized, but the real, the tragic truth is that the book is not too long, but too short. I am not talking of page-length, word-length, or anything like that—as I told you many times, I did not care whether the final length of the book was 300, 500, or a 1000 pages, so long as I had realized completely and finally my full intention—and that was not realized. I still sweat with anguish—with a sense of irremediable loss—at the thought of what another six months would have done to that book—how much more whole and perfect it would have been. Then there would have been no criticism of its episodic character—for, by God, in purpose and in spirit, that book was not episodic but a living whole and I could have made it so—the whole inwrought, inweaving sense of time and of man's past conjoined forever to each living present moment of his life could have been made manifest —the thing that I *must* and *will* get into the whole thing somehow.

Again, people will talk of the book having taken five years to write, but the real truth of the matter was that it was written practically in the whole in a year—it was written too fast, with frenzied maddened haste, under a terrible sense of pressure after I had written two other antecedent books [6] and found I had not got back to a true beginning. It is the work of frenzied, desperate, volcanic haste after too much time had slipped away, and no one will know that. Even now, I [can] not read the book, save for a page or two at a time—at every point the deficiency of my performance compared with the whole of my intent stares me in the face—the countless errors in wording and proof-reading—for which *I* alone am utterly to blame, but which in my frenzied state of mind I let pass by—stab me to the heart. I was not ready to read proof, I was not through *writing*—the fault is my own. I fell down on that final job, the book was written and typed and rushed in to you in such frantic haste day after day that I did not even catch the errors in wording the typist made in an effort to decipher my handwriting—there are *thousands* of them. I don't know where to begin, but for God's sake, if it should be vouchsafed us that *more* editions will be printed, try to catch these:

Page 506 "The Hudson River drinks from out *of* the inland slowly"— Cut out *of*.

Page 509 "our *craving* flesh"—for "craving" print "waning."

Page 510 "mining against the sides of ships"—for "mining" print "moving."

Page 665 "The *minute-whirring* flies buzz home to death"—for "minute-whirring"—put "minute-winning."

Page 663—"Battersea *Lodge*"—put "Battersea Bridge."

Page 678—"I can *list* to nothing else"—put "listen."

Page 678—"right across the character of my brain"—for "character" put "diameter."

Page 678—"Hummel Vee"—put "Hummel Bee."

Page 680—"I am as naked now as *sorry*"—put "sorrow."

[6] *The October Fair* and *The Hills Beyond Pentland.*

Page 517—"at this *gigantic* moment" substitute "'*propitious*" for "*gigantic*."

Page 519—"*ah* petty"—"so petty."

Page 545 "*envy* and departure"—"error and departure."

Page 545 "race of African *beings*"—"African *kings*."

Page 545—"leonic"—"leonine."

Page 545 "the *bad* and almost brutal *volume*"—"the *hard* and almost brutal *violence*."

Page 545—"*marked* his pain"—"*masked* his pain."

Page 546—"shaking his *beard*"—"shaking his *head*."

page 549—"And nothing finally but night and dullness"—"night and darkness."

page 576 (a horrible error) a hiatus between sentences, utterly meaningless—". . . smiling his radiantly gentle and good-natured smile, 'I don't agree with you spoke with a crisp—' etc." Change to

"'I don't agree with you.'"

She spoke with a crisp but obstinate conviction, 'Joel, I *know* I'm right!'

'All right,' he said quietly, 'Perhaps you are—about the gold—but about the pavilion—I'd like to argue with you about that'"

(Or better still, Max, since I can't remember, why not look up the manuscript and find out what I really did say!)

Page 588—"*ever-long* immortality"—put "ever-living immortality."

Page 596—"dyed hair of straw-*blade* falseness"—"straw-blonde falseness."

Page 662—"ate cinq cent mille"—"et cinq cent—"

Page 662—"a fond d'artichant *moray*"—"a fond d'artichaut mornay."

page 669—"the man who wrote *Batouale*"—"*Batouala*."

page 671—"the great mirrors reflecting *these*"—"reflecting *them*."

page 672—"the veteran of a million *lives*"—"a million *loves*."

page 673—"the flat heavy *mark*"—"the flat heavy "*smack*."

page 673—"*Light* up your heart"—"*Lift* up your heart."

page 676—"with mean and *senile* regret"—"the mean and *servile* regret."

Max, Max, I cannot go on, but I am sick at heart—we should have waited six months longer—the book, like Caesar, was from its mother's womb untimely ripped—like King Richard, brought into the world "scarce half made up."

Before I went away, you wrote me, in reference to the introduction I wanted to write, that you were trying to "save me from my enemies." Max, my enemies are so much more numerous than you expect—they include, in addition to the Henry Harts, Wassons, and others of that sort, the Benéts, the I.M.P.'s, the F.P.A.'s, the Morleys, the Nathans, the Mark Van Dorens, the Mike Golds, and others of that sort—they include also . . . the Lee Simonsons, the Theatre Guilders, the Neighborhood Playhouses, the Hound and Horners, the Kirstens, Galantières, and all that crowd with all its power and wealth—and I fear we have played directly into their hands by our carelessness and by our frenzied haste— our failure to *complete* just when completion was in our grasp. I gravely fear that by the time this reaches you the reaction will have set in—the enemy will have gathered itself together and the attack begun. I can't go through five more years like this last five—my health is gone—my youth is gone—my energy is gone—my hair is going, I have grown fat and old—and for all my agony and anguish—the loss of my youth and health—what have I got? I've got to have some security and repose— I've got to be allowed to finish what I've begun—I am no longer young enough, I have not energy or strength enough to go through it again.

For God's sake, try to kill false rumors

This is *Fourth* and Last Section

when you hear them. Before I left, I saw that they were beginning to make another rubber stamp under the name of "criticism." Apparently they had discovered that I was six and a half feet tall, and very large: therefore it follows that all my characters are seven feet tall—bellow and roar when they talk—that I can create nothing but a race of gigantic monsters. Max, for Christ's sake, I beg and plead with you, don't let this horrible god-damned lie go unanswered. I have never created a monster in my life, none of my people are seven feet tall. The *fault*, the *fault* always, as *you* should know, is not that we exceed the vital energy of life but that we fall short of it—and that a horrible misbegotten race of anaemic critics whose lives have grown underneath a barrel call out "monster" and "exaggeration" at you the moment you begin to approach the energy of life.

You yourself told me you took one of your daughters through the Grand Central Station and showed her twenty people who might have stepped out of the pages of Dickens, and not a day of my life passes— a day spent in the *anguish of intense and constant speculation* and not at *literary cocktail parties*—that I do not see a hundred—no, a thousand— who, if you put them in a book, would immediately bring down upon your head the sneers of the Patersons, the Benéts, the Van Dorens, and all their ilk, of "monsters," "seven feet tall," "untrue to life," etc.

In Christ's name, Max, what is wrong with us in America? The whole world—not myself alone—wants to know. The English ask me, everyone asks me, why do we cry out that what we want is life, and then try to destroy and kill the best people that we have? Why do our best writers, poets, men of talent turn into drunkards, dipsomaniacs, charlatans, cock-tail-cliquers, creators of Pop-eye horrors, pederasts, macabre distortions, etc.? I tell you, it is not I alone who ask the question, but everyone here—all of Europe knows it. Why is it that we are burnt out to an empty shell by the time we are forty, that instead of growing in strength and power we are done for—empty, burnt-out wrecks at an age when men in other countries are just coming to their full maturity? Is it because the seeds of destruction are *wholly* in ourselves—that there is something in the American air, the weather of the American life that burns the lives of men to rust as quickly as it rusts iron and steel? Or is it perhaps that there is in us a sterile, perverse, and accursed love and lust for death that wishes to destroy the very people that we set up—the people who have something to give that may be of value and honor to our life? Is it because we take a young man of talent—a young man proud of spirit, and athirst for glory, and full with the urge to create and make his life prevail—praise him up to the skies at first, and then press in upon him from all sides with cynics' eyes and scornful faces, asking him if he can *ever do it again* or is done for, finished, no good, through forever? Is it because we deal this hand of death to young proud people, telling them they are the lords of the earth one year, and the glory of their nation's country, and the next year sneering, jeering, laughing, reviling, scorning and mocking them with the very tongues that sang their praises just a year before? Is this the reason why we fail—the reason that our finest artists are destroyed? Tell me, is this the reason—men in England also ask me; they all want to know. And then how easy for them all, when we *are* done for—when we have been driven mad, when we are drunkards, dipsomaniacs, perverts, charlatans, burnt out shells—how easy it is for the whole pack to pull the face of pious regret, to sigh mournfully, to say: "What a pity!—We had hoped once —He looked so promising at one time!—What a shame he had to go and waste it all!"

I know your answer to these questions—that the strong man is as Gibraltar, that all these assaults will fall harmlessly against his iron front, the impregnable granite of his invincible soul—but, alas, no man is strong as that—it is a pleasant fable—his great strength is needed, to be concentrated on the work he does, and while his brows and every sinew of his life is bent to the giant labor of creation, what shall protect him from these coward-hordes who come to destroy his life from every side? Why should the artist—who is life's strongest man, earth's greatest hero— have to endure this in America of all the countries of the earth, when his task alone is so cruel hard there: the need for a new language, the creation of a new form so stern and formidable? Why should he have to do this great work, and at the same time withstand the murderous attack of death-in-life when in every country in Europe the artist is honored, revered, and cherished as the proudest possession that a nation has?

Take this for what it is worth. If you think it extravagant, then take it so, but see the core of truth in this as well. I have given my life to try to be an artist, an honor to my country, to create beauty, and to win fame and glory, and the honor of my people, for myself, what has it got me? At the age of thirty-four I am weary, tired, dispirited, and worn out. I was a decent looking boy six years ago—now I am a bald, gross, heavy, weary-looking man. I wanted fame—and I have had for the most part shame and agony. They continue to speak of me as a "writer of promise"—and if I only do 197 impossible things—which they doubt that I *can* do—something may come of my work in the end. The Paterson woman [7] says my people are all seven feet tall and talk in bellowing voices—she says take away his adjectives, nouns, verbs, pronouns, words of violence, height, altitude, colour, size, immensity— and *where* would he be? The Mark Van Dorens [8] say take away his own experience, the events of his own life, forbid him to write about what he has seen, known, felt, experienced—and where would he be? The Fadimans say take away his apostrophes, declamations, lyrics, dreams, incantations—and where would he be? [9] The Rascoes [10] say he has no

[7] In "'Turns with a Book Worm" in *The New York Herald Tribune Books* for Sunday, February 24, 1935, I.M.P. said: "Mr. Wolfe is a lavish writer. He steps up the scale of everything—all his principal characters are highly exaggerated. They are seven feet tall with megaphone voices. We don't mind; he does manage to keep up the excitement. But it might be an interesting experiment to take one of his chapters and eliminate all the superlatives, the adjectives indicating altitude, volume, and violence. Step it down again to life size and see what would remain."

[8] Mark Van Doren did not review *Of Time and the River* but in *The Nation* on April 25, 1934, he had said: "Thomas Wolfe's one novel to date, *Look Homeward, Angel,* needs to be followed by others before anybody can know whether Mr. Wolfe is an artist in anything beyond autobiography. . . . The public is justified in asking Mr. Wolfe whether he can keep himself out of the picture in books to come."

[9] Clifton Fadiman in *The New Yorker*, March 9, 1935 said: "It is open to debate whether he is a master of language or language a master of him; but for decades we have not had eloquence like his in American writing. His declamations and apostrophes . . . are astounding and even beautiful; and even when mere rhetoric, they are mere gorgeous rhetoric. . . . At their best these tempests of poetic prose . . . are overwhelming, and at their worst they are startlingly bad. . . . Thus it is impossible to say any one thing of Mr. Wolfe's style. At its best it is wondrous, Elizabethan. At its worst, it is hyperthyroid and afflicted with elephantiasis."

[10] Burton Rascoe, in *The New York Herald Tribune Books* for Sunday, March 10, 1935, said: "He has no evident sense of humor; nor any true sense of comedy. Even when he attempts to be playful or funny the effect is the disconcerting and uncomfortable one of a rictus, an attack of giggles, or the fantastic laugh of 'L'homme qui rit.' "

sense of humour—this, to the man who created old Gant, wrote the lunch room scenes in the *Angel*, Bascom Hawke in the *River*, *The Web of Earth*, Oswald Ten Eyck, the Countess, the Englishmen at the inn and all the others. The Communists say he is a romantic sentimentalist of the old worn-out romantic school, with no Marxian code; and the Saturday Reviewers [call him] a depicter of the sordid, grim, horribly unpleasant and surrealistic school—and so it goes—in Christ's name what do these people want?

Apparently, I would be a good writer if I would only correct 3,264 fundamental faults, which are absolutely, profoundly and utterly incurable and uncorrectable—so what in Christ's name am I to do?—In God's name how am I to live? What's before me? I tell you, Max, I cannot put in another five years like the last—I must have some peace, security, and good hope—I must be left alone to do my work as I have planned and conceived it, or the game is up. I am tired and ill and desperate, I can't go on like this forever. I got hurt somehow in Paris —how I don't know—during one of those three days I can't remember. I don't know whether I'm ruptured or not—I haven't the faintest idea, memory, or recollection of what happened, whether I got slugged in some joint or ran into something—but I woke up with a bruise above my groin the size of a saucer, and ever since it's felt as if something has been torn loose inside me.

Forgive these wild and whirling words—you are the friend I honor and respect more than anyone else. I hope and pray to God you may have some use and credit from my life in return for all you have done for it, just as I hope that I can make it prevail—as by God's will, I hope and trust I yet may do.

This is all for the present. If there is any great good news, for God's sake send it to me. At any rate stay with me, be my friend, and all may yet be well. Take this letter—or rather this chronicle, this history— for what it is worth—weed the good from the bad—and consider what truth is in it. I'm sending it to you in three or four instalments because I can't get it in one letter. Goodbye, good luck and good health, and love to all the family.

XI

THE SUCCESS OF OF TIME AND THE RIVER,
AND PUBLICATION OF FROM DEATH TO MORNING

1935

To MAXWELL E. PERKINS

[Postcard: *Hogarth's Servants*]

London

April 10, 1935

Dear Max:

This is the way people ought to look—and the way they always have looked—I see them around me every day. This is the only thing that *beats* time—if I could ever do it in a book I'd die happy. You didn't know I knew a lot about pictures, did you? Well, I do—about this kind. The "old masters," Titian, Veronese, etc. mean nothing to me—only these men like Hogarth who had the sense of life that could speak to me in a language I know. This is one of the most *moving* pictures I ever saw.

To MAXWELL E. PERKINS

[Postcard: Marinus' *The Ursurers*]

London

April 10, 1935

And maybe this is the way they always *have* looked too. The real title of this picture is "Two Bankers" or "The Usurers." Does it look like anyone you ever saw? [1]

[1] There is a very slight resemblance to Robert Cross, head of the accounting department at Scribners.

451

The following letter was addressed to Mrs. Maxwell E. Perkins.

To LOUISE S. PERKINS

St. George's Court
26 Hanover Square
London W. 1.

Thursday, April 18, 1935

Dear Louise:

I was surprised and delighted to get your cable and the news that you and Elizabeth and Peggy [1] are coming over here in June. . . . Nothing would give me more pleasure than to meet you and the children and if anything I knew or could show you would be of interest to you, the occasion would give me the greatest happiness.

But as I told you in my cable I may not be in Europe when you arrive in June: my plan was to return to America sometime in May. I don't know what publishing plans Max may now have in mind concerning me, but he originally intended to publish a volume of my stories in the Fall,[2] and if he does that, I want to come back and try to make the book as good as I can before it is published. I wish you could persuade Max to take a short vacation *now*—in May—bring Elizabeth with you, if she can come, and have Peggy meet you in June when school is out. If Max felt he could not stay away for long, you could get a fast boat and he could spend three or four weeks over here and have a vacation—which he sorely needs. He could still get home by June, in ample time to make his preparations for the Fall season. I mention this, not only because the weather and the country is now getting lovely and would be beautiful in May, but also because, as I understand it, the Spring publishing season slackens up at about this time, and it seems to me, from Max's point of view, there could not be a better time to take such a vacation—particularly since I shall want his help so much a little later.

I don't think there is anyone in the world—particularly at Scribners —who would not enthusiastically approve of a holiday for Max, so I wish you'd all do it. If Elizabeth couldn't come now, or if you'd rather have her come with Peggy, you and Max could come, and the girls could meet you later. Personally, I see no reason why two grown-up girls are not perfectly capable of making a five day journey by themselves in a transatlantic liner—and that's all it would amount to. You could meet them in Paris, London, or Berlin, or at the boat—there's

---

[1] Two of the Perkins' daughters.
[2] *From Death to Morning,* which was published on November 14, 1935.

no trouble at all about it. I am urging this plan, not because I have much hope that it will happen, because frankly I do not believe Max will agree to it, but because, by one of those sudden and blinding flashes of intuition which (whether it sounds boastful or not) *have rarely played me false,* I feel profoundly that he *ought* to agree to it, that a *wise instinct* on his part would make him agree to it, that if he came now, this trip would have a good and fortunate result, which he would never regret. The one thing I have observed in Max in the last few years which worried me and which seemed wrong was a growing tenacity in the way he stuck to business—what seemed to me some-times an unreasonable solicitude and preoccupation with affairs which might be handled by proxy or in less exhausting ways. It is surely a sort of vanity, even in so modest a man as Max, to feel that a business cannot run itself if he is absent from it for a few weeks. No one on earth —and I, as you know, have reason to know this better than anyone— no one on earth can do the kind of work Max does, no one could take his place in doing that, and if it were a question of some valuable work that *had* to be done now, there would be nothing for him to do but stay and do it. But my guess is that at just this moment, this season, there really is no such work, and that such a journey as I have proposed, brief as it is, would give him a spiritual and physical refreshment that in the end could work nothing but *the greatest good.* Max is now at the summit of his powers—the best work is still before him: it would be a tragedy if he in any way blunted or impaired his great faculties at this time simply because he failed to take advantage of a chance to recuperate and replenish his energies.

Another reason I wish you could come now is this:—I think, from certain things I have seen, that this is not only a critical and immensely interesting period in the life of Europe, but also this particular time, the month of May, has several events of extraordinary interest. Here in England, for example, they are making preparations for the King's Jubilee—if you could possibly get to London by May 6th you would be able to see a kind of stupendous pageantry that the world may never see again, and that certainly none of us are likely to see in our lifetime. It should be an immensely interesting thing. I shall not be here myself to see it unless you and Max decide to come, because I have got to go to Berlin in a day or two and from there propose to go to Russia (in time for May Day if possible) and back to Copenhagen, and so home. But if you and Max could come, I could meet you anywhere you like. . . .

Of course, in all of this, outside of my earnest conviction that such a trip could do Max nothing but good, there is also some special pleading for myself. Nothing could possibly give me greater happiness than to meet you and Max and spend some time, however brief, with you over here. The blunt truth of the matter is that none of us are chickens any more. Max is getting on to fifty and I am almost thirty-five, and this thing I have often dreamed of—of looking at some of these old societies and civilizations with him, and seeing together some of what they have to offer—this pleasant dream, I say, will probably remain forever just a dream unless it is now realized.

This is all I can say, and of course I fear my arguments are useless.[3] At any rate, I think it's grand that you and the girls are coming. If I am here I should be delighted to see you, and if I miss you, I wish you the happiest and most interesting kind of journey. . . . Meanwhile, with best wishes and love to all,

To MABEL WOLFE WHEATON

St. George's Court
26 Hanover Square
London W. 1

Tuesday April 23, 1935

Dear Mabel:

I was delighted to get your letter—it was the first news I'd had from home. My mail is being held for me at Scribners until I get back, and outside of a letter and a couple of cables from Mr. Perkins, your letter, and one from Fred which came the same day yours did, is about all the mail I've had. I was sorry, however, to hear that Mama had not received my long letter at the time you wrote—I wrote her just a day or two after I got to England a month ago . . . but she must have it now. . . . The last few weeks in New York were frantic: everyone in the world, not only people I knew but people I didn't know, seemed to be on my trail. I was going crazy what with fools, freaks, bores, and the attentions of well-meaning friends, and having to pack up and sort out tons of manuscript, books, store my furniture, buy some clothes—I was in rags—etc. Our dear old pal and well-wisher Mr. ——, by the way, wrote me a letter just before I sailed and it was one of the most horrible, venomous, and dishonourable productions I ever read. He seemed about to strangle with gall and venomous hatred because I had not answered his letters, because I had not read his novel—the one he gave me and

---

[3] As Wolfe suspected, Perkins did not go abroad. For approximately the last twenty years of his association with Scribners, he never took a vacation for more than a few days, except for trips to see Hemingway or other Scribner authors.

then demanded back when I confessed I had not had time to read it—because, in short, I had resisted in every way his efforts to make use of me to worm his own way around here and there among places and people he wanted to know. In particular he demanded the instant return of a letter he sent me three or four years ago, a letter containing notes and impressions of the mountains of western North Carolina. I haven't, of course, the faintest idea where the damned letter is. Now, apparently, he claims it is very precious to him and contains precious notes which he must have—the whole truth, however, being that he wants another outlet and excuse for his venomous hatred. He spoke of what "a pitiable fool" he had been ever to "delude himself" with the hope that I would read his book, or, I suppose, accept the so-called "friendship" he tried to pour down my throat. He spoke of what a deluded fool he had been even to "believe in Tom Wolfe's genius" and—this was the most horrible thing he did—he then deliberately, just out of sheer malignant hatred and a desire to hurt me in any way he could, concocted a dirty and despicable lie to this effect:—that day, he said, he had been to the offices of one the leading New York literary reviews, and talked to the distinguished woman editor in charge about reviewing my book for this paper. The woman told him, he said, that the book had already been given to Sinclair Lewis for review (all of this information, of course, easily identified the review as The New York *Herald Tribune* Sunday Book Section, which along with *The Times* is one of the two most important, and *vitally* important to the success of the book)—but the woman had told him that she didn't think he'd care to review the book anyway, particularly after he saw what Sinclair Lewis had said about it. She then went on with a cold and dispassionate analysis of my book, he said, and as she did he felt his last deluded enthusiasm and belief in "the genius of Tom Wolfe" oozing away, etc.

Mabel, I almost got sick at the stomach—not only because of the horrible display of venom . . . but also because I thought it was really true what he said about the *Tribune* and Sinclair Lewis and, after all these years of work, to have my book ruined at the beginning and to have a man like Lewis turn on me seemed about as rotten a break in luck as I could imagine. Well, I called up Max Perkins immediately and told him I had bad news for him, and then told him the contents of this horrible reptile's letter. I was in a pretty excited state—in addition to the disappointment and bad luck of it, I thought that if a high class publication like *Herald-Tribune Books* could stoop to reveal the contents of an unfavorable review two weeks or more before publication and to run the book down two weeks before it was published, it was almost as rotten and unfair a trick as I had ever heard of. Max was very quiet and calm and told me to come in later in the day. When I got to Scribners later in the day, they had telephoned the *Herald Tribune,* explained the contents of the letter, and asked if it was true. The reply was this: That —— was known at the office as Public Nuisance and Bore Number 1; that he was constantly coming in and pestering them; that they never gave him books to review; that there was not the remotest possibility of his reviewing my book for the *Tribune;* that no one there had ever discussed my book with him; that it had *not* been given to Sinclair Lewis to review, but to Burton Rascoe, and that no one knew whether Rascoe's review was favorable or unfavorable. Incidentally, although I have read none of the reviews myself as yet, I understand indirectly—through Max Perkins' letter—that Rascoe's review was favorable.

I am sorry to take up so much space over this. . . . Perkins read the letter and said correctly: "It is the letter of a venomous old woman," but maybe you will understand a little better now the kind of price a man sometimes has to pay for public notice, and the kind of horrible slanderous lies unscrupulous and embittered people will stoop to in an effort to injure him. I am learning more about life and people all the time—I have met some wonderful and fine people these last few years but I have also met some of this sort, too. The incredible thing is that I have never injured this man in any way—was grateful and somewhat embarrassed by his letters of gushing praise, thanked him as courteously as I could, and have wronged him in no way save by my failure to read his book and to allow him to thrust his friendship forcibly upon me, make himself a part of my life, my friends, etc.—and any man alive has a right to defend himself in this way.

One amazing thing I have learned in the last few years is the number of people there are in the world who can do nothing for themselves, have no real friendship for you but who, once you achieve a little success, try forcibly to thrust themselves into your life, and when you repel them, no matter how courteously, turn on you in envenomed gall and hatred.

No, I promise you I shall try not to be too much troubled this time by what you call "rot from Asheville." I hope to God there is none— there is absolutely no reason for it from *this* book—but if there is, I went through my first baptism of fire five years ago, and should be able to stand it better now. I know that you and the family, as you say, "are with me"—and that's good enough for me. I am grateful from the bottom of my heart to all of you and I hope that I shall always live and work honorably in such a way as will bring credit to the family—and to grow better and deeper always in my work. I also hope that this book has had a creditable success, not only for myself, but for the sake of the fine man and true friend—Max Perkins—who has stood by me and believed in me and whose heart is in my work as much as my own. I know that if we have "come through" the strain and stress of the last five years, I can now go on and *far surpass*—with the confidence and experience I have gained—anything I have done before. This is all for the present. I am leaving London today, . . going to the country for a day or two, and then direct to Berlin to see my German publisher who wires he will pay expenses. Hope he does. . . . Love to all,

To ELIZABETH NOWELL

St. George's Court
26 Hanover Square
London W. 1

April 23, 1935
Easter Monday! And how! When they have
Easter here, it lasts four days—Sunday
all the time.

Dear Miss Nowell:
. . . I'm leaving London to-day after being here a month—going up to Norfolk for a few days and then to Germany via Harwich and Hook of Holland. My German publisher has wired saying he wants my book and for me to come on over and he will pay expenses, but coyly refrains from mentioning terms. I understand, however, that whatever money I get from the Germans will have to be spent there in the country—so it looks as if I'll have to go there and live riotously for a week or two or get nothing at all. I have a most humorous plan whereby I'll use Herr Hitler's currency to pay the expenses of a trip to Russia, but friends here say they think I'll strike a snag. Anyway, there's no harm trying. . . .

Have had little news from U.S.A. . . . But heard indirectly (through letter Max wrote Frere-Reeves, my English publisher) that "Tom's agent [1] has sold four stories." [2] Darling, I am torn between joy and

---

[1] Miss Nowell had left the Maxim Lieber office in September, 1934, and had started her own agency in January, 1935.

[2] "Gulliver" which appeared in the June, 1935, issue of *Scribner's Magazine*, "In the Park" which appeared in the June issue of *Harper's Bazaar*, "Arnold Pentland" which appeared in the June issue of *Esquire*, and "Cottage by the Tracks" which appeared in the July issue of *Cosmopolitan*. All four of these stories were included in *From Death to Morning*, but "Cottage by the Tracks" was retitled "The Far and the Near." These had been among the portions of manuscript cut from *Of Time and the River* which Wolfe had given to Miss Nowell when he was moving out of Brooklyn, and which she had not been able to cut and edit until after he had sailed.

trepidation. The news, if true, is swell, but I don't know where the hell you *found* the four stories. . . . Anyway, upon the strength of rumor, counting my chickens before I've seen them, and my purely hypothetical wealth, I've gone and had several suits of clothes made by the Prince of Wales' own royally-appointed pants-maker, and am now the damndest fop and triple-gazzaza dude that American literature has ever known. So for God's sake don't tell me when I get back home it ain't true! . . .

Hope this finds you well and not staying up nights writing stories for ungrateful authors. Take care of yourself, and since I'm wishing *you* good luck, why, good luck to *both* of us. Will see you, I hope, in May.

Irma Wyckoff, to whom the following letter was written, was Mr. Perkins' secretary for twenty-seven years up to the time of his death. She is now Mrs. Osmer F. Muench.

To IRMA WYCKOFF

University Arms Hotel
Cambridge, England
Wednesday, April 24, 1935

Dear Miss Wyckoff:

I've wanted to write you for a long time to say hello, and tell you again how much I appreciate all your services to me, so generously and cheerfully given even when you had other work to do, and to hope that all goes well with you and with the others at Scribners. Imagine you have quite a parcel of mail for me—hope it hasn't been too great a bother—and if not too much extra trouble will you kind of keep it in a chronological order? Also, if any beautiful women come in and ask for me, get their name, address, and telephone number and tell them I'll be back very soon and will get in touch with them immediately; but if they look and talk mean, ugly and vicious, tell them you don't know where I am, but that the last you heard I sailed from the Skaggeraks of Norway on a very slow sailing vessel for a polar expedition and that you expect me back in about five years. Good-bye and good luck and best wishes to all.

To MAXWELL E. PERKINS

The Wartburg
Germany
May 23, 1935

Dear Max:

I meant to write you before but for the last two or three weeks at any rate writing anything has been impossible. I don't know what my status quo may be in New York but in Germany I have been the white-haired boy. I don't think I could stand another two weeks of it but the last two weeks have been an extraordinary and wonderful and even enchanted period of my life because I have never known such a time before. I am so glad to have known it, so grateful, I shall never forget it. I have heard it said that Lord Byron awoke one morning at twenty-four to find himself famous. Well, I arrived in Berlin one night, when I was thirty-four, and got up the next morning and went to the American Express and for the last two weeks at least I have been famous in Berlin. I found letters, telephone messages, telegrams etc., from all kinds of people, including Rowohlt, publisher here, and the daughter of the American Ambassador, Martha Dodd.[1] For two weeks I have done nothing but meet people of all sorts, go to parties, have interviews, get photographed by the Associated Press—and I have literally lived at the Ambassador's house. I have taken most of my meals there and if I didn't have my room there—it did not matter much because I have had no time for sleeping, and since daylight now comes at three o'clock in the morning anyway in Berlin and Miss Dodd, her brother[2] and I have sat up most of the night talking, I have almost forgotten how to sleep. It did finally get a little too much for us so yesterday Miss Dodd and I and a couple of others left Berlin and all through a wonderful sunlit day drove down southwest through this magnificent, beautiful and enchanted country. We spent the night in the old town of Weimar and today we went about the town and saw first, Goethe's Gartenhaus in a wonderful green park and the rooms where he lived and worked and the saddle he sat on when he wrote, his high old writing desk and many other things that he used and lived with, that made his life and work seem real and near to us. Then we went to the fine old house in Weimar where he lived later on and where all the evidences of his great and illimitably curious intelligence—his laboratories, his workshops, his

[1] Martha Dodd, now Mrs. Alfred K. Stern, has described Wolfe's visit to Germany in her book, *Through Embassy Eyes.* She is also the author of a novel, *The Searching Light,* as well as various articles and stories.

[2] William E. Dodd, Jr.

great library, his rooms for his experiments in physics, chemistry, electricity and optics—have been exactly and truly preserved. Then we went about the town some more and visited the crypt where Goethe and Schiller are buried side by side, and finally with regret we left that wonderful and lovely old town that seems to me at least to hold in it so much of the spirit of the great Germany and the great and noble spirit of freedom, reverence and the high things of the spirit which all of us have loved. Then we came here through one of the most indescribably lovely and magical landscapes I have ever seen. And tonight we are staying here in the Wartburg, a great legendary kind of hill from which came the legend that inspired Richard Wagner to write *Tannhaüser*. We are going back to Berlin to-morrow through the wonderful Harz Mountains, and I have not space or power enough here to tell you how beautiful and fine and magical this trip has been.

I am telling you all this because you and I have often talked about Germany and the German people whom you do not like as much as I do and about what has happened here in recent years. But I want to tell you that I do not see how anyone who comes here as I have come could possibly fail to love the country, its noble Gothic beauty and its lyrical loveliness, or to like the German people who are, I think, the cleanest, the kindest, the warmest-hearted, and the most honorable people I have met in Europe. I tell you this because I think a full and generous recognition must be made of all these facts and because I have been told and felt things here which you and I can never live or stand for and which, if they are true, as by every reason of intuition and faith and belief in the people with whom I have talked I must believe, are damnable.

Now I so much want to see you and tell you what I have seen and heard, all that has been wonderful and beautiful and exciting, and about those things that are so hard to explain because one feels they are so evil and yet cannot say so justly in so many words as a hostile press and propaganda would, because this evil is so curiously and inextricably woven into a kind of wonderful hope which flourishes and inspires millions of people who are themselves, as I have told you, certainly not evil, but one of the most child-like, kindly and susceptible people in the world. I shall certainly tell you about it. Someday I should like to write something about it, but if I now wrote even what I have heard and felt in two weeks, it might bring the greatest unhappiness and suffering upon people I have known here and who have shown me the most affectionate hospitality. But more and more I feel that we are all of us bound up and tainted by whatever guilt and evil there may be in this whole world, and that we cannot accuse and condemn others without in the end coming back to an accusal of ourselves. We are all damned together, we are all tarred by the same stick, and for what has happened here we are all in some degree responsible. This nation to-day is beyond the shadow of a vestige of a doubt full of uniforms and a stamp of marching men—I saw it with my own eyes yesterday in one hundred towns and villages across two hundred miles of the most peaceful, lovely and friendly-looking country I have ever seen. A thousand groups, uncountable divisions of the people from children eight years old to men of fifty, all filled beyond a doubt with hope, enthusiasm and inspired belief in a fatal and destructive thing—and the sun was shining all day long and the fields are greenest, the woods the loveliest, the little towns the cleanest, and the faces and the voices of the people the most friendly of any I have ever seen or heard, so what is there to say?

I have felt a renewed pride and faith in America and a belief that somehow our great future still remains since I came here to Berlin and met some of the Americans here, particularly Ambassador Dodd. He is a historian, a man who was born on a farm in my own state of North Carolina and who had spent his whole life before he came here in teaching and in the contemplation of history. He is, I believe, what is known as a Jeffersonian Democrat and believes in the society of free men and the idea of democracy which he thinks has never been given a fair and practical experiment anywhere on earth. I don't know whether he is right or wrong in this . . . but their home in Berlin has been a free and fearless harbor for people of all opinions, and people who live and walk in terror have been able to draw their breath there without fear, and to speak their minds. This I know to be true, and further, the dry, plain, homely unconcern with which the Ambassador observes all the pomp and glitter and decorations and the tramp of marching men would do your heart good to see. I wish you could have been there the other night in his house when he came back from attending Hitler's two hour and forty minute speech which was delivered to that group of automatic dummies that now bears the ironical title of the "Reichstag," and which was broadcast all over Germany. It was wonderful to hear him tell his wife "the way the Jap looked and the way the Englishman looked and how the Frenchman looked pretty hot about it and how he himself shook hands with the Dutchman on the way out and said 'very interesting but not entirely historical' and how the Dutchman grinned and agreed." It was Emerson who said that if you heard the pop of a popgun not to believe it was anything else but a pop of a popgun, even if all the captains and kings of the earth told you it was the roar of a cannon—he said it better than this but that was the substance and I always felt it was an American thing to say and was glad that an American said it. I think the Ambassador here is a man like this.

I cannot tell you any more now but I will tell you all I can when I come back. This has been in many ways an extraordinary and wonderful trip. I have remembered so many vivid and exciting things about it, I have seen so many different kinds of life and people, I feel myself welling up with energy and life again and if it is really true that I have had some luck and success at home I know I can come back now and beat all hollow anything I have ever done before, and certainly I know I can surprise the critics and the public who may think they have taken my measure by this time—and I think I may even have a surprise or two in store for you. If this sounds like bragging, let me feel this way until I try to put it to the proof—in any case it can do no harm.

After leaving London I went up to the county of Norfolk in England, a somewhat remote and out of the way place but a real blunt and good England I had never seen before. I lived around the little towns in the countryside for a week or two and saw some wonderful things and people, and then I went to Holland for a week, and then came on to Germany and Berlin and am writing you to-night from the Thuringian forest. I am going on to Scandinavia next week, will stay a short time in Denmark and think I will come home from there. Anyway I hope to see you the first part of June.

Please don't go too far with the stories before I get there. There are things I can do that will make them much better, and if you will only wait on me I will do them and we will have a fine book of stories and unlike any I know of. I think "The October Fair" is going to be a grand book and we will try to meet the criticism of the critics and to show them that I am improving and learning my business all the time. The book I am living for, however, is the Pentland [3] book—it is swelling and gathering in me like a thunderstorm and I feel if there is any chance of my doing anything good before I am forty it will be this book. I feel such a swelling and exultant sense of certitude and such a feeling of gathering power and fulfillment that I tremble when I think about it and I hope to God that nothing happens to me or to my life—that I do not ruin myself with alcohol or some other craziness that can be avoided—before I get to it.

Of this I am resolved: that if there has been any stir and public interest in this book I shall become more private and withdrawn in my life than ever before when I get back home and will allow myself in no way to be drawn out of it. I will go down deeper in myself than I ever have before and you must try to help me in every way to do this. It has been a great thing for me today to go to Goethe's house in Weimar and to see the way he lived and worked. I may never be able to be a great man like

[3] *The Hills Beyond Pentland.*

this—the life of a great man always fills me with hope and strength and gives me a renewed faith and makes me despise all the cheap and low little lives and base aspirations that you see about you in the lives of so many men today.

Goodbye for the present, Max. This letter, like its author, is too long. I hope the letter will not exhaust you as the last one must have. . . . It will be good to see you again. . . .

P.S. Saturday, May 26—Dear Max—I got back to Berlin last night at midnight after a magnificent and beautiful trip. Today I went to the American Express Co., and found there a letter from one Harry Weinberger, "counsellor at law" etc. of 70 West 40th St., New York, who says he represents Mrs. Madeleine Boyd in reference to her "claim for agent's commissions on royalties on your books published by Scribners." He threatens suit, and wants to know when I will return, etc. This was the thing you said could not "happen," the thing "she would not dare to do" . . . , etc. Well, she has done it, as I told you she would, because we were foolish, benevolent, soft-hearted, weak—call it what you like. . . .

The Amended Complaint *filed against Wolfe by Weinberger for Madeline Boyd with the Supreme Court of the State of New York on August 12, 1935, alleged that "on or about and prior to the month of January, 1929, defendant entered into an agreement with the plaintiff whereby defendant employed plaintiff as his literary agent and agreed to pay her ten percent of whatever royalties he may earn from the publication and sale of his literary works, in any part of the world. That pursuant to said agreement and on or about the month of January, 1929, plaintiff procured from Charles Scribner's Sons, publishers, a contract whereby said Charles Scribner's Sons agreed to publish the novel,* Look Homeward, Angel, *written by defendant, and agreed to pay defendant royalties on the sale of said novel. On information and belief at the time of the making of said contract between Charles Scribner's Sons and defendant, plaintiff procured from said Charles Scribner's Sons a separate contract providing that said Charles Scribner's Sons were to have an option for publishing the next two books written by defendant." The complaint then alleged that Mrs. Boyd had secured contracts for the publication of* Look Homeward, Angel *from William Heinemann of London and Ernst Rowohlt Verlag of Berlin, and that the contract procured from Heinemann contained options "for publishing the next two works written by defendant," and the contract with Rowohlt gave Rowohlt an option on Wolfe's next work. After making allegations concerning other foreign publishers, the complaint then alleged "on information and belief, that defendant has been paid, or there has become payable to him, as royalties on the sale of* Look Homeward, Angel *and* Of Time and the River, *a sum amounting in the aggregate to at least One Hundred Thousand Dollars. On information and belief, that by reason of the aforesaid, there has become due and payable to plaintiff by defendant a sum amounting in the aggregate to at least Ten Thousand Dollars.*" This first part of Mrs. Boyd's Amended Complaint then concluded with the statements "*that defendant has failed and refused to pay to plaintiff her commission as his literary agent although the same has been duly demanded,*" and "*that plaintiff has duly performed all the conditions on her part to be performed.*"

Next, "*as and for a Second Cause of Action,*" Mrs. Boyd's complaint alleged "*that defendant wrote* Look Homeward, Angel, *the first of a trilogy of which* Of Time and the River *is the second. That pursuant to said agreement and on or about the month of January, 1929, plaintiff procured from Charles Scribner's Sons, publishers, a contract whereby said Charles Scribner's Sons agreed to publish a novel written by defendant as heretofore stated, consisting of a trilogy of which* Look Homeward, Angel *was the first and* Of Time and the River *the second, and the said Charles Scribner's Sons are proceeding with the publication of the third, and the said Charles Scribner's Sons agreed to pay defendant royalties and advances on the sale of said novels.*" After virtually repeating these allegations in regard to the contract made with William Heinemann, the complaint concluded by demanding "*judgment against the defendant in the sum of Ten Thousand Dollars, together with the costs and disbursements of this action.*"

In the answer to Mrs. Boyd's Amended Complaint which was filed for Wolfe by his attorneys, Mitchell and Van Winkle, Wolfe admitted that he employed her as his literary agent for the purpose of procuring the publication of Look Homeward, Angel, but denied that he employed her to act any further for him. He admitted that she procured from Scribners a contract for the publication of that book, but denied that she procured from them a separate contract which gave them options on his next two books. He also admitted that Mrs. Boyd procured contracts for the publication of Look Homeward, Angel from Heinemann, Rowohlt, and other foreign publishers, but denied "that at present he has any knowledge or information sufficient to form a belief as to any of the other allegations" made by her concerning the existence of options in these contracts for his future works. He admitted that he had been paid or that there had become payable to him royalties on the sale of Look Homeward, Angel and Of Time and the River, but denied Mrs. Boyd's allegation that they amounted in the aggregate to at least One Hundred Thousand Dollars, and he also denied her allegations that he had refused to pay her her commission as his literary agent and that she had "duly performed all the conditions on her part to be performed." Finally, as an answer to her "Second Cause of Action," he denied that Look Homeward, Angel and Of Time and the River were the first two books of a trilogy, or were considered as such in the contracts made with Scribners and Heinemann.

After thus replying to Mrs. Boyd's allegations, Wolfe's answer launched

*into "A First and Separate and Distinct Defense" which said in part that
"Defendant is informed and verily believes that in or about the month of
January, 1931, plaintiff, as literary agent for defendant in connection with
the publication of* Look Homeward, Angel, *sold to Ernst Rowohlt Verlag of
Berlin, Germany, the right to publish said book in the German language and
at that time received from Ernst Rowohlt Verlag, as a payment on account,
the sum of One Thousand Reich Marks, all of which was unknown to defendant at that time. That thereafter and in or about the month of January,
1932, defendant for the first time learned, from sources other than the plaintiff, of the said sale of the right to publish said book,* Look Homeward, Angel,
*in the German language, and that this sale had been made by the plaintiff as
his literary agent for the publication of said book and that plaintiff had received on account of said sale the sum of One Thousand Reich Marks. That the
defendant thereupon immediately charged the plaintiff with breach of her obligation under her literary agency for the publication of said book,* Look
Homeward, Angel, *in failing to disclose the making of said German contract
and withholding of his portion of said One Thousand Reich Marks. Plaintiff
thereupon admitted the defendant's charges and eventually, but not immediately, paid to the defendant the U.S. money equivalent of his portion of
said One Thousand Reich Marks. That at some time in or about the month of
January, 1932, and prior to January 28, 1932, plaintiff requested the defendant for authority to act as his literary agent in the securing of the publication of defendant's works other than the book* Look Homeward, Angel, *and
the defendant thereupon and on or about January 28, 1932, informed the
plaintiff that she would not be his literary agent for the securing of the publication of any of his works then existing or future, other than the book*
Look Homeward, Angel."

A settlement of this case was finally made in 1936.

To MAXWELL E. PERKINS

[Postcard: Room in Goethe's House, Weimar]

Eisenach, Germany

May 24, 1935

Dear Max: Goethe died in this little room while sitting in the chair
beside the bed. His study, laboratories, work rooms and library are just
outside. He made his wife and children live upstairs—out of the way.

To MAXWELL E. PERKINS

[Postcard: Statue of a Young Egyptian
Girl Carved in Wood]

Berlin
Tuesday, May 28, 1935

Dear Max: I'm just about 2500 years too late to have known this girl but she's pretty grand, isn't she? I must leave here in a few days although everyone is urging me to stay. I have never known such friendship, warmth, good will and affection as these people have shown me—hate to leave.

To MAXWELL E. PERKINS

Hotel Am Zoo
Berlin

Saturday, June 8, 1935

Dear Max:

These photographs were made by *Die Dame*—a German magazine that corresponds to *Vanity Fair*. I have written a piece [1] for them and they are using one of these pictures—the one with the fist—when they publish the piece. I thought the photos pretty good and am sending you one of each. Am leaving here for Denmark in day or two and expect to sail for New York about June 20. . . .

The gay social whirl continues. . . . When I come back to my hotel room I find it filled with magnificent flowers which beautiful women have brought here in my absence. It has been wonderful, thrilling—and very comical. There have been all sorts of stories in the papers—my name has been mentioned in connection with Sinclair Lewis and for that reason, I think, they think I'm very rich. Last week one of the papers came out with a photograph of a magnificent sailing yacht upon the Wannsee—a fashionable lake resort a few miles from town. It said the yacht belonged to "the famous American novelist Thomas Wolfe" and that I was lavishly entertaining a party of beautiful moving-picture

---

[1] Efforts to find this piece in *Die Dame* have met with no success, since the files of that magazine were destroyed during World War II. Probably the piece was never published there, since it concerned Ernst Rowohlt who was under Nazi trial soon after it was written. Fifteen years later, on March 19, 1950, a short humorous article by Wolfe, "Begegnung mit Rowohlt," appeared in *Der Kurier*, published in the French Zone of Berlin. This probably was the piece written for *Die Dame* but how it survived the war and turned up in *Der Kurier* is not known.

actresses aboard her. Of course I had never seen the damned yacht and
someone told me I had met one beautiful moving-picture actress at a
night club, but I didn't know who she was. . . . I'll tell you all about
everything when I come back.

To MAXWELL E. PERKINS

[Picture Postcard: Pieter Breughel's *Die Niederlandischen
Sprichworter,* with key to the proverbs illustrated]

Berlin

June 12, 1935

Dear Max: I don't know if the U.S.A. postal authorities will let me send
this card to you, but if you get it, please keep it for me—this is the
painter I like best.

*The following postcard to Mrs. Bernstein breaks off unfinished and was
never mailed. It probably refers to the suicide of Emily Davies Whitfield in
Santa Fe, New Mexico, on May 25, 1935.*

To ALINE BERNSTEIN

Copenhagen

[June, 1935]

Dear Aline:

I read in the paper some weeks ago that a friend of yours had shot
herself through the head or heart. I always knew she would. And do
you know why? Because, like poor Raisbeck, she tried everything in life
but living, she knew about everything in life but life itself. I was sad
for two whole days after I read it, then forgot it—did you do as well,
who knew her so much better?

I think about you a great deal and all the people I met through you
and your group ten years ago. . . . It was a lie of life, false, cynical,
scornful, drunk with imagined power, and rotten to the core. And
through that rottenness, through that huge mistaken falseness and corruption, there will run forever the memory of your loveliness—your
flower face and your jolly and dynamic little figure on my steps at noon
—the food, the cooking, and the love, and in the little boarded city yard
the [faint?] [so?] more than forest

To MAXWELL E. PERKINS

[Picture Postcard: 21 Fredericksborg. Slot. Copenhagen]

Copenhagen
June 18, 1935

I found the girl all right, Max—not here, but in Berlin. I miss her so much it hurts. I've got to come back home and work. For God's sake keep people away from me if there are any.

To MAXWELL E. PERKINS

[Postcard: photograph of Wolfe
in front of City Hall, Copenhagen]

[Copenhagen]
[June 21, 1935]

Dear Max:

I have a letter from a New York publisher—with quoted excerpts—which informs me that *Scribners* last month carried 3 *printed attacks* on me—one from Miss Evelyn Scott, one from Mr. Ernest Hemingway—the Big Big He Man and Fighter With Words who can't take it—and one from Professor Wm Lyon Phelps.[1] He wants to know why I should still consider Scribners my friends. Can you think of an answer? This is a good picture, isn't it?

---

[1] In the June, 1935, issue of *Scribner's Magazine*, Evelyn Scott reviewed *Of Time and the River* under the title of "Colossal Fragment," saying: ". . . Thomas Wolfe . . . is representative of our national individualistic bent at its faulty but often splendid best. . . . In *Of Time and the River*, his concern is with the adventuring ecstasies of Eugene Gant only. . . . The sum of this turbulent writing, in which sentimentalities blend with authentic cries of agony, is an impression of young, inexhaustible vitality, by which, with the violence of his own will to beauty, the author almost convinces us of a universe made in his image. . . ." In an installment of *The Green Hills of Africa*, appearing in the same issue, Ernest Hemingway said: "Dostoevsky was made by being sent to Siberia. Writers are forged in injustice as a sword is forged. I wonder if it would make a writer of him, give him the necessary shock to cut the over-flow of words and give him a sense of proportion, if they sent Tom Wolfe to Siberia or the Dry Tortugas. Maybe it would and maybe it wouldn't. He seemed sad, really, like Carnera." William Lyon Phelps, in his selected list of 100 new books in the same issue, merely listed *Of Time and the River*, saying: "I include it because of its universally enthusiastic reception. I have not had time to read so long a book. I hope it is all 'they say' it is."

To MAXWELL E. PERKINS

[Postcard: photograph of Wolfe
in front of City Hall, Copenhagen]

Copenhagen

June 23, 1935

"Although both (Wolfe and the late D. H. Lawrence) were sprung from
the socially obscure, neither shows any feeling of *class* resentment"—from
a review.[1]

*The following postcard from Wolfe to Mrs. Jelliffe was in reply to sugges-
tions from her about the repairing of his furniture which he had stored at her
house.*

To BELINDA JELLIFFE

[Postcard]

[Copenhagen?]

[June 1935?]

Fixing the chairs etc. is fine, but I don't believe it would be worth $17
to me to have the chest of drawers fixed. It is a fine piece but I am
not a furniture antiquarian and I don't much care if all the handles are
on or not. What I *would* like to get fixed is my beautiful and beloved
and cigarette-scarred gate-legged table! Whatever you do will be all right
with me. Will write later.

No, I've got to admit that I've fallen down badly on *my* homework
—the typewriter—and all I can mumble into your cynical ears is that
someday I'll show you. But I'm beginning to eat and sleep regularly
again—no cracks now about the eating—to feel more like a member
of the so-called human race. The old pencil-itch has got into my fingers
again—I've made fifty thousand words of notes.

[1] From the Review of *Of Time and the River* by Evelyn Scott in the June, 1935,
issue of *Scribner's,* which Wolfe had been told was an "attack" on him.

To ALFRED DASHIELL

[Picture Postcard: Steckelhornflet and Nikolaikirche, Hamburg]

Hamburg, Germany

June 29, 1935

I'm crammed to the gills with kultur, küche, and antiquity, so I'm coming home again.

To ROBERT RAYNOLDS

[Picture Postcard: Nikolaiflet, Hamburg]

Hamburg

June 29, 1935

Dear Bob: This is my last night in Europe and I want to write you a word of greeting before I go, even though this card may get there after I do. I am sitting here on the terrace of a little hotel that overlooks the harbor of Hamburg. It is almost dark and I can see a great tangle of cranes and derricks against the sky—and big freighters all alight and lovely—and the rattling of a winch. Somehow it makes me think of Brooklyn and is comforting.

On returning to New York from Europe, Wolfe found waiting for him an invitation to attend the Writers' Conference at the University of Colorado as a "visiting novelist." He was asked to deliver one lecture there, to participate in round table conferences on the novel with other writers, and to confer with the students, for which he would receive a fee of two hundred and fifty dollars. In the following letter of acceptance to Edward Davison, he suggests the subject of his speech, which was based on the discarded introduction to Of Time and the River *and which finally was published as* The Story of a Novel. *Davison, a well-known poet both here and in England where his reputation was originally established, was at this time Program Director at the University of Colorado.*

To EDWARD DAVISON

New York, New York
July 8, 1935

Dear Mr. Davison:

I returned from Europe just two or three days ago and found here an enormous stack of mail which has been accumulating for the last four months, and I am hastening to answer your own letters first of all.

I am looking forward to the Colorado trip and to meeting all of you with the greatest delight. I am very proud to have been invited and I shall do the best I can. In one of your letters I think you said you were yourself going to talk on the making of a poem and suggested that I might talk on some such topic as the making of a novel. If you still feel that that is a good idea, it would suit me splendidly.

Last night I was with Fritz Dashiell, of *Scribner's Magazine,* who spoke at Boulder two or three years ago, and he said his own impression was that the people there prefer a plain, straightforward way of talking rather than a more involved and technical discussion. As you may know, among the many faults and imperfections which the critics have spoken about in my own work, is the fault of overabundance and a general too-muchness out of nature. I realize this fault, I think, more keenly than anyone and have sweated blood in an effort to correct it. How would it do if, so to speak, I "shot the works"? That is, if I just got right down into the sawdust and told the people out there the plain, straight story of what happened in the writing of this last book and of the other two books which are to follow it but which have not yet been published. Max Perkins here at Scribner's, the great editor without whose help I might have been sunk, said that the making of this book constituted the most interesting problem of his editorial experience. I believe it really might be interesting and perhaps of some value to the people at the conference if I just told about the way it happened and how the three books, over a period of five years, began finally to emerge out of the great creative chaos, and what happened to me during that time, and what mistakes I made, and what I hope I have learned from the experience, and also what a great editor can do in his relations toward a writer and an enormous manuscript.

Don't you think if I told about this in as plain and direct a way as I can, it might be interesting to the people out there? I suggest it because it is a piece of my own life, of my own direct and immediate experience; it is something I know of my own life and something I have learned with my own life; and it seems to me that for this reason it might be more interesting and valuable than a lecture of a more detached and impersonal character. But if you don't think so, won't you please write and let me know and make another suggestion?

I am so happy at the prospect of coming out there and seeing a little of the West and its people that I want to do my best, and I shall be sincerely grateful for any advice you can give me. . . .

Thanks again for your generous invitation and your letters.

Among the many letters praising Of Time and the River *which Wolfe found waiting for him on his return from Europe, was one from Sherwood Anderson which said: "Dear Thomas Wolfe: As I read it I have a hunger to write you a word about your new novel. It is such a gorgeous achievement. It makes me a little sad too. Here I've been struggling all these years, trying to write novels, and along you come and show me very simply and directly that I'm no novelist. Some things I can write but you—you are a real novelist."* [1] *The following was Wolfe's reply.*

To SHERWOOD ANDERSON

New York City

July 8, 1935

Dear Mr. Anderson:

I just got back here from Europe a few days ago and found a great stack of mail which had piled up during the past four months and in it was the letter you wrote me from Greensboro some time ago.

I want to tell you how proud and happy your letter made me. You are one of the American writers whose work I have admired most and whose work has meant a lot to me. It seemed to me ever since I first began to read your books when I was a kid of twenty that you got down below the surface of our lives and got at some of the terror and mystery and ugliness and beauty in America better than anyone else. This comes from the heart; I mean it, and for that reason I will always have the proudest and most grateful remembrance of your generous letter.

Max Perkins knows you, and he tells me he sometimes sees you when you come to New York. When you do come here next time, if you are going out to lunch with Max, I wonder if you wouldn't let me come along too? I should like to meet you. Meanwhile, with thanks again and best wishes,

[1] Copyright, 1956, by Eleanor Copenhaver Anderson.

The following letter to James Boyd was also written in reply to one praising
Of Time and the River.

To JAMES BOYD

New York City

July 8, 1935

Dear Jim:

I just came back the other day and found a great stack of mail here
with your letter of May 29 in it. I can't write you much here, nothing
that is fit to be an answer to your wonderful letter. Will you let me tell
you how much it has meant to me to have known a man as true and
straight and high grade as you are, and how proud it makes me to
have had such a letter from the artist of fine and high integrity I know
you to be. The last two or three days since I came back have been pretty
wonderful. I shall never forget them.

When I went away, I was exhausted, emptied out, and desperate, and
I did not have much hope, and now I've come back filled up, strong
and ready, and I find myself a little famous, and the whole damn thing
is wonderful, and if it makes a difference to me or my work, except to
make it better, please come up here to New York and kick me in the
pants the whole way from Scribners to the Battery.

Your letter, and a few others, fill me with such a sense of joy and
confidence and power that I'll swear to you I'm going to hit this next
book like a locomotive, and I know I can ten times surpass all that
I have done before. Jim, if this be foolish bragging, let me do it for
a day or two; the real thing is I'll never forget your friendship or your
letter, and I'll use every energy in life to live up to it. Good-bye now,
and I send my love and best wishes to all of you. It is wonderful to
hear how well "Roll River" [1] is going. I read the first part of it in
Scribner's Magazine, and I wrote you what I felt about it then. It
was, I thought, your best and highest. The second part is still before
me. I don't know what I'll find in it; I only know you'll grow and
prosper in your power forever.

*J. G. Stikeleather, to whom the following letter was written, was a promi-
nent Asheville real estate man, and had known the Wolfe family for many
years. He had written Wolfe a letter about his books, in which he had re-*

[1] *Roll River* had been published by Scribners in April, 1935, after being serialized in
Scribner's Magazine.

*proached him for being "too hard on your family and not just to Asheville,"
but which was friendly and fatherly in tone.*

To J. G. STIKELEATHER

New York City

July 8, 1935

Dear Mr. Stikeleather:

. . . I want to thank you for the spirit of friendship and kindness
which prompted you to write me as you did, and to assure you that I am
sincerely grateful for your letter. I should also like to tell you that I
know I have made mistakes in the past, that I have said and written some
things which I now regret, but I should like you to believe that a great
many of these things were due to the inexperience, the intemperance,
and the oversensitivity of youth rather than to a desire to hurt and
wound people that I have known all my life. May I not tell you also that
I have in my heart not one atom of bitterness or resentment towards
the town and the people from which I came and which, I think, I shall
always be proud and happy to acknowledge as my own.

Mr. Stikeleather, may I give you one little illustration of what I think
may have happened between myself and the people in Asheville? Have
you ever tried to pass a man in the street and the moment you stepped
to the right to go around him he would also step the same way, when
you step to the left, he would follow you, and so the thing would continue until it became funny and you both stood still and looked at each
other and yet all the time all you were trying to do was to be friendly
to each other and to give the other fellow a free passage? Or, better still,
have you ever met some one that you knew you liked and you were
pretty sure he felt the same way about you and yet, figuratively speaking,
you "got off on the wrong foot" with each other? Now I think that something of this sort may have happened between Asheville and myself.
When I wrote "Look Homeward, Angel" several years ago, I can honestly
assure you I had no notion that the book would arouse the kind of comment and response and cause the kind of misunderstanding in my home
town that it did do. I should like you to believe that I, myself, was just
about the most surprised person in the world when I finally understood
the kind of effect my book was having in Asheville.

I cannot go back to "Look Homeward, Angel" now nor tell you what
I felt about that book or what my purpose and intentions were in
writing it or how I feel about it. In fact, although this statement may
surprise you, I no longer have a very clear memory or idea of what

was in "Look Homeward, Angel" nor do I know exactly what I said
there or what the total content of the book may be. The reason for this
is pretty simple, and yet it is awfully hard to explain. It is hard to explain
because the thing that makes a man write a book and the thing that
makes him read a book are two such different things that it is really
like the North Pole pointing toward the South. If this sounds too involved
and complicated, what I am trying to say to you is that a reader reads
a book in order to remember it and a writer writes a book in order to
forget it. For that reason a writer, after he has got the whole thing off
his chest, wants to forget it utterly, and yet he wants fame, too. He wants
people to read his book, to like his book, to admire his talent as a writer.
This is the thing he writes and sweats for, and yet when he meets people,
and they tell him they have read his book and praise him for it or say
that they have not read his book and apologize for it, he has a terrible
feeling of embarrassment and constraint and wishes that they would
just say nothing about it and does not know what to say himself.

It's a strange situation, isn't it? It seems very complicated and difficult,
and yet it is quite simple at the bottom, and I know that a man of your
experience will understand it. I suppose it boils down to this: you want
to be a famous man and a great writer, and yet you want to lead an
obscure, simple, and plain kind of life like other men. I have told you
all these things just to indicate—I can't do anything more but indicate
them because if I ever started explaining the whole thing, I could go
on until tomorrow morning—but just to indicate the kind of difficulty
that arises when a man tries to tell how he felt when he wrote a book, not
when a man tells how he felt when he read one.

Now, having said all this, I would like plainly and frankly to admit
something—something which I have already mentioned. I do think that,
as you say, there may have been something of the bitterness and intolerance and hot temper of youth in "Look Homeward, Angel." And yet
may I say to you—it is pretty difficult to say this because no man likes
to be put in the position where he must seem to defend his own book
or to point to the praise and success which it may have had—may I
say to you that although the youthfulness and a certain intemperance in
the book was recognized by critics elsewhere, these imperfections were
on the whole considered only incidental to a book which was read, I
assure you, not as a savage and vitriolic attack upon the citizens of Asheville, North Carolina, but as a young man's vision of his childhood and
his youth and the world from which he came—a world which in its
general humanity could have been as true of Peoria or Spokane or
Berlin or any place as it was of Asheville. Anyway, Asheville and I got
off on the wrong foot with each other because of that book. I think there

may have been some bitterness in it but not as much bitterness as Asheville thought there was, and as for this last book, which is also finished, over, published, and out of my system as the first one was, I think I can really assure you that no matter what its many faults and imperfections may be, so far as Asheville is concerned, there is no bitterness at all.

I just ask you to believe this, and if you cannot believe it, I would hope that you have time to go back to the book and examine it for yourself. This is all I can write you at present, and I know you will understand I am writing this out of my heart because you and I come from the same town, the same people, and because I want to answer your kind and friendly letter in a way that will, I hope, bring about a better understanding between the people of my native town and myself.

I am certainly coming home to see you all some day. I don't know when that will be. I have much work to do, many things to learn and to experience, but when I do come home, I hope you will all understand that I am a man who, whatever errors he may have made, has tried to grow and learn and increase in strength and wisdom and humanity, and who would have grown beyond malice and resentment in the end. Certainly I hope the last is now true and that all of you will come, in time, to understand it and believe it.

Meanwhile with all my best and friendliest wishes, and with thanks again for your good letter, . . .

Harold Calo, who had been one of Wolfe's students at New York University, had written him, saying: "Of all my . . . friends, I am the only one who, fortunately, was a member of your first class . . . at N.Y.U. Consequently, when one of the boys charged you with intolerance and anti-semitism, inferred from a criticism of Of Time and the River, *I could not concede that. You never gave me that impression and I do not believe that to-day. . . . I cannot help wondering, however, if you have not been unduly harsh in your criticism of the students and perhaps should give them a chance to explain their reactions . . . towards the University and towards yourself." The following was Wolfe's reply.*

To HAROLD CALO

New York City
July 10, 1935

Dear Mr. Calo:

I just got back from Europe the other day. It was good to find your letter here among the stack of mail which had been accumulating during the four months which I was away. I certainly do remember very well our meeting in Europe and the pleasant talk we had together, also the days when you were a student in one of my classes at N.Y.U.

I have many, many letters to answer right away, and, therefore, I cannot give your letter the kind of answer it deserves, but I do want you to know, and I ask you to believe, as I am sure you do, that if anyone charged me with anti-semitism because of anything in the last book, that charge was absolutely groundless. I have not time to go into the matter fully here, and of course I should like to know upon just what evidence that charge is based, but I think you will believe me when I tell you that some of the best and most valued friends I have ever had here in New York have been Jews, and I believe a careful reading of the book will bear me out in that point. As for the rest of it, all I ask you to remember are the days I taught you at New York University and then to consider fairly whether you ever saw or heard me do anything that was unfair, intolerant, or unjust to any member of your faith.

This is all for the present. Yes, I should certainly like to see you again and renew our acquaintance and hear what you have been doing during the years that have passed since I last saw you. I am going West in a week or two, but shall be back here to stay later on. You can always reach me by writing me here at Scribner's.

To MARTHA DODD

New York City

July 10, 1935

Dear Martha:

. . . I have thought of you and my other friends in Berlin very often, and I have missed seeing you all. It was a wonderful trip, a wonderful crowded experience for four months, and although I did not get much rest, it did me a world of good. Copenhagen was also fine, and I met some nice people there and had a good time, but I was ready to come home.

It is wonderful to be back. Reporters met me at the boat; there were pieces in the paper; everybody here at Scribners seems excited and happy about the way the book has gone. It still keeps on, and they say it's not going to stop—not this year anyway. It's the first time in my life I've been a little famous, and the experience has been very wonderful and happy, but if it affects me or my work, please heave a brickbat at me.

Last night I stayed up until five o'clock reading hundreds and hundreds of reviews from all over the country. They took some nice, cheerful, wholehearted pokes at me, but they seemed to love me, and the total effect is overwhelming. The letters have been wonderfully moving and exciting. In addition to the regular sort of fan mail and autograph letters and flirty-girl kind of thing, there have been wonderful letters coming from people everywhere, all the way from hotel clerks to school teachers to ordinary men and women of all sorts, who said they had never written a writer before and don't want an answer and just wrote to tell me so the moment they finished the book. Among other things, I got a grand, generous letter from Sherwood Anderson who said he knew why he could never write a novel after finishing the book. The whole thing has made me pretty happy, and it also makes me feel a little guilty and ashamed. If they think this book is good, I know I am going to beat it forty ways with the next two. I failed in this book, not in the ways the critics said I did, but in another way that Max and I know about. In spite of their talk about its tremendous energy and so forth, I wrote it in less than a year before it was published, at a time when I was horribly tired and when I had exhausted myself in writing the two books which are to follow.[1] Perhaps I should have taken another year, but so much time had gone by without publication that I agreed with Max that it was more important to get it out and to go on to all the work that awaits me than to spend more time perfecting this one.

I feel grand. I am strong and happy and confident as I haven't been in several years, and if I failed last time, the time is coming when I may not fail. Anyway, I will use every energy of my life—and my life itself if need be—to justify what Max and my friends and some of the people in these letters have said and felt about what I do.

I am going to Colorado in a couple of weeks and intend to explore the West this summer, but I shall be back here in September, and I think I am ready to work this coming year as I have never worked before. We have a book of stories which are ready and which are coming in October.[2] And with six months' work on "The Fair"[3] the way I am now, I shall have far and away the best book I have written. The Pentland book comes later, and for that I am saving the best of everything I have in me.

New York these days is hot, sweaty, sticky, sweltering, and the most wonderful, terrible, gaudy and stupendous wench you ever saw. It is grand to be here. This is my air and my weather, and somehow—I don't know how or why—my kind and my people. It is good to have had

[1] *The October Fair* and parts of *The Hills Beyond Pentland*.
[2] *From Death to Morning* was actually published on November 14.
[3] *The October Fair.*

this success. I intend to use it so that it will bring me added power and wisdom and achievement. Good-bye for the present. Please give my love to your father and mother, and thank them again for all their generous kindness and hospitality which they showed me when I was in Berlin, and let me know if there is anything I can do for you ever here.

With all my best and warmest wishes to you and all the family,

The following letter was written in reply to one from Lewis Gannett of the Herald Tribune *asking Wolfe for a list of the books he had recently enjoyed reading, for publication in that paper's daily book column.*

To LEWIS GANNETT

New York City
July 10, 1935

Dear Mr. Gannett:

I have just returned from Europe and found . . . your letter of June 6 in which you ask me if I would jot down and send to you the names of six or a dozen books which I have enjoyed reading recently. If it is not too late, I should be glad to do so, but I think I ought to tell you that during the last four months that I have been traveling and seeing a great many new things, I have not had time for much reading. Consequently I am not very well informed on current books. And before this recent journey for a period of four years, I was working very hard in Brooklyn and, for the most part, read the books which belonged to me and which I had had for some time.

It is a curious fact that during my student years and for years thereafter I read prodigiously and gobbled up everything I could lay my hands on, but during these past four years when I have worked harder than any other time in my life, I must confess that I found myself more and more drawn back to find comfort and stimulation in a few books which I had read many times and to which in this period I referred again and again. For this reason I am afraid my list will not be a very contemporary one and I am afraid it may seem a little too stern and rare for some of your readers, but it is literally true that these are some of the books to which I returned again and again during that time and of which I have never grown tired and which have given me some of the best and finest moments of my life.

1. "The Book of Ecclesiastes," which it seems to me is as great a single piece of writing as I have ever read and which I must have read at least

a dozen times a year for the past four or five years. To this I should like to add the "Book of Job" and the "Songs of Solomon."

2. "King Lear," "Hamlet," second part of "King Henry IV," which I think is one of the best plays ever written, "King Richard III," "Othello," and "The Tempest."

3. A great deal of poetry, which for me, at least, is the one form of writing to which it is possible to return again and again without weariness and with a constant wonder and discovery. I cannot at the moment think of any book which I have read as often as a half dozen times, but there are scores of poems which I have read hundreds of times and which are now more wonderful than when I first read them. I cannot name them all, but some of the poets I like best and to whom I have gone back most often are Milton, Donne, Wyatt, Herrick, Herbert, Blake, Coleridge, Wordsworth, Keats, and Robert Browning, and in the last few years, Walt Whitman.

4. "The Oxford Book of English Prose."

5. Burton's "Anatomy of Melancholy," which no man, I think, could read from start to finish, but which is certainly one of the most difficult books to crack that was ever written but which, once cracked and experienced, will give the reader an unending store of pleasure, wisdom, and delight. You can read it forever. You can open it at any place and read; you will never get tired of reading it. It is certainly one of the greatest books that was ever written.

6. "War and Peace," which I have read two or three times in the last four years and which, so far as I can know or judge, is the greatest novel I have ever read.

7. I cannot leave out "The World Almanac," which, with its wonderful, hard and certain figures, its statistics concerning the population of cities, counties, towns, and states; World Series records; batting and pitching averages, etc., gave me again and again, at times when my energies were exhausted and my mind numb with fatigue, a kind of ease and comfort that no other volume on the shelves could give.

I am afraid that this is much too long, but these are honestly some of the books which I have read most often for the last four years and which have helped me most. If you care to make any use of it, please do so.

The following letter was found in Wolfe's own files, and evidently never mailed. It was addressed to an Asheville woman who had repeatedly complained that Wolfe had portrayed her in Look Homeward, Angel, *and who had now written that a friend of hers had heard a strange man in a hotel say that she was represented by a certain character in that book, and that Wolfe himself had told him so.*

To —— ——

New York City

July 18, 1935

Dear ——:

. . . I want to tell you again how terribly sorry I am to hear that you have been caused any further distress because of "Look Homeward, Angel," and I want to repeat now, as I told you before in my other letter, I had no intention of portraying you under the character of Mrs. ——, and if that character had any actual basis in fact, the basis was not only very slight but was influenced by a person I knew long after I left Asheville. As for this latest version of the story which you mention in your letter, I want to brand it here and now as an absolute and deliberate falsehood. This man, ——, who, you say, was doing the talking, is so far as I can know or recollect an utter stranger to me. I do not assert this for a positive fact because ——, as you know, is a fairly common name in western North Carolina, and it is possible that I may have met or known some one by that name. But of all the ——s that I can remember at the present moment—and I have tried hard since reading your letter to remember all of them—I can call to mind no —— ——. Further, I want to add this: if any person named —— who lives in Asheville or Hendersonville asserts that I ever discussed "Look Homeward, Angel" with him or identified any character in the book or asserted that you or any other living person are intended as the Mrs. —— in the novel, or that I ever told him or anybody else that you were a notorious woman, each and every one of these assertions is an absolute falsehood.

There is no difficulty at all in proving the truth of this. In the first place, my last visit to Asheville was in September, 1928 before "Look Homeward, Angel" was published. Although it was known at that time that the book was scheduled to appear later on that autumn, no one in Asheville knew anything about the book or what was in the book, nor could anyone have possibly known at that time what the nature of the book might be. If I talked to anyone about the book at that time, it was only in the most casual and general way because it is absolutely impossible to give a reader a clear and coherent idea of a book like "Look

Homeward, Angel" before he has read it; but I assure you that I discussed neither the plot nor the story nor any of the characters in the
book with anyone while I was in Asheville. I have no recollection of
meeting or talking to anyone by the name of ——, and if I did meet
and talk to such a person, I certainly made no such vile and abominable
statement about any person as the one you mention in your letter as
having been made, and I hereby once again brand it as a complete and
infamous lie.

Naturally I understand your great distress because of this outrageous
story, and I not only sympathize with your distress, but I share it with
you, and I want to assure you that I will do everything in my power
to help you and, if need be, to denounce and expose this story for the
ugly lie it is. I should also like to add this: I don't know how or by
what sinister and devious ways these stories spring up and gain currency, but I suppose you know as well as I do that in addition to the
many fine and honorable people one knows, there are also unfortunate
people who are so warped and twisted and so full of hatred and bitterness that they will not scruple to start a malicious and slanderous story
even when they know it will cause innocent people distress and pain.
I say that there are unfortunately such people as this in the world and
that if such a story as this has been told, it undoubtedly comes from such
a source. As I said before, I cannot at the moment remember having
known a person by the name of ——. I certainly know no one of that
name here in New York, and if I did know anyone by that name in Asheville or Hendersonville, I certainly did not discuss my book with him or
make the statement you describe in your letter, and I know that if such a
person as —— does exist and I could meet him and talk to him about this,
he would deny that I had ever made such a statement.

This is all for the present. I have tried to tell you just exactly how I
feel and think about this whole matter, and I assure you that if such
a story ever appears again, I will give you my heartiest and most
energetic support in your effort to expose it.

And now with all my best and friendliest greetings to you and your
family,

*The following postcard was mailed by Wolfe from Greeley, Colorado,
where he had stopped off to give one lecture at the Colorado State College
of Education before going to the writers' conference at the University of
Colorado in Boulder.*

To MAXWELL E. PERKINS

[Picture Postcard: Estes Park to Grand Lake,
Rocky Mountain National Park, Colorado]

Greeley Colo.

July 30, 1935

Dear Max: I've seen no mountains yet but the West is wonderful—
blazing hot, but crystal air, blue skies. The journey across the country
was overwhelming—I've never begun to say what I ought to say about it.

To MAXWELL E. PERKINS

University of Colorado
Boulder, Colorado
Writers' Conference

August 12, 1935

Dear Max:

Thanks for your letter of August second. This is the first letter I have
written since I came out here, and the first chance I have had to write
you. The Writers' Conference is over, and I am leaving here to-day for
Denver and expect to be on my way for Santa Fe and the Southwest
in another day or two. This has been, and is going to be, an extraordinary trip. The West is like something that I always knew about. I
feel good and have been immensely happy ever since I came here. The
country is magnificent. I took a long trip yesterday up into the Rocky
Mountain National Park and saw some of the most glorious scenery
from a height of thirteen thousand feet that I have ever seen. The people
here have been wonderfully kind and hospitable, and between the
Writers' Conference lectures, talks, reading manuscripts, conferences,
and being taken around to parties, I am pretty well tired out to-day.
We're almost a mile high here. I have been constantly exhilarated and
ravenously hungry ever since I came here.

Some remarkably interesting things happened out here at this Writers'
Conference. It is the first one I ever attended and perhaps the last,
but I have been astonished at the quality of the talks that have been
made and the instruction that has been given, and I think something
very interesting and important may come from here. A number of the
people who attended gave me their manuscripts to read, and I have
taken the liberty of suggesting to three people that they send their
manuscripts to you immediately for a reading. I don't know if anything

will come of it or not. Because of the pressure of time and the great amount of manuscripts to be read, I was unable to judge just what possibilities the manuscripts had, but it seemed to me that these three at any rate were interesting enough to justify a reading. . . .

Now, as briefly as possible, a few words about other things. I note what you say about the Boyd matter, and I hope you are right in believing her case has been destroyed and that we shall hear no more from her. Nevertheless, Mr. Mitchell[1] has written me by air mail and has very urgently requested me to try to find the letter she wrote in answer to my own letter dismissing her as my agent, and is further asking me to get in touch with the Czechoslovakian publishers of "Of Time and the River"—to cable them if necessary—in an effort to get a copy of their correspondence with Mrs. Boyd establishing from their side as well the fact that she wrote them saying she was no longer my agent. It is also said that Mrs. Boyd's attorney speaks of some mysterious third person who was "a mutual friend" of both of us, and who is willing to testify that, at a time subsequent to the time I wrote the letter dismissing Mrs. Boyd as my agent, he had a conversation with me in which I agreed to a reconciliation and to retain her services as my agent for future work. As you know, this is an absolute and utter falsehood, and not only have I never seen nor written to Mrs. Boyd since I wrote the letter of dismissal, but I have never had any word of communication with her through any other person in any way whatever, and of course I have no idea who this mysterious third person may be.

Upon the basis of all these things, Mr. Mitchell informs me that he has entered a notice of appearance, whatever that may be. Whatever it is, I fear it means the long, involved, and costly operation of the courts of law and of lawyers, and although I feel confident that we can eventually defeat this woman's . . . claims, I am bitterly indignant over the fact that my own honesty and pity for her, . . . my failure to secure an absolute release [from her], have now put me in a position where these people can threaten me with suit and try to take from me a portion of my earnings. It is an ugly and intolerable situation, and what is most shameful about it now is the fact that even if I defeat her claims, I can do so only at the cost of a large sum of money for legal services and of an utterly shameful waste of my time, my energy, my temper, and what is most important, of human faith in other people and in the integrity of their intentions. This business of pawing through stacks and bales of old letters, trying to find every little scrap of writing which a person once wrote to you, is a disgusting one. I worked for three days

---

[1] Cornelius Mitchell of Mitchell and Van Winkle, Wolfe's attorney in this suit.

going through great stacks of letters in an effort to find everything the woman had ever written to me and everything which seemed to me to bear on the case, till finally I had succeeded in collecting a great mass of evidence, including my letter of dismissal—everything in fact which Mr. Mitchell said he wanted. Now he wants this letter which she wrote to me, and of course I have no idea where it is and will have no opportunity to look for it until I get back to New York and have to go through the whole accumulation of years of letters again. I am not going to let my life be eaten up and consumed . . . I have my work to do, and as my friend and publisher, I ask you in the future to try to help me in every way possible to keep me from this kind of shameful and ruinous invasion.

Finally, you must not put the manuscript of a book of stories in final form until after my return to New York. If that means the book of stories will have to be deferred till next spring, then they will have to be deferred, but I will not consent this time to allow the book to be taken away from me and printed and published until I myself have had time to look at the proofs, and at any rate to talk to you about certain revisions, changes, excisions, or additions that ought to be made. I really mean this, Max. I have money enough to live on for a while now. I do not propose to trade upon the success of "Of Time and the River." I propose rather to prepare my work in every way possible to meet and refute, if I can, some of the very grave and serious criticisms that were made about the last book, and as my friend and the person whose judgment I trust most, you must help me to do this.

I am coming back to New York in September. My mind is swarming with new material and the desire to get back and finish up "The October Fair" as soon as possible, but before we do that, we must first do a thorough, honest and satisfactory job upon the book of stories, "From Death to Morning"; we must get the Boyd matter settled; we must get the deck cleared for action; otherwise another shameful and revolting waste of talent right at the time of its greatest fertility and strength is likely to occur. And if this happens, I am ready to go to Siam, Russia, Timbuctoo, or take out citizenship under the benign and democratic governance of Adolph Hitler where, by comparison, the rights of men and of freedom and integrity of the individual are respected.

This is all for the present. I will be in the Southwest next week and then on to California, the Northwest, back through Idaho, Wyoming, and St. Louis and so back east again. And if they don't kill me out here with hospitality, or in New York with . . . lawsuits and so forth, I'll have some good stories to tell you and a lot of work to do in the winter. . . .

P.S. Max, forgive my ill temper—I am *exasperated* beyond measure by this Boyd thing—and I must work now—please help me in every way. . . .

To MAXWELL E. PERKINS

[Picture Postcard: Prehistoric Cliff Dwellings,
Pueblo of Puye, near Santa Fe, N.M.]

Santa Fe, N.M.

August 26, 1935

Dear Max: This is the most magnificent country—wild and fiendish, magnificent—just the way I always knew it would be. I had a fight with Mabel Luhan the moment I walked into her house and left immediately [1] but everyone else seems to like me.

To MAXWELL E. PERKINS

Hollywood-Roosevelt Hotel
Hollywood, California
Send mail to General Delivery, San Francisco

Sunday Sept. 1 [1935]

Dear Max:

I am sending you with this letter the proposed dedication for the book of stories. Will you and Jack please read and consider it carefully and decide whether you think it should be used? I had originally intended to dedicate "The Hills Beyond Pentland" to my brother, Ben, but because of the nature of the book of stories, and the subject matter involved, it has occurred to me that the present book might be a more fitting subject for the dedication. What do you think? At any rate, here's the dedication—I will abide by your judgment.

Finally, please let me urge on you again the desirability of getting *a good order* in the arrangement of the stories. I mean . . . the arrangement really should, so far as we can make it do so, illustrate the title, "From Death to Morning"—that is, they should progress in a general way, beginning, say, with "Death—The Proud Brother," and ending perhaps, with such a piece as "The Web of Earth."

[1] Mabel Dodge Luhan had invited Wolfe to come and see her at Taos, and he had been torn between friendliness and a fear of being lionized. He finally arrived there very late at night with two society girls who had driven him there from Santa Fe. When they were not received too cordially, Wolfe became angry and left with them.

Max, I think you might be surprised to know of the interest people out here have taken in the stories. I met Miss Edna Ferber, the novelist, in Santa Fe, the other day, and had lunch with her. She spoke most generously of everything I had done, but said she thought the stories were the finest things I had yet written. In the same way, a number of these moving picture people here in Hollywood—directors and other executives—know all about my work and are *collecting* it! I have met several who have a copy of every story I ever wrote, including the college stuff of Chapel Hill days—furthermore, they've read it. I met one director yesterday who began to rave about "The Web of Earth"—others about "Death—The Proud Brother." As for myself, I feel there is as good writing as I've done in some of the stories—it represents *important* work to me, and I think we should spare no pains to present it in as important and impressive a way as possible. I think you may be a little inclined to underestimate the importance of arrangement and presentation, and may feel that the stories can go in any way, and that the order doesn't matter much. Perhaps you are right—my own feeling, however, is that in a general way the stories do have a kind of unity and should be presented with an eye to cumulative effect, as the title "From Death to Morning" indicates. There is so much more that I want to say to you—so much more I want to do, include, write—and I know I have done little. There are at least half a dozen big stories I should have written and that should be included, and all kinds of minor things: the scene in the railway station, some of the night scenes, so many things bearing upon death and night and morning that could be put in to weave the whole thing together—in particular a scene where old Bascom (in "The Hills Beyond Pentland") looks down from the mountain in the town of Altamont and tells his twelve-year-old nephew about the Pentlands.[1] This could be used wonderfully to lead right into "The Web of Earth," and by doing a few things like this I know *the whole book* could be woven together and given a tremendous feeling of unity and cumulative effect that you almost never find in a book of stories. But please consider them carefully, Max. I could say much more, but you know what I mean, and as the drunken top-sergeant in "What Price Glory" yelled after his commanding officer—"Wait on me, Captain—Baby's Coming!"

Yes, I agree with you, I've had six months vacation, and that ought to be enough for any man. And it is—I feel guilty as hell, and eager to get to work again. But Max, it has been a thrilling wonderful experience—these last six months—I am filled to bursting with the pictures and variety of it, and as for this trip to the West, I have no words here to tell

[1] This was not included in *From Death to Morning* but finally appeared in *The Web and the Rock* on pages 160–170.

you of the beauty, power and magnificence of this country. Thank God, I have seen it at last!—and I know that I did not lie about it; I know I have not yet begun to put it down on paper; my store of wonderful subject matter has been enormously enriched.

I have some amazing and fantastic stories to tell you [about] this moving picture world, as well. I have met the famous stars, directors, producers, writers etc., have seen them at work—this is simply incredible —and in the midst of all the false and unreal world, the technical, building, working world is simply amazing in its skill and knowledge. Good God! I could write a magnificent book even about this place if I lived here a year. They want me to stay, have offered me a job, and mentioned huge sums, but perhaps I shall resist.[2] Everyone has been wonderfully kind all through the West—lavish generous hospitality. I am almost worn out by it—here as well. Dorothy Parker seems to like me, swears she does, and last night told a room of people that I was built on a heroic scale and that there was no one like me. Maybe the old girl is laughing at me behind my back and making wicked jokes about me but I think she meant what she said. She and her young husband are living in a magnificent imitation Colonial house and just bought a new Packard the other day, and the liquor and hospitality flows like the Mississippi—I am going there again this afternoon.

Yes, I know I have stayed too long, but Max, Max, you *must* wait on me—I've *got* to see San Francisco—above all, I must see that wonderful town—in the end, we shall not lose by it. Then, if you like, I'll cut it short and come straight home, only I'd hope to see a little of Oregon, Salt Lake City, and stop off a day in St. Louis to see where Grover died on my way back.[3] I'll be home in two weeks. Now, Max, please wait on me— don't take the book away before I get back. I've some wonderful things to tell you. Are Louise and the girls home yet?

[2] Wolfe was approached as to the possibility of his working as a writer for Metro-Goldwyn-Mayer by Sam Marx, the Story Editor there at that time, and with the approval of Irving Thalberg, Head of Production. However, he replied quite candidly that he had "a lot of books to write" and so could not accept. Since the making and declining of the offer was only oral, there is no record of it, but according to Marx's recollection, it was either on a week-to-week basis at $1000 to $1500 a week, or on a yearly basis at $30,000 to $50,000.

[3] Wolfe described the death of his brother Grover in *Look Homeward, Angel* on pages 51–60. He also described both Grover's death and his own visit to "St. Louis to see where Grover died" in a short story, "The Lost Boy," which appeared in the November, 1937, issue of *Redbook* and is included in *The Hills Beyond*.

To MAXWELL E. PERKINS

> The Riverside,
> Reno, Nevada
> Thursday, Sept. 12, 1935

Dear Max:

I am a little worried about something, and if you see fit, won't you take steps about it right away? It is this: at various times during the last month—at Boulder and elsewhere—I have discoursed very eloquently and persuasively about my book of the night, which is beginning to interest me more and more all the time. I have told how much of my life has been lived by night, about the chemistry of darkness, the strange and magic thing it does to our lives, about America at night: the rivers, plains, mountains, rivers in the moon or darkness (last night, by the way, coming up here through the Sierra Nevadas there was blazing moonlight, the effect was incredibly beautiful)—and how the Americans are a night-time people, which I have found out everywhere is absolutely true. Now, I'm afraid I've talked too much—please don't think I'm fool enough to think anyone is going to, or can, "steal my ideas," but people have been immensely and instantly absorbed when I told about my book, and have at once agreed to the utter truth of it. I have got hold of an immense, rich, and absolutely true thing about ourselves, at once very simple, profound, and various—and I know a great and original book, unlike any other, can be written on it—and I don't want some fool to get hold of it and write some cheap and worthless thing. The idea is so beautiful and simple that some bungler could easily mutilate it.

It will be years before I do it, but it keeps gathering in me all the time. I don't know yet exactly what form it will take, or whether it can be called a "novel" or not. I don't care—but I think it will be a great tone-symphony of night—railway yards, engines, freights, dynamos, bridges, men and women, the wilderness, plains, rivers, deserts, a clopping hoof, etc.—seen *not by a definite personality,* but haunted throughout by a consciousness *of personality.* In other words, I want to assert my divine right once and for all to be the *God Almighty* of a book—to be at once the spirit to move it, the spirit behind it, never to appear, to blast forever the charge of "autobiography" while being triumphantly and impersonally autobiographical.

Can't you do this, if you think best—and something tells me that it may be best: make an announcement to this effect: that I have for years been interested in the life of night (*not* nightclubs) and have been slowly acquiring an immense amount of material about it; that the book is slowly taking form, but will not be ready for years when these other books are out of the way; and that it is at present called "The Book of The Night." [1] You might put in something about "Saturday Night in America" (When I get back, I'll tell you about Longmont, Colorado on Saturday night. I've told you before what Saturday night does to us here in America and one part of the book has to do with this). At any rate, Max, I've talked to other people about it, and since this is one of the most precious and valuable ideas I've ever had, do what you can to protect it for me now. Why can't we do this? You could even say that I am so interested in the book that I am now at work on it, and that it *may* appear before the other books of the "Of Time and the River" series come out. This would do no harm, would arouse interest and discussion, and might serve the purpose of throwing some of my various ——s off the track for the present.

As for the Brooklyn lecture thing [2]—answer for me, as you think best. I could certainly do it, I could probably do it well, the talk at Boulder went over beautifully. But let us first consider this: do you think it is well for me to get into the lecture habit—I am getting offers now all the time—and do you think it is good for my *special* writing reputation to become known as a public lecturer? Also, what are we to work on next—"The October Fair," the Pentland book, "The Book of the Night," short stories—or what? When do you want to publish next, and when do we begin to work again? I am just mentioning these things for your consideration—I could probably do the lecture without great difficulty—and if law suits and crazy women are going to destroy my work, and take up my time again, I might as well pick up what extra money I can. But you be judge and answer the Brooklyn people as you see fit—whatever you say will be all right with me.

Other matters rest until I see you in few days. I've stopped off the day to see this town—incredible little 15,000 one-street place with gambling halls and bars and dance halls open all day and all night; gray faced faro and roulette men, silver dollars stacked up by the tons. Catching Overland Limited at 5 o'clock in morning in order to see Nevada and Utah deserts by day—then in Salt Lake for day—then St. Louis for few hours—then back home.

[1] Wolfe later gave this material the title of *The Hound of Darkness*. He never wrote much of it, but portions of it appear in "A Prologue to America" in the February 1, 1938, issue of *Vogue*, and are scattered through *The Web and the Rock* and *You Can't Go Home Again,* as on pages 474–475 of *The Web and the Rock,* and pages 429–431 and 506–508 of *You Can't Go Home Again.*

[2] The Brooklyn Institute of Arts and Sciences had phoned Perkins to ask if Wolfe would give the opening lecture of a series they were planning for that fall.

The following two letters were written to John Hall Wheelock about the galley proofs of From Death to Morning, *which Wolfe read and corrected with great care.*

To JOHN HALL WHEELOCK

[New York City]

[September, 1935]

Dear Jack:

Here are the remainder of the proofs for "Death the Proud Brother," which I have now read and corrected.

Now, about what is probably the most important matter first—your comment on galley 22 that my story really lacks there and that what follows is another thing. I see your point and feel a break myself, but wonder if the inclusion of a phrase at the very beginning of this passage which would refer it to the death scene that has gone before would not help? What do you think?

A much more serious question however, is this: the passage that follows to the end of the story is really one of my most ambitious apostrophes—to Loneliness, and Death and Sleep. It is the kind of thing that some of the critics have gone gunning after me for—but it is also the kind of thing that many people have liked in my writing, and that some say they hope I never lose. This passage in peroration—about Sleep and Death, etc.—has made friends. Now, what do you think? It's a pretty serious matter to me, because if it really is better that I cut out this *kind* of writing entirely, it is a fundamental thing and I must seriously change my whole method and style everywhere. *But I want you to say what you think!*

About other things: please note the changes I have made in galley 12 —taking out the word "Esther" and substituting "the woman." Do you think it is now clear, and also a change for the better?

I note your red marks on galley 14. . . . This passage now refers to "the woman" rather than to Esther. Do you want it cut? I have indicated several paragraphs on galley 20 with a line and question mark. I feel something a little stiff and inept here—it is part of a much longer part that was cut out. Will you read it, and tell me if you can find the trouble, if any?

Galley 23: you marked several phrases and sentences, as having been duplicated in "Of Time and the River." That's true, they are—this was written first. Do you think their inclusion here would be a serious error? The trouble is, I have trouble thinking of an adequate substitute for the passage "They come! Ships call!—etc."

Finally, in apostrophe to Sleep I have capitalized *Sleep* throughout save in the concluding phrase, "Sleep, sleep, sleep." I did this to avoid confusion—but do you think in the phrase "In *Sleep* we lie all naked and alone," would arouse obscene comment?

As to shorter phrases, which I had repeated in other stories, I have either modified them here, or let them stay, preferring them to go in here rather than in the other stories.

I'll try to get in before closing time to see you.

To JOHN HALL WHEELOCK

[September, 1935]

Dear Jack:

Here is the proof of the only story left (except "The Web"). Note that I have changed the title to "The Far and The Near." Also observe changes on galley 82 which have been done with a view to changing the attitude of the two women to a *timid* and *uneasy unfriendliness* rather than surly hostility. Also last sentence. If you think changes good, let them stand—if not, erase them.

Harry Woodburn Chase, to whom the following note was addressed, had been President of the University of North Carolina from 1919–1930, and had come to New York University as its Chancellor in 1933. He had sent Wolfe an anonymous poem about the University which had been published in the Year Book of the School of Architecture.

To HARRY WOODBURN CHASE

Charles Scribner's Sons
597 Fifth Avenue
New York

Oct. 30, 1935

Dear Chancellor Chase:

Thanks very much for your note and the enclosed poem. I am sorry to say that I am not working twenty-four hours a day as I feel I should be, but I hope to get started soon. I had a wonderful vacation of more than six months which took me all the way from Denmark to San Francisco, and I am back here now, ready to work and desperately eager to get at it, but somehow I find it terribly hard to break through my own inertia and get started. I wonder why people are like that. No one knows better than I that I must work, and that my life is nothing without work, and yet I do everything in the world to avoid it—that is, before I get started. . . .

Thank you for sending me the poem. Yes, I think it decidedly does say something, and is eloquent and true. As time goes on, and I have been able to get more detachment and perspective on my years at New York University, I have realized that being there is one of the most valuable and fruitful experiences of my whole life. I can think of no other way in which a young man coming to this terrific city as I came to it, could have had a more comprehensive and stimulating introduction to its swarming life, than through the corridors and classrooms of Washington Square. In April of this year I had the opportunity to revisit the great English university at Cambridge. It is gloriously beautiful, even more so than I had remembered it, but somehow it seemed remote from the life of the world around us, and my thoughts kept going back to Washington Square and to all the eager, swarming, vigorous life I knew there, and it seemed to me without making comparisons, that whatever happens to our universities in the future, Washington Square was somehow closer to reality than Cambridge. So thanks again for sending me the poem. . . .

The following note was written in a presentation copy of From Death to Morning *for Henry T. Volkening. The unfavorable review to which it refers was undoubtedly the one by Ferner Nuhn in the Sunday, November 17, 1935, issue of the* Herald Tribune Books, *which was released on Saturday, November 16. Nuhn's review was headed: "Thomas Wolfe, Six-foot-six. These Stories Reveal Again the Exuberance of an Over-sized Man in a Standard-sized World," and said in part: "The advantages of an oversized view of the world are obvious in Thomas Wolfe's work: the heightened color, mood, sweep, rush which can so easily carry lesser organisms along. But there are disadvantages too. The bulge of an excess of emotion is as flabby in the end as the slack of an insufficient one. Readers swept off their feet have a way of picking themselves up and rejecting further rides, and this would be a pity."*

To HENRY T. VOLKENING

New York City

November 13, 1935

Dear Henry:

I'm a little sad as I write you this. I've just read the first review of this book—in next Saturday's *Herald Tribune*—which pans it and sees little in it except a man six foot six creating monstrous figures in a world of five feet eight. I do not think this is true, but now I have a hunch the well-known "reaction" has set in against me, and that I will take a pounding on this book. Well, I am writing you this because I believe that as good writing as I have ever done is in this book and because my faith has always been that a good thing is indestructible and that if there is good here—as I hope and believe there is—it will somehow survive. That is a faith I want to have, and that I think we need in life, and that is why I am writing you this—not in defense against attacks I may receive but just to put this on record *in advance* with you, who are a friend of mine. So won't you put this away—what I have written—and keep it— and if someday it turns out I am right, won't you take it out and read it to me?

The following letter to Clayton Hoagland was occasioned by Hoagland's review of "From Death to Morning" in the New York Sun, *on November 14, 1935, which said: "This book of stories has in it all of Wolfe's realism, the ribaldry, the humor, the lyrical prose ascending to poetry, the gift of vitalizing a character until it stalks from the page."*

To CLAYTON HOAGLAND

865 First Avenue
New York City
[November, 1935]

Dear Clayton:

I want to tell you how moved and grateful I am about your magnificent and generous review of "From Death to Morning." I felt overwhelmed and a little guilty, too, when I read it, because in addition to being my reviewer you are also my friend; but I reflected, then, that it was because of some of these stories that we first got to know each other and become friends, and that your liking for my work really preceded your meeting with me. In spite of this, I know I am not wholly worthy of such praise as this, but perhaps a wonderful review like this will have one of the finest effects that any criticism could have—the effect of making me want to live up to it, and of making me exert every energy of my life in order to do so. I will call you up in a day or two, and hope to see you and Kitty [1] and all the family soon. Meanwhile, with love to all of you, and with all my heartfelt thanks,

[1] Mrs. Hoagland.

XII

THE BEGINNING OF THE WEB AND THE ROCK *AND* YOU CAN'T GO HOME AGAIN

1936

Stark Young, author of The Three Fountains, Heaven Trees, River House, So Red the Rose, *etc. had written Wolfe to clarify a conversation they had had about William Faulkner, and had also congratulated him on* From Death to Morning, *saying: "The dedication struck me almost down. I have never felt like intruding about your brother Ben. But though people are always telling me that time heals these things into oblivion or peace, I know better. Not many of the living are so real as the dead that are beloved." The following was Wolfe's reply.*

To STARK YOUNG

865 First Avenue
New York City
Saturday, March 7, 1936

Please excuse pencil and paper—
no pen or ink available.

Dear Stark:

Thanks for your letter. I don't think I misunderstood you at all in what you said about Faulkner, and certainly no one who was present could have failed to understand that everything you said came from a feeling of true friendliness and admiration. And I agree utterly with your estimate in your letter—that what he writes is not like the South, but that yet the South is *in* his books, and in the spirit that creates them.

And I think you're right in what you say about death—there's very little in life that's as real—and I think I like to live as well as most people. I've had a curious experience concerning this in recent years, and I

believe the same thing has happened to most people: I discovered a year
or two ago that it was not the people one has known *least* who are hardest to remember, but the people one has known *most,* and loved the best.
For example, I can remember faces seen on subway trains, a pretty girl
seen for a moment on the street, a waiter in a little town in France, or
the features of Wild Bill Hart, the old time movie stars, Edna Purviance,
Fatty Arbuckle—thousands of faces like these. I can see them at once
just the way they were, and I think the reason is that they had—for me,
at least—just that one face. But a few years ago I discovered that when
I tried to remember the face of someone who had died, whom I had
known well, or a woman I had been in love with, it was almost impossible
to remember how that person looked. There was not one person then,
there were a *thousand,* and they changed and interfered with the instancy
of light—and suddenly they would be there like a stroke of lightning—
upon an intonation of the voice, a familiar movement of the hand, a
moment's burst of laughter—but not *all* of them: just one face out of the
thousand faces, one life out of their thousand lives. It is a hard thing for
a novelist to solve. My own tendency, perhaps, is to try to fill books with
a universe of life—hundreds of characters—making each of them as real
and living as I can. And then I have the overwhelming desire to make
just one person live the way he was—or anyway, the way I knew him:
to restore, compare, and bring to life again all of his thousand faces and
his thousand forms. And then I realize that even the pages of the largest
book are far too short for such a universe as *that!*
    Thanks for writing me: I hope to see you soon.

The following telegram to Perkins marks the beginning of The Vision of
Spangler's Paul, *which finally became* The Web and the Rock *and* You Can't
Go Home Again.

To MAXWELL E. PERKINS
[Telegram]

Boston, Mass.

March 17, 1936

Tell Calverton [1] out of town. Wrote book beginning. Goes wonderfully.
Full of hope.

---

[1] V. F. Calverton, the editor of *The Modern Monthly.*

The following letter to V. F. Calverton, (familiarly called George) editor of the Modern Monthly, *was written as the result of one of the minor understandings which invariably arose to upset Wolfe and distract him from his work.*

To V. F. CALVERTON

865 First Avenue
New York, New York

April 3, 1936

Dear George:

I am sorry there has been a misunderstanding about my speaking at the *Modern Monthly* dinner. The first definite information I had about it came the other day when Nina [1] called me up and asked me to come to a cocktail party and then told me I was on the program to speak and that notices to that effect had been sent out to the press. If anything I said myself was responsible for this misunderstanding I regret it very much, but my own clear recollection is that when I had dinner with you and Nina a month or so ago, a *Modern Monthly* dinner was mentioned and you both told me you hoped I would be there. As I remember it, I told you that if I were in New York at the time and I had no other engagement that I had to meet I should be glad to attend. I don't remember how, or whether, the question of my speaking at the dinner came up, but if it did I am sure I expressed myself pretty vigorously as not wanting to speak at the dinner, or for that matter at any dinner, as I felt very strongly on the subject at the time because I had just been wangled into speaking at a dinner and it is my one and only such performance— I attended only on the belief and assurance that I would be present anonymously and at the most only get up and say hello to the people and then leave immediately. The off-shoot of that assurance was that I eventually found that it was being announced in large bulletins and post-cards that I was going to talk to the gathering on "The Story of a Novel." [2] That experience, as I say, was my first of this kind in which I found myself involved through no fault of my own.

If I had known that there could be any possible misunderstanding on your part or on Nina's about the way I felt on the whole business of

[1] Nina Melville, Calverton's wife.

[2] *The Story of a Novel* had been published serially in the December 14, 21, and 28, 1935, issues of *The Saturday Review of Literature,* and was to be published in book form on April 21, 1936.

public speaking, or that you were going to print announcements and send them out with my name heading the list of several speakers, I should certainly have called you up and asked you not to do it. Believe me, I will cause you no embarrassment whatever, but there has been a misunderstanding here and I am compelled to tell you that I do not want to talk at the *Modern Monthly* dinner or at any other dinner. My reasons for feeling this way are many and positive but the chief of them is that I am a writer and not a public speaker and if I have anything at all to say to people I will have to say it through writing or not at all.

Perkins and I agreed upon this months ago when the question of lectures and lecture tours came up. In the last year I have repeatedly turned down offers to give lectures or to go on lecture tours which would have paid me thousands of dollars. I did this because I made the decision to stick to writing for the present at least and not to turn aside for anything else. I am telling you this simply because I wish to make wholly clear what I had hoped was clear before: I am not a public speaker. I have never in my life gone around making speeches at public gatherings and I do not intend to begin it now. I am sorry, therefore, that there has been a misunderstanding, and sincerely regretful if anything I said or didn't say was in any way responsible for the misunderstanding. But I do think that before announcements were printed and sent out I should have been informed, because I certainly had no knowledge that I was listed definitely to speak and that announcements had been sent out to the press until Nina telephoned me the other day.

I don't think Max Perkins understood this either. You said in your letter that he was glad that I had consented, but I asked him about it and he said that he had not understood that I was to speak.

If, as I told you before, I am here on Friday, April the 17th, and you want me to attend the dinner I shall be glad to come. If I have to go away, as I indicated I might have to, of course I can't attend, but the speaking is out in any event.

And now let me repeat, in conclusion, that I am genuinely sorry if I have in any way upset your plans or been the cause of any misunderstanding, but if I have done so it was because I did not myself clearly understand the nature of your plans or that you intended to put me on your printed program as one of the speakers.

Believe me I have, as you know, now as in the past, every good wish for the success of the *Modern Monthly* and I send you those good wishes now, together with all good wishes for the success of the dinner.

To V. F. CALVERTON

865 First Avenue
New York, N.Y.
April 9, 1936

Dear George:

I got your Special Delivery this morning, and am replying at once. I cannot wholly agree with you that the success of the *Modern Monthly* depends so much on my being there and speaking as you seem to think it does. But in view of what you say in your letter about the embarrassment you will be caused if I do not attend and how important you consider my attendance is to the welfare of *The Modern Monthly,* I agree to come.

I do want you to understand this, I never agreed to make a speech, I do not intend to make a speech, I have no speech at all to make, and I should heartily, earnestly, sincerely prefer to attend the dinner along with the other guests and say nothing at all. But if you really feel that you are so committed now, that it is up to me to say something to save you embarrassment, I agree to get up and say that I am glad to be there and meet the other members of the *Modern Monthly* public, or something to that effect. I am not trying to make any issue of this, or to act stubbornly and obstinately about a minor thing, but the truth of the matter is that I have been so hounded and wangled into one thing and another, ever since I came back here last October, that I have finally decided that if I am to have any peace of mind or try to find time to work in at all hereafter, I must now take a stand. As I say, I am genuinely sorry if anything I said or implied that last time I saw you and Nina, lead to this misunderstanding.

I won't go into the matter again and I will go through with this because you seem to feel so strongly that my not doing it will put you in a serious predicament. But while regretting deeply the whole misunderstanding, I feel that you did not have sufficient justification from anything I said to warrant your sending the announcements to the press and having programs printed. I am not going to harp on this any more. I hate to have to mention it all, but I am speaking about it now, simply because I want it to be understood from now on, that I am not going into the public speaking business and I have to earn my living through what I write and that I have got to be given time enough to do my own work. I wish to God that it were still possible for me not to have to speak at the dinner. If I do, I promise you that what I say will be extremely brief. I want you to understand that you can depend on my not being bad tempered about it and that the thing is settled. It may not be much of a talk and it probably will not be; but at any rate, I shall do it in good will and we will hope that the next time a thing of this sort comes up, we will both have a clearer understanding of it and so avoid this difficulty.

I will call you up before the dinner to get any other information you may care to give me about it. In the meantime, best wishes to you and Nina.

The following note was in answer to one from A. Y. C. Powers, who had written Wolfe from England to praise Of Time and the River *and* Look Homeward, Angel, *saying: "It seems to me that in your prose you are discovering something which I have always been looking for and hardly ever found except in poetry."*

To A. Y. C. POWERS

865 First Avenue
New York, N.Y.
April 9, 1936

Dear Mr. Powers:

. . . I cannot give your kind and interesting letter the thanks it deserves, but I want to thank you most sincerely for having written as you have, and for what you say about my work. I think the knowledge that a reader feels the way you say you do about something one has done, is the greatest reward a writer can have and it makes me want to exert every energy to fulfill and justify your good opinion. It is especially good to know that what one writes in one country, on one side of the ocean can waken recognition and appreciation in some one living on the other side of the ocean. I suppose it proves that no matter who you are or where you live, the fundamental material and design of human experience is everywhere the same.

I appreciate also your saying that I see life as a poet sees it: that I get the whole picture all together and that some times accounts for the super abundance of detail. I don't know whether you are right about this or not, but I hope you are right because it seems to me that what every man would like to be if he could be, is a poet. And I suppose the reason we write prose instead of poetry, is simply because the power to write poetry is not in us.

Your letter and what you say about my writing awoke many interesting and I believe, helpful speculations. Thank you again for having written as sincerely and warmly as you did.

To MABEL WOLFE WHEATON

865 First Avenue
New York, N.Y.

April 19, 1936

Dear Mabel:

I was glad to get your letter because I have been thinking about you and wondering what you were doing and even tried to get you on the telephone two or three weeks ago. I don't know what the trouble was, but the operator told me she could find no phone listed under your name, and I couldn't find your old number, which I remember was Metropolitan something. I didn't know what you were doing or whether you had temporarily or permanently gone out of the rooming-house business or not.[1] Fred and Mama had written me and said that they thought you might go back to Asheville or to Florida. I am glad to know where you are and if I could take a day or two off a little later on when the weather gets better, I will come down and see you. . . .

Several weeks ago I got a letter from one of our Westall relatives, who lives in Washington. His name is William G. Westall, he is one of the Yancey County members of the family[2] and is thirty-two years old. From what he told me, I figured out that we were second or third half cousins, if such a degree of relationship exists. His father was a half brother of Mama's father, and his grandfather was our great-grandfather. I figured that this made this young fellow and Mama first half cousins, which would mean, wouldn't it, that he is a second half cousin of ours? He wrote me an awfully interesting and intelligent letter, telling me about his own branch of the family, saying that he had read "Look Homeward, Angel" and "Of Time and the River," and he was sure I was sometimes talking about his Asheville relatives. He wanted to know if this was so and in what way we were related, and I wrote him back at considerable length and told him. I also told him that you and Ralph were living in Washington and that I wished he would go to see you. . . . He tells me he is married, and since he wrote me about what I have written in a much more friendly and understanding spirit than some of the members of the family have shown, I thought it would be a great idea to look him up if I come down. . . .

I was awfully sorry to hear about Mrs. ——. Your letter was the first news I had of her death. I always liked her and, as you say, as you get

---

[1] Mrs. Wheaton had been obliged to move out of her former rooming-house in Washington, the Gramercy, and was trying to get settled in another.

[2] William G. Westall is the son of John Westall who was a half-brother of Wolfe's grandfather, Thomas Casey Westall. This branch of the family lived, and still lives, in Burnsville, Yancey County, North Carolina.

a little older you begin to overlook some of a person's faults and remember more of their good and generous qualities, and I think she had lots of them. I don't know whether I ever told you that she had written me several times, two or three anyway, in the last few years and seemed to be disturbed and upset about "Look Homeward, Angel." I wrote and answered her at considerable length and tried to make it as emphatic as I could that I had the greatest liking and affection for her, as we all did, and I was sincerely sorry and regretful if anything I had written had caused her, in no matter how mistaken a way, any embarrassment or worry. She wrote me again not so long ago, within the last year or so anyway, and to this letter it seemed to me I could make no reply. It dealt with rumors, hearsay, and things she said she had heard from people I didn't know and had never heard of. And it seemed to me, after thinking it over, that the wisest course was not to become involved in a situation I knew nothing about. I know we shall always remember her, and with affection. I suppose hers was a pretty sad and difficult kind of life and I can easily see that with her great beauty of person and of character, she might have found happiness and success if circumstances had been different. . . .

This is all for the present that I have time to write. I have had almost every kind of worry, threat and annoyance this winter from suits and lawyers to . . . even blackmail letters, and I let it bother me a good deal, but I've about gotten used to the fact now that everyone who gets some public notice is likely to be the victim of this sort of thing. And I have also about come to the conclusion that if worst comes to worst, I would rather have the crooks and shysters get what little means or property I have than to let them so destroy what peace of mind or power of concentration I may have that I will be unable to work. Anyway, I am back at work—that's the main thing—and getting a good deal done, and I can only hope that no matter what happens, I will be able to go right on now day after day until I finish another big piece of work. You are dead right about work: it makes all the difference between having a happy life and an unhappy one, between taking a drink with a friend and enjoying it, or between seizing a gallon jug and trying to drown the essential horror of so much in life around you in oblivion. As long as I can work, I am all right. If I ever lose the power or capacity for work, I don't know what I would do. But I don't intend to lose it, if I can ever help it.

Write me when you feel like it, and . . . if I can get away in the next few weeks, I may come down for a day or two. Meanwhile, with love to you and Ralph and all,

P.S. I have a little book coming out to-morrow called "The Story of a Novel" and I will send you a copy. It is just a very short account of the experiences I had getting started as a writer and what happened, the mistakes I made, etc. But people seem to think it is quite interesting and, of its kind, unique. I don't think it will have much sale or get out to a very wide public, because it is a special kind of thing and likely to be of interest mainly to people who have some special interest in my own work, or who are themselves interested in writing. But it is very simply written and you can read it in an hour or so, and I thought you might want to see it, so I am sending it on to you.

The following letter to Perkins was written by Wolfe during his first serious quarrel with Scribners.

To MAXWELL E. PERKINS

865 First Avenue
New York

April 21, 1936

Dear Max:

I want to tell you that I am sorry I got angry last night and spoke as I did. The language that I used was unjustifiable and I want to tell you that I know it was, and ask you to forget it.

About the matter I was talking to you about [1] however, I feel just as strongly to-day as I did last night. I don't want to re-hash the whole thing again—we have talked and argued about it too much already—but I do want to tell you honestly and sincerely that I am not arguing about the two or three hundred dollars which would be involved if I were given my old royalty of 15%, instead of the reduced one of 10%. I admit that there can be no doubt that I agreed to this reduction of my royalty before the publication of the book and at the time when estimates of cost of publication were being prepared, I told you that I hoped the book could be published at a very moderate price of 75¢ or a dollar, not only because I thought it might be better for the success of the book itself, but also because I am not willing to make use of any past success I may have had, or take advantage of any present reputation I may have in the eyes of the public to publish so short and small a book at a high price. Now I don't want you to think that I am trying to dictate to my publishers the price for which I think my book ought to be printed. You told me an author had no right to dictate such prices and that in fact, the price the publisher put on his books was none of his business, and al-

[1] The retail price and royalty rate on *The Story of a Novel*.

though I think the subject is open to debate, I am, on the whole, inclined to agree with you and was really not trying to dictate any prices, except what I told you when the publication of the book was discussed that I hoped personally, it would be brought out at a low price of 75¢ or a dollar.

You told me that it would be impossible to bring it out for as low a price as 75¢, but we all had hoped, I believe, that it might be brought out for a dollar. Later, when estimates on the cost of publication came in, it was agreed that the price would have to be $1.25 and either then at that time or previously, I had agreed to a reduction of my customary royalty from 15% to 10% and I believe the 10% was to cover the first three thousand copies and that if the book sold more than that, I would get an increased royalty. The reason that I agreed to this reduction was because I knew the publisher was not likely to profit very much by the publication of so small a book and because I agreed with you the publication of the book was, nevertheless, probably a good thing, and finally because you told me that even at the $1.25 price, the margin was very small and you thought I ought to accept the royalty of 10%, which I agreed to do.

Now the book has been published and the other day when I got my own advance copy, I saw that the price had been still further raised from $1.25 to $1.50. This was the first knowledge that I had that the price had been raised. I agree with you that I probably have no right to argue with you about the price of a book or to have the say as to [the] price it ought to sell for. I also agree that if the book is successful and sells, I stand to profit in my share of the royalties at the increased price as well as does the publisher; but I don't think that either of these facts is the core of the matter, and they are certainly not what I am arguing about.

What I am arguing about is this: that I agreed to accept a reduced royalty upon the basis of a dollar or dollar and a quarter book, and the reason that I agreed to accept the reduction was because it was presented to me that the cost of making the book was such that it would be difficult for the publisher to give a higher royalty and have him come out clear. Then after agreeing to this reduced royalty, upon my understanding that the book would be published at a dollar and a quarter, and having signed a contract accepting the reduced royalty, I find that the price of the book, without my knowledge, has been raised to $1.50, and is being published at that price. When I discussed that fact about a week ago, when I got my own advance copy, I told you that in view of the increase in price, I thought you ought to restore my former royalty of 15%. I still think that you ought to do so and have told you so repeatedly, and you feel you ought not to do so, and have refused to do so.

You have been my friend for seven years now and one of the best friends that I ever had, I don't think anyone in the world is more conscious than I am of what you have done for me, of how you stuck to me for years when I was trying to get another book completed and when so much time elapsed that people had begun to say I might never be able to write again. I think you stuck to me not only with material aid and support that Scribners gave me during a large part of the time when I had no funds of my own, but you stuck to me also with your own friendship and belief and spiritual support, and you not only gave me these priceless things, but you also gave me unstintedly the benefits of your enormous skill and talent as an editor and a critic. I do not think a debt such as I owe you can ever sufficiently be repaid, but I have tried to do what I could through work, which I know you do value, and through public acknowledgment which I know you do not want and on which you don't put the same value as you do upon the more important fact of work. So having said all this, and feeling this way toward you, and about what you and Scribners have done, I want to repeat again that I do not think it is right or proper for you to withhold from me my full and customary royalty of 15%, the circumstances being what they are.

I do not question your legal and contractual right to do this. I agreed to the reduction at the time and for the reason I have mentioned. I signed the contract and I am, of course compelled to abide by it. But I think it is up to you now, in view of the facts I have mentioned, and since the reason of the reduction of the royalty, namely, the low price of the book, is no longer true—I think it is up to you and Scribners of your own accord to give me my 15%. It will not amount to much, even if you sell the entire three thousand copies, which the 10% royalty covers. I don't think it will amount to more than two or three hundred dollars and I am not arguing with you about that. But just because you have been generous and devoted friends, and because my feeling toward you has been one of devotion and loyalty, I do not want to see you do this thing now which may be legally and technically all right, but is to my mind a sharp business practice. I know that you yourself, personally, do not stand to profit one penny whether I get 10% or 15%. I know that you yourself, probably did not suggest the reduction in royalty or fix the price of the book, but I also know the way I expect and want you to act now as my friend. It seems to me that it is imperative that you do this just exactly for the reason that I consider you all my friends and have always lived and felt and thought about you in that way, and not as people with whom I had business dealings and who were going to use whatever business advantage they considered legitimate in their dealings with me.

You know very well that I am not a business man and have no capacity for business and that in matters of this sort, I am not able to cope with people who are skilled at it; but where it concerned you and Scribners, I have never thought for one moment, that I would have to cope with it. The thing I really feel and believe is that at the bottom of your heart, . . . you agree with me and my position in this matter and know that I am right as I know you agreed with me in the matter of almost $1,200, which I was charged for corrections in the proof of *Of Time and the River*. I'll admit that there, too, I am legally responsible and signed the contract which had a clause in it stipulating the cost to the author if the changes and corrections in the proof exceed a certain amount. But the truth of the matter is, as you know and as you said at the time when the bill was first shown to me, that a great many of these corrections came as the result of the work we were both doing on the manuscript, and as a result of the editorial help and advice and the suggestions you made which were so generous and so invaluable. For this very reason perhaps, I ought not to harp upon the subject or complain about having to pay almost $1,200 for corrections that helped the book, but you said at the time the bill was shown to me that in view of the circumstances and the way the corrections were made and done, you didn't think I ought to have to pay as much money as that, and I understood you even to say that if I felt too strongly that I ought not to pay and that the bill was unfair, I would not have to pay it. Well, I don't feel that strongly about it—I think I made a lot of corrections on the proof on my own hook and I think that if these corrections were excessive, I ought to pay for them like anyone else. But I do feel that the bill of almost $1,200 is excessive and that I am being made to pay too much for corrections which I'll admit helped me and the book, but which were partly done with your collaboration. . . .

I want to ask you this; if your refusal in this matter is final and you insist on holding me to the terms of the contract I signed for *The Story of a Novel*, don't you think that I, or anyone else on earth for that matter, would be justified henceforth and hereafter, [in] considering my relations with you and Scribners were primarily of a business and commercial nature, and if you make use of a business advantage in this way, don't you think I would be justified in making use of a business advantage too if one came my way? Or do you think it works only one way? I don't think it does and I don't think any other fair-minded person in the world would think so either. As you know, I never gave a moment's serious consideration to any offers of persuasions that were made to me by other people and I think that you know very well that such offers were made. And that in one case at least, a very large sum of money was mentioned at a time when I, myself, had nothing.[2] You not only knew of the occasion, but I telephoned you of it just as soon as the person telephoned and asked if he could talk to me. I informed you of the telephone call at once and told you I didn't know what it meant and you told me what it did mean, and furthermore told me I had a right to meet the man and listen to what he had to say and even consider what he had to offer. Well, I suppose that's business practice and everyone agrees that it is fully justified and that a man has a right not only to listen, but to take the best and most profitable offer. That's business practice, maybe, but it has not been my practice. I did meet the man, I did listen to what he had to say and I paid no attention at all to his offer. What do you think about this any way? If people are going to get hard-boiled and business-like, should it all be on one side, or doesn't the other fellow have a right to get hard-boiled and business-like too?

I understand perfectly well that even publishers are not in business for their health, even though you have said that none of them make any great amount of money out of it. And I don't expect my relations with my publisher to be a perpetual love feast, into which the vile question of money never enters, but I do say that you cannot command the loyalty and devotion of a man on the one hand and then take a business advantage on the other. I am sorry to have to say all this. I want to repeat how much I regret my language of last evening, but I also want to say that about this matter of the royalties, I feel as strongly and deeply now as I did then. I am writing this letter to you as a final appeal. You may think I am kicking up a hell of a row over nothing but I do think it is something, a great deal, not in a money way but in the matter of fair dealing, and I am writing to tell you so.

Perkins' reply to the above was written on April 22, 1936, and said in part: "I am giving directions to reckon your royalties on The Story of a Novel at 15% from the start. . . . I would rather simply agree to do this and say nothing further, but I should not have the right to do it without telling you that the terms, as proposed, on the $1.50 price are just and that if the matter were to be looked upon merely as business we should not be justified as

[2] Between 1930 and 1934, Wolfe was informally approached by several publishers, one of whom, he told Miss Nowell and others, offered him an advance of ten thousand dollars against royalties on his next novel. In 1937, after he had left Scribners, when he was first approached by Houghton Mifflin and Harper's, he again referred to this offer as a gauge of what he could expect as an advance against his new book.

business men in making this concession. You are under a misapprehension if you think that when we suggested a reduction of royalty . . . we were basing the suggestion on the question of price. . . . We could not, at that time, know what the price would have to be. We found that the price had to be higher because of the question of basic costs which come into every phase of the handling, advertising, promoting, and making of a book. . . . The terms we proposed were therefore, in my opinion, just.

"You return to the question of the excess corrections. . . . I once said to you in Charles Scribner's presence that you had a good technical argument for not paying these corrections because you did not make them . . . since you did not read your proof, but, if you had done so, is there any doubt but what these corrections would have been much larger? . . . They were rightly author's corrections, and why should the author not pay for them? I think we began wrong by making no charge in the case of excess corrections on the "Angel," which amounted to seven hundred dollars. . . .

"As to the other matter you speak of . . . I certainly would not wish you to make what you thought was a sacrifice on my account, and I would know that whatever you did would be sincerely believed to be right by you, as I know that you sincerely believe the contentions you make in this letter to me to be right. I have never doubted your sincerity, and never will. I wish you could have felt that way toward us."

For the full text of this letter, see Editor to Author, The Letters of Maxwell E. Perkins, page 110. (*Scribners, 1950.*)

To MAXWELL E. PERKINS

865 First Avenue
New York, N.Y.

April 23, 1936

Dear Max:

I got your letter this morning and I just want to write you back now to tell you that everything is settled so far as I am concerned, so let's forget about it. Now that you have told me that you would restore my old royalty of 15%, I want to tell you that I don't want it and want to stick to the contract I signed. That goes for all my other obligations as well. I really made up my mind to this yesterday, and that was the reason I called you up last night and went around to see you.

I wanted to tell you and I am afraid I didn't succeed [in] telling you very well that all the damn contracts in the world don't mean as much to me as your friendship means, and it suddenly occurred to me yesterday that life is too short to quarrel this way with a friend over something that matters so little. But I do want to tell you again just how genuinely and deeply sorry I am for boiling over the way I did the other night. We have had fireworks of this sort before and I am afraid they may occur again, but every time they do, I say something to a friend that is unjust and wrong, and sweat blood about it later. So just help me along with this by forgetting all about it, and let's look forward to the future.

I suppose it is a good thing for me to have had this experience in the last year but there is something a little grotesque and tragic in the fact that the success I wanted and looked forward to having as a child should have brought me so much trouble, worry, bewilderment and disillusion, but I am going to try to add the whole experience to the sum of things I have found out about all through my life, and I hope that I will be able to make use of it, instead of letting it make use of me. I see now what a terribly dangerous thing a little success may be because it seems to me the effort of an artist must always aim at even greater concentration and intensity and effort of the will where his work is concerned, and anything that tends to take him away from that, to distract him, to weaken his effort, is a bad thing.

I am now started on another book. I need your friendship and support more than I ever did, so please forget the worst mistakes I have made in the past and let's see if I can't do somewhat better in the future.

A bitterly critical article on Wolfe, "Genius Is Not Enough" by Bernard De Voto, had appeared in the April 25, 1936, issue of The Saturday Review of Literature, *purportedly as a review of* The Story of a Novel. *The following reaction to it was written by Wolfe to Julian Meade, who had protested against it both to Wolfe and to Henry Seidel Canby, editor of* The Saturday Review of Literature.

To JULIAN MEADE

865 First Avenue
New York, N.Y.

May 4, 1936

Dear Meade:

Thanks for your letter. It was very generous of you to feel the way you did about the *Saturday Review* piece and to register such a vigorous protest. I was over at the Canbys' for dinner last night and of course, made no reference to the article but finally Mr. Canby himself brought it up. I think your letter had made quite an impression. He didn't mention your name but said he had got a pretty vigorous letter a few days ago denouncing the article and asking why a man's book should be reviewed by his enemies and so on. So I figured it was your letter he was talking about. I told him that personally I had no hard feelings and that although I read every scrap that was written about me in the way of a review or criticism, provided I saw it, and still took the whole thing very much to heart, it didn't bother me quite as much as it once did. I added that I had my living to earn, and that the only way I have of earning it is through what I write, and that if a reviewer says I am no good, it's just too bad for me and perhaps occasionally for him, but that nevertheless, I was going to keep right on writing. This was all I said, and then got off the subject.

I think really my only objection to the *Saturday Review* piece was that it didn't review the book. It seems to me that it was hardly a review at all, but rather a kind of general denunciation of all my deficiencies as a writer, some of which, of course, I am prepared to admit and have done so already. I don't think a writer has any right to dictate to the editors of a literary review who shall review his book or what form the review should take, but I do think he has a right to expect a *review* of his book, whether hostile or favorable, rather than a mass assault on every other book he has ever done. And as I understand the remarks of our *Saturday Review* friend, he said at the beginning that the book he was reviewing was a good book. I think he called it one of the most appealing books of our generation—ahem, ahem, here he cleared his throat, low growls began to rumble from his diaphragm, smoke began to issue from his nostrils and he surged forward to the attack—an attack which by the way, an author has no chance of defending himself against unless he resorts to what seems to me the very unwise and ineffectual practice of writing a letter in reply, which of course gives the other fellow a chance to write a letter in reply to this, and so on, I suppose, ad infinitum, save that the man who has been attacked in this way and who answers in this way, is always in the undefended position, controls none of the means of publication and must yield to the attacker the privilege of delivering the final volley. Is it worth it?

And in this case at least, it seems to me that it doesn't matter enough. I do think this, and I suppose this is the most sensible way of looking at these matters in the end: I think you will find, if you have not found out already, that one of the pleasantest occupations of a great many people in this world is to shoot down a whole regiment of wooden soldiers, and then return triumphant from the wars, saying, "we have met the enemy and they are ours." This kind of warrior does exist. It is very comforting of course, to create a straw figure of your enemy and then shoot it full of holes, but it is not a very substantial victory and in the long run means nothing. . . .

As you say, there are far too many people who will seize the opportunity of making a review of a book about the introduction of plumbing into Venezuela the basis for vituperations of all the works and words and creations of any novelist, playwright, poet or historian whom they do not like. But I have been pretty well through the mill now; I guess I'll get a lot more of it before I'm done, but at any rate it doesn't come exactly as a surprise. I have found out that a man who writes anything, no matter what it is, or where he gets it published, whether in *Scribner's Magazine* or in book form or in the Oregon Fur Traders' Quarterly, lays himself open to almost any form of attack or personal abuse known. It is not only the erstwhile friends and neighbors of his native town, benevolent old ladies and Christian deacons who will threaten him with tar and feathering, lynch law or shooting at sight if he ever comes back home, but he must be prepared also to receive letters carrying tirades of abuse from young one-eyed boys from Bethlehem, Pa., expectant mothers in Wichita, Kan., the parents of pure young girls from Tulsa, Okla., who have just come back home from Miss Burkewell's finishing school, bringing with them a copy of his accursed book, to every other form of execration and abuse imaginable. Moreover, as you yourself should know by now, if the aspiring young author has any illusions concerning the temperate, reasonable and coolly impartial tone in which the matter of book-reviewing and literary criticism is carried on, it won't take him long to have this pleasant daydream kicked out of him. Under the guise of high-toned criticism and impartial literary judgment, he must be prepared to hear himself described as a manic depressive, a pathological item of the specialist in criminal psychology, a half-wit, or the grandson of Wordsworth's idiot boy, the bird that fouls its nest, a defiler of the temple of religion, a political reactionary, or a dangerous red, or a traitor to his country.

I have lived through it all, I have known it all, I have had it all happen to me, and although, as you may infer from this letter, I am not yet exactly resigned to it, in a state of philosophic benevolence, I am at least a little prepared for it and not google-eyed with astonishment when it happens. Nevertheless, I thank you for your letter. But I suppose things like these will always happen; they seem to be baser elements of the human animal.

Only the other day in fact, I was reading a review that appeared in one of the higher toned English journals a hundred years or more ago, shortly after the publication of some of William Wordsworth's best poetry. The review begins somewhat as follows: "It is now apparent that young Mr. Wordsworth's malady is incurable. We had hoped for a while that the disease might be checked and controlled before it spread to dangerous proportions, but since it is evident that this is now impossible, we can only do what we can to prevent the malady from spreading farther, etc. etc. etc."

Don't these words have a familiar ring to you? Haven't you read them in one form or another a thousand times or more? Aren't they still being written by thousands of squirts who palm off their own hatred and venom under the guise of critical inquiry? So why worry about it too much? All we can hope for is to make things a little better. Personally, I have no panacea to use against dishonesty, injustice or hatred, masking behind a specious guise of critical utterance. These things have always been in nature and I suppose they always will be, but I do think that letters and efforts such as yours tend at all times to make things a little better, to direct things a little more in the direction of justice; and in addition, it is, of course, one of the most warming and heartening things that can happen to a man to know that anyone feels deeply enough about his work to feel indignant when he thinks that work has been unfairly dealt with. So thanks again for writing me and also for writing *them.*

Let me hear from you sometime when you are not too busy and of course, come to see me if you come to New York. I've got started on another book and have been blazing out manuscript at the rate of three thousand words a day for several weeks now. I don't know yet what will come of it, but it looks as if I may have dug in and got ahold and that I shall probably be here through the summer. Meanwhile, until I see you, with warm thanks again and all good wishes.

The following letter to Henry Seidel Canby was written in reply to a note from him which said: "If I had been on the Pulitzer Prize Committee there would have been only one question in my mind:—whether to vote for Ellen Glasgow's long established and (by then) unrecognized talent; or for your 'Of Time and the River' as the one real exhibition of new and original power of the year."

To HENRY SEIDEL CANBY

865 First Avenue
New York, N.Y.
May 7, 1936

Dear Henry:

Thanks for your letter. It is very kind and generous of you to feel the way you do and I appreciate it, but honestly, I didn't feel badly about not getting the Pulitzer award. It really didn't occur to me very seriously that I might get it and I have only the best and most cheerful good wishes in the world towards all the winners save that, like you, I should also like to see Miss Glasgow's long and impressive career fittingly recognized.

As for myself, I have been pretty fortunate during the past year. I don't need a prize and I can even see how getting one might be a very bad thing for me at the present time. The main thing is I am back at work. I did over five thousand words on Monday and I hope to get in another big day to-day. But thanks again for your kind words. I deeply value them, and send my regards to you and Marion.[1] I hope to see you again soon.

Peter Monro Jack had favorably reviewed three of Wolfe's books in the New York Times: Of Time and the River *in the March 10, 1935 issue;* From Death to Morning *in the November 24, 1935, issue; and* The Story of a Novel *in the May 3, 1936, issue. As a result of this last review he had received a letter from an unknown woman which listed, in implied protest, various episodes dealing with sex in* Look Homeward, Angel. *He therefore had forwarded it to Wolfe.*

To PETER MONRO JACK

865 First Avenue
New York, N.Y.

May 18, 1936

Dear Jack:

I came back to New York just last night after a short holiday and found your letter with the enclosed clippings from our lady friend. It is amazing, isn't it? If it were the first time this kind of thing had happened, I wouldn't believe it, but it is simply astonishing the number of people there are running around loose in this broad land who apparently spend a large part of their time in concocting this kind of thing.

There was one man in Brooklyn a few years ago, perhaps he has died a peaceful and merciful death since then, but I doubt it; anyway, I was enjoying life in Paris one fine day in May, five or six years ago after the publication of "Look Homeward Angel," when a great fat letter arrived in an envelope about eight inches long and a half inch thick. I opened it with considerable hope, thinking that some benevolent old

[1] Mrs. Canby.

gentleman or wealthy old maid had mentioned me handsomely in their will. Instead, I found twenty-eight pages of close type, which began as follows: "Dear sir: I have just finished a hasty reading of your interesting novel, 'Look Homeward, Angel.' Permit me however, to point out to you a few errors in grammar, spelling, punctuation, construction, usage, idiom, etc., which I jotted down as I was skimming through the book." There followed a staggering and appalling list of my alleged grammatical errors. I felt that I could never hold up my head again and look the world in the face, that I was ruined, done for, ditched. And in somewhat this frame of mind, I wrote the editor at Scribners who had helped me with the proof reading and asked him how in God's name, we had ever let proof go through our hands which was as full of shocking errors as apparently this one was. He wrote back and told me not to take it quite so seriously. The man, he said, who wrote the letter was noted for this kind of thing: in fact, very few authors of recent years had escaped his devilish scrutiny—even old Galsworthy was one of his victims.

This lady's interest however, seems to be somewhat more moral than grammatical. I should think that the inside of a person's mind who remembers entirely out of their context and often falsely and inadequately sentences such as those which she has quoted, would not be a very pretty thing to look at. About the other items, which she sent you, they were apparently concerning her own literary efforts, and I don't know what to say. I wish I had kept a collection of these things. All of them were astonishing, and the sum total of them perhaps indicate something appalling, I am not quite sure what, except that I doubt that any other country in the world can produce quite so many of this type of crack-pot as we can. . . .

Jack, I have tried to think of a way of thanking you without thanking you, but there seems to be none. I want to tell you how deeply I appreciated your wonderful review of my little book [1] in The New York Times. It set me up tremendously. I have had a great many letters from people who have read it and who all felt good about it. And all I can tell you is that I shall try to live deserving of some of the things you said. Anyway, I am back at work again.

"Of Time and the River," by the way, seems to have gone well in Germany. I found a great batch of press cuttings when I got back here last night and a letter from the publisher saying there had been a great deal of excitement about the book and that although it costs more than $5.00, in German editions, and was just out in April, they had already sold more than twelve hundred copies and that there were indications

[1] The Story of a Novel.

that the sale would pick up. The amount of space they gave it in their reviews was really surprising. There were two and three page articles about it and although my German limps heavily, I have read enough to judge that the reviews are extremely favorable. The publisher earnestly assures me that by some kind of international legerdemain which I can't quite follow, I will be able to get my money, and I hope he is right about it. I don't like to be too coarsely commercial about these things, but it is rather tough to have to sweat away for years at a book and then to get nothing from it. I am, of course very glad if my book has had a good reception in Germany, but there is so much hatred against the country here in New York at present that I doubt if it would do me any good if the news got out.

This is all for the present, and much too long a letter to inflict you with. I will call you up in a few days and then if you and Jane[2] have a free evening, perhaps we can all get together as we did before. Meanwhile, with all good wishes,

The following letter was written to the wife of A. S. Frere (formerly A. S. Frere-Reeves), who had sent Wolfe some photographs which she had taken of him during a visit to New York earlier that spring.

To PATRICIA FRERE

865 First Avenue
New York, N.Y.

May 19, 1936

Dear Pat:

I was delighted to get the photographs, and even though I shouldn't say so, they are awfully good, aren't they? I know now that the way to get a good photograph in America is to have friends from England come and make them.

What you say about your place at Aldington makes me very homesick. I will never forget the day I came there with Frere from the channel boat, just after two or three wretched weeks in Paris. I felt better right away and kept on feeling better from that time on.

Last year this time I was in Germany and this year I have just come back from Pennsylvania, where my father was born. It is perfectly glorious country. I wish you and Frere could come here sometime in the

---

[2] Mrs. Jack.

Spring or in the Autumn: there is so much I would like to show you, even within a few hours of New York. I suppose when you think of Pennsylvania, you think of places like Philadelphia or Pittsburgh, but it is really one of the most beautiful states in the Union. It has lovely mountains and a lovely rolling, undulating landscape, and in the country of the Pennsylvania Dutch, great red barns that dominate the landscape exactly as they should, like powerful and comfortable bulls. It has the most lavish and fertile farms I have ever seen. A lot of the people still believe in witches and witchcraft, and the barns have signs and symbols painted on them to scare off the devils. Perhaps you can come sometime in May or October. The young Spring wheat was just coming up. It is the greenest thing on earth, and then there were enormous sweeps of ploughed bronze earth and lovely woods just beginning to come out good. I went almost a thousand miles in five days, travelling back roads most of the way. The whole thing was simply magnificent and the variety of it is astonishing: hills, mountains, a perfect river called the Delaware that cuts through the most magnificent gap, and all the farm lands, the tiny little Pennsylvania Dutch villages.

I wish you and Frere could come here at some time of the year when you could see some of these things. Most American people, of course, never do. They get in their cars on Sundays and go out from New York on great crowded concrete highways and roar along with a million others, past filling stations and hot dog stands. But it is a nice country, if I do say so myself. And there are some wonderful things to be seen here, and some day I should like to show them to you and Frere.

I am back at work again—whenever I begin to moan and groan about working, I think of your father [1] and shut up and try to get started again—and this time I hope to do something good.

Please come back and see us again when you can. Meanwhile, with thanks again for the pictures and love to you and Frere,

On May 11, 1936, Margaret Roberts had written Wolfe for the first time since their estrangement because of Look Homeward, Angel, *saying: "I have written because I suppose that being actually in New York, the scene of your struggles and triumphs, my mind has gone back, first to the boy I loved, and next, to the eagerness with which I read your letters detailing the progress of your book—back to joy in seeing you grow; back, too, to the tide of misery caused to us by what you did to us—as you say in* Of Time and the River, *'it's all there.' I have not changed in thinking that the wounding was needless . . . I am not so dumb as not to believe that an artist has a right to get his*

[1] Edgar Wallace.

material where he pleases and twist it as he pleases, but I maintain that he has no right to twist or invent, making a pen-picture, and then write under it the name of a living person [1]. . . ."

The following was Wolfe's reply. Perhaps he was afraid of becoming involved in an argument about Look Homeward, Angel, *or perhaps he was simply too busy working: in any case, he did not see the Robertses until May, 1937, when he returned to Asheville.*

To MARGARET ROBERTS

865 First Avenue
New York, N.Y.

May 20, 1936

Dear Mrs. Roberts:

I had hoped to answer your letter sooner, but I was just on the point of going away for a few days' vacation when I received it and I decided to wait until I came back. I have been working hard and got pretty tired. I find that you reach a point in writing when you cannot go on farther: no matter how much the heart and soul may want to, the body and brain will not respond. So I went down to Pennsylvania for a few days. . . . I wonder if you know the state? It is one of the most beautiful places I have ever seen. It has almost every variety of landscape and the finest farms in the world. I went with a friend, we avoided main highways as much as we could and drove along back country roads. We drove a thousand miles in four days and saw some astonishing and beautiful things in the country of the Pennsylvania Dutch. . . . Everything in that part of the country has an air of thrift and of tidiness, of solid and prosperous substance. In the city here, you see such shocking contrasts of wealth and poverty, and often you hear such sad and tragic stories of human suffering and injustice and oppression. Going out to a place like the country I have just come from restores your faith, not only in nature but in man.

We got as far as York Springs, the little village a few miles from Gettysburg near which my father was born. I went out to the little country graveyard where his father and mother and a good many of his people are buried, and talked to a lot of people who remembered them all, and visited some relatives of mine who live in York Springs.[1]

Isn't the beauty of this country simply astonishing? I had never seen

[1] Copyright, 1956, by The Estate of Margaret Roberts.

[1] His first cousin Edgar E. Wolf, the son of Gilbert John Wolf, and his mother and his wife. The Pennsylvania branch of the family has always spelled their name without the final e.

the West until last summer, and I remembered that you and Mr. Roberts lived there for some time. I loved the West; I felt instantly at home the minute I got off the train in Colorado. The people were wonderful to me: there is something so spacious and free and generous in this hospitality. I had just come from Denmark. You must admit that from Denmark to New Mexico at one jump is a pretty large order. It was a wonderfully valuable and informing experience that seemed to crystallize things I have been feeling and thinking about America and Europe for years now. I wish I could see you and tell you about it.

I am back at work now. It is going to be another very long, hard pull. I am already beginning to be haunted by nightmares at night. I am probably in for several thousand hours of hell and anguish, of almost losing hope utterly, and swearing I'll never write another word and so on, but it seems to have to be done in this way and I have never found any way of avoiding it. I am both fascinated and terrified by this new book.[2] It is a thing which has been going in my mind for years and it is not one of the books that have been announced. It is a much more objective book than any I have yet written. Sometimes I am appalled by my own undertaking, and doubt that I can do it.

The best friend I have in the world, who is also the best editor this country has produced, and who has never been wrong in his judgment yet, told me at once, when I described the book to him, . . . by all means to do it at once with all my might. I think it is a good thing for several reasons. In the first place, if I succeed, it will meet the objections which some of the critics have posed about my being an autobiographical writer. In the second place, I think that one of the things that is likely to happen to the artist when he gets a little older, is that he may tend to become cautious and conservative and to stick to the thing which he has learned or is learning to do. There is a good deal to be said for this, but I do think it is a pity if a man is to lose the enthusiastic eagerness, the desire to experiment and find out new ways, the fearlessness of conception and effort which he has in his twenties. I don't want to lose it and my friend tells me I never will, and that there is no question about my being able to do this thing if I see it through. I wish you knew him, his name is Maxwell Perkins. He is not only a wonderful friend, he is also a great man and a great person with the finest qualities of character, spirit, and intelligence I have ever known. He has often asked me about you and I know he would like to meet you.

This last year has been a very extraordinary one. I have seen some wonderful things and met a great many people. I took too much time

---

[2] *The Vision of Spangler's Paul* which finally became *The Web and the Rock* and *You Can't Go Home Again.*

away from work, but I was desperately tired and had in fact been writing steadily for almost five years, and I have found that a man's energy and the way he uses his talent is like a reservoir: when it gets depleted, you have got to let it fill up again. Well, I think it is full again, full to overflowing. I hope and believe that I may have learned something from all the mistakes and errors of the past and that I will be able to work hereafter without quite so much useless waste and confusion and agony of spirit. I don't think by any means that I can wholly avoid these things yet, but I do think you learn something from every piece of work you do and that every piece of work you do adds something to your stature, increases the power and maturity of your experience, and helps you to use your talent with greater certainty. . . .

I am sorry you didn't see Mabel when you came through Washington, I know she will be disappointed when I tell her you couldn't find her. Yes, I think they did have their telephone taken out, but they are still living there. They have had a terribly hard time and she has suffered a great deal, but somehow, I always believe that she has it in her to pull herself together in a time of crisis or necessity and meet the situation no matter how hard or bitter. Mr. Wheaton, as you know, is a fine man in many ways. He has devotion and loyalty and great staunchness of character, but I think—and this of course is confidential—that he is a most tragic individual case of the effects of this tragic depression. I am sometimes accused by the Communist writers here in New York, of lacking what they call "social consciousness" and of not showing in my writing sufficient resentment towards the present system. Well, there are several answers to that. When I am told that I do not appreciate or understand the lot of the worker, I remember and am proud to remember that I am the son of a stonecutter, that I come from people in Pennsylvania and in the hills of Western North Carolina who have had to work hard and long for two hundred years or more by the sweat of their brow, the strength of their hands, to earn their daily bread. I am not talking of the more prosperous members of the family whom you may have known in Asheville, yet even they, my mother's brothers and my mother herself, knew poverty and want in their childhood in the years after the Civil War, and my father worked all of his life. So I think you will agree with me there is no particular reason for me to be very much impressed by the assertions of young gentlemen calling themselves Communists, whose fathers provide them with a comfortable allowance which enables them to indulge their political fancies without knowing a great deal about some of the things or people of whom they write.

What I am really telling you, and I think you agree with me in your own feeling, is that by instinct, by inheritance, by every natural sympathy and affection of my life, my whole spirit and feeling is irresistibly on the side of the working class, against the cruelty, the injustice, the corrupt and infamous privilege of great wealth, against the shocking excess and wrong of the present system, the evidences of which are horribly apparent I think, to anybody who lives here in New York and keeps his eyes open. I think that the whole thing has got to be changed, and I'll do everything within the province of my energy or talent to change it for the better, if I can, but I am not a Communist, and I believe that the artist who makes his art the vehicle for political dogma and intolerant propaganda is a lost man. I think almost every great poet and every great writer who ever wrote and whose works we all love and treasure has been on the side of the oppressed, the suffering, the confused and lost and stricken of the earth. Do you know of a single exception to this? But really isn't this just another way of saying that every great man or any good man is on the side of life, and although I am myself the son of a working man, I go so far as to say that an artist's interest, first and always, has got to be in life itself, and not in a special kind of life. His devotion, his compassion, his talent has got to be used for man and for the enrichment of man's estate and not for just one class or sect of man. Finally, I think that insofar as any artist would turn against a man because that man is rich or would have no understanding or tolerance of the lot of a man who belongs to a certain class, the artist who would feel this way is by just this much a smaller man than he should be.

To get back to Wheaton. I think he has been crushed by the catastrophe of recent years. Furthermore, although I never had much feeling one way or another about great corporations until this thing happened, I think the way he was treated by the great corporation that employed him after he had given his life, his strength, his youth and all his best energies since his fourteenth year, was simply damnable and I for one do not propose to sit around silent and acquiescent in a society where such a situation exists and where such things happen. Wheaton knows how to do nothing except to sell cash registers. His father died when he was a child and it was up to him to contribute to the support of his mother and his sister without delay. He left school at the age of thirteen or fourteen, went into the cash register factory, learned the business and finally became an agent as you knew him in Asheville. Now he is no longer a young man, he has been in poor health for many years, his reserve of physical strength and energy is very short, and he was kicked out ruthlessly, brutally, and without notice by the employers to whom he had given his life and who for thirty years or more had profited by his efforts. I suppose the cold-blooded answer to this would be that he profited too, and that he was paid well for his services, and that when the period of his usefulness waned as far as the company was concerned, they owed him nothing more, they were free to dismiss him as they chose. I say to hell with all such reasoning; it is probably in accord with the ruthless code of business procedure, but it is not in accord with human life, with human justice, with human decency, do you think so? . . .

In the face of this situation, it has been up to Mabel to keep the whole thing going, to keep body and soul together for both of them. Frankly, I think she has done amazingly well. The whole thing has been a terrible blow to her, the loss of everything they owned, the uprooting of her whole life in Asheville where, as you know, she knew everyone, and to which she was so much attached. I don't think she has ever gotten over it; for her it was really almost like being sent into exile in Siberia. She has cracked under the strain time and again, but she has always pulled herself together and kept things going. She is running, as you know, a kind of lodging house in Washington . . . Of course the strain, the anxiety of this kind of life on a person of her temperament is terrific: furthermore, as you know, in spite of her railings and tirades against this or that, she would give anyone, as the saying goes, the shirt off her back, if she thought someone needed it. As a result, she is constantly being victimized by unscrupulous and dishonest people who will stay in her place for months and then go away without paying her any of the money they owe her. So many of the other people with little gray lives and no particular color or personality of their own, will swarm about a person like Mabel as flies swarm about a sugar bowl, feed upon her vitality, use up her time and exhaust her energy. Of course, I suppose this cannot be helped: she is the kind of person who gives herself out as naturally as the sun shines, and I don't think this will ever change. But it has been a severe strain. . . . Anyway, they are still there in Washington; the address is 920 17th Street, N.W., and I know if you are in Washington she would be delighted to see you. . . .

I did not mean to write you so long a letter. But I was so glad to hear from you after all these years. I want to see you and Mr. Roberts. If you want to talk to me about some of the things you speak about in your letter, I will talk to you about them, if you think it will make for clarification and better understanding, but if it causes greater pain and confusion in the lives or hearts of anyone, I'd rather not say anything. I do believe from your letter that you want to see me again and all I can say sincerely and honestly is that that means a great deal to me. About so many other things—could I just say this: that I know I have done things that I ought not to have done, and left undone things that

I should have done, but that my hope and faith is that I grow a little in knowledge and experience and in understanding all the time, and that I shall, accordingly, do better in the future. I am digging in here for a great burst of work and may not pause for a week or two, but I shall call you up and hope you will be able to arrange a time for meeting, and perhaps you can also meet Mr. Perkins, if you feel like it.

Meanwhile, thanks again for your letter and with all good wishes to all of you,

To A. S. FRERE-REEVES

865 First Avenue
New York, N.Y.

May 28, 1936

Dear Frere:

I am glad you want to do "The Story of a Novel" in England.[1] I don't suppose the book will have any great sale over there, but I am glad you are doing it just the same. The ten percent royalty that you mention, upon the basis of a 3/7 book, is satisfactory to me and you may take this letter as confirming my agreement. I talked to Max about it over the phone a few minutes ago. He, too, was glad that you were going to do the book and I think he said he had already sent you a sheet quotation you asked for. . . .

To-day, I believe, that little ferry boat of yours, the "Queen Mary" is starting her dash across the Atlantic. There is great excitement and interest about it here, great pieces about it in the papers this morning. I suppose a goodly gathering will be at hand to cheer her as she comes in, provided New York harbor is big enough to get her in. I read the usual statements from officials of the line to the captain, etc. to the effect that they were not out to break any records, etc. which means, I suppose, they are not trying to get more than forty knots an hour out of her.

The big German zep, "the Hindenburg," has been flying back and forth over New York, star-like, recently with appalling frequency. If this kind of thing keeps up, our tired business men will be spending a weekend in London before long. I feel like a tired business man myself at present, and wish I were going back in the "Queen Mary" to pay you all a visit. I have dug into work, however, the last month or two, have done a tremendous amount of writing, and think I will keep at it until I get something accomplished.

[1] *The Story of a Novel* was published in England by Heinemann on November 9, 1936.

The Boyd matter, thank God, seems to be finished. The lawyers are still haggling over terms of the agreement, but the main argument seems to be settled. I finally gave her $500., for which she signs an agreement relinquishing all claims to everything except "Look Homeward, Angel," about which, of course, there never had been any argument . . . In addition, they told me she was hard up. I gave her $150 as a present. Of course, the whole thing was outrageous. It has caused me a year of worry, trouble, bother of consulting lawyers, digging up old letters and reading about myself in Mr. Winchell's column, and about one thousand dollars of actual expense by the time I am finished; but I suppose this is the best way out of it. At any rate, this present agreement pays her off, saves me the additional expense and worry of a court trial, and leaves me completely free for the future. Now that it is over I feel sorry for the woman and wonder why she did it. . . . As it is, there has been a year of wrangling, threats, conferences between lawyers, and I suppose from letters which she wrote Max and things I have heard elsewhere, a great deal of bitterness and bad feeling; and now that it is over, I wonder how much good it has done her. I am afraid there won't be much left after her lawyer gets through taking out his share. Anyway I am free of that particular bit of trouble. There are others, of course. It seems that once you get started on them, there always are.

Well, I am going to try to buckle down to work now and get something done. Some of the English reviews of the book of stories [2] seemed awfully good to me. I hope you managed to sell a few copies. Well, we may come through yet. I am back at work. One year of so-called success has not killed me; and if anyone has as much vitality as I, he stands a fair chance of surviving. They will be howling for my blood before long —in fact, there are blood-thirsty growlings now—but I think if I can keep on working, I will be all right.

Write me when you get a chance. Meanwhile, with all good wishes to you and Pat, and the people at Heinemann's,

The following letter was written to Heinz Ledig, now Heinz Ledig-Rowohlt, who is the son of Ernst Rowohlt and the editor at Rowohlt Verlag most closely concerned with Wolfe's books. At this time, Rowohlt was thinking of publishing The Story of a Novel *in Germany. This was finally decided against, but parts of the book were serialized in the November, 1936, issue of* Die Neue Rundschau.

[2] *From Death to Morning* had been published in England on March 16, 1936.

To HEINZ LEDIG

865 First Avenue
New York, N.Y.

June 10, 1936

Dear Heinz:

Mr. Wheelock sent me this morning a translation of your letter to
him, in which you ask for photographs, copies of "The Story of a Novel,"
and other material. I am delighted to know that you are interested in
"The Story of a Novel," and hope that you may find it possible to publish
it in Germany, although of course the demand for such a book will
probably be quite limited. . . .

I am glad to know that there will be no great difficulty in sending
me the royalties from my books. I think you understand very well that I
am not trying to make hard terms or hold you up. As you know, I am
not a business man, but an artist. It is rather hard, however, to have
to work the way I have to work and then to get no financial return whatever. I have to earn my living through what I write. There is no one
in the world who helps me and I do not want help, anyway. During
the past year I have turned down offers to go to Hollywood and write
for the movies, offers to go on lecture tours, etc., which would have
paid me a great many thousand dollars, a great deal more than I will
ever earn from writing, and I'll turn them all down, simply in order
to do the work I really want to do. I have the utmost sympathy for the
difficulties of your position, and I think I understand something of the
complicated nature of international publishing arrangements at the
present time. I certainly do not intend to add to your difficulties if I
can help it, and I am delighted to know that you want to publish a
book of stories.[1] I do want to ask you this final question and I will try
to cause you no further delay about the contract. I have never haggled
with anyone yet about royalties, but I do want to ask you if you think
it is absolutely unreasonable and impossible to restore to me the original
royalty of 10%, which you gave me for "Look Homeward, Angel." You
may remember that this royalty was cut to 7½% in the contract that
Ernst [2] gave me for "Of Time and the River." It was presented to me,
as you know, that the reason for this reduction in royalty was that
the size of the book made the cost of production very high and that [it]
would furthermore necessitate a price for the book that would make its
sale in large quantities doubtful. For these reasons, of course. I con-

[1] *From Death to Morning* was published by Rowohlt in 1937.
[2] Ernst Rowohlt.

sented, but I wonder if these reasons still apply to a book of such moderate length as the book of stories. Of course, I don't know how long my future books are going to be—some of them will certainly be quite long and others, I hope, will conform more to average proportions —but I don't think my royalty should be cut, unless there is some valid reason concerning production costs, sales, etc. What do you think? It doesn't seem to me that I am being unreasonable here and I wish you'd let me know right away how you feel about it.

I do think that, in fairness to myself, as time goes on I ought to try to be a little more business-like. I am not a money-making kind of man; I have no idea how to make a deliberate popular appeal to the writing public; I am really trying to get something out of myself as well as I can and, as time goes on, I hope to do better work, work of which I can be proud and I can feel represents the best and finest use of my talent. Feeling this way, it is not very likely that I will ever become a huge popular success. I was very fortunate with "Of Time and the River." The book had a good sale over here—over 40,000 copies—but you must remember that when I published it I had not published a book for over five years: I owed my publisher a great deal of money, which of course had to be paid back out of the profits of "Of Time and the River," and during the past year since I came back here I have been hounded, worried, and tormented . . . by almost every kind of parasite. . . .

I am learning many things about the world, dear Heinz, some of them not very pretty ones, but I have not lost faith in people. I have met many fine and honorable people as well as all those other ones—some day I shall put it all in a book. I am beginning to do so now, and really I think it may be a very extraordinary book, even though I do say so myself. I want to tell you something about it in a minute; but to finish the other matter about the contract for "From Death to Morning": I have told you some of these unhappy experiences of the past year just in order to let you understand that I am really not rolling in money, that I have very little left and that people hereabouts show an amazing talent for taking money away from me as fast as I can make it. I know that I have got to earn my living and support myself with what I write, so it has occurred to me during the last few months, as a result of all these unhappy experiences, that perhaps I have the right to be a little more businesslike in the matter of contracts and royalty arrangements than I have been in the past. You know me, we have been together, we have talked together, we have had some wonderful times together, and I think you will understand I would never take a business advantage of anyone or ask anyone to give me more than was my due; so please just try to understand the questions I have raised about the contract in the

spirit in which I ask them and then don't hesitate for a moment, don't
be afraid, to give me your frank and honest opinion right away.

Now, before I close, I want to tell you something about my new
book. . . . Briefly—I can't tell you much about it now but the general
conception of the book is this: it is not one of the books that have been
announced as part of [the] "Of Time and the River" series, it is by far
the most objective book I have ever written, although of course, like
anything that is any good, it comes right out of my own experience,
from everything I may have learned or found out during the course
of my life. If I succeed in it, I want it to be a kind of tremendous fable,
a kind of legend composed of all the materials of experience. The
general idea, so far as I can tell you here in the limits of a letter, is
the idea that so many of the great men of the past, each in his own
way, has used as the fundamental idea of his book. That idea as I
conceive it is the story of a good man abroad in the world—shall we say
the naturally innocent man, the man who sets out in life with his own
vision of what life is going to be like, what men and women are going
to be like, what he is going to find, and then the story of what he really
finds. It seems to me that this is the idea behind "Don Quixote," behind
"The Pickwick Papers," behind "Candide," behind "Gulliver," and even
it seems to me behind such works as "Faust" and "Wilhelm Meister." I
am putting everything into this book of mine. Of course it has got to
be the book of an American, since I am an American. Parts of it are
going to be savage, parts fantastic, parts extravagant and grotesque, and
some of it very coarse and very bawdy and, I think, wonderfully comical
and funny; and of course I also want the book to be full of faith and
poetry and loveliness and my own vision of life and of America. I know
it sounds like a tremendous order, but Perkins says he knows I can do
it, so I have taken the plunge. If I succeed, it ought to be a wonderfully
exciting and interesting book to read. It will be another tremendously
long book—God knows how long—longer perhaps even than "Of Time
and the River," but I am not worrying about that at present.

I have begun to go again like a locomotive, and I am trying to get it
out of me, down on paper, as fast as I can. I don't know how to write yet
but I think I am learning something all the time. I think I am becoming
more sure and certain of my purpose and I believe I will avoid some of
the mistakes and pitfalls in this book that I fell into in the other.

Tentatively, I have called the book "The Vision of Spangler's Paul." It
has a sub-title:

"The Story of His Birth, His Life,
His Going To and Fro in the Earth,

His Walking Up and Down in It:
His Vision also of the Lost, the
Never-Found, the Ever-Here America.

With an Introduction
by
A Friend."

The following quotation, which I have taken from "War and Peace" and which I intend to use as a kind of legend at the beginning of the book, may make it a little clearer:

"Prince Andrei . . . turned away . . . His heart was
heavy and full of melancholy. It was all so
strange, so unlike what he had anticipated."

I don't know whether you want to say anything about this in Germany or not. Scribners have not announced it here as yet. It is generally assumed, of course, that I am at work at present upon one of the remaining books of the "Of Time and the River" cycle, and we are going to surprise them. There is a tendency here among the critics to assume the kind of writing I do best is what they call "autobiographical," and we hope through this book to show them once and for all that this is not true. Perkins says I can create freely, invent and tell a story as well as anyone in the country—and I hope he is right. The "Of Time and the River" books, of course, are still waiting. I can't lose them because so much of them is already written, and really I think I am doing a very wise thing now to do this completely new kind of book at a time in my life when I am still young and full of energy and have the enthusiasm and the fire to do it.

I had not meant to write you such a long letter, and hope it has not fatigued you. Please write me at once in answer to my enquiries about the contract and give me all the news you have about "Von Zeit und Strom." Meanwhile, with all good wishes to you and Ernst, and Mrs. Rowohlt and all the other people at the Verlag,

The following letter was written in reply to one from Kent Roberts Green-field which praised Of Time and the River *and protested against Bernard De Voto's article, "Genius Is Not Enough," in* The Saturday Review of Literature. *Greenfield was at this time Professor of Modern European History and Chairman of the Department of History at Johns Hopkins University, and is now Chief Historian of the Department of the Army and General Editor of* The U.S. Army in World War II.

Wolfe never mailed the letter but kept it in his own files. Evidently the

*legal difficulties to which he refers in his postscript had made him extra-
cautious.*

To KENT ROBERTS GREENFIELD

865 First Avenue
New York, N.Y.

June 23, 1936

Dear Mr. Greenfield:

Your letter came this morning. It was sent over from Scribners, and
before I begin my day's work I want to write a few lines to tell you that
it is one of the best letters I ever got, and thank you for writing it. It makes
me very proud to know that anyone feels the way you do about something
I have done. I don't know whether I can yet live up to what you say in
your letter, but it makes me want to try. I don't think anything else in
the world—any other reward—can be as valuable and precious to the
artist as the kind of reward he gets from a letter like that.

As to Mr. De Voto, I think I feel equal to all the De Votos in the world
—and I guess there are a good many—after reading your letter. No, that
piece of his in *The Saturday Review* didn't hurt me, and didn't worry me.
My hide is by no means as tough as it should be, I still take all these things
pretty hard, and so far from pretending to ignore reviews, I think I'd stay
up all night to get the morning paper if I knew an old lady was going to
write me up or down in the *Akron Ohio Bee:* but I have been through
a good bit of it in the last seven years since I wrote my first book and
the people in my home town informed me that the Vigilantes would be
out with tar and feathers if I ever came back. At that time I took it pretty
hard and I think I sweat as much blood in living the book backwards and
forwards and every other way after I had written it as I had spent writing
it, but I have been pounded on enough since to find out that these matters
are not as desperate as I thought them, and what has been most valuable, I
think I have really found out for myself that it is the truth that hurts. So
usually when something gets in under my hide and hurts, I have found
there is a measure of truth in it, and in the end have usually managed to
derive some profit from it. The De Voto thing didn't hurt me—it just made
me mad. I am not pretending to laugh it off, nor to dismiss utterly everything the man says as false, but I am grateful to you for thinking that
the total amount of what he said was false because, even though I do say
so myself, I thought so too. Truth has a thousand faces, hasn't it? For my
own part, I have never been convinced that Pilate jested. It is a strange
perplexing thing, isn't it, to see how a number of true things can be put
together to frame a lie? I think Mr. De Voto used the subtle method of

indirection in his previous remarks about me, but so far as I know, this is the first time my carcass has been delivered into his custody for a central onslaught. . . .

A year ago . . . this same man began a review of a book in *The Saturday Review of Literature* with another virulent attack upon my work.[1] This is all very well, I suppose, except that the book he was reviewing was not my book and had no possible connection with my book that I can see, except that Mr. De Voto thought that the book was a better book than mine, that the author was a better writer, all of which may be true. I think the author of the book in question, which was "Roll River" by James Boyd, is certainly a very fine artist, and the book a very fine book. The author is one of the finest people I know and a friend of mine. I told him later that if I was going to be taken for a ride, I'd rather be taken for a ride on his account than for almost anyone I know. But aside from the fact that De Voto thought that Jim Boyd's book was better than mine and that both books are for the most part about America (which, by the way, is a fairly extensive place, isn't it?) and that the word "River" occurred in both titles, it seemed to me that the reviewer exercised considerable ingenuity in getting me into the picture at all.

Well, what is there to say? . . . I still take it hard; I still get mad about it; but if there is anything true in what they say, I have got a good memory and I don't forget it; and if what they say is not true, then how can a man be hurt by it? I have had some pretty bad times when I didn't think what I did was any good, I was inclined to agree with almost anyone who felt the same way, but I have held on to this conviction, and in fact the conviction grows stronger as I go along—I genuinely believe that if a thing has something good in it, the good in it is indestructible and will be saved, no matter what anyone says or does; and if a thing has no good in it, it cannot be saved, no matter what anyone says or does, and if it is no good, the man who did it ought not to want it to be saved, anyway. Furthermore, if what a man does is good, and another man is false about it and goes on record with his falseness, then it seems to me there is no need of doing anything to him. He has done the job himself. Usually I find when our hides get nailed up to the wall, we not only supply the hide, but we also supply the hammer and the nails. It is our own job. Well, I

[1] De Voto's review of *Roll River* by James Boyd in the April 27, 1935, issue of *The Saturday Review* began as follows: "There are a number of ways to write that undefined entity, the American novel. Mr. Wolfe has recently exhibited one way: to print the word 'America' ten thousand times, to depict young Faustus as a victim of manic-depressive insanity, to fill the stage with Mardi Gras grotesques who suffer from compulsion neuroses and walk on stilts and always speak as if firing by battery, to look at everything through the lens of an infantile regression . . . and to fluff up the material of fiction, one part, with ten parts of bastard blank verse ecstasy."

am not going on record myself as saying what I do is either good or bad. I suppose if I didn't really feel there was some good in it, it would be hard to keep on working as I do, in hope of betterment, and I think that the conviction that I have just expressed to you is something more than a mere desire to believe. I believe it is a fact that the good thing can't be hurt, and that knowledge helps me a lot as I go on writing. As you can see from this letter, I don't pretend that I didn't take the De Voto thing seriously. . . . I   am not trying to laugh it off, but it didn't hurt me, it doesn't rankle, I have no vengeful feelings; in the end I may even get some good from it. The main thing is I am working like a horse and I don't see how anyone, not even Mr. De Voto, is going to do anything about that.

The other thing is that I think I will learn a little, slowly, all the time; that I hope to profit by my own mistakes and errors of the past and grow in wisdom, in power, in maturity; and that whenever I get a letter like the one you wrote me, it makes me want to exert every energy of my life and talent to do so. So thanks again. Your letter meant a lot to me, and I want you to know that it did and that I am deeply and sincerely grateful. Please forgive me for writing you such a long one in return—as you may have heard, brevity is not one of my most noticeable gifts; but maybe I can do something about that too. Anyway, I'm going to try. Meanwhile, with all best wishes and thanks,

Dear Mr. Greenfield: I wrote this *ten* (10) days ago, and just failed to mail it. The letter, of course, is written to *you*—and is confidential. It does not matter about De Voto, Canby, or the rest—but I am just through with legal trouble and not through with it yet—they have got all my money, all my manuscripts—so don't give this to them.

The following letter to Hamilton Basso was called forth by Basso's article, "Thomas Wolfe," in the June 24, 1936, issue of The New Republic. *Basso is the author of* Beauregard, Courthouse Square, Days Before Lent, Wine of the Country, Sun in Capricorn, The Greenroom, Mainstream, The View from Pompey's Head, *etc., and had first known Wolfe through Scribners. His article on Wolfe ended with the following words: "In* The Story of a Novel *he . . . says, in effect, . . . that he is going to renounce his former ways and try to do better in the future. This is all very fine but I like the declaration contained in a letter I had from him much better. 'I have something I'd like you to see but it ain't wrote good yet. You wait—I'll learn 'em!' And learn 'em I think he will."*

To HAMILTON BASSO

865 First Avenue
New York, N.Y.

June 24, 1936

Dear Ham:

I want to write you a few lines just to thank you for writing that fine piece in the New Republic. People began to call me up and tell me about it last week, so I went out and got a copy at once. The whole thing has warmed me up more than I can possibly tell you, and if I was fired with the ambition to "learn 'em" before, that piece of yours has set off a bonfire. It is pretty hard for me to say everything to you I would like to say, because I am not only the recipient of the honor but in a way the subject of it; but I do think that I learned something valuable from the piece, in addition to the happiness it gave me. I think you hit the nail on the head with what you said about the railroad trains in my books and how the feeling of space is probably derived from the childhood of a man who grew up in the confinement of a mountain town. That is the truth. As I look back on it now, my whole childhood was haunted by the ringing of train bells at night, the sound of whistles fading away somewhere along the French Broad River, the sound of a train going away down the river towards Knoxville and the West. I certainly hope you are right when you say that I have been able to take materials of localized regional experience and give them communication of universal interest. That is what I should like to do. I suppose that is what every writer, with his own special material, would like to do.

I won't say any more about it, but just let me thank you again and tell you how grateful I am, and assure you that an experience of that kind can do nothing but good to a writer and his work.

"Of Time and the River," by the way, seems to be a crashing success—critically at any rate—in Germany and all through Central Europe. The reviews have been coming in by the dozens. Some of them are of immense length—six and eight-paged articles in magazines and critical reviews, column after column in newspapers. They say tremendous things. I can't believe it when I read them. The publishers write me that there has been a great deal of excitement and some of the most magnificent reviews they have ever seen. Well, I am vulgarly commercial enough to hope that some of this excitement gets translated in the sales and that the Germans find a way of getting the money out of the country to me, which they say they will be able to do.

The German Book Society, by the way, after the publication of "Of

Time and the River" have arranged with the publisher to bring out an edition of 8,000 of "Look Homeward, Angel" for their subscribers, and, although I get only a very small royalty for this, the total result ought to be good, because they may succeed in creating additional interest in "Of Time and the River." "Of Time and the River" is awfully expensive in the German edition—that's the main difficulty. They've done a grand job of printing and publishing and translating. It comes out in two volumes and costs fourteen marks, which is over five dollars at the present rate of exchange, and I understand is more than a good many working men in Germany can afford to pay for a suit of clothes. I am a little sorry it costs so much, but I suppose they did the best they could.

I am back at work again, after a year which has had everything packed into it. Everything happened to me except homicide, and I am knocking on wood. The experience of having a so-called literary success in these here parts has put some gray hairs in my head, but on the whole, I am glad I went through it and found out what it was like. Parts of it have been pleasant, parts of it grotesque, fantastical, unbelievable, and rip-roaringly, side-splittingly funny. Unfortunately, the bird who gets crowned with a brick-bat while he is smelling a rose, or is kicked in the seat of the pants when he bends over to retrieve a cigar butt is at the moment not in a favorable position for appreciating the humor of the situation, so my laughter has at times been deferred and I have got a notion that it will take years for my full enjoyment of the experience to mature. Maybe I will be like those Englishmen I have heard about whose parents told them jokes when they were young, in order that they might have a good time in their old age. I can't tell you the whole story here, it's too long and fantastic, but if we can ever get together over a jug or a bottle, I think I can give you an earful. . . . Until a year ago, I still had some lingering and naive belief that law and the courts had some connection with human justice. . . . It is, of course, not true. . . . I finally got my suit settled out of court, and I suppose you might say I won out. I simply paid a sum of money, a very trifling sum compared to the amount they were asking, in order not to be hounded, worried and tormented by the thing any more. Also I have a complete and everlasting quittance "from the beginning of the world to these presents," henceforth and forever. All in all, by the time I get through paying my lawyer, the whole miserable business will cost me a thousand dollars, to say nothing of all the other costs of time and care. . . . Well, maybe the experience has been worth a thousand dollars. It has introduced me to that fantastical never-never land of the law, and provided me with the material some day of some bawdy chapters, a half-dozen characters that most people wouldn't believe existed outside of the pages of Dickens.

I have also had innocent-looking little boys, the sons of gentle Irish families . . . with whom I was friendly, and who all solemnly assured me their friendship for me was beyond price and of undying fidelity—I have had their youngest and most holy representative walk off with my manuscripts, sell them in various parts of the country, . . . and solemnly assure himself that he had done nothing wrong in the eyes of God and of his own moral conscience, no matter what mistaken notions men might have about his conduct.[1] Some of the rest of it, the other things that have happened, is unprintable here. . . . If you give me a chance I'll confide it to you some day; but it is simply astounding to discover how many people there are in this world, and particularly in this City, who exist through some form of parasitism, who seem to have no life of their own, except as they hope to get their life from someone else—whether by taking someone's money, or his property, or his labor; or what is even more costly—trying to take his life, somehow to attach themselves to it, to stake a claim on it, chain themselves to it, somehow to get their own life from it. Well, I went through it all in less than a year. I don't suppose I am wholly out of it yet, but I am out as far as my knowledge of the situation is concerned. I was getting pretty desperate, stewing around in this huge web, trying to get myself out of this snarled tangle of dishonest scheming, insane congeries of parasites, crack-pots and hysteric neurots—most of the latter, I am afraid, being women, who write the longest, frequentest and most incredible letters.

Well, I had to get back to work, or I think I would have gone crazy myself, and I finally found, as old Daniel Webster said, that the way to resumption was to resume. Accordingly, about three months ago, I decided that if the worst came to the worst, they could take what money I had —I could probably make more money; they could steal my manuscripts— I could certainly write more manuscripts; but if they took away from me the concentration and the power of work, they had taken everything I had. In other words, I said "To Hell with it" and got busy, and since then I have

---

[1] Wolfe's legal difficulties about his manuscripts had begun in February, 1936. He had given several pieces of manuscript to a young man with the understanding that he would act as his agent in selling them in the rare book and manuscript market, but after various difficulties and misunderstandings they had quarrelled on February 10, and Wolfe had dismissed him as his agent. However, the young man claimed that his agency for Wolfe could not be terminated unless by mutual consent, had refused to return the unsold manuscripts still in his possession, and had threatened to sue Wolfe unless he paid him $1900 for services rendered and for commission on the appraised value of the unsold manuscript of *Of Time and the River*. Wolfe finally instituted suit against him on September 14, 1936, to reclaim his manuscripts and obtain an accounting of all transactions made by the young man as his agent. After many difficulties, the case was finally tried before Vice-Chancellor Kayes in Jersey City on February 8, 1939, and the judgment awarded to Wolfe.

written between 150,000 and 200,000 words. It is a new book—I can't tell you much about it here, but it is a pretty daring venture, completely different from anything I have ever attempted. . . . It came boiling to the surface all of a sudden. Of course, it had been stewing around down there for a great many years, but when I told Max about it, he snapped his fingers and said at once, "Do it, and do it now." He then told me that he had known for years that I would have to write such a book, it was unquestionably a thing I ought to do now at this period of my life. He told me to get busy on it at once. I expressed doubts to him whether I would be able to achieve such a book, and he told me there was no doubt at all, if I would go at it and keep going, that I could undoubtedly do it and that I was the only person who could.

Well, I hope the doctor is right. He has been right most of the time so far, and I hope he is right now. At any rate, we are both excited about it, and I am going to "let 'er rip." God knows how long a job it is going to be, a very long one I am afraid, but if I can do something good, if I have begun to learn to use myself, at least, it doesn't matter how long it will be.

Well, Ham, you see what happens when I set out to write a few lines. I hope you haven't sprouted whiskers while reading this letter. I just wanted to thank you for having written that fine piece and to tell you how grateful I am for it, but I managed to throw in a large part of the American continent as well. Please write me when you get a chance and tell me what you are doing. Is there any chance of your getting up here this summer? I may go away for a short vacation, but so far as I know, I will be here plugging away most of the time. I hope it won't be too long before we see each other again. Meanwhile, with love to all,

The following letter was written in answer to one from William Polk who was at this time President of the North Carolina Literary and Historical Association, and had invited Wolfe to speak at its meeting in Raleigh in December.

To WILLIAM T. POLK

865 First Avenue
New York, N.Y.

June 25, 1936

Dear Bill:

Thanks for your letter. Honestly, it is good to know that at least I have a chance of coming home without being escorted to the outskirts of the town by the local Vigilantes and told never to darken their public square again. Seriously, I am very much interested in your invitation and would like to ask for a little more information. Just how historical does a speaker have to be when he talks to the Historical Association? Knowing you as I do, I know you'll gladly give me all the rope I need to hang myself; but if I spoke, would I be tongue-tied with terror every time I looked around and found the cold and fishy eye of the experts upon me? As I mounted to my peroration, would I be checked in my full flight by the presence of J. G. de Roulhac Hamilton,[1] his face fixed on me with a very fishy look, as though to say: "If this be history, I'm a horse"?

Now you also say something about speaking for a half-hour. Think fast, Captain; as you may have heard, brevity is not one of my notable gifts, although I try to do a little better all the time. I made a speech out in Colorado last summer. It took me the first fifteen minutes to quit stuttering, hemming and hawing, and fiddling around for an opening, but after that, if I do say so as shouldn't, I did the job up pretty brown. Prepare yourself for a shock—it took one hour and forty minutes, and they were hanging on by their eyelids when I finished. Really, though, if I had to face an audience of the home folks, I'd probably be ten times as scared as I was out there, and God knows that was bad enough until I got going. If I got going in Raleigh, the Lord knows what would happen—I've got too much to tell them—in fact when I think of it, I feel like that fellow in the Leacock Nonsense Novel who jumped on his horse and went galloping off madly in all directions.

I wonder if we couldn't do this: I know you want to get your program settled as soon as possible, but couldn't you write me and tell me a little more about the thing, the kind of gathering I would have to face and the kind of talk they usually get? The real gist of the thing is simply this: I still procrastinate, I think—I try to avoid making engagements six months in advance because they weigh upon me and seem to put a sort of check and restraint upon me, to tie me down much more than I should let them. So far as I know, I'll be right here in New York in December, plugging away at a new book. If I am still here and it was still possible for me to come to Raleigh, I'd probably do it. I know this is no good to you, because you have a definite program and you've got to plan it now. There wouldn't be any chance of this, would there—it sounds pretty brazen, I know, but all this is confidential between you and me and I know you won't expose my effrontery—but could you go ahead and get another speaker, announce him and put him on your program, and if you like, say that I didn't know definitely whether I would be able to be present at the

---

[1] J. G. De Roulhac Hamilton had been Professor of History at the University of North Carolina when Wolfe and Polk were students there.

date of the meeting? Then, without my feeling obligated, if I was here and you wanted me to come down, perhaps I could come and without interfering with the other fellow, just attend the meeting or get up and talk for ten or fifteen minutes. I know it all sounds cockeyed, and perhaps it is against all the rules of the old noblesse. If it is, don't give me away. The main thing, really, Bill, at the present time is that I have got started working on another big piece of work. I finally got myself clear of the whole snarl of engagements and complications that were beginning to get me this last year, and am back at work, and I want to keep at it as hard as I can without feeling that I am tied down by anything outside.

I think this makes it plain, and I know you will understand. Just write me and tell me how you feel about it, and if what I suggest is in any way possible. Meanwhile, with all good wishes and regards,

P.S. Dear Bill: Rereading your letter, I notice you say there is a chance of your being in New York in July. I live at this address: 865 First Avenue, and the phone number is Plaza 3 4583. . . . I've got a fine place here, fourteen stories up, overlooking the East River, about three sticks of dilapidated furniture, but one of the coolest places and one of the most wonderful views in New York. Let's get together.

XIII

THE BEGINNING OF THE BREAK WITH SCRIBNERS
1936–1937

The reasons for Wolfe's growing conviction that he must leave Scribners were too many and too complex to describe adequately here. However, the most obvious of them was the necessity to disprove the implication made by Bernard De Voto in "Genius Is Not Enough" that Wolfe could not write his books without the help of "Mr. Perkins and the assembly-line at Scribners."

Another reason was Wolfe's realization that Perkins was opposed to his writing about Scribners and the people who worked there. The following letter was probably written because of Perkins' unfavorable reaction to Wolfe's story, "No More Rivers," which described characters similar to those of various editors at Scribners. At Wolfe's request, Miss Nowell had shown this to Perkins and one of his associates, neither of whom objected to his having written about themselves. However, Perkins told Miss Nowell that if Wolfe "wrote up" certain things which he had told him in confidence about his associates, he felt it would be his duty to resign from the firm.

This letter is the first of the many, approaching other publishers, which Wolfe wrote and never mailed, and it was accompanied by a list of firms to whom he evidently thought of sending it: "Macmillan, Harper, Viking, W. W. Norton, Little Brown, Houghton Mifflin, Longmans Green, Dodd Mead, Doubleday Doran, Harcourt Brace"—and also by a rough draft of an announcement which he may have momentarily considered sending out: "An author, Thomas Wolfe, being now without a publisher, would like to have a publisher."

"To ALL PUBLISHERS"
[Other than Scribners]

865 First Avenue
New York, N.Y.

July 15, 1936

To All Publishers:
Gentlemen:
I am the author of four published works, of which two are novels, one

a volume of stories, and one a very short book about the experiences a writer has in beginning to write.

All of these books have been published by the same publishing house, with whom my relations have been satisfactory.

At the present time, I am engaged upon the composition of a long book, and since I have no obligation, whether personal, financial, contractual, moral, or of any kind soever to any firm of publishers, I am writing to inquire if you are interested in this book, and if so, upon what conditions, terms, proposals, and contractual alliances you are so interested. I am going abroad next week and should appreciate an answer now.

In all fairness, I should here state that I think my physical resources, which have been generous, are at the present moment depleted; that the kind of vital concentration which has at times in the past attended the act of creation, is diffused. But I think these things may come back, and that there is a possibility I will do better work than I have yet done. That, of course, is my hope: and despite this present depletion of my energies, I am of cheerful mood and resolute temper, and I have strong hopes that the energy and power of such talents as I have will return.

Frankly—with no disparagement of any connection I have had—I feel the need of a new beginning in my creative life.

[THE LETTER BREAKS OFF HERE]

To FRED W. WOLFE

865 First Avenue
New York, N.Y.

July 23, 1936

Dear Fred:

I am sailing in a few hours, and this letter has to be a lot shorter than I wanted it to be. Anyway I am sending you back your check.[1] I do not need any money, I won't take any money from you, so please just forget about it and make me happy. Everything is fine. This is the cheapest trip I have ever made, in fact am standing a chance to make some money out of it before I am through. The North German Lloyd has given me a credit of $150.00, or more than half my tourist class passage, on my promise to write them a piece or two for their travel magazine, and my German publishers have cabled me that they will have one thousand marks waiting for me when the boat docks at Bremerhaven. In addition to this, a couple

---

[1] During the depression, Wolfe had sent his brother Fred money to help support certain members of the family. The check was in repayment of the balance of this.

of New York magazines have promised to take travel pieces if I will write them, so you see I am sitting pretty.

I shall write you a long letter on the boat or after I get there, telling you about recent events. I have been pretty upset and wrought up by some of these things that happened in the last few months, and I was pretty badly disappointed when Mabel did not show up the other night. I had come in from the country. Mr. Perkins had driven me eight miles to make a train through the worst rain and lightning storm I have ever seen, and I guess I got a little worked up when I got home and found a telegram from her saying she was not coming after all. It is all right, of course. It is no one's fault. Everything is fine as far as the family is concerned. I was just a little excited. I had absolutely no right to call you up, but you were the first one I thought of. I wanted to get it off my chest to you, so please forget about it now. You will make me a lot happier if you do.

I hope to be back here about August 20th, and if I do, I would like to come to Asheville for a few days, but don't say anything about it. They were pretty mad at me a few years ago but I understand they feel a bit better about it now, but I do not want either one thing or the other. If I come home I would like to come as I always did without any fuss.

I have been reading about the murder [2] in the papers the last few days. It has been on the front page of all the papers here and it may amuse you to know that one of the New York papers called Mr. Perkins up and wanted to have an interview with me upon the ground that I come from Asheville. I told him to tell them that so far as this particular crime was concerned, my alibi was secure, that they did not have a thing on me. Anyway, of course I would not give such an interview. The folks back home have had hard feelings in the past. I hope most of it is over now, but I would not do anything to cause any more trouble if I could help it.

This is all for the present. Just please forget about the whole blow-up. I am sorry I bothered you. I was just tired and worried, but everything is fine with me. I am going to be better than ever when I come back. I shall try to write Mama on the boat to-night. Anyway, I shall write you all in a few days.

[2] This probably refers to the murder of a Miss Helen Clevenger, of Staten Island, in an Asheville hotel. A Negro employee of the hotel was executed for the crime the following December.

To ROBERT RAYNOLDS

[Postcard: Blick auf Rathaus und Frauen Kirche, München]

Munich

July 29, 1936

This is a wonderful city. I looked at the Durers, the Cranachs and the Grunewalds in Alte Pinothek again to-day for first time in eight years. It seems very natural to be back.

To MAXWELL E. PERKINS

[Postcard: Pariser Platz mit Blick auf Tiergarten u. Reichstag: Berlin]

Berlin

August 7, 1936

Dear Max: I've had a good trip—seen all my old friends here and lots of new people—also newspaper interviews, drawings, etc. The town is crowded with Olympic visitors, and the Germans have done their job beautifully. Wonderfully cool and clean after New York.

To MAXWELL E. PERKINS

[Postcard: Alpbach mit Galtenberg]

Alpbach
Austrian Tirol

August 26, 1936

I climbed that big mountain (the highest one) yesterday. It damned near finished me but I did it. It makes all your New England mountains look like toad-stools. This is a beautiful country and good people. On my way back to Munich and Berlin to-day. Will sail next week if I can get passage.

To ROBERT RAYNOLDS

[Postcard: Pariser Platz und Brandenburger Tor: Berlin]

Berlin

September 4, 1936

Dear Bob: All this was massed with flags and packed with people during the Olympiad but that hysteria is past now—but the Partie Tag will be here in a day or two.

To ELIZABETH NOWELL
[Postcard: München, Feldherrnhalle]

Munich

September 8, 1936

This is a wonderful city—after eight years it seems very natural and friendly. Frankly, after what happened last year, I don't very much want to come "home"—but I will.

To MAXWELL E. PERKINS
[Postcard: Die Wachtruppe am Brandenburger Tor, Berlin]

Berlin

September, 1936

We can never learn to march like these boys—and it looks as if they're about ready to go again.

To ELIZABETH NOWELL
[Postcard: La Place de l'Opera, Paris]

Paris

September 16, 1936

Dear Miss Nowell: Don't do anything about the stories until I get back. I've written a good piece [1] over here—I'm afraid it may mean that I can't come back to the place where I am liked best and have the most friends, but I've decided to publish it. So wait on me.

To FRED W. WOLFE

865 First Avenue
New York, N.Y.

October 5, 1936

Dear Fred:

Just a note to tell you I am back at this address, that I have your note saying you may be up here about the middle of October and that I am

[1] "I Have a Thing to Tell You" which was published in the March 10, 17, and 24, 1937, issues of *The New Republic*, and appears in *You Can't Go Home Again* on pages 634–640, 641–651, 655, 663–704.

delighted. I have two rooms here, with two comfortable couches in one and a good double bed in the other, so the matter of putting you up with me is easy. Will you just do this, please?—because, as you know, our family is not noted for punctuality: let me know *exactly* when you are coming, so that I can be here, and there will be no confusion or mistake in our meeting arrangements. . . . Meanwhile, until I hear from you, with love to all and best wishes,

P.S. There is a poor, desperate, unhappy man staying at the Grove Park Inn.[1] He is a man of great talent but he is throwing it away on drink and worry over his misfortunes. Perkins thought if Mama went to see him and talked to him, it might do some good—to tell him that at the age of forty he is at his prime and has nothing to worry about if he will just take hold again and begin to work. His name, I forgot to say, is Scott Fitzgerald, and a New York paper has just published a miserable interview with him— it was a lousy trick, a rotten . . . piece of journalism, going to see a man in that condition, gaining his confidence, and then betraying him. I my- self have suffered at the hands of these rats, and I know what they can do. But I don't know whether it's a good idea for Mama to see him—in his condition, he might resent it and think we were sorry for him, etc.—so better wait until I write again.

The following brief note to Irma Wyckoff was evidently written after Wolfe's renewed quarrel with Perkins about the latter's unfavorable reaction to the story "No More Rivers." When Wolfe had gone abroad in July, he had told Miss Nowell to delete some of the material which Perkins had objected to in that story, and to show it to him again. Perkins had then written her on August 26, saying: "I think this story could do no one any harm now—except perhaps Thomas Wolfe. I do not think it is up to his usual level." Wolfe had quarrelled with Perkins about this on his return to New York in October, charging him with personal bias and with attempting to censor what he wrote. From this time forth, he avoided going to Scribners almost entirely, instead of coming in every few days to talk to Perkins and pick up his mail, as he had been in the habit of doing for the past seven years. His note to Miss Wyckoff was, in effect, a notice of his determination to stay away, since he had been living at 865 First Avenue since October, 1935, and she knew his address very well.

[1] In Asheville.

To IRMA WYCKOFF

New York City
October 5, 1936

Dear Miss Wyckoff:

From now on, will you please address and send any mail that may come for me to 865 First Avenue, New York City?

The following letter was in reply to one from Elsa C. Serfling, editor of the North German Lloyd magazine, The Seven Seas, who had written Wolfe to remind him that he owed that magazine two short articles on Germany in return for the $150 credit he had received on his passage on the Bremen. In accordance with Wolfe's suggestion made here, the North German Lloyd accepted his check for $150 in place of the articles.

To ELSA C. SERFLING

865 First Avenue
New York, N.Y.
October 12, 1936

Dear Miss Serfling:

Please excuse me for my delay in answering you. I did not get your letter of September 9th, sent to the American Embassy in Berlin, until I returned home, where it was forwarded on to me. I got back about two weeks ago.

I wanted to write you while I was in Germany, telling you I'd changed my plans for sailing and would not be home as early as I had originally planned, but my whole summer, from the time I left here until I returned, was so crowded with events—seeing the Olympics, meeting old friends again, talking to my German publisher about contracts, going to the Tyrol, and becoming intensely interested in what is going on in Europe to-day—that I did not have much time for writing letters.

Now about the proposed articles for *The Seven Seas*. First of all, I want to tell you how genuinely sorry I am for any delay or inconvenience I may have caused you. Then I ought to explain my present situation to you frankly, and ask you if you would kindly agree to what I am going to propose.

This was one of the most intriguing summers, one of the most extraordinary and interesting trips I've ever made. I am boiling with ideas and with plans for work. There is no question but that I got material, not only for three articles but for thirty, during the summer. The only difficulty that I contemplate in writing such articles as you suggest for *The Seven Seas Magazine* is this: everything I do, everything I create, comes from the whole texture of my experience—from everything I have seen, thought, felt or known. As I think of these proposed articles, I find it very difficult to isolate them from this whole fabric, to separate them from lives and events and feelings which would be proper and essential in a work of the imagination but which I feel would not only be improper but decidedly unwise in a series of travel articles for a travel magazine.

May I tell you that I have the deepest and most genuine affection for Germany, where I have spent some of the happiest and most fruitful months of my life, and for the German people, among whom I have some of the best and truest friends I know. For that very reason, above all others, I want to be scrupulous now not to abuse your own generosity or to make any commitments that would not be in full accordance with certain deep and earnest convictions of my own or with anything I might write or say hereafter.

I cannot go into detailed explanation here, but I leave it to your intuition to understand what is in my mind. Briefly, what I should like to do and what I hope you will understand and agree to is to send you a check for the one hundred and fifty dollars which you advanced me upon my passage as payment for the proposed articles, and so allow me to discharge my obligation in this way.

Believe me, I am sincerely sorry for any inconvenience or delay I may have caused you, but if you can understand my desire to settle our arrangement in this way, you will greatly relieve me and I shall be sincerely grateful for your consideration. Please write me as soon as you can.

Thea Voelcker, to whom the following letter was written, had met Wolfe in Berlin in the summer of 1936, when she had made a drawing of him to illustrate an interview for the Berliner Tageblatt. *Wolfe, at first, had disliked the drawing and said that it made him look "piglike," but he and Frau Voelcker evidently fell in love, later quarrelled, and finally made up. When he first came back to America that autumn, he announced that he was going to bring her to America and marry her, but they drifted apart. She is rumored to have committed suicide some years later, after another tragic love affair.*

The letters to her which appear in this volume were dictated by Wolfe to his secretary and found in carbon copies in his own files. If he wrote her more personally in longhand, those letters are now lost.

To THEA VOELCKER

865 First Avenue
New York, N.Y.

October 13, 1936

Dear Thea:

I am writing you just a short letter this morning to let you know I'm safely at home again and to thank you for your two letters and the wonderful book you sent me for my birthday.[1] I'll write you at greater length later on and I hope you'll be able to decipher my scrawl. I am having this letter typed so you shouldn't have much trouble with it.

I was wonderfully happy to get your letters. They are fine letters and very eloquent—especially the last one, which you wrote in English. In spite of your difficulties with a foreign language, you expressed yourself beautifully and I understood and valued everything you had to say.

I am back at work again and tremendously eager to plunge into the heart of it now. I think the trip this summer, and all I saw and learned, has done me a great deal of good. For one thing it took me far enough away from my work to give me the kind of detachment I needed. And although my conscious mind was busy with all the things and places I was seeing and the people I was meeting, I think my unconscious mind must have been busy at my book, because now that I am back, the whole plan, from first to last, has become clear to me, and I think I know exactly what I want to do. It is going to be a very long and tremendous piece of work and I suppose I shall feel defeated and desperate many times before I come to the end of it. But with the knowledge that I have the belief and friendship of a few people, including yourself, I think I can accomplish it.

There's so much I should like to tell you, but I think I'd better reserve that for another letter. Your birthday book is wonderful. It has in it some of the most magnificent heads I've ever seen. This is the Germany I love and believe in—the great Germany of the mind and heart and spirit. You are very good to say that my head belongs with these. I should be only too proud if it were true. I am very happy if you think so.

After the well-kept cleanliness of Berlin, Paris stank; and the French— well, they're still the French, aren't they? And they're forever with us. Yet I am glad there is a Paris and a France, and that we have the French. If we did not have them I think it would be necessary to invent them. I have always been a stranger there. I have lived and endured some of the most bitter and lonely times of my life among those little strange dark French-

[1] She had sent him a book called *Grosse Deutsche*, an illustrated catalogue of an exhibit of portraits of great Germans, saying that his head belonged with these.

men, who are only for themselves. But I am glad I have known them, too.
I have learned much from them, even though I can never be one of them.
And although every time I go, the old conflict begins again—that strange
mixture of like and dislike, of contempt and admiration, of disgust and
affection—although I am always glad to leave them—I should be sorry if
I could never come back again.

I came back on a French ship and, after the beautiful and well-run order
of the *Europa*, it seemed a rather haphazard and perilous experiment.
However, we got here. I am unjust, of course. I knew that we should get
here. I have no doubt but that they are really good and able seamen. But I
could never quite believe it. All Frenchmen on a ship look a little seasick
to me and I always remember the answer of one of our wits, who, when
asked why he always chose to travel on a French boat, instead of an English or a German one, replied, "Because on a French boat, if anything
happens, there's none of this damn nonsense about women and children
first."

I think you would have enjoyed the voyage, however. There was a
terrific hurricane raging up and down the whole American coast and it
caught us when we were three or four days from New York. The storm
lasted for two days. It was one of the most violent and savage storms I've
ever seen but if one did not get sick it was beautiful and magnificent also.
Most of the people were sick but I don't think you would have been. New
York also seemed very dirty, noisy and disorderly after the comparative
quiet and order of Berlin, but it was good to be back here too. We are
different from the French and, after all that I saw and felt this summer—
the feeling of pressure and of tension, the feeling that those tragic and
apparently incurable hatreds of Europe were going to explode at any
minute—it is good to be here where, whatever we lack, we still have space
to move in, freedom to expand.

I am still at my old apartment on First Avenue. I write you this looking
out my window on the fourteenth floor—looking out upon the river, a river
which is busy at almost every moment of the day with its wonderful and
thrilling traffic of boats, great and small: the busy little tugs, the great
barges, freighters and ships. We are now having our grand October
weather. This is the best part of our autumn, one of the best times of the
year. The air is clear and sharp and frosty, and out in the country the
trees are burning with flaming and magnificent colors, which I think you
do not have in Europe. You would like it here now.

This is all for the present. I shall write you later on and talk to you more
personally about the things you speak of in your letters. Meanwhile, with
all my sincerest and most affectionate greetings, with all good wishes to
you for happiness and success in all you do, I am, ever sincerely,

                              Your friend

P.S.: I shall never forget Alpbach. No matter what happens in the world, no matter what sorrow, strife or trouble we may go through, it will always be good to know that there is in the world a place like that quiet and enchanted Alpine valley.

To HAMILTON BASSO

865 First Avenue
New York, N.Y.

October 14, 1936

Dear Ham:

I was glad to get your letter and to hear what you were doing. I've been back here two or three weeks and have been expecting a copy of "Courthouse Square," but it hasn't yet arrived. I've been too busy to read the book news, so I don't know what date the publication is scheduled for. But I suppose Bill Weber will send me a copy when the time comes.

I had a wonderfully interesting trip this summer and I am glad I went. I did a good deal of travelling, saw a great many exciting things, met a lot of people, talked to a lot more and was able to get almost completely away from things back here. As a result, I was able to think the whole situation out clearly—the whole jam of trouble, law suits, interruptions, etc., that I got into last year—and make up my mind what I was going to do about it. And what was best of all, I think I got my book straight in my head—the whole plan of it from beginning to end. At any rate I've begun to work again.

Like you, I feel pretty bad about Scott. I wish something could be done about him, but I don't know what. I had thought of asking my mother to go round and see him, and also of asking some people I know, but I don't know how much good it would do. He might resent it, especially if he thought any one was trying to help him or felt sorry for him.

I don't know whether you saw the interview which appeared here in *The New York Evening Post*. It made me sick, and I felt and still feel that some one ought to do something about him. I told Max Perkins so. His attitude, of course, and the Scribner attitude, apparently, is that any attempt at answering a thing like this, or of denouncing such journalistic practice, only adds fuel to the flames and makes the situation worse than ever. I suppose there is a lot of truth in this but I wonder just how much longer we've got to sit by meekly and submissively in the world while the scavengers, the shysters, the traducers and the filth-purveyors of every sort are allowed to go their way unchecked. It almost makes me long for dear old Adolph and his S. S. men. They at least could put a stop to a good many of our own accepted forms of thugdom. Of course, in doing so they would establish another and much more powerful one of their own, and there's the rub.

As you say, it looks as if Scott were bent on committing professional suicide, but if a man in his present condition is determined to destroy himself, I think it is a vile and cowardly act on the part of other people to help him along in his intent. From what I have heard from Max, the interviewer got in to see Scott, played him up sympathetically with conversation, gained his confidence and let him spew the whole thing out—all about being lost, done for, defeated, unable to get back and, what was worst of all, all about Zelda being in the sanitarium and all the rest of the miserable business. From the very tone of the interview it was evident what condition Scott was in at the time, and that he could not have been fully aware of what he was saying. . . .

The whole thing was smeared all over the first page of the paper and, like your pal Sherwood,[1] I want to know why. I can't see what possible news value it has—what possible public service it can achieve—why the illness, alcoholism, mental ill health of a writer, together with the mental illness of his wife, is a matter that should be aired for the instruction of the American public. It was a cheap, sensational piece of journalism, and the thing that gets me sore is that I have met the man who owns the paper, and met his wife, and had dinner in their home, and they preened themselves upon their liberalism. His paper is forever attacking Hearst for his vicious and unprincipled methods, and now this great liberal, this spokesman of decent journalism, perpetrates a thing like this. As Perkins said, one of the bitter and disheartening things in life is to find out how many of these people who set themselves up as liberals, as champions of decent living, turn out in the end to be just as filthy a flock of vultures as the worst of them.

Well, the thing is done now, and there's no use talking about it any more. Like you, I want to do something for Scott but when I think about it I come up against a blank wall and end by thinking that maybe I'll give him a good swift kick and tell him, for God's sake, to come out of it. And, of course, I know that would do no good either. I was thinking of his career the other day and, in a way, it seems to me that his greatest misfortune in life has been that he was a child of fortune. Most of us stick around and plug ahead hoping that Lady Luck may hit us with a spare horseshoe. But Scott, at the beginning, had horseshoes rained on him by the whole damn cavalry. I think that this, in a way, unfitted him for what was to follow. He not only had one of the best breaks that any one ever had, he got a very tough break too. I hope that, in a way, I got a bit prepared for it after my experience with "Look Homeward, Angel."

[1] Sherwood Anderson.

Knowing what I did about the career of the book, how the entire population of my home town wanted to draw and quarter me, how eminent reviewers, such as Mr. Harry Hansen, headed their reviews with such master strokes of sarcasm as "Ah, Life, Life," [2] etc., how everybody asked if I could ever write another book and how quickly they began to say I never would—I say I was able to smile a trifle grimly a year ago after the publication of "Of Time and the River," when I read that my career had been a bed of roses from the beginning, that "Look Homeward, Angel" had been greeted with a hurricane of applause, that my path from that time on had been as smooth as velvet. I know what happened then. I think I know what is likely to happen to me now until I get another book done. It's not going to be easy to take. But it's not going to be quite the bitter and disillusioning experience that it was five or six years ago. You know, as well as I do, how quickly they can turn, how desperately hard it is to prevail, when they make up their minds about you.

I had that happen to me a year ago, when a volume of stories came out and I am certainly not bitter about the reception of the stories. I am not sore about it. I'm only telling you that most of the criticism was as the minds made up in advance saw it. The things they'd begun to go for me for in "Of Time and the River," were carried right over and plastered on my book of stories. The stories, it appeared, were not stories at all but sections that Max Perkins and I had scissored out of the manuscript of "Of Time and The River." There was a page or two which described the movement of a regiment of negroes through a pier at Newport News during the war, and the great Mr. Chamberlain, in his critique, inquired, "We have negroes here, negroes in the mass, a regiment of negroes. But where is Booker T. Washington, where is Joe Louis, where is Father Divine, etc.?" [3] Where indeed? Where, oh where? For that matter, where is the Queen of Sheba, where is Leonardo Da Vinci, where is Tiglath Pilezar? Gone with the wind, I suppose. The thing that made me tough, however, saved me from apoplectic strangulation, and, in fact, gave me a sort of haughty indifference, was the earnest and no doubt pigheaded belief shared in by Max Perkins and a few other people that the best single

[2] This was the title of Hansen's Review of *Look Homeward, Angel* in the October 26, 1929, issue of *The New York World.*

[3] John Chamberlain's review of *From Death to Morning* was in *The New York Times* on Friday, November 15, 1935. What it actually said was this: "In 'The Face of the War,' one sees the black troops, 'powerful big men, naive and wondering as children, incorrigibly unsuited to the military discipline.' But one does not see W. E. B. DuBois, or Abram Harris or Joe Louis, strongly marked individuals, marching by in the column of black troops. Yet the column must have contained men closer to DuBois or Harris or Joe Louis than to the generalized portrait that emerges from the Wolfe pages."

piece of writing, the truest, the most carefully planned, and in the end the most unassailable that I've ever done is in that book.[4] I'm not going to tell you what it is. Apparently, most of the critics didn't take the trouble to read it, and those that did, for the most part, dismissed it as chaotic, formless, a river of incondite and meaningless energy. Well, I'll stick to the piece and I'm willing to wait. I don't believe it's gone with the wind. I think the time will come when some one will really read it. So I don't feel bad about it or about the book.

Scott, I think, had a similar experience but a much more bitter one. My own feeling is that he never got justice from the critics for "Tender Is the Night." I admit deficiencies and weaknesses in the book, but I still think that he went deeper in the book and did better writing in it than in any of his previous books. But their minds, of course, were for the most part made up in advance. For years they've been saying that he would never write anything else and accordingly he suffered.

I still feel he has it in him to do fine work. I still feel something ought to be done about him and for him. But when he himself is so set against doing anything for himself, so bent, apparently, upon announcing, publishing and consummating his own ruin, who in the name of God can help him?

I did not mean this letter to be so long or take on such a melancholy hue. I wish I could be down there for a few days, to talk to you and see the mountains at this time.[5] I know how lovely they are. I'm afraid I can't make it at present, but will you do this for me, Ham? When you write me, and I hope it will be soon, will you tell me something about New Orleans, give me the names of a few people there? I've never gone around carrying letters of introduction. I promise not to bother your friends, but there is just a chance that during the winter I might get down there for a few days, and if I should I'd deeply appreciate any advice or information you could give me. So far as I'm concerned you are the greatest living authority on New Orleansiana.[6]

This is all, now. I pray for the success of "Courthouse Square." I know you have put your heart and your life in it. I know how deeply your integrity is involved in everything you do, and I hope that now you will get your true and fitting reward. It is bound to come sooner or later but I hope you get it while you still have the mischievous twinkle in your flashing eye.

Meanwhile, with love to you and the Missus, and to them thar hills,

[4] "The Web of Earth."

[5] Basso was living at Pisgah Forest, N.C.

[6] Basso was born and grew up in New Orleans, and began his career as a newspaper reporter there.

The following letter was in reply to a note from Jonathan Daniels inviting Wolfe to dinner when he came to Raleigh for the meeting of the Literary and Historical Association. Daniels had attended the University of North Carolina with Wolfe and been a member of The Carolina Playmakers with him, appearing in the cast of two of his early plays. He is now editor and part-owner of The Raleigh News and Observer, *and the author of* A Southerner Discovers The South, A Southerner Discovers New England, Tar Heels: A Portrait of North Carolina, Frontier on the Potomac, The Man of Independence, The End of Innocence, *etc.*

To JONATHAN DANIELS

865 First Avenue
New York, N.Y.
October 23, 1936

Dear Jonathan:

Thanks for your note. Bill Polk wrote and asked me if I could speak at the meeting of the State Literary and Historical Association, and I wrote him the other day and told him not to count on me as a speaker, because the chance of my being able to go to Raleigh is so uncertain, but that I would try to come just to see and talk with some of you again if I can make it. It is certainly one of the things I'd most like to do and, of course if I do, I shall be delighted to have dinner with you and Mrs. Daniels on December 4th. . . .

I have heard everywhere of the fine work you are doing with the *News and Observer*. Jim Boyd spoke to me about it last, and he said you were producing one of the finest newspapers in the country. I'm delighted to hear it. May I also take this belated opportunity of telling you how deeply I value the fine and generous notice that was given my work in the *News and Observer* a year or more ago, after "Of Time and the River" appeared. It was not only a notice which any one would have been proud and happy to receive, but of course I valued it all the more because it came from my own state. . . .

I went abroad this summer, mainly because I had royalties awaiting me in Germany and saw small prospect, in view of their present law against letting money get out of the country, of using my royalties unless I went there and spent them. So I did this. It was a good trip—a wonderfully exciting and interesting one but not always a happy one. I like Germany. It is a wonderful country. I like the German people, who have such magnificent qualities of fortitude, of indomitable effort and devotion. But I deeply fear that these grand qualities, all this devotion and fervor and self-sacrifice, has now been given to a misdirected purpose, a false ideal. Europe this summer was a volcano of poisonous and constricted hatreds which threatened to erupt at any moment. The great engines of war are ready, are on the rails, are being constantly enlarged and magnified, and it is hard to see how, if they continue in this way, they can control these tremendous machines they have created. It is good to be back home again and to feel that, whatever we may lack, we are free of these constricting national hatreds, that we still have space and air to move in.

I think you'd be surprised if you saw how politically-minded I've become. I've become enormously interested in politics for the first time in my life, not only in Europe, but even more here at home. I think what did the trick, more than anything else, was my trip across this summer on the *Europa.*

I travelled tourist class. My room-mate, an elderly liquor salesman of kindly and generous impulses, was a delightful travelling companion until he asked me who I was going to vote for. Very innocently, presuming that such matters could still be mentioned without the instant and complete severance of diplomatic relations, I answered, "Roosevelt." At that my erstwhile friend let out a squawk you could have heard on Sandy Hook, and from that time on there was no more peace or rest for me. He began to chase me around the boat. Wherever I went I could hear him pounding after me, like the Hound of Heaven, breathing stertorously and blowing hoarse and hot upon the back of my neck, panting out all the time that such an action as I proposed was nothing short of treason to my country, that the only means of salvation was to help elect that great American, that defender of the constitution and restorer of the system of free enterprise, Governor Langdon of Kansas. Still pounding ahead in my effort to escape, I paused long enough to look over my shoulder and suggest that it might not be a bad idea if he would learn how to spell and pronounce properly, before election day, the name of his hero.

After that I began to duck when I saw him coming, hid behind life boats, tried to look like a life preserver, etc., and finally, to my enormous relief, got invited up to first class, where I felt the story of my adventures might amuse my hosts. Not so. The moment that I told my little story and announced, innocently again, my dark electoral intention, the squawk that went up made the disturbance in tourist class sound like the cooing of a dove. Their boiled shirts began to roll right up their backs like window-shades. Maidenly necks that but a moment before were white and graceful as the swan's became instantly so distended with the energies of patriotic rage that diamond dog collars and ropes of pearls were snapped and sent flying like so many pieces of rock and string. I was informed that if I voted for this vile Communist, for this sinister Fascist, for this scheming and contriving Socialist, and his gang of co-conspirators, I had no longer any right to consider myself an American citizen. I was doing my share to help destroy the country, etc.

Well, the upshot of it was that the more they talked, the less I believed them. Seriously, it was astounding. I have never, so far as my own experience and observation is concerned, seen such bitterness of feeling, such distorted prejudice, such downright hatred as I saw among these people on the *Europa*, and as I have seen among other people in this class since then. If the election of November third were to be determined by the first class passenger list of a crack trans-Atlantic liner, I have little doubt what the result would be. But fortunately, it will not be determined there. As you know yourself, there are still a lot of us truck-drivers left in the world.

Anyway, I've got all het up over politics for the first time and I agree with Mr. Dodd, whom I'm sure your father knows, and who is our ambassador in Berlin. He is a historian, and he told me that he thought this was the most important national election that had been held in this country since 1860. I want to do something about it. In spite of all the mistakes that have been made, in spite of all the formidable and disquieting expenditure of money, the grievous errors that I believe few intelligent people would deny, I nevertheless feel the worst calamity that could happen [to] this country at the present time would be the election of a reactionary government, and that this present administration, whatever its errors of commission or omission may have been, has made the only decisive movement that has been made in the direction of social progress and social justice since the administrations of Woodrow Wilson.

So I want to take the stump. I want to write letters to the newspapers. I should particularly like to riddle the editorial columns of the *New York Herald Tribune* with cannister and grape. Except, what is the use of bringing your guns up and cutting loose upon a graveyard?

In your capacity as editor of the *News and Observer,* you must have read the editorial columns of a good many newspapers. Well, honestly, have you ever known the state of journalism to sink to such an abyss of imbecilic foolishness as it has in some of these papers in recent months? I can't believe it when I read it. Such irreconcilable things and systems and ideas as Communism, Fascism and Socialism are lumped together in one indiscriminate wad and hurled wildly in the direction of the President. The other night on the radio I heard a speaker accuse Mr. Roosevelt of all three of them in the same breath. About the only thing I have not yet heard him accused of is of plotting and conspiring with the King of England and Herr Hitler to restore the ex-Crown Prince of Germany and establish an autocratic monarchy. In the name of God have these people lost their reason utterly or do they have such contempt for the public intelligence, the understanding of the ordinary man, that they think he will swallow anything regardless of the meaning or implication, so long as they shout it loud and long enough?

Herr Hitler gets up one day and makes a speech in which he attacks the idea of democracy, and the *Herald-Tribune,* by some fantastic and unfathomable editorial process, converts Herr Hitler's attack upon democracy as an evidence and a warning of what Roosevelt will do. The next day some one in Russia answers Hitler's attack and this too is translated as an overwhelming evidence that the program and ideas of the Communists and of the President are identical. This morning the *Herald-Tribune* heads its alleged account of the President's recent tour through New England with this headline: "Roosevelt Trip in Connecticut Snarls Traffic." I think, considering all its implications and all that has gone before, this is the most astoundingly funny headline I've ever read. One sees the motored cavalcade of the New Deal making its sinister way through the New England states, causing automobiles to bump each other and innocent women and children to faint in the crowds that gathered. It is all, one gathers, part of a deep, dark and sinister conspiracy to undermine American institutions, to scrap the constitution and to stamp out the spirit of rugged individualism which we inherited from our forefathers.

These are strange and disquieting symptoms for me but perhaps I shall recover my normal temperature after November third. Meanwhile I am back at work again on a new book. It's all coming with a rush and, believe it or not, for several weeks now I've done more than 5000 words a day.

I didn't mean this letter to be so long, Jonathan, but it was good to hear from you and I suppose that, remembering some of the all-night sessions we all used to have at Chapel Hill, I couldn't resist temptation to let a little of it roll out on paper.

With the hope of seeing you all soon, and with best wishes for you and Mrs. Daniels,

XIV

THE BREAK WITH SCRIBNERS

1936–1937

In November, 1936, Wolfe's conviction that he must leave Scribners was heightened by a disagreement with them concerning the suit which was brought against him and them by Marjorie Dorman, William Samuel Dorman, Louise Dorman Leonard and Mary Roberta Dorman from whom Wolfe had rented his apartment at 40 Verandah Place, Brooklyn, in 1931, and who now claimed that they had been libelled by certain passages in "No Door" in From Death to Morning. *Scribners, and the attorney whom they had retained to represent themselves and Wolfe, were in favor of settling the suit, but Wolfe was violently opposed to settlement, although he finally unwillingly consented.*

The following rough draft fragments to Perkins and the note to Charles Scribner III were found in Wolfe's own files and never mailed. They may have been written at almost any time or times during 1936 or 1937, but because they contain similarities to other letters written to Perkins in November–December, 1936, they are included as of that date.

To MAXWELL E. PERKINS

[New York City]

[November or December, 1936?]

Dear Max:

I am writing to tell you that I have at last taken the step of communicating formally to other publishers the severance of my relations with Charles Scribner's Sons. It is true that no formal relation between us existed, and that both you and Charlie have told me I was free to go. But I think the relation existed in our minds at any rate, and for me—I believe for you, as well—it existed in the heart.

555

If any apprehensions concerning my letter to the publishers may exist in the minds of any of you—and I know they will not exist in yours—let me assure you at once that I spoke of my former publisher in such a way as left no doubt as to my own earnestness and sincerity, or as to my own belief in the integrity and [high capacity?] of your house. No one could read that letter without understanding that the necessity for this severance is a matter of deep and poignant regret to all of us.

I am sick and tired, but I believe that I shall rise again, as I have done before—I know that for a time now the world will say that you and I have fallen out, that the great sounding-board of rumor and malicious gossip that echoes round and round the granite walls of this little universe, the city, will frame its hundred little stories and all of them, as usual, will be false. I know that they will say this and that—well, *let* them say. That is honestly the way I feel now.

The editorial relation between us, which began, it seems to me, so hopefully, and for me so wonderfully, has now lost its initial substance. It has become a myth—and what is worse than that, an untrue myth—and it seems to me that both of us are victims of that myth. You know the terms of the myth well enough—it was venomously recorded by a man named De Voto in *The Saturday Review of Literature* during this past summer—and the terms of the myth are these: that I cannot write my books without your assistance, that there exists at Scribners an "assembly line" that must fit the great dismembered portions of my manuscript together into a semblance of unity, that I am unable to perform the functions of an artist for myself. How far from the truth these suppositions are, you know yourself better than anyone on earth. There are few men —certainly no man I have ever known—who is more sure of *purpose* than myself. There are very many men, of course, who are more sure of *means* —but that assurance, with such men, is just a small one—with me it is a hard and thorny one because my means must be my own.

I know you will not be uncandid enough to deny that these differences and misunderstandings have been profound and fundamental.

Plainly may I tell you that I think that looking like a plain man, you are not a plain man; that speaking like a simple man, you are not a simple man: that speaking in words and phrases that as time went on [indicated and assured me?] by their simplicity and [————?] directness, so that they seemed to be the very [charter?] of your soul, I do not now believe that they were so.

In fact, I now believe you are not a plain man—you are an un-plain man—I do not believe you are a simple man—you are an un-simple man —I do not believe your words. . . .

I impeach your virtues and your conduct: may I tell you frankly, plainly, that I do not believe they have achieved and maintained always the quality of [unconditioned innocence?], faith, good will, and simple and direct integrity that you have always claimed for them.

The fault, I think, is here: that having so much that belonged to humankind, you lacked—or you with-held—what makes us one. And therefore I renounce you, who have already, for so long a time, renounced me and got so safely, with no guilt or wrong, so freely rid of me.

And I am writing therefore now to tell you that I am, upon the date of these words, dissolving a relationship that does not exist, renouncing a contract that was never made, severing myself and of my own accord a bond of loyalty, devotion and self-sacrifice that existed solely, simply and entirely within my own mind, and to my own past grief of doubt, my present grief of sorrow, loss, and final understanding.

With infinite regret, my dear Max, with the deepest and most genuine sorrow, with an assurance—if you will generously accept it—of my friendship for yourself,

Faithfully and sincerely yours

I understand that you have been afraid that some day I might "write about" you— Well, you need not be afraid any longer. The day has come—and I am writing about you. Your fears have been realized—I think you will find that your fears, like most fears, have been exaggerated.

This is one of the saddest and most melancholy occasions of my life. To say now that I have "thought about" this thing, or "arrived at certain conclusions" would be ludicrous. I have not thought about the thing—I have sweat blood about it: I have carried it with me like a waking nightmare in the day time, and like a sleeping torment in the night. I have not "arrived" at my conclusions: I have come to them through every anguish that the brain, heart, nerves and soul of man can know—and I am *there* at last. I can't go on in this way: it is a matter of the most desperate uncertainty whether I can go on at all. For seven years I have been increasingly aware of the seepage of my talents, the diminution of my powers, the dilution of my force—and I can not go on.

I am therefore asking you to send me at once an unqualified and unequivocal statement to this effect: that I have discharged all debts and contractual obligations to the firm of Charles Scribner's Sons, and that I am no longer under any obligation to them, whether personal, financial, or contractual on my part.

I want you to make this statement in your own language, but according to the terms I have mentioned, if you think them just.

In the name of honesty and sincerity, I can write no more than here I have written: in the name of justice and of fairness you can, and will, write no less.

I beg and request you to send me at once, without intervention of personal conversations or telephone call, this letter that I am asking you to write.

TO CHARLES SCRIBNER III

[New York City]

[November or December, 1936?]

Dear Charles:

I have upon this present date written a letter to Maxwell Perkins in which I have told him that the firm of Charles Scribner's Sons are no longer, for any publication save those which have previously been published by Charles Scribner's Sons, my publisher. It is a painful and chastising experience to renounce an agreement that does not exist, an understanding for the future that, however undefined, was mine alone, and in my mind alone; but in order that there may be no misunderstanding of my purpose, or of the meaning of this letter, I do state here and now that you are no longer my publisher, that you will never again be my publisher for anything that I may ever write; that I hereby renounce, adjure, abrogate, deny and terminate any requests, claims, offers, inducements, obligations, commitments, or persuasions which you have made formerly, shall make now, or in the future make.

The following is the letter which Wolfe actually sent to Perkins in November, 1936.

To MAXWELL E. PERKINS

865 First Avenue
New York, N.Y.

November 12, 1936

Dear Max:

I think you should now write me a letter in which you explicitly state the nature of my relations with Charles Scribner's Sons. I think you ought to say that I have faithfully and honorably discharged all obligations to Charles Scribner's Sons, whether financial, personal or contractual, and that no further agreement or obligation of any sort exists between us.

I must tell you plainly now what you must know already, that, in view of all that has happened in the last year and a half, the differences of opinion and belief, the fundamental disagreements that we have discussed so openly, so frankly, and so passionately a thousand times, and which have brought about this unmistakable and grievous severance, I think you should have written this letter that I am asking you to write long before this. I am compelled by your failure to do so to ask you, in simple justice, to write it now.

I think it is unfair to put a man in a position where he is forced to deny an obligation that does not exist, to refuse an agreement that was never offered and never made. I think it is also unfair to try to exert, at no expense to oneself, such control of a man's future and his future work as will bring one profit if that man succeeds, and that absolves one from any commitments of any kind should he fail. I also think it is unfair that a man without income, with little money, and with no economic security against the future, who has time and again in the past refused offers and proposals that would have brought him comfort and security, should now, at a time when his reputation has been obscured and when there are no offers and little market for his work, be compelled to this last and sorrowful exercise of his fruitless devotion. And finally, I do not think that life is a game of chess, and if it were, I could not be a player.

I have nothing more to say here except to tell you that I am your friend and that my feeling toward you is unchanged.

For the full text of Perkins' three answers to this letter, see Editor to Author: The Letters of Maxwell E. Perkins, *pages 115–117. The first was a personal note dated November 17, in which Perkins merely promised to answer Wolfe's letter the following day, and added: "I never knew a soul with whom I felt I was in such fundamentally complete agreement as you. . . . I don't fully understand your letter, but I'll answer it as best I can. You must surely know, though, that any publisher would leap at the chance to publish you. . . . You have with us at present a balance of over $2,000, all but about $500. of which is overdue."*

The second was also a personal note dated November 18, enclosing a more formal business letter, and saying in part: "On my part there has been no 'severance.' I can't express certain kinds of feelings very comfortably, but you must realize what my feelings are toward you. . . . Your work has been the foremost interest in my life and I have never doubted for your future on any grounds except, at times, on those of your being able to control the vast mass of material you have accumulated and have to form into books. You seem to think I have tried to control you. I only did that when you asked my help and then I did the best I could. . . ."

The third, more formal letter was also dated November 18, and said in part: "You have faithfully and honorably discharged all obligations to us, and no further agreement of any sort exists between us with respect to the future. Our relations are simply those of a publisher who profoundly admires the work of an author and takes great pride in publishing whatever he may of that author's writing . . . We do not wholly understand parts of your letter, where you speak of us as putting you in a position of denying an obligation that does not exist, for we do not know how we have done that; or where you refer to 'exerting control of a man's future,' which we have no intention of doing at all, and would not have the power or right to do. There are other phrases, in that part of your letter, that I do not understand, one of which is that which refers to us as being absolved from any commitments of any kind, 'should the author fail.' If this and other phrases signify that you think you should have a contract from us if our relations are to continue, you can certainly have one. We should be delighted to have one. You must surely know the faith this house has in you. There are, of course, limits in terms beyond which nobody can go in a contract, but we should expect to make one that would suit you if you told us what was required."

The following letter to a reader who had accused Wolfe of anti-Semitism was never mailed.

To ————

865 First Avenue
New York, N.Y.

November 18, 1936

Dear Sir:

I have read your letter of November 15th. While I agree and sympathize with your feeling about anti-Semitism, I cannot agree that my little book, "The Story of a Novel," shows any trace of that hostile and ugly feeling which, I am sure, we both abhor. Certainly, nothing of the sort was intended in that little book and if anything in it is possible of such interpretation, I, for one, would be the first to regret it and to deprecate it.

I do not have a copy of the book here at the present time but I am sending for one because I want to read it again and see if I can find out what it is that you object to. Meanwhile, may I not say this, in all kindness and in a spirit of fair reasonableness—that while I understand and sympathize with your deep feeling, it seems to me that your own remarks, about "untutored Southerners" or Gentile students whom you have encountered in various large Eastern universities where you taught and who were, you say, far more "boorish and rapacious, conceited and arrogant, more utterly repulsive culturally than any Jew that moved in the circles I frequented," are not, it seems to me, conducive to the promotion of the spirit of racial liberty and tolerance that, I am sure, we both share.

I know that you will join me in my very sincere hope that this spirit of tolerance will become universal.

To WILLIAM T. POLK

865 First Avenue
New York, N.Y.

December 2, 1936

Dear Bill:

By now you have my telegram telling you that it is impossible for me to come to the meeting. I want to follow it up with this word of explanation which I hope you will get before the meeting opens. I have been working here two months now as hard as I can go, and because I am now finishing something which I have promised to have ready for reading, and I hope for publication (not in book form) within another week or two,[1] it seems to me that I ought to keep going at this job until I finish it. In addition to that there have recently been more legal complications. Charlie Scribner and I are having to consult a lawyer on a matter of common interest to both of us.[2] I think they feel I'd better be on hand until we decide on action.

I am pretty tired. I've just stayed in and worked for two months now and I haven't even had a haircut, which of course won't be news to you. No, it wasn't the fact that I'd have to get a haircut that kept me from going to North Carolina: it was all the other things. I'm going to keep on here as hard as I can go until Christmas and then I'm coming South for a week or ten days' holiday. If you are there at that time, I hope to see you.

Bill, I am genuinely proud to know the Historical Association wanted me to appear upon their program. The only thing that distresses me is that a program arrived last night and I see that I'm really listed to appear on the same evening with you. It troubles me very much to think that my failure to come may cause you embarrassment, or to think that the Association really believed I'd given you a definite promise to be there. I did try to make it plain to you all along that it was doubtful whether I could attend the meeting and that my attendance was understood to be tentative. If there is any misunderstanding about this, won't you please explain it for me to the members of the Association and tell them how grateful I am for their invitation and how sorry I am that these present circumstances have prevented me from accepting it. Also, I hope that I get invited again.

I'm coming down to North Carolina in a few weeks for the first time in seven years to see a few of you again. It means a great deal to me— I think you understand how much. I think also the time is coming when I may have something to say to North Carolina that will interest it. But I'm not sure that I am ready yet. When I do feel ready, I hope you will give me another chance to say my piece.

Meanwhile, I send all my warmest wishes for a successful meeting, and my friendliest greetings to you and to the Literary and Historical Association.

[1] "I Have a Thing to Tell You."
[2] The libel suit brought against them by the Dorman family.

To FRED W. WOLFE

865 First Avenue
New York, N.Y.
December 7, 1936

Dear Fred:

Thanks for your letter. Yes, the pecans came in good condition and I have been devouring them with great relish for a week or so. I am glad to know that Mabel and Ralph are now at home. . . . I am very sorry to hear of all their hard luck and of Mabel's injury and, like you, I hope this new move will mark the beginning of a better time. My troubles still continue. There have even recently been additional legal complications but I hope somehow to live through all this trouble and to achieve some harbor of my own. At any rate I am faced with the stern necessity of working with all my strength and energy now, if only for the payoff of the lawyers' bills to defend myself against the crooks and try to keep my head above the water. Of course, in this hard time, so full of trouble and peril and injustice, I can only hope those who say they are my friends and who say they wish me well will stand by me, and where their own emotional or personal demands or interests are concerned, will just try to go as easy on me as they can. Few people who have never experienced the strain of creating anything, who do not know the terrible exhaustion of energy and of nervous endurance, the need for peace and concentration, and all the elements of publicity, parasitism, sensationalism, slander and treachery that strike at the very vitals of the artist's life, can understand just what it is the artist is up against and how desperately he hopes that his friends and family will try to act as thoughtfully, as humanely and as unselfishly as they can. And if they cannot help him, that they will at any rate try to refrain from doing anything that will add to the troubles he already has, or betray him into the hands of the people who would ruin and defeat him if they could.

I plan to come South Christmas for the first time in seven years. Whether I shall get to Asheville or not, I do not know. I am desperately tired and need a rest. At the present moment I do not feel that I can endure to be pawed over, talked to nineteen hours a day, pulled and tugged and yanked until every separate nerve is screaming with exasperation, and otherwise maddened or exhausted by people who are, I suppose, well-meaning, but whose total effort seems to be to try to kill you with what I suppose must be described as well-intentioned but inconsiderate and thoughtless kindness. I hope to get to Chapel Hill, and if I have time, I may go even farther South to New Orleans. As for Asheville, in my present frame of mind, my present need for peace and rest, I don't know that I can stand it.

I am neither a criminal nor an angel. I am just an honest man. I have no desire either to be sneered at or reviled by rascals, or fawned upon by fools. If I ever came back to the town in which, through accident of birth, I first saw the light of day, I could only hope that I would be met neither by a lynching mob nor by a brass band. If and when I do come back, I want to come back my own way, to be exhibited, shown about and exploited by no one. And if and when I do come back, I shall come back in that way—as my own man, my own master, and very quick and strong to resent any intrusion upon my own liberty and my private life.

This is all for the present. There is very little news to tell you except that in spite of all the sinister and exhausting troubles which have come to me during the last year, in view of what I may ironically describe as my "success," I still keep on working and shall continue so to work as long as I have strength to draw a breath or lift a hand. I hope this finds all of you well and enjoying some success. With thanks again for the pecans and with best wishes for everyone,

To THEA VOELCKER

865 First Avenue
New York, N.Y.

December 15, 1936

Dear Thea:

This will only be a very short letter because I want to get it off to you in time for Christmas and the *Bremen* sails to-night. I am going back to my home in the South for several days at Christmas and I shall try to write some better answer to the letters you have sent me. Just let me tell you now how much I value your letters and how much I thank you for having written me as you have. The reason, really, that I haven't had a chance to answer you is just that I have been working as hard as I can since I came back, and even when I stop working my mind keeps on. I have done a tremendous amount of work, over 200,000 words since October. I know you will be glad to hear it. Of course, I'm a long way off from having anything completed, but I have the whole thing shaped and working in my mind now and pouring from me in a tremendous flood. I am very tired and when my mind gets very tired it is stimulated to terrific activity, so that my sleep at night is broken by hundreds of dreams, but everything will be all right as long as I work.

I am looking forward to my trip home. You know, I was practically an exile for years in my native state, they became so angry at me because of the first book I wrote. But now, I think, they feel better and they want to see me again.

I just want to get this letter off to you in time for Christmas, to wish you a happy Christmas and all happiness and joy for the New Year. I shall probably write you from New Orleans, where I intend to spend a few days with friends during the holidays. It is a lovely old town, deep in the South, at the mouth of the Mississippi River, where the river joins the Gulf of Mexico. The population is composed largely of old French settlers. The life has been dominated by this French influence, by the negro and by the almost tropical climate. It is one of the most interesting cities in America and I hope some day you'll be able to see it.

This is all for the present as I want to take this letter out and mail it in time for the *Bremen*. And now good-bye, good luck, and may Christmas bring all happiness and good cheer to you.

Norman H. Pearson was editing The Oxford Anthology of American Literature *in conjunction with William Rose Benét, and had asked Wolfe's permission to include in that book a section of his work, preferably the portion of* Look Homeward, Angel *which describes the death of Ben. He finally used instead the section from* Of Time and the River *describing the death of Gant, in accordance with Wolfe's preference expressed in the following letter. Pearson at this time was a graduate student in American Literature at Yale, and is now a member of the Department of English there.*

To NORMAN H. PEARSON

865 First Avenue
New York, N.Y.

December 18, 1936

Dear Pearson:

I told you I would write you in a day or two after I'd had a chance to talk to Mr. Perkins about the matter we were discussing the other night. I saw Mr. Perkins last night and his own feeling, I think, is that if you had space, the best selection would be the series of scenes which deal with the death of Gant in "Of Time and the River." I have looked these up in the printed edition and they extend from page 210 to page 273 inclusive, and cover chapters XXI–XXXIV.

This, I know, is a very long selection and I don't know whether you can print it, although in a book of the dimensions you describe to me, with double columns, it would not, of course, take up as many pages as it does in mine. I think you yourself rather prefer the death of Ben scenes in "Look Homeward, Angel," and I am glad you like them because I have always liked them too. I can certainly not urge any scene upon you. It is difficult enough to recommend one's own work, particularly when one has been away from it and has not looked at it for months or years. He is likely to forget, and besides a writer's private judgment on what he has written may be valid for him without being valid for the reading public. The only reason, therefore, I should be inclined to second Mr. Perkins' selection is that I have never yet known him to err in judgment. His discriminating faculty is, I think, by all odds the most accurate I've ever known, and I would therefore accept his judgment about a piece of writing rather than my own.

I think I understand some of your own reasons for preferring the scenes about the death of Ben in "Look Homeward, Angel." I think you felt . . . that these scenes have a quality of poignant sharpness, a kind of bitterness even, which the scenes about the death of Gant in "Of Time and the River" may not have, and in this I think you are probably right. It's awfully hard to talk about one's own work, Pearson, but I would suggest this to you, relying as I do upon Mr. Perkins' judgment, that regardless of what may or may not be the better book—I, of course, am not the person to decide that—I do think "Of Time and the River" was more properly my *own* book. "Look Homeward, Angel" was a young man's book, a first book. I believe and hope I succeeded in making it completely my own book before I got through: the fact remains, however, that I was far more under the influence of writers I profoundly admired—notably, of course, Mr. James Joyce—than in the work which I was to do later. For that reason I suggest to you that "Of Time and the River" is probably more myself and more indicative of the direction in which I may go than "Look Homeward, Angel."

I suggest further—and in this I am simply following out what I believe to be Mr. Perkins' feeling as he explained it to me last night—that the sections dealing with the death of Gant in their entirety perhaps have greater sweep, include greater variety of what Perkins called "the different kinds of things you can do" than the death of Ben. . . . More briefly, I might explain it this way: the death of Ben is a tragedy; the death of Gant is not a tragedy. The death of Ben is a tragedy because Ben is a young man, little more than a boy, who has missed, has never found, has never gotten in life, any of the things he longed for and that he should have had. The death of Gant, manifestly, is not a tragedy in this way because Gant is an old man, ridden with disease and pain. His death has been awaited for years. When it comes, it comes almost as a blessed relief to everyone.

Therefore, the quality and purpose in the two scenes, although each of them deals with the death of a man, are entirely different. The important and valuable thing, I think, in the death of Ben is the personal tragedy of the death of Ben. The important thing in the death of Gant . . . is the effect of the death of the old man upon a large number of people—his friends, his children, his family, the people of the town. I would suggest to you, therefore, that although the death of Gant may lack a quality of intensity and tragedy which the death of Ben has, the death of Gant covers a wider and more varied sweep of life and character. Its implications, I believe, are greater.

I inferred from our conversation the other evening—which, by the way, I thought was a mighty good evening: I hope you enjoyed it and that we can repeat it some time—that you may have felt there was some indication in "Of Time and the River" that I had changed my position, modified my feeling, compromised my integrity with regard to some of the characters in the death of Gant scenes who also appear in the death of Ben scenes. Well, Pearson, all I can tell you is that I think I have somewhat changed my position, I have somewhat modified my feeling, but I have compromised not one atom. I do not have the same feeling of anger and bitterness about these people as I may have had in my first book, but this certainly does not mean compromise. It rather means, I think, that I may have been full of anger, of fury and of bitterness towards some of these characters, towards the whole vexed and tragic scheme of life, in my first book as I was not to the same degree in the second. But I suggest to you that is not compromise. I will not be vain enough to suggest it is growth, but at any rate I was a young man when I wrote "Look Homeward, Angel": I am approaching middle age now. I think I know more about life, more about living, more about people now than I did then. I know that I have a deeper understanding, more sympathy, more compassion, than I had ten years ago. I hope it is reflected in what I do. But I can tell you definitely that I think it would be improper and false if I attempted now to write the way I did in "Look Homeward, Angel," because I do not feel just that way now. This is a kind of integrity the artist has got to maintain: he has got to change, he has got to grow, and at the same time he has got to try to keep true.

I hope this makes my own feeling in the matter plain. Forgive me for having written at such length or for seeming to argue in this matter. I have merely tried to indicate my own feelings and what I believe is also the feeling of Mr. Perkins, who knows more about me and what I can do than anyone on earth, and whose judgment I assure you you can rely upon.

But whatever you do will be all right. I am only too proud to be represented at all in a book of the sort you described to me. I know that any selection you make would be a good one—the death of Ben, the Bascom Hawke piece—I should not be sorry to see any of these pieces included in the book. As a final suggestion, Perkins told me last night that he had been surprised that no one yet had used the death of Gant scenes. He suggested—and I recommend this to your consideration—that the reason . . . was not only one of length (the Bascom Hawke is longer, by the way) but that, being a part of the fabric of the whole book as they are, few people yet realize how complete the scenes dealing with the death of Gant are in themselves.

This is all for the present. I hope it helps you. At any rate, I've tried to indicate some of my own opinions and those of Mr. Perkins, and I hope you find them useful. Drop me a line and let me know what you are going to do and call me up when you come to town. I enjoyed the other evening and hope to see you again.

Marjorie C. Fairbanks, to whom the following note was written, had first known Wolfe in the early 1920s when he was at Harvard.

To MARJORIE C. FAIRBANKS

865 First Avenue
New York, N.Y.

December 24, 1936

Dear Marjorie:

Thanks for your Christmas card. I'm terribly sorry to hear you've been so ill. Please write and tell me what the trouble was.

I hope I'm going to survive—I've never been as tired as I am now. I've done a quarter of a million words in less than three months. I'd like to sleep solid for about a week but I want to get away from here, out of this room, away from the manuscript, try to forget it. I'm going home the day after Christmas for the first time in seven years. Yes, I think they'll let me come back now. I don't know that all is forgiven but they asked me to make a speech,[1] which is something, isn't it? Of course, I didn't make it. I'm going the whole way to New Orleans first, after a day's stop-off in Richmond, where your pal Hank Canby assured me the other day he will be guzzling egg-nogs at Miss Glasgow's house. If I can get past the egg-nogs I'll be in New Orleans for New Year's. I wish you could be there too to drink absinthe with me—if they still serve it. I

[1] The speech at the meeting of the North Carolina Literary and Historical Association in Raleigh.

haven't been there since I was nine years old. It was a lovely old town then. It ought to be a good trip.

Goodbye, Marjorie, for the present. I'll be back here after New Year's. I think I'll be fine after a few days' rest. I've a grand book coming if I live to finish it. Please write and tell me how you are and call me up when you come to town. Meanwhile, all my best for a happy Christmas and a good New Year.

Ever since the exchange of correspondence between Wolfe and Perkins of November 12, 17 and 18, Wolfe had continued to write, but never to mail, letters to complete his severance from Scribners. He had taken these letters with him when he had gone south to New Orleans, and was still brooding over them when, in early January, 1937, he became enraged at Perkins for having given his probable New Orleans address to Cornelius Mitchell, his attorney in the case over his manuscripts.

The defendant's attorney had suggested a settlement of this case whereby Wolfe would pay the sum of $500. This Wolfe had refused to do. Now the defendant, in reply to this refusal, had threatened to make public certain "salacious matter" in the Wolfe manuscripts still in his possession, to aid the Dorman family in their libel suit, and to stir up other suits in Asheville. These latest developments had been communicated to Mitchell by the lawyers acting for Wolfe against the defendant in New Jersey, and Mitchell had urged upon Perkins the necessity of communicating with Wolfe in New Orleans to ask him to return immediately to New York.

To Wolfe, in his state of exhaustion and irritation, this was the last straw. He blamed Perkins not only for divulging his address, but also for having given what he considered weak and pusillanimous advice in the matter, and this, in turn, brought to a head all his earlier complex grievances against Perkins and Scribners. The following letters and telegrams, sent and unsent, mark the climax of Wolfe's severance from Scribners, although he did not actually complete the break by approaching other publishers until eight months later.

The following letter to Perkins was written by Wolfe in New Orleans but never mailed.

To MAXWELL E. PERKINS

> The Roosevelt
> New Orleans, La.
> [January 5(?), 1937]

Cornelius Mitchell has written me an astounding letter in answer to one I wrote him in [the] —— matter. I had supposed the evidence

against —— to be complete and overwhelming, but now, instead of telling me what we are going to do, he tells me of fantastic threats that ——
is making, and requests my instant return to New York. This I unconditionally refuse to do. I have come here for a rest of which I was in desperate need; this amazing letter has caused me the most intense distress; I have been hounded by this shameful business for a year and a half now—and it has got to stop! I am an honorable man and an artist—and the cursed thing now is that my work and talent are being destroyed. Mitchell says he got my address here from you. In the name of God, knowing the state of my health and the utter exhaustion I was in when I left New York, how could you do it?

Max, I have begun to lose faith in your power to stick or to help when a man is in danger. I know now that I must fight this whole horrible business out alone—the whole vicious complex of slander, blackmail, theft and parasitic infamy that . . . usually destroys the artist under this accursed and rotten system that now exists in America. You are going to get out from under when you see me threatened with calamity—but, in the name of God, in the name of all the faith and devotion and unquestioning belief I have had in you—if you cannot help me, for Christ's sake do not add your own influence to those who are now trying to destroy me. Under *no* conditions, save the death or serious illness of a member of my family, give my address hereafter to anyone. Before I come back to that black and vicious horror again, I must restore myself. I shall fight to the end, but for Christ's sake have manhood now not to aid in the attack until I can try to mend a little in energy and health.

The following fragment to Cornelius Mitchell was found in Wolfe's own files. It may or may not have been recopied into the letter which Wolfe actually sent to Mitchell from New Orleans.

Probably to CORNELIUS MITCHELL

[New Orleans, La.]

[January 7(?), 1937]

. . . heretofore—and it is gone. They may exhaust my energy and my youth—they have done so heretofore, and they are *almost* gone. But they shall not take my life from me. They shall not take my power to work from me—I shall now fight with all the strength left in me to save my talent—

my work—my creative integrity. You tell me that I must now return to New York by January 7th to discuss the ways and means of meeting the threats. . . . I tell you that in these conditions—if this is your final proposal, all you have to offer—I can not return.

I know I am alone now. You suggest that we can talk with Perkins. We can not talk with Perkins any more. The house of Scribners has now unmistakably indicated a desire for the complete severance of their publishing relations with me. As for Mr. Perkins—he is the greatest editor of this generation. I revered and honored him also as the greatest man, the greatest friend, the greatest character I had ever known. Now I can only tell you that I still think he is the greatest editor of our time. As for the rest—he is an honest but a timid man. He is not a man for danger—I expect no help from him.

The following wire sent at 6:57 A.M. on January 7, was the first communication which Wolfe actually sent to Perkins from New Orleans. Many versions of longer but similar wires which were not sent are still among Wolfe's papers, written in a hasty and almost indecipherable scrawl.

To MAXWELL E. PERKINS
[Telegram]

New Orleans, La.

January 7, 1937

How dare you give anyone my address?

Perkins did not answer this wire, but on January 9, Wolfe sent him another.

To MAXWELL E. PERKINS
[Telegram]

New Orleans, La.

January 9, 1937

What is your offer?

To this Perkins wired: "If you refer to book we shall make it verbally when you return as arrangements will depend on your requirements. Gave no one your address but suggested two possibilities to your lawyer who thought it important for you to communicate." Scribners never did make Wolfe a definite offer, probably because Perkins felt that Wolfe's desire for a severance was too deep and too complex for him to stay with Scribners anyway.

Meanwhile Wolfe had mailed the following letter of January 9, together with the letter which he had written on December 15, but postponed mailing.

To MAXWELL E. PERKINS

[The Roosevelt]
[New Orleans, La.]
Saturday, January 9, 1937

Dear Max:

I'm sorry I telegraphed you as I did. And I don't even know now exactly what I telegraphed you. But maybe you can understand a little when I tell you that all this worry, grief, and disappointment of the last two years has almost broken me, and finally this last letter of Mitchell's was almost the last straw. I was desperately in need of rest and quiet—the letter destroyed it all, ruined all the happiness and joy I had hoped to get from this trip—the horrible injustice of the whole thing has almost maddened me. I can understand none of it any more—first the Boyd thing, then Mrs. Bernstein and the [——s?] of last year, then the libel suit, then this latest . . . threat of ——'s . . . most of all your own attitude.

Max, I simply can't understand: you yourself urged—not only urged but indignantly insisted—that I take action against —— at a time when I was practically decided to let these ——s take what they could rather than let them take my life—my work—my talent. Now, you speak of paying him off—you told me only a few weeks ago that you would pay the $500 and be done with it—this after insisting at first that I take action, recover the manuscripts and that there should be no compromise. In God's name, what is your meaning? Are you—the man I trusted and reverenced above all else in the world—trying, for some mad reason I can not even guess, to destroy me? How am I going to interpret the events of the past two years? Don't you want me to go on? Don't you want me to write another book? Don't you hope for my life—my growth—the fulfillment of my talent? In Christ's name, what is it, then? My health is well-nigh wrecked —worry, grief, and disillusionment has almost destroyed my talent—is *this* what you wanted? And why?

As for Mr. Mitchell I have given up trying to fathom his motives or his reasoning. When I last saw him a few weeks ago, it seemed to me that our course was clear—that we were in entire agreement—that the evidence against —— was complete and overwhelming. At this time he gave me ——'s offer of compromise for $500. . . . My own feeling was absolutely against such a settlement, particularly since the offer was couched in such ambiguous and obscure phrases that it was impossible to know just what I was going to get in return for my money. I understood that Mr. Mitchell felt this way, too, and that it would be improper to agree to such a settlement. In addition, I wrote him a very long and very clear letter about the proposal of settlement . . . pointed out numerous ambiguities in phrasing, and said that I wanted to go ahead and compel ——, if I could, to return the manuscripts. . . . At the time of my conversation with Mr. Mitchell, he also mentioned ——'s threat to publish "salicious matter" from the manuscripts. I told Mr. Mitchell that this threat was blackmail pure and simple—and, regardless of the proposal of settlement, it would be the height of folly to yield to such a threat now. Well, the result is that this latest letter from Mitchell, instead of saying what *we* are going to do, is an apprehensive account of ——'s . . . threats from beginning to end. In addition to the publication of the alleged "salacious matter," he is going to aid and abet the libel suit of the Brooklyn woman, and "stir up" libel suits in North Carolina. As for the statement that I opened a trunkful of manuscripts and told him to help himself, this is just a lie. . . .

And you—where are you, Max? Have you, too, become terrified at these threats of libel suits? Are you going to advise me to yield . . . simply because the interests of Scribners might be involved? What are we going to do? This thing is like death to me. Have we really reached the end? I fear desperately we have—it is all so tragically sad—and as for that powerful and magnificent talent I had two years ago—in the name of God is that to be lost entirely, destroyed under the repeated assaults and criminalities of this blackmail society under which we live? *Now* I know what happens to the artist in America. *Now* I know what must be changed. *Now* truly, henceforth and forever after, I shall work with all my strength for revolution—for the abolition of this vile and rotten system under which we live—for a better world, a better life.

And you? You are in very many ways the best person I have ever known, the person for whom I have had the greatest reverence and devotion—but in some few ways, perhaps, I am a better man than you. Forgive me these wild telegrams. Even if we have now come to the end of our publishing connection—a connection for which I have sacrificed everything—a connection that is now being severed when I have nothing left, when no one wants me—for God's sake let us try to save our belief and faith in each other—a belief and faith that I still have—that I hope you have not lost. I would to God I were a better man, but I will not cease trying to be a better one—and for you, I cannot bear to see you just a good but timid man. I am in deadly peril, but right or wrong, I want you to go into battle with me—I see you as the noble captain, strong and faithful, and no matter what the cost, right to the end. I have no right to ask it, but you must be the great man that I know you are. Don't give up the ship. I am leaving here tomorrow, I think. Some friends are taking me to the country in an effort to get me some quiet and rest.[1] I hope to be in North Carolina in a few days—although now, feeling as I do, I doubt the [approval?] of my friends. But if you want to write me, you might address the letter in care of Mr. Garland Porter, *The Atlanta Georgian*, Atlanta. But whatever you do—unless it is something involving the serious sickness or death of a member of my family—don't give my address to anyone. I'm in a wretched state, and I've got to get on my feet before I come back to New York to fight. . . .

P.S. I was worn out yesterday when I wrote this. To-day I feel a little better—and I am assured now of my course. Further words, arguments, entreaties are useless. We are either at the end or we shall go on. I am sending two letters which I wrote some weeks ago and which, hoping against hope, I have withheld. These letters in a general way put the story of my relation to you and Scribners upon the record. There is nothing in either of them that can do you any harm. But, in case anything happens to me, I am sending duplicates to a friend. I think this is proper.

Wolfe actually ·sent only one of the two letters referred to above, the one dated December 15, 1936, which he called "the personal letter," but not the one dated December 23, 1936, which he called "the business letter" and of which the original is still in his own files. The friend to whom he sent duplicates of these letters remains unidentified in spite of queries to the most likely people. Perhaps he never actually sent duplicates to anyone at this time. However, in the fall of 1937, he gave a copy of the letter of December 15, 1936, to Hamilton Basso, after writing the following words in pencil on the bottom of the last page: "To my friend, Hamilton Basso: Dear Ham—I've gone upon the record here—this is not perhaps the whole story—but in a general way it says some of the things I felt had to be said. I am leaving this copy of the letter in your care and, if anything should happen to me, I leave it to your discretion what should be done with it."

[1] Mr. and Mrs. Allan B. Eldred had invited Wolfe to their house at Ocean Springs, Mississippi, for a few days' rest. Before her marriage, Mrs. Eldred was Margaret Folsom of Asheville: she and her brother, Theodore W. Folsom, had been childhood friends of Wolfe's.

The following is "the personal letter" which Wolfe mailed from New Orleans on January 10.

To MAXWELL E. PERKINS

865 First Avenue
New York, N.Y.

December 15, 1936

Dear Max:

I am sorry for the delay in answering your three letters of November 17th and 18th. As you know, I have been hard at work here day after day and, in addition, have recently been beset by some more of the legal difficulties, threats and worries which have hounded my life for the last year and a half. And finally, I wanted to have time to think over your letters carefully and to meditate my own reply before I answered you.

First of all, let me tell you that for what you say in your own two personal letters of November 17th and November 18th I shall be forever proud and grateful. I shall remember it with the greatest happiness as long as I live. I must tell you again, no matter what embarrassment it may cause you, what I have already publicly acknowledged and what I believe is now somewhat understood and known about in the world, namely, that your faith in me, your friendship for me, during the years of doubt, confusion and distress, was and will always be one of the great things in my life.

When I did give utterance to this fact in print [1]—when I tried to make some slight acknowledgment of a debt of friendship and of loyalty, which no mere acknowledgment could ever repay—some of my enemies, as you know, tried to seize upon the simple words I had written in an effort to twist and pervert them to their own uses, to indicate that my acknowledgment was for a technical and professional service, which it was not, to assert that I was myself incapable of projecting and accomplishing my own purpose without your own editorial help, which is untrue. But although such statements as these were made to injure me, and perhaps have done me an injury, I believe that injury to be at best only a temporary one. As for the rest, what I had really said, what I had really written about my debt to you, is plain and unmistakable, clearly and definitely understood by people of good will, who have a mind to understand. I would not retract a word of it, except to wish the words were written better. I would not withdraw a line of it, except to hope that I might write another line that would more adequately express the whole meaning and implication of what I feel and want to say.

[1] In *The Story of a Novel.*

As to those statements which were made, it seems to me, malevolently, for what purpose I do not know, by people I have never met—that I had to have your technical and critical assistance "to help me write my books," etc.—they are so contemptible, so manifestly false, I have no fear whatever of their ultimate exposure. If refutation were needed, if the artist had time enough or felt it necessary to make an answer to all the curs that snap at him, it would not take me long, I think, to brand these falsehoods for the lies they are. I would only have to point out, I think, that so far from needing any outside aid "to help me write my books," the very book which my detractors now eagerly seize on as my best one—the gauge by which the others must be measured, and itself the proof and demonstration of my subsequent decline—had been utterly finished and completed, to the final period, in utter isolation, without a word of criticism or advice from any one, before any publisher ever saw it; and that whatever changes were finally made were almost entirely changes in the form of omission and of cuts in view of bringing the book down to a more publishable and condensed form. That book, of course, was "Look Homeward, Angel," and I believe that with everything else I ever wrote, the process was much the same, although the finality of completion was not so marked, because in later books I was working in a more experimental, individual fashion and dealing with the problem of how to shape and bring into articulate form a giant mass of raw material, whose proportions almost defeated me.

The very truth of the matter is that, so far from ever having been unsure of purpose and direction, in the last five years at any rate I have been almost too sure. My sense of purpose and direction is definite and overwhelming. I think, I feel and know what I want to do: the direction in which, if I live and if I am allowed to go on working and fulfill myself, I want to go, is with me more clear and certain than with any one that I have ever known. My difficulty has never been one of purpose or direction. Nothing is more certain than this fact, that I know what I want to do and where I want to go. Nothing is more certain than the fact that I shall finish any book I set out to write, if life and health hold out. My difficulty from the outset, as you know, has never been one of direction, it has only been one of means. As I have already said and written, in language that seems to be so clear and unmistakable that no one could misunderstand it, I have been faced with the problem of discovering for myself my own language, my own pattern, my own structure, my own design, my own universe and creation. That, as I have said before, is a problem that is, I think, by no means unique, by no means special to myself. I believe it may have been the problem of every artist that ever lived. In my own case, however, I believe the difficulties of the problem may have been increased and complicated by the denseness of the fabric, the dimensions of the structure, the variety of the plan. For that reason I have, as you know, at times found myself almost hopelessly enmeshed in my own web.

In one sense, my whole effort for years might be described as an effort to fathom my own design, to explore my own channels, to discover my own ways. In these respects, in an effort to help me to discover, to better use, these means I was striving to apprehend and make my own, you gave me the most generous, the most painstaking, the most valuable help. But that kind of help might have been given to me by many other skilful people— and of course there are other skilful people in the world who could give such help, although none that I know of who could give it so skilfully as you.

But what you gave me, what in my acknowledgment I tried to give expression to, was so much more than this technical assistance—an aid of spiritual sustenance, of personal faith, of high purpose, of profound and sensitive understanding, of utter loyalty and staunch support, at a time when many people had no belief at all in me, or when what little belief they had was colored by serious doubt that I would ever be able to continue or achieve my purpose, fulfill my "promise." All of this was a help of such priceless and incalculable value, of such spiritual magnitude, that it made any other kind of help seem paltry by comparison. And for that reason mainly I have resented the contemptible insinuations of my enemies that I have to have you "to help me write my books." As you know, I don't have to have you or any other man alive to help me write my books. I do not even have to have technical help or advice, although I need it badly, and have been so immensely grateful for it. But if the worst came to the worst—and of course the worst does and will come to the worst—all this I could and will and do learn for myself, as all hard things are learned, with blood-sweat, anguish and despair.

As for another kind of help—a help that would attempt to shape my purpose or define for me my own direction—I not only do not need that sort of help but if I found that it had in any way invaded the unity of my purpose, or was trying in any fundamental way to modify or alter the direction of my creative life—the way in which it seems to me it ought and has to go—I should repulse it as an enemy, I should fight it and oppose it with every energy of my life, because I feel so strongly that it is the final and unpardonable intrusion upon the one thing in an artist's life that must be held and kept inviolable.

All this I know you understand and will agree to. As to the final kind of help, the help of friendship, the help of faith, the help and belief and understanding of a fellow creature whom you know and reverence not only as a person of individual genius but as a spirit of incorruptible integrity—that kind of help I do need, that kind of help I think I have been given, that kind of help I shall evermore hope to deserve and pray that I shall have. But if that too should fail—if that too should be taken from me, as so many rare and priceless things are taken from us in this life— that kind of dark and tragic fortitude that grows on us in life as we get older, and which tells us that in the end we can and must endure all things, might make it possible for me to bear even that final and irreparable loss, to agree with Samuel Johnson when he said: "The shepherd in Vergil grew at last acquainted with Love, and found him a native of the rocks."

You say in one of your letters that you never knew a soul with whom you felt that you were in such fundamentally complete agreement as with me. May I tell you that I shall remember these words with proud happiness and with loyal gratefulness as long as I live. For I too on my own part feel that way about you. I know that somehow, in some hard, deep, vexed and troubling way in which all the truth of life is hidden and which, at the cost of so much living, so much perplexity and anguish of the spirit, we have got to try to find and fathom, what you say is true: I believe we are somehow, in this strange, hard way, in this complete and fundamental agreement with each other.

And yet, were there ever two men since time began who were as completely different as you and I? Have you ever known two other people who were, in almost every respect of temperament, thinking, feeling and acting, as far apart? It seems to me that each of us might almost represent, typify, be the personal embodiment of, two opposite poles of life. How to put it I do not know exactly, but I might say, I think, that you in your essential self are the Conservative and I, in my essential self, am the Revolutionary.

I use these words, I hope, in what may have been their original and natural meanings. I am not using them with reference to any of the political, social, economic or religious connotations that are now so often tied up with them. When I say that you a Conservative, I am not thinking of you as some-one who voted for Governor Landon, for I can see how an action of that sort and your own considered reasons for doing it might easily have revolutionary consequences. When I say that I am a Revolutionary, I know that you will never for a moment think of me as some one who is usually referred to in America as a "radical." You know that my whole feeling toward life could not be indicated or included under such a category. I am not a party man, I am not a propaganda man, I am not a Union Square or Greenwich Village communist. I not only do not believe in these people: I do not even believe they believe in themselves. I mistrust their sincerity, I mistrust their motives, I do not believe they have any essential capacity for devotion or for belief in the very principles of Revolution, of government, of economics and of life, which they all profess.

More than that, I believe that these people themselves are parasitic excrescences of the very society which they profess to abhor, whose destruction they prophesy and whose overthrow they urge. I believe that these people would be unable to live without the society which they profess to abhor, and I know that I could live if I had to, not only under this society but under any other one, and that in the end I might probably approve no other one more than I do this.

I believe further that these very people who talk of the workers with such reverence, and who assert that they are workers and are for the worker's cause, do not reverence the workers, are not themselves workers and in the end are traitors to the worker's cause. I believe that I myself not only know the workers and am a friend of the worker's cause but that I am myself a brother to the workers, because I am myself, as every artist is, a worker, and I am myself, moreover, the son of a working man. I know furthermore that at the bottom there is no difference between the artist and the worker. They both come from the same family, they recognize and understand each other instantly. They speak the same language. They have always stood together. And I know that our enemies, the people who betray us, are these apes and monkeys of the arts, who believe in everything and who believe in nothing, and who hate the artist and who hate the living man no matter what lip service they may pay to us. These people are the enemies to life, the enemies to revolution. Nothing is more certain than that they will betray us in the end.

I have said these things simply to indicate to you a difference of which I know you must be already well aware. The difference between the revolutionary and the "radical," the difference between the artist and the ape of art, the difference between the worker and those who say they are the worker's friend. The same thing could be said, it seems to me, on your own side, about the true conservative and the person who only votes conservative and owns property and has money in the bank.

Just as in some hard, strange way there is between us probably this fundamentally complete agreement which you speak of, so too, in other hard, strange ways there is this complete and polar difference. It must be so with the South pole and the North pole. I believe that in the end they too must be in fundamentally complete agreement—but the whole earth lies between them. I don't know exactly how to define conservatism or the essential conservative spirit of which I speak here, but I think I might say it is a kind of fatalism of the spirit. Its fundaments, it seems to me, are based upon a kind of unhoping hope, an imperturbable acceptation, a determined resignation, which believes that fundamentally life will never change, but that on this account we must all of us do the best we can.

The result of all this, it seems to me, is that these differences between us have multiplied in complexity and difficulty. The plain truth of the matter now is that I hardly know where to turn. The whole natural impulse of creation—and with me, creation is a natural impulse, it has got to flow, it has got to realize itself through the process of torrential production—is checked and hampered at every place. In spite of this, I have finally and at last, during these past two months, broken through into the greatest imaginative conquest of my life—the only complete and whole one I have ever had. And now I dare not broach it to you, I dare not bring it to you, I dare not show it to you, for fear that this thing which I cannot trifle with, which may come to a man but once in his whole life, may be killed at its inception by cold caution, by indifference, by the growing apprehensiveness and dogmatism of your own conservatism. You say that you are not aware that there is any severance between us. Will you please tell me what there is in the life around us on which we both agree? We don't agree in politics, we don't agree on economics, we are in entire disagreement on the present system of life around us, the way people live, the changes that should be made.

Your own idea, evidently, is that life itself is unchangeable, that the abuses I protest against—the greed, the waste, the poverty, the filth, the suffering—are inherent in humanity, and that any other system than the one we have would be just as bad as this one. In this, I find myself in profound and passionate conflict. I hold no brief, as you know, for the present communist system as it is practiced in Russia to-day, but it seems to me to be the most absurd and hollow casuistry to argue seriously that because a good Russian worker is given a thicker slice of beef than a bad one, or because a highly trained mechanic enjoys a slightly better standard of living and is given more privileges and comforts than an inferior mechanic, the class system has been reestablished in Russia and is identical with the one existing in this country, whereby a young girl who inherits the fortune of a five-and-ten-cent-store king is allowed to live a life of useless, vicious idleness and to enjoy an income of five million dollars annually while other young girls work in the very stores that produce her fortune for ten dollars a week.

It is all very well to say that the artist should not concern himself with these things but with "life." What are these things if they are not life— one of the cruelest and most intolerable aspects of it, it is true, but as much a part of the whole human spectacle as a woman producing a child. You, better than any one, have had the chance to observe during the past year how this consciousness of society, of the social elements that govern life to-day, have sunk into my spirit; how my convictions about all these things have grown deeper, wider, more intense at every point. On your own part, it seems to me, there has been a corresponding stiffening, an increasing conservatism that has now, I fear, reached the point of dogged and unyielding inflexibility and obstinate resolve to try to maintain the status quo at any cost.

Since that is your condition, your considered judgment, I will not try to change it, or to persuade you in any way, because I know your reasons for so thinking and so feeling are honest ones. But neither must you now try to change me, or to persuade me to alter or deny convictions which are the result of no superficial or temporary influence, no Union Square, Greenwich Village cult, but the result of my own deep living, my own deep feeling, my own deep labor and my own deep thought.

Had I given full expression to these convictions in "Of Time and the River" I believe it would have been a better book. You do not think so. But I will say that these feelings, these convictions, are becoming deeper and intenser all the time, and so far from feeling that the world cannot be changed, that it cannot be made better, that the evils of life are un-remediable, that all the faults and vices at which we protest will always exist, I find myself more passionately convinced than ever of the necessity of change, more passionately confirmed than ever in the faith and the belief that the life and the condition of the whole human race can be immeasurably improved. And this is something that grows stronger with me all the time. It has been my lot to start life with an obedient faith, with a conservative tradition, only to have that faith grow weaker and fade out as I grew older. I cannot tell you all the ways in which this came about, but I think I can indicate to you one of the principal ones.

I was a child of faith. I grew up in the most conservative section of America, and as a child I put an almost unquestioning belief and confidence in the things that were told me, the precepts that were taught me. As I grew older I began to see the terrible and shocking differences between appearance and reality all around me. I was told, for example, in church, of a Sunday morning, that people should love one another as their brothers, that they should not bear false witness against their fellow-man, that they should not covet their neighbor's wife, that they should not commit adultery, that they should not cheat, trick, betray and rob their fellows. And as I grew older and my knowledge of life and of the whole community increased until there was hardly a family in town whose whole history I did not know, I began to see what a shameful travesty of good-ness these lives were. I began to see that the very people who said on Sunday that one should not bear false witness against his neighbors bore false witness all the time, until the very air was poisonous with their slanders, with their hatreds, their vicious slanderings of life and of their neighbors. I began to see how the people who talked about not coveting their neighbors' wives did covet their neighbors' wives and committed adultery with them. I saw how the minister who got up and denounced a proposal to introduce a little innocent amusement in the Sunday life of the people, a baseball game or a moving picture show—upon the grounds that it not only violated the law of God but was an imposition on our fellow-man, that we had no right to ask our fellows to do work on Sunday —had, at that very moment, two sweating negro girls in the kitchen of his own home, employed at meagre wages to cook his Sunday dinner for him. . . .

Well, it is an old, old story, but to me it was a new one. Like every other boy of sense, intelligence and imagination, who ever first discovered these things for himself, I thought I was the first one in the world to see these things. I thought that I had come upon a horrible catastrophe, a whole universe of volcanic infamy over which the good people of the earth were treading blissfully and innocently with trusting smiles. I thought I had to tell this thing to some one. I thought I had to warn the world, to tell all my friends and teachers that all the goodness and integrity and purity of their lives was menaced by this snake of unsuspected evil.

I don't need to tell you what happened. I was received either with smiles of amused and pitying tolerance or with curt reprimands, admonitions to shut up, not to talk about my betters, not to say a word against people who had won a name and who were the high and mighty ones in town. Then slowly, like some one living in a nightmare only to wake up and find out that the nightmare is really true, I began to find out that they *didn't* mean it, they *didn't* mean what they said. I began to discover that all these fine words, these splendid precepts, these noble teachings had no meaning at all, because the very people who professed them had no belief in them. I began to discover that it didn't matter at all whether you bore false witness against your neighbor, if you only said that one should not bear false witness against his neighbor. I began to see that it didn't matter at all whether you took your neighbor's ox or his ass or his wife, if only you had the cunning and the power to take them. I began to see that it did not matter at all whether you committed adultery or not, so long as it did not come out in the papers. Every one in town might know you had committed it, and with whom, and on what occasions—the whole history might be a matter for sly jesting, furtive snickerings, the lewd and common property of the whole community—and you could still be deacon of the church provided you were not sued for alienation of affection. I began to see that you could talk of chastity, of purity, of standards of morality and high conduct, of loving your neighbor as yourself, and still derive your filthy income from a horde of rotting tenements down in niggertown that were so vile and filthy they were not fit to be the habitation of pigs. You could talk to a crowd of miserable, over-worked and under-paid shop-girls about their moral life and the necessity of chastity even though your own daughter was the most promiscuous, drunken little whore in town. And it didn't matter, it didn't matter—if you had the dough. That was all that mattered.

I discovered very early that people who had the money could do pretty damn near anything they wanted to. Whoredom, drunkenness, debauchery of every sort was the privilege of the rich, the crime of the poor. And as I grew older, as my experience of life widened and increased, as I first came to know, to explore, to investigate life in this overwhelming city, with all the passion, the hope, the faith, the fervor and the poetic imagination of youth, I found that here too it was just the same. Here too, if anything, it was more overwhelming because it was so condensed, so multiplied. Here too, if anything, it was even more terrible because the privileged city classes no longer pretended to cloak themselves in the spurious affirmations of religion. The result has been, as I have grown older, as I have seen life in manifold phases all over the earth, that I have become more passionately convinced than ever before that this system that we have is evil, that it brings misery and injustice not only to the lives of the poor but to the wretched and sterile lives of the privileged classes who are supported by it, that this system of living must be changed, that men must have a new faith, a new heroism, a new belief, if life is to be made better. And that life can be made better, that life will be made better, is the heart and core of my own faith and my own conviction, the end toward which I believe I must henceforth direct every energy of my life and talent.

All this, I know, you consider elementary, and I agree with you. It is. These evidences of corruption in the life around me which I have mentioned to you, you consider almost childishly naive. Perhaps they are. But if they are, the anterior fundamental sources of corruption which have produced them are certainly neither childish nor naive. You have told me that you consider the . . . life of a young girl who, without ever having done a stroke of work herself, is privileged to enjoy an income of two million, or five million, or ten million a year, only a trifling and superficial manifestation and of no importance. With this, of course, I am in utter opposition. If these people, as you say, are only flies upon the tender of a locomotive, they are locomotive flies, and the locomotive that produced them should be scrapped.

I have gone into all this not because these bases of contention are even fundamental to you and me, but because they are indicative of all the various widening channels of difference that have come up between us in recent years. Just as my own feeling for the necessity for change, for essential revolution in this way of life, has become steadily deeper and more confirmed, so too have you, hardened by the challenge of the depression, deeply alarmed by the menace of the times to the fortune of which you are the custodian—not for yourself, I know, for you yourself I truly believe are not a man who needs material things, but alarmed by the menace of these times to the security and future of five young and tender creatures who, protected as they have been, and unprepared as they are to meet the peril of these coming times, are themselves, it seems to me, the unfortunate victims of this very system you must now try to help maintain —you have accordingly become more set and more confirmed in your own convictions. With these personal affairs, these intimate details of your fine family, I have no intention to intrude save where it seems to me to have resulted in a bias that challenges the essence of my own purpose and direction.

What I really want to say to you most earnestly now is this: there has never been a time when I've been so determined to write as I please, to say what I intend to say, to publish the books I want to publish, as I am now. I know that you have asserted time and again that you were in entire sympathy with this feeling—that, more than this, you were willing to be the eager promoter and supporter of this intention, that you were willing to publish whatever I wanted you to publish, that you were only waiting for me to give it to you. In this I think you have deceived yourself. I think you are mistaken when you say that all you have waited for was the word from me, that you would publish anything I wanted you to publish. There are many things that I have wanted you to publish which have not been published. Some of them have not been published because they were too long for magazine space, or too short for book space, or too different in their design and quality to fit under the heading of a short story, or too incomplete to be called a novel. All this is true. All this I grant. And yet, admitting all these things, without a word of criticism of you or of the technical and publishing requirements of the present time that make their publication impracticable, I will still say that I think some of them should have been published. I still think that much of the best writing that a man may do is writing that does not follow under the con- venient but extremely limited forms of modern publication. It is not your fault. It is not Scribners' fault. It is just the way things are. But as I have been telling you, the way things are is not always the way, it seems to me, that things should be; and one fact that has become plain to me in recent years and is now imbedded in my conviction is that in spite of the rivers of print that inundate this broad land, the thousands of newspapers, the hundreds of magazines, the thousands of books that get printed every year, and the scores of publishers who assure you that they are sitting on the edges of their chairs and eagerly waiting, praying, that some one will come in with a piece of writing of originality and power, that all they are waiting for, all they ask for, is just for the opportunity of discovering it and printing it—the means of publication are still most limited for a life of the complexity, the variety, the richness, the fascination, the terror, the poetry, the beauty and the whole unuttered magnificence of this tremendous life around us: the means of publication are really pitifully meager, ungenerous, meanly, sterilely constricted.

Which brings me now to an essential point, a point that bears practically and dangerously on every thing that I have heretofore said to you.

About fifteen years ago, as you know, an extraordinary book was produced which startled the whole critical and publishing world. This book was the "Ulysses" of James Joyce. I know that you are well aware of the history of that book, but for the sake of the argument I am presently to make, let me review it again for you. "Ulysses" was published, if I mistake not, in 1921. I have been informed dozens of times in the last few years by reputable and well-known publishers, including yourself, that they are eagerly waiting a chance to produce a work of originality and power, that they would produce it without question, without modification, if it were given to them. What are the facts concerning "Ulysses"? Was it published by Charles Scribner's Sons? No, it was not. Was it published by Harper's, by Macmillan, by Houghton Mifflin, by one of the great English houses? It was not. Who published it then? It was published privately, obscurely, by a woman who ran a book shop in Paris. And at first, as you know, it was treated by most critics as kind of literary curiosity—either as a work of deliberate pornography or as a work of wilfully complicated obscurity, of no genuine value or importance, save to a little group of clique adepts. And as you know, the book was taken up by clique adepts everywhere and used, or rather misused, in their customary way, as a badge of their snobbish superiority. But in addition to both these groups there was also a third group, I think a very small group, composed of those people scattered throughout the world who are able to read and feel and understand and form their own judgment without prejudice of the merits of a powerful and original work. It seems to me that almost the best, the most fortunate thing in life—in a writer's life at least—is that these people do exist. A great book is not lost. It does not get done to death by fools and snobs. It may be misunderstood for years. Its writer may be ridiculed or reviled or betrayed by false idolatry, but the book does not get lost. There are always a few people who will save it. The book will make its way. That is what happened to "Ulysses." As time went on, the circle widened. Its public increased. As people overcame their own inertia, mastered the difficulty which every new and original work creates, became familiar with its whole design, they began to understand that the book was neither an obscene book nor an obscure book, certainly it was not a work of wilful dilettante caprice. It was, on the contrary, an orderly, densely constructed creation, whose greatest fault, it seems to me, so far from being a fault of caprice, was rather the fault of an almost Jesuitical logic which is essentially too dry and lifeless in its mechanics for a work of the imagination. At any rate, now, after fifteen years, "Ulysses" is no longer thought of as a book meant solely for a little group of literary adepts. The adepts of this day, in fact, speak somewhat patronizingly of the work as marking "the end of an epoch," as being "the final development of an outworn naturalism," etc., etc. But the book itself had now won an unquestioned and established place in literature. Its whole method, its style, its characters, its story and design has become so familiar to many of us that we no longer think of it as difficult or obscure. It seems no more difficult than "Tristram Shandy." For my part, I do not find "Ulysses" as difficult as "Tristram." Certainly it is nowhere near as difficult as "The Ring and the Book." Moreover, "Ulysses" can now be published openly in this country, sold over the counter as any other book is sold, without fear of arrest or action by the law. And at the present time, as you know, it is being sold that way, in what is known as "large quantities," by one of your fellow publishers. This man told me a year and a half ago that the sale up to that time, I believe, was something like 30,000 copies. "Ulysses," therefore, has made its way not only critically but commercially as well. These are the facts. I do not recall them in order to accuse you with them. I know you did not have the opportunity of publishing "Ulysses." Perhaps no other well-known publisher, either in England or America, had that opportunity. I suppose furthermore that at that time it would have been impossible for any reputable publisher to have published that book openly. But the fact remains it did get published, didn't it—not by Scribners, not by Houghton, not by any known publisher in England, but privately, by a little obscure bookseller in Paris.

And the reason your associates, the Modern Library, Inc., can now publish this book in large quantities, openly, and derive a profit from it now, is because some private, obscure person took the chance fifteen years ago—took the chance, I fear, without the profits.

What then? You say you are waiting eagerly to discover a manuscript of originality and power. You say that you are waiting eagerly to publish a manuscript of mine—that you will publish anything I want you to publish. I know you believe what you say, but I also think you deceive yourself. I am not going to write a "Ulysses" book. Like many another young man who came under the influence of that remarkable work, I wrote my "Ulysses" book and got it published too. That book, as you know, was "Look Homeward, Angel." And now, I am finished with "Ulysses" and with Mr. Joyce, save that I am not an ingrate and will always, I hope, be able to remember a work that stirred me, that opened new vistas into writing, and to pay the tribute to a man of genius that is due him.

However, I am now going to write my own "Ulysses." The first volume is now under way. The first volume will be called "The Hound of Darkness," and the whole work, when completed, will be called "The Vision of Spangler's Paul." [2] Like Mr. Joyce, I am going to write as I please, and this time, no one is going to cut me unless I want them to. Like Mr. Joyce, and like most artists, I believe, I am by nature a Puritan. At any rate, a growing devotion to work, to purpose, to fulfillment, a growing intensity of will, tends to distill one's life into a purer liquor. I shall never hereafter—I hope that I have never heretofore, but I shall never hereafter—write a word for the purpose of arousing sensational surprise, of shocking the prudish, of flaunting the outraged respectabilities of the middle-class mind. But I shall use as precisely, as truthfully, as tellingly as I can every word I have to use; every word, if need be, in my vocabulary; every word, if need be, in the vocabulary of the foulest-mouthed taxi driver, the most prurient-tongued prostitute that ever screamed an obscene epithet. Like Mr. Joyce, I have at last discovered my own America, I believe I have found my language, I think I know my way. And I shall wreak out my vision of this life, this way, this world and this America, to the top of my bent, to the height of my ability, but with an unswerving devotion, integrity and purity of purpose that shall not be menaced, altered or weakened by any one. I will go to jail because of this book if I have to. I will lose my friends because of it, if I will have to. I will be libelled, slandered, blackmailed, threatened, menaced, sneered at, derided and assailed by every parasite, every ape, every blackmailer, every scandalmonger, every little Saturday-Reviewer of the venomous and corrupt respectabilities. I will be exiled from my country because of it, if I have to. I can endure exile. I have endured it before, as you well know, on account of a book which you yourself published, although few—among them, some of the very ones who betrayed me then either by silence or evasion—now try to smile feebly when I speak of exile, but it was the truth and may be true again. But no matter what happens I am going to write this book.

You have heard me talk to you before. You have not always been disposed to take seriously what I say to you. I pray most earnestly that you will take this seriously. For seven years now, during this long and for me wonderful association with you, I have been increasingly aware of a

---

[2] By this time, Wolfe had decided to include the material and title of *The Hound of Darkness* in *The Vision of Spangler's Paul* (which finally became *The Web and the Rock* and *You Can't Go Home Again*). The title, *The Hound of Darkness*, is used for Book II of *The Web and the Rock*, but most of the original material was omitted or used elsewhere in that novel or in *You Can't Go Home Again*.

certain direction which our lives were taking. Looking back, I can see now that although "Look Homeward, Angel" gave you pleasure and satisfaction, you were extremely alarmed even then about its publication, and entertained the hope—the sincere and honest hope, directed, I know, to what you considered my own best interests—that the years would temper me to a greater conservatism, a milder intensity, a more decorous moderation. And I think where I have been most wrong, most unsure in these past seven years, has been where I have yielded to this benevolent pressure. Because I think that it is just there that I have allowed myself to falter in my purpose, to be diverted from the direction toward which the whole impulsion of my life and talent is now driving me, to have failed there insofar as I have yielded to the modifications of this restraint. Restraint, discipline—yes, they were needed desperately, they are needed badly still. But let us not get the issues confused, let us not again get into the old confusion between substance and technique, purpose and manner, direction and means, the spirit and the letter. Restrain my adjectives, by all means, discipline my adverbs, moderate the technical extravagances of my incondite exuberance, but don't derail the train, don't take the Pacific Limited and switch it down the siding towards Hogwart Junction. It can't be done. I'm not going to let it happen. If you expected me to grow conservative simply because I got bald and fat and for the first time in life had a few dollars in the bank, you are going to be grievously mistaken. Besides, what is there longer for me to fear? I have been through it all now, I have seen how women can betray you, how friends can sell you out for a few filthy dollars, how the whole set-up of society and of justice in its present form permits the thief, the parasite, the scavenger, the scandal-monger to rob, cheat, outrage and defame you, how even those people who swear they are your sincerest and most enduring friends, who say they value your talent and your work, can sink to the final dishonor of silence and of caution when you are attacked, will not even lift their voices in a word of protest or of indignation when they hear you lied about by scoundrels or maligned by rascals. So what am I now to lose? Even the little money that I had, the greater part of it, has now been taken from me by these thieves and parasites of life. Well, they can take it, they can have it, they have got it. They can take everything I have, but no one henceforth shall take from me my work.

I am afraid of nothing now. I have nothing more to lose except my life and health. And those I pray and hope to God will stay with me till my work is done. That, it seems to me, is the only tragedy that can now stay me.

The other day you were present when we were having an interview with a distinguished member of the legal profession. I wonder what was going on in your mind when you saw that man and when you looked at me. When you saw that man, secure in wealth, in smugness, in respectability, even though all these authorities had come to him from his accursed profession, from shuffling papers, peering around for legal crevices, seeking not for truth or justice but for technical advantages. When you heard this man ask me if I had lived in certain neighborhoods, in certain kinds of habitation, if I ever drank, etc., and when you heard him cough pompously behind his hand and say that although he of course had never led "that sort of life" he was—ahem, ahem—not narrow-minded and understood that there were those that did. Understand? Why, what could he understand of "my kind of life"? He could no more understand it than a dog could understand the books in his master's library. And I have been forced to wonder of late, after some of the sad events of this last year, how much of it you understood. What I am trying to tell you, what I am forced to say because it is the truth, is that I am a righteous man, and few people know it because there are few righteous people in the world.

But from my boyhood, from my early youth, I have lived a life of solitude, of industry, of consecration. I have cost few people anything in this world, except perhaps the pains of birth. I have given people everything I had. I think that I have taken from no one more than I have given them. Certainly, I suppose that not even my bitterest enemies have ever accused me of living or working or thinking about money. During the time that you yourself have known me you have had ample demonstrations of that fact. I know you have not forgotten them, and I hope that if anything should happen to me, if I should die, as indeed I have no wish to do, there would be some one left who had known me who would say some of these things I know to be true.

Please understand that I neither intend nor imply any criticism of you, or of your friendship when I say these things. I know you are my friend. I value your friendship more than anything else in the world: the belief that you, above all people, respected my work and found happiness in being able to help me with it has been the greatest spiritual support and comfort I've ever known. I think further that if I ever heard you slandered or defamed or lied about, I would assault the person who defamed you. But I know that that is not your way. You believe that silence is the best answer, and perhaps you are right. At any rate, I want you to know that as long as I know you are my friend to the very hilt, to the very last—if need be, and I hope it never need be, to your own peril and security—that is all that matters. And that is the way I feel about you.

I do not know if you have always been aware of how I felt about these things; of what a naked, fiercely lacerated thing my spirit was; how I have writhed beneath the lies and injuries and at times, [been] almost maddened to insanity at the treachery, the injustice and the hatred I have had to experience and endure; at what a frightful cost I have attained even the little fortitude I have attained. At times, particularly during the last year or two, the spectacle of the victim squirming beneath the lash has seemed to amuse you. I know there is no cruelty in your nature. I do suggest to you, however, that when one is secure in life, when one is vested with authority, established in position, surrounded by a little world of his own making, of his own love, he may sometimes be a little unmindful of the lives of people less fortunate than himself. There is an unhappy tendency in all of us to endure with fortitude the anguish of another man. There is also a tendency among people of active and imaginative minds and temperaments, who live themselves conventional and conservative lives, to indulge vicariously their interest in the adventures and experiences of other people whose lives are not so sheltered as their own. And these people, I think, often derive what seems to be a kind of quiet, philosophic amusement at the spectacle of what is so falsely known as the "human comedy." But I might suggest to such people that what affords them quiet entertainment is being paid for by another man with blood and agony, and that while we smile at the difficulties and troubles in which an impulsive and generous person gets involved, a man of genius or of talent may be done to death.

I suppose it is very true to say that "every one has these troubles." I do think, however, that a man in my own position, of my own temperament, whose personality seems to penetrate his work in a peculiarly intimate way, so that he then becomes the target for intrigues and scandals of all sorts—such a man, I say, may have them to an exaggerated degree and through no essential fault of his own. Certainly, I do not think he could expect to be protected wholly from them. Certainly no one has the right to expect that his own life will be wholly free from the griefs and troubles that other people have. But I think a man who has not injured other people, who has not interfered with other people's lives or solicited their intrusion, has a right to expect a reasonable and decent amount of privacy—the reasonable and decent amount of privacy that a carpenter, a truck driver or a railroad engineer might have.

At any rate, in spite of all these things, I shall push forward somehow to the completion of my work. I feel that any more confusion or uncertainty might be ruinous to my purpose. There has been too much indecision already. We postponed the completion and publication of "The October Fair," with some intention, I suppose, of showing the critics and the public I could create in a different vein, in a more objective manner than I had yet done. We also deferred completion and publication of "The Hills

Beyond Pentland." I know you said you were willing to go ahead and publish these books. You have always assured me on that point. But I did feel that your counsel and your caution were against their publication now.

I believe you may have allowed your apprehensions concerning who and what I might now write about at the period I had now reached in my writing to influence your judgments. I don't like to go into all this again. The thing that happened last summer, your reaction to the manuscript Miss Nowell brought to you while I was in Europe,[3] and your own comment as expressed to her in a note which she sent to me and which said, after she had cut all the parts you objected to in the manuscript out of it, that "the only person it can now possibly hurt is Thomas Wolfe," was to me a shocking revelation. I am not of the opinion now that the manuscript in question was one of any great merit. I know that I've done much better work. But the point, as I told you after my return from Europe, the point that we discussed so frankly and so openly, was that your action, if carried to its logical conclusions and applied to everything I write from now on, struck a deadly blow at the very vitals of my whole creative life. The only possible inference that could be drawn from this matter was that from now on, if I wished to continue writing books which Charles Scribner's Sons were going to publish, I must now submit myself to the most rigid censorship, a censorship which would delete from all my writings any episode, any scene, any character, any reference that might seem to have any connection, however remote, with the house of Charles Scribner's Sons and its sisters and its cousins and its aunts. Such a conclusion, if I agreed to it, would result in the total enervation and castration of my work—a work which, as I have told you in this letter, I am now resolved must be more strong and forthright in its fidelity to purpose than ever.

Again, in this whole situation there is a display of an almost unbelievable vanity and arrogance. It was first of all, the vanity and arrogance that would lead certain people to suppose that I was going to "write about them," and then the vanity and arrogance of people who said that, although it was perfectly all right for me to write about other people "in humble walks of life," it was an unpardonable affront to all these important high-toned personages to be "written about" freely and frankly by a low scribbling fellow, who is good enough no doubt to supply a publisher with manuscript, to give employment to his business, to add prestige to the reputation of his firm, but who must be put in his place when he overstepped the bounds of human sanctity.

Now, in the first place, as I told you before, whoever got the idea that

---

[3] "No More Rivers." This was never published, but small portions of it are scattered through *The Web and the Rock* and *You Can't Go Home Again*.

I was going to write about him or her or them anyway? And in the second place, whoever got the idea that I was not going to go ahead and write as I damned pleased, about anything I wished to write about, with the complete freedom to which every artist is entitled, and that no one in the world was going to stand in the way of my doing this? I am certainly at the present time not interested in writing about Charles Scribner's Sons or any one connected with Charles Scribner's Sons. It has at the present time no part of my creative plan or of my writing effort. And as you know very well, I don't "write about" people: I create living characters of my own—a whole universe of my own creation. And any character that I create is so unmistakably my own that anyone familiar with my work would know instantly it was my own, even if it had no title and no name.

But, to go back to this simple, fundamental, inescapable necessity of all art, which I have patiently, laboriously, coherently, explained a thousand times, in such language that no one can misunderstand it, to all the people in this country, to all the people who, for some strange and extraordinary reason, in America and nowhere else that I have ever been on earth, keep harping forever, with a kind of idiot pertinacity, upon the word "autobiography"—you can't make something out of nothing. You can either say that there is no such thing as autobiographical writing, or you can say that all writing is autobiographical, a statement with which I should be inclined to agree. But you cannot say, you must not say, that one man is an autobiographical writer and another man is not an autobiographical writer. You cannot and must not say that one novel is an autobiographical novel and another novel is not an autobiographical novel. Because if you say these things, you are uttering falsehood and palpable nonsense. It has no meaning.

My books are neither more nor less autobiographical than "War and Peace." If anything, I should say that they are less, because a great writer like Tolstoi who achieves his purpose, achieves it because he has made a perfect utilization of all the means, all the materials at his disposal. This Tolstoi did in "War and Peace." I have never yet succeeded in doing it completely and perfectly. Accordingly, Tolstoi is a more autobiographical writer than I am, because he has succeeded better in using what he had. But make no mistake about it: both of us, and every other man who ever wrote a book, are autobiographical. You are therefore not to touch my life in this way. When you or any man tries to exert this kind of control, to modify or shape my material in an improper way because of some paltry, personal, social apprehension, you do the unpardonable thing. You try to take from the artist his personal property, to steal his substance, to defraud him of his treasure—the only treasure he has, the only property and wealth which is truly, inexorably, his own.

You can take it from him, but by so doing you commit a crime. You have stolen what does not belong to you. You have not only taken what belongs to another man, but you have taken what belongs to him in such a way that no one else can possibly claim ownership. No one owns what he has as does the artist. When you try to steal it from him he only laughs at you, because you could take it to the ends of the earth and bury it in a mountain and it would still shine straight through the mountain side like radium. You couldn't hide it. Any one on earth could find it and would know at once who the proper owner was.

That is what this final argument is about. I'm not going to be interfered with on this score. I get my material, I acquire my wealth, as every artist does, from his own living, from his own experience, from his own observation. And when any outer agency tries to interpose itself between me and any portion of my own property, however small, and says to me "hands off," [or] "you can't have that particular piece there," someone is going to get hurt.

You told me when I discussed these things with you in October, after my return from Europe, that you agreed with me, that in the last analysis you were always with the man of talent, and that if the worst comes to the worst you could resign your executive and editorial functions. Well, don't worry, you'll never have to. In the first place, your executive and editorial functions are so special and valuable that they can not be substituted by any other person on earth. They could not be done without by the business that employs them. It would be like having a house with the lights turned out. Furthermore, no one is going to resign on my account. There are still enough people in the world who value what I do, I believe, to support me freely, heartily and cheerfully, with no sense that they are enduring martyrdom on my account. So if there is ever any situation that might indicate any future necessity for any one to resign anything on my account, that situation will never arise, simply because I won't be there to be resigned about.

This business about the artist hurting people is for the most part nonsense. The artist is not here in life to hurt it but to illuminate it. He is not here to teach men hatred but to show them beauty. No one in the end ever got hurt by a great book, or if he did, the hurt was paltry and temporary in comparison to the immense good that was conferred.

Now, at a time when I am more firmly resolved than ever before to exert my full amount, to use my full stroke, to shine my purest and intensest ray, it is distressing to see the very people who published my first efforts with complete equanimity, and with no qualms whatever about the possibility of anybody getting "hurt," begin to squirm around uncomfortably and call for calf-rope and whine that their own toes are being stepped upon, even when nothing has been said, nothing written. They have no knowledge or declaration of my own intention except that I intend in my own way to finish my own book. What are you going to do about it? You say you are not aware that there have been any difficulties or any severance. If these things I have been talking about are not difficulties, if this is not a threatened severance of the gravest nature, I should like to know what you consider difficult and what severance is? We can not continue in this irresolute, temporizing "Well now, you go ahead for the present—we'll wait and see how it all turns out" manner. My life has been ravaged, my energy exhausted, my work confused and aborted long enough by this kind of miserable, time-serving procrastination. I'm not going to endure it any longer. I'm not going to pour my sweat and blood and energy and life and talent into another book now, only to be told two or three years from now that it would be inadvisable to publish it without certain formidable deletions, or that perhaps we'd better wait a few years longer and see "how everything turns out."

We stalled around this way with "October Fair," until all the intensity and passion I had put into the book was lost, until I had gone stale on it, until I was no longer interested in it—and to what purpose? Why, because you allowed your fond weakness for the female sex to get the better of your principle, because you were afraid some foolish female, who was inwardly praying for nothing better than to be a leading character in a book of mine, and who was bitterly disappointed when she was not, might get her feelings hurt—or that the pocketbook of the firm might get touched by suits for libel. Well, there would have been no suits for libel. I never libelled anybody in my life. Certainly, there was no remote danger of libel in "The October Fair," but because of our weakness and irresolution the news got around that we were afraid of publication for this reason. The rumor was spread around in the column of a . . . gossip-writer,[4] and the result now is that we have a libel suit on our hands from a person who was never libelled, who doesn't have a leg to stand on, but who is willing to take the chance and make the effort to get something because we were not firm and resolute in the beginning.

Let's make an end of all this devil's business. Let's stand to our guns

---

[4] In *The New York Daily Mirror* for Monday, September 21, 1936, Walter Winchell wrote: "Thomas Wolfe, author of *Of Time and the River* and *Look Homeward, Angel,* has held up publication of his latest novel until all the people in it die. His last two slightly autobiographical tomes brought several libel suits." This is probably what Wolfe refers to here.

like men. Let's go ahead and try to do our work without qualification, without fear, without apology. What are you willing to do? My own position is now clear. I have nothing to be afraid of. And my greatest duty, my deepest obligation now is to the completion of my own work. If that can not be done any longer upon the terms that I have stated here, then I must either stand alone or turn to other quarters for support, if I can find it. You yourself must now say plainly what the decision is to be, because the decision now rests with you. You can no longer have any doubt as to how I feel about these matters. I don't see how you can any longer have any doubt that difficulties of a grave and desperate nature do exist.

I can only repeat here what I have told you before, that the possibility of an irrevocable and permanent severance has caused me the greatest distress and anguish of the mind for months, that if it occurs it will seem to me like death, but that whatever happens, what I have said and written about the way I feel towards you will remain.

I'm going South in a few days for the first time in seven years. It is a tremendous experience for me. Those seven years to me have been a lifetime. So much has been crowded into them—exile and vituperation from my own country, modest success and recognition, then partial oblivion, years of struggling and despairing to conquer a new medium, to fashion a new world, partial success again, added recognition, partial oblivion again. It seems to move in cycles. Now I'm up against the same grim struggle, the same necessity for new discovery, new beginning, new achievement, as before. It will be strange to be back home again. I had but recently met you when I was there last. I was unknown then, but within a few weeks after my visit home a storm of calumny and abuse broke out that made me long for my former oblivion. Now that storm apparently has died down. They are willing to have me come back. So much has happened in those seven years. I've seen so many people that I know go down to ruin, others have died, others have grown up, some have lost everything, some have recovered something. People I knew well I no longer see. People who swore eternal love are now irrevocably separated. Nothing has turned out as we thought it would turn out. Nothing is the way we thought it was going to be. But Life, I now begin to see, moves in a great wheel; the wheel swings and things and people that we knew are lost, but some day they come back again. So it is a strange and wonderful event for me to be going back home. I knew so little of the world and people then, although I thought I knew so much of them. Now I really think I know a little more about the world and people than I knew then, and I think all of us understand a little more about one another.

I'm sorry this letter has had to be so long. It seemed to me there had to be some sort of final statement. I hope, now the statement has been made, the problem is more clear. I send all of you now all my best wishes for Christmas and for a New Year which I hope will bring to all of us an accomplishment and fulfillment of some of those things we most desire.

Meanwhile, with all friendship, all good wishes,

—Max, this is not a well-written letter, but it is a genuine and honest one. If you still have any interest in me, please attend to what I say here carefully!

P.S. New Orleans, Jan. 10, 1937: I have withheld this letter as long as possible. I had hoped against hope not to have to send it. But now, after the shocking events of the past two weeks since I left New York— Mitchell's letter conveying the blackmail threats of —— — the growing peril of my situation in a mesh of scoundrelism—and your own telegram—the increasing ambiguity and caution of your own statements— I have read the letter through again and decided that *it must be sent.* In spite of its great length there is much more to say—but let this stand now for a record!

For Perkins' full replies to this letter, see Editor to Author: The Letters of Maxwell E. Perkins, *pages 119-126. Perkins wrote three letters in reply. The first, dated January 13, said in part:* "My belief is that the one important, supreme object is to advance your work . . . What impedes it especially is . . . the harassment . . . of outside worries. When you spoke to me about the settlement . . . it was only because of that that I gave the advice I did. . . . As to my own self: I stand ready to help if I can, whenever you want. You asked my help on Of Time and the River. . . . No understanding person could believe that it . . . was much more than mechanical help. . . . Apart from physical or legal limitations not within the possibility of change by us, we will publish anything as you write it."

The second was a short note dated January 14, saying in part: "I've read your letter carefully. . . . I have no quarrel with any of it, except that you have greatly misunderstood some things I must explain. . . . Your position is right. I understand and agree with it."

The third letter, dated January 16, is too long and too complex to represent adequately by brief quotations, but says in part: "In the first place, I completely subscribe to what you say a writer should do. . . . But there are limitations of time, of space, and of human laws which cannot be treated as if they did not exist. I think that a writer should, of course, be the one to make his book what he wants it to be, and that if . . . it must be cut, he should be

the one to cut it. . . . It would be better if you could fight it out alone—
better for your work, in the end, certainly. . . . I believe the writer, anyway,
should always be the final judge, and I meant you to be so. . . .

"I certainly do not care—nor does this House—how revolutionary your
books are. I did try to keep you from injecting . . . Marxian beliefs into
Time and the River, because they were . . . not those of Eugene in the
time of the book. . . . It seems as if you must have forgotten how we
worked and argued. You were never overruled . . . I do not want the passage of time to make you cautious or conservative, but I do want it to give
you a full control . . . over your great talent.

"Tom, you ought not to say . . . that I find your sufferings amusing . . .
I do try to turn your mind from them and to arouse your humor, because to
spend dreadful hours brooding over them . . . seems . . . only to aggravate
them.

"Then comes the question of your writing about the people here . . . I
agree that you have the same right to make use of them as of anyone else.
. . . When I spoke of resigning after we published—and the moment I in-
advertently said it I told Miss Nowell she must not repeat it . . . I did not
mean I would be asked . . . to resign. But . . . it's up to you to write as
you think you should. . . .

"There remains the question of whether we are in fundamental agreement.
. . . I have always . . . felt that it was so. . . . But I believe in democracy
and not in dictators . . . and that violence breeds more evils than it kills.
. . . I believe that change really comes from great deep causes too complex
for contemporary men . . . fully to understand and that when even great
men like Lenin try to make over a whole society suddenly the end is almost
sure to be bad, and that the right end, the natural one, will come from the
efforts of innumerable people trying to do right, and to understand it, because
they are a part of the natural forces that are set at work by changed conditions. . . . But this is getting to be too much of a philosophy of history or
something, and I don't think it has anything to do with fundamental agreement. I had always felt it existed—and I don't feel, because you differ with
me . . . on such things . . . that it does not. . . .

"Anyway, I don't see why you should have hesitated to . . . send the letter. . . . There were places in it that made me angry, but it was . . . a fine
writer's statement of his beliefs . . . and . . . it gave me great pleasure
too—that which comes from hearing brave and sincere beliefs uttered with
sincerity and nobility."

The following is "the business letter" which Wolfe never mailed. In it he
is quoting from his own letter of November 12 and Perkins' reply of November 18.

To MAXWELL E. PERKINS

865 First Avenue
New York, N.Y.
December 23, 1936

Dear Max:

I have already written you a long answer to your two personal letters of November 17th and November 18th which you should have received by the time you receive this. Now, before I go away, I want to write an answer to your formal business letter of November 18th, in which you state the relations that now exist between myself and Charles Scribner's Sons.

First of all, let me thank you for acknowledging that I have faithfully and honorably discharged all obligations to you and that no further agreement of any sort exists between us with respect to the future. Then I want to tell you that I am sorry you found parts of my letter obscure and did not wholly understand them. I am sorry, because it seemed to me that the letter was clear. But if there has been any misunderstanding as to what I meant, I shall try to clarify it now.

You say you do not wholly understand the part where "you speak of us as putting you in a position of denying an obligation that does not exist, for we do not know that we have done that." Well, what I said in my letter was "I think it is unfair to put a man in a position where he is forced to deny an obligation that does not exist, to refuse an agreement that was never offered and never made." That is a little different from the way you put it, but I thought it was clear, but if further explanation be needed, I can tell you that what I meant to say by "I think it is unfair to put a man in a position where he is forced to deny an obligation that does not exist" is simply that no one has a right in my opinion to mix calculation and friendship, business caution with personal friendship, financial astuteness with personal affection. The artist cannot do that. Where his friendship, affection and devotion are involved he cannot say, "I think the world of all of you but of course business is business and I shall make such publishing arrangements as shall be most profitable to me." That is what I meant by "I think it is unfair to put a man in a position where he is forced to deny an obligation that does not exist." For, although you have acknowledged that no obligation does exist, after two years of delay since the publication of "Of Time and the River" no concrete proposal has ever been made to me concerning my novel or novels which were to follow it. I have waited in vain, with growing anxiety and bewilderment for such a proposal to be made until the matter has now reached a point of critical acuteness which compelled me to write you as I have written you and say "I think it is unfair to put a man in a position where he is forced to deny an obligation that does not exist."

As to the next phrase, "to refuse an agreement that was never offered and never made," I think the meaning of that phrase is now sufficiently clarified by what has been already said.

To proceed: You say you also do not wholly understand the part of my letter where I "refer to 'exerting control of a man's future' which we have no intention of doing at all, and would not have the power or right to do." What I said was "I think it is also unfair to try to exert, at no expense to oneself, such control of a man's future and his future work as will bring one profit if that man succeeds, and that absolves one from any commitments of any kind should he fail." I thought that sentence was clear too. But if you require additional explanation I can only say that what I meant was that I did not think it fair again to play business against friendship, to accept the loyalty and devotion of an author to the firm that has published him without saying precisely upon what terms and upon what conditions you are willing to publish him in the future. In other words, if I must be still more explicit, I am now in the undeniable position of being compelled to tell people who ask me who my publisher is, that my publisher is Charles Scribner's Sons, while Charles Scribner's Sons on their part, without risk, without involving criticism of any sort, are undeniably in the position where they are able to tell any one that they are my publishers, provided they want to be, but are not my publishers if they do not want to be.

You continue in your letter by saying "there are other phrases in that part of your letter that I do not understand, one of which is that which refers to us as being absolved from any commitments of any kind 'should the author fail.'" I do not see why you should have found this statement obscure or puzzling, but if you did I think that what I have already said in this letter precisely and exactly defines my meaning.

You continue by saying "if this and these other phrases signify that you think you should have a contract from us if our relations are to continue, you can certainly have one. We should be delighted to have one. You must surely know the faith this house has in you. There are, of course, limits in terms to which nobody can go in a contract, but we should expect to make one that would suit you if you told us what was required."

I think it is now my turn to be puzzled. I do not wholly understand what you mean when you say "we should expect to make one" (a contract) "that would suit you if you told us what was required." This really seems almost too good to be true. I have never heard of an author before being able and privileged to tell a publisher "what was required" in the terms of a contract. I cannot believe that is a practice of the publishing business. Authors do not dictate terms of a publisher's contracts. The publisher states the terms himself, and the author accepts them. For my part, so far as my relations with Scribners are concerned, I have always accepted what was offered to me instantly and without question. It seems now a delightfully unexpected, overwhelming privilege to be suddenly told that it is now up to me to state "what is required" in the way of a contract.

Well, then, if I am to be allowed this privilege, may I ask for information on these specific points? When you say in your letter that "our relations are simply those of a publisher who profoundly admires the work of an author and takes great pride in publishing whatever he may of that author's writings," in what sense and meaning am I going to understand the word "may"? I hate to quibble about words, but since you have yourself found it difficult and hard to understand phrases and sentences in my own letter which seem absolutely clear to me, it seems to me that the interpretation of even a little word like "may" may be important. Neither of us surely is so ingenuous as to believe that this statement means that Scribners is eagerly waiting my gracious permission to publish any and all manuscript that I may choose to give to them. We both know that such an interpretation as this would be ridiculous. We both know that in the past six or seven years I have written several million words of which Scribners has published approximately seven or eight hundred thousand. We both know that you have seen and read millions of words of my manuscript which have never been published, which you rejected for publication flatly, or whose publication you advised against. We both know that I not only accepted your advice gratefully but that I also accepted your decision without question, even though it sometimes caused me grievous disappointment when I found that something I had thought good and worthy of publication was not thought good or worthy of publication by the person in whose judgment and critical authority I had and still have unqualified belief. We both know that there was never a time, there has never been a moment since I first walked into your office eight years ago, when I have been in a position to hand you a piece of manuscript and arbitrarily demand that you publish it. The right of selection has always been yours. The right of rejection has always been yours. The right to say what you would or would not publish has always, and to my mind, properly, been finally and absolutely your own privilege. It seems manifest therefore that what you mean by the word "may" as used in your sentence must be interpreted as what you "may see fit" to publish. To this interpretation I have certainly never objected, but now that this misunderstanding and the danger of possible misinterpretation has arisen,

I must ask you, secondly, if you won't try to specify, insofar as you are able, what it is you may see fit to publish of mine. I understand, of course, that there are obvious limits to what a publisher may be expected to publish—limits imposed by law and custom. But within those limits, how far are you willing to go?

You say in one of your personal letters that you "have never doubted for my future on any grounds except, at times, on those of being unable to control the vast mass of material I have accumulated and have to form into books." Alas, it has now become evident that this is not the only difficulty. It is not even any longer a fundamental one. As I have explained in my long letter to you, no matter how great a man's material may be, it has its limits. He can come to the end of it. No man can exceed his own material. It is his constant effort to surpass it, it is true—but he cannot spend money when he has not got it, he can not fish coin from the empty air, he cannot plank it down across the counter when his pockets are empty. No man has more than his one life, and no man's material is greater than his one life can absorb and hold. No man, therefore, not even the artist, can become the utter spendthrift with what he has. It is spitting straight in the face of fortune, and in the end he will get paid back for his folly. You say you have been worried about my being able to control my vast masses of material. May I tell you that in the past year one of my own chief and constantly growing worries has been whether I shall have any material left that I could use if you continue to advise against my present use of it, or if these growing anxieties and perturbations in the year past as to what I should use, as to what I should write about, continued to develop to the utter enervation and castration of my work. Therefore, having as you do some approximate knowledge, a far better one than any one else at any rate, of the material at my command, can't you try, in view of all these doubts and misunderstandings, to specify what you think you may be able to publish and how much of it?

Third, at about what time would you now desire and expect to publish it, if I fulfilled my work in time? I know that I have been grievously at fault in meeting publication dates heretofore, but you know too it has not been through lack of effort or of application but rather through the difficulties imposed by my own nature and my imperfect understanding of the writer's art and the command of the tools of my profession. Nevertheless, and in spite of all these imperfections on my part, I should like to get some fairly definite notion of when it is you next expect to publish me, if ever. The reason that I am so earnestly and seriously concerned with this is that in former years, before the publication of "Of Time and the River," you did show the greatest anxiety on this score. You were constant in your efforts to spur me on, to get me to complete and finish something for publication. Now, although almost two years have gone by since the publication of my last long book, you no longer show any anxiety whatever and, so far as I can judge, no immediate interest.

Finally, if you do want to publish another book of mine, if you can try to tell me what it is you think you want to publish, what you will be able to publish, and when you would like to publish it—what, finally and specifically, are these terms of which you speak?

You say "there are, of course, limits in terms to which nobody can go in a contract, but we should expect to make one that would suit you if you told us what was required." I suppose, of course, that when you say that there are "limits in terms to which nobody can go in a contract" you mean that there are limits in terms beyond which no one can go. I understand this perfectly. But what, specifically, are these limits? What, specifically, are these terms?

Now I'm awfully sorry, Max, to have to try your patience with another long letter, and I am sorry if I seem to quibble over words and phrases, but I really do not think I quibble, since all these matters are of such vital and immediate concern to me and since we both have seemed to have trouble understanding sentences and phrases in each other's letters. I have gone to extreme lengths in this one to make everything I say as clear as possible. I shall be on my way South when you get this letter. I intend to be in New Orleans New Year's day, but since I am still uncertain whether I shall stay with friends or in a hotel, I suggest that you write me, if you have time and feel like writing, in care of General Delivery.

Meanwhile, until I hear from you, or until I see you again, with all my best and friendliest greetings to everyone at Scribners,

Max: This letter is imperative. I must have an answer—a definite one—at once.

I have deferred sending this, and accordingly am sending it from Richmond, Va. (But I deferred that too!)

P.S. I am writing you this from Richmond. Frankly, I think we are at the end. I am sending this to you now. I should have sent it to you long ago, in view of the agony, the despair, the utter desolation this thing has cost me—but I must send it to you now. As to the other letter—the enormously long letter I wrote in answer to your two personal ones [1]—I shall hold

[1] The "Personal Letter" dated December 15, 1936 and mailed on January 10.

on to it a day longer—reread it—perhaps make little revisions here and there. Anything! Anything!—to try to temper the sorrow and the grief of this final decision into which I—God knows—have been compelled without even the power of saying whether I wanted it or not. You must answer this *straight!*

Additional P.S. As to your statement that anyone would *want* me—that, as you must *now* know, is not true. I am almost penniless—this suit for libel has appeared with almost sinister immediacy in the last month or two—I have turned down fortunes—$10,000 *is* a fortune to me, and you knew of *that* one at once, the one that was made me two years ago when I was really penniless, and when you asked me to tell you what the offer was. I am broke—I have lost everything—I do not think we can go on. Who, then, are these eager publishers? Answer at New Orleans.

P.S. Max: You'd better send the answer air mail to New Orleans. I am afraid you did not take this thing seriously but, as I told you, it is like death to me. You'd better answer by wire. Atlanta, December 29, 1936. You'd better say *precisely* what you can offer. Atlanta December 29, 1936.

To ELIZABETH NOWELL

[Chapel Hill, N.C.]
Sunday, January 24, 1937

Dear Miss Nowell:

I have been unable to do much to this first installment [1] since coming here. People have swarmed around me—old friends I have not seen in seventeen years or so—and there has been no time for anything. I went over the first half of this installment and made—or rather indicated—a few cuts. If you and *The New Republic* think them good, make them: if not, you can leave it as it stands. This first section is something over 5,000 words but I have found it very hard to cut. I intend to be back in New York Wednesday, and will call you then.

I wish you could wait with this till Wednesday. Wouldn't *The New Republic* let you? I'm worried about a lot of things—phonetics, accents, etc. I'm not yet sure what to do about all the "zis," "zese," "zem" business.

[1] The first installment of "I Have a Thing to Tell You" which was to be published in the March 10 issue of *The New Republic*.

I want to use as little as possible and yet to be consistent. I must either do without them entirely—or use them constantly. Please go through the manuscript and, if you think best, make it consistent—that is, get all the "th" words consistent: "fazzer," "mozzer," "zis," "zat," etc. The character I had in mind really did not speak with such a marked or broken accent: yet he *did* have an accent and I had to suggest it somehow. Have I overdone it? Wait till Wednesday if you can.

Garland B. Porter, to whom the following letter was written, had known Wolfe at the University of North Carolina. They had met by accident in Atlanta when Wolfe was on his way to New Orleans, and Porter had invited Wolfe to visit him on his way back. At this time, Porter was national advertising manager of The Atlanta Georgian *and southern manager for the Hearst Advertising Service. He is now general manager of* Southern Advertising and Publishing.

To GARLAND B. PORTER

865 First Avenue
New York, N.Y.

February 1, 1937

Dear Garland:

I should have written you before this, but since I left you I haven't had much time. I got back here a week ago and had to plunge into work right away getting a long piece, which *The New Republic* is going to publish, cut down to printable proportions. It was a wonderful trip and one of the nicest things about it was seeing you again and meeting the family. Please give them all my love and tell them how much I want to see them all again.

I stayed three or four days with Jim Boyd after leaving Atlanta and had a grand time there. They are fine people. They have a beautiful place right in the pine woods. I can't tell you how good it was to be back in my own state again and just to get my number fourteens down on North Carolina clay. I went up to Chapel Hill and stayed four or five days. It was a great experience. It took me about two days to get used to the place. They've created another world since you and I were at school there, but down below I think the people are much the same as they always were. I saw Horace [1] twice and had long talks with him,

[1] Professor Horace Williams.

and also met dozens of other people I had known. Horace holds his own, I think, amazingly well. He is older, of course, and a little feebler, than when we sat in his classes, but the old man can still flash like a rapier. He can talk as he always could. I think he may be lonely now. His active connection with the University has almost ceased, and of course the greatest part of his life, for almost fifty years, was with his students. I suppose with the present student generation he is more or less of a legend, and I don't believe they'd beat a path to his door the way they used to do.

I saw Paul Green [2] and Phillips Russell,[3] Jonathan Daniels, Albert Coates and a host of other people we both know. I stayed with Shorty Spruill [4] and his wife. It was wonderful to find that so many people I had known still lived in Chapel Hill. Then I went up to Warrenton for two or three days and stayed with Bill Polk and his family. I don't know if there's any chance of you and the missus coming up here within the next few months, but if you do please let me know. . . . I'm still short on sleep, but otherwise I had a much-needed change and the wonderful stimulation of seeing old friends, home folks, home soil again. I'm getting back to work as soon and as hard as possible. I hope to do another big job this spring and to come back to North Carolina for another visit late in April. I send you all my love and best wishes. Please write me when you get a chance.

Ever since his return to New York at the end of January, Wolfe had avoided Scribners, but he still frequented Perkins' house on East 49th Street. Both men knew that his complete severance from Scribners was almost inevitable, but they continued to argue endlessly about it in some faint hope that it could be averted. The following telegram, scrawled in pencil in Wolfe's pocket notebook, was evidently written soon after his return from New Orleans but was never sent.

[2] Paul Green had attended the University of North Carolina with Wolfe and been a member of The Carolina Playmakers with him. He is the author of *Lonesome Road, In Abraham's Bosom, Tread the Green Grass, This Body the Earth, Hymn to the Rising Sun,* and other plays and novels.

[3] Phillips Russell had graduated from the University of North Carolina earlier but returned there as a teacher in 1931. He is now Professor of Journalism there, and the author of *Benjamin Franklin: First Civilized American; Emerson: The Wisest American; The Glittering Century, The Woman Who Rang the Bell,* etc.

[4] Corydon P. Spruill was in Wolfe's class at the University of North Carolina and closely associated with him. He returned to the university as Professor of Economics, and is now Dean.

To MAXWELL E. PERKINS
[Telegram]

[New York City]
[February ?, 1937]

Dear Max Perkins:

Does Scribners want my next book? Please answer immediately.

XV

THE RETURN TO ASHEVILLE AND THE FINAL
BREAK WITH SCRIBNERS

1937

To FRED W. WOLFE

> 865 First Avenue
> New York, N.Y.
> February 23, 1937

Dear Fred:

I have been wanting to write you before, but I've been down with flu and also had to do a lot of work and spend a lot of time with the lawyers since I returned from the South. I got a long letter from Mama this morning in answer to one I wrote her a week or so ago. She tells me something about her affairs in it and about the suit which the Wachovia Bank is bringing against the family.[1] I gather that, since I am a member of the family, I am also mentioned as one of the parties in the suit. If this is true, I should like to have a little more specific information about it. I've had a good deal to do with suits and lawyers in the last two years, and, although this is one branch of human activity I never wanted to take part in and never sought out on my own account, it is just possible I may have learned a little and might be able to help out now with suggestions. So why don't you write me now and try to tell me what it's all about?

---

[1] The Wachovia Bank and Trust Company of Asheville had brought suit against Mrs. Wolfe, her heirs, itself as her trustee, and various individuals who held liens on her property. They alleged that she had borrowed various sums of money from them since 1927, for which she had executed certain deeds of trust and had put up various pieces of real estate as pledges of security. They petitioned that since she owed them various amounts of money as principal and interest on these loans, the property be foreclosed and sold to settle her indebtedness to them. A court settlement of the case was finally made in 1939.

I read Mama's letter carefully two or three times, and although I do understand certain things in it, I don't understand why she, or particularly the children—for certainly I knew nothing about it—are being sued. According to Mama's letter, the Wachovia, about ten years ago, persuaded her to make out what she calls a "living trust." She says she signed the trust, but that she did not fully understand what was in it, or just what it was she was signing. The gist of the letter from then on, as I understand it, is that the bank . . . sold property at prices far lower than the property was worth, etc. I can follow all this, and can understand how, if these facts are true and could be substantiated in court, we would have cause for action against the Wachovia Bank. But why has the Wachovia Bank cause for action against Mama, and, more especially, against her children? . . . I'd like to know what their side of the story is, what do they claim, upon. what contention do they base their suit against Mama, you and me and all the rest of us? And the reason I ask for this information is because your side of the case and Mama's side of the case is also my side of the case. So far as possible, I should like to get the facts clear in my mind.

I now intend to come to Asheville and to go out into the mountains for a few days at the end of April or the early part of May, and perhaps I may be able to be of some assistance to you then. I hope so, because of course I am wholeheartedly on Mama's side. I think it is shameful to see them take her house away from her, and I shall do whatever I can to prevent it. Therefore, I think you ought to take me into your confidence. I know that none of you ever thought I was much of a business man and I would cheerfully agree with all of you that I am not. But I think I can also point out to you that whatever money I've lost has been lost because I have been the victim of rackets to which, my lawyers inform me, almost everyone of any public reputation here in America is exposed and against which there seems at the present time to be no defense save a defense that would cost more time and money and worry than the racket itself. There is nothing that I can do about this condition except to hope and pray that it will change, and to do whatever I can in my own individual capacity to bring it to light, to make people aware of it, and to try as a good citizen to change it. But I've never been taken in by any get-rich-quick schemes yet. I never had much belief in them. The most I have hoped for is the chance to earn a decent living, get some security against the future, and have peace and time in which to do my work. On this ground, I'm pretty sound and sure of myself, so I wish you'd try to tell me in a little more detail just what this suit against *us* is all about.

I'm just getting over flu and it's left me feeling pretty weak, but

I keep on working. I'm getting a little better every day now. The trouble with the lawyers was about to get me down, but I didn't let it happen. There's not going to be much left when I get through paying the rascals off, or what amounts to just the same thing, paying lawyers to defend me against the rascals. But I shall get through it somehow and do another big piece or work, and some day, perhaps, get a rip-snorting book out of this whole experience, which I imagine you could throw in under the general title of "Life" and not be far wrong about it.

I had a good trip through the South but didn't get much rest. People were after me all the time and, just to make things pleasant, the lawyers wrote informing me . . . that I'd better come back right away. I should have liked to come to Asheville and intended to do so, but when I called you up from Atlanta there seemed to be some excitement and confusion about my coming, or whether I wanted to come or not, so I was too tired to argue the point and decided to pass my visit up until some other time.

Yes, I got your gift of neckties, and your box of nuts and raisins. I'm sorry that I did not acknowledge them before, but let me thank you for them now.

I have tried to do the best I could towards everyone. I've had to deal with a lot of trouble. I've gone through a lot of worry and suffered a lot of disillusionment, and of course, with me as with every other man, one of the main troubles of life, one of the chief worries, is how to get a job and keep on doing it. Maybe my own experience is a little different from most people's. I have a job and a big one too—more work than I can possibly do. But the last year or two, it has sometimes seemed to me that there is a general plot abroad not to keep people like myself out of work but to keep them from doing the work they already have. Not many people realize very well what a man is up against if he has been unfortunate enough to get his name in the papers a few times, and it sometimes seems that one's old friends and acquaintance know it least of all. It sometimes seems that whenever a man gets a little public notice the very people who have known him longest show the least understanding of all the problems he has got to meet. I'll get through this somehow and, meanwhile, there's always the hope I'll get a chance to work, to get an even break, to earn enough from what I write to get rid of the lawyers and the rascals and to earn my living without getting into debt.

This is all for the present. Mama tells me she is going to Miami for a a week or so. I know the change will do her good. I am enclosing a little check for her. . . . I'd be much obliged to you if you'd send it right along to her and tell her please to try to have a little fun. . . . Write me when you can, and tell me something if you can about Mama's difficulties. With all best wishes, as ever,

On the afternoon of February 17, 1937, Wolfe and Charles Scribner had a long discussion on the telephone about the advisability of settling the libel suit, in the course of which Wolfe evidently reiterated his demand for a complete release from Scribners. Accordingly, the following day, Mr. Scribner wrote him, saying: "You can feel assured that we have no option or moral claim on any of your future books. We should like to continue as your publishers as we have every faith in your work and feel certain that you are due to write even finer books than those which we have published. On the other hand, if you find that the connection with us is not to your liking, I certainly do not wish to press you to continue. With regard to the present libel suit, we agreed at luncheon to go fifty-fifty on this, and you agreed to settle it for not over $2500. . . . The more I think of it, the more certain I am that it would be the wise thing to get this out of the way, for your own peace of mind. I fully appreciate the fact that you do not wish to be held up, but it would certainly take a lot of time and money to fight it out. If you decide, however, that you would rather not settle, I am perfectly prepared to back you in seeing it through to a finish."

A few days after this, Wolfe reluctantly agreed to settle the suit. Accordingly, his half of the settlement and lawyer's fees, which half amounted to $2745.25, were paid by Scribners from his royalty account in three separate installments on February 23, April 1, and May 3. He was horrified to see his savings thus wiped out, blamed the whole affair on Scribners, and took Charles Scribner's letter of February 18 as proof that he was "free to go." The following letter approaching publishers other than Scribners was probably written as a result of all this, in March, 1937, but was never mailed. However, in December, 1937, Wolfe handed it to Edward C. Aswell of Harper & Brothers, saying that it would explain the nature of his severance from Scribners.

To ALL PUBLISHERS

[OTHER THAN SCRIBNERS]

865 First Avenue
New York, N.Y.
[March, 1937?]

Gentlemen:

I am the author of four published books, of which two are novels, one, a book of stories, and one, a short volume about my experience as a writer. Since I am no longer under any obligation, whether financial, contractual, or personal, to any publisher, I am writing to inquire if I could talk to you about my future work.

In order that there may be nothing in this letter capable of misinterpretation, I want to state here with the utmost candor my reasons for writing you. First of all, I want to say most earnestly that I am not approaching any publisher at the present time in an effort to secure good terms and get a contract, but in the genuine hope that this letter will reach some person of critical judgment and understanding who will be interested—and disinterested—enough to listen to my story, allow me to lay the matter before him, with all its difficulties and complexities, and then, if he can, give me the benefit of his advice.

This would involve the discussion of unpublished manuscript that runs into millions of words, and projects for work that will occupy me for years. I realize that to ask for advice and guidance of this sort from people that I do not know, when I have at the present time no completed work to offer for examination, is a strenuous and perhaps unwarranted demand upon the generosity of a stranger, but necessity of the gravest kind has compelled me to this course as being the only one that is now left open to me.

May I say here that so far as my relations with my former publishers are concerned, they have been characterized from beginning to end on both sides by feelings of the deepest affection and respect. I have been fortunate in having for my publishers a firm which not only enjoys a public and professional standing of the highest order but which, in all its dealings with me has been eminently just and fair. Moreover, the nature of our relationship has been so peculiarly intimate and personal that no one can possibly know, better than myself, the gravity of the step I am now taking, or the peril with which it is charged.

For seven years or more I have enjoyed the friendship of an editor of extraordinary character and ability, who at a time when I needed help desperately, when I was trying to learn how to write, when I was involved with gigantic masses of material and struggling with a task of such magnitude that at times I almost gave up in despair, stood by me and gave me without stint not only the benefits of his great technical and editorial skill but also the even more priceless support of his faith and belief, a spiritual sustenance of the grandest and most unselfish kind. To this man I owe a debt of gratitude so deep and lasting that I feel I can never repay it, or never sufficiently testify to it by anything I say or write. And the prospect of this severance of our relations—professionally, at any rate— not only with this man but with many other people in that house, is for me not only a prospect of the utmost gravity, but it is like having to face the prospect of making a new, and perhaps disastrous, beginning in life.

But I can see no other course before me. For months now, perhaps for a year, or more, there has been a steady widening of the ground between us, a difference of opinion, of conviction, of belief, even a spiritual severance that is so profound and grave that it touches the very heart of my life and work, and if I remain I see no prospect before me but the utter enervation of my work, my final bafflement and frustration as an artist.

I should like to say here further that the necessity which compels me to write this letter is, I believe, understood and appreciated thoroughly by my former publishers, has been examined and discussed so thoroughly in the conversation and correspondence of several months that there is now nothing more to say on either side, except that this necessity is a matter of the most genuine and profound regret to each of us.

Now I can only say, with utter candor, that I hope that I am prepared to do the best work of my life, but that, if I am to do any work at all, I can now do it only by making no compromise of artistic integrity, by making rather the most full, free, honest, and final use of my talents and of my materials that I have ever made.

Finally I should like to say that these differences, I believe, were inevitable and inescapable, that they have been honorably and honestly arrived at on both sides, and that the feeling of friendship and respect between my publishers and myself is as deep as it always was. I believe that they would confirm me in all I say.

To have to write in a formal letter, and at such length, explanations of such intimate and personal concern to myself and other people, is a painful and difficult task. But it seemed to me that, circumstances being what they are, to write less explicitly than I have might lay open to misinterpretation not only my own position but my relations to other people whose conduct has been generous and high.

As I have no wide acquaintance in the publishing profession I have taken this means, as difficult as it is, as being the only one by which I could state my problem and establish contact with someone who might help me. Accordingly, I have addressed this letter to several publishers. But, so far as possible, within these limitations, I hope that the contents of this letter will be treated as personal and confidential.

I believe that I am now engaged upon the most important book that I have ever written. But the book is far from complete: a great task is before me. Now I should like to talk to some editor of critical understanding and judgment, for the purpose of laying the matter before him, with complete frankness and with all the difficulties and perplexities it entails.

If there is such a person in your house who is willing to give me an evening's time, with no commitments on either side, I should be grateful for his courtesy in doing so. I can be reached at this address, and any evening after March twenty-fifth would be convenient.

Dixon Wecter had first met Wolfe at the University of Colorado where he was an assistant professor of English when Wolfe attended the Writers' Conference there in 1935. On Wolfe's recommendation, he had taken his book, The Saga of American Society, to Scribners who were to publish it soon after the date of the following letter. He had therefore written Wolfe saying: "I have an impulse to write and tell you how everlastingly grateful I am for your introduction to Maxwell Perkins. As Thornton Wilder told me some time ago, he is 'the last of the great paternal editors.'" The following was Wolfe's reply.

At the time of his death in 1950, Wecter was a professor of English at the University of California, Literary Editor of the Mark Twain Estate, and author of The Saga of American Society; Edmund Burke and His Kinsmen; The Hero in America *(with William Matthews)*; Our Soldiers Speak; When Johnny Comes Marching Home; The Age of the Great Depression, *etc. His* Sam Clemens of Hannibal *was published posthumously in 1952.*

To DIXON WECTER

865 First Avenue
New York, N.Y.

March 5, 1937

Dear Dixon:

I was delighted to get your letter, and so glad to know you have at last finished your long labor on the book. I don't get around to Scribners nowadays, but I can tell you out of my own knowledge that Perkins is delighted with the book and with the job you have done, and in his reticent fashion displays as much hope of the book's success as I can remember his showing over anything. He has told me repeatedly what a fine book it is, and he told me recently that there was no doubt that it would receive a fine critical reception, but that he also hoped and believed it might have a good popular reception too. At any rate, I can assure you that you are in the hands of people on whom you can utterly rely.

I was so happy to read what you said about Perkins, because that is the way I feel too. I agree absolutely with everything you say, except your too modest estimate of your own abilities, which Perkins certainly rates very highly. But I don't believe his like is to be found anywhere in the editorial world. In fact, I think he has a faculty of intuition and understanding that amounts to genius. He has certainly done more, I think, not only to discover but to stimulate new talent than any man of his time. I called him up this morning when I got your letter and told him I'd heard from you, but I could not read him what you said because it would bring the blushes to his face. But he was awfully pleased about it, and he said again what a fine book you had written and how interested and excited they all were about it. He wanted to know if you had gone to Switzerland and I told him you were apparently just on the point of going when you wrote the letter. I suppose you're there now and I somewhat enviously wish you a most happy holiday. . . .

There's not much news that I can give you. I went South just after Christmas—my first trip back home in seven years—and was overwhelmed, in fact almost exhausted, by hospitality. I keep plugging away here and have done a lot of writing, although I have gotten pretty tired. *The New Republic,* beginning with this week's issue, is publishing three installments of a long story that I wrote about Germany.[1] They are advertising it rather lavishly as "a new short novel," but it is not a novel, long or short, and I never said it was. I think it may be pretty good. At any rate I've crossed the Rubicon as far as my relations with the Reich are concerned. It cost me a good deal of time and worry to make up my mind whether I should allow the publication of the story because I am well known in Germany, my books have had a tremendous press there, I have many friends there, and I like the country and the people enormously. But the story wrote itself. It was the truth as I could see it, and I decided that a man's own self-respect and integrity is worth more than his comfort or material advantage. . . .

I wish I could accept your invitation to spend the weekend with you at Oxford. There's nothing I'd like better. I'm sorry if anything I wrote gave you any other impression,[2] but I really love the place and thought the few weeks I spent there some of the happiest of my life. Unfortunately, I don't see much prospect of taking another long voyage until I get another big piece of work done. I sometimes wonder, when I pick up the paper and read about the vexed and tragic state of Europe as it is to-day, whether it would not be wise for all of us who have a chance to see it now, without further delay, before the big explosion comes. Of course, I hope it doesn't happen. But it sometimes seems that only a miracle could avert it now.

I had not meant to write you such a long letter, but it was good to hear from you, and I am delighted to know that your book is finished and that everyone is so hopeful about it. I shall await its publication and its reception with great eagerness. Meanwhile congratulations and all my best wishes for your success and happiness.

[1] *I Have A Thing to Tell You.*

[2] Wecter was at Merton College, Oxford, at this time and had written to Wolfe: "The only thing with which I disagreed in your last novel was the section on Oxford, and I shall undertake to convince you of a different aspect if you will spend a weekend or a week with me here next term."

P.S. On my trip South after Christmas I stopped off at Richmond and had not been there a day before I ran into Red Warren, Allen Tate, Caroline Gordon, John Crowe Ransom [3] and many others who were there for a meeting of The Modern Language Association, I think. I spent a very pleasant evening with the Warrens, the Tates, the Brooks [4] and Mr. Ransom. In fact I did almost everything except become a Southern Agrarian. I suppose I don't understand enough about that. But it was good to see Red again and to meet all the others. Red asked about you and I told him about your book and how hopeful people were about it. This is all for the present. Good-bye and good luck. Write me when you can.

To HAMILTON BASSO

Roanoke, Virginia

April 28th, 1937.

Dear Ham:

I wanted to answer your letter before but to tell the truth, this is the first letter writing or writing of any sort that I have done in a month. I have been loafing down the beautiful Shenandoah Valley all the way from Pennsylvania for the last week or ten days and have seen a great deal of flood and rain but very little of the beautiful Shenandoah Valley. The weather is fine today. I am going on to Bristol, Virginia, tomorrow, then over to Yancey County [1] for a few days, then on to Asheville and then I hope to see you and Toto either at Asheville or on your own estate.

In short, I am beginning to perk up again and I think I shall survive the wars. For a change I have begun to sleep. Every one tells me I do everything to excess and now nothing less than fourteen hours a day of slumber will suffice me. I am beginning to worry about not working again, which is also an ominous symptom.

[3] Robert Penn Warren is the author of the 1946 Pulitzer Prize novel, *All the King's Men,* and other novels, biographies and poems, and had been a "visiting novelist" at the University of Colorado Writers' Conference with Wolfe in 1935. Allen Tate, a contemporary poet and critic, is the author of *The Mediterranean and Other Poems, The Fathers, Reason in Madness, Poems, 1922–1947,* etc. Caroline Gordon (Mrs. Tate) is the author of *Penhally, The Garden of Adonis, The Women on the Porch, The Strange Children,* etc. John Crowe Ransom is the author of *God Without Thunder, The World's Body, The New Criticism, Poetics, Selected Poems,* and other books. This group of writers contributed largely to *The Southern Review,* of which Warren was an editor, and were leaders in the Southern Agrarian movement.

[4] Cleanth Brooks was then co-editor of *The Southern Review* with Warren.

[1] Burnsville, Yancey County, North Carolina, had been the home of Wolfe's maternal ancestors, the Westalls, for many years before his grandparents had moved to the mountains outside Asheville and finally to Asheville itself. John Westall, a half-brother of Wolfe's grandfather, still lived in Burnsville, and it was to see him that Wolfe was going there.

Yes, Max Perkins and I are all right. I think we always were, for that matter. Periodically I go out and indulge in a sixty-round, knock down and drag out battle with myself but I think Max understands that. I am afraid it is likely to happen again but in the end I believe I may pull through. I read somewhere that no writer has ever yet been known to hang himself as long as he had another chapter left.

Sherwood Anderson came to New York two or three weeks ago and we all had dinner together at Cherio's—Anderson, Max and I. I thought he was fine—he seems to have picked up a lot of real wisdom and real mellowness and real understanding along the way. I think there is just a shade too much of resignation in it—he told me, for example, that we writers didn't count for much anyway in the scheme of things, a statement which I am vociferously prepared to deny—but, of course, all this is probably just the effect of his age and experience and a certain sense of completion. But I liked him very much. We had a good time and I hope I shall see him again. He spoke of you with great affection.

This is all for the present. I am going to have my sleep out and mosey along in my own way until I am ready to come to town. When I get there I will let you know. Meanwhile, with love and all good wishes to you and Toto,

To CORYDON P. SPRUILL

865 First Avenue
New York, N.Y.

May 20, 1937

Dear Shorty:

I found your letter informing me that the dogwood had arrived in Chapel Hill waiting for me when I got back from Asheville the other day. I knew that you would be punctual to the dot, and my own delay in answering you is occasioned by the fact that, during all the time I was in Asheville, I did not have time to write a line to anyone.

If I can say so with any modesty, the homecoming of the prodigal was a crashing success. Everything apparently, to my enormous relief, is forgiven. At any rate, they were glad to have me back again and I do not have to tell you how glad I was to be back. I wish you would tell Julia [1] that even though I missed the Chapel Hill dogwood, I saw whole mountains full that was from North Carolina. It was one of the loveliest springs I have ever seen and I never really knew just how homesick I had been until I got back again.

[1] Mrs. Spruill.

I should have come by Chapel Hill on my way back to New York except for the fact that I so far over-stayed my visit in Asheville that I had to come back here in a hurry, but it may interest you to know that I now belong to the landed gentry. I have rented a cabin on top of a hill a few miles out of Asheville, complete isolation and fifteen or twenty acres of my own woods all around it.

I do not know where you are going this summer, or what you plan to do, but if your plans should lead you up in the direction of Asheville, I should be proud and happy to show you my estate, and to put you up. I will be here in New York until the end of June, but plan to be back in North Carolina for the beginning of July. Please let me know your own plans, and meanwhile, with best wishes and love to you all,

To FRED W. WOLFE

865 First Avenue
New York, N.Y.

May 24, 1937

Dear Fred:

Your note came this morning. I am back at work. There is little news to record except that I stopped off for a day at Washington on the way up and saw Virginia and Frederica.[1] . . .

Yes, George McCoy sent me the clippings of the piece in the *Citizen*.[2] I am glad you like it. They made a few mistakes, typographical errors in words, and left out a sentence or two, but on the whole I think it turned out all right. What worries me most at present is the row that seems to have broken out at home after my visit there had passed off so well. George McCoy and Annie Westall [3] are apparently squabbling over what shall be done with the manuscript, and my chief interest is to settle it peaceably and not be bothered about it any more. Of course, I had no idea that there would be any controversy of any sort. The whole thing came up casually. I saw Annie in the street before I left and, in the course of our conversation, she mentioned that she was a director or trustee of the Randolph Macon library and that they were making a collection of autographs and manuscripts and would I contribute something. I told her I should be glad to. This suggested to me that I had promised to write the *Citizen* a piece, and I told her I could give her this or something else if she preferred. She said this would be all right, and so the matter rested. I wrote the piece and gave it to George McCoy

[1] Wolfe's nieces, the daughters of Effie Wolfe Gambrell.

[2] "Return" in the May 16, 1937, issue of *The Asheville Citizen-Times*.

[3] Annie Westall is the daughter of Mrs. Wolfe's brother, James M. Westall.

just an hour or so before I caught the train. I told him to give it to Annie as soon as he had finished with it for the *Citizen,* and he then said that he had intended to give it to the Sondley Library and that he thought, since it was about Asheville, written on the occasion of my return, it ought to stay there. I told him I thought this was all right and to call up Annie and tell her I would send her another piece—that is, if the Randolph Macon library did not want this one. That, I thought, was the end of the whole matter. But in the last few days I have had letters from George McCoy and Miss Dickey [4] of the Sondley Library, and apparently a row has broken out in which everyone except myself is taking part. George said he called up Annie and she expressed herself at first as being perfectly satisfied, saying that as she was on the board of both libraries, it was turning out well both ways. Then Jack Westall [5] called up and, according to George, laid him out, saying that his conduct was "gratuitous." George took the manuscript to the Sondley Library and left it. Miss Dickey, the librarian, wrote me and said that Annie came around later and took it back, apparently telling her that she had promised it to Randolph Macon for commencement and was, therefore, in an embarrassing situation, all of which was news to me since I do not remember her mentioning commencement in our conversation. Then Mama apparently called up Miss Dickey and gave her version of the affair and Miss Dickey wrote me saying that she felt this particular manuscript ought to stay in Asheville at the Sondley Library and that she was sure Annie would be satisfied just as well if I gave her something else. I have written both George McCoy and Annie and tried to make peace and offered to give both of them a piece of manuscript for both libraries. I hope they get the matter adjusted to their mutual satisfaction and that it does not wind up, as these things so often do, by an innocent party, in this case myself, being heartily damned by all sides. I did not get a penny for the piece or for the manuscript, nor did I expect one. Now I just don't want to get embroiled in any petty and useless argument.

I had a letter from Max Whitson [6] this morning telling me he is fixing up the road and making repairs in the cabin and putting it in good order, and that he would be delighted to have Mama look at it when he gets it ready. He said he would take her out himself, but if you are in Asheville one Sunday soon and have time, I wish you would call him up

[4] Miss Philena A. Dickey was director of the Sondley Library.

[5] James Westall (familiarly known as Jack), the son of James M. Westall and brother of Annie Westall.

[6] Max Whitson, the cartoonist, was the owner of the cabin at Oteen which Wolfe had rented.

and get the key and drive Mama out and look the place over and let me know what you think of it. I thought it was a right nice place, and Max, who went to school with me, assured me that he was putting it in good order and that I would find it a very comfortable place to live in. . . .

Mr. Perkins has moved out to his place in the country for the summer, but of course he comes to business every day and I am seeing him this week. He called up and asked about you all, and seemed very pleased when I told him my reception at home had been such a warm, hospitable one. I was pretty tired when I left there. I certainly want to see my friends this summer, and get away from some of the troubles and worries and interruptions that have harassed me in the last year or so. I hope people will understand this and not come breaking in on me at all hours and moments of the day. Anyway, I am going to try it, and I have high hopes that it will work out well.

This is all for the present. . . . Let me know if there is any news. Meanwhile, love and best wishes to you all.

To FRED W. WOLFE

865 First Avenue
New York, N.Y.

June 26, 1937

Dear Fred:

I have wanted to answer your letter before this, but I have been driving as hard as I could go ever since I got back here five or six weeks ago in an effort to get as much work done as possible before I leave here. I am trying to wind it up to-day and to-morrow. I have been working every day, and often at night also with Miss Nowell, my agent. She is coming here again tomorrow, Sunday, for another go at it and I hope then to finish up the work I have been doing. . . .

According to my present plans I hope to leave here for Asheville some time next week, possibly around Tuesday or Wednesday. I am dog-tired, just about played out, and dreading the big job of packing, getting ready, that is before me. My main concern is, of course, my manuscript. There is an immense amount of it, millions of words, and although it might not be of any use to anyone else, it is, so far as I am concerned, the most valuable thing I have got. My life is in it—years and years of work and sweating blood—and the material of about three unpublished books. I am going to bring it with me to North Carolina, but I have not fully decided yet just what means of transportation I shall use. I hate to take the chance of letting it go out of my sight. I suppose the Railway Express is safe enough. What I should prefer to do would be to take it right with me in the train, but unfortunately there is so much of it that nothing less than a good-sized packing-case would hold it. In addition, I have to buy some clothes and supplies and take along my bedding and towels. Mama has written me that she will need all that she has this summer so, as you can see, I have quite a problem in moving upon my hands.

I got a letter from Max Whitson this morning in which he informs me that he has put the cabin in good shape, waxed the floors, fixed up the road that leads to the place, and has put in some new furniture, and that everything is now comfortable and ready. If this is so, I think I ought to find it a good place to live and work, if too many people don't start coming out and paying me casual and unexpected visits.

People, of course, don't seem to be able to get this into their heads. Most people don't realize that writing is not only hard work, but that a writer, when he works, works several times as hard as the average business man. Moreover, when a writer is working he ought not to be interrupted, and few people are able to understand how big a difference that makes. A great many people apparently think that they can drop in on a man while he is writing and spend an hour or two in conversation—that it does not matter very much—that he can make it all up later. Well, this is not the way it goes: he ought not to be interrupted: if he is, it sometimes throws him completely off the track and he cannot make it up.

My experience has been that most business and professional people do not work very hard, not nearly as hard as they think they do. This is particularly true of a town like Asheville. I have always noticed in Asheville, even in my childhood, how much time nearly everyone has to waste. Lawyers and bankers and business people are always coming in and out of the drug store, fooling around and talking to one another: apparently they have time to burn. I noticed this again when I was home in May: a lot of the boys I know who are now lawyers would invite me up to their offices in the Jackson Building and we would spend an entire afternoon talking, and no one would come in. The point I am trying to make here is that, as much as I should like to, I have not got time to burn this way. I have got my living to earn: I have got an immense amount of work to do, and I sincerely and earnestly want to see my friends and members of my family this summer, but I do hope they will have understanding and consideration enough to see the problem I am faced with and to allow me privacy and peace to get my work accomplished.

I am appealing to you to help me in my purpose in any way you can. I know that Mama does not wholly understand how hard I have to work and how desperately serious I am when I say I have to work and must be given time and quiet in which to do it. I don't think that Mama has ever fully understood that writing is not only hard work, but harder work than she has any idea of. From what she said to me once or twice, I gathered that she may not even understand that it is work at all but rather a kind of lucky trick which the person lucky enough to possess can use when and where he chooses in his off moments and at absolutely no expense of time and trouble. Well, it is not a lucky trick. It is a desperate, back-breaking, nerve-wracking and brain-fatiguing labor. And, in addition to this, it is often a very thankless and heart-breaking labor because a man may give years of his youth and best effort to a piece of work and then get nothing for it except abuse. Of course, I am making no criticism of Mama whatever: her point of view is a familiar one among people who have had no experience with such work and who get a very romantic idea about it, but I am sure that I can explain it to you and that you will understand what I say and will help me in any way you can to get the peace and quiet that I so much want and need.

I don't think anybody quite understood when I was home just how tired I am and how much I need now a period of quiet and seclusion. But I do need it very badly, and that is the reason that I have taken the little cabin out near Asheville in the hope and belief that I can get it there. If I fail to get it there, it is going to be a bitter disappointment, but I really have high hopes that it will turn out well. I think my friends in New York all understand how much I need it now, and are earnestly hoping I shall get it this summer. Of course, you have not seen a great deal of me since the publication of "Look Homeward, Angel," almost eight years ago. But there has really been almost no rest or relaxation for me since then. First of all, as you know, there was the great stir and rumpus in Asheville about "The Angel," all of the talk and feeling of perturbation, and I got a full share of that. Then I was faced with the problem and task of getting another book done, of meeting the challenge of the critics, who praise you one month and revile you the next, and who keep pressing all the time to get another book out of you. I had very little money, and after the royalties on "Look Homeward, Angel" were exhausted I had to depend for my living on an occasional story or on money that Scribners advanced to me. Thus I was under the constant strain of knowing that I was in debt to my publisher and that I ought to try to do something to pay that off.

The book that I was writing developed into a project of such tremendous size that it turned out to be four or five books instead of one, and five years or more went by before I was able to get the first of these books completed and published. During most of this time I lived in Brooklyn and worked like a dog. In addition, there were personal troubles which I believe are all settled now, but which took from me a heavy toll in time, worry and anxiety. When "Of Time and the River" was published a little more than two years ago, I thought that my troubles were over. But it seems now as if they were just beginning. I went abroad to rest. I was as close to utter physical and nervous exhaustion as I had ever been in my life. There was a time there when I was seriously afraid that I might not be able to pull myself back again, but I managed to. And then, as you know, the storm broke. I returned to America feeling sure that now, at last, I had a secure position, a very modest income, the independence and, for the first time in my life, the peace and comfort that would enable me to continue my work hereafter in tranquility. I found instead that I had been thrown into a whirlpool. I was set upon by every kind of parasite, every kind of harpy, every kind of vulture, every kind of female egotist that had a string to pull, or that thought they could get something out of me—whether money, manuscript, royalties, percentages, or simply a sop to their vanity. Since I was—and this is the truth—a more or less unsuspecting and believing person who responds very quickly to people and to apparent overtures of friendship and good will, I was taken for quite a ride.

I am not kicking or complaining about this at all. On the whole, I came through it all right. I think I shall always be glad I had the experience and that it taught me something. But I am merely telling you that, instead of the peace and security I thought I should now get, I found myself in the lions' den, and I have fought it out with the animals for over two years now. On the whole, I do not think I have done badly. They have taken me for quite a promenade: . . . I have learned a good many very hard and bitter and disagreeable facts about life and about some of the adventures and people one could meet in it, but I have not lost my faith either in life or in people, I am more grateful than I have ever been for my true friends and for the many fine people I have known, and I have kept on working. So, with all humility and deference, I think I will come out all right.

However—and this is the point of the whole matter, the reason I am writing you this letter, the reason I am explaining all these things to you, knowing that I can depend on your help and understanding—the point, I say, is: I am now damn tired—and I want to get a rest. I am not merely saying I am tired, I am not just pretending I am tired—I am, actually, honestly and genuinely—nervously, physically and mentally. I believe a few weeks out there in the cabin will fix me up again. I am eager—more eager than I have ever been—to work, and I believe

I will get a lot of work done out there. But I do know how I feel now; I do know what has happened to me and what I have been through these last seven or eight years; and I do know exactly what I want to do now—which is to get out to my cabin, to get some rest and relaxation, and to work—and I can only earnestly pray that all my friends and members of my family will understand this extremely normal, sensible desire, and help me every way they can. And that is why I am writing you this letter—because I know I can appeal to you and that you will understand exactly my problem when I put it before you—and that I can depend on you, tactfully and diplomatically, without hurting anyone's feelings, to get other people to understand it too.

Of course, I had a good time when I was home in May. It was wonderful to be home again after so long an absence, and it was fine to see all of you and to resume contacts with so many people that I had known. It was for me a wonderful home-coming: I am glad I got to see so many people and to talk to them, but I was pretty well fagged out when I left. My desire now, I think, is a pretty sensible one. I do not want to go out in the country and become an utter hermit; I hope that all these people who were so nice to me in May will not have forgotten they know me by the time I come back; I hope to see many of them this summer and that they will visit me at the cabin. But I also hope that they show some discretion and won't overwhelm me, and that I get a chance to rest up and to do some work. I think all of this is perfectly plain and sensible and that any intelligent person would see my point immediately and agree with me.

This is all for the present. I am sorry that the letter is so long, but I thought it would be a good idea if I wrote you and told you something of my present problems and difficulties before I come down. Of course, I should like to come to Spartanburg and meet your friends, but just at the present time, feeling as tired as I do, it seems to me it would be a better plan if I got out in the country and rested up a week or two before meeting anyone you know. At any rate, I will let you know when I arrive. Meanwhile, with all good wishes to you until I see you.

To HAMILTON BASSO

[Box 95]
[Oteen, N.C.]
July 13, 1937

Dear Ham:

I got your letter without any serious confliction with the Postal Authorities in spite of your alarming instructions to the Post Master; [1] but this

[1] On the envelope of his letter to Wolfe, Basso had written: "Postmaster: Will you

is almost my first opportunity to answer you. I have been seeing a lot of people in town including the family, and have been busy moving in out here. I wish I could see you, and very soon. If the mountain won't come here then I will have to go to the mountain, but I hope you come here because I would like you to see the place.

First of all, here are the directions; I am about 6 miles from Asheville and if you come through town the best way to get here is through the tunnel. When you get to the Recreation Park you take the road to the right that leads up around the lake at the Park. This is a gravel road but not a bad one. The entrance to my place is about two-thirds of a mile from the place where you turn off at the Recreation Park. You can recognize the place by two large wooden gates which have lanterns on top of them. If I know you are coming, the gates will be open and the lanterns lit. I am on top of the hill at the end of this road: it is a cabin completely hidden from sight by tremendous trees. It is really a good place and I hope to do a lot of work here. So far I have done little except sleep—after New York it has been a blessed relief to be out here. About the only human sound I hear out here is the wail of the train whistle going by the foot of my hill in the azalea bottoms and occasionally very faint music from the Merry-Go-Around at the Recreation Park. Of course I love the trains and I don't mind the Park a bit.

I was dog-tired when I got here but I am beginning to feel a whole lot better already. As usual I am aching to get to work again, although it might be better if I waited a bit. After I saw you in May I returned to New York and worked like fury for eight weeks in an effort to make some money. I wrote six stories [2] of which one is still in rough draft and must be worked on some more. But Miss Nowell took the other five and so far has succeeded in selling three. One to *The New Yorker*—not the Malone piece which they published some time ago but a new one—

---

be good enough to hold this until the arrival of the addressee whose presence will be made known, probably, by an earthquake or some other violent upheaval."

[2] " 'E,' " which was published in the July 17, 1937, issue of *The New Yorker* and appears with some changes in *You Can't Go Home Again* on pages 513–527; "April, Late April" which was published in the September, 1937, issue of *The American Mercury* and appears with many changes and additions in *The Web and the Rock* on pages 441–452; "Katamoto" which was published in the October, 1937, issue of *Harper's Bazaar* and appears with many cuts and changes in *You Can't Go Home Again* on pages 28–36; "Chickamauga" which was published in the Winter, 1938, issue of *The Yale Review* and is included in *The Hills Beyond*; "No More Rivers" which was never published in a magazine but small portions of which are scattered through *The Web and the Rock* and *You Can't Go Home Again*; and the first rough draft of "The Party at Jack's" which was finally published in the May, 1939, issue of *Scribner's Magazine* and appears with many changes and additions in *You Can't Go Home Again* on pages 196–322.

one to *The American Mercury,* and one a few days ago to *Harper's Bazaar.* She still has the two best—and longest—and says she is sure she will sell them somewhere. But the ways of commercial editors are very strange and hard to fathom; when I was here in May, Miss Nowell sold a story to *The Saturday Evening Post.*[3] Of course we were both delighted. We had never been paid so much before and they seemed eager for more. It looked as if we had a ready market.

When I got back to New York, I wrote a story called "Chickamauga" and if I do say so, it is one of the best stories I ever wrote. I got the idea for it from an old, old man, my great-uncle, John Westall, who lives over in Yancey County and who is ninety-five years old. When I saw him this spring, he began to tell me about the Civil War and about the battle of Chickamauga, which was, he said, the bloodiest, most savage battle he was ever in. He told about it all so wonderfully and in such pungent and poetic language, such as so many of the old country people around here use, that I couldn't wait to get back to New York to begin on it. My idea was simply to tell the story of a great battle in the language of a common soldier—the kind of country mountain boy who did so much of the fighting in the war. The *Post* heard that I was writing it and they liked the story they had bought so much and were apparently so eager to get some more stories from me, that they telegraphed Miss Nowell even before I had finished and asked that they be allowed to see it before anyone else. Well, we sent it off to them and Miss Nowell and I thought it was a cinch. The story was so good, really much better than the one they had taken, and it simply crackled with action from the first line and besides that, it was so real, so true—it was all told in the old man's language and when you read it, it was just as if he was there talking to you. What do you suppose happened? In a week's time the story came back with a regretful note from *The Post* to the effect that although they appreciated its "literary merit"—I wonder by the way what the Hell people mean by "literary merit." Is there any other kind of merit where a piece of writing is concerned? I have never been able to see that there was, although so many people seem to think there is . . . that there really are two kinds of books, books that are good in a "literary sort of way," and "good" books, but of course . . . it is all nonsense— at any rate, The Post rejected "Chickamauga," apparently with the idea that it was good "in a literary sort of way," but that it did not have enough of the "story element." Nowell and I were absolutely flabbergasted. What in the name of God do these people mean by "story element"? And what is a story anyway? All this piece had was the whole

[3] "The Child by Tiger" which was published in the September 11, 1937, issue of *The Saturday Evening Post* and appears in *The Web and the Rock* on pages 132–156.

Civil War, the life of a common soldier and his account of one of the bloodiest battles that was ever fought. If it had had any more of the "story element" it would have exploded into electricity.

Of course I am not mad about it, I know we will sell it somewhere —but I am puzzled and curious to find out what they mean or what kind of standards they have. I think I have an idea: it is something that has to do with a kind of accepted and recognizable formula which is familiar to their readers, but really it does not have very much to do with story. A piece of writing might be one of the most thrilling and exciting stories ever written and still be rejected by these people if it did not fit in with one of their established patterns. Curiously enough, they are now very much interested in another piece I wrote called "No More Rivers." I would have sworn that this story was of such a quiet and unexciting kind that *The Post* would not even have considered it. But the editor wrote Miss Nowell quite a long letter and showed the most surprising interest in it: in fact he practically promised to take the story if I would condense the first twenty pages to four or five. I do not know whether or not it can be done—but there you are: the only action in this story is a telephone conversation between a man and a girl—and *there* is "story element."

Anyway, I am making enough, I hope, to pay expenses and keep going for a while and I am getting back to work immediately on my Gulliver book. I brought most of the manuscript of the last five or six years down with me—millions of words of it—and I hope to write several hundred thousand more this summer. Eventually I hope it will begin to take shape, like another monster of the deep, and I will have another tremendous book. I believe I learn a little something about writing all the time; but I am not so sure that I will be worried so much this time by apprehensions over size and length. The very nature of a book like this is that everything can go into it—to tell such a story is to try to loot the whole treasure of human experience. Well, we shall see what we shall see; there are so many things to find out. I do not even know yet whether I can work here.

It has been so long since I have really lived at home and almost all of my creative work has been done somewhere else—in New York, or in London, or in France. And already I have encountered certain learned, local psychologists, who hint darkly that I will find it impossible to work here: one even said that I would find these surroundings "allergic"—I believe that is one of the new words isn't it? At any rate the sum and substance of it is that a man like myself could write in a room in a city with a Hell of life and traffic roaring along beneath him, but that he could get no work done in the peace and quiet of the country and among people that he knows, and in the place where he was born. All of which I hold to be ridiculous: work, as you yourself know, is a desperate necessity; and if the need is desperate enough nothing will stop us—not even our own lazy bones or natural indolence of which I have so much more than a fair share—not even, by God, allergic conditions. It is going to be an interesting experience. It is the first time in almost twenty years since I left college that I have come back home with the intention of actually staying a while; and I have come back here after so many years of strife and wandering, after so much turbulence and chaos, after so much work and hope and failure and success, after such a packed and crowded life in which I have always dreamed and hoped of achieving a state of serenity and repose without ever having found it.

I have come back here as the result of a very powerful and deep-rooted instinct, which has grown slowly and steadily for years. No matter what happens or how this experience may turn out, I know the instinct was right. That is to say, this time it was inevitable; it had gathered for years and I was utterly convinced that it was right for me to come home again, to make the old connections and resume myself; and if I had done anything else at this time, this feeling in me was so strong and single I should never have been satisfied. Feeling so, of course, there was nothing else for me to do. I cannot fairly tell you that I am "through" with New York; but I have realized in recent months that I am "through" with it at this present period of my life. In other words, with the same powerful and inevitable instinct, I began to realize that I had taken all of it that I could possibly absorb at this period, and to stay there longer now would not only be foolish but barren.

I believe I must have lived through almost the whole vast kaleidoscopic range of experience that the city can give to the young man. I went there a kid from a little town, with all the fierce and passionate eagerness that such a boy could know. I had built the enchanted vision of the city in great flaming pictures in my brain from my childhood and I believe it is not too much to say that to the very end some portion of that enchantment remained—that I always saw New York, not only with all its cruelty, its ugliness, its loneliness and horror, not only with its harsh and sordid poverty and its obscene wealth; but also with all the magic of its special weather, its fierce exultant pulse, its hope, its passion and its unrecorded loveliness, seen so, pulsed so, flaming in all these hues of magic, and so built and so imagined there in the proud and flaming vision of a boy. I brought these things to it, just as you did, and just as every other boy that ever lived who came there from the little towns across America, who came burning with a fierce desire that all men know in youth, which is to be loved and to be famous.

Well, I got what I was looking for. I had both of them and none of it turned out the way I thought it would, and all of it was so different from the way we thought it would be; and yet I had it all and I would not have missed it and am glad that I have had it now. But I can have no more of it. I have got to the end of that road. I have squeezed that orange dry. It belongs there now in the province of things done—in the domain of the irrecoverable—that whole experience of youth, desire and love and fame, in the unceasing city. I knew that it was over—that no matter what may come hereafter, I shall never go along that way again; and that if I do go back, it will be now from a different point, another vision and, I hope, with a deeper purpose.

So I have come back here to "set a spell and think things over;" to rebuild here in my brain again these past fifteen years or more of youth, of conflict and of wandering. And from this substance, this accumulation of a life worn down—I pray, a little brighter, and freer, I hope, in some substantial measure, from the degrading egotisms all men know in youth —here to strike out, I hope to God, a living word: to do out of the substance of my one life, my single spirit, a better and a truer work than I have ever done.

I did not mean to load upon you all things in this way; but I did want you to understand what I believe you may have guessed already, that my coming back was not haphazard and that there was behind it a deeper sense of purpose than many people know.

Good-bye for the present, Ham. Write as soon as you can and let me know if you and Toto can come over and when you can come. Or if you prefer, I will come over and see you, if you just name a date. I got a letter from Sherwood Anderson just before I left New York. But I have had no time to answer it yet. He invited me to visit him and I believe the address is Troutdale, Virginia; but I left the letter in New York and shall not be able to accept his invitation. But I am going to ask him to let me know if he is coming here, and if he does I think it would be fine if all three of us could get together. I do not know where Scott is, but I suppose he is around here somewhere. He was in New York a month or so ago. I didn't see him, but Max told me that he seemed to be much better. He had written some stories and had plans for new work and Max believed that he was going to pull out of the hole all right. With all my heart I hope so.

I was too busy in New York to keep up with current movements which were having an especially furious career this spring and I suppose by doing so, I have lost what is called prestige. This is too bad of course; however, like you and every man, I only have what I have, I am what I am. I don't believe there is much to report, except that the boys are having meetings, congresses and demonstrations all over the place and were carrying on the Spanish war with unabated vigor, using, it seemed to me, essentially the same appeals to idealism, democracy, civilization, etc., as were current among the propagandists whose similar activities they so much abhorred twenty years ago and have so bitterly denounced since. However, let them argue and deny as they please. It is the same old business—"Plus ça change plus c'est le même chose." It's the old army game. What I say is, "it's spinach and to Hell with it." But I suppose you know all about these things and have kept informed on all these important doings. Spain and Marx have made some strange new bedfellows. . . . So runs the world away.

I hope you are getting a lot of work done and most of all, that we can wear a whole night out in talking, before long. Meanwhile I send my love to you and Toto.

The following letter was written in reply to one from Fred B. Millett asking Wolfe for biographical material for use in Millett's book, Contemporary American Authors. *Millett at this time was a member of the Department of English at the University of Chicago, and is now Professor of English at Wesleyan University and Director of the Honors College there.*

To FRED B. MILLETT

[Box 95]
[Oteen, N.C.]
July 14, 1937

Dear Professor Millett:

I am sorry for the delay in answering your letters of March and June. I was very busy in New York trying to put through a great deal of work that had to be finished by a certain time, and recently I have been moving down here and into a cabin, where I am living for the summer.

I should be glad, of course, to give you any information concerning my life and interests which might be of some use to you in the preparation of your book, and which might not be available elsewhere. But I do not know very well just what kind of information might be of value to you. May I suggest, if you are not familiar with it already, that you look at a very short book called "The Story of a Novel" which was published by Scribners last year. I think it may tell as much about some of my experiences as a writer trying to learn his job as anything else I could tell you. It contains more or less my writing experience between 1929 and 1935, after the publication of my first long book, "Look Homeward, Angel," and up to the publication of "Of Time and the

River." . . . As to the new book, the following facts about it may be of some interest to you: I have written perhaps a million words of manuscript for it in the past two years. Of course I shall use only a part of this. Furthermore the book is not one of the series that was announced with the publication of "Of Time and the River," but an entirely separate book. It is hard in a brief space to give you any comprehensive notion of it, but I think you might get some idea of it if I tell you it is a kind of modern fable or legend, and that it sets forth the chronicle of a kind of modern Gulliver—an American Gulliver—someone, let us say, that in our own special time and phrase we might call Joe Doaks. For me, the conception and creation of the book has been an exciting and, I believe important experience. I hope it has enabled me to make use of the materials of experience, of what a man is able to see, feel, hear, know and comprehend in a life-time, more wholly and fully than I have ever been able to use such experience before. But at the same time I hope and believe that through the medium of this new book and its more "fictional" quality, I have been able to gain a greater objectivity than I have known in my previous books, and to detach myself more completely from the purely personal elements of what is generally, and I believe mistakenly, referred to as "autobiographical" fiction. At any rate —and I believe this may have some special interest to you—I think this may have been happening to my work: as I have grown older and a little more experienced and, I hope, a great deal more aware of my purpose, of my materials and of the work I want to do, I think my interests have turned more and more from the person who is writing the book to the book the person is writing. I do not know whether I have said this well or plainly, but I hope that I have, because I believe that it may indicate the change of development that has occurred in my work. I am immersed in work and I hope that it goes well.

I do not know that this information will be of any use to you, but I shall be very glad if it is. With all good wishes for the success of your book . . .

To HAMILTON BASSO

(Oteen, N.C.)

July 22, 1937

Dear Ham:

I would be delighted to make the trip up to see Sherwood [1] in August, but are you sure he's going to be there? As I remember it when I had

[1] Basso had suggested that he and Wolfe drive up to see Sherwood Anderson in Marion, Virginia.

dinner with him in New York two or three months ago he told me he had accepted an invitation to go out to Boulder, Colorado where I was two years ago and give some lectures at the Writers Conference. If he does this I think he might be away at the time you mention. . . . Anyway I'm all for the trip if he is going to be there. But if he's not, I wish you'd come over here and spend the week-end with me anyway. My only plans for the present besides work are a trip down to South Carolina to see my older sister [2] and her family a week from this Saturday or Sunday. I could put you up here comfortably at the cabin. There is lots of room for both you and Toto if she wants to come, and I have a man here now who cooks for me and looks after the place and I believe he is going to turn out all right. There has been a lot of family, old friends and social activities so far—a good deal too much, but it was unavoidable and I believe there is going to be a lull now. I am working again on a very long, difficult and closely woven story called "The Party at Jack's." I don't know how it's going to turn out, but if I succeed with it, it ought to be good. It is one of the most curious and difficult problems I have been faced with in a long time and maybe I shall learn something from it. It is a story that in its essence and without trying or intending to be, has got to be somewhat Proustian—that is to say its life depends upon the most thorough and comprehensive investigation of character—or characters, for there are more than thirty people in it. In addition, however, there is a tremendous amount of submerged action which involves the lives of all these people and which includes not only the life of a great apartment house but also a fire and the death of two people. I suppose really a whole book could be made out of it but I am trying to do it in a story. After that, of course, I don't know what will happen. It has got to be a very long story. It is all very well to talk of classic brevity etc. but this story cannot be written that way: if it is it becomes something else. And if I do it right it is certainly worth doing. But to get it published? I don't know. All this talk about there being a market or a publisher nowadays for any good piece of writing is nonsense. A writer's market, unless he chooses to live and work and publish like James Joyce or to be one of the little magazine precious boys, is still cabin'd and confined to certain more or less conventional and restricted forms and mediums. I kick against it constantly because I know it just ain't right and because I know that the familiar answer that is made to my objection—namely that the true artist will learn to do it in the "accepted" way—is the easy and dishonest answer of people who are themselves interested in doing it in the lazy, convenient or temporarily commercial one. There is no accepted way: there are as many art forms as

[2] Effie Wolfe Gambrell.

there are forms of art, and the artist will continue to create new ones and to enrich life with new creations as long as there is either life or art. So many of these forms that so many academic people consider as masterly and final definitions derived from the primeval source of all things beautiful or handed Apollo-wise from Mount Olympus, are really worn out already, will work no more, are already dead and stale as hell.

I know—I believe I know this one thing better than most other people! The thing we have got to fight for constantly and unflaggingly in America is utterance. I don't know why but it is a curious and baffling paradox of our mind that it tends to conventionalize and harden, much more so, it seems to me than in many other countries. I don't know for certain the answer yet and the ones they tried to make me swallow ten or fifteen years ago—that is, "puritanism" "Babbittry" etc.—never meant very much to me, never gave me an essential answer. These things themselves were effects, I thought, much more than causes. And these effects are, I feel somehow powerfully sure, associated with so many other effects that we are all familiar with and which no one ever mentions in connection with these things—that is, the dry neck of the American, a kind of prognathous set and bleakness of the face and jaw, the way he moves and walks, a kind of meagerness around the hips, the nasality of the voice, a kind of dry precision in the speech—for example here in western North Carolina we say "Lee—ces—ter" and not Lester (for Leicester). At any rate the whole matter is deeper, stranger and subtler than the pedants think: it is a thorny paradox, a kind of weather of our lives conjoined of all our space and light and our immense and superhuman distances.

It has occurred to me that perhaps one fundamental reason for this conventionalizing and hardening of our thought and speech and art and life processes is that every American in a fundamental sense is a surveyor. Have you ever thought, by the way, of the great number of Americans who actually were surveyors? George Washington was one. My grandfather,[3] who was a great variety of things, a carpenter, a contractor, a hatter and a trapper, was also a surveyor. I believe you would find that millions of the pioneer Americans had some knowledge of surveying and of how to handle surveying instruments. What I am trying to say here is that America has really never yet, in any profound and essential way, been *explored*—it has rather been *surveyed*. The first problem of the people who settled in this immense and spatial continent was not to explore it but to "lay it out" —to find the shortest distance between two points, to get the best and easiest grade across the continental divide—to give, in short, a definition of the wildnerness. We have hunted always for the short cut, the practicable way, and I think the effect of this—it does not seem to me at all far-

[3] Thomas Casey Westall, Mrs. Wolfe's father.

fetched so to think—has been to hunt for the short cut, the easy and practicable way, the neat definition, everywhere: hence the neat glib finish of the O. Henry type of short story, the "punch at the end," the "gag," and many other kinds of gimcrackery.

In New York now whenever they talk of starting a new magazine, of making a new publication go—they do not talk of getting out a good magazine, of making a magazine so good, so much better than any other, that people will have to buy it. They talk of getting out one with a "new idea," of getting a new concoction that will "click" as *Life, Time, Fortune, The New Yorker* click. Well this is surveyordom—it is not exploring. In my own humble opinion they have done damn little exploring yet, and those of us who intend to do some are going to have to fight grimly and constantly from beginning to end against the conventional set in order to accomplish what we want to do.

A German—an ex-Prussian cavalry officer whom I met last summer and who had spent the last eight years trapping in Canada—told me that the most characteristic attitude of mind he had noticed in America was indicated by the phrase "that will do." He said that he had never heard this phrase used in the same way in Germany. If a reaping machine broke down, he said, he had noticed that instead of taking it apart, giving it a thorough overhauling and making new parts for those that were worn out, the tendency was to patch it up with twine, solder it together, get it to running again in the quickest possible time—do something to it, no matter what, so long as it would "do." In many respects all this is admirable, but it is surveyordom. It is the resourceful attribute of a people who are forced to meet emergencies and to meet them quickly, of people who had to fence in and house the wilderness and who could not afford to be too nice, or neat, or dainty while they were about it. In another way as well, our love of neat definitions in convenient forms, our fear of essential exploration, may be the natural response of people who had to house themselves, wall themselves, give their lives some precise and formal definition in that enormous vacancy. Anyway all of these things have seemed to me to be worth thinking of and I know that we still have to fight and fight hard to do our work the way we want to do it—not only against the accepted varieties of surveyordom—that is, book publishers, most of the critics, popular magazines, etc.—but against even deadlier and more barren forms, because they set up as friends of exploration when they are really betrayers and enemies: I mean little magazinedom, Hound and Horners, young precious boys, esthetic Marxians and all the rest of it.

Come over and talk to me sometime. I think I'm going to get some work done here and it would be good to see you and talk to you while I am doing it. I got a letter from Max praising a piece I have just written for the

New Yorker [4]—also a notice from the publishers to the effect that all of my remaining royalties have been wiped out [5] in the settlement of a suit which, if truth and justice and common honesty are at all to be defended, should never have been settled; and in the payment of lawyers' fees which were far more ruinous than both suit and settlement, and who for all they did or accomplished besides the pompous superfluity of their costly presence and the frightening eminence of their great name—an eminence which frightened Charlie Scribner but not the people who were suing us —might just as well have been supplanted by Glickstein and O'Toole, or by any little tough and combative attorney, and better so, it seems to me. At any rate, my profits on the books are not only all wiped out but I am also heavily in the red with Scribners. I suppose it's all a part of the price we have to pay for experience, but the price is a heavy and a bitter one.

As to friendship in the modern business world—well, it exists: they will bleed and die for you in conversation, but they will not lose money. In fact the principle of modern business friendship seems to be not to let the right hand know what the left hand is doing—one hand is warm and open and extended in the clasp of love, but the other is clenched grimly around a handful of accursed papers. This is the way things are, and I suppose we are fools to think it could be different. Besides, why protest? What right or justice is there in our argument? Who has defrauded me? Who has stolen my ox and my ass or committed adultery or lain with my maid servant or done any of the other things that we were brought up to believe were wrong? And since none of these things have been done, why then it follows, doesn't it, that all else that is done in life, in business and in friendship are right, and it is unfair and unjust of us to kick against the traces or to protest against the ordered scheme of things as they are.

I'm not really bitter about it. I simply know more about it than I knew or suspected two years ago. As for Max Perkins, my feeling toward him of course is the same as it always was. I used to wish the world was shaped and made more to his own measure, his high stature; but since it is not, I am glad he is here to give it the improvement of himself.

Good-bye for the present. Let me know if you can come over and when. Meanwhile, with all good wishes to you and Toto.

[4] " 'E."

[5] As of August 1, 1937, Wolfe's royalty account at Scribners showed a deficit of $1,225.40 after payment of half the settlement and attorneys' fees in the libel suit.

To ELIZABETH NOWELL

[Oteen, N.C.]

[July 22 (?), 1937]

Dear Miss Nowell:

Thanks for your letter and for the check for "Katamoto" ($360.) which came yesterday. I am sorry "Chickamauga" got turned down by *American* but after our initial preparation it was not a great surprise. I thought this story would be the easiest to sell but it is turning out the hardest. However, go ahead and try *Harper's* if you like and let me know what happens. If Perkins really wants it for *Scribner's*, we have always got that to fall back on but it might be a good idea to try the remaining possibilities first. I've had so many pieces in *Scribner's* and I really don't think it would hurt to be spread around a little more. I am also willing, if necessary, to revise the story and perhaps to bring it back more to its original purpose— that is, the story of an old man telling about the war and the battle. I think I may have put in a little too much Jim Weaver and his love affair in an effort to make it palatable to the big magazines. I don't feel yet that all of this should be cut out, but I might reduce it and make it play a less important part than it now does.

As to the enclosed letter . . . asking for permission to translate "I Have a Thing to Tell You," [1] I am not so sure. I wouldn't mind at all having it done if it were not for the suggestion of propaganda that might attach to it. And frankly I do not think the story ought to be used in that way. It is a straight story; so far as I know, it has no propaganda in it save what the reader wishes to supply for himself by inference, and its greatest value, it seems to me, lies in that fact—that I wrote it as I wrote all my other stories about a human situation and about living characters. I think it ought to be published and read in that way, and I should be against its being read or used or published in any other way. However, I'll think about it and let you know if I change my mind. Meanwhile, you can handle the matter with your customary diplomacy.

I am working on "The Party at Jack's." I have changed and revised it a great deal with an effort to weave it together better and to get it to move more quickly. However, it is bound to be very long and the problem of finding a market for it is one I'd rather not think about now. If all goes well, it may turn out to be a very interesting piece of work; but of course there is the question of its length. However, if I get it in shape I'll send it to you and you can read it over and see what you think.

I think I may have another piece for you that from a commercial point

[1] Into Yiddish.

of view may be much more practicable. I put it down in rough draft the other day: it's only an outline yet but I have called it tentatively "A Great Idea For a Story"—and it might really be that. I got the idea a few days ago from a waiter in Asheville who has been hovering around my table whenever I go in and showing me a great deal of attention. The other day, after clearing his throat a good many times and looking cunningly around to make sure that he was in no danger of being overheard and that his priceless secret would be safe, he bent over and coyly whispered that he had had in his brain for years "A Great Idea for a Story." It's a little habit waiters have: all of a sudden I thought of at least a dozen of them who in exactly the same way, with the same air of hopeful secrecy, had confided to me that they had a great idea for a story which would make us both a fortune, if only a guy like me who knew all the tricks could help him out on it. Of course, as a reward for this expert supervision, yours truly will get cut in on the profits, movie rights, etc., which will be simply staggering.

Well, I composed my soul to patience, put a fixed grin on my face and murmured that I was simply dying to hear it—and you know the rest. You can imagine the kind of stories that they tell—or perhaps you can't. They make Cecil B. De Mille in his most fantastic moments look like a stern realist. This one, which he assured me had been given to him by a Greek— a fact which he evidently felt gave it at the outset a sensational value— was all about "a dame in Assyria" and her love affair. She was, the waiter assured me, the richest dame in the country, and her old man used to lock her up on the top floor of her house, which was, the waiter said, thirty stories tall. So help me God, I'm not making up a word of this: I'm even understating it. Well, "the guy" comes along then and falls for the dame and climbs up to the thirtieth floor every night to play his banjo to her and to carry on his courtship of her in other ways. The old man dies conveniently and the happy pair are married. The marriage, however, is short-lived. The guy, the waiter said, turns out to be a booze hound—these phrases are the waiter's—begins to stay out late at nights, and to run around with a bunch of hot blondes. Finally he deserts her utterly, vanishes in thin air, taking with him a lot of her dough and "joolry." She is still nuts about him, however—apparently they are gluttons for punishment in Assyria—so she hunts for him for the next two years: private detectives, rewards, advertisements in the newspapers, and all the rest of it.

And then she had "her great idea"—the waiter was really getting warm now. "The dame," he said, "opens up a swell night club, the biggest, swellest night club that anybody ever heard of in Assyria. And then she puts an ad in the paper informing the public that anyone who comes to her joint the next day will be given a ten-dollar gold piece and as much liquor as they can drink or carry away—all free for nothing." The waiter cunningly explained the cunning pyschology of this move to me. "The dame," he said, "knew that such an ad would inevitably [attract] all the booze hounds in Assyria—including her erring husband. And she was not mistaken. And when she goes downstairs the next morning she finds a line of bar-flies three blocks long, and sure enough, there is friend husband, first in line. Well, she jerks him out of line right away, tells the cashier to pay off the others but tells [friend] husband that she has her suspicions about him, that she doubts whether he is really a genuine, bonafide, high grade, number 1, 18 carat Assyrian booze hound: that he will have to come upstairs with her and convince her before she allows him to cash in. Well, he goes with her, of course, and when she gets into her boudoir, she takes off her veil." (The waiter explained to me carefully that the reason the husband didn't recognize her was because she was heavily veiled.) Well, I waited and then asked "Then what? What happens then?" and the waiter, after giving me a look of great disgust, answered: "Then nothing. That's all: she's got him back, see? And isn't it a wow?"

Well now, I got to thinking it all over and decided I might make something of it. And here is my own idea. I have talked with literary waiters of this kind before and always they have some preposterous, fantastic and utterly worthless yarn like this, which in some strange way they are all convinced will make them a fortune if only someone like me will help them put it down. Apparently the more far-fetched and preposterous the story, the less it has to do with life, the better it seems to them, simply because, I suppose, it has so little to do with the life that they have seen. And yet they all see so much; they hear so much—the material of a dozen living stories is going on around them all the time, but it never occurs to any of them that anyone would be interested in the real stuff. So that's the way I framed it. I drew upon my experience with a dozen waiters, a hundred restaurants, and let it tell itself. I told what was going on around the waiter all the time that he was talking: the people coming in and out; the other waiter who is a communist and who argues violently for revolution with any customer who will talk with him; the little waitress who has had an illegitimate child a few months before and who has put it in a Home and goes to see it every Sunday; and other human things and episodes like this—the whole weave and shift and interplay of life and comedy and tragedy that goes on in a place like this. And all the time, the waiter is earnestly telling this preposterous fable—his "Great Idea for a Story"— to the customer.

That's roughly the idea that I had in mind for it. I guess you might call it a kind of study in unconscious irony—the stuff of life, the materials for a thousand stories all around one, while someone tells a preposterous fable of far away that never could have happened anywhere. I may revise it and send it on to you.[2]

I hope you have some good news soon about "No More Rivers." If *Redbook* turns it down and you think it's worth trying, I might try to revise and shorten it to fit the length requirements of *The Saturday Evening Post.* I'd have to look at it again to find whether I could do it, or whether anything of my original story would be left if I cut the twenty pages to four or five to meet Mr. Stout's [3] requirements. At any rate, let me know what happens and what you think about it. I saw " 'E" in *The New Yorker* but have heard nothing yet of the *Post* or *Redbook* stories. Of course I like to get paid for them, but it is also nice to have them come out.

Goodbye for the present. I'm still hoping things will turn out well here —that is, that I'll get some work done. I think I shall, but I'll let you know when I am more sure about it. Meanwhile, with all the best,

To FRED W. WOLFE

Oteen, N. C.

July 22, 1937

Dear Fred:

To-morrow, Friday night is, I think, the night of the supper out at Shope's cabin. I have written Jimmy Howell and promised to be present.[1] I told him that I could not answer for you because you were busy and if you came to it, it would involve coming all the way up from Spartanburg and probably going back the same night. Of course I know that all of them would be delighted if you came and it's for you to decide, but it doesn't seem to me to be worth all that time and travel unless you actually had business up here that would make it worth your while. I suppose people will have a good time and I promised to go simply because it would be less trouble for me to go and get it over with than have to put it off till some other time. I appreciate all this hospitality, but I am trying to work also, and social activity is about to get me down. After this week I hope there is a lull.

Things at the cabin have gone pretty well. I have a new man here now and I think it is going to turn out okay. The pests have not bothered me

[2] This appears on pages 414–423 in *You Can't Go Home Again.*

[3] Wesley Winans Stout at this time was editor of *The Saturday Evening Post.*

[1] James S. Howell had arranged for Wolfe and some of his boyhood friends to meet for a steak supper at the cabin of William Shope in the Reems Creek section of Buncombe County. Howell had known Wolfe from early childhood and roomed with him one year in Dr. Kemp Brattle's cottage at Chapel Hill. He is now an attorney in Asheville.

much as yet, but of course I'm still praying. Donald MacRae, who is of course my friend and always welcome, drove out last night and took me into town to see Mabel. . . . We got back out here at about eleven or eleven-thirty and as we drove up there was a loud sound of revelry in the night. One of my Yancey County cronies, the gent who was with me on the night of the shooting scrape,[2] had turned up with a gang and made himself at home. I suppose he felt a little shooting makes the whole world kin—at any rate he had some other fellow with him I had never seen and two wild looking females, all of them more or less under the influence and playing the victrola as hard as it would go. I managed to keep polite but also to plead fatigue and presently got rid of them, all of them vowing enthusiastically that they would be back soon . . . [which?] will be sweet.

This is all for the present. I am trying to get a story done and will push on in spite of hell and high water. I was tired when I got here and I probably have seen too many people and tried to get to work again too soon. But on the whole, I think I feel better, and if our friends will neither forsake me nor consume me, I believe I'll pull out all right. . . . If I can get some work done, I hope to see you . . . as planned in Spartanburg a week from Saturday or Sunday. Meanwhile, with best wishes . . .

The following letter was in reply to a note from Mrs. Roberts asking Wolfe if she could bring to call two young admirers of his work, a Mr. E. E. Miller and Miss Eula Person, who wanted to come from Nashville, Tennessee, to meet him. A reconciliation between Wolfe and Mr. and Mrs. Roberts had taken place during his first visit to Asheville in May, 1937.

To MARGARET ROBERTS

Oteen, N.C.

July 26, 1937

Dear Mrs. Roberts:

I did not get your letter until Saturday night when I was in town and went out to Mabel's house. And as it was then rather late, I did not call you but decided to write you and call you up when I am next in town. Of course I have no telephone out here and that is why I have not called you earlier. I know you must understand that I should have tried to see you or communicate with you before if I had not been so busy. I have been

[2] The shooting of James Higgins in Burnsville on May 8, which Wolfe had witnessed and about which he was to testify in the trial of Philip Ray and Otis Chase in August.

away from home so long and there have been so many connections to make, so many threads to pick up, so many people, family, relatives, friends, acquaintances and even people I had never seen before, to talk to. A great deal of it, of course, has been very pleasant and a great deal of it has been exhausting and perhaps useless but unavoidable. . . . But that is the way things have been thus far and I know you can understand it. . . .

Of course I'd be delighted to meet the two young people from Nashville, and I think the meeting could be arranged at almost any time. I don't believe this coming Saturday is a good time because I have tentatively promised my sister Effie, who was up here last week and whom I have not seen for eight years, to take the bus and come down to visit her over the week-end in Anderson, South Carolina. . . . Excepting the trip down to South Carolina this weekend, I have no definite engagements and it seems to me you might arrange the meeting with your friends at almost any other time.

The only other thing that worries me is the feeling of personal responsibility. I wish you would do what you could to ease that up a bit. It is very flattering, of course, to be the object of anyone's adoration but it is also a very hard and trying role to live up to. And I am so genuinely, so profoundly grateful for the good will and belief of people. It seems to me that the knowledge that something one has written has meant so much to anyone ought to make a writer proud and happy, and is more than anything else the reward for which he lives and works. But I was a very tired man when I left New York and I am not rested yet. . . . I don't want to disappoint your two young friends but I should like to feel relieved of the strain and pressure of having to try to live up to their image of me. I know that you can arrange the whole thing simply and without complication—get them to understand that I am no longer a wild-eyed boy or a flaming youth or anything like that, but just a man who has done a lot of work and a lot of living at high pressure, and is now trying to relax and think it over. If they will take me like this, I am sure we will all be more comfortable and have a better time. . . . I am sorry these young people are going to make the trip all the way from Nashville just to meet me. I wish they too just "happened in" so to speak—it gives me a feeling of tension and anxiety to know they are going to the expense and trouble of such a journey just to see me. But since they are, I want them to enjoy themselves; I wish they'd come out here and spend the day with me—on some Sunday if it could be arranged. Then if they like we could go in and visit Mama and Mabel or any other members of the family.

As to where they are going to stay, you will have to decide that later. Mabel and Ralph have been living in a very nice house on Kimberley Ave., but they have just rented it for the summer and they are moving to a very much smaller one, and I don't know until I see it how much extra room they have. As for Mama's house, there is certainly room there, but it is frankly in a dilapidated state—an old house in a state of disrepair, which has long since passed its palmy days. Of course it is Mama's home and she loves it and sees it with a different eye, but these are the facts and I don't know whether it would be advisable for the young people to stay there or not. However . . . all these things can be arranged. I'd keep them here if there was room. But we can easily find a place for them somewhere. . . .

I shall call you up and talk with you further about it in a day or two when I come to town. Meanwhile with all good wishes to you and Mr. Roberts,

On July 19, 1937, Scott Fitzgerald had written to Wolfe from Los Angeles, saying:
"Dear Tom:

I think I could make out a good case for your necessity to cultivate an alter ego, a more conscious artist in you. Hasn't it occurred to you that such qualities as pleasantness or grief, exuberance or cynicism can become a plague in others? That often people who live at a high pitch often don't get their way emotionally at the important moment because it doesn't stand out in relief?

Now the more the stronger man's inner tendencies are defined, the more he can be sure they will show, the more necessity to rarefy them, to use them sparingly. The novel of selected incidents has this to be said that the great writer like Flaubert has consciously left out the stuff that Bill or Joe (in his case Zola) will come along and say presently. He will say only the things that he alone sees. So Mme. Bovary becomes eternal while Zola already rocks with age. . . .

That in brief is my case against you, if it can be called that when I admire you so much and think your talent is unmatchable in this or any other country.

Ever your Friend, Scott Fitzgerald" [1]

The following was Wolfe's reply.

To SCOTT FITZGERALD

[Oteen, N.C.]
July 26, 1937

Dear Scott:

I don't know where you are living and I'll be damned if I'll believe anyone lives in a place called "The Garden of Allah" which was what the

---

[1] Copyright, 1956, by the Estate of Scott Fitzgerald.

address on your envelope said. I am sending this on to the old address we both know so well.[1]

The unexpected loquaciousness of your letter struck me all of a heap. I was surprised to hear from you but I don't know that I can truthfully say I was delighted. Your bouquet arrived smelling sweetly of roses but cunningly concealing several large-sized brickbats. Not that I resented them. My resenter got pretty tough years ago; like everybody else I have at times been accused of "resenting criticism" and although I have never been one of those boys who break out in a hearty and delighted laugh when someone tells them everything they write is lousy and agree enthusiastically, I think I have taken as many plain and fancy varieties as any American citizen of my age now living. I have not always smiled and murmured pleasantly "How true," but I have listened to it all, tried to profit from it where and when I could, and perhaps been helped by it a little. Certainly I don't think I have been pig-headed about it. I have not been arrogantly contemptuous of it either, because one of my besetting sins, whether you know it or not, is a lack of confidence in what I do.

So I'm not sore at you or sore about anything you said in your letter. And if there is any truth in what you say—any truth for me—you can depend upon it I shall probably get it out. It just seems to me that there is not much in what you say. You speak of your "case" against me, and frankly I don't believe you have much case. You say you write these things because you admire me so much and because you think my talent is unmatchable in this or any other country and because you are ever my friend. Well Scott I should not only be proud and happy to think that all these things are true but my own respect and admiration for your own talent and intelligence are such that I should try earnestly to live up to them and to deserve them and to pay the most serious and respectful attention to anything you say about my work.

I have tried to do so. I have read your letter several times and I've got to admit it doesn't seem to mean much. I don't know what you are driving at or understand what you hope or expect me to do about it. Now this may be pig-headed but it isn't sore. I may be wrong but all I can get out of it is that you think I'd be a good writer if I were an altogether different writer from the writer that I am.

This may be true but I don't see what I'm going to do about it, and I don't think you can show me. And I don't see what Flaubert and Zola have to do with it, or what I have to do with them. I wonder if you really think they have anything to do with it, or if it is just something you heard in college or read in a book somewhere. This either-or kind of criticism seems to me to be so meaningless. It looks so knowing and imposing but

[1] Care of Scribners.

there is nothing in it. Why does it follow that if a man writes a book that is not like "Madame Bovary" it is inevitably like Zola? I may be dumb but I can't see this. You say that "Madame Bovary" becomes eternal while Zola already rocks with age. Well this may be true—but if it is true isn't it true because "Madame Bovary" may be a great book and those that Zola wrote may not be great ones? Wouldn't it also be true to say that "Don Quixote," or "Pickwick" or "Tristram Shandy" "becomes eternal" while already Mr. Galsworthy "rocks with age."? I think it is true to say this and it doesn't leave much of your argument, does it? For your argument is based simply upon one *way*, upon one *method* instead of another. And have you ever noticed how often it turns out that what a man is really doing is simply rationalizing his own way of doing something, the way he has to do it, the way given him by his talent and his nature, into the only inevitable and right way of doing everything—a sort of classic and eternal art form handed down by Apollo from Olympus without which and beyond which there is nothing? Now you have your way of doing something and I have mine; there are a lot of ways, but you are honestly mistaken in thinking that there is a "way."

I suppose I would agree with you in what you say about "the novel of selected incidents" so far as it means anything. I say so far as it means anything because every novel, of course, is a novel of selected incidents. There are no novels of unselected incidents. You couldn't write about the inside of a telephone booth without selecting. You could fill a novel of a thousand pages with a description of a single room and yet your incidents would be selected. And I have mentioned "Don Quixote" and Pickwick and "The Brothers Karamazov" and "Tristram Shandy" to you in contrast to "The Silver Spoon" or "The White Monkey" as examples of books that have become "immortal" and that *boil* and *pour*. Just remember that although "Madame Bovary" in your opinion may be a great book, "Tristram Shandy" *is* indubitably a great book, and that it is great for quite different reasons. It is great because it *boils* and *pours*—for the *unselected* quality of its selection. You say that the great writer like Flaubert has consciously left out the stuff that Bill or Joe will come along presently and put in. Well, don't forget, Scott, that a great writer is not only a leaver-outer but also a putter-inner, and that Shakespeare and Cervantes and Dostoievsky were great putter-inners—greater putter-inners, in fact, than taker-outers—and will be remembered for what they put in—remembered, I venture to say, as long as Monsieur Flaubert will be remembered for what he left out.

As to the rest of it in your letter about cultivating an alter ego, becoming a more conscious artist, by pleasantness or grief, exuberance or cynicism, and how nothing stands out in relief because everything is keyed at the same emotional pitch—this stuff is worthy of the great minds that review books nowadays—the Fadimans and De Votos—but not of you. For you are an artist and the artist has the only true critical intelligence. You have had to work and sweat blood yourself and you know what it is like to try to write a living word or create a living thing. So don't talk this foolish stuff to me about exuberance or being a conscious artist or not bringing things into emotional relief, or any of the rest of it. Let the Fadimans and De Votos do that kind of talking but not Scott Fitzgerald. You've got too much sense and you know too much. The little fellows who don't know may picture a man as a great "exuberant" six-foot-six clod-hopper straight out of nature who bites off half a plug of apple tobacco, tilts the corn liquor jug and lets half of it gurgle down his throat, wipes off his mouth with the back of one hairy paw, jumps three feet in the air and clacks his heels together four times before he hits the floor again and yells out "Whoopee, boys, I'm a rootin, tootin, shootin son of a gun from Buncombe County—out of my way now, here I come!" —and then wads up three-hundred thousand words or so, hurls it at a blank page, puts covers on it and says "Here's my book!"

Now Scott, the boys who write book-reviews in New York may think it's done that way; but the man who wrote "Tender Is the Night" knows better. You know you never did it that way, you know I never did, you know no one else who ever wrote a line worth reading ever did. So don't give me any of your guff, young fellow. And don't think I'm sore. But I get tired of guff—I'll take it from a fool or from a book reviewer but I won't take it from a friend who knows a lot better. I want to be a better artist. I want to be a more selective artist. I want to be a more restrained artist. I want to use such talent as I have, control such forces as I may own, direct such energy as I may use more cleanly, more surely and to a better purpose. But Flaubert me no Flauberts, Bovary me no Bovarys, Zola me no Zolas, and exuberance me no exuberances. Leave this stuff for those who huckster in it and give me, I pray you, the benefits of your fine intelligence and your high creative faculties, all of which I so genuinely and profoundly admire.

I am going into the woods for another two or three years. I am going to try to do the best, the most important piece of work I have ever done. I am going to have to do it alone. I am going to lose what little bit of reputation I may have gained, to have to hear and know and endure in silence again all of the doubt, the disparagement, the ridicule, the post-mortems that they are so eager to read over you even before you are dead. I know what it means and so do you. We have both been through it before. We know it is the plain damn simple truth.

Well, I've been through it once and I believe I can get through it again. I think I know a little more now than I did before, I certainly know what to expect and I'm going to try not to let it get me down. That is the reason why this time I shall look for intelligent understanding among some of my friends. I'm not ashamed to say that I shall need it. You say in your letter that you are ever my friend. I assure you that it is very good to hear this. Go for me with the gloves off if you think I need it. But don't De Voto me. If you do I'll call your bluff.

I'm down here for the summer living in a cabin in the country and I am enjoying it. Also I'm working. I don't know how long you are going to be in Hollywood or whether you have a job out there but I hope I shall see you before long and that all is going well with you. I still think as I always thought that "Tender Is the Night" had in it the best work you have ever done. And I believe you will surpass it in the future. Anyway, I send you my best wishes as always for health and work and success. Let me hear from you sometime. The address is Oteen, North Carolina, just a few miles from Asheville. Ham Basso, as you know, is not far away at Pisgah Forest and he is coming over to see me soon and perhaps we shall make a trip together to see Sherwood Anderson. And now this is all for the present—unselective, you see, as usual. Good bye, Scott, and good luck,

Ever yours,

To HAMILTON BASSO

[Oteen, N.C.]

July 29, 1937

Dear Ham:

Pick out a week end, any one you like,[1] and I'll make it fit with my own plans which are very simple ones. I intend to keep at work, and so far as I know, except for the hordes of thirsty tourists who just happen in casually to look at the elephant, I have no definite engagements. . . . Except for casual intrusions—people driving up to demand if I've seen anything of a stray cocker spaniel, gentlemen appearing through the woods with a four-pound steak saying their name is McCracken and I met them on the train four weeks ago and they always bring their own provisions with them, and the local Police Court judge and the leading hot-dog merchant, and friends of my shooting scrape in Yancey County with bevies of wild females—all of which has and is continuing to happen —I have practically no company at all out here. At any rate it's all been very interesting and instructing and in spite of Hell and hilarity I am pushing on with my work. You come on over anyway: I can't promise you

[1] Basso had written that he would come and spend a weekend at Wolfe's cabin.

long twenty-four hour periods of restful seclusion while we meditate upon the problems of life and art, but you may have an instructive and amusing time, and of course I'd love to see you and talk it over with you.

I had a letter from Scott, and the surprise of hearing from him was so great you could have knocked me over with a brick bat. It was, for him, an amazingly long letter and a very earnest one. It was all about Art— and more especially my own lack of it. He passed out some very graceful compliments about my "unmatchable talents" and so on, and how he wouldn't be doing all this if he wasn't my friend, etc.—and then let me have it. It was all very much like those famous lines of my favorite poem:

> "It was all very well to dissemble your love
> —But why did you kick me downstairs?"

I couldn't make out very well what he was driving at and told him so. There was a whole lot in it about Flaubert and Zola and "Madame Bovary" and how much greater Flaubert is than Zola, etc.—all of which may be true, but like the celebrated flowers that bloom in the spring, have nothing to do with the case. I let him have it with both barrels when I answered him, and I hope the experience will do him good. I know he will understand I wasn't a bit sore and enjoyed writing a letter and a chance of ribbing him a little. He has come out apparently as a classical selectionist and was telling me that Flaubert would be remembered as a great writer for the things he left out. I answered, not, I thought unneatly that Shakespeare and Cervantes and Tolstoi and Dostoievsky would be remembered as great writers for what they put in and that a great writer was not only a great leaver-outer but a great putter-inner also. Anyway I had some fun and I know Scott won't mind it. His letter was postmarked Los Angeles and I don't know whether he has got a job at Hollywood or not. His letter sounded more stable and cheerful, and I hope that everything is going better with him.

My Chickamauga story, which I liked so well myself, has now been honored with rejection slips by most of the nation's eminent popular magazines. Harper's also turned it down the other day with a pompous note from Mr. Hartman [2] to the effect that they would like a *real* Wolfe story, but they supposed this was impossible since *Scribner's* had a stranglehold on the author's best work. Well the comical pay-off on this is that *Scribner's* have no hold at all, not even a feeble clasp. I have had only one piece in the magazine in three years, and that not one of the better ones, and Perkins has been panting to get hold of "Chickamauga" which Harper's has just rejected. I don't know whether his pants will

[2] Lee Hartman was editor of *Harper's Magazine* at this time.

cease when he has read the story, but I hope not.[3] At any rate I'm gathering experience. Mr. Stout of *The Saturday Evening Post* allows as how my "No More Rivers" is a good story after page twenty and that they'd be very seriously concerned if I'd agree to cut the first twenty pages to four. As I remember it, the beautiful girl with the husky voice makes her appearance on page twenty—so that's that.

I've just taken time out to have pictures of myself, the cabin and all three of us made by a beautiful lady and her escort, Judge Phil Cocke, who weighs 340 on the hoof and is one of Asheville's famous and eminent characters. I like the Judge and the Judge curiously seems to like me; certainly I've never had as devoted and accurate a reader—he hasn't forgotten a comma or a semicolon, he annotates my book with the names of the "real" characters, and I have heard that he was especially touched and delighted because he thinks I referred to him and a very celebrated lady in Asheville who bore the name of Queen Elizabeth and who at one time was the Empress of the Red Light District. Of course, I admit nothing, I just look coy and innocent—but if that's the way they want to have it, I suppose no one can stop them. Anyway we are having fun, you must come over. This is all for the present, write and let me know what time suits you. Meanwhile, with love to you and Toto,

To ELIZABETH NOWELL

> Box 95
> Oteen, N.C.
> July 29, 1937

Dear Miss Nowell:

It looks as if no one's right about "Chickamauga" except thee and me— and maybe even thee is a little peculiar. Anyway, we are finding out something about those great minds that direct the editorial policies of our leading magazines, aren't we? . . .

I am going on with "The Party at Jack's," but it is turning out to be a terrifically complicated and difficult job. But it is a very interesting one and if I work and weave and rework long and hard enough I may have something very good. The market is a different matter: my plan when I get through is to have a complete section of the social order, a kind of dense, closely interwoven tapestry made up of the lives and thoughts and destinies of thirty or forty people, and all embodied in the structure of the story. It is an elaborate design; it has to be: it is, I suppose, somewhat

---

[3] The editors of *Scribner's Magazine*, which by this time was virtually independent of the publishing house of Scribners, declined "Chickamauga" soon after this.

Proustian but this also has to be and the interesting thing about it is the really great amount of action. This action is submerged and perhaps not at first apparent, but if the reader will stick with me, if I can carry him along with me, it will be apparent by the time he finishes the story. In spite of all kinds of interruptions—there have been droves of thirsty tourists out here to look at the animal, all the way from a police court judge to the leading hot-dog merchant—I have done a lot of *work* and hope to see where I stand with it in another two weeks. . . .

The weather is fine, the country is beautiful, I am sleeping at night and I think I feel better than when I left New York four weeks ago. My plans for the future are still uncertain. I don't know where I'll be next year, or where I'm going to live. All I hope for is to go on with my work and get something done and to escape somehow the ruinous calamities of the last two years. . . . I am afraid some of the old connections may be worn out: there are too many scars now, too much disillusionment and disappointment. At any rate, no matter what happens, I hope to go on working and get something done. I am sorry we have had such bad luck with the two stories, but I hope to get some good news soon. Meanwhile, with all good wishes,

The following letter was in reply to one from Mrs. Anne W. Armstrong offering to rent to Wolfe, for a purely nominal sum, a cabin belonging to her brother-in-law and sister, Major General and Mrs. Philip Peyton, on her property near Bristol, Tennessee. Mrs. Armstrong had first met Wolfe when he had passed through Bristol on his way to Asheville in late April, 1937. She is the author of two novels, The Seas of God *and* This Day and Time, *a play,* Some Sweet Day, *and various magazine articles, including "As I Saw Thomas Wolfe" in the Spring, 1946, issue of* The Arizona Quarterly.

To ANNE W. ARMSTRONG

Box 95,
Oteen, N. C.,

August 4, 1937.

Dear Mrs. Armstrong:

Thanks very much for your letter. The rent you mentioned for General Peyton's cabin was not only reasonable but ridiculously cheap for the place. I pay more than that for my own modest little place, which, of course, is nowhere near as comfortable and as elaborate as the Peyton place. But I think I shall try to stick it out here, at least for the present. I have taken the cabin here for another month, and should like to stay at home until I have the satisfaction of getting some work done and finding out that I can really work here. . . .

I brought down with me from New York an enormous crate containing millions of words of manuscript, the material for half a dozen books and notes and ideas and sketches and stories and dozens of other things. Another tremendous piece of work has been shaping itself in my mind and in my writing for two or three years now, and now I think I have it fully articulated and a plan clear from beginning to end. But I lose heart sometime when I think of the magnitude of the task that lies before me. I hope that my health continues and that my will will remain firm. If only things didn't take so long! If only I didn't almost always bite off more than I can chew! It's my own fault, I suppose, but I don't know what I can do about it. It really seems that such talent as I have has to realize itself through a process of torrential production—that is, by pouring it out in a Niagara flood, millions and millions of words. After that, of course, comes the ghastly and heart-breaking labor of cutting it down, shaping and re-weaving it. It's all very well for these fellows who write forty and fifty thousand word books to talk to you about Flaubert and classical brevity: you can try honestly to mend your ways, to learn through experience and work to correct some of your most excessive faults—but what's the use of talking to a man about Flaubert if his talent—such modest talent as he has—is really more like Dickens or Rabelais? Anyway, all I can do is to learn what I can and to do my work, I pray, the best I can.

Well, this is all for the present and too much as usual. If things get too much for me in my own neighborhood, I may come over to find out if that wonderful cabin is still unoccupied. Anyway, I hope to see you before the summer is over. . . . Meanwhile, I send you my thanks again for all your generous interest and consideration. . . .

To HAMILTON BASSO

Oteen, N.C.

August 21, 1937.

Dear Ham:

Thanks for your note and for the enclosed clipping on the Hemingway-Eastman matter.[1] It was all very interesting and instructive. It is good of

[1] Probably a clipping from one of the New York newspapers of August 14, 1937, referring to the encounter between Ernest Hemingway and Max Eastman in the Scribner offices on the preceding day.

you to say that you enjoyed the weekend, but I'm afraid you found it a very hectic one. However, it was quiet compared to what has happened since.

I had to attend a murder trial in Yancey and testify. It was a fascinating and thrilling and exhausting experience. I got off fairly lightly compared to some of the witnesses, but I was denounced by one of the defense lawyers in his final plea to the jury as the author of an obscene and infamous book called "Look Homeward, Angel," who had held up his family, kin-folk, and town to public odium, and whose testimony, I therefore gathered, was not to be taken into account. Also when I returned to my cabin I found that William [2] had disappeared. He showed up finally on Thursday afternoon, confessed that he was afraid of the dark and of staying alone at night, and said he wanted to quit. I looked forward to coming back and working here, but maybe it will not work out as I had hoped. I may go over and visit some friends in Virginia in a few days and perhaps see Sherwood [3] who has written me again and asked me to come. Anyway, I'll try to think my way through it and let you know how it works out.

There is not much other news to tell you. I wish I could see you, and no matter whether I go or stay, I hope to have another talk with you before you go abroad. Meanwhile, with love to you and Toto and with all good wishes,

The following fragment of a letter, found in a carbon copy in Wolfe's own files, was almost undoubtedly written to Elizabeth Nowell about the manuscript of "The Party at Jack's." The person who had told Wolfe "that the thing is a unit in itself" was probably Hamilton Basso who read the manuscript at Wolfe's request and then sent it to Miss Nowell from Pisgah Forest. The "friend in New York" to whom Wolfe intended to send another copy would seem to have been Perkins: certainly the friend referred to in the subsequent paragraph was he. However, there is no record at Scribners of the receipt of the manuscript, and no recollection of it among Perkins' close associates. Moreover, it was at about this time that Wolfe took the final step of breaking with Scribners by putting in long distance calls to various other publishers. Perhaps worrying about Perkins' possible reaction to "The Party at Jack's" was what finally brought things to a head and impelled him to complete the severance.

---

[2] The colored house boy who was working for Wolfe.
[3] Sherwood Anderson.

Probably to ELIZABETH NOWELL

[Asheville, N.C.]

(August 22 (?), 1937.)

. . . It is still only a draft, but as you will see, in a very much more complete and finished form than what you saw in New York. I have completely rewritten it and rewoven it. It was a very difficult piece of work, but I think it is now a single thing, as much a single thing as anything I've ever written. I am not through with it yet. There is a great deal more revision to be done, but I am sending it to you anyway to let you see what I have done, and I think you will also be able to see what it may be like when I'm finished with it.

As to the final disposition of it, I do not know. Someone has told me that the thing is a unit in itself and could be, when I am finished with it, published as a unit without further addition. I have not made up my mind about this yet. The whole thing belongs, as you know, to the entire manuscript of "The October Fair," of which sections and fragments have been published for years—"Death—The Proud Brother," "April, Late April," etc.—and many other things, of course, which have not been published. "Mr. Malone," by the way, belongs in the piece that I am sending you, "The Party at Jack's," but since "Mr. Malone" has already been published, I did not think it advisable to include it here. All the other parts which you have seen: the whole long section called "Morning," that is, Mr. Jack waking up and feeling the tremor, faint and instant, in the ground beneath him; Mrs. Jack and the maid; the "April, Late April" piece which the *Mercury* is publishing; the scene in the station; the long section called "The Locusts Have No King" [1] which I do not think you ever saw; "Death—The Proud Brother"; and other matter which perhaps you never read, also belong with this piece. I, therefore, kept a copy and put it all together with some tentative idea in my mind of making a complete book of all of it—a book which would occur within the limits of a single twenty-four hours, beginning [with] midnight of one day and ending with the midnight of the next, and bearing probably the title "The October Fair." I have not made my mind up definitely about this yet, but I am sending the manuscript to a friend in New York to get his opinion.

[1] This title taken from Proverbs, 30:27, was later used by Dawn Powell for her novel published by Scribners in 1949.

As you know, the whole thing has been a very vexed and perturbed part of my writing experience and it has cost me the utmost worry and difficulty because it seemed to me that so much labor, so much effort, and so much that I really think is valuable and good and needs to be saved was in danger of dying the death, of being in so many various and complicated ways—all of which apparently sprang out of a friend's [2] desire to help and perhaps some instinctive timidity and caution—suppressed and killed. I cannot say definitely as to all this, but I do know that a man must not be thwarted in the process of his creation, and I feel very strongly that this has happened to me with this piece of work.

As to this piece I'm sending you, "The Party at Jack's," I feel that whatever else may be said about it, it escapes entirely the objections that were raised about the purpose of "The October Fair." I really think that the purpose of "The October Fair" was misunderstood, and [that] people whose judgment I respected were too quick and willing to assume that the book would be a sequel to the first two books and thus lay me open to the old charges of autobiographical literalness and romanticism, etc. and not as I intended it to be: the progression of my life, the maturing of my experience and my talent. At any rate, "The Party at Jack's," I believe, escapes these feared qualities. I don't believe the charge of "autobiography" can be brought against it, except in so far as they must be brought against the work of any man. I have simply taken the lives of thirty or forty of the people I knew during my years in New York and revealed them during an evening at a party in the city.

As to the matter of action, it seems to me that the piece is crowded, although perhaps it is not apparently so. But I don't see how any intelligent reader could read it without understanding that almost everything has happened before the piece is ended. As to the rest of it, the social implication that, I fear, would make the piece anathema to almost any of the older publishers, I simply cannot help it. It is simply the way I feel and think: I hope and believe there is not a word of conscious propaganda in it. It is certainly not at all Marxian, but it is representative of the way my life has come—after deep feeling, deep thinking, and deep living and all this experience—to take its way. And I believe and hope, also, that this piece will show the energy of life, a genuine and reverent love of life, and a spirit of understanding and compassion for all the characters. I hope and believe that it has passion in it, indignation and denunciation, and I hope also it has pity and love

[2] Wolfe undoubtedly meant Perkins here. See his letter to him dated December 15, 1936.

and comprehension in it. You are seeing the thing in its first blocking out: if all these qualities that I hope for it are not fully revealed now, I hope they will be when I get through working on it. It is in concept, at any rate, the most densely woven piece of writing that I have ever attempted.

There is not much more that I can tell you about it except that I wish you would read it as it is, in and for itself, without too much reference to these other portions I have mentioned, of which it is also a part. But just read it, if you can, as a story in itself and see if you think it carries the unity and direction of a single thing. Because I am not certain that I shall be here more than a day or two longer, I am sending you the piece in its present unrevised and uncorrected form. Travelling around with great bags of manuscript—and I've written sixty or eighty thousand words since I came down here—is a precarious business, and I would like to know that even in its present form, you have a copy in your hands. Another copy will be in the keeping of a friend in New York, and I hope to keep the final one intact for myself. . . .

It's pretty hard to tell you what I shall do about staying here in Asheville. I wanted to come back: I thought about it for years. I think I should like still to stay and work if it were possible. As you know, I have never put much stock in looking for "places to work." It seems to me that a man can work almost any place he wants to. But my stay here this summer has really resembled a three-ring circus. I think people have wanted to be and have tried to be most kind, but they wore me to a frazzle. My cabin outside of town was situated in an isolated and quite beautiful spot, but they found their way to it, and in addition I found out that it is, to say the least, terribly difficult to keep a negro servant in such a place. They are afraid of the dark: that is about what it amounts to. As a result, they were always disappearing at night and not coming back until the next morning. . . . Of course, it's not their fault, but just the way they are.

As to living in town here, I don't know whether that can work out or not. I know so many people here and the place is really very small. People know everything you do, even before you do it—it's always that way, isn't it—and they are still, in a friendly way, living over the whole vexed experience of "Look Homeward, Angel" and of having the culprit back in their midst. It is a beautiful country here. I shall always miss it, but perhaps what I had thought possible cannot happen. At any rate, the summer has not been lost. I have established the connection again and, of course, completed gathering all the materials for perhaps the most tragic incidents of our collapse—which happened to the entire nation—in the history of our country. I don't think anything else like it could be found! The whole thing, intensified and specialized, is here. And since it is my own home place, of course I have the deepest interest, the profoundest sympathy with all of it.

I may go up to Virginia for a day or two to see Sherwood Anderson. As to mailing addresses for the present, I don't know what to tell you. I still have my cabin at Oteen until September, and I am still trying to think my way through this, to find out what I am going to do. I think for the present if you would send any communication you may have to General Delivery, Asheville, N.C., that would be the quickest and safest address. Then if there is any change, I can leave word there where the mail should be forwarded. This is all for the present, and too much as usual. Please let me know if you receive the manuscript of "The Party at Jack's" safely, and what, if any, you think the prospects are. Meanwhile, with thanks and all good wishes,

To SHERWOOD ANDERSON

[New York City]

Wednesday, September 22, 1937

Dear Sherwood:

Thanks for your letter. It was not only fine to hear from you—what you said did me a lot of good. What you say is true—I do, and have all my life gone for *everything*—not only writing—hell for leather. I seem to wrestle each experience as if, in circus talk, I am "now about to engage in a hair-raising, spine-freezing, gravity-defying duel to the death with the universe." I suppose that's why that shrewd and wise and nice mother-in-law of yours told you I was [——?] pretty hard on myself. I went home this summer for the first time in almost eight years to fight it out, talk it out, live it out, with the city of Asheville as if I was a regiment of storm troops going into a decisive battle. And of course it took it out of me. I was pretty tired when I saw you—but maybe also I was coming away with a lot of tar on my heel and large fistfuls of the native earth. I hope so, anyway.

I don't think really I'm so much worried about the bulk and flood of my writing as I once was. I've got a *feeling* about some things, after long mulling and thrashing about with them, that often turns out right —and my feeling is that I shall probably always have to do essentially about as I do now—that is, pour it out, boil it out, flood it out. I realize myself through a process of torrential production. Perhaps there are better ways but that is my way—I believe essentially my way—and it would be wrong to worry about doing it Flaubert's way, or Hemingway's way, or Henry James' way. Nevertheless, I do worry, as we all do, about my improvement: I want to be a better writer, a less wasteful writer, a surer writer, a cleaner writer, a more disciplined writer—and I believe and hope that may come through work. As to the rest of it—my death-defying duel with the universe—just the business of living which I make so damned hard but out of which I do believe I have managed to get a good deal—I think it is pretty closely bound up with my work. In fact, living and working are so close together with me that it seems to me they are damned near the same thing. I do carry my work too much with me—when I'm doing it, I take it into bars, restaurants, railroad trains, parties, upon the streets, everywhere. I guess many a row or quarrel or dispute in some joint with a sanded floor began somewhere hours or days or weeks before upon a page of manuscript, but I hope some of my better moments started there as well.

I'm wrestling with a huge leviathan of work—three monstrous books, all worked upon and sweat upon and prayed about and dreamt and cursed upon for years.[1] I'm caught in the Laocoön coils of this too-muchness. I get maddened like Tantalus with the feeling of having everything almost within my grasp and of starving to death.

For one thing, I think I am starving for publication: I love to get published: it maddens me not to get published: I feel at times like getting every publisher in the world by the scruff of his neck, forcing his jaws open, and cramming the manuscript down his throat—"God damn you, here it is—I will and must be published."

You know what it means—you're a writer and you understand it. It's not "the satisfaction of being published." Great God! it's the satisfaction of getting it out; of knowing that, so far as you're concerned, you're through with it; that—for good or ill, for better or for worse—it's over, done with, finished, out of your life forever and that, come what may, you can at least as far as this thing is concerned, get the merciful damned easement of oblivion and forgetfulness.

My troubles with Scribners are deep, grievous, and, I fear, irreparable: I'll have to try to find someone else, if anyone will have me. I can't tell you the anguish this thing has cost me: these things get deep hold of me, and this has been almost like death. But I *will* be published, if I can: I've got to be—and I will have my own picture of life, my own vision of society, of the world as, thus far, I have been able to live, sweat, feel and think it through! And my disagreement with these people with

[1] He probably meant *The October Fair, The Hills Beyond Pentland,* and *The Vision of Spangler's Paul.* However he usually thought of these as one great mass of manuscript.

whom I have been so close, with whom my life has been so deeply knit, has become so great, so complex and so various!—I don't see how it can be patched up now!

Really, I don't think I'm either muddled or confused. I don't think I know anyone who knows—or thinks he knows—so clearly and so desperately what he wants to do. I want to do my work and to get it published. I want to find a place where I can feel at home and to which I can go back. (Incidentally, I think there are such places, but I don't think they're either Asheville or New York.) I want to get married and try to have a family.

I'll probably always go through this kind of struggle with my work, but honestly I don't see why I shouldn't get all these things I have spoken of. At any rate, I shan't give up trying yet.

May I also say that I want to be your friend—as I am—and I want you to be mine, as I believe you are. When I told you how I felt about you and your work, I was not laying it on with a trowel. I don't think of you as a father, as an elderly influence, or anything of the kind. So far as I know, your work has not "influenced" me at all, save in the ways in which it has enriched my life, and my knowledge of my country. I think you are one of the most important writers of this country, that you plowed another deep furrow in the American earth, revealed to us another beauty that we knew was there but that no one else had spoken. I think of you with Whitman and with Twain—that is, with men who have seen America with a poet's vision, and with a poetic vision of life —which to my mind is the only way actually it can be seen.

I appreciate your letter and all you say to me. I'll have to work the whole thing out for myself, but I feel there is wisdom in you, and we never perhaps give up the wonderful image of our youth—that we will find someone external to our life and superior to our need, who knows the answer.

It does not happen—"is not my strength in me?"—but it comes, I think, from the deepest need in life, and all religiousness is in it.

Good-bye for the present, Sherwood. I hope I'll be here when you come. At any rate, I'll look forward to seeing you again before too long. Meanwhile, with love to all,

XVI

THE SEARCH FOR A NEW PUBLISHER AND FINAL CHOICE OF HARPERS

1937

In late August or early September, 1937, Wolfe had finally completed his severance from Scribners by putting in long distance calls to several other publishers to inquire whether they would like to publish him. Nothing definite came of these first queries, either because the other publishers could not clearly hear what he said and were not sure that he actually was Thomas Wolfe, or because they hesitated to take him away from Scribners, or, because he himself decided against going with them. A few weeks later, after Wolfe had returned to New York, Robert N. Linscott of Houghton Mifflin heard the rumors that he had left Scribners and wrote him to ask if this was true. The following was Wolfe's reply.

To ROBERT N. LINSCOTT

[Prince George Hotel]
[New York City]
[October 16, 1937]

Dear Mr. Linscott:

Thanks very much for your letter. By an unfortunate coincidence I was in Boston last week at the time your letter was written and might have seen you then. I did try but found a whole column of Linscotts when I looked in the telephone book, and I couldn't decide which was you. As it was then Saturday afternoon I knew there was no use trying Houghton Mifflin.

I'm sorry there have been "rumours"; as you know New York is a pretty rumourous place, but I want to assure you that I don't go around in the groups where these presumably originate, and in fact have not seen a publisher in almost four months. I am telling you this because to my great and deep regret my former publishers and I have separated. It is not true that I have "left" them; I am simply without a publisher. I want you to know that this severance is not the result of a temperamental explosion on the part of an author who is now trying to make terms with someone else, and get the best terms that he can; but that it is, for me, at any rate, one of the most grievous and sorrowful experiences of my whole life; it involves deep and complicated differences which touch, it seems to me, my whole life and work—differences that are by no means recent, but that began two and a half years ago. I know there are people at my former publishers who could tell you that this is true —chiefly, the man who has stood closest to me for eight years now and who knows more about my life and the problem of my work than anyone else, Maxwell Perkins.

I am telling you all this to let you know that I can honorably talk about these things to other people now, and other people can talk to me about these things. And honestly, Mr. Linscott, what I need most of all right now is someone I can talk to—someone who understands the problems of publishing and of a writer's work. I do feel earnestly that this ought to be done first, because the problem is really so complex, the differences that brought about this severance are so involved that I need to lay them before someone and get the opinion and perhaps the guidance of a more detached mind. I can not go into them here, I can only tell you that the whole problem is one that involves several million words of manuscript, the material of at least three big books, and a great many stories and novelettes, and what I am going to do with this material, how I am going to use it, and whether anyone is going to support me and encourage me in my use of it.

That is why I need so badly to talk to someone. It will take a long talk, a lot of talk, maybe a whole series of talks, but that is what is needed first. And I know I can make the whole thing clear: I am completely certain of my purpose. I am very happy and grateful to know that people in your office feel as you say they do about my work. I am proud to know that a house of your standing is interested in me. I don't know if you would care to assume a publishing responsibility of this nature after I have explained it to you, or whether your house is the best one for a problem of this sort. But I do think that it would help a lot if we could talk about it, and if I could say my piece to you. And please understand, Mr. Linscott, that there is nothing underhanded about this situation: it is a sad business for me and I am sick at heart because of it, but it is a trouble that has been developing for almost three years, and that my publisher and I have debated and worked on from every side until there was no more to say. Naturally, I think they are wrong about many things, and I should like to tell you about them, and then, if you like, you can talk to the publisher—to Max Perkins—yourself. But please understand that I have no intention of indulging in bitter recriminations towards people with whom for years I had the deepest and closest relations, whose intelligence and ability I so deeply respect, and for whom I shall always have a feeling of warmth and affection. As I told you, it's a sad and bitter business for me: it's damned near got me down, I'm trying to rest up a little, but I want to get back to work. I'm staying here at this hotel, probably only for a few days until I decide where I'm going to live. You can reach me by writing me, or telephoning, care of my agent, Elizabeth Nowell, 114 East 56th St., New York City—Wickersham 2-1262. If you are coming down to New York and want to see me, please let me know through her. And excuse this long letter—like everything I do it's too long—but I wanted to give you some idea of what's in my mind.

After talking with Wolfe and also with Perkins, Robert Linscott had asked Wolfe to let him read some of his manuscript, especially that of The October Fair, *which Wolfe now thought he wanted to publish first. Wolfe had some of his manuscript with him, some was still at Scribners and some in a storage warehouse, and when he explained the difficulty of sorting and assembling it all in a small hotel room, Linscott arranged for him to take it to Houghton Mifflin's New York office. On October 22, 1937, Linscott wrote him a note acknowledging receipt of "one packing case and nine packages of manuscripts," and continued: "I am a little worried by the fact that we have no fire-proof safe in which to store material of this value, and I hope you realize that, under the circumstances, it will have to be held entirely at your risk. Let me take this opportunity to tell you how much I enjoyed our evening together and how greatly I appreciate the chance to read this manuscript."*

Wolfe became upset by this disclaimer of responsibility for the manuscript and wrote Linscott the letter which appears below; then thought better of it and never mailed it, but kept it in his own files and finally handed it to Edward C. Aswell of Harper & Brothers as a partial explanation of the situation that existed between himself and Houghton Mifflin.

Shortly after writing this letter, Wolfe went to the New York office of Houghton Mifflin and took his manuscript away. At this time he talked with LeBaron Barker, who was then New York editor of Houghton Mifflin, about their disclaimer of responsibility, but as Barker now remembers it, he did not seem as much upset as amused by the whole thing. In all fairness to Linscott, it should be pointed out that the general policy of all publishers is to disclaim responsibility for manuscripts submitted to them. Perhaps Linscott was over-conscientious in making this clear, but Wolfe had no real reason

to take offence. However, he was totally ignorant of this general policy, be-
cause Scribners had stored his crates of manuscript many times without ever
mentioning the matter of responsibility for them.

To ROBERT N. LINSCOTT

[Prince George Hotel]
[Fifth Avenue and 28th Street]
[New York City]

October 23, 1937

Dear Linscott:

I did not read the letter you gave me yesterday at your office until
I returned home. You said it was an acknowledgment of the manuscript
I had left at your New York office, but when I read it I found that you
also disclaimed responsibility for the material and said that it would
have to be held at your office entirely at my risk.

It had not occurred to me that any risk was involved in view of what
you had said to me in our previous conversations, and when I brought
the manuscript to your New York office, people there assured me there
was no risk. I wish you had let me know of this before I took the manuscript out of safe-keeping in a storage warehouse because, as I told you,
it represents the work of several years and is almost all I own in the
world. In view of your letter, however, I am removing the manuscript
from your office and shall try to put it in a place where no risk is involved.

I am sorry about all this, but just to keep the record straight, you wrote
me on October 8 saying that you had heard I was looking for a publisher
and that Houghton Mifflin was interested in my work. I wrote back on
October 16 and said that I was without a publisher and would like to
talk to someone about the matter of publishing my future work. You
telephoned Miss Nowell, my agent, from Boston and made an appointment with me. When I saw you I tried to explain the situation as far
as my manuscript was concerned, and you suggested that I give you
first for reading a part of the manuscript which was called "The October
Fair." I told you that all the manuscript was packed and stored in a
storage warehouse and that I should have to go there and take it out,
and that I had no apartment here, no place to take it. You told me I
could bring it to the Houghton Mifflin office here in New York, and you
repeated this offer in a subsequent conversation on the telephone, and
told me Mr. Barker of Houghton Mifflin would go with me and help me
get it. Mr. Barker and I did go immediately and get the manuscript

from the warehouse and bring it to the Houghton Mifflin office here. This completes the record of the transaction until your letter of October 22.

In view of the fact that I had already begun to arrange the manuscript which you had asked to read, and since the necessity for moving the manuscript now from your office to a place of safe-keeping means a further delay, I must ask you to let me know right away what you want to do as far as the manuscript of "The October Fair" is concerned. Since I promised to get it out and arrange it, I am still willing to abide by that promise, but in view of your letter that the manuscript you were keeping is entirely at my risk, I want to know what responsibility, if any, you are willing to assume for the safe-keeping, the protection, and the safe-return of the manuscript you asked to see.

If you are willing, as you say in your letter, to assume no risk, our agreement concerning this manuscript is ended. It seems to me that you must assume the risk, that the entire and whole responsibility of safe-guarding an author's property, once you have requested it, is yours and yours alone. If you can not agree to this, then I do not know why I should entrust my property into your care.

I am sorry about all this, but since you have yourself raised a question of "risk" which it never occurred to me would be raised, I must request that you explicitly state to me immediately just what, if any, you conceive as your responsibility toward the property I entrust into your care. If you do not feel you have a responsibility, then I request that you write me to that effect immediately so that I can make further efforts to find people who will assume that responsibility, and will offer me a chance of obtaining the two things I lack and that I need now more than anything in the world—a good publisher and a decent living.

I want you to understand that there is not a particle of anger, misunderstanding, or ill-feeling in this letter. But I do insist now on getting things straight. It is vitally important to me at what is to me a very critical and vitally important time. I know you are a business man, and I want you to know that I respect the rules of business so far as the rules of business respect the rights of general humanity. But I am a creating man, and hence a very practical man, and therefore can not agree that there is one set of rules that apply to business and another set that apply to general humanity. In other words, you can not talk to a man over the dinner table and a drink about your belief and interest and enthusiasm for his work, and how your organization supports and upholds such people in failure or success, and then talk about who is to take the risk, or whose responsibility is whose when he brings his property into your office and entrusts it to your care. I do not say that either set of chips is wrong, but you've got to play one or the other. You can't play both against the same man, when he has got only one set of chips and intends to use only one. I am telling you this because I've been through this whole thing before, and so far as I am [able] I shall avoid hereafter dealing with people who have two sets of chips.

I know that this, together with my previous long letter and my conversations with you, makes my own position plain.

Please let me know what you want to do about the manuscript I was to give to you. Meanwhile, with all good wishes,

To CORNELIUS MITCHELL

[New York City]
November 15, 1937

Dear Cornelius:

I have your letter of October 26th, and also a recent communication from Miss Nowell, my agent, to the effect that the New Jersey lawyers, Lum, Tamblyn & Fairlie,[1] have been trying to communicate with me through Scribners. I should like to inform you that my forwarding address is no longer Charles Scribner's Sons, as they have severed their relations with me, and are no longer my publishers. My present address for mail and for telephone calls, if it can be possibly kept this way, is in care of

Miss Elizabeth Nowell,
114 East 56th Street,
New York City

If there is really any urgent need to communicate with me in a hurry, I can be reached by a telephone call to Miss Nowell, which will be relayed to me within five minutes. All I can finally tell you with the utmost earnestness is that unless there is a real and urgent need for me and the prospect of something being done in my own behalf, I hope that I may be left to do my work, because my livelihood depends on it.

My funds are almost exhausted, and after two years of constant, nerve-racking interruptions of all sorts, I am faced now with the necessity of getting on with my work without further delay, if I am going to support

---

[1] Because of Wolfe's dissatisfaction with the handling of his case against ——, Mitchell had retained new counsel in New Jersey, where the case was to be tried. Lum, Tamblyn and Fairlie were the new counsel retained, and brought the case to a very successful conclusion in February, 1938.

myself at all. And if I don't support myself no one else is going to do it for me, because I have no income other than what I can earn by my own hands. I have at present an understanding with a publisher [2] to the effect that he is interested in my work and if I will push on now as hard as I can and try to get another big book finished this winter, he is willing to consider the manuscript with a view to publication. If I don't do this, the time is very soon coming when there will not be any money left for anything—to pay lawyer's bills or, what is certainly more to my own immediate purpose, to pay the rent. For that reason I am living here in New York in a rented room, and have so far as possible cut myself away from all contacts and all interruptions just in order to get my work done. I have wanted to explain all of this to you to let you know why I am doing this, that I am not hiding from any one or anything save for the one end and purpose in mind: to be allowed to work and earn my living. . . .

Economically and in every other way, I am right up against the wall. My eyes went back on me this summer and I've got to wear glasses now when I work, but I'm working as hard as I can here, day and night, and I'll get through somehow if I can only be spared the costly experience of these past two years. I have been loyal to my friends and tried to stick with the representatives I started out with. But I think you know where that led in one case: we both agreed we thought the representatives were in error in their judgment of the case, failed to take . . . decisive action, and we were compelled to seek counsel elsewhere. . . . I simply can't afford to go on like this. . . .

I have to work desperately hard for every dollar that I earn and that is why I am now putting this situation to you as I have, and I am putting it to you not as to a lawyer but as to a man who has told me that he has my interest and my welfare at heart. And that is why, Cornelius, I have not minced words here and have spoken bluntly to you about the whole situation. I know that, with the facts and circumstances being what they are, that is the way you would want me to speak. I know also that you can be depended upon to answer the same way. Meanwhile, until I hear from you, with best regards and with all good wishes,

The following letters to Fred W. Wolfe and to Maxwell E. Perkins, were written after reading the correspondence between Fred Wolfe, Mrs. Wolfe and Perkins concerning the severance with Scribners. Fred Wolfe had first

[2] Houghton Mifflin.

written to Perkins on October 28, 1937, saying: "Inasmuch as Mama seems a little perturbed because she has not heard from Tom . . . I thought it best to learn from you if he is O. K." To this, Perkins had answered on November 1: "I can tell you at any rate that Tom is all right. He has left his apartment on First Avenue, and has been living in different hotels until he finds a place to settle, I understand. He has also turned his back on me, and Scribners, so I have not seen him at all, though I would very much like to. I never could understand about all the trouble, but I hope in the end it will smooth out, at least so far as personal relations are concerned." Mrs. Wolfe herself had also written Perkins on November 3, saying: "Will you kindly give me Tom's address? . . . For his sake, I'm ashamed to let anyone know that we have not heard from him since he left September 5. I have worried, thought he might be sick . . ." To this Perkins answered that the quickest way to reach Wolfe would be in care of Miss Nowell, and referred Mrs. Wolfe to his letter of November 1 to Fred Wolfe. Meanwhile, Fred Wolfe had replied to Perkins on November 3, saying: "It is . . . a relief to know that Tom is all right. I am sorry he is having to live around in hotels and I hope he will soon make up his mind and settle and also make up his mind who his friends are. It is regrettable to be told he has turned his back on you and Scribners although I can't help but feel that there is a mistaken idea here on perhaps your part and your company's. Tom's warm statements of his affection to you personally at all times and while he was at home at Asheville are in direct . . . contradiction to your apprehensions in this direction. I rather think he is lost in a spell of worry or indecision. . . . When he gets back down to earth and realization, he will be around. If there is any trouble, I likewise fail to understand what it is all about. I can not see any reason why he should have any chip on his shoulder towards you or any members of his family, unless he is suffering from mental hallucinations. There is no normal reason for anything at all."

Upon receiving these letters from his brother, Wolfe evidently became very angry and upset and wrote him the following letter, but never mailed it. Probably when he had calmed down somewhat, he realized that it was inadvisable to involve his family in his difficulties with Scribners. Perhaps he also realized that his long metaphorical description of Scribners as an ice-cream company and himself as one of its salesmen had distorted the actual facts too far from truth and justice. It would be difficult to define just where and how he did this. However, the reader is referred to the actual correspondence between Wolfe and Perkins of November, 1936, and January, 1937, quoted in this volume as of those dates.

At any rate, after a two-day period of reflection, he wrote the letter below to Perkins and sent a copy of it to Fred Wolfe with a brief note simply saying: "I hope [this] clarifies the situation somewhat in your own mind. I think he's a fine man and that everything is bound to work out all right in the end."

To FRED W. WOLFE

[New York City]
November 17, 1937

Dear Fred:

I got your letter last night with the two enclosed letters from Mr. Perkins and the letter you wrote him on November 3rd. I am glad, at any rate, you told Mr. Perkins that you had never heard me say anything but good about him, for this is true, not only in your case but in the case of everyone that I have ever talked to. Miss Nowell, who has been, I believe, a true friend to me through all this trouble and is also a friend of Mr. Perkins', informed me the other day that he had told her I was going around "talking about him." This is so far from the truth that nothing could possibly be more wrong. The truth apparently is that of all the people in New York, I am the only one who has done no talking whatever about this whole situation—whatever talking has been done by me has been done within the past few days to publishers who have heard the rumors, and then whenever Mr. Perkins' name was mentioned, [it] was always mentioned by me in such a way as to do him nothing but honor. Moreover, in these conversations with other publishers I have been scrupulous to avoid making any statement that could be interpreted as showing bad feeling toward Scribners. All I have said was that I am no longer with a publisher, that the cause of this separation was not a recent one but a matter that had its beginnings at least two years ago, and that the situation finally reached such a state that it was understood on both sides months ago that I could not continue. Mr. Perkins' statement in his letter to you that I have "turned my back" on him and Scribners could not be further from the truth. The truth of the matter is that it was not my back that was turned, or if it was, it was because I looked for my friend and found that he had already walked away from me. Eight months ago at least, Charles Scribner Jr., [Charles Scribner III] the head of the firm, wrote me a letter in which he told me that I was now free to go if I wanted to, that they would be sorry to lose me, but if I felt that the time had come when we could no longer continue, I was free to go anywhere I liked. And about the same time, Mr. Perkins came to see me at my apartment on First Avenue, and with what I thought was deepest sincerity, told me that if I felt I had to leave Scribners, to leave, but that what was really important to him was that he and I continue to be friends. And that is what I have tried to do. Whatever talk has been done—and God knows, I suppose from what I have heard, there has been plenty, for when they start in this town they are just as bad as they are in a smaller town—has been done by others, and not by myself.

For two months after my return here in September, I stayed absolutely to myself, trying to think things out. It has been one of the saddest and most painful experiences of my whole life. To remember the devotion and loyalty and friendship that I had for all of these people for eight years, all the work I did for them, all the years of my life I gave to them, [and to have it] come to this, has been like death, like the death of a friend you can never forget. But there was simply no other way out. It had got to the point where it seemed I could no longer get them to publish the work I had done—the great mass of unpublished work on which I have expended years of effort in planning—but also it was becoming more and more a question of whether I could get them to publish anything in the future. When Perkins speaks about my "leaving" them, I can only ask you to remember that I had absolutely no contract of any sort with Scribners for any future work, nor had they offered me one.[1] I resent, therefore, the idea that I have left something that I did not even have.

I don't think you would consider an employer of yours justified in accusing you of leaving him, if he had quit paying you two years ago, had never spoken of a renewal of his employment, and had even taken away from you the work you had to do. Also, if someone had bumped into you at a cross-section, if no one in either car had been hurt and you had not even scraped any paint off anyone's fender, what would be your own feeling if the people in the other car thought they saw the chance of a little easy money and [got a] lawyer and brought suit against you and your employer for $125,000, saying that you had completely demolished their car, almost killed all the people in it, ruined the health of their sisters, their cousins and their aunts so that they will never be able to walk again, and so on. How would you feel about all of this if your own employer, not only for himself but for you, sought out not some good competent hard-boiled lawyer who would take a $50 fee and then deal with a shyster as he ought to be dealt with, but instead engaged the most expensive firm of attorneys in the South and paid them a retainer of $2,000 before they even lifted a finger. Suppose, also, that these attorneys laughed at the notion of there being any case, assured you that it was nothing but a nuisance suit and would be thrown out of court, and that you would on no account settle for anything. Then suppose within ten days or two weeks, your employer called you

[1] See Wolfe's letter to Perkins of November 12, 1936, and Perkins' formal answer of November 18, 1936; also Wolfe's wire of January 9, 1937, and the appended commentary.

into his office and the great attorneys are there and they tell you that they have now got the other people down so that they are willing to "compromise" for $2500 or $3000. Suppose you say you don't believe there ought to be any compromise whatever, even for a penny, and your employer calls you aside and tells you that he thinks a compromise is the best way out because the lawyers have already cost so much money that it will be cheaper to accept the compromise than to go on and fight the crooks and see it through. Suppose you tell the man that for your own part, although you have only a few hundred dollars in the bank, you are willing to put every penny that you have into fighting the case rather than yield to an outrageous holdup, and suppose he asks you to yield on his account.

Then suppose that the next time you ask for your salary, and for some back money which he has been keeping for you, the cashier tells you that you haven't got any salary or any back money, that you've been charged $3,000 as your share of the legal expense and compromise, and that you are in debt to them. If all of these things happened to you, wouldn't you feel that the people you worked for had let you down, had sold you out at a time when plainly the only right thing to do was stand up and fight against injustice?

Suppose, at about this time your employer wrote you a letter, saying that although he was sorry to lose you, you were now free to go. Suppose you hung on like grim death, out of your loyalty to the man and your long association with him, tried not to break off relations, did everything in your power, begged and entreated to be allowed to keep on working. Suppose he said that of course he would be glad for you to keep on working, but when you went down to the plant on Monday morning you found that they had taken your car away from you and locked it up in the garage and told you that maybe you'd better forget about all of that business in Greenville or Anderson on which you had been working for the last three years, and which gave promise, you thought, of developing into the best business you had ever done, and why didn't you instead just take a walk around the corner and see the fellow who has just opened up a little hole in the wall up there, and see if you can't persuade him to buy a few gallons of ice cream.

Suppose you were getting no more salary, no more pay, but that everyone still thought that you were, and that when another rival employer said to you one day: "I think you are the best salesman in the business, and if you'll just name the figure Jones pays you, I'll top it in a minute, but I know it's no use, because you two are such good friends and you are getting along so well there." Suppose you kept your mouth shut out of loyalty, even in the face of this—don't you think the time would come when you would have to give up, when your money was almost gone—when you were faced with the actual problem of paying the rent and keeping a shelter over your head—and you realized finally that you were left dangling in the air, and that although everybody assumed you were still working for Jones, the fact was that you were no longer being paid a cent of wages, had no understanding or contract of any sort with Jones, or [were] not even allowed to do your work any more, since he had taken away from you the equipment you had to work with—the machine you had to have to make calls fifty miles away? Do you think you could go on like that forever? Don't you think the time would come when you would be forced to realize that so far as Jones is concerned, you were through?

Suppose when that time came the knowledge was so hard to face, the memory of your past friendship with Jones and other members of his firm meant so much to you, that for four long and bitter months you did nothing except try to think your way through the thing, ached your heart out about it, were too decent and loyal and honorable to talk to anyone about it, although the time had long since passed when you were bound by any obligation of any sort. Suppose that during all that time Jones and all the members of his firm know the truth, know they do not employ you any more and yet never breathe a word to anyone to the effect that now you have no job, although they know there are many other firms which would be glad to offer you a job if you were free.

Suppose finally the news got out that you no longer work for Jones, and that then some of the other firms begin to seek you out. Wouldn't you be a bit surprised in view of all of these things to hear that Jones was pulling a long face, pretending to be terribly surprised, and going around saying that you had "turned your back on him" and the other members of his firm?

Well, this may seem to you to be some kind of devilish nightmare, or some wild invention of the fancy, but I can assure you that it is the simple truth. It is not part of the truth; it is not half of the truth; it is the whole truth. It was not something that I imagined in my mind; it was something that happened; that was done to me by Jones and his associates; that cannot be denied. The only thing that I have left out is additional evidence tending to the same end and all piling up to a staggering total. Furthermore, even in view of all that has happened, I want you to know that I have no bitterness in my heart either for Jones or his associates—that I have spoken of them all with friendship and respect.

I want you to understand also that I do not think that Jones and his associates are as bad as their conduct—their callous and indifferent treatment to [the] loyalty and devotion of a man—would indicate. I think rather that some of them may be a little hurt now, wounded to know that at last it has happened. I think also that Jones and his associates were a little bit inclined to think that they had been given special privileges by God Almighty—that to question the essential rectitude and finality of their opinions on any matter smacked of sacrilege—that there was nothing else on earth so infallibly right as everything they did as Jones and Company. I think that Jones and Company may have got to a very dangerous point where it believed that there was no other company in the world that could touch it: that it not only made good ice cream but that the ice cream that it made was so good that no one who had ever tasted it could possibly be persuaded to try another brand. I think they find it pretty hard to believe now that the old hand is really going to work for another concern: perhaps he cried "wolf, wolf" too often, and they opened the gate too many times and told him to take a walk, and at last he did. That's the story.

As for Jones's old hand, I think he was considerable of a fool—and did a lot of things he should not have done. But I know that in his heart he has nothing to be ashamed of, except the words spoken in haste and anger now and then. And I think Jones and Company know this too, and they realize at last that loyalty and devotion doesn't come a dime a dozen, and maybe next time there won't be so good to get at the gate. And so far as the old hand is concerned, I know he hopes for the time when he can see Jones again, and when he and Jones can again come together as friends. I know he is still Jones's friend and I hope and believe Jones is also his friend, and is man enough when this thing is over to forget his temporary hurt pride, and to give his friend his hand again and tell him that everything is all right as long as they are still friends. If Jones is the man I think he is, he'll do this. If he thinks he's got a [Holy?] life and that an unpardonable sin has been committed against the Holy Ghost, he won't. Whatever happens, I've got a notion that Jones's old hand will probably continue to feel about his old boss as he has always felt as long as he lives. And that's the story.

Now, I would just like to be left alone for a while. I don't think I'm going to be helped much by any of you, and I no longer expect it, but if you can't help, for God's sake when I am fighting for a living, don't rush in and shoot off your mouth about matters you know nothing of. And also, why assume, because a man happens to be your brother, he is bound to be wrong? I assure you there are many people who don't think so, and by and large, I think, my reputation among people who know me and also through the country, is a good one.

I understand that Mama wrote Perkins that because she couldn't tell people who called up my address, she felt "ashamed for me." It seems to me that's getting ashamed too easily and in the wrong direction: there are so many other more important things that I have nothing whatever to do with, that people could get ashamed about if they want to. And if my keeping my address a secret is a cause for shame, that's just too bad. It's going to stay a secret, if I can keep it so, and people will just have to keep on being ashamed. I've been through hell enough the past two years, and all I ask now is a chance to do my work and earn my living. Meanwhile, if there is any real occasion to communicate with me, I can always be reached through Miss Nowell. And that is the way things are going to stand.

About the summer I spent at home, my first return in seven years or more, the less said the better. I'd like to forget about it if I could. I went home a very tired man, not only with all of this trouble of Scribners gnawing, but the pressure and accumulation of everything that has happened in the past two years. And when I left home I was as near to a breakdown as I have ever been. My eyes began to go this summer in Asheville and I am now compelled to wear glasses. Nevertheless, if I can be left alone now to do my work, I believe I'll pull through somehow. All I ask now is to be left alone to work without letter hindrance.

It's too bad things had to turn out the way they did this summer: I had hoped that things would have changed: I had been away so long that I thought maybe they would be different. But I found out that they were just the same, only worse: so I guess that's the end of me in Asheville. I'm sorry that you felt that I did not go around to the house enough this summer. I went all I could, but the situation there was such that I could not have gone more often than I did. I am sorry for afflicted and unfortunate people and I tried to do what I could to help: I was willing to go to the wall to use what money I have, or to borrow money to help when I was appealed to. But it all turned out as it always has. I've certainly not tried to save myself: on the contrary [I] allowed my time, strength and health to be used up by all kinds of worthless people. But now I am up against it, economically, physically and in every other way, and I don't see why a good life should be thrown away for a bad one. I have something in me that people value, that has given some people happiness and pleasure, and that people think is worth saving. I think so too, and that is why I'm going to try to save it.

I'm willing to do anything I can to help any one of my own kin in any way I can, but I'm not willing to waste my life and talent in an atmosphere of ruin and defeat, among people who can't be helped and who have been so defeated that they hate anything in life that has not been, and want to drag it down. I'm sorry to have to talk this way, but I have been driven to it. I've felt pretty sick and sore at heart when I left home, as it has all been so sad and so different from what I had hoped it would be. But I'm getting better now, and I know that it will all slip into its true proportion as time goes on. And of course, I have no ill feeling toward anyone. I've just found out a man must stand alone.

If there is anything I can do for anyone, let me know. I think I'm going to get through this present trouble. I hope soon [to] find another publisher, and begin to earn some money again. Meanwhile, all I can do is keep on working.

It has been a hard thing having my eyes go bad on me, because they are just about the most important asset that I have. But if I watch my health, perhaps they will get better. The doctor told me that a good deal of it was probably nervous strain. At any rate, I hope the worst is over now, and that things will look brighter in the future. Also, I hope this finds all of you well, and that you will let me know if all goes well and if there is anything I can do. Meanwhile, with all good wishes to everyone,

To MAXWELL E. PERKINS

[New York City]

November 19, 1937

Dear Max:

My brother Fred has just written me enclosing two letters that you wrote to him and to my mother, and a copy of a letter he wrote to you. I want to go upon the record right now about several things. You told Fred that I had turned my back on you and Scribners. You told Miss Nowell that I had been going around town talking about you. And you told Basso that you were afraid now I was going to "write about" you and Scribners, and that if I did this, you would resign and move to the country. I think that if you have said or felt these things, you have been unjust and misleading. But what is a whole lot more important to me, I think they may have had an effect upon our friendship, which is the thing that matters to me most, and which I am willing to do anything I can to preserve.

Now, I am going to answer these specific things at once. In the first place, I did not "turn my back" on you and Scribners, and I think it is misleading and disingenuous for anyone to say this was the case. The facts of the matter are that the misunderstanding and disagreement between us had grown in complexity and difficulty for the past two years and perhaps longer, and you and everybody else there at Scribners have known the situation as well as I. Furthermore, you have known for at least a year, and I think longer, that the possibility of this severance in our relations was a very real and imminent one, and we have talked about the situation many times. More than this, Charlie Scribner wrote me a letter last spring, at the time of the libel suit, and told me that although he would be sorry to lose me he would not try to hold me, if I wanted to go, and that I was free to go. Further, you told me once last winter to go, if I wanted to, but not to talk about it any more. Later you came to see me in my apartment on First Avenue and told me to go if I wanted to, but that the important thing was that you and I be friends. That is exactly my own position now. Finally, you have known for at least three months, since August, that my going was no longer a possibility but an actual fact. You told Miss Nowell that I had communicated with various publishers and you asked her if it was true that I had signed up with Little Brown and Company. It was not true.

Now that's the record. It is absurd for anyone now to pretend that he is surprised, and that it has all come suddenly and is news to him.

You said in your letter to Fred that you could never understand about all this trouble, and that is the way I feel, too. But I do know that we both understood very definitely, and over a long period of time, that there was trouble, and I think it would be misleading and untruthful for either of us to say that he had absolutely no conception of what it was all about. We did have a conception, and a very clear conception, too. There are so many things about it that are still puzzling and confusing to me, although I've spent a good part of the last year, and the better part of the last four months, trying to think it out. But there are certain things that you knew and that I knew very clearly, and without going into the whole painful and agonizing business all over again, which we threshed out so many hundred times, beginning with "Of Time and the River" and continuing on with "The October Fair" and what I was going to do with it, and on to the book of stories and "The Story of a Novel," and the lawsuits and the lawyers, culminating in our final disagreement about the libel suit, the proper course to be taken, and the possible implications of the whole thing concerning my whole future life and work and the use of my material—there has been one thing after another, which we talked about and argued about a thousand times, so how can either of us truthfully say now that he has absolutely no idea what the misunderstanding is about?

You know that as a man and as a writer, I had finally reached a state of such baffled perplexity that I no longer knew what to do, what to try to accomplish and finish next, or whether, if I did finish and accomplish something, I could ever have any hope under existing circumstances, of getting it published. You know and I know that beginning with "Look Homeward, Angel," and mounting steadily, there has been a constantly increasing objection and opposition to what I wanted to do, which phrased itself in various forms, but which had the total effect of dampening my hope, cooling my enthusiasm, and almost nullifying my creative capacity—to the work that I had projected, to the use I should make of my material, and even in some cases going so far as to oppose my possible use of material on personal rather than on artistic grounds. I am not trying to put all the blame for this on someone else, either. I know that I have often been unfair and unjust, and difficult to handle, but I do think that all this difficulty came out of these troubles I have mentioned. I felt baffled and exasperated because it really seemed to me I had a great creative energy which was being bottled up, not used, and not given an outlet. And if energy of this kind is not used, if it keeps boiling over and is given no way of getting out, then it will eventually destroy and smother the person who has it.

So that is why I think you are wrong when you tell my brother Fred and other people that I have turned my back on you and Scribners, and you don't know why. I am not going to do anything to carry on the debate of who left whom or whose back was turned, but I do know that there was no agreement of any sort between us concerning future work, no contract, and no assurance except perhaps that if I did something that satisfied you and that avoided the things you were afraid of, you would publish me. But, at the very least, under those same conditions any other publisher in the land would publish me, and I can't see that a connection is much of a connection when all the risk and obligation is on one side and there is none whatever on the other. This condition has persisted and developed for at least two years and I have said nothing to anyone about it outside of Scribners until very recently. If you are going to tell people that I turned my back and walked out on you, why don't you also tell them that three years ago when I didn't have a penny and was working on "Of Time and the River" I was approached by another publisher [1] and offered what seemed to me a fortune. You know that I not only called you up and informed you of the matter instantly just as soon as it happened, but even asked you if I should even meet and talk to the people, and that with great fairness you told me that it was certainly my right to meet and talk with them and listen to what they had to offer and then submit the offer to you and Scribners and give you a chance to meet it or to say you couldn't. You know when I did meet

[1] See the footnote on page 507.

and talk with these people and heard their offer and rejected it on my own accord, and told you all about it, I never once asked you or Scribners to meet the offer, although most writers apparently, and even publishers, would have considered that entirely fair and businesslike. So if you are going to say now that I walked out on you, why not tell some of the rest of the story too, and admit that I not only never tried to hold you up about anything, but never made approaches to anybody else, and rejected all that were made to me, even when I didn't have a cent. That is just the simple truth and I think in justice to me you ought to say so. But there is no use trying to go through all of this again: we have talked about it so many times, and both of us may be partly right and partly wrong, but how can either of us deny now that a situation has existed for months which had got into such a hopeless complex snarl that at the end there was absolutely no way out of the mesh except by cutting it. That is the truth, and you know that is the truth. You have understood for a long time that it is the truth and that it existed, and I think you are now unjust to me if you pretend to anyone that you did not know it was the truth.

About your statement to Miss Nowell that I was going around "talking about you" in an injurious sense, I want to assure you that there is not an atom of truth in it. In the first place, I do not "go around": I am not a gossip monger: I have no stories about anyone to trade around. I am afraid that most of the gossip has come from the other side of the fence. You know better than I do that the profession in which you are employed and the circles in which you have to move are productive of rumor and much false report. I would injure myself before I injured you, but grim justice here compels me to remind you that those who live by the sword shall perish by the sword, and those who contemplate too often the play of the serpent's fangs and find the spectacle missing must run the risk some day of having those swift fangs buried in their own flesh.

I want to tell you now, if there were any further need of my going on the record, that if I have ever spoken about you to any man or woman, no one could have possibly construed my speech and meaning in any other way except in such a way as did you honor. And that was not only true when you were my publisher, but it is even more true now, when you are my publisher no longer.

Fred told you in his letter that he had never heard me speak of you in any way except in such a way as to plainly indicate the affection and respect I felt for you. And I can assure you that has been true not only with Fred but with everybody else, and not only in Asheville this summer but in New York since I returned to it in September; and if anyone has really given you any different idea, he has either deliberately lied, or wickedly, wilfully and maliciously twisted or perverted something I said out of its context and its plain meaning for some bad purpose of his own.

You owe me nothing, and I consider that I owe you a great deal. I don't want any acknowledgment for seeing and understanding that you were a great editor even when I first met you, but I did see and understand it, and later I acknowledged it in words which have been printed by your own house,[2] and of which now there is a public record. The world would have found out anyway that you were a great editor, but now, when people solemnly remind me that you are, with an air of patiently enlightening me on a matter about which I have hitherto been unaware, I find it ironically amusing to reflect that I myself was the first one publicly to point out the fact in such a way that it could not be forgotten—that I, as much as any man alive, was responsible for pulling the light out from underneath the bushel basket, and that it is now a part of my privilege to hear myself quoted on every hand, as who should say to me: "Have you read Wolfe?"

About the rest of it, I came up here in September and for two full months I saw no one and communicated with no one except Miss Nowell. During all this time, I stayed alone and tried to think this whole thing out. And I want to tell you that one reason I now resent these trivialities and this gossip is that this may be a matter which is only important enough to some people to be productive of false and empty rumor or nonsensical statements, but to me it has been a matter of life and death. I can only tell you straight from the heart that I have not had anything affect me as deeply as this in ten years, and I have not been so bereaved and grief-stricken by anything since my brother's death. To hear, therefore, that at a time when I have eaten my heart out thinking of the full and tragic consequences of this severance with people with whom I have been associated for eight years, who printed my first work, and for whom I felt such personal devotion, the thing that chiefly was worrying you was the tremendous question of whether I am going to "write about you" and whether you could endure such a calamity is enough to make me groan with anguish.

I cannot believe you were very serious about this when there were

[2] In *The Story of a Novel*, and in the dedication of *Of Time and the River:* "To Maxwell Evarts Perkins, a great editor and a brave and honest man, who stuck to the writer of this book through times of bitter hopelessness and doubt and would not let him give in to his own despair, a work to be known as *Of Time And The River* is dedicated with the hope that all of it may be in some way worthy of the loyal devotion and the patient care which a dauntless and unshaken friend has given to each part of it, and without which none of it could have been written."

so many more important and serious things to think about. But, if it will relieve your mind at all, I can tell you "writing about you" is certainly no part of my present intention. But what if it was, or ever should be? What possible concern, either as friend or editor, ought you to have, except to hope that if I ever "wrote about" you, I would write about you as an artist should, add something to my own accomplishment, and to the amount of truth, reality and beauty that exists. This I thought was your only concern when you considered "Look Homeward, Angel," and not whether it was about possible persons living in a specific little town. This I thought was also, with one or two reservations, your chief concern with "Of Time and the River." This, I think, has been less and less your concern ever since—with "The October Fair," with perturbations about other work that I have projected since, and finally with the crowning nothingness of this. I don't know how or why this thing has come about, or what has happened to you—but I know my grief and bewilderment have grown for two years and are immense.

Like you, I am puzzled and bewildered about what has happened, but in conclusion can offer this: that maybe for me the editor and the friend got too close together and perhaps I got the two relations mixed. I don't know how it was with you, but maybe something like this happened to you too, I don't know. If this is true, it is a fault in both of us, but it is a fault that I would consider more on the side of the angels than the devil's side.

I think, however, that what is even more likely to be a fault in modern life is when the elements of friendship and of business get confused, and when there is likely to be a misapprehension on the part of one or both of the parties as to which is which. I won't pretend to be naive about business, or to tell you that the artist is a child where business matters are concerned. The artist is not a child where business is concerned but he may seem to be so to business men, because he is playing the game with only one set of chips, and the other people are sometimes playing the game with two sets of chips. I don't want you to understand by this that I think playing the game with two sets of chips is always wrong and wicked, and playing the game with one set of chips is always right. I do not think so. But I do think that when the players sit down to play, each of them ought to know what kind of game is being played—with one set of chips or two. I think this is important, because I think most of the misunderstanding comes from this.

To give you a simple hypothetical example, which, let us say, I invented for purposes of illustration, and which I assure you certainly does not dig into the past or concern my relations with my former publishers: a publisher, let us say, hears an author is without a publisher and writes him. It is a very nice and charming letter and says that the publisher has heard that the writer no longer has a publisher and tells him, if that is the case, he would like to see him and to talk to him. He goes on further to say that everybody in his office feels as he does personally about the work that he has done and about the work that he is going to do, and that it would be a privilege and an honor to publish him.

Do I suppose that this letter is hokum and that it is only a part of a publisher's formula when approaching an author? By no means: I think the publisher is sincere and honest and means what he says.

But to proceed with this hypothetical case. The author replies to the publisher that it is true he is without a publisher, but that he is in a great state of perplexity and puzzlement about his work, about a great amount of manuscript involving the material of several books and the labor of several years, and about what he is going to do next. He tells the publisher that what he needs most of all first is someone of editorial experience and judgment he can talk to. He tells him further that he is not at all sure that the work he has in mind would be the kind of work the publisher of this house would care to publish. But he asks the man if he wants to talk it over and find out what the situation is.

The upshot of it is the publisher telephones and comes to see him right away. They go out to dinner together, they have a good meal and some good drinks, and they talk the situation over. The publisher tells the author again how he and his house feel about the author's work, and repeats and emphasizes his warm interest. The author then lays the matter before the publisher, tells him so far as he can the problems and perplexities that have been bothering him about his work and his manuscript. The publisher then asks which part of this manuscript the author thinks is nearest to completion. The author tells him that the manuscript is packed up and in storage, and the publisher asks the author to get it out and show it to him. The author replies that he would like to, but that he is living in a small rented room and that the bulk and magnitude of the manuscript is such that it would be impossible to get it out and work on it in his own place. The publisher replies that in the offices of his company there is loads of space and that he would be delighted if the author would make use of it: he can move his manuscript here and be free to work without disturbing anyone. The author agrees to this proposal, and before they part, the publisher addresses the author by his first name.

Now, so far so good. This hypothetical story must have a very familiar sound to you, and you must agree as I do that so far everything is fine. Both parties are not only sincere and mean everything they say, but both sides are also playing with one set of chips.

Now to proceed: in a day or two, the publisher calls up again and tells the author that a young man in his publishing house is free and would be very glad to help the author move the manuscript that very afternoon. The author agrees to this, meets the young man, and together they go to the storage warehouse, get the manuscript, and bring it back to the publisher's office, where it is left. The next day, the author goes to the publisher's office, the crates and boxes of manuscript have been opened up, everything is ready, and the author sets to work. The publisher comes in, jokes about the size and bulk of the manuscript, and repeats again his eagerness to see it and his desire to get at it as quickly as possible, and asks the author if he may call him by his first name, Jim. The author replies that this is his name and that he would be delighted if the publisher called him Jim. The publisher is catching a train in a few minutes; the two men shake hands very warmly; just before he leaves, the publisher says: "Oh, by the way," and hands the author an envelope. When the author asks him what the envelope is, the publisher says it is nothing, just an acknowledgment that he has received the manuscript, and to put it away among his papers. The author sticks the envelope into his pocket without looking at it. That night, however, in his room, he sees the envelope upon his table and opens it. It reads as follows:

"Dear Smith:—This is to acknowledge that we have received one large packing case of manuscript, nine pasteboard cartons, and two valises, which are now stored in our offices. In view of the possible value of this material, we wish to inform you that this house can assume no responsibility for it, and that you leave it here entirely at your own risk."

Now, what is the truth about this situation? Is the publisher wrong? By no means. Apparently, he is justified in writing such a letter by all standards of good business practice, and it would be hard to find a business person who would say that he was anything except exactly right. Furthermore, the publisher may have acted as he did out of scrupulous observance of what seemed to him the rules of business fairness and honesty. Nevertheless, the author cannot help remembering that the publisher asked if he could call him Jim when they were having drinks together over the dinner table, but calls him Smith when he writes a business letter. The author also cannot help remembering when the publisher talked to him over the dinner table, he told him it was not the money he hoped to make out of the author's books or the sales he hoped the books would have that concerned him principally, but rather the pride he would have in publishing the author's works, the privilege and the honor it would be to publish them, regardless of any commercial advantages that might accrue. He has told the author also that he can rest assured that if he comes to his house, he need not worry about the economic future—that no matter whether his next book sold or not, the house was a house which would stand by its authors through disappointments and vicissitudes and was willing to back its faith with its support. Furthermore, I believe that the publisher was sincere and meant what he said.

But the author is puzzled, and I think he has a right to be puzzled. Any business man would tell you the publisher was right, not only about what he said over the dinner table, but right also when he wrote the letter about who should assume the risk and responsibility for the manuscript. The author can understand both conversations, but what he cannot understand is both conversations together. What he objects to is "Jim" over the dinner table and in editorial relations, but "Smith" where business is concerned. From my own point of view, the author is right. The publisher did not tell him that it was going to be Jim in friendship and in editing, but Smith in business. He led the author to believe, with his talk of faith and belief and support and the privilege and the honor of publishing the author, that it was going to be Jim all the time.

Now from my own point of view, Max, I think the publisher was wrong. I know that many people will not agree with me and will say that the publisher was right, that it was business, and that he was justified in everything that he did. I do not think so, and I think that much of the misunderstanding between publishers and authors comes from just this fact. I think the trouble comes when one side is playing with one set of chips, and the other side with two. Please understand that I am not accusing the side that plays the two of dishonesty or of unscrupulous practices. But I do think they are wrong in not making it clear at the beginning—the kind of game they are playing. And I have used deliberately a trifling and relatively unimportant example to illustrate my meaning. When you multiply this example by scores of much more important and vital examples, and when Jim finds that it is always Smith when a question of business advantage, of profit or loss, is concerned —when Jim finds that friendship and business are not equal and [do not] balance each other, but that business always gets the upper hand when a question of advantage is concerned—then there is likely to be trouble.

I want to say also that I think Jim was wrong in the very beginning when he allowed his personal feelings to get so involved that he lost his perspective. I think Jim was wrong in that he based his publishing relationship too much on friendship—on feelings of personal loyalty and devotion, no matter at what cost to himself. I think in doing this, Jim was unfair to himself and unfair to his publishers. I think that perhaps the best publishing relation would be one in which Jim felt friendship and respect and belief for his publishers, and they for him, but in which neither side got too personally involved. In the end, it is likely to involve too great a cost of disillusionment and grief and disappointment for someone, perhaps upon both sides. Please believe that I have offered this not by way of criticism of anyone, but just as possibly throwing some light upon a confused and troubled problem.

Now I am faced with one of the greatest decisions of my life and I am about to take a momentous and decisive step. You are no longer my publisher, but with a full consciousness of the peril of my position and the responsibility of the obligation I am now about to assume, I want to feel that you are still my friend, and I do feel that, in spite of all that has happened. I feel that you want me to go on and grow in merit and accomplishment and do my work; and I believe that you would sincerely wish for my success and high achievement, and be sorry for my failure, no matter who became my publisher. I believe other people there at Scribners feel the same way. You said a year ago that the important thing, regardless of who published me, is that we remain friends. That expresses my own feeling now, and I am writing to tell you so, and to tell you that I hope it is the same with you. This letter is a sad farewell, but I hope also it is for both of us a new beginning, a renewal and a growth of all the good that has been.

You told Fred that I had not been to see you but that you would like to see me. I want to see you, but I do not think that now is the right time. I think you ought to see by now that I am not "sore" at anybody, but I am sore inside, and I want to wait until things heal. And my whole desire now is to preserve and save, without reservation, without any ranking doubt or bitterness, the friendship that we had, and that I hope we shall forever have. This is about all that I can say. I have felt pretty bad, and for a time my eyes went back on me but I am wearing glasses when I work now, and am now back at work again. If I can keep on working, without interruptions and the costly experiences of the last two years, I think everything may yet turn out all right.

You don't need to answer this letter. I wrote it to you just to go upon the record, to tell you how things really were, and let you know what was in my mind and heart. I hope that I have done so.

With all good wishes to you, to Louise and the children, and to Scribners,

I am your friend, Max, and that is why I wrote this letter—to tell you so. If I wrote so much else here that the main thing was obscured—the only damn one that matters—that I am your friend and want you to be mine—please take this last line as being what I wanted to say the whole way through.

For Perkins' answer of November 20, 1937, see Editor to Author: The Letters of Maxwell E. Perkins, *page 133. He said in part: "I am your friend and always will be, I think. . . . Of course I had to tell Fred and others, when they asked me about you, what the situation was. . . . I could not properly, even by silence, let it be assumed that things were as they had been. I told Fred truly too when I said I did not understand about it. I don't, but that need make no difference between us, and I won't let it on my side. Miss Nowell should never have told you of my concern as to your writing about us—it was not [about] me. . . . I know the difficulty of your problem and I never meant this point to come up to confuse you. But don't you see that serious injury to this House and to my longtime associates here, for which I was responsible, would make me wish to be elsewhere? I've missed you and felt badly about it. . . . Anyhow, I'm glad to have seen your handwriting again."*

To ROBERT N. LINSCOTT

[Hotel Chelsea]
[222 West 23rd Street]
[New York City]
November 17, 1937

Dear Mr. Linscott:

I had lunch with Mr. Barker yesterday and last night had dinner with Mr. Aswell and Mr. Saxton of Harpers. Also, I talked with Mr. Canfield.[1] Apparently some word has gotten around that I am no longer at Scribners and in the last week or two members of two publishing houses, Harpers and Doubleday, have spoken to me. Both of them made specific proposals: I cannot state definitely, as yet, with what authority the Doubleday proposal was made, but people from that house are coming to see me again on Thursday. The Harper proposal was specific, and was made with the authority of the whole house.[2]

[1] Cass Canfield was President of Harper & Brothers, and Eugene F. Saxton was Editor-in-Chief. Edward C. Aswell was Assistant Editor to Saxton and succeeded him as Editor-in-Chief on his death in 1943. He is now editor and vice-president of McGraw-Hill and administrator of the estate of Thomas Wolfe.

[2] The Harper proposal was for an advance of $10,000 against a straight royalty of 15%, to be paid immediately on signing of a contract for Wolfe's next novel. Harper's did not ask to see any of the manuscript before signing of the contract. Linscott, for Houghton Mifflin, had tentatively suggested an advance of $10,000 against a 15% royalty, to be paid in monthly installments of $500 for twenty months, but the contract was not to be drawn until Houghton Mifflin had read at least a portion of the manuscript. James W. Poling, who was Managing Editor at Doubleday and Company at that time, conferred with Wolfe several times and told him they would equal any offer from another publisher, but Wolfe was so intent on trying to choose between Houghton Mifflin and Harpers that he did not enter into any definite negotiations with Doubleday.

It has been a very puzzling and troubling situation, because I have been getting on with my work very rapidly and these developments, of course, mean that I may have to think a great deal about all the questions that have been raised. So far, I have not decided anything except that the best course is for me to get on with my work, and to think about the matter until I reach some clear conclusion. Of course, I told both the Harpers and Doubleday people about my conversations with you, and the outcome of them. I told them also that no commitments had been made on either side, and that after talking the situation over we had agreed that I should give you a piece of manuscript to read without commitment on either side. Barker suggested yesterday at lunch that I try to send you the manuscript now and then talk to you when you come down to New York in about two weeks. I told him that I should like to do this, but that I still think that it would be better if I kept on working as I have been working until I get the manuscript in some more definite shape, and that if it is satisfactory to everybody, it is what I propose to do.

I wanted to inform you of these events, and of what I have myself been doing. It is a puzzling and perplexing situation but I think it is better to think about it very carefully now rather than come to a hasty decision.

[IF THERE WAS A SECOND PAGE TO THIS LETTER, IT HAS BEEN LOST]

In answer to Wolfe's letter of November 17, Linscott wrote him on November 19: "Don't you think the common sense of the situation is to concentrate on one thing at a time and cross each bridge as you come to it? If, as I gather, you're in the writing mood now, I'd go full speed ahead until you reach a place where it will be helpful to have it professionally read. Then, and not till then, I'd cast about for the perfect publisher, giving us first shot at it, in accordance with our understanding, but with complete freedom to turn later to any other publisher if our reaction or proposal is not entirely to your liking. I'm still hoping you'll be able to send me a sizable chunk of manuscript and an outline soon enough so that I will have something tangible to say about it when I next see you. . . ." The following letter of November 29 was Wolfe's reply.

To ROBERT N. LINSCOTT

[Hotel Chelsea]
[New York]
November 29, 1937

Dear Mr. Linscott:

Thanks very much for your letter of November 19th, which I had intended to answer before this. Matters still stand very much as they did when I wrote you on November 18th. I have had some additional conversations with various people, but have come to no definite decision yet. However, I agree entirely with your suggestion that the sensible course for me at present would be to continue with my writing at full speed. I have thought about this a great deal and have had several conversations with Mr. Barker.

Mr. Barker wants me to send you a portion or portions of the manuscript before you come down here from Boston. I tentatively agreed to this when I saw him the other day and suggested that I might even try to select a few scenes or episodes, which, although they might not give any coherent idea of what the book is about, would perhaps serve to indicate what I hope the final texture will be. Mr. Barker seemed to think this was a good idea. But thinking it over I have more and more my doubts, and I will tell you what they are.

I have been writing pretty steadily ever since I saw you, and it was really not until just the other day that my secretary and I opened up the big case and bundles of manuscript and began seriously to set about the task of sorting it out, disposing of that which has already been printed, or for which I shall have no need in this book, and taking the material that I may need and arranging it in an orderly fashion. As you can imagine, it has been a big job and we are not yet done with it.

I am also aware, as I re-examine this material with a fresh eye after having been away from most of it for three or four years, that what I have is material for an enormous book, a great deal of which is not even yet in rough draft form, and a good deal more that really approaches final completion. At any rate, the stuff of the book is there and the book will also be there if I continue at the present pace and with the whole purpose that I have in mind. For that reason also I am less and less inclined to monkey with it now: I not only do not want to impede my own progress, but I should also like anyone who might be interested in reading it to see it in some form that would more nearly, as I think, do it justice. As I have said, there are parts which I am ready to have read now, but taking all of these various things into consideration, I do not really believe that is the way it ought to be read, do you?

The other thing is this: I am deeply and sincerely grateful to you for your helpful interest and your desire to read and estimate this manuscript. But, after thinking this question over from every possible angle and taking into consideration everything that has happened in these past few weeks, it doesn't seem to me that it would be fair either to myself or to the other people who have committed themselves to the extent of making specific proposals concerning the publication of this manuscript, to tie this manuscript up in any way that might imperil its chances with people who have already signified their interest to the extent of making a concrete offer, or in any way that might impede me or other people from coming to a final decision. I really think that the justice of the whole matter, with a view to the rights of everyone, is just there.

I am going to suggest to you, therefore, that instead of sending you portions of the manuscript in fragmentary form I'll wait until you come to New York when I hope we can talk together and perhaps come to a clearer decision. This seems to me to be the best course now and I believe it will seem so with you, also. Meanwhile, of course, I propose to go on working.

With all good wishes and with hopes of seeing you soon.

On December 3, 1937, Mrs. Bernstein had returned some photographs to Wolfe through Miss Nowell, with a note saying that she did not want him to write to her about them. Wolfe therefore dictated the following letter and asked Miss Nowell to send it over her signature. It was so obviously his that she rewrote it in her own words.

To ALINE BERNSTEIN

[New York City]
[December 5(?), 1937]

Thanks very much for your note and for the photographs which you are returning to Mr. Wolfe. I know he will appreciate them and will be glad to get your message. I have heard him speak of you many times with affection and respect, and I know that it will cheer him up now to hear that you too have heard of his trouble and are shocked by it. It is a matter of which I do not care to speak except to say that it has caused him the greatest distress and anguish.

He has very little money, but he is hard at work again and I know that you, like all his other friends, will be glad to hear this and will hope, as we all do, that he will succeed in finding a publisher who believes in him and who will encourage him to fulfill himself and do the work of which he is capable. He has gone through a hard time the past two years, but I believe he has been through the worst of it and that things will go better now. At any rate, I want to assure you that he has learned, as a result of these experiences, to know true friends from false ones, and to distinguish between those who have sought to exploit him for their own purposes and those who value him and believe him for his own sake.

I know he counts you among this latter group, and for that reason I know he is going to be happy to hear that you have inquired about him with such affectionate concern. I shall give him your message and photographs when I next see him.

To ANNE W. ARMSTRONG

[Hotel Chelsea]
[New York]
December 6, 1937

Dear Mrs. Armstrong:

I was so glad to get your letter. I was really just on the point of writing you and finding out if you had received my letter of several weeks ago, or if anything had happened to it. I am glad to get your new address in care of General Peyton, at Fort Sheridan. Of course if I am out that way, I'll come to see you pronto. I don't really see much prospect of it at present, because I am back at work again on the big book [1] and I am going to try to keep at it if I can until I finish.

My new address, by the way, is

Hotel Chelsea,
222 West 23rd Street,
New York City.

It is an old old place with great big rooms, and I have two of them: and all my manuscript is out and again I am on the job. It's been a pretty nerve-racking experience and in so many ways a sad one too. Breaking off relations with people one has known so well, for so many years, is never

[1] *The Vision of Spangler's Paul* which finally became *The Web and the Rock* and *You Can't Go Home Again.* By this time Wolfe had given up his earlier idea of working on *The October Fair,* realizing that *The Vision of Spangler's Paul* was always foremost in his mind.

an easy thing, and I think they are particularly hard for me because things get rooted in me so. However, it's over now and I believe things are going to be better. I think from what I heard there was at first a good deal of wounded feeling, but now that seems to have gone away, and I have just heard the man I know best in all the world wants to see me, and is my friend. I knew it was going to be that way, I never had any doubts about it, but it was pretty tough at first.

About definite publishing connections, I have made no new one yet. I wanted to take plenty of time thinking the whole thing over, so I didn't go around soliciting people, and on the whole, I think it is just as well that I did not. At any rate, at least three publishing houses have heard that I am without a publisher, and have signified their interest. Two of them have actually gone so far as to make specific offers, mentioning terms, and the firm of Harper and Brothers has made what seems to me a very generous and fine one. At any rate, the amount of the advance they offered was so large that I was rather overwhelmed by it. And what I think is a whole lot more important than this is that they actually seem to be intensely and deeply interested in me as a man and as a writer, which, in a publishing connection, I think is a pretty important thing.

What you said in your letter about my not going back to Asheville also shoots straight to the mark, because it is exactly what I have been thinking myself, and of course at first the knowledge of it was pretty hard to face. But you are right: *You can't go home again.* I found this out this summer, of course I had to go home to find it out, it was hard to face, but I have faced it now and I feel better. But don't be surprised some day if you see a piece, *You Can't Go Home Again.* I guess we all find this out as we go along, but it's a pretty tremendous fact and revelation in the life of any man, isn't it? But as long as I know that there are people like you, and that one meets a few of them in the course of a life time, it doesn't make things too bad. Maybe it's just there that eventually a man comes to look for home.

Dear Mrs. Armstrong, please take care of yourself and have a good winter at Fort Sheridan. And please tell General Peyton and his wife for me how much I appreciate the use of their magnificent cabin down by the Holston River in September. I think those few days there gave me more peace and quiet and rest than I had had in years, and to you, of course, I shall be everlastingly grateful. And now goodbye for the present. I hope this finds you well, and, as usual, enjoying life.

On December 19, Wolfe informed Linscott on the telephone that he had decided to accept the offer of Harper & Brothers. The next day he wrote the following letter to express his genuine regret at having disappointed him.

To ROBERT N. LINSCOTT

[Hotel Chelsea]
[New York]
December 20, 1937

Dear Bob:

I would just like to write and add this to what I said yesterday. It was one of the hardest decisions I have ever had to make, and I think last week was one of the hardest weeks I have ever been through. Now it is all settled, and I am relieved to know it is over. However, the only thing I have to regret is that in making the decision, I perhaps had to disappoint someone I like and admire very much.

I want to tell you again how sincerely I appreciate the interest you have shown in me and my work from the beginning, and I am happy to think now that although I may not have you as a publisher, I do have you as a friend—that, at any rate, is a big gain.

It may not be possible for me to go to Boston for Christmas, but I am hopeful that the next month will see me there. If I do come, of course I want to see you and shall look you up. Meanwhile, with all best wishes to you and your family for this and many future Christmases.

The following letter, of which a carbon copy was found among Wolfe's own papers, was written as the result of the quarrel which Wolfe had with Sherwood Anderson at the Hotel Brevoort on December 17, 1937. On December 1, Wolfe had gone to a dinner party given by the Andersons at the New York apartment of Mrs. Mary Emmett whom they were visiting. As Mrs. Anderson remembers, everyone was talking about the South, saying that if a person was a liberal, people in the South never attacked him for his liberalism but on some entirely different and often spurious grounds. Simply as an example of this, she said to Wolfe that she had been in North Carolina the week before, and had heard it said that he was Jewish. She says that Wolfe took violent offence; said he was going to get on a train and go right down to see his mother; that the Wolfe family was as good as Mrs. Anderson's (which came from the same part of Pennsylvania) etc. After a general discussion of anti-Semitism, Wolfe calmed down, but the incident evidently rankled in his mind.

On December 17, Anderson wrote Wolfe saying: "I do hope you didn't take seriously the queer row we seemed to have got into that night at Mary's house," [1] *and asking him to come to a cocktail party for the benefit of the Spanish Loyalists and to have dinner with him afterward. Meanwhile, however, Wolfe was drinking heavily and brooding over his severance from Scrib-*

[1] Copyright, 1956, by Eleanor Copenhaver Anderson.

ners and the necessity of choosing between Houghton Mifflin and Harpers for his future publishers. Before he received Anderson's note, he happened to go into the Brevoort and found Anderson lunching there. According to what Wolfe told Miss Nowell later, he called Anderson out into the lobby and "told old Sherwood off," saying that Winesburg, Ohio *had meant something important to him and his entire generation of writers, but that Anderson had "failed them," that he was "washed up," and that "this business of sitting around and talking, naked, on parlor sofas was no good." (This was probably a reference to Anderson's* Many Marriages *and his similar later writings which showed the influence of D. H. Lawrence.)*

The following day, Anderson wrote Wolfe a second note, saying: "When I wrote you yesterday, suggesting that you have dinner with me Tuesday evening, I had no notion how you felt. As you have expressed such a hearty desire to chuck our acquaintance—why not." [2] *In answer to this, Wolfe evidently wrote the following letter, which he may or may not have actually mailed.*

To SHERWOOD ANDERSON

December 20, 1937.

Dear Sherwood:

I am sorry that you felt you had to write that last note. I was pretty rough the other day, but my clear impression was that at the end we shook hands and meant it, and not only that, but also said that we were going to stick together, and not let anything come between us. I should have written you anyhow, but I thought that I would wait until it was a little closer to Christmas, but since you wrote this note I want to tell you that if this is the way it stands, it's got to stand this way—only I don't feel "Why not?"

I guess you thought it over—about what I said the other day—and changed your mind. If you did, I am not blaming you and I am not trying to get away from the point—but I would like to say that a good deal of what happened and what was said was just accidental. I wasn't thinking about it or you so much when it happened, as about something else—a matter to the conclusion of which I have been working slowly for the past two years, and which involved one of the most grievous and painful decisions of my life.[1] I have decided it now, and ought to be happy, but I am not. I think I am going to be happy later on, but I am worrying for the dead this Christmas and for a lot of things that can't be helped. You must have felt that way some time in your life, and you must know what

[2] Copyright, 1956, by Eleanor Copenhaver Anderson.

[1] The break with Scribners which was made irrevocable by Wolfe's agreement to sign with Harpers.

I am talking about. Anyway, I'm trying to tell you that the immediate thing that happened—the flare-up, explosion, or whatever it was—was really not about you at all, but about something else. You just happened to be present when it happened.

About the other thing, the more immediate personal thing,[2] I'd like to tell you that I am willing to forget about it. As you said the other day, it was an ugly party, there was somehow a pretty ugly feeling there which you felt. I did too, I don't know where it came from, I only know it didn't come from me, and I would be willing to bet it didn't come from you. I have my streaks of violence and passion, but I never took ugliness to a party in my life: I always went with faith and hope as I went to that one, and all I can tell you is that nobody ever had a bad time or felt anything ugly at a party that I gave. I believe it must have been the same with you, too.

About the other thing [3]—the thing that seems to have caused so much pain and misunderstanding, I would like to forget about it too, and I certainly don't want to labor a thing that is probably trifling and that has made too much trouble already. I do have to tell you this, however, and then I hope I am done with it: I just can't agree that it is something that should not be taken seriously, because it seems to me the implications not only to myself, but to a lot of obscure decent people are pretty serious, and whether you will agree with my point of view or not, you must have understanding enough to see that such a thing would affect them pretty tragically in so many of the fundamental relations of life and their marital relations, their social and business relations, and so on. And I think also it would affect me pretty seriously too. I have been mighty fortunate as a writer, people have said some mighty fine things about me. I don't know whether they were right or not, or whether it means anything, but apparently a lot of people have thought I was a pretty American sort of writer, and what I did was indigenous to this country. I hope this is true. At any rate, I am pretty proud of it, and I would like to live up to it, and I say this honestly without a word or thought of prejudice toward any people, any race, or any creed.

So I don't think, Sherwood, it's shooting straight to the mark to say these [things] don't matter: I think I found out a lot about life in the last two years that I never knew about before, and I've seen in our own country, which we both love and believe in so much, forces that seem to me to be ugly and vicious, that I never knew about before. At any rate, I am now prepared to fight them to the death, if I need to, and the only

---

[2] The mentioning of the current rumor that Wolfe was part Jewish and the subsequent argument at the Andersons' party on December 1st.

[3] Wolfe is still talking about the mention of the rumor that he was part Jewish.

thing that I expect of any man who is a friend of mine is that he is prepared to fight them too. If they attack me, and [tell] other vicious lies about me or mine, with a purpose to discredit us or destroy us, I expect a friend of mine to stand his ground and to brand the lies for what they are, not only for me or mine, but for the human race as well, and I promise any friend I'll do the same for him. Maybe that's asking too much for friendship, but I don't think so, and I don't think I am taking anything too seriously now: there are some things you don't laugh off, or flash your celebrated sense of humor over and a dirty sell-out in the human race is one of them. You know where I stand now, and if you are the man I think you are, you'll stand there too.

About the rest of it the other day [4]—put it down to a lot of things which I hope this letter will help make clear, but don't put it between you and me. I said some things which were out of order—the business of going to parties, female companionship, your own aesthetical leanings is all your own affair, no business of mine, and something I don't know much about anyway. The main thing is I always strung with you as a writer, and since I met you a year ago I also strung with you as a man. I not only do not think that you are washed-up as a writer—but if I said so the other day you can put that down as another of those things. I told you when we shook hands and parted that I thought you had done the best writing that had been done in this country in this century. I still stick to that and honestly, as far as you are concerned, I have no other idea except that the best is yet to be.

This is going on the record as well as I can just now. If as your note indicates, you feel, as a result of what happened the other day, [that] you want to "chuck our acquaintanceship" that's up to you, and I'll do nothing else to try to persuade you differently, but I shall be sorry about it. At any rate, you've got the story now as far as I am concerned. I have been wrong about many things, but I think I had a point to make, and no matter how you feel, I wouldn't let this Christmas go by without telling you that I wish you and all your family nothing but the happiest and best for Christmas and for years to come.

I think you will also remember that even when I spoke the hottest the other day I also told you that whatever I had to say to you I'd say to you man to man. You spoke of other people, here in New York or elsewhere, trying to come in and poison our minds and turn us against each other. Well, as far as I am concerned, that will never happen. Nobody's going to do that. Nobody has a chance to: I am a hard working and a serious person and I lead as hard working and as quiet a life right here in New York as you do down in Marion, Virginia. So whatever you have heard,

---

[4] Wolfe's outburst at the Brevoort.

for good or bad, you have heard straight from me, and that's all there is. I hope you will want to see me again, but if you don't, you don't need to bother to answer this letter. Meanwhile, I would like to wish you a happy Christmas with all my heart.

To FRED W. WOLFE

December 20, 1937.

Dear Fred:

I got your letter this morning and the two enclosed post cards from Mamma. Also by the same mail a long letter from Mamma from Florida. I just want to shoot the immediate news to you now, so will not pause to give you the contents of her letter except to tell you that she seems to be well and in good health, and of course the details of the case you know all about anyway. She seemed anxious to get home, but I hope she stays for awhile—I'm writing her right away and sending her some money and I shall see that she gets it before Christmas, if I have to send it airmail.

The other news is that after two or three agonizing months in making up my mind, I have gone to the old publishing house of Harper and Brothers. The news has not been announced yet, so don't say anything about it until there is some kind of an announcement. I haven't signed a contract either, but they have offered me a tremendous advance. It's funny, but the thing that worries me now is that I don't know whether I should take it all or not, the income tax will probably be so high, etc.

I wish I could tell you that I'm happy. I believe I'm going to be because they seem to be fine people—it was not only the money that they offered but the fact that they seemed to want me with all their heart. The fellow I have had the most to do with, although I have met them all, is a young fellow named Aswell, who is exactly my own age, and who comes from Nashville, Tennessee. The rest of the story about him is that he is married and has a kid one year old, and lives out in the country. When I called up the other day to tell him that I had made up my mind, he was not at home, but his wife cried and told me he was on the way to town and to get him at Harpers. He told Miss Nowell that if necessary he was willing to change his whole life if he had to, and if he became my publisher. Of course he won't have to: the only point is the man thinks I am the best writer in the country—which he is wrong about—and he thinks I am going to get better, which I think he is right about. At any rate, I feel I am leaving the greatest editor in America, and a man of genius to boot, and maybe this young man Aswell is none of these, but I am playing a hunch—I feel he is a good man, and an able man, and if anybody's got this much faith in me I'll kill myself if I have to to live up to it.

I wish I could tell you I felt happy, but I don't. I am worn out, have been torn up about this thing coming to a point for over two months now, and of course there were two or three people interested in me, [and] all of them I liked. I had to make up my mind between them. If you've ever had to do this, you'll know how hard it is, and I'm still mourning for the dead. I mean for the people that I knew, with whom I worked so many years. I will see them again some day, but it is a pretty sad business just now. Maybe this will really be a new year. Harper's think it is going to be, both for them and for myself, and I believe they may be right. Anyway, it is a new beginning.

This is all for the present, Fred. I'll get a letter off to Mamma by airmail tomorrow morning and I will try to write to everybody before Christmas. I think you will understand the way things have been, but let's all hope it will be smoother sailing now. Please let me know right away if anything is needed, or in what way I can be of help about anything. Meanwhile, until I hear from you, with love to all and best wishes for a happy Christmas,

To MAXWELL E. PERKINS

[Hotel Chelsea]
[New York]
December 27, 1937

Dear Max:

I have had a talk at last with Mr. Ralph Lum, who is now representing me in that —— manuscript case over in New Jersey, and I am glad to say that at last it looks as if something is going to get done, and that I have a man on the job who knows how to do it. He told me the present state of affairs, outlined the situation very clearly, and asked me if I would get in touch with you to see if there was any help you could give us. I told him that I knew you would be glad to, if there was anything you could do, so to put the whole thing briefly, here is the way things stand now: the case comes up in the Court of Chancery in Jersey City early in February, and Mr. Lum seems to think it will go right through in an hour or two. He told me that I would recover my manuscripts—those that are left—and that disposes of this end of it. About the other end, Mr. Lum did not seem to be worried very much, and apparently does not believe —— has much of a case. In fact, he said that —— had gone so far with his contentions and allegations that he might find himself in a precarious and dangerous situation if he attempts to press them. He is suing me for the sum, I believe, of $2600—which Mr. Lum said might just as well be $26,000—basing his suit apparently on the contention that I owe him the money for his services as a "manuscript appraiser"—whatever that may mean—and for his services as a manuscript agent.

—— contends that a verbal agreement or contract existed between us, that there were no witnesses present to the agreement and that it is what is known as "an unlimited agreement"—which means that I gave him complete and absolute authority over all of my manuscript without reservation of any sort, to do with as he saw fit, from now on, henceforth and forever after. This, of course, as you know, is preposterous—and Mr. Lum believes it will seem to be preposterous to the Chancellor when the case comes up before him. If —— really contends this, I suppose it will simply come down to the question of his word against mine, but Mr. Lum feels that if I can now enlist the aid of some other people—yourself, Chester Arthur,[1] Ruder, the manuscript man,[2] or anyone else who might have dealt with —— or been present at conversations that I had with him—it would help.

I told Mr. Lum that the only part you had in the matter was that of a friend and adviser, but that you had been present on several occasions when I talked to ——, and I thought you would be able and willing to say that from your own observation and what you yourself saw and heard, there was no suggestion of "manuscript appraising," unlimited agreements, etc., but that rather my whole connection with —— was entirely provisional and tentative, and that I was simply letting him "try the market" with certain pieces of manuscript to see what luck he had and what came of it. This, of course, as you know, is just exactly what happened, but I do think, Max, if you could say so—that is, tell Mr. Lum that that was your understanding of the situation from what you saw of it—it would help us.

I am just as sorry as I can be to have to trouble you again about this thing, or about anything else. But I do believe we are beginning to see light at last, and I know you have always wanted me to get this thing settled and thought I ought to see it through. I agree with you absolutely, and Mr. Lum not only agrees but he says that it is imperative now that I see this through, and I think you will feel so more strongly than ever when I tell you the kind of answer —— has made. You remember he wrote some threatening letters to my former lawyers in New Jersey, revealing to them certain alleged obscene phrases and expressions which he threatened to make public if we continued with the suit. . . . As you and I both

---

[1] Chester Arthur had lived at 865 First Avenue and had been in Wolfe's apartment on one occasion when Wolfe and —— were discussing what manuscripts might or might not be sold.

[2] Barnet B. Ruder, the rare book and manuscript dealer, had bought some of Wolfe's manuscripts from ——, the defendant.

know, the threat is ridiculous: I have now seen the alleged words and phrases, and I think it may perhaps make you smile that most of them have already been printed in "Look Homeward, Angel" anyway. Nevertheless, it was intended to be an ugly threat, and Mr. Lum thinks on that account that I must go through with this thing now. . . . What —— has done in his answer is this: he apparently tried to get around the legal responsibility in which he may be involved by saying in his "Answer" that he cannot exactly describe the following manuscripts except by these phrases which he *happens* to remember. . . . : then follows, of course, a list of the alleged obscene phrases. As Mr. Lum says, he is skating on pretty thin ice. Beyond that, it's pretty ugly, isn't it?

Anyway, I wanted to describe the situation to you because I thought you would be interested to know how matters now stand, and also to ask you if you won't call Mr. Lum up or write him, and contribute anything you can by way of additional information that might help us. I think you understand the whole situation now, and will see what Mr. Lum is driving at. And honestly, Max, I hate like hell to bother you, but I do think this is one of those cases where people ought to stand together if they can, not only for personal or friendly reasons, but just because it's taking a stand in favor of the human race. But anyway, I am your friend as I told you in my letter, and I know that whatever you do will be all right.

I hope you have had a good Christmas, and I send you all my best wishes for this coming year. By the way, Martha Dodd just called up, and in behalf of all of us I gave her the hearty welcome of the American nation. I told her that old man Dodd from a diplomatic point of view might not be a good ambassador, but he was something a whole lot better than that—a good man and a good American, and that we were proud of him. She told me to go out and get to-day's *World-Telegram* because she had written a piece about the Nazis. If she can write, she certainly ought to have material for a tremendous book.

Goodbye for the present, Max. I hope that I shall see you soon. And forgive me for troubling you this time. With all good wishes,

To ANNE W. ARMSTRONG

[Hotel Chelsea]
[New York]
December 27, 1937

Dear Mrs. Armstrong:

Thanks for your letter which came last night. I am so glad you spoke as you did about Harper's, because I gave them my answer a week ago. I am going to be with them, and I believe somehow it is going to be one of the most fortunate and happy experiences of my life. They are giving me a great advance, if I want it. But really I was playing a personal hunch. They want me so much, they believe in me so utterly, and there is no doubt they meant everything they said. Moreover I will be associated with a young man just exactly my own age, who is second in command.[1] I am playing this hunch, too: I think it is going to turn out to be a wonderful experience—I feel that the man is quiet, but very deep and true: and he thinks that I am the best writer there is. I know he is wrong about this, but if anyone feels that way, you are going to do your utmost to try to live up to it, aren't you?

I spent Christmas with him, his wife and child out in the country. A lot of other people were there too—a young professor from the Harvard Law School, and his wife and sister, who has just won a great case for Roosevelt in the gold business.[2] I have never seen a higher group of people and I know if I'm going to live up to this, I've got to go some. And I believe you will be happy with me. However, I am still a little sad thinking about the past—Scribners, all of that—but you can't go home again, can you?

Now I am facing toward a New Year and a new, I hope, and greater piece of work. If you ever, of all things, see *Vogue*, please look at the, I believe, February issue, because that is where I have, of all places, written a piece about America.[3] I think it is good.

Now all the best to you and yours for this coming year.

To ELIZABETH NOWELL

[Hotel Chelsea]
[New York]
December 29, 1937

Dear Miss Nowell:

Thanks for your letter. There is nothing much to report except that Aswell brought me the contract and I took it up to the Authors' League which I joined, yesterday afternoon, and I am going back to the Authors' League to-day. . . .

[1] Edward C. Aswell.

[2] Professor and Mrs. Henry M. Hart, Jr. of Cambridge, Mass., and Mrs. Hart's sister, Miss Louise White, now Mrs. John William Willis. Professor Hart was on leave of absence from the Harvard Law School in the academic year 1937–1938, working as head attorney in the Office of the Solicitor General in Washington. He had been responsible for the briefs in the case of Smyth v. United States, 302 U.S. 329 (1937) which were argued and won by Solicitor General (now Mr. Justice) Reed.

[3] "A Prologue to America" in the February 1, 1938, issue of *Vogue*.

There were one or two . . . things in the contract that bothered me in any reference they might have to you [1]. . . . In other words, no one is going to take one little red penny of the ill-gotten gains which have enabled you thus far to wallow in luxury at my expense—no sir, by gum, not if I can help it. . . .

Ed suggested to me that it would be a good idea for me to get it settled up as quickly as possible before the first of the year, because of the income tax. That is, he suggested that I might get half the advance this week before the year is out, and half next month or at some later time, so that the tax would be divided in two years. What do you think? The trouble is, I always want to talk to you, and the little problem that is bothering me now is whether it will be cheaper to get it divided or have it all paid next year.[2] I think practically all of my so-called income this year has passed through your own fair hands, but I believe it amounts to considerable, so I am not sure whether it would be cheaper to tack half the advance on to it now, or let the advance go until next year. On the other hand, it will not hurt my feelings a bit if you succeed in selling the *Redbook* and *The Saturday Evening Post* a dozen stories next year, in which case—well, you get the point.

I think on the whole this describes the situation, and if anything does occur to you, I wish you would call me up to-morrow morning (Thursday) just as soon as you get this letter. And I guess this is all for the present—I've got to hike it now to The Authors' League—except to say I know I've been a pain in your neck for the last two or three weeks, but that I think a better day is dawning for us both. Anyway, "that is no agent, that is my friend" is the way I really feel, and in one way or another I'll try to live up to it.

We really did have a swell Christmas out at Ed Aswell's—I think it was the best one I have had since I was a kid. There were a lot of nice people and everyone was really very happy and very moved, and as we finished dinner Mary Lou whispered to me and asked me if it was "all right to tell them" [3] and I said "yes" so we got out your bottle of champagne and Mary Lou told them, and I tried to say something and Ed tried to say something, and neither could very well, and everyone had tears in their eyes, and I think they meant it, too. That's why it is a little

---

[1] Miss Nowell was never agent for Wolfe's books: only for his short stories and for some foreign rights, subsidiary rights, etc. which he could not conveniently handle for himself.

[2] Wolfe finally decided to divide his advance between the two years, and accordingly received $2,500 of it on December 31, 1937. The balance was paid in three installments of $2,500 each on February 1, March 1, and April 1, 1938.

[3] Mrs. Aswell was asking if it was all right to announce that Harpers were to be Wolfe's publishers.

tough to have to wrangle about contracts now, but I guess that's life, isn't it? And we were right both times. Anyway, dear Agent, I send you my love and with all my heart my wishes for nothing but the best for both of us next year. . . .

Wolfe had sent Charles Scribner a Christmas card and had received from him a short personal note thanking him for it and saying that he hoped they could have a drink together sometime. The following note was Wolfe's reply.

To CHARLES SCRIBNER

[Hotel Chelsea]
[New York]
December 29, 1937

Dear Charlie:

I can't tell you how happy I was to get your letter. Believe me, nothing was further from my intention in not writing or seeing any of you before than hurting the feelings of people who mean so much to me. As I told Max in the letter I wrote him, the reason I didn't come around was for no other reason except to think things out for myself, and to try to spare everybody pain, including myself.

Whatever happiness I had this Christmas was mixed in with a lot of sadness, too. Without going into the past, hashing it all up again, trying to thread back through the whole tangled snarl—like Max, I am still confused about so many things—just let me tell you that I think you are not only the finest publishers, but among the finest people I have ever known. Whatever comes of all of this, I know we will be friends; and now that I am committed to a new and, for me, very lonely and formidable course, that knowledge gives me the deepest comfort.

Some time soon, I look forward to seeing you again. Meanwhile, with affectionate greetings to you and all of your family, and with all good wishes for the coming year,

Mary Louise Aswell was the wife of Edward Aswell and at this time a member of the editorial staff of The Reader's Digest. *She had sent Wolfe an article from the December, 1937, issue of the* Digest *entitled "One Small Unwilling Captain," a very moving letter written by a captain in the Japanese Army deploring the necessity of war. The following was Wolfe's reply to her.*

To MARY LOUISE ASWELL

Hotel Chelsea,
222 West 23rd Street,
New York, N.Y.

December 31, 1937.

Dear Mary Lou:

Ed has just left, and I am winding up the old year with a touch of grippe, and am not much to look at, but very hopeful.

The final grim technical details of business and contract signing have been attended to, and now I am committed utterly, in every way. It gives me a strangely empty and hollow feeling, and I know the importance of the moment, and feel more than ever the responsibility of the obligation I have assumed. But I guess it is good for a man to get that hollow empty feeling, the sense of absolute loneliness and new beginning at different times throughout his life. It's not the hollowness of death, but a living kind of hollowness: a new world is before me now; it's good to know I have your prayers.

Thanks so much for your letter and for the enclosed story about the small Japanese Captain. It was moving and beautiful, and the pity is, it's all so true. It's so wrong to hate people, isn't it? And yet I feel that there are times when we have got to hate *things*. Everywhere you look and listen nowadays there is so much hatred. I hear it on every side every day. I even hear that the Germans are organically different from other members of the human race; the Trotskyites hate the Stalinites, and tell you they are not as other men: the Stalinites reply with equal hatred.

I've been reading Huxley's book which you gave me for Christmas. He's a brilliant writer, isn't he? His mind is so clear and penetrating, and sees so many things, and yet I got the impression he was puzzled and confused, too. To be partisan about anything almost implies hatred. Apparently Huxley's ideal is a kind of non-partisan man—or rather, a man who is partisan only in his belief in life. And yet, I wonder if in this world of ours to-day we can be non-partisan. Of one thing I am sure: the artist can't live in his ivory tower any more, if he is, he is cutting himself off from all the sources of life. Tremendous pressure is brought to bear from all sides upon people like myself: we are told that we must be partisan even in the work we do. Here I think the partisans are wrong; and yet a man does feel to-day a tremendous pressure from within—a kind of pressure of the conscience. There are so many things that are damnable, and which must be fought—we all ask ourselves the question: can we be free and be effective at the same time? I think nearly all of us have a pretty strong and clear feeling in our hearts about the larger humanity we would like to achieve. But when we see such wrong and cruelty and injustice all around us we ask ourselves if we have any right to refrain from taking sides and joining parties, because taking sides and joining parties are likely to limit and distort us so. I wish it were also possible for me to feel like Candide that the best thing in the end is to tend one's garden. A tremendous lot can be said for that, a tremendous lot of good, but somehow garden tending doesn't seem to be the answer either, the way things are to-day.

I wish it were possible for people to hate the thing that has the small Japanese Captain in its power without hating the small Japanese Captain, but you know what happens. Men start off by hating things and wind up by hating people. Well, I don't know the answers, but I'm looking for them and I think I am learning a little all the time. At any rate, there is friendship and love and faith and work. They are not just words: I have known and had them all.—Now, in a new and thrilling way, I feel that I know and have them all again. That is why I send you all my love, and all my deep and heartfelt wishes for your happiness and success this coming year.

The following letter is included in a longhand draft of "A Statement" which Wolfe wrote for Harpers to use in announcing his signing of a contract for his new book with them. The "Statement" was too long for Harpers' purposes, so they rewrote it, quoting only brief excerpts from it.

To EDWARD C. ASWELL

[Hotel Chelsea]
[New York]
[Late December, 1937]

This is a time of year that has some sadness in it for us all. But we can feel happy too, in the knowledge that nothing gets lost, and that the people we have known will still be our friends, no matter where we are, and that although we can't go home again, the home of every one of us is in the future. And that is why I am looking forward to next year.

It has been my fortunate lot always to have as publishers in this country people of the finest ability and the highest integrity. For that reason, I am glad to know that with the New Year I shall be associated with a house like yours.

As you know, like many other young men, I began life as a lyrical writer. I am no longer a very young man—I am thirty-seven years old—and I must tell you that my vision of life has changed since I began to write about ten years ago, and that I shall never again write the kind of book that I wrote then. Like other men, I began to write with an intense and passionate concern with the designs and purposes of my own youth; and like many other men, that preoccupation has now changed to an intense and passionate concern with the designs and purposes of life.

For two years now, since I began to work on my new book, I have felt as if I was standing on the shore of a new land. About the book that I am doing, I can only tell you that it is a kind of fable, constructed out of the materials of experience and reality, and permitting me, I hope, a more whole and thorough use of them than I have had before. The book belongs in kind with those books which have described the adventures of the average man—by this I mean the naturally innocent man, every mother's son of us—through life.

Anyway, for better or for worse, my life, my talent, and my spirit is now committed to it utterly. Like Martin Luther, I can't do otherwise—"Ich kann nicht anders"—I have no other choice.

Now I can only hope the end for both of us will be well.

XVII

THE COMPLETION OF THE FIRST ROUGH DRAFT
OF THE WEB AND THE ROCK AND
YOU CAN'T GO HOME AGAIN

1938

To NORMAN H. PEARSON

> c/o Miss Elizabeth Nowell
> 114 East 56th Street
> New York, N.Y.
>
> January 21, 1938

Dear Norman:

This is a letter of thanks and also of contrition. Just to get it off my chest, let me confess the whole sordid and humiliating business to you at once: I got your fine Modern Library Hawthorne [1] just as I was setting off to Virginia for a little trip, and I took it with me. [2] On the way down to Washington, I read your fine introduction. And that was as far as I got. Because when I got to Washington, I stopped over the night at a small hotel near the station. And there your book vanished. I had it under my arm when I entered the hotel, they showed me a room that had not been made up, and then they put me in another one. I am pretty sure that I left your book on the dresser of the first room. At any rate, the next morning when I discovered my loss and inquired about it, they could not find the book. So a genuine first edition Pearson with an autographed inscription from the author is floating around somewhere, or possibly has

---

[1] *The Complete Novels and Selected Tales of Nathaniel Hawthorne,* edited and with an introduction by Pearson.

[2] Wolfe had gone to Virginia for the weekend of January 9, then come up to Baltimore for a few days.

already found its way into the greedy clutches of a collector. Whoever has it, I hope he chokes.

Now I am going to propose this to you: if I go out and buy a Giant Hawthorne, will you put your scrawl in it when you come to New York? It may interest you to know that I have a large new supply of South Carolina paper shell pecans, [and] much more floor space than I had a year ago, so the possibilities of cracking nuts and strewing the shells all over the floor are practically unlimited. If this does not seduce you, what may? I think I have told you that I am staying at the old Hotel Chelsea, which is on 23rd Street between 7th and 8th Avenues. Also I am trying to get on with my big Doaks book.[3] There is still one more bout with the lawyers, one more session of the almost endless litigation which has made my life a nightmare for the past two years—this comes up in February— but after that I hope what is left of me may be left in peace. . . .

I've written a piece which is coming out, by gum, in *Vogue*, the ladies' corset and hosiery encyclopedia.[4] But I think it's a good piece even so, and I hope you get a chance to look at it. They told me to write five thousand words about America and that's what it's about. It comes from a book, or a section of a book I hope to write some day called *The Hound of Darkness*, but the ladies at *Vogue* thought this was not sunny enough, so we called it "A Prologue to America." I also had a piece in the *New Masses* —my initiation.[5] It's been published but I've never seen the copy it appeared in. There's one thing to be said about getting published in the *New Masses*: you never have to bother about an income tax.

This is about all the news I can think of at the present. Oh yes, I attended the annual meeting of the National Institute of Arts and Letters on Wednesday night. I got elected to it a year ago, but this was the first time I had been around. Walter Damrosch was presented with a gold medal and Jonas Lie was the toastmaster and Arthur Train was the treasurer and got up and read an account of the year's finances, and Henry Seidel Canby was the secretary and got up and read the annual report and a list of the members who had died during the year and the new members who had been elected, and there were four proposed amendments to the constitution which people got up and talked about and finally it was decided to reject them because the constitution said the same thing anyway, and Robert Nathan was there and Van Wyck Brooks and Stephen Vincent Benét and many other older ones whose names I did

___

[3] By this time Wolfe was considering discarding the title "The Vision of Spangler's Paul" and calling his book "The Lives of the Bondsman Doaks," or "The Ordeal of the Bondsman Doaks," or "You Can't Go Home Again."

[4] "A Prologue to America."

[5] "The Company" was published in the January 11, 1938, issue of the *New Masses*, and appears with many changes in *You Can't Go Home Again* on pages 129–140.

not know, and it was very sad. I went away and drank, and wished some-one like yourself had been with me that I could talk to. And yet, what is there to say? Walter Damrosch, who, Mr. Robert Nathan whispered to me, was "a grand old lion" was full of years and honors and gold medals, and Jonas Lie read a long very touching letter from Deems Taylor regretting he could not be there in person to present the gold medal to the grand old lion, and recounting all the things the lion had done. And Mr. Jonas Lie was very smooth and cold and polished and he had a little tufted goatee that stuck out of the hollow of his underlip and he, too, was full of years and honors and I believe he referred to Walter Damrosch as "our beloved master." And there were a lot of others there who were also full of years and honors, and, it seemed to me, of straw. Didn't Eliot write a poem beginning "We are the hollow men"? Maybe I'm being unfair and un-just—I know that I ought to be grateful to be a member of such a famous body—but I'm just telling you what ensued, and it was a sad, depressing evening.

It was a little terrifying too: I think there's nothing in life quite so tragic and desolate as the artist who has gone dead. I haven't seen this recent moving picture, "Zola," that people say is very fine, but I know something of Zola's life; and in the picture, I am told, it is shown how Zola, after the stern integrity of his earlier years, gets fat and prosperous and turns away from life, but then in his last years, when the Dreyfus Case finally breaks through his consciousness, becomes an artist and a liv-ing man again and gives his life, his talent and his courage for freedom and for truth. It seems to me that is the way an artist's life should be com-pleted, but the other night I looked at them and—well, Dr. Canby read the annual report and Mr. Damrosch got a gold medal.

Hendrik Willem Van Loon was one of the new members to be elected: he came in late and made a funny speech. He is a practical, diligent, hard-working Dutchman: I think he will do well among them. Mr. Robert Nathan is also, I feel, slated for great things. He is still young and yet, as the saying goes, "he has the wisdom of one twice his years." In these strident times, it is good to know that a writer of such delicate, whimsical talents is still true to the canons of pure art: as one cultivated lady is reported to have said recently, "I can't waste my time reading the dull and gloomy works of Hebrew writers like Thomas Mann and Theodore Dreiser. I want to read someone who knows how to write beautiful Eng-lish prose like Robert Nathan, for example."

Well, this is all for the present. And really, I assure you, with charity to all. I send you all good wishes for the coming year. I hope it will be a good year for me too, and that I'll be a better writer, which also means a better man. Come to see me soon.

To FRED W. WOLFE

January 22, 1938
114 E. 56th Street
New York, New York

c/o Miss Eliz. Nowell

Dear Fred:

. . . I was unfortunately unable to write Mama in time before she made her deposition,[1] but I am glad to know that she came through all right. I was away in Virginia when your letter came—anyway, it was too late to do anything about it. Let me know how it all turns out. Of course, I have known for years that things were in a bad way and that there would not be much left, but I do hope the lawyers can save her house for her. As I found out in the last two years, litigation is a costly and gruelling process, and I am not sure that anyone wins out in the end except the lawyers. . . .

. . . I don't know much about this suit the family is bringing against the Wachovia Bank, or they against us, because no one told me very much about it when I was home this summer, but I suppose you have thought everything over carefully and know where you stand. I understand that you and Mabel have named me as one of the parties to the suit, and therefore I wish you'd keep me informed about it and let me know what happens, and just exactly what it is we arc suing for. Just to get the matter straight for the record here and now about what happened, so far as I was concerned, in its connection to Papa's estate, the facts are these:

When I was graduated from Chapel Hill in 1920, I was nineteen years old. As you know, I decided then to go to Harvard and do graduate work. It was my intention to go to Harvard for a year, but as it eventually turned out I stayed three. Papa, of course, was still alive in 1920, but very feeble and very ill, and no longer able to take an active interest in what was going on around him. When I decided to go to Harvard I went to Mama and talked to her about it. We all knew, even at that time, that Papa had made a will, and that according to the terms of the will each of the children was to receive the sum of five thousand dollars, and that the remainder of the estate would go to Mama. I proposed to her, as I remember it, that I be allowed to go to Harvard for a year, and that the expenses of this year at Harvard should be deducted from my share in the estate. At the time, I believe that the matter rested there, but, as you know, I remained at Harvard for three years instead of one. Papa died

---

[1] Her deposition in the case brought against her by the Wachovia Bank and Trust Co.

in 1922: When the question of settlement finally came up, somewhere around 1923, which was my last year at Harvard, or shortly after that, it was proposed to me that I cancel any claim I had in the estate in recognition of the expenses of my three years. To this I readily agreed, and for that matter, have never made any objection to that arrangement since. But Mama did object. She said, as I recall it, that it was fair to deduct the expenses of one year from my share, but that she had herself agreed to bear the expense of the additional two years, and that she did not think it was fair to charge me the whole amount.

I certainly do remember signing a document at about this period which you and Ralph [2] gave me your capacity as executors to the estate and that document, as I remember it, was a release to the estate of my share in the inheritance.[3] And I also remember clearly within recent years, within the last three or four, I believe, receiving letters and another document from you, which was also in the form of a release. You asked me to sign it, saying that it ought to be filed as a matter of record at the Court House, as one of the final things to be done in settling up the estate. I was perfectly willing to sign this paper, as I had the first, but my recollection is I mislaid it, and never returned it to you, and I believe later on you wrote me about the matter again.

Now, Fred, I've gone in to all this just to go upon the record, and to make my own part in the whole business as clear as I can. I know you understand that I make absolutely no claim to anything besides what I have received. But this is what happened. From a technical point of view, I suppose I really did not receive a full share in the estate. But I always consider that I actually did, since the help I received at Harvard during the three years I was there was approximately equivalent to what a full share would have been. I don't know whatever became of the paper I signed, but you may have it somewhere. Of course, as far as this present litigation is concerned, I am absolutely with the family and with Mama

[2] Ralph Wheaton.

[3] This was done because, although Mr. Wolfe had willed $5000 to each of his five children, his estate at the time of his death had shrunk to less than half of its original amount. In reply to this letter, Fred Wolfe wrote on January 26, 1937: "Your statements are all correct about the papers signed, etc. with the exception that you are wrong that the signing of said paper signed away your right in your supposed inheritance. Your paper was merely an acknowledgment of having received $5000 cash on account, by terms of will, but not "all your inheritance." At that time I also signed one for $5000. . . . It all was merely the juggling of two inexperienced people, Ralph and I, to attempt to make $11,000 in cash and Liberty Bonds cover the ground in terms of $25,000 (5 x $5000) as set forth by the will."

Shortly after this exchange of letters between himself and Fred, Wolfe signed a waiver to any claim upon his inheritance from his mother, which excluded him from being named in the suit of the Wachovia Bank and Trust against her and her heirs.

where their interests are involved. But I thought it better at this time just to make it clear to you personally what actually happened as far as my own part in it was concerned. It is better to have a clear understanding of all these things.

Now, I can only hope that everything turns out in favor of our own best interests, and above all, that the bank does not succeed in taking away from Mama her house, and what remaining property she may have. If they do, I consider it an outrageous injustice, and I am willing to do what I can to help you prevent its happening.

This is all for the present. I am getting back to work again, and hope to be able to work uninterruptedly now on my new book. It certainly seems that I deserve that measure of quiet and security after the past two years. Please write and tell me the news when you get a chance. And let me know if there is anything I can do. . . .

When Wolfe's New Jersey attorney, Ralph E. Lum, had asked him to obtain witnesses for the —— case, he had written to Mrs. Jelliffe, asking if she could testify for him since she had been present at one interview between him and ——. She had replied that on that occasion she had heard Wolfe and —— arguing about what manuscripts —— could or could not take and try to sell, and that she would be glad to testify as much in denial of ——'s claim that he and Wolfe had had "an unlimited agreement." After consultation with Mr. Lum, Wolfe wrote her the following letter.

To BELINDA JELLIFFE

> 114 East 56th Street
> New York, New York
> c/o Miss Elizabeth Nowell
> February 1, 1938

Dear Mrs. Jelliffe:

I heard from Mr. Lum to-day and he told me he was writing you and telling you he would like you to come over and be present in Jersey City when the case comes up. He is not sure that he will actually need you to take the stand as a witness at all, but he thinks your very presence there would be helpful "psychologically"—I suppose just by way of showing the court what nice people I know—you and Mr. Perkins, etc. Personally, I hope he puts you on because I think you would be a swell witness: anyway, I want you to know how much I appreciate your willingness to help.

I am seeing Mr. Perkins to-night in order to talk the whole thing over with him, and let him know how matters stand. He too, is going to be present; but what moves me most of all is that to-night will be my first meeting with Mr. Perkins in seven months. A whole lot has happened since then, a kind of definition and articulation of belief and conviction in my life. I have burned some great bridges behind me: I have been grieving for the dead a lot this past year, and I have found out something which is, I think, the most important discovery of my whole life, and that is this: you can't go home again, back to your childhood, back to your town, your people, back to the father you have lost, and back to the solacements of time and memory. I found that out through exile, through storm and stress, perplexity and dark confusion. I found it out with blood and sweat and agony, and for a long time I grieved as a man grieves for a brother who is dead.

But I think I am through the jungle now, and I feel naked and alone, and maybe a little scared too, and with a kind of dryness in the throat and in the mouth, and like a man that is standing all alone upon the shore of a new land, and knows that a whole new world is there before him, and that he has to face it for himself, and that his only help is in him now.

But I am grieving for the dead no longer: I know now that you can't go home again, but I know also that our home, yours and mine, and every mother's son's of us, is in the future, and I believe in it and trust in it as I believe and trust in life, and think that it is valuable, as life is valuable, and must be won and saved, and to that end I am now willing to devote all the energy, talent, faith and hope that in me are.

And I have also found out that although you can't go home again, there are certain things you do not lose, but that grow and flourish as the years go on, and one of them is the love and belief of a friend. And that is why it means so much more to me than I can ever utter here to know that in another hour I shall meet again and hear the voice again of the wonderful and noble man who has been, I think, the greatest, best, and most devoted friend that I have ever had; of whose friendship and belief I hope I may be forever worthy. Great bridges may be burned, and there is a path which we can never take, a road down which we never shall go back again; but there is also a fire that once lighted will always burn, and that never while life lasts can be put out.

And now—here is to good citizens like you and me, and a plague to all conspirators, here or abroad, or in the Jersey swamps, who plot the ruin of honest folk like you and me. As the British national anthem has it, "Frustrate their politics, confound their knavish tricks"—or hasn't it? Anyway, you get the idea, and I am sincerely grateful to you for the help you offer to that end.

Mr. Lum informs me that the hearing will be held in Chancery

Chambers, 1 Exchange Place, top floor, Jersey City, New Jersey, before Vice-Chancellor Kays on Tuesday, February 8, 1938. He does not say at what hour of the day it is to be held, but from what he told me before, I believe we should be there by ten o'clock in the morning, and he also hoped the whole matter would not take up more than an hour or two of time. Anyway, I will find out the time exactly and let you know, and maybe all three of us, you and Mr. Perkins, can go over together. There will also be one or two others who have agreed to go, but with two such as you and Mr. P. I do not feel I lack for comfort or for strength.

Meanwhile, until you hear from me, with thanks and all good wishes,

To MARGARET ROBERTS

> 114 East 56th Street
> New York, New York
> c/o Miss Elizabeth Nowell
> February 14, 1938

Dear Mrs. Roberts:

I have wanted to write you for a long time, but many things have happened to keep me busy, including courts and lawyers, and a long and ugly business of trying to recover manuscripts which a man had taken, and which he had not returned. I won the thing the other day, completely and overwhelmingly—that is, if one ever does win anything when the lawyers have taken out their pound of flesh. Anyway, for the first time in three years I am out of the woods—out of the legal woods, at any rate —the long, exhausting and complicated series of legal difficulties with which I shall not weary you here. . . .

. . . Now I want you to help me if you can, and I know that I can depend on you to keep this confidential. I am also writing to my cousin, Jack Westall, with a similar request for information and help. . . . What I want is this: I am writing a long book, and I want to put everything that I have in it: and this time the book is not about a town, nor about any certain group of people, but it is about America and what happened here between 1929 and 1937. I think you will agree with me and see what I am driving at when I tell you that what happened in Asheville in that period seems pretty important and significant in the light it throws on what happened to the whole country. So, to get down to brass tacks: first of all, do you know what is the best and completest newspaper account of the events—the bank trials, the affairs of the city, etc.—which occurred between 1930 and 1932? And do you know where I can get a copy of them? I would be willing to buy them, if I could do so at a fair price: or if you know anyone who has kept such a record and would be willing to let me have it for several weeks, I would make every guarantee to preserve it and to see that it is returned to its owner safely. And if anything else occurs to you—if there are any people you think I could write or any other information that might be useful—I should be grateful if you would let me know about this too.

There is so much that I would like to tell you now of what has been happening to me, and so much that I would like to tell you about this book. But if I ever got started here, I would never finish. . . . Please help me if you can. And please write soon. Meanwhile, with all good wishes to you and Mr. Roberts for your health and happiness,

On January 19, 1938, Charles Scribner III had written Wolfe saying: "I have been having quite a time with our cashier's department straightening out the report that they are obliged to make to the United States Government . . . regarding the money that you received from us in the year 1937. . . . I have regarded the payments on the libel suit charged against your account as a loan. . . . The royalties earned . . . subtracted from the deficit on your account leave a debit balance of $826.38. In the course of a year and a half this amount will probably be met by the royalties on the books we published and I do not wish to embarrass you by pressing you to pay the debit balance owing to us, at this time, if you cannot conveniently do so. On the other hand if you have the money that you can spare, it would seem just as well to wind this up, and as I understand you will probably receive during the year a considerable payment on your new book, it might work out better for you from the income tax point of view. . . . I hope you agree with me now that you did the sensible thing in settling this suit, as you are now free to go ahead with your work without interruption, whereas you would otherwise be tied up with us for an indefinite time in fighting the thing out at probably a considerably larger cost and all of the payment would have fallen on your shoulders."

The following was Wolfe's reply.

To CHARLES SCRIBNER III

> 114 East 56th Street
> New York, New York
> c/o Miss Elizabeth Nowell
> February 14, 1938

Dear Charlie:

I am sorry to have delayed answering your letter of January 19th so long, but, as you know, I have been wrestling with a law suit—the last I pray I may ever have—and doing my level best to help the lawyer and protect myself against a series of legal outrages that included practically everything except arson. As you know, I won the case, or at least it will seem as if I won it until I begin paying the lawyer bills.

Now about your own letter and your suggestion that I pay you now the deficit which stands against my account in your books: I have thought this over very carefully, and I want to ask you to let the deficit remain unpaid for the present, and to allow it to be absorbed, as you suggest it can be, by future sales of my books which you publish.

Yes, it is true that I did receive a considerable advance from Harpers, but it was money which I hope to keep, so far as possible, for my own use, to support me until I get another piece of work done. The lawyers are already swarming around, flapping their wings and emitting blood-thirsty caws, and if I am going to begin the new year in the same way as the two or three before it, paying out large sums of money in suits and settlements and lawyers' fees, the advance is not going to stretch too far. So, if you understand my position, I should prefer it if you will agree to let the deficit be paid off by further, and, I hope, continued sales.

I hope you are right when you say that settlement of the libel suit has left me free to do my work in peace. At any rate, I shall now find out. The experience of the past three years has been a very costly one, in time, in energy, and in money: I can only hope now that I may derive some future profit from it. Please let me know if my proposal here about the deficit is agreeable to you. Meanwhile, with all good wishes,

The following letter to Edward C. Aswell was begun in the first person, then given the title "A Statement of Purpose" and changed to the third person, using the words "the author" and "the editor" instead of "I" and "you." For the sake of consistency and directness, it has all been changed back to the first person here. It was never finished and was not sent to Aswell until Perkins and Miss Nowell found it among Wolfe's papers after his death.

To EDWARD C. ASWELL

> 114 East 56th Street
> New York, N.Y.
> c/o Miss Elizabeth Nowell
> February 14, 1938

Dear Ed:

I am doing the synopsis of the book which I told you I would make out for you, and I hope to give it to you in a day or two. First of all, so far as I can now make out—and the reason for any dubiety that may be apparent here is not due to any doubt on my own part, or any lack of conviction as to purpose or direction, but rather to the enormous masses of material with which I am working, and the tides and planes and forces which shift and vary constantly while still holding the same general direction—here is my latest stage of definition as clearly as I can put it to you, and what I think the book is about:

It is about one man's discovery of life and of the world, and in this sense it is a book of apprenticeship. As I told you before, I had in mind the doing of a kind of American "Gulliver's Travels." I used this comparison deliberately, but I also likened the book to those books that had to do with the adventures of what I call "the innocent man" through life —and mentioned, in addition to "Gulliver," such books as "Don Quixote," "Pickwick," "Candide," "The Idiot," and "Wilhelm Meister." As you know, I am using these names not as examples of literary models which I intend to follow, but merely as indications of the direction I am taking. And I now think that the illustration that comes closer to the kind of book I want to do is "Wilhelm Meister's Apprenticeship" rather than "Gulliver." And the reason for this is that I now believe, as the definition of the book grows clearer, that the illustration I made to you about "Gulliver" might mislead you in that, as the name "Gulliver" implies, it might indicate to you that I was contemplating a book about a man who was "gulled," who was expecting one thing from life and found another, etc.

Well, all of this element is certainly in the book, but it does not define as directly as it should my position and direction at this time about the book. The book will have satire in it, I hope swingeing and scalding satire, but it is not essentially a satiric book. It is a book, as I have said, about discovery—about discovery not in a sudden and explosive sense as when "some new planet breaks upon his ken," but of discovery as through a process of finding out, and of finding out as a man has to find out, through error and through trial, and through fantasy and illusion, through falsehood and his own damn foolishness, through being mistaken and wrong and an idiot and egotistical and aspiring and hopeful and believing and confused, and pretty much, I think, what every damned one of us is and goes through and finds out about and becomes.

And, in order that there may be no doubt as to what this process of discovery involves, the whole book might almost be called "You Can't Go Home Again"—which means back home to one's family, back home to one's childhood, back home to the father one has lost, back home to romantic love, to a young man's dreams of glory and of fame, back home to exile, to escape to "Europe" and some foreign land, back home to lyricism, singing just for singing's sake, back home to aestheticism, to one's youthful ideas of the "artist," and the all-sufficiency of "art and beauty and love," back home to the ivory tower, back home to places in the country, the cottage in Bermuda away from all the strife and conflict of the world, back home to the father one is looking for—to someone who can help one, save one, ease the burden for one, back home to the old forms and systems of things that once seemed everlasting, but that are changing all the time—back home to the escapes of Time and Memory. Each of these discoveries, sad and hard as they are to make and accept, are described in the book almost in the order in which they are named here. But the conclusion is not sad: this is a hopeful book—the conclusion is that although you can't go home again, the home of every one of us is in the future: there is no other way.

I hope you will keep this description of the purpose of the book in mind and read it pretty carefully, and think about it a lot, because I am depending on you now so much. I want you to be thoroughly convinced at the outset that I know what I am doing and where I am going; and although there are many, many doubts in my mind, there is no doubt; and although there are many, many confusions, there is no confusion. To get right down to cases now, even, as it has to be here, in the most broad and general way, here is what I have in mind:

I intend to use my own experience absolutely—to pour it in, to squeeze it, to get every damn thing out of it that it is worth. I intend for this to be the most objective book that I have ever written, and I also intend by the same token, for it to be the most autobiographical. I have constructed a fable, I have invented a story and a legend: out of my experience I have derived some new characters who are now compacted not so much from specific recollection as from the whole amalgam and consonance of seeing, feeling, thinking, living, and knowing many people. I have two important ones, for example, named Alsop and Joyner—who, each in his own way, is pretty much what the name of each signifies—but each, I believe, are as convincing and living people as I have ever created. I now think I may be wrong in calling the central figure, the protagonist, Joe Doaks, but Alsop and Joyner can probably stand as they are—that is, both are real names, both are fairly familiar and common names. The objection to Joe Doaks, of course, is that it may carry with it too much a connotation of newspaper cartooning, slap-stick, the fellow in the bleachers, and so on. The way I feel now, I have got to get more of a Wilhelm Meister kind of name—an *American* Wilhelm Meister kind of name.

To get still further down to cases, as you will remember, when I first met you and we talked together about what I had to do, I spoke to you of the book which I had called "The October Fair," and told you something of the conflict in my mind between this book and the other book which I have been describing here. I told you, for example, of the time several years ago when all my heart and life and energy were absorbed by "The October Fair" and how, at that time, I thought this was the book I had to do and had framed it in a sequence to follow "Look Homeward, Angel" and "Of Time and the River." I told you how I had written and striven on this book for two or three years, how "Of Time and the River" finally grew out of it and preceded it, and of how finally I had gone cold on "The October Fair": that is, it was no longer the burning, all-absorbing thing I had to do.

But I described also the feeling of incompletion and discontent in my mind because of this book which had been projected and never published —the feeling that it had in it some of the best and truest work I had ever done, and the feeling that this work ought to receive the consummation and release of print. I still feel that way except—and that is what I am trying to explain about my whole position here as concerns my book—my position has changed: I no longer wish to write a whole book about a woman and a man in love, and about youth and the city, because it now seems to me that these things, while important, are subordinate to the whole plan of the book I have in mind. In other words, being young and in love and in the city now seem to me to be only a part of the whole experience of apprenticeship and discovery of which I am talking. They are also a part of the knowledge that you can't go home again.

That plan, as I now see it in my mind, as I am shaping it in the enormous masses of manuscript which I have already written, and as I am trying to clarify it for you in the synopsis, is as follows:

The protagonist, the central character, the Wilhelm Meister kind of figure—really the most autobiographical character I have ever written because I want to put everything I have or know into him—is important now because, I hope, he will be or illustrate, in his own experience every one of us—not merely the sensitive young fellow in conflict with his town, his family, the little world around him—not merely the sensitive young fellow in love, and so concerned with his little universe of love that he thinks it is the whole universe—but all of these things and much more insofar as they illustrate essential elements of any man's progress and discovery of life, and as they illustrate the world itself, not in terms of personal and self-centered conflict with the world, but in terms of ever-increasing discovery of life and the world, with a consequent diminution of the more personal and self-centered vision of the world which a young man has.

In other words, I have sometimes thought of the book as a series of concentric circles—that is, you drop the pebble in the pool—the Wilhelm Meister pebble or whatever we shall ultimately call him—but instead of pebble and pool simply in personal terms of pebble and pool, you get a widening ever-enlarging picture of the whole thing—the pebble becomes important, if important at all, only in terms of this general and constant pattern of which it is the temporary and accidental stimulus. In other words, any other pebble would produce the same effect. The important thing is to tell about the thing itself, the thing that happens. The pebble, if you like, is only a means to this end.

THE PROTAGONIST.

I feel that the figure of the protagonist may be, technically and in other ways, the most important and decisive element in this book. As I have told you, this book marks not only a turning away from the books I have written in the past, but a genuine spiritual and artistic change. In other words, I feel that I am done with lyrical and identifiable personal autobiography; I am also seeking, and hope now to obtain, through free creation, a release of my inventive power which the more shackling limitations of identifiable autobiography do not permit.

In other words, the value of the Eugene Gant type of character is his personal and romantic uniqueness, causing conflict with the world around him: in this sense, the Eugene Gant type of character becomes a kind of romantic self-justification, and the greatest weakness of the Eugene Gant type of character lies in this fact.

Therefore, it is first of all vitally important to the success of this book that there be no trace of Eugene Gant-i-ness in the character of the protagonist; and since there is no longer a trace of Eugene Gant-i-ness in the mind and spirit of the creator, the problem should be a technical one rather than a spiritual or emotional one. In other words, this is a book about discovery, and not about self-justification; it hopes to describe the pattern that the life of Everyman must, in general, take in its process of discovery; and although the protagonist should be, in his own right, an interesting person, his significance lies not in his personal uniqueness and differences, but in his personal identity to the life of every man. The book is a book of discovery, hence union with life; not a book of personal revolt, hence separation from life. The protagonist becomes significant not as the tragic victim of circumstances, the romantic hero in conflict and revolt against his environment, but as a kind of polar instrument round which the events of life are grouped, by means of which they are touched, explained, and apprehended, by means of which they are seen and ordered.

Autobiographically, therefore, he should bear perhaps about the same relation to the life of the author as Wilhelm Meister bears to the life of Goethe, or as Copperfield bears to the life of Dickens. As to the story itself—the legend—it should bear about the same relation to the life of the author as the story of Wilhelm Meister bears to Goethe's life; even perhaps as Don Quixote bears to the life of Cervantes, although this book is perhaps more in the vein of satiric legendry than the book I have in mind.

But the book certainly should have in it, from first to last, a strong element of the satiric exaggeration of Don Quixote, not only because it belongs to the nature of the legend—"the innocent man" discovering life—but because satiric exaggeration also belongs to the nature of life, and particularly American life. No man, for example, who wants to write a book about America on a grand scale can hardly escape feeling again and again the emotion of the man when he first saw a giraffe: "I don't believe it!"

So, the book certainly must have this element, and it seems to me the figure of the protagonist must have it too. He must have it because the very process of discovery, of finding out, will be intensified and helped by it.

For example—and this may serve to illustrate the *special* way I hope to use autobiography in this book—one of the facts which has played an important part in my own life, which has been of immeasurable value to me in my own voyage of discovery, has been my great height. And it has been valuable to me for none of the reasons people usually assign: that height gives a man a commanding appearance, attracts attention to him, gives him a psychological advantage in the affairs of life over other men. This is not true: any marked variation from the type of average humanity is unfortunate—the midget, or the man of dwarfed figure, the excessively fat man, or the extremely tall man must encounter every moment of the day all kinds of sizes, patterns, shapes and measures of Things as They Are, which cause him discomfort and inconvenience. The value of his own variation, if any, is psychological—in the kind of increased awareness it gives him of the structure of life, and the pattern of the world. Again, in his discovery of life, he is so strongly and passionately drawn to life because, in a sense, life rebuffs him: in his youth, he is often in passionate and angry conflict with the world and people because of these rebuffs, usually unintentional, or the result of type customs and type prejudice—(maybe a girl, for example, hesitates to dance with a man of great height because she is afraid the comparison will excite laughter and ridicule)—but later on, a man learns tolerance and wisdom and understanding out of the very discomfort and pain his own variation has caused him. He comes to realize that he is in no fundamental sense different from other people: he is compacted of the same clay, filled with the same blood, breathes the same air, has the same passions, appetites, joys, fears, hopes and aspirations as the rest of humanity. He sees that people are not often intentionally cruel, but merely myopic in their understanding of him—that they think he is different simply because his physical dimensions are not quite the same as theirs. And when he understands this, a man's vision and knowledge of life is increased immeasurably: the very handicap that once caused him so much pain and conflict now becomes an asset: instead of being driven away from life by it, he is drawn ever closer to it: now that he understands the reasons why people act as they do, he responds to them naturally, accepts all the jokes and gestures, as banal as they often are, good-naturedly, and instead of being an outcast from the fold, he now draws people to him. Once they see he is one of them, and really not one whit different from themselves, they cluster around him: they reveal themselves to him, talk to him, even when they have just met him, as they would rarely do to another stranger. The very handicap that caused him so much pain in youth has now become one of the most valuable possessions that he has.

This fact—this tremendous discovery in my own life—has been such an important part of my own experience that several years ago when the outlines of this legend began first to shape themselves in my mind, I was convinced that I ought to use this fact somehow—for it is a veritable gold-mine—in the figure of my protagonist.

But how? Obviously, to create in the character of the protagonist, a figure which is six feet and six inches tall—my own height—would be to incur the very danger of personal autobiography and personal identity I am so anxious to avoid. The danger would be not merely that the reader and the critic would tend to identify such a character literally with me, but that I myself might tend to identify myself too personally with such a figure. Certainly, in the tremendously important fact of physical experience I could not help more or less duplicating my own experience—of being six feet six—with that of my protagonist.

It seemed then, as it does now, that the really important thing—the *truly* autobiographical thing—was the fact of physical variation: to create a figure who would illustrate that variation and all the great human experience that attends it.

Thus, as the legend of the book began to shape, as I began to create and invent the boyhood friends, the family, the town, the events and characters, the whole geography of the legend, around the character of the protagonist, the appearance of the figure, from his childhood on, began to shape itself until it is now more indelibly written in my mind than the face and figure of anyone I have ever known.

The figure may seem at first a little grotesque—it will quickly become apparent he is not so at all, he is only a little off the usual scale. These differences sometimes awake laughter in those who see him for the first time. As the book opens, he is still somewhat in the ugly duckling stage of his career, a little truculently resentful of remarks on his appearance, still over-sensitive, not yet at the stage where he is able to forget himself, accept jokes and badinage good-naturedly, and welcome his body for the loyal, if ugly, friend that it is.

And his appearance, as the author has conceived it in his imagination, is as follows:

He is somewhat above the middle height, say five feet nine or ten, but he gives the impression of being somewhat shorter than that, because of the way he has been shaped and molded, and the way in which he carries himself. He walks with a slight stoop, and his head, which is carried somewhat forward, with a thrusting movement, is set down solidly upon a short neck between shoulders which, in comparison with the lower part of his figure, and his thighs and legs, are extremely large and heavy. He is barrel-chested, and perhaps the most extraordinary feature of his makeup which accounts for the nickname he has had since childhood—the boys, of course, call him "Monk"—are the arms and hands: the arms are unusually long, and the hands, as well as the feet, are very big with long spatulate fingers which curve naturally and deeply in like paws. The effect of this inordinate length of arms and hands, which dangle almost to the knees, together with the stooped and heavy shoulders, and the out-thrust head, is to give the whole figure a somewhat prowling and half-crouching posture.

Finally, the features, the face, are small, compact, and somewhat pug-nosed, the eyes set very deep in beneath heavy brows, the forehead is rather low, and the hair begins not far above the brows. The total effect of this, particularly when he is listening or talking to someone, the body prowling downward, the head thrust forward and turned upward with a kind of packed attentiveness, made the Simian analogy inevitable in his childhood; therefore the name of "Monk" has stuck.

In addition to this, it has never occurred to him, apparently, to get his figure clothed in garments suited to his real proportions: he apparently has walked into a store somewhere and picked up and worn out the first thing he could get on. In this way, a way of which he is not wholly conscious, the element of the grotesque is exaggerated.

The truth of the matter is, he is not really grotesque at all: that is to say, his dimensions, while unusual and a little startling at first sight, are in no sense of the word abnormal. He is not in any way a freak of nature, although some people might think so: he is simply a creature with big hands and feet, extremely long arms, a trunk somewhat too large and heavy, the legs and features perhaps somewhat too small and compact for the big shoulders that support them. Since he has added to this rather awkward but not distorted figure, certain unconscious tricks and mannerisms of his own, such as his habit of carrying his head thrust forward, and peering upward when he is listening or talking, it is not surprising if the impression he first makes should sometimes arouse laughter and surprise. Certainly he knows of this, and he has sometimes furiously and bitterly resented it; but he has never inquired sufficiently or objectively enough into the reasons for it.

The truth of the matter is that although he has a very intense and apprehensive eye for the appearance of things, he does not have an intense and apprehensive eye for his own appearance: in fact, the absorption of his interest and attention in the world around him is so passionate and eager that it rarely occurs to him what kind of figure and appearance he is himself making. In other words, he does not realize the kind of effect he has on people, and when, as sometimes happens, it is rudely and brutally forced upon his attention, it throws him into a state of furious anger. He is young: and he has not learned the wisdom and tolerant understanding of experience and maturity. In short, he does not see that these things are accidental and of no great consequence—that personal beauty is probably no very great virtue in a man anyway; and that this envelope of flesh and blood in which a spirit happens to be sheathed, has been a very loyal and enduring, even though an ugly, friend.

THE STORY

The Story Begins With a Prologue

Prologue

The prologue as the author now sees it is to be called "The Hound of Darkness"—and states [1] the setting. The setting is America. This is followed with "Old Catawba," a description of the place from which the protagonist comes.

This was followed originally by The Doaksology: a satiric genealogy of the great Doaks family since the earliest times.[2] If the name Doaks is changed, perhaps the genealogy could still be used. Then follows

[1] This was the first chapter, now entitled "The Quick and the Dead" of "The Hills Beyond," which appears on pages 201–210 in the book of that name.

[2] Wolfe first wrote "The Doaksology" in 1936–37, and was rewriting it and changing the name Doaks to Joyner just before he started on his trip west in May, 1938. It is not included in *The Web and the Rock* but appears as chapters 2–6 of "The Hills Beyond" in the book of that title.

an account of the town of Libya Hill: how it got its name from the first Joyner who settled there, the connection of the Joyners with the family of the protagonist: a description of Libya Hill and the people there. All of this save the part about Libya Hill has been completely written. The Libya parts are incomplete.

THE DIRECT NARRATIVE

To Be Called
The Station or
The one and The Many or
The Pebble and The Pool.

The direct narrative begins with the pebble (the protagonist) rolling home. The chapter bears the title of "The Station." Perhaps a better name for it would be "The Pebble and The Pool." Another, and perhaps the best of all, would be "The One and The Many." For the purpose of this beginning—this setting—is to show the tremendous and nameless Allness of The Station—ten thousand men and women constantly arriving and departing, each unknown to the other, but sparked with the special fire of his own destination, the unknown town, the small hand's breadth of earth somewhere out upon the vast body of the continent— all caught together for a moment, interfused and weaving, not lives but life, caught up, subsumed beneath the great roof of the mighty Station, the vast murmur of these voices drowsily caught up there like the murmurous and incessant sound of time and of eternity, which is and is forever, no matter what men come and go through the portals of the great Station, no matter what men live or die.[3]

And our protagonist is introduced: he is here among them, the one and the many, the pebble and the pool.

From here on, Wolfe began writing not only the synopsis of his book but portions of the book itself: the scenes in car K 19 which appear in Chapter V of You Can't Go Home Again. *Since this portion of the letter is really not a letter at all, but an already-published section of his book, it is omitted here.*

Arthur Mann, the sports writer, had taken Wolfe to the 15th Annual Dinner of the New York Chapter of the Baseball Writers Association of America at the Commodore Hotel on January 30, 1938, and had now invited him to spend Washington's Birthday at his home in Cherry Plain, N.Y. The following was Wolfe's reply.

[3] This material appears on pages 48–51 of *You Can't Go Home Again*, in Chapter V which is entitled "The Hidden Terror."

To ARTHUR MANN

114 East 56th Street
New York, New York
c/o Miss Elizabeth Nowell
February 16, 1938

Dear Arthur:

I really have been intending to write you day by day, but now your long letter has arrived to make my protestations look a little phoney. But I have been wrestling with the law, with law courts, and with another guy who is trying to indulge in the grand old national pastime of shaking-down—in my own case of being shook—and I just got through with it a few days ago. At least I hope to God I am through with it. My lawyers assured me it was a famous victory, and the newspapers said I had won: I do not know how I will feel about it when I see the lawyer's bill.

Some people tell me that life is too short to waste one's time and energy in bickering with the courts, and my own experience of the last three years has certainly been a very costly one in both time and money. But there are times when you simply have to fight, just to protect yourself, this was one of them: the case involving a little fellow who had walked off with some of my manuscripts a year ago, sold some of them and pocketed the money, and refused to return the rest: in addition, he had mixed the whole thing up charmingly with blackmail, threatening my first set of lawyers—for be it known by all these present, I have lawyers in sets, squadrons and platoons representing me in all the American states—that if I carried the case to court he would make public certain vile and obscene and unmentionable words with the avowed object of—or—ruining me.

All of this made me yawn long and loudly when I heard it, but my first set of lawyers, whose reading experience apparently ended with the works of the late Bulwer-Lytton, and who had never heard of such word-users as Joyce, Hemingway, Faulkner, etc.—were undone: they paled at the news, and sent me a hurry-up call to New Orleans to return at once, that our affairs were teetering on the brink of ruin, etc. The result was that I had to pay them off for their own ineptitude—and I find that misrepresentation in the law costs just as much as being represented. I managed to get another lawyer who is not intimidated by the threats of a naughty little boy, and the other day we went to town.

The court instructed him to return all the manuscript which he still had, to pay me in full, without commission, the money he had received for all the manuscripts he had sold unlawfully—you can figure for yourself what a fat chance I have of getting this—and further denied all of his claims for being an agent and of being due the huge sum—two thousand dollars or so—which he said was coming to him in agent's commissions.

It was a fine proceeding: the fellow cut his own throat every time he opened his mouth—and what he did not do for himself, his lawyer completed for him. When the Judge asked him for an accounting of the manuscript, for example, he testified that he had burned some of it because of its "filthy and obscene character." When the Judge asked him if he had my letter dismissing him as agent, he said he had, but that he had not brought it to court because he was holding it in order to sell the autograph. It was an astounding proceeding. . . .

When people ask me how I got into a mess like this, I confess I do not clearly know the answer. I suppose I should have been more careful, but it is so easy to point out one's mistakes after the mistake is evident. All these experiences of the last three years, for this has only been one of a whole Pandora's box of troubles, have made me think of a lot of things concerning a man's relation with the world and of people he knows in a way I never thought about them before.

The lawyer will tell you to let this be a lesson to you, not to enter into casual and genial conversations with people you meet in elevators, barrooms, observation cars, etc., and never to have anything to do even with your own blood brother in a business way unless you have the whole thing drawn up in a contract and gone over by a lawyer in advance. And the cynic will tell you that it ought to be a lesson to you because it ought to teach you that everyone is out to do you, that life is really just a vast and complicated system of Gyp, that the sooner you place this hardboiled information in your hat, the better it will be for you.

I think that both of them are wrong: of the two evils I think it is better to be gypped than to go through life with your fangs bared in a snarl; and I would rather remain the present incomplete work of nature that I am than go to dinner at my friend's house with a dictaphone concealed in my vest pocket, my attorney in the right hand, and a court stenographer in the left. Maybe everything that happened would then be according to Hoyle, but somehow I believe I would fail to meet a lot of interesting people.

This whole experience of the last three years—ever since "Of Time and the River" came out . . . has been a painful but an interesting one. I do not know what the hell it has to do with writing, but something tells me it might have a great deal to do with it: I now see that the late

Charles Dickens by no means exhausted the subject in his observations on the law and on the courts—I think we could teach him a few new tricks nowadays that would make him rub his eyes—down below, of course, the old, old business of delay, technicality, charge and counter charge, the weaving of that unreal spider's web that is the law, goes on as it has gone on since the beginning of history.

You learn some pretty sad things about people—one is, how many people there are who say they are your friends cannot be depended on when a question of profit is involved. . . . It makes you wonder about people—maybe there is something in what the Communists say about the profit motive corrupting life. Anyway, I am out of the woods—of this kind of woods—for the first time in three years—and I am knocking on wood as I make this proud boast.

I cannot tell you how much I enjoyed the Baseball Writers' Dinner, and how much I think I got out of it. Not that I learned so much, but I think there was a big value in verification—in seeing the animal at first hand, and in communication with his fellows. The point is, one of the characters in this immense long book that I am writing is a baseball player,[1] and I realize from past observation how easy it is for a writer to go wrong when writing about a professional athlete: the sporting writer, or the writer of baseball fiction, does it best of all, I think, because they put him in a certain limited setting—on the field, or on the bench, or at the training camp. My problem is a different one: I think I may have told you that one reason I have always loved baseball so much is that it has been not merely "the great national game," but really a part of the whole weather of our lives, of the thing that is our own, of the whole fabric, the million memories of America. For example, in the memory of almost every one of us, is there anything that can evoke spring—the first fine days of April—better than the sound of the ball smacking into the pocket of the big mitt, the sound of the bat as it hits the horse hide: for me, at any rate, and I am being literal and not rhetorical—almost everything I know about spring is in it—the first leaf, the jonquil, the maple tree, the smell of grass upon your hands and knees, the coming into flower of April. And is there anything that can tell more about an American summer than, say, the smell of the wooden bleachers in a small town baseball park, that resinous, sultry and exciting smell of old dry wood.

Well, I could go on indefinitely: the point is that one of the characters is out of this weather, from this setting: he becomes a Big League player, but it is of this kind of man—strong, simple, full of earth and sun, and his life in relation to other lives that I want to write: I have got the man,

[1] Nebraska Crane.

I knew him as a child—he never made the Big League, but he could have. I mean, he would have looked real in a Big League uniform because, as I saw at the dinner, it was from just such fellows that the Big League players come. And I am not making the mistake of trying to write about him too professionally—too technically in relation to his merits as a player—I am simply trying to write about him as a living man.

Now after this unexpected deluge, about your invitation. Your description of the mad abundance has me hanging on the ropes. I would take up your invitation like a shot, here and now, if it were not for this overwhelming necessity of work. I not only feel that I ought to work now, but after all these thwarting delays of law and lawsuits, I want to work: at the present time I am trying to get done a long and very detailed synopsis of the book; and I have also been working on a piece telling what I have seen of Fascism not only in Germany, but in this country, which I think may be good, and which I want to try and get published somewhere.

At any rate, my plan for the immediate future is just to keep at it. I do not believe I can get up there for Washington's Birthday, but if you will give me a raincheck I would certainly like to know that I can come up later. Anyway, that is the way I am going to feel about it until you tell me differently.

I probably would not get much work done if I came up, nor would I try to. I suppose you are one of those fortunate people who have found out that you can work anywhere. I think I can too, except with me it takes time; that is, I like to settle into a place of my own, get used to the idea of staying there and working there. And right now for the present, while the spirit is willing, I think I had better go to it with all my might. Maybe, after getting rid of the weary burden of all these lawsuits I feel like the fellow with the toothache who said to the man who stepped on his corns in the subway train: "Do it again, it feels good."

It was grand meeting you and getting to know you, Arthur, and I guess the reason you are now the victim of this torrential deluge is that I hope to continue and proceed from where we left off. I certainly do hope to see you soon, either here or on your own acres. Meanwhile, with thanks and best wishes to you and all the family,

On February 15, Charles Scribner had written to Wolfe: "I am willing to allow your obligation on the suit we had to run along for the time being, although it is not customary to carry such accounts for an author for whom you are no longer acting as publisher, and our contract which is similar to that of other publishers and agents, calls for a settlement on the part of the author for any suits of this kind which may be brought." Wolfe's reply was as follows.

To CHARLES SCRIBNER

114 East 56th Street
New York, New York
c/o Miss Elizabeth Nowell
February 18, 1938

Dear Charlie:

I don't want to inconvenience you a bit, and if you say the deficit has got to be paid now I will pay it. My only point was that since my books made almost twenty-three hundred dollars last year, according to the royalty statement you sent along with the letter, I therefore felt they would naturally be expected to make good the eight hundred dollar deficit within a reasonable time.

I notice that you refer in your last letter to the deficit as an "obligation on the suit." Well, I am not going to argue with you about the suit. I never have. I told you last year how I felt, and I still feel the same way. I am sorry as hell that you got involved in it through something I had written which you published. But as you know and I know, and as the lawyers knew, I did not libel anyone.

You say in your letter you hope I do not have any more libel suits, and I second the motion with all my might. But I do not know what you or I or any man can do about people suing you. It is a racket, a part of a great organized national industry of shaking-down—in my case, of being shook—and you and I and every other decent citizen ought to do everything we can to stop it. And the only way to stop it is to fight it, because it lives by threat and flourishes on submission. As long as we submit it will continue to flourish.

I think that when a writer willfully, deliberately and maliciously writes something for the purpose of insulting and injuring a living person, or a dead one for that matter, he ought to be punished for it. But I do not think he ought to be punished for being honest and decent and doing his work, and having been unfortunate enough, maybe, to attract some public notice and get his name in the press. And you know that is what happened. You are yourself an honest and a decent man, and you know as well as I do that it was a shake-down. I am not going to harp upon it any more, but you have mentioned the thing several times in your letters, and I have got to tell you what I told you a year ago. I think we should have fought it out.

I want you to know, and I am sure you do know, that there is not an ounce of resentment in my heart, and that particular thing is all over now. But we should have fought it out. I do not think it is sticking to the real point to talk about publishers' contracts, and what the clause of the contract says concerning libel suits, and who is to be responsible for them. The point is, it seems to me, that a publisher ought to stick to a writer and fight with him when he knows that that writer is loyal and honest, has injured no one in his writing, and is being unfairly taken advantage of, and, believe me, Charlie, I am not saying this because I have any rankling memory of the past. I just hope that I will profit by the experience, and I also hope that in the future publishers and writers will stick together and fight for each other in matters of this sort. For, as any decent person knows, that is the only thing to do. When you publish a man, when you put the imprint of your name upon a man's book, you are for him, and not against him. I think you have always been for me, and what is more, I think you always will be, no matter who is my publisher. But I think that in that particular matter we were wrong in not fighting it, and furthermore I think we were licked before we started, because our lawyers cost so much that we were practically forced to settle to protect ourselves against our own lawyers' bill if we went on. Frankly, so far as I can see we would have done as well if we had had Abie Glickstein and paid him fifty bucks. In the end, the three floors of office space . . . the magnificent private offices, regiments of slick-looking assistants, etchings of Abraham Lincoln, etc., did not mean a damn thing except trouble and money: it was a sorry job.

I know you took it on the chin on account of something that I wrote, but Charlie, all that suit proved to me was that a man might write "The cat has whiskers" and then get sued for libel by an old maid in Keokuk. I am sorry as all hell you had to be involved, but I still think we should have fought it out. You took it on the chin to the extent of about three thousand bucks, but so did I—and maybe you have got some idea of how much three thousand bucks is in my young life. It is just about ten per cent of all the money I ever earned from the beginning out of writing. Those facts are correct, and people tell me I am a well-known writer.

So the only reason I am harping on it is not because I have got an atom of soreness or resentment in me: you did what you thought was right, but I am only saying that if guys like you and me do not stick together and fight it out sometimes when people try to shake us down, it is not only going to be too bad for writers, but too bad for publishers too. And that is that. I have spoken my little piece and I know you will take my word for it, I am not sore: I am your friend.

And now about the eight hundred dollar deficit: if you say I have got to pay it now, I will pay it. But honestly I do not think you are running much of a risk in letting it run on, in view of the fact that the work of mine which you publish earned almost three times that much last year. But if you do feel that it ought to be paid now, it seems to me that a simple and decent arrangement of the matter would be one in which we square the whole account, and you relinquish to me the rights of my books which you publish.

Frankly, I think you ought to do it. They are my books, they belong to me because I created them and because they mean something to me they cannot mean to anyone else. I would like to see you and talk to you about this, and I think we could reach an agreement that would be satisfactory to both of us, and which would clear the whole situation up in such a way that the deficit would not only be wiped out, but you would also be relieved of all the risks and responsibilities attendant on suits, publication, and keeping the books in print.

And now that is all in a business way, but I am sorry to have to protract the discussion of a matter which must already have grown tedious to you. For my own part I can only repeat what you said to me in your fine letter of Christmas, when you heard that I had definitely gone with another house—it has always seemed to me that there has been something more between us than a business connection, and, as you say, friendship is considerably more important.

I know that you will always hope for my success, and that if my next book is a good one there will be no one in the world more genuinely pleased about it than you. For that reason, I am grateful for the kind inquiry you make in your last letter about the progress I am making. I see no reason, now that the legal difficulties which have beset my life for the last three years have been settled, [why] I should not get ahead with my work very rapidly. I have collected an immense amount of material and done an immense amount of writing, and the scheme and pattern of the book is all clear. An immense labor still remains to be done, but I believe it is worth doing, and naturally I hope that the result will be one that all of us can be proud of.

I know there may be some pretty dark times ahead, times when I may almost lose hope, but when I do I shall always remember the letter you wrote a year ago, when you told me that I was free to go if I liked, but that whatever happened you would be my friend, and you expected me to go and grow and prosper in my work, as time went on. Naturally, I can only hope that you are right, and the knowledge that you feel that way will always be a source of comfort and inspiration to me. I still have that letter and shall always treasure it as a token that no matter who publishes me, or what business connections I form, I shall always have your friendship. And I still hope that some night when you have nothing else to do, and feel like having a drink, you will call me up. Meanwhile, with all good wishes to you all,

> *In his reply of February 24, 1938, to this letter, Charles Scribner said: "I told you not once but several times that I was perfectly prepared to go ahead with you in fighting out the libel suit, if that was what you wished to do. The lawyer advised that the cheapest and safest way was to settle, and personally I was inclined to agree with him, . . . but I distinctly left the final decision to you. . . .*
>
> *"I would also like to say a word on the other point you raise with regard to our giving up to you the publishing rights on your books. I do not believe that you have thought through the whole of the partnership relationship which you say should exist between author and publisher. . . . When the libel suit came up, we waived at once our contract rights as publishers to dump the entire cost of the suit and any damages that might result on you as the author, and agreed to go into it fifty-fifty, as we felt we had entered a more or less permanent relationship. . . . With regard to the books published, it is true that they are your creation, but we made a mutual agreement to invest our money as publishers in making the plates, printing them and selling them, your share being the royalty we agreed to pay on sales, and our share being any profit we might realize after our investment was met. . . . We like your books and are proud to have them on our list, and . . . we have a right to . . . make our share of the profit from their sale. We do not wish to sell our rights, but if this should come about, it would then be up to any publisher who might take them over to buy out our rights, and they would have to pay a damn high price, as I have every faith that they will go on selling for years. . . ."*

To WALTER WINCHELL

114 East 56th Street
New York, New York
c/o Miss Elizabeth Nowell

February 21, 1938.

Dear Mr. Winchell:

In your column "On Broadway" in *The Daily Mirror* for Monday, February 21, you state: "Thomas Wolfe, the novelist, is at war with

Scribners and Harcourt, Brace—both of whom rejected his new book."

This statement is wholly incorrect: my new book is not finished, Scribners did not reject it, Harcourt, Brace did not reject it, and no publisher has ever seen the manuscript. Your statement is injurious and I ask you to correct it.

In his column in The Daily Mirror *for February 25, 1938, Winchell said:* ". . . Thomas Wolfe, the book writer, called. Said his manuscript isn't finished so how could it be rejected?"

To MARGARET ROBERTS

114 East 56th Street
New York, New York
c/o Miss Elizabeth Nowell

March 7, 1938

Dear Mrs. Roberts:

Your letter is full of good news, except, of course, poor —— ——.[1] I felt, of course, last summer that there was something wrong; and yet, I liked him. He seemed to have a genuinely good heart and good feeling. I do hope he can be cured. I wonder what is wrong with the set-up, anyhow. I suppose Asheville is no worse than other communities in this respect, and that the average of catastrophe is no higher there than anywhere else. And yet, that was one of the most disturbing revelations that I got last summer, going back as I did after an absence of eight years and with the sharp and fresh impressions that such absence gives to one. It seemed as if the whole landscape was strewn with the shipwrecks of people I had known: I inquired about person after person only to be told that they were at Dix Hill, or had just returned; or at Morganton,[2] or that they had gone completely to pieces through drugs or drink, or a combination of both. And looking back over my childhood and early youth in Asheville, it often seems to me now that the people who went down, who became these shipwrecks, were not the worthless litter of humanity, but often the best, the brightest, and the most intelligent we had.

It occurred to me that if such things happen to such people there must be something wrong with the background that produced them, something in the life around them that did not give them enough to employ their talents or waken the deepest interest in their lives. Am I wrong about this? I want to keep a clear perspective, and I think the answer

[1] An Asheville man who had gone insane.

[2] Dix Hill and Morganton are North Carolina state hospitals for the insane.

may be that my own life in so many special and intimate ways is bound up with the life of Asheville. I know so many people there—in a sense, when I go home, I inherit the life of the whole community.

Here, in this vast city, it is, of course, different: the number of people that one knows or can know is relatively small. I know that one can find every kind of human wreckage here, because I have seen it myself, but it does seem to me, among most of the people that I know best, such catastrophe does not happen with the appalling frequency it does at home. The big wicked city that one hears so much about is also a very busy and hard-working place. It would be ironic, wouldn't it, if one eventually discovered that he had come here to keep out of mischief?

Anyway, the whole problem to my mind is a pretty serious one: if there is anything in it, I would like to find out why—it seems to me that that, too, is a legitimate subject for fiction. For example, often when I have heard the learned economists talk about the boom—how and when it began, how it got going, why it collapsed, what was fundamentally wrong about it—I have kept silent, because there were so many human and spiritual things about it as well that never get mentioned. I think that one of these things—remembering my own childhood—is a deep and intense hunger in people for "something to happen"—waiting for something, they are not sure what, but something that is full of excitement, movement, color, sudden wealth.

Whatever use I make of anything you or Mr. Roberts or Jack Westall give me, I assure you it will be the best and most serious use. It is going to be a tremendous labor, but when I am done with it—at any rate, when I have set it down—I shall not only be delighted but I shall appreciate it if you will look it over to find out if I have done the job. I've bitten off a tremendous hunk to chew on this time—maybe more than I can—but as you say, we shall see. . . . The book covers a tremendous panoramic sweep of places, people, events, and times—I may be a doddering old man before I am done with it, but meanwhile I am giving it everything I have. So everything you do, together with all the trouble and labor I know this entails, is deeply and genuinely appreciated.

I don't know whether I shall come home this summer. If I do it will only be for a short visit. I have to work now at the top of my bent, and last summer I found out that one's home town is not always the best place to do it. But I can't tell you what a tremendous experience that was. I'd like to tell you all about it some day, for in a way I think it may have been one of the great turning points in my life. It crystallized a feeling, a conviction, a discovery that I had been slowly coming to for years. And I suppose that discovery and conviction might be best summarized by these words: "You can't go home again". . . .

That trip to Asheville crystallized that discovery, and I believe was one of the most important things that ever happened to me. For years, I had thought about my long absence from Asheville; I felt a sense of exile until it began to eat on me, haunt me in dreams. It became so oppressive and overwhelming that that return was inevitable—and it was a cleansing flood. I know you won't misunderstand me: I was more deeply touched and moved than I can tell you over the overwhelming reception I received, the great kindness and friendliness and interest of almost everyone I saw. And it is comforting to know that whenever I want to I can go back to my own town, and find friends there who will be glad to see me.

But my discovery that "you can't go home again" went a whole lot deeper than this: it went down to the very roots of my life and spirit— it has been a hard and at times terrifying discovery because it amounts to an entire revision almost of belief and of knowledge; it was like death almost, because it meant saying farewell to so many things, to so many ideas and images and hopes and illusions that we think we can't live without. But the point is, I have come through it now, and I am not desolate or lost. On the contrary, I am more full of faith and hope and courage than I have been in years. I suppose what I am trying to tell you here is a spiritual conviction that will inform the whole book—you could almost call that book, "You Can't Go Home Again," although I don't think I shall call it that. But I do want you to understand that it is not a *hopeless* book, but a triumphantly *hopeful* one. I've tried to tell you a little about it now, and I hope you see something of what I have in mind. Like you, like Mr. Roberts, like the late Mr. Shakespeare, I, too, believe in the brave new world, and I hope now that I am on the way to find it.

Meanwhile, until I hear from you again, with all good wishes to you and Mr. Roberts,

P.S. . . . I live here in a very old Victorian style hotel with enormous rooms and lots of other strange critters like myself. Mr. Edgar Lee Masters also lives here and has for years. I see him from time to time; in fact, he set me up to a glass of beer yesterday afternoon—but for the most part I just work.

I wish you'd tell me how to sleep as you used to. It is not a question of health, it is just a plain damn question of writing—and that is a plain damn question. I work every day from about ten in the morning until about six at night, but after that I can't stop thinking about it: it goes rumbling and roaring around in my head, or what serves me for a head. The result is there is usually no sleep until long after midnight. I don't know what to do about all this, it has always been the same—at least every time I start to work. The only satisfaction I get from it is the rather gloomy one that I must be really at work again. I don't think, otherwise, it means an early catastrophe. As "The Tempest" says, "His complexion is perfect for hanging." I may be wrong, but something tells me my time is not yet. And now good-bye.

To MABEL WOLFE WHEATON

> 114 East 56th Street
> New York, New York.
> c/o Miss Elizabeth Nowell.
>
> March 19, 1938

Dear Mabel:

I was glad to get your letter and very interested in all the news it contained. I am very sorry to hear Ralph has not been well and that you have not been up to scratch yourself. I think the worry and the nervous strain attendant on this trial [1] and in having to do with lawyers and the courts may have something to do with it. I speak as one who has also been through the mill again and again during the past three years. Lawyers and court rooms are bad business: they take it out of you like nothing else, and in the end I do not know who wins. . . .

I was very much interested to hear what you had to say about the trial. I hope you succeed in keeping the bank from confiscating what remains of Mama's property, and in compelling them to make some restitution to the heirs. I want you to know also that I am with you heart and soul in your effort and desire to save something for the family, and if I am able to help I want to.

But now, since the family is involved in this legal dispute and certain things are going on record in the courts, I want to go on record personally with you and the family. That means that I am going to have to say some things that we all know about pretty bluntly. It may not be pleasant while it lasts, but there has been too much self-deception and evasion and rationalizing which makes for misunderstanding in the end. So believe me, it is better to get the whole thing straight now, once and for all, so that there can be no misunderstanding in the future. And I believe there is no need telling you that there is not an ounce of resentment in me over anything that ever happened, nothing but genuine good will and a desire to help and stand by all of you.

As far as I am concerned, what is past is past: if I ever had any grievance, real or imagined, at any time, or ever thought that in any way I had a tough time as a kid, that is all over now. It is all washed up, I got

---

[1] The case brought by the Asheville Wachovia Bank and Trust against Mrs. Wolfe and her heirs.

it off my chest, and whatever things I may ever have said about it in anger or in hurt that were unfair, I am sorry for. I am sorry for some things I may have said in my first book: they were written in the heat of creation and of youth, and some of them may have been exaggerated and unfair. And I am sorry for some of the things that were said at home and that came back to me, and that I heard last summer. But that is all over, too. I think the intention of everyone was at the bottom good: as far as I am concerned, it has been wiped off the slate. Now, I want to get off to a fresh clean start with everyone, and it seems to me that the best way to do it is to start off by us all being straight with one another, and not by continuing to tell a lot of old fairy tales.

When I was a kid, I was forever having it hammered into my head and pounded into my ears about how good and great and noble and self-sacrificing somebody was and what a selfish little brute I was myself. That kind of bunk used to get me down as a kid, and I guess it got me sore later on. But I am not down and I am not sore any more. I do not think I was a selfish little brute, I think I was a decent little kid, and I have tried to be decent ever since. And I do not think there was anything particularly great or noble or self-sacrificing or unselfish about anyone except insofar as we were all members of the human race, and in the bottom of my heart I have always thought we were, on the whole, pretty decent ones and pretty good ones. I think that now just as much as I ever did.

But let us not go on with the old blarney. Nobody stayed at home and made sacrifices because of some great self-sacrificing loyalty and devotion to the family, or to Mama, or to someone else. They stayed home because they wanted to stay home and could not be happy anywhere else. And I am also tired of being told that I was the "lucky one" because I "got away." I did no such thing. I got away because I had to get away, there was no place for me at home, which is the simple brutal truth. As for being lucky, I have lived alone and fought my way alone for fifteen years, and if anyone thinks that is being lucky they are invited with my permission to try it, and see how it fits.

As to the present situation, it is a little surprising now to be assured that I got nothing when I used to have it pounded into me all the time that I was getting everything—God knows why—when everyone else was getting nothing. The truth of the matter seems to be that I got about as much as everyone else, and I have no complaint to make. I do not like to dig into an old sore which is certainly as painful to me as it could be to anyone, but I have a good memory and I remember what happened right after Papa's death in 1922, and almost, it seems to me, before he was buried—the bitterness and the suspicions and the recriminations and who had had the most and who should have it.

It is all over now, and I for one want to forget it, and I hope to God it is over forever, and never comes to life again, for of all the forms of human ugliness, money-ugliness is the most hateful and most damnable, and when it gets into families, there is hell to pay. The way I feel now, I would sooner have someone I thought was my friend betray me because of envy, jealousy, hatred, a desire to get revenge, or because he was in love with my girl, than sell me out for a few dirty dollars. You can get over the other things and still retain your faith in life, because at least what was done was done in human passion—but when they do a job on you because of money you feel like turning your face to the wall and admitting you have seen enough.

And that is the reason that I do not like it when the question of money comes up, and I want to go on record now about the future. I did not get more than my share in 1922, neither did I ever consider that I got less: I was not a martyr then and I am not a martyr now. I always considered that I got the equivalent of my five thousand dollars in the three years I went to Harvard: I signed a paper to that effect and gave it to Fred and Ralph right after Papa's death, I believe. So let us keep that straight. As to anything that may come out of this trial, or that you may recover, I do not expect anything, and if there is anything, I would like to see it applied first of all to Mama's support, then to helping you and Ralph, then to helping Effie and her children.

As to my own presence and testimony being of any help to you now, as you suggest, I am certainly willing to help you if I can, but I do not see what there is that I can do. I was never asked to take any part in the matter fifteen years or more ago. As far as Papa's will is concerned, I never saw it, I do not know what is in it. Fred and Ralph were appointed executors of the estate, which it seems to me was bad, for I think in a matter where emotion and personal feeling are involved, as they were in this case, members of the family should not be given such authority; and furthermore, I think it should never be given to members of a family like ours where, so far as I have been able to see, there is not a grain of business ability, except an almost unfailing instinct for doing the wrong thing. These are stern words, but you have got to admit that in view of everything that has happened, they are deserved: and I am saying them now because I wish for nothing but your success and the family's success in this trial, and because I hope to God that if anything comes of it and you recover anything, you will salt it down somewhere where the first plausible crook who comes along with a get-rich-quick scheme, or a project for making all of you fabulously rich by selling you Florida real estate, will not get it away from you. . . .

I am back at work again—this is the first time in almost three years when I have been left uninterrupted to do my work. I got no rest at home last summer, I have had none since then, in fact, I cannot remember when I did have any rest to amount to anything in the last six or eight years. But if I can go on and get my work done, all will be well. I had to pay my income tax the other day which is a joke—the income, not the tax. Scribners returned a report to the government that they had paid out to me in royalties, etc., something over three thousand dollars last year. They did not mention the fact, however, that I never saw a penny of this sum—that all of it was used up in the form of lawyer fees and payments in a suit which we should have fought, but which they were eager to settle. I suppose our lawyers in the bank case are working on a contingent basis: if they are, I hope you find out in advance how great the contingency is, and how big a portion they propose to take.

This is all now. I hope this finds you and Ralph feeling better, and the rest of the family well. Aside from being tired, I think I am all right. My new book is all clear in my mind, I know what it is all about from beginning to end, and in the last two years I have done a lot of writing on it. I work like hell, drive myself to the point of exhaustion, but of course I am a long-winded cuss and I write hundreds of thousands of words that I never use, and go through hell before I get through. But I will get through somehow, never fear. I do not think my time has come yet, maybe I'm being saved for cannon fodder when the Fascists try to take America, which is where I'll grab a musket and go to town; but I believe I will be able to hang on until this job is done. . . .

I hope this finds Mama well, and I send love and best wishes for success to all of you. Please let me know if there is anything you want me to do.

Frieda Kirchwey, editor of The Nation, *had written to Wolfe and various other authors, asking for statements as to "How to Keep Out of War." The following is Wolfe's reply which was published in the April 2, 1938, issue of* The Nation. *The covering letter, if there ever was one, has been lost.*

● To THE EDITOR OF *THE NATION*

[New York City]

[March 20(?), 1938]

Aside from the question whether even peace can be worth any price that we can pay or that can be demanded of us—a view which was seriously maintained by many people until a year or two ago—I do not think that peace can ever be won and kept in such a way. I further think that "isolation" is a rhetorical concept, useful to politicians for the purpose of strengthening the majorities at home and of reassuring their constituencies, and perhaps useful to other people who project the metaphysical idea that it is possible for a nation of one hundred and thirty million people to live scaled up hermetically in peace in a world that is ravaged by war. Beyond this, I do not believe "isolation" has any real meaning in fact, because it has no existence in reality. It is a King Canute–Christian Science kind of word, which says, there is no sickness, there is no death; or if there is, let us ignore them. The peace of the whole means the peace of every one of its parts; and the sickness of the whole means the sickness of its parts.

Because I believe in individual security, I believe in collective security, and do not think it is possible to have one without the other. And, in view of the events of the past two years, it seems manifest that the only way to get security is through collective action. And, although I hope, together with most other people, that the necessity for force may be avoided, it cannot be avoided by denying that such a necessity may exist. It becomes increasingly apparent that the only effective way to meet armed aggression may be armed resistance: the wheels of a great war machine, such as that which Germany has today, are not going to be stopped, once they have begun to roll, by a handful of reproving phrases, or by a batch of diplomatic protests. Just as the foundations of Fascism are rooted in the hopelessness and despair of a bankrupt and defeated people who, having nothing more to lose, submit to any promises of gain —this would have been apparent to anyone who visited Germany as I did in 1928 and 1930—so does the success and growth of Fascism depend upon submission, and flourish upon compromise and vacillation.

All these facts have been apparent for years, and should have surprised no one: the only thing that is surprising now is that anyone should be surprised. Where have these surprised people been living for the past ten years? If anyone ever furnished the world with a blueprint of his intentions in advance, it was Adolf Hitler. Now, since he has checked his announced objectives off the list one by one with the precision of a riveting machine, it seems reasonable to suppose that he will continue to do so as long as he is unimpeded and as long as he realizes that there is no formidable and united force that will, if necessary, resist him.

I do not know any more than any man what form that force will take, or what will be the composition and alignment of its elements, because at the present moment it does not exist; but it is evident that if Fascism is to be checked, such a force will have to exist. The failure of the major democratic powers thus far effectively to oppose the aggressions of Germany, Italy and Japan has not weakened my belief in the possibility of collective action and has not destroyed my faith in the power of the major democratic powers to act effectively. Sooner or later, it seems to me, they will have to. They will have to when they decide that democracy is valuable enough to be saved, and is worth fighting for, if need be, by those who believe in it. In the end, I think we may all have to make that decision. For Fascism is a creature that thrives but is not appeased by compromise.

To MARGARET ROBERTS

114 East 56th Street
New York, New York
c/o Miss Elizabeth Nowell

April 6, 1938

Dear Mrs. Roberts:

I was mighty glad to get your letter and sorry to know that you had been put to so much trouble and bother to get the material I asked for. I shall appreciate it all the more on account of the labor you have expended, and I can repeat my assurances that I shall take the greatest care of anything that is entrusted to me and see that it gets returned in good condition to its owner when I am done with it.

It is an immense undertaking that I have embarked on. A week or so ago I was so tired that I simply could not force myself another foot; so I went out in the country for several days, all of which did me a lot of good, but I have about reached the conclusion that when a man gives himself completely to a tremendous piece of work, there is just no such thing as rest, and he had better reconcile himself to it.

I saw an extraordinary Russian film the other night called "Lenin in October" which brought out that point very compellingly. In a scene where Lenin is in hiding in the furious days just preceding the Revolution, Lenin is pictured as saying to one of his associates who had been appointed to guard him and who had been on the job day and night without rest: "You ought to get some sleep." The man says that he will get some sleep after the Revolution. "After the Revolution," says Lenin, "we won't sleep at all." And maybe that is the way it has got to be.

It is curious how many hard and thorny things we find out about life, and how strangely palatable they become to us. It is all so different from what we imagined it was going to be when we were children, and curiously in so many ways it is so much better. I suppose like so many other boys, I pictured a future life of brilliant works crowned by success and fame and ease, and surcease from labor; but it does not work out that way at all. Work gets harder all the time because as one digs deeper one goes into the rock. And there is no rest—those periods of delightful relaxation as a kind of reward for work accomplished that I used to look forward to with such eagerness simply do not exist. Now I would say that almost the worst time in a writer's life are those periods between work— periods when he is too exhausted and feels too empty to attempt a new piece of work, or when a new piece of work is still cloudily formulating itself in his mind. It is really hell, or worse than hell, because writing itself is hell, and this period of waiting is limbo—floating around in the cloudy upper geographies of hell trying to get attached to something.

It just boils down to the fact that there is no rest, once the worm gets in and begins to feed upon the heart—there can never after that be rest, forgetfulness, or quiet sleep again. Somewhere long ago—God knows when, or at what fated moment in my childhood—the worm got in and has been feeding ever since and will be feeding till I die. After this happens, a man becomes a prisoner; there are times when he almost breaks free, but there is one link in the chain that always holds; there are times when he almost forgets, when he is with his friends, when he is reading a great book or a great poem, when he is at the theatre, or on a ship, or with a girl—but there is one tiny cell that still keeps working, working; even when he is asleep, one lamp that will not go out, that is forever lit.

It sounds pretty grim, but like so many other grim discoveries, it is not so grim once you recognize it, accept it, make up your mind to it. In fact, when I think of all the dreams I had as a boy—my idea of "happiness," "fame," and so on—I do not know that I would have them back again, even if I could recapture them; and as for this thing I used to call happiness, I am not so sure but that it, too, is a very hard and thorny thing, and not the smooth and palatable thing I thought it was. And I am perfectly sure that whatever it is, if it exists at all, it cannot exist without work—which would have been a strange doctrine indeed when I was twelve years old. As far as I am concerned, there is no life without work —at least, looking back over my own, everything I can remember of any value is somehow tied up with work.

What to do? Like you, I have become in the last few years tremendously involved with the state of the world—as my consciousness of life has enlarged, my consciousness of self has dwindled; there are things now that so afflict me in the state of man that I think I would take up arms against them, or give my life to stop them—but what to do? There is hardly a day goes by now but what people—for the most part, I think, sincere and genuine people—call me up or write me, and ask me to sign my name to a petition or proclamation of some sort, to go to Washington with a group to protest to the President about the state of things in Spain; to appear with a group at the French Consulate and protest to the French Consul about the state of things in Spain; to serve on committees of protest about the condition of the sharecroppers in the South— about the imprisonment of Tom Mooney—about the violation of civil liberties in various places—about the Scottsboro boys—about the Moscow trials—for or against the Stalinites or Trotskyites—but what to do, what to do?

To reject these pleas for help and demonstration often seems callously indifferent and self-centered, particularly when so many of them are about things with which my mind and conscience are now seriously involved; but in the name of God, what is a man like myself to do? The observation of Voltaire in *Candide* that at the end of all the best thing is for a man to tend his garden used to seem cynically and selfishly callous to me, but I am not so sure now that it does not contain much deep wisdom, and much humanity as well. Perhaps the best thing that a man can do is just to do the work he is able to do, and for which he is best fitted, as well as he can. And perhaps his greatest service to other men can be rendered in such a way as this.

I am solicited and persuaded on all sides now by worthy people to take sides and to make proclamations on all manner of things—there are so many writers and leagues of writers who are involved in all of this, but although I admire their energy and do not question their sincerity, I do not know when these writers write—or how they can possibly find time to write: one does not write books by carrying placards in front of the French Consulate, or having interviews with President Roosevelt. It is hard enough for me to get anything done anyway, because everything comes out with such a tremendous superflux, and calls for such infinite boiling down and rearrangement—but it seems to me the best course for me is to stick at it somehow, somehow by the grace of God to get it done, somehow to get it all wrought into a single and coherent vision of life, not just as a series of explosive and isolated protests.

I think I have ploughed to the bottom now as far as this present work is concerned. It has been going on for years and it has been hell because it involved, perhaps for the first time in my life, the creation of a whole universe of the imagination into which I could pour all the materials I had gathered. Now I think I have accomplished it, I have the whole thing launched and floated in my mind, and I believe I am the master of it: an enormous labor of completion and fulfillment is before me, but if I stick to it I shall get there. . . .

Just do the best you can for me about getting the material I asked you for, and I will try to deserve it by the use I make of it. . . . I suppose it is wise, as you say, to go about the business as discreetly as possible; but I do want to assure you again, and everyone else, that I have no intention of doing a job on Asheville. God knows, after what I have known and seen and lived through myself in the last few years, I am in no mood to exult and mock at the afflicted and tormented soul of man, particularly when it comes as close to home as this does. Time and again last summer I could have groaned in anguish at the things I saw: most pitiful and moving of all, perhaps, was the pretense—people with naked terror in their eyes still whistling to keep up their courage, still speaking the old words, the old spurious phrases that had lost whatever meaning they may once have had because they referred to something that was gone forever. And I think the people knew it. I could give you an account of a meeting of the Associated Civic Clubs at which I was present —a concerted effort or "drive," as it is called, to raise funds for a Convention Hall—it would be howlingly funny if it were not for the underlying tragedy and pathos of the situation.

There has been a good deal of talk about "the lost generation," meaning the young men who came up during and after the last war, but I wonder if the real lost generation is not these men of middle or advanced middle age, who keep saying the old phrases, trying to whoop it up in the old way over something that is gone forever. It made me think of a pep meeting in a morgue, a kind of cheering squad of ghosts. And, in the name of God, what are these men going to do? They have only one language, only one set of values: the language and the values were false to begin with, but now that they know that they were false, they have not even the conviction of their previous delusion to give them hope.

I am not lost because I accept and am ready to meet the future that is before us; but what are people to do when they cannot accept it, cannot face it, are looking forever backward at the image of a world that is gone? Do not think that I could be happy at the tragic spectacle, or take pleasure in flaying the hide off something that is already quivering and raw.

I wish I could come home quietly, as you suggest, and talk to some of the people you mention, but you know what happened last summer.

A prophet may be without honor in his own country, but he is also without privacy. I shall get out of town during the hot weather and go somewhere to work; but I simply cannot go through another summer like the
last one, as interesting and overwhelming as it was, particularly now that
I have plunged into this thing and must go on. . . .

Let me hear from you as soon as you are conveniently able. Meanwhile,
I send you and Mr. Roberts all my good wishes and best regards.

P.S. There is a popular song called "Roses in December"—well, someone
ought to write one now called "Snow in April." It is the sixth day of the
month, and as I look out my window at the present moment the whole
world—the roofs and buildings of New York—are white and blind with
snow. It looks like a blizzard, the first we have had in this nothing-of-a-
winter. April, April, laugh thy girlish laughter!

To BELINDA JELLIFFE

> 114 East 56th Street
> New York, New York
> c/o Miss Elizabeth Nowell
>
> April 11, 1938

Dear Mrs. Jelliffe:

I was delighted to read the wonderful review you sent me of your
book [1] from *The London Observer*. You should be very proud of it, and
since I feel I had some share in making possible the publication of your
book, I feel proud of this fine recognition, too.

I believe you are prone to overestimate the importance of those people
who, you say, are eagerly waiting to see what I shall do without Mr.
Perkins. I hope, indeed, that I shall never be without him; for I believe
he is genuinely my friend, and will continue to be, and certainly he would
himself, I think, be the first to regret such small and irresponsible talk.
He is not a man who would allow vanity or wounded pride to obscure
his sense of justice and fair play.

I do not know where such talk comes from, and do not believe there
can be very much of it. As you may know, I have been through the mill
for almost ten years now, and I am as familiar as anyone with all these
manifestations, and am not inclined to let them affect me as deeply as
they once did. Besides, the thing to which they refer is so completely
and sorrowfully over that it can never be brought to life again; and now,
since I have finally won through to a strength and repose that I have

---

[1] *For Dear Life.*

never had before, it can surely serve no good purpose on the part of those who count themselves my friends—and I know you are one of these—to attempt to revive them.

Therefore, since you yourself are so sure in your faith in me—a faith which I value—I hope you will not allow yourself to be troubled by such a report. As for myself, I should prefer not to listen to it, since I have so much else of deep importance to me now, and I know that you yourself wish only to join with my other friends in the hope that I will be allowed to proceed now to my accomplishment without further, and too often, ignoble interference.

For you, of course, and for your own work and accomplishment, I wish you now what I have wished you from the beginning, when I brought you and your manuscript to your present fine publisher [2]—only the highest and the best that you yourself could wish.

With all good wishes,

[2] Scribners.

XVIII

THE TRIP WEST AND FINAL ILLNESS

1938

On March 31, 1938, Professor S. A. Cummings of the Department of English at Purdue University had wired Wolfe, asking him to speak at the Literary Banquet to be held at that university on May 19. Wolfe had accepted, and had then received a letter from Professor Herbert J. Muller, also of the Department of English at Purdue, inviting him to stay at his house while he was there. The following was his reply.

Professor Muller is still in the English Department at Purdue and is the author of Thomas Wolfe *in the* Makers of Modern Literature *series; also of* Modern Fiction: A Study in Values; Science and Criticism; *and other books.*

To HERBERT J. MULLER

Hotel Chelsea
222 West 23rd Street
New York, New York

April 11, 1938

Dear Professor Muller:

Thanks very much for your letter and kind invitation to stay with you and your wife while I am at Purdue.

I have had a telegram from Mr. S. A. Cummings confirming our agreement, and he said also that he was writing me. Thus far I have not had his letter, but I suppose when he writes he will explain to me more fully just what the nature of the University occasion is, and what I should prepare for. I sent him quite a long telegram expressing my interest and my appreciation in his invitation, and I also asked him if he would not let me know more fully what he had in mind. I explained to him that I was hard at work on a new book and that I would not, therefore, be able to take time off now for the preparation of a formal speech. But I also tried to explain that I thought what I had to say might be more interesting if I talked informally, and out of my own working and writing experience. That is really what I have in mind. Since my present life is largely writing—for even when I am not actually engaged on it, I am thinking about it—it seems to me that anything I had to say might be more interesting if I drew it out of my own experience, and from the work I do. I should deeply appreciate it if you could write me and let me know your own opinion on this, and give me what advice you can, and tell me what I can expect when I get there.

It is most kind and generous of you to offer me the hospitality of your home while I am at Lafayette, and I hope you can hold the offer open; but I should prefer not to answer definitely now until I hear from Mr. Cummings, or until I find out how long I shall be there. I am looking forward to my trip with great interest and expectation. I have been pretty steadily at work, and shall continue to be until I leave for Lafayette, and the break in routine will not only be a most welcome one, but I think will be a most refreshing one, too. Please write me if it is convenient, and give me what advice you can on the questions I have raised. Meanwhile, with renewed thanks for your kind invitation, and with all good wishes,

To HERBERT J. MULLER

Hotel Chelsea
222 West 23rd Street
New York, New York

April 15, 1938

Dear Professor Muller:

Thanks very much for writing me so promptly and giving me an idea of what is ahead of me. I feel much easier about the whole thing now, and believe I can swing it well enough. Of course, I am no sort of public speaker, but I did speak to a gathering similar to this at the University of Colorado two or three years ago and, after the first few minutes of fumbling and stumbling around, I got hold of what I wanted to say and did very well. The only trouble was that after I did get wound up it was hard to stop: I offered to at the end of three-quarters of an hour, but they very generously told me to go on. But I know what a bore a long-winded speaker can be on an occasion like this, at a banquet; so I will try to hold myself down within reasonable limits.

I hate to bother you again, but since you have so kindly given me such useful and reassuring information already, perhaps you would enlighten me on one or two other details. My wardrobe at the present time is decidedly threadbare and scanty, but I do have one pretty good blue suit and a tuxedo. I thought I would bring both along, and hope these will meet the sartorial requirements of the occasion acceptably.

Yes, I certainly would like to get together with you before the dinner and have a cocktail or two, not only for convivial reasons but because of the moral fortification they may supply. And after it is over, I am looking forward to relaxing and enjoying myself, and it would be a great pleasure to meet and talk to some of you.

I have mislaid the first telegram that Professor Cummings sent me, but I am sure that he said the date of the meeting is May 19. At any rate, I am making plans to be in Lafayette on that date, and shall arrange to leave here in sufficient time. Thank you again for all your kind assistance. With all good wishes,

Because of his new conviction that "You Can't Go Home Again," Wolfe had begun looking for a place in which to spend the summer in New York State, New Jersey, Pennsylvania or New England. Marjorie Fairbanks had suggested that he rent the Shaker House at Harvard, Massachusetts, and the following was his reply.

To MARJORIE C. FAIRBANKS

Hotel Chelsea
222 West 23rd Street
New York City

April 23, 1938

Dear Marjorie:

By all means find out about the Shaker house. I do not know what I would do with twenty rooms, unless I wrote a chapter in each of them, and some of the things I may write would give even the Shakers the Shakes, but the big meeting room as a place to work sounds wonderful, and, in fact, the idea of the whole thing sounds good if there are not too many complications and if it does not cost too much. I certainly appreciate your finding out about things so promptly, because now is the time, if ever, I should be getting things settled.

Ed Aswell, my friend at Harper's, and his wife are starting out with me next weekend in our jaunt around the countryside to look the terrain over. He is himself a Harvard University man, and he also has been to

Harvard, Mass., which he says is beautiful. But I do not know whether he is going to be able to swing it into his circle next week, for he has several things in mind, and we will only have two days to do it in. But if you find anything that looks good, let me know and I will come up some Saturday or Sunday between now and the time I go out to Purdue and look it over.

And again, thanks for all the trouble you are taking. It really means a lot to me to find a good place now, because last summer was a disappointment as far as work is concerned and now that I have got going again on a tremendous job—by far the biggest I have ever undertaken—a good place to work is mighty important. I think you understand pretty well what I want and need, and certainly I do not want to be pampered —but I have not time now to learn cooking, striking a fire between two flints, or other boy-scout tricks. Aside from the time I am taking off in May for my jaunt to the Middle West, I hope to keep going right through the summer, and anything anyone can do to further me in that design will be deeply and sincerely appreciated.

Thanks for writing the people at Olivet.[1] I am pretty tired and I do not know how much speaking I am going to be up to, but anything that would help out on expenses would be worth considering. And let me know also if you are going to be out there at about the same time as I am. You should not miss the Chicago stockyards. I have been through twice, and so far from being shocked, I found it a very wholesome and edifying spectacle, as a good many forceful and natural physical things are apt to be.

This is all for the present. It is a beautiful day here, and I envy you Single Tax plutocrats of Harvard, Mass. But I have got to work now, and so good-bye.

P.S. And by the way, if the Shaker house is available, what kind of complications are there—if any? That is, would I have it to myself, or do they still hold meetings there on Sunday etc.?

Over the weekend of May 1st, the Aswells had driven Wolfe through upper New York state and had taken him to stay at the house of their friends, Dr. and Mrs. A. P. Saunders, of Clinton. The following is his bread-and-butter letter, written the day after he returned. Dr. Saunders was Professor of Chemistry and formerly Dean at Hamilton College, and a horticulturalist specializing in the propagation of rare peonies.

[1] Mrs. Fairbanks had written to Joseph Brewer, who was President of Olivet College, to suggest that Wolfe might speak there after his talk at Purdue.

To DR. AND MRS. A. P. SAUNDERS

Hotel Chelsea
222 West 23rd Street
New York, New York

May 3, 1938

Dear Dr. and Mrs. Saunders:

We all got back in good condition yesterday afternoon, and I am writing to tell you both what a delightful and extraordinary trip it was, and that I shall never forget it.

Your house is amazing and beautiful—and I think of the whole place, the country, the campus, the trees, the flowers, and the people, as if I had just returned from a visit to the Elysian fields. Was it not Wordsworth who said: "A primrose by the river's brim, a simple primrose was to him," etc.—well, if it was, I have been telling people since I got back that one cannot even take primroses for granted at Hamilton—if he does, he will find that a primrose by the river's brim is really a rare and precious plant on which a whole encyclopaedia of knowledge, culture, love and tender care has been expended. It did me an amazing amount of good to be there and to see it all—no matter how often I come back (and I hope I have the opportunity again), I shall never forget the magic of this first trip.

Our ride down was also beautiful—the weather was glorious, everything turned out beautifully, we even found the fish place in Catskill and had Hudson River shad. We made good time, and Ed delivered me to the Harmon train yards four minutes after five o'clock. I was home shortly after six, and the Aswells, I am sure, got home before that time.

I am now about to be guilty of the supreme immodesty of sending you a photograph of the undersigned in his most recent state of dilapidation. You said you wanted it, so henceforth the consequences are on your own head. If it wilts the flowers, darkens the cheerful atmosphere of your household with its all-pervasive gloom, or causes the other photographs to shudder and withdraw and turn their faces to the wall, I accept no further responsibility. I am sending it to you in a separate envelope, and I hope this does not put me under the penalties of the acts for using the mails to defraud.

I am back at work again, it is past twelve o'clock, and I have not even been out to get my breakfast yet. Even breakfast is something that they only have at Hamilton.

With love and all good wishes to you both,

P.S. I did not sign the photograph, because I did not know if you wanted it that way. If you do, I will sign it the next time I see you.

The following letter was written in answer to one from Mrs. Roberts saying that a prominent citizen of Asheville would lend Wolfe the complete files of The Asheville Advocate, *the publication of the Asheville Taxpayers' League, if he would put up a thousand dollar bond to ensure their safe return.*

To MARGARET ROBERTS

114 East 56th Street
New York, New York
c/o Miss Elizabeth Nowell

May 3, 1938

Dear Mrs. Roberts:

Thanks very much for your letter and for the information in it. I am deeply sorry to think that you have been put to so much trouble in this matter, but I want you to know how much I appreciate it.

Now about Mr. T——'s proposal. Frankly, I am afraid what he suggests is out of the question. It may be possible, as he says, to secure a thousand dollar bond at no greater expense than five dollars to myself. But that is not the point. The point, it seems to me, lies in the responsibility he asks me to assume, and the value he attaches to his papers. It may be perfectly true that he "would not take a thousand dollars for them." But it is also true that probably no one else would give a thousand dollars for them. Certainly I would not, and I would not, therefore, care in any way, however hypothetical, to involve myself for any such amount. What he has may be very rare and precious. Not having seen it, I cannot judge. But I have also learned, from past experience, that there are many people who put an utterly unreasonable value on something that may be of very little worth.

For example, after "Of Time and the River" appeared, I received a long and rambling letter from an apparently illiterate man in Florida, who announced that he was a "doctor" who would like to build a new house and office, and take some graduate work in medicine, and would, therefore, very generously sell me his life story (which would make me fabulously rich and famous, of course) at the knock-down price of twenty-five thousand dollars. I was also besieged, tormented, interrupted, and interfered with last summer by hordes of people who could obviously do very little more than write their own names, if their literary talents went so far, but who were generously trying to cram down my throat wads of manuscript, life stories, "great ideas" and so on, that would make me immensely wealthy—and would result in "a greater book" than "Gone With the Wind." God knows why that immortal piece of bilge was invariably selected as the almost ne plus ultra in literary achievement, but invariably it was. There is also the kind of person—seven million, two hundred and sixty-seven thousand, by the most recent and conservative count—who, unsolicited, send manuscripts of poems, plays and novels, and what-not to a defenseless author, and offer to split the staggering royalties, fifty-fifty, if he will only "write it up good" for them— I presume, in his off moments from carousing around with the Bohemian literary gang, on a quiet weekend.

All this is pretty brutal, but I have suffered from it for years. There was one painted hag last summer who wormed the location of my cabin from my sometimes too garrulous mother, hunted me out, and then demanded that I read a manuscript of one thousand, four hundred and sixty-two handwritten pages, rewrite and revise it for her, tell her "what to do with it," find a publisher for her—all within two weeks' time. The plain truth is, the more worthless the material, the more deluded is its possessor in his estimate of its priceless value.

I had thought perhaps that I might be willing to pay as much, say, as twenty-five dollars for the loan of the papers for a few weeks—which certainly strikes me as being munificently and extravagantly generous for a file of newspapers in an obscure weekly sheet, in a small town. Mr. T—— has other notions, apparently, and while not disputing his own personal sense of their value, I simply cannot agree with him. Moreover, his frantic haste for their return is decidedly perplexing: if they had any value, to get them back within ten days or two weeks, or thirty days, would be absurd. I am a serious and hard-working man, I am engaged upon a tremendous piece of work—whatever value such information as this might be, it would only be a portion of the whole, and I cannot agree to such unreasonable demands. So we will have to call this portion of it off.

As to —— ——. I am perfectly willing to write him, and should be grateful for any information that he might give, but if he has as many sore toes to be stepped on as you say he has, perhaps I had better not try. Frankly, I am a little tired of taking it on the chin from these small-town liberals, these leaders of enlightened thought, these Buncombe County . . . Socialists who are all for social reform, world revolution, and what-not, but who are all undone when you mention casually some good old Anglo-Saxon four-letter word that can be found repeatedly in Shakespeare or in the King James version of the Bible.

When I was a child, the poet, the artist, the creative man was held up to me as an ideal of the highest and the best in human life—the man who bravely and truthfully wrought out his vision of the world, at no matter what the cost to him, according to the dictates of his conscience and his talent. In later years, when I tried to do the same thing myself, it was shocking and bewildering to find out that I was most bitterly denounced and execrated by some of the very people who had held this ideal before me—to find out that it is noble to tell the truth, so long as the truth is not too close at home, and does not refer to the wart upon Aunt Nellie's chin.

I am not bitter, but I am through with apology. The only apology I have now to make is to my conscience, to the knowledge wherein I may have failed, to the things to which I may have been unfair, to the things in which I did not fulfill myself and my work as completely as I should. I lived out my exile for more than seven years and then went back, and I saw what I saw, I know what I know. I know now that you can't go back—there is no turning back; with that knowledge also came a deeper feeling of compassion and of understanding for stricken people. But no apologies—they are not needed, they are not due. I was a citizen of Asheville, and I am now a citizen of mankind—there is my loyalty, and that is where it must go.

I know you can help me in this thing more than anyone I know at home, for I believe you understand better than anyone else what I am after. There is nothing very complex or mysterious about it; I know some other people who, I think, may help out, too, and who may have kept the records that I want, and I shall write them. When I was home last summer, I was given to understand that it would be very simple to provide them, but of course, as so often happens, results are harder to achieve than promises. If I cannot get them, I shall have to do without; but I have done without before, and I shall get along.

I do not want to harass you or Mr. Roberts with a matter that has already, I know, cost you so much of your generous time and care. But if you will keep trying and let me know what you find, I shall be grateful, and, as I said before, I think the result may be worth it in the end. Do not offend T——, simply tell him that I appreciate his position, but did not feel that I could obligate myself in so large a sum; and that I appreciate his interest and his offer.

This is all now. I have been pretty tired, for I have gone through a long, hard winter here with publishers, law suits, and finally, with the thing I want to do—work. . . . I am going out to Purdue University in about two weeks to talk to a student gathering there, and then I am going to take a short vacation. When I get back here in June, I am going somewhere out of town, and get back to work again. If I do not hear from you before then, I hope to hear from you when I come back. Meanwhile, with all good wishes to you and Mr. Roberts,

To ELIZABETH NOWELL

Hotel Chelsea
222 West 23rd Street
New York, New York
May 3, 1938

Dear Miss Nowell:

I came back last night and got your note with the letter from *The New Yorker*.[1] I think you are handling it just right—and we undoubtedly will have something sooner or later that we want to send them—perhaps even good "Dr. Turner"[2] if I get around to giving him another go. But there will be many others as well.

Anyway, I want to see you very soon now before I go West and go over the whole business with you. I have only got an even two weeks from today, and I think it would be a good idea if we could get together sometime this week—say, Saturday or Sunday. The most immediate thing of interest I want to talk to you about is this: I finally wrote *The Nation* and rejected the proposal for the "Living Philosophies" piece,[3] on the ground that it would take too much time, and would take me away from my work. At the same time I made another suggestion to them. I told them about the Purdue engagement, and told them that I proposed to go out and talk to the students right out of the workshop, so to speak —to tell them what I thought and felt about writing, what I think I have learned about it, what change and development has come about in me, and what convictions and beliefs I now have, not only about writing, but about the life around me from which I draw the sources of my material, and the writer's place in the whole world today.

As you know, this has been the principal thing that has interested me for at least a year now, it is at the bottom of everything that has happened—beginning with the *New Republic* piece,[4] leading up through all the Scribner trouble to the place where I now am, and the work I am now doing. I believe the time has come when I am ready to say it, and if the time has come and I can say it, it will knock the *New Republic* piece into a cocked hat because it will shoot the works.

[1] A letter from the editors of *The New Yorker* saying they would be glad to see more stories by Wolfe.

[2] The piece about "Dr. Turner" was published under the title "Portrait of a Literary Critic" in the April, 1939, issue of *The American Mercury*, and is included in *The Hills Beyond*.

[3] Frieda Kirchwey of *The Nation* had written Wolfe asking him to write a 3,000 word essay on his philosophy of life for publication in *The Nation* and later inclusion in a book to be published by Simon and Schuster under the title of *Living Philosophies*.

[4] "I Have a Thing to Tell You."

What I did, therefore, first of all, was simply to dictate a very plain and simple account of things to use at the Purdue gathering. Of course, it is immensely too long, and besides towards the end there are many, many things in it of too personal and complex a nature for an occasion of that sort. However, it did serve the purpose of getting certain things on record, and as for the Purdue thing, I do not think I shall have any difficulty with that at all, nor even to refer to a typed sheet, because I know pretty clearly in my mind now what I am going to say to them, and what will probably be most appropriate for an occasion like that.

The Nation suggested that I show them the Purdue thing pretty much as I have it for the students, but I do not want to do this, because I think the final outcome may be so much better. Briefly, what I am trying to do, as with everything in which I am most deeply interested, is to give the piece at the end the depth and permanence of imaginative truth. I hope this does not make you smile—for that is the idea.

For months now, it has occurred to me that I would conclude the tremendously long book on which I am working with a kind of epilogue that takes the form of personal address—to be called, "You Can't Go Home Again" or "A Farewell to the Fox," or perhaps by still another title.[5] That epilogue, as I have conceived it, would be a kind of impassioned summing up of the whole book, of everything that has gone before, and a final statement of what is now. The book will certainly close in some such way as this, although it may turn out at the end that the method of personal address, even in high poetic terms, is not the best way to conclude a book in which the whole narrative, hundreds of characters, and the events of more than a hundred years are stated objectively. However that may be, it is not important here, for if I succeed in doing "You Can't Go Home Again," or "A Farewell to the Fox," as I want to do it, it will stand most tremendously on its own legs. Anyway, that is what I am doing now: transforming the material for the simple Purdue statement into the terms of poetic and imaginative fact—into the truth of fiction—because it seems to me that is really my essential job. What do you think of it?

I have written *The Nation* and more or less committed myself to letting them see it, but of course, three thousand words is nonsense—thirty thousand probably will be likelier, if I can hold it down to that —they realize, although I have not explained to them what it is as I have to you—that the thing is probably out of the question for them—unless they want to pull a big one, and match their distinguished rival[6] of a

---

[5] This appears as the seventh and final portion of *You Can't Go Home Again* under the title of "A Wind Is Rising, and the Rivers Flow."

[6] *The New Republic.*

year ago. This, of course, in case it is good. Sooner or later, it will be good, it must be, because it is so deep in me—but I hope it is good now. I have only two weeks more to work on it—and if I was fresh, I believe I could almost put it through, because usually the length of time a piece of writing takes—the best writing, that is—can never be reckoned except in terms of the days and months and years it has been coming to a head. That certainly has happened with this one—and I know that I am ready; but it may be I have to take another breather before I put it through. I suppose I may take the Purdue trip as the chance to get one—the chance to get away by myself on a streamlined train for a week or two—before I come back and settle in for the summer. . . .

This is all now, and I hope this finds you well. With best wishes,

To FRIEDA KIRCHWEY

Hotel Chelsea
222 West 23rd Street
New York, New York

May 4, 1938

Dear Miss Kirchwey:

The attached letter was "wrote sarcastical," and if you have space for it and think it good enough, you can print it.[1] If you do, I wish you would check up on one or two details of fact. I have been unable to find the newspaper which contained an account of Franco's efforts to encourage the tourist trade this summer, but I am quite sure it was in *The New York Times* within the past two weeks, in a dispatch written by a man named Carney. If you use the letter, I would like to check up on this detail in advance, and since you probably have a file of *The Times* for the past two or three weeks, someone in your office could check up on it without much difficulty.

To the Editor of *The Nation*

Sir:

A recent dispatch in *The New York Times* announces that General Francisco Franco is making arrangements for the reception of the tourist trade in Spain this summer, and I am writing to inquire if someone in your Travel Department could inform me if there are going to be any personally conducted tours.

I have never been to Spain, but like many other Americans, its ro-

[1] This letter was published in "Letters to the Editor" in the May 21, 1938, issue of *The Nation*.

mantic charm has always exerted a strong influence upon my imagination, and since I have read with great interest the recent remarks of Mr. Ellery Sedgwick, and his account of what General Franco is doing in the interests of his people, my desire to visit Spain has naturally been increased.

For what could be more delightful than the charm of the old Spain, so to speak, now so happily combined, as Mr. Sedgwick describes it to us, with the progressive and liberalizing leadership of the new. It is certainly a proposition that should excite the imagination of every good American because to the prospect of ancient customs and historical relics—a prospect always fascinating to citizens of our own young country—is added the healthy and invigorating assurance that Spain, under General Franco's leadership, has not allowed herself to lag behind in the pit of medievalism, but is going forward. Indeed, what could be a better indication of this new progressive spirit in modern Spain than General Franco's efforts to stimulate and encourage, in a businesslike and yet attractive manner, the healthful and peaceful propagation of the tourist industry.

According to the account I read in the reliable *Times*, no effort or expense has been spared to make Spain an agreeable resort this summer for the hordes of tourists from across the Atlantic who will flock there. General Franco, for example, has ordered sixty new and brightly painted charabancs, which will swiftly and comfortably transport the tourists from one end of his beautiful country to the other. In addition, it is understood that he has not only taken considerable pains in the work of restoring and preserving the most notable of the ancient ruins, but he has also shown extraordinary ingenuity in the creation of new ones, all of which will now be within easy and delightful access of the inquiring tourist, through the avenues and agencies that General Franco has so thoughtfully opened.

For my part, although I by no means share the too general lack of interest and veneration for the monuments of antiquity, I must confess that on the whole the evidences of the modern spirit are more exciting to me. In other words, if I had to choose between two sets of ruins, I should be inclined to visit the new ones rather than the old.

To mention but a few that have already suggested themselves to my awakened curiosity—I should like, if opportunity presents itself, to visit the various craters and ruined masonries throughout the town of Barcelona, paying particular attention to the subway entrance where a bomb exploded, and where one hundred and twenty-six men, women and children were killed in one economical gesture. I should like to visit the ruins of Madrid, the ruined villages around Teruel; and being of a religious turn of mind, I should like to pay a visit of devotion and respect to the Chapel, a photograph of which was recently reproduced in the press, where General Franco's wife and daughter go to offer prayers for the success of the Defender of the Faith. There are many other places of historic and memorable interest which I should also like to visit, but I will not try your patience with a further record of them.

Anyway, if someone in your own Travel Department could inform me what arrangements have been made for the conduct of these tours, I should be grateful to him.

To MARJORIE C. FAIRBANKS

Hotel Chelsea
222 West 23rd Street
New York, New York

May 4, 1938

Dear Marjorie:

Thanks for all the additional trouble you have gone to in my behalf.[1] I do not know whether I will be able to get up to explore your findings before I go West, because I have only two weeks more, and I have just come back from the luxury of a long weekend. But I will be grateful if you just keep plugging, and if you find anything you could tell me about it if you come West.

I had a very nice letter from Mr. Brewer,[2] inviting me to come to Olivet, and even suggesting a fee, although he did not say how much. I have just written him and thanked him for his invitation, but decided it was best not to make any more commitments as far as speaking engagements are concerned. I suppose I might do it and get several of them, and make some money, but I am fagged out, and am really using this Purdue thing as a kind of springboard to a holiday. Since I have to come back here later on, move out of town somewhere and get to work again, I think I had better make the most of the short vacation time I have. But I do hope to see you if you go out to Olivet, it would be nice to see the others, too.

Brewer tells me Ford Madox Ford is staying with him and is "most anxious" to see me again, and although our acquaintanceship was very brief—a cocktail party, I believe, in Paris years ago—I might be able to do something to relieve an anxiety that has extended over all these years.

---

[1] Mrs. Fairbanks had written him further about places which he could rent for the summer.

[2] Joseph Brewer, who at that time was President of Olivet College.

I certainly have read some of Ford's books, and deeply respected the craftmanship and skill that was in them, because they contained so much that I myself could wish to attain; but otherwise, I imagine we are at different ends of the writing stick. I am awfully tired, it will all come out all right with a few days' rest and a complete break-away, but I am simply not up to the higher reaches of Left Bank or Left Wing dialectics at the present time; something simple and corn-fed with large open spaces in it is more in my present line.

From what Brewer says, Olivet cannot be very far from Purdue. He did not know where Purdue is, but you might tell him it is a sizeable institution of ten or twelve thousand students, located at Lafayette, Indiana, which is sixty miles northwest of Indianapolis, and I judge no more than a hundred and fifty from Olivet.

Please write and let me know what you are going to do, Marjorie. That invitation to take you on a personally conducted tour through the stockyards of Chicago still holds. After that, I know a place where you can really get a wonderful thick and juicy sirloin. . . .

With best wishes,

To S. A. CUMMINGS

Hotel Chelsea
222 West 23rd Street
New York, New York

May 5, 1938

Dear Professor Cummings:

Thanks very much for your letter. I am glad you got the photograph and biographical material from Harper's, and hope you found the material useful.

I think that everything, thanks to you and Professor Muller, is now perfectly clear in my mind, about the nature of the occasion, and what I am to do. I shall probably come out a day in advance, and spend the night in Indianapolis, and although I am pretty tired just now, having put in a long stretch of work, I think I will be in good shape for the talk, for I am really approaching it in a kind of holiday spirit, and with a sense of anticipation. In fact, I think it is going to give me the stimulus and relief of a much needed change.

I am pretty clear in my mind about what I am going to say. I am delighted to know that I shall have as much as fifty minutes or an hour to speak in and I shall try neither to misuse or over-use my time. About the talk itself: I have already written down in very simple form what I want to say—just for the sake of getting it objectively stated. But I do not think I will even refer to a typed page, when I get up to talk, because I think I may do better without it. Now this is what I have in mind:

As I told you in a previous letter, I want to make this a kind of "workshop talk"—that is, a very simple account of a writer's work and his beliefs and convictions about writing, drawn directly from his own experience. I am glad to know you have read "The Story of a Novel," and that it interested you—and that you would not object if I drew on it for material. That will be very helpful—I also had this in mind: "The Story of a Novel" was written almost three years ago, and was a kind of summary or record of my writing experience up to that time. I think there has been another development since then, and with your permission I should like to try to tell about it in my talk. It is this:

In the past three years, in particular, I have thought more and more of the writer's relation to the world around him, and what effect it has, or ought to have, on his own work. Briefly, my own experience, which I think is fairly typical of the experience of many writers, has been this: I began life, as many young men do, as a lyrical writer. That is, I wanted to express my vision of life and of the world largely in terms of my own youth and my own personality. At college and later on, when I first began to write, I went through one of the usual periods of aesthetics—that is, seeing the life of the artist and his work in aesthetic terms: perhaps you could call it a somewhat "ivory tower" view of things. As I grew older, and as I continued to work, my view began to change, and I think this, too, was natural and inevitable. That is to say, as I grew older, I think I was not so much preoccupied with the concerns and purposes of my own youth. The field of my objectivity widened—with greater maturity and experience, I believe I began to look at the life around me more objectively—to see things and people and the world in a more objective way.

This, briefly, is what I should like to tell the students. I believe I may be able to do it in very clear and simple terms. I may have something to say about the "ivory tower" view of things in terms of a writer's work and whether it now seems to me that a creative writer's work ought or ought not to reflect an interest in the political and economic life of his time, but I assure you that my talk will be in no sense of the word political, nor do I have any axe to grind for propaganda.

I might describe the talk I have in mind as a series of concentric circles, tracing briefly and simply the stages of my own development. I suppose the root of the thing is that I want to tell the students about the writer and his life not merely in terms of writing, but in terms of living also. In other words, humorously we might call the talk, "Are Writers Human?" (please do not use that one, though). But I do want to show them if I can that the writer is not a strange and mysterious creature, but very definitely a citizen of mankind, a living, breathing, acting member of the human race, with work to do, a place to fill, a function to perform like everyone. What do you think of this for a title: Writing and Living [1] —or does that seem too general and diffuse to you? That is really what the talk is about, if it meets your approval, and I can put it over clearly—and if you think the title is all right, you can use it.

I think this clears up everything. You have all been very kind and helpful, and I think it is very generous of Professor Muller to offer to drive me over from Indianapolis. I will let him know by telegram when I am arriving, and I am looking forward to meeting all of you in about two weeks' time. And if my outline of what I want to say does not satisfy you, please do not hesitate to write and let me know what you think.

With all good wishes,

To EDWARD C. ASWELL

> Hotel Chelsea
> 222 West 23rd Street
> New York, New York
>
> May 6, 1938

Dear Ed:

. . . I have only about ten days more here before I go out to Purdue, and I hope to see you again before I go. I shall certainly call you up and talk to you. I think we [1] are going to be pretty busy for several days next week assembling the manuscript and packing away the other manuscript I shall not use. I wonder if it would be possible for you to take the assembled manuscript and put it in a place of safekeeping there at Harpers until I come back from the West. It is going to make a very large and bulky package, or possibly a series of them, but we will try to devise some means for getting it together in its present form in the most logical and accurate sequence.

Although I have not begun this work yet and cannot say for sure, I have a very strong conviction that I have now reached about the same state of articulation as I had reached with "Of Time and the River"

[1] This was the title finally used.

[1] Wolfe and his secretary at that time, Miss Gwen Jassinoff, now Mrs. Peter Campbell.

in the month of December, 1933. It was at this time that Mr. Perkins saw that manuscript in its entirety for the first time. What he saw, of course, was only a kind of enormous skeleton, but at any rate, he was able to get some kind of articulate idea of the whole. It was at that time that we went over the whole thing together, decided in general terms on the cycle of the book and on the immediate labor that remained to be done. From that point on, I moved very rapidly to completion. The whole book was written and finished within the course of the following year: although it did not appear until March, 1935, we were getting the proofs of it in November and December, 1934, within a year after we had gone over the first skeleton carefully together.

I mention all of this to you not because I think we established any kind of historic precedent that has to be invariably followed, but as indicating to you the state of things as they now stand. From the first, I have been very careful not to commit myself to any promises as to when the manuscript will be finished and ready for publication, and you have been very fair and generous in understanding this and in not asking me to make such commitments. I shall not do so now, but I can tell you that I hope with a good year of steady uninterrupted work, to complete the job. Please do not take this as a promise, but only as an expression of a reasonable hope.

The book will be a much bigger book—at least, in its first completed form—than "Of Time and the River." It will deal with a much greater sweep of time—over one hundred years, in fact. It will deal with a much greater variety of scenes, of characters, of events than "Of Time and the River," and it will present a narrative that is much more continuous and closely-woven, and that has, therefore, made a much more exacting demand upon my powers of invention and creation than anything I have done before.

I ask you to bear this in mind, because I want you to be aware of the magnitude of the task before us. I know, and deeply appreciate, your patience and your desire to help in any way you can. It would perhaps be a good idea if you could familiarize yourself, so far as possible, with this first great batch of manuscript when I give it to you, but I am not sure about that yet until I have seen it all together myself. However, we shall see what we shall see.

My own very strong conviction at present is this: I have never been so clear in my mind before as to what I am after, and what I want to do. The analogy to "Of Time and the River" is a physical one rather than an artistic one. In other words, my very strong hunch at present is that it may be best to allow me to proceed with my work without any great assistance until I have brought it to a further state of development and completion. At the same time, it might be a good idea if the editor did get a general idea of the whole thing now.

I do not believe that I am in need of just the same kind of editorial help at this moment as Mr. Perkins so generously and unselfishly gave me in 1933, 1934. At any rate, since the whole process [is that] of trying to learn, like little Duncan,[2] to stand erect, to toddle, and then to walk by myself, it might be better for me to go on by myself for awhile, and see what happens. It is, of course, comforting and of immense value to me to know that when I do need help it will be generously and patiently given. At any rate, I hope that is the program for the present, and that you can take care of the manuscript for me until I get back.

I really do feel it is pretty important for me to get some rest now, because such a tremendous job is before me—and for the past three years at least, what with law suits, publishing troubles, and an effort to get my work accomplished, there has been no let-up. I am due at Purdue on May 19, and where I shall go from there I shall try to keep my little secret. But I will not be gone for long and will see you early in June, at any rate. . . .

With best wishes,

To MABEL WOLFE WHEATON

114 East 56th Street
New York, New York
c/o Miss Elizabeth Nowell

May 10, 1938

Dear Mabel:

I was glad to get your letter and to have the news. I certainly hope that the bank case turns out favorably and that if the lawyers make a compromise it will be a worthwhile one. I am glad you went to see Carter and tried to get some definite idea from him what he would charge, or how big a cut he expects to take. You will find that is pretty important. It is not just mere bitterness, but actual experience, that makes me say that lawyers are out, first and foremost, for themselves. This is the truth. I have found that it is a kind of great closed corporation that exists primarily for the benefit and profit of those who are engaged in it as against the rest of the world.

From my own point of view, in its present form, the profession of law as it exists in this country ought to be abolished. But it can't because the system we have produced and under which we live has created the

[2] Aswell's son, Edward Duncan Aswell, who at this time was 20 months old.

lawyer. He is a kind of parasite with a recognized established position. Our system makes it possible for a great many unscrupulous and dishonest people to take advantage of other people—to sue them, or to threaten them, or to try to worry and harass them in such a way they will pay out money to be left alone. For this reason we have the lawyer.

The lawyer works both ways, either as a representative of dishonest and unscrupulous people who say "here is a chance to get some money," or as a representative of honest people who have to defend themselves. In both cases, obviously, it is the lawyer who wins out: the so-called good lawyer gets in touch with a so-called shyster, they put their heads together and try to work out a compromise—a compromise for everybody but the lawyer. The reputable lawyer will tell you that it is all a great pity and that he himself, of course, is a very honest, noble, upright citizen, there to protect your interests against the practices of the shyster. But I am afraid that most of them—even the so-called good and upright ones—have a good deal of the shyster in them—for they are always trading and bargaining with shysters, and it is their fault, more or less, that shysters exist—that is, they all play in together: the good lawyer gets a large part of his living from the fact that the crooked lawyer is allowed to exist and menace people. He can, therefore, hold himself up as a model of righteousness and a guardian of one's interest against the forces that prey on one. But he, too, is a member of the whole bad system.

You and I were never taught this when we were children, and we were never taught a whole lot of things we should have known, and that might have been a great deal more useful to us than a great many things we were taught. We were never taught, for example, to question the life around us, which was the little world of Asheville, which in its turn is the whole world of America. If we questioned the essential and beautiful rightness of anything, we were labeled a "radical," "queer," a "freak," and all the rest of it. As a result, you are to-day in middle age a baffled person, and I am having to begin my education all over again. But I am not baffled and I am not defeated, and I think it would be a great pity if anyone with as much intelligence and energy as you have continue to allow yourself to be baffled and defeated. You and I are not going to change the world, but we can both work for a better one, and in that direction lies hope and new life, and not defeat.

Just to reassure you, and to let you know where I stand, I would like to say that I like people everywhere and my own country, America, much more than I ever did before. But I think that people everywhere have been generally misused and exploited, and I think that America, which is such a beautiful and wonderful country, has been taken away from the people to whom it should belong and given largely into the hands of a few of the exploiters.

I am afraid you will consider this "queer talk" or "radical talk" or "communistic talk," and for that reason I have felt very sorry about you all. You have been chewed up by the existing order and system of things —I will just mention the Asheville boom, the way the —— —— —— Company treated Ralph, etc.—and it never occurred to you to question or resent the thing that was chewing you up. It was right because it happened to exist, and you accepted it. Well, that's no reason for accepting anything—and you are not a radical or queer because you question and resent it and want to change it. Unless you do, I don't think you can have much hope in the future. You will go on feeling more and more defeated, vainly pining for what is gone and will never come back again—Asheville during the boom, insane speculation, Grove Park, Biltmore Forest, and all the rest of it—which was never much good in the beginning.

I think you are wise in wanting to get out of Asheville. I have known what happened to it for years, but I had a good chance to sum it all up when I went back last summer. It is a ruined and defeated town, and it is full of ruined and defeated people. If you think that I am happy about this, you do me an injustice. After all, it was my town, I was born there, and some of the people I care for most on earth still live there. But I found out last summer that you can't go home again, and now I know why.

You say that you hope I am as happy as any of our family ever get to be. Well, I think I am as happy as I have been in years, and a great deal happier than most people ever get to be, because I believe in something. And let's not get to believe about ourselves [that] there is something in us so special and different that we can't be as happy as ordinary people are. In that way also lies nothing but defeat. We are not different from other people, we are all members of the same human race, and we can hope for as much and achieve as much as other people can.

I don't know what you mean by the scandal you referred to in your letter, but I am afraid you allow yourself to be worried too much by what you think people around you are saying about you, or in what kind of estimation you are held by people in your own town. I assure you that doesn't matter very much, and if you really want to be "happy" you'll never be as long as you allow it to worry you. You will only be when you learn to feel the courage and self-respect and dignity that comes from the strength you have in you. I am sure you have it in you. Why not rely on it and be true to your own self? And for God's sake, don't let defeat get you. . . . It's not going to happen to you, it's not going to happen to me, and it's not going to happen to Fred; so let's not even mention the possibility of its going to happen. We won't be defeated, because nothing can defeat people who refuse to acknowledge defeat.

You told me one time that it almost killed you to think that people were "talking about" you. For God's sake, get over it. Get over worrying about what people say. I have been through the whole mill a lot more than any of you ever have, I have read and heard and had brought back to me every kind of lie, myth, fairy tale and legend—some vicious and malicious, some just stupid—it used to burn me up, but it doesn't any more. Why should you care or worry about such lies, as long as you know in yourself what the truth is. Love life and love people, but don't be afraid of foolish little tongues. To be afraid is also defeat.

And don't apologize for yourself, or for me, or for any of us. We don't need it. I think you're going to be all right, and that Ralph is going to be all right, and that we're going to pull out of the swamp. But we're not going to pull out of the swamp by staying in it and brooding about it and thinking of the good old days when we thought it wasn't a swamp. Keep your head up, and have faith and courage and belief in yourself and in people and in life, and don't worry about Bingville and what the Women's Club is saying about you, and you're going to be all right.

Don't worry about Papa. Don't forget him, but don't brood over him. He lived seventy-one years, he made his own life, he died sixteen years ago, and in general he got about as much as most men ever get. Don't live in the past in a sad defeated way. We've got our own home to find or make, and our home is in the future. Don't forget it. Believe in this, live for it, work for it—and you will achieve the happiness you speak of.

The old world that you knew is largely gone—I mean Grove Park, stucco houses, boom-town speculation, Wall Street,* 1929—and all the rest of it. It's not coming back, Mabel. Most of those poor defeated devils in Asheville hope that it is coming back. But it's not. And most of them have nothing else to cling to, no other language to talk, because it is the only language they ever knew. I saw that last summer, and from the bottom of my heart I feel sincerely and compassionately sorry for them all.

But I don't want you to be one of them: you've still got plenty of stuff in you, and enough to face the future. It's always harder to go through the woods, remember, than to take the beaten path, but you sometimes get places going through the woods that you never see or know about if you stick to the beaten path. And the old beaten path, I am afraid, is no good any more: it doesn't lead to anywhere: it's like that great glittering tunnel through Beaucatcher Mountain that cost a million dollars. You get through, and there you are, just where you always were—in Chunn's Cove. Except you find that Chunn's Cove isn't even there—it's just something you used to think was there when you were a kid. I am going places—better places than Chunn's Cove—and I invite you to come along. And let me know if I can help you. I am your friend.

I'm dog-tired, got no rest last summer, and have had none since. But I feel good. Did you ever read a story of mine that came out about a year ago called "I Have a Thing to Tell You"? Well, I have a thing to tell you now: that is you can't go home again, but there are other places you can go. So why not try to find them?

I'm going West in a few days on a speaking engagement, and after that, I'm going to hit for the wide open spaces—probably northwest—and look at geysers and big trees and mountains and such like. I'll only have two or three weeks for it, but it's going to be a swell trip and do me a lot of good.

This is a grand country. I wish you could see it all, and could be along with me. We'd have a swell time. But meanwhile, until I come back, I send you all my love and best wishes for success and for the future.

To ELIZABETH NOWELL

Hotel Chelsea
222 West 23rd Street
New York, New York

May 12, 1938

Dear Miss Nowell:

. . . It was awfully good of you to write me as you did. Naturally, it makes me feel good, and somehow, although I am appalled at the job I have cut out for myself, I think it is going to be all right. I am tired, but otherwise I have not felt such hope and confidence in many years. It may be that I have come through a kind of transition period in my life—I believe this is the truth—and have now, after a lot of blood-sweat and anguish, found a kind of belief and hope and faith I never had before.

At any rate, I am going to try to put it all into the book, and if you stand by and put in an occasional comforting word to people who may be getting restive,[1] that would be swell. I am sorry that you didn't see more of it the other night, but nowadays I am a little too fagged to do the whole thing at once. There has not been much let-up since I went to Germany two years ago, and there wasn't much then, because I found out that I couldn't go back to Europe again as if I were taking a trip on a Coney Island pleasure boat. Anyway, it's all gone into the mill, and I hope it comes out the right way.

This is packing-up day—I approach with considerable fear and trembling the job of assembling a good part of the manuscript I have done in the last three or four years. We are trying to arrange and audit it, so to speak, in some convenient form. Aswell is going to keep it for me until I get back, but I don't know whether it would be a good idea to let him read it now or not. I know where I stand, but it is like presenting someone with the bones of some great prehistoric animal he has never seen before—he might be bewildered. Anyway, I will know in a few days when I get it together. . . . I have written and explained the situation to him, and I think he understands it. I have a very strong hunch that I know where I am going a lot more clearly than I ever did before, and for that reason, I am not sure that it would be the best thing to have editorial advice and revision at this present time.

I hope also that he is able or will consent to take care of the rest of my stuff at Harpers until I get back. This business of being a vagabond writer with two tons of manuscript is not an easy one, particularly when one is going off somewhere, and does not want and cannot afford to keep on paying rent for an establishment he is no longer using. I had a letter from an autograph and manuscript dealer this morning, and I suppose he would gladly volunteer to keep it *but*——

This is all now. I will call you up if I have time before I leave on Tuesday night. If not, I'll see you when I return. . . . Meanwhile good luck and all good wishes,

To HERBERT J. MULLER

Hotel Chelsea
222 West 23rd Street
New York, New York

May 16, 1938

Dear Professor Muller:

Thanks again for letting me know that you will meet me. I have made

[1] Wolfe probably meant Harpers, though they had showed no signs of "getting restive."

reservations on the Southwestern Limited, which leaves here tomorrow night (Tuesday) at 8 o'clock EST, and arrives in Indianapolis, I understand, at noon on Wednesday. I gratefully accept your generous offer of hospitality and am looking forward to staying with you and Mrs. Muller while I am at Purdue.

Because you have been so kind, I am going to be completely frank and tell you what the situation is. I have driven myself without limit steadily for seven months now, and with only a brief interval for a long time before that. For the past week, my secretary and I have been engaged on the labor of assembling, putting in sequence, typing and binding the manuscript of my new book. It has been an enormous task, for it involved sorting and going over piece by piece a large portion of the manuscript I have written in the past four years—I should judge several million words.

I was up until five o'clock this morning working on it, and although there is still a tremendous quantity of manuscript left, I begin to see light, and feel a tremendous amount of comfort and satisfaction as the thing begins to shape up. Of course, the book is not finished yet—a tremendous labor of writing and revision is before me—but for the first time since I began it, I begin to feel a sense of wholeness: I have at least articulated a tremendous structure. All of this will be bound and minutely titled, section by section, and given to the editors at Harpers tomorrow to read and to hold for me until I come back and go at it again, and the remainder will be boxed up and kept in storage.

I have been thus tedious in telling you about all of this because I wanted to explain to you that I am not only very tired, but very happy, also. This trip is really a kind of momentous celebration for me, and that is why I am looking forward to it with so much pleasure. But just because I am looking forward to it with so much pleasure, I would like to spend the night in Indianapolis after I get there, and then, if it is convenient, meet you Thursday and drive over to Lafayette with you. That will give me a chance to rest and relax a bit, and get the memory of these millions of words out of my head, also to get a haircut, which I much need, and such like. I think you will find me fit and ready Thursday, after a night's sleep. I shall wire or telephone you from Indianapolis and let you know where I am, and you can tell me then where and when to meet you.

And I do want to thank you again for your patience and kindness in this whole matter. With all good wishes,

To ELIZABETH NOWELL

Auditorium Hotel
Chicago, Ill.
Monday, May 23, 1938

Dear Miss Nowell:

. . . Everything went off beautifully at Purdue—I talked and I talked, there was great applause, and everyone seemed very satisfied. Also met some very nice young people, teachers and instructors and their wives who took care of me. We all drove up to Chicago together Friday night,[1] and we spent two very pleasant days together, eating, drinking, driving all over Chicago, visiting the *stupendous* University, exploring the magnificent Lake Front and the not so magnificent slums. I really got it to a T in the *Vogue* piece: all of the grandeur and the misery of America is here—and yesterday we spent the whole day at the Brookfield Zoo, which is superb! I fed packages of crackerjack to the polar bears who wave their paws at you coyly and beat anything for charm you ever saw.

My friends left last night, and I am on my way West this afternoon —don't quite know where yet, but probably to Colorado first by one of the streamlined Zephyrs (it's only overnight this way—1100 miles across the continent and the plains in 15 hours—how's that?)—and later on perhaps to the North West. I hope nothing comes up that I have to be bothered about. Everything's going to be O.K. now if I get a little uninterrupted rest.

The Middle-western thing—Indianapolis, Purdue, and all of it—was swell! People say you'd get tired of it, but it was fat as a hog and so fertile you felt that if you stuck a fork in the earth the juice would spurt —one thousand miles of fat, flat, green, hog-fat fertility—barns, houses, silos, towns—the whole repeating in the recessions of a gigantic scroll —very restful, somehow, after the torment of New York and four million words of manuscript. (Aswell got the manuscript before I left— I finished completely and was completely finished! He wanted very much to read it. I had misgivings but he swore I could trust him to understand the unfinished state of things and to *feel* what I am about—and I hope to God he does, and that it is all right for him to read it now. It would be a crime if I were interrupted or discouraged now!)

Goodbye for the present, and try to take care of anything that comes up. I'll let you know where I am.

[1] The Herbert Mullers, the Kendall Tafts, Albert Fulton, William Hastings and William Braswell. Braswell later described this trip in "Thomas Wolfe Lectures and Takes a Holiday," in the October, 1939, issue of *College English*.

P.S. I'm staying here in an old hotel—not unlike the Chelsea—which I've always wanted to stay at because we had a book when I was a child called "Wonders of Science" or "The Marvels of the Modern Age" with a picture of the hotel. Have a good big room overlooking the Lake Front with the whole great system of parks, esplanades, drives, museums and freight trains right before me. Weather has been in and out—mostly good—but today awful. Sick of rain and fog from the Lake. Hope it changes before I go west. . . .

To ELIZABETH NOWELL

> The Brown Palace Hotel
> Denver, Colo.
>
> Thursday, May 26, 1938

Dear Miss Nowell:—

Got here yesterday after an all night ride at eighty miles per hour across the continent in the Burlington Zephyr. No sleep, but couldn't quiet down at this altitude of one even mile. Looked up my Denver friends, they gave a swell party for me last night, and I'm afraid I talked and ate and drank them all into a state of exhaustion. Both newspapers were on my trail thirty minutes after I hit town, and I am sending you a sample of their arts.[1] I'm heading Northwest from here towards Oregon—may miss the Yellowstone because I understand it doesn't open until June 20th. Can't give you any forwarding address, because I don't know any myself at present. Am driving over to Boulder tomorrow to see my friends there—and am leaving here, I think, day after tomorrow (Saturday). Sending this air mail to you—if anything important turns up, wire me here. Meanwhile good luck and best wishes,

To HERBERT J. MULLER

> Denver, Colorado
>
> May 31, 1938

Dear Herb:

I'm late in writing you to say hello and thanks again, and to let you all know that I think about you and the good time we had together, and hope that we will do it again. I've been here almost a week—I came for just a *day!* The whole town has been swell to me—so swell that for the first few days we just eliminated sleep as a despicable

---

[1] These were probably an interview with Frances Wayne in the May 25, 1938, *Denver Post* and one with Miriam Wise in the May 26 *Rocky Mountain News.*

luxury. But I'm beginning to feel ironed out again, and if I can only keep my fingers off the cursed quill for another week or two—which I doubt!—I should be in fairly good shape for the struggle when I go back East. Am still resolute in my intention to push on to the Northwest, although my friends here now lift their eyebrows and smile sceptically when I speak of it! And I'm still hoping to stop over in Chicago long enough to see you all again. Meanwhile, I send love and best wishes to you all.

P.S. Take care of the polar bears!

To ELIZABETH NOWELL

> Hotel Boise
> Boise, Idaho
> Monday, June 7, 1938

Dear Miss Nowell:

Just a line to tell you I'll be in Portland to-morrow night. Stopped off here to-day in order to see country to-morrow by daylight. To-morrow should be wonderful because I get the Columbia River and Oregon, but to-day—Idaho. What I saw of it to-day is the abomination of desolation: an enormous desert bounded by infinitely-far-away mountains that you never get to, and little pitiful blistered towns huddled down in the most abject loneliness underneath the huge light and scale and weather and the astounding brightness and dimensions of everything—all given a kind of tremendousness and terror and majesty by the dimension. And this?—their pride and joy, I guess, set in a cup of utterly naked hills, a clean little town but with a sparseness, a lack of the color, open-ness, richness of Cheyenne. I've tried to find Fisher: [1] people know him here but he's not in the telephone book. Anyway, what I've seen to-day explains a lot about him.

---

[1] Vardis Fisher, the author of the Vridar Hunter tetralogy, *Children of God, The Testament of Man*, etc., had first known Wolfe in 1928 when they had both been assistant professors in the English Department at New York University. Fisher's articles, "My Experiences with Thomas Wolfe" and "Thomas Wolfe and Maxwell Perkins" appeared in the April and July, 1951, issues of *Tomorrow*.

To ELIZABETH NOWELL

University Club
Portland, Oregon
Wednesday, June 15, 1938

Dear Miss Nowell:

I'm on my way to Seattle in a few minutes after a most wonderful week here. I'll be back here Saturday but am leaving again Sunday morning on what promises to be one of the most remarkable trips of my life. It means I'll be away about two weeks longer than I intended, but it is the chance of a lifetime and after long battlings with my conscience, I have decided I'd be foolish not to take it. Here's the program: a young fellow I know on one of the local papers [1] is starting out Sunday morning in his car on a tour of the entire West, and he has asked me to come with him. We leave here Sunday and head south for California stopping at Crater Lake on the way down; we go down the whole length of California taking in Yosemite, the Sequoias and any other national parks they have; then we swing east across the desert into Arizona to the Grand Canyon, etc., north through Utah, Zion and Bryce Canyons, Salt Lake, etc., then to the Yellowstone, then North to the Canadian Border, Montana, Glacier Park, etc., then west again across Montana, Idaho, Washington, then Ranier Park, etc.—in other words a complete swing around the West from the Rocky Mountains on, and every big national park in the West. The cost will be very little as we are stopping at roadside cabins, etc. He's writing a series of articles to show the little fellow how inexpensively he can see the West. [2] The whole thing will take two weeks to the day—perhaps a day or two less for me, because I intend to leave him at Spokane, and head straight for N.Y.

I've seen wonderful things and met every kind of person—doctors, lawyers, lumberjacks, etc.—and when I get through with this I'll have a whole wad of glorious material. My conscience hurts me about this extra two weeks, but I believe I'd always regret it if I passed it up. When I get through I shall really have seen America (except Texas).

Why didn't you write? I'm worried. I'll be back here at the University Club for a day Saturday, and if you want to reach me, use this address. Wish I could tell you more about this wonderful country, but that will come later. Meanwhile, best wishes.

[1] Edward M. Miller, who was at this time the Sunday Editor of *The Oregonian* and is now Assistant Managing Editor, and Ray Conway, Manager of the Oregon State Motor Association, had invited Wolfe to go on this tour of the Western national parks.

[2] Miller's articles, "Gulping the Great West," appeared in the July 31 and August 7, 1938 issues of *The Oregonian Magazine*.

The following letter to Elizabeth Nowell was written in answer to a letter from her which is now lost. In it, she said that she had had lunch with Maxwell Perkins at Cherio's; that he had asked about Wolfe; that he had seemed old, tired, tragic, and terribly depressed about the spread of Fascism in Europe; and that they had had a long and very enjoyable argument about the world in general. Evidently her letter reached Wolfe when he also was tired and depressed and had been brooding over certain literary gossip concerning his leaving Scribners which he had heard out West. Certainly Perkins never "instructed" anyone to "pass around" derogatory stories about Wolfe, and certainly Wolfe didn't seriously think he had, as is shown by his final letter to Perkins of August 12, 1938.

When, in 1945, Perkins began collecting Wolfe's letters for this present volume, he asked Miss Nowell to send him all the letters she had received from Wolfe. She did so, including the following letter of June 19, 1938, explaining to Perkins that she knew it would hurt him but that she had no right to suppress it or any letter of Wolfe's. Perkins answered her on August 7, 1945, saying: "Were you capable of believing—I know Tom could believe anything when his imagination got working—that we would instruct our salesmen to damage him? Besides, we should betray our profession, and everything we believe in, if we tried to injure a great talent. It's incredible that even Tom could believe that. It is possible that some of the men were so aggrieved at Tom's leaving us, that they expressed derogatory opinions of him as a man. Very likely they did, because many salesmen haven't the faintest understanding of literature, or of writers, and they might have interpreted Tom's decision in the most obvious way. But you must know that I never said much of anything about the whole matter, and that when pressed, I spoke in Tom's defence. Anyhow, a man who has spent his life as an editor, and insisted that the function of a publisher was to help bring out the truth by publishing whatever pertained to it, could never for an instant approve the suppression of a letter just because it ran against him."

To ELIZABETH NOWELL

University Club
Portland, Oregon
Sunday, June 19 (1938)

Dear Miss Nowell:

I got back here from Seattle last night and was delighted to find your letter. Our trip has been postponed until tomorrow morning—the little girl of one of the men was sick, but she's O.K. now, and by cutting a few corners we'll be back on schedule in a day or two. It ought to be a grand trip.

Washington and Seattle were wonderful, and I discovered all of my

Westall kin, the progeny of old Bacchus [1] who came out here in the '90s. There are thirty-seven of them now—I have the whole family tree and talked to three of them and have the record—I'd like to go back again and get the whole story. To me, it's mighty interesting.

This part of the country is almost fabulous. The streams and creeks and rivers swarm with fish—not 6 inch, 12 ounce ones—but great salmon, steelheads, etc., that weigh from 10 to 30 pounds. The forests are dense with enormous fir trees four and six feet through; the lumberjacks cut them down; the great lumber mills—I visited one of them—tear and slash and plane them into boards; and the enormous forests keep producing them—they keep growing everlastingly in spite of everything. The people are wonderfully good and open—I think a little too simple, maybe, and uncomplicated and *away* from the rest of the world—but it's a swell place and you're willing to believe that almost anything can happen here.

I was glad to get your letter and to know you'd seen Ed Aswell. I'll see him when I get back. I'm looking forward to the trip as a great thing in every way and shall try to put work out of my head till I get back.

I'm sorry about M. P. Everything you tell me about him touches and grieves and hurts me like hell. Please—*please* don't tell him about me, or anything about me, if you can avoid it. For six years he was my friend—I thought the best one I ever had—and then, a little over two years ago he turned against me. Everything I have done since was bad, he had no good word for it or for me, it's almost as if he were praying for my failure. I can't understand or fathom it, but it is a sad strange thing. Max still tells people that he is my friend, and then he runs me down; and out here in the West I have run on one or two stories that the Scribner salesmen apparently have been instructed to pass around that sicken me. It's like a nightmare, but I won't let it get me down. What is this thing in life anyway that causes people to do things like this? The hell of it is, the people who say they love you are often the ones who do the most to injure you. . . . I can't make it out, and now Perkins, under this mask of friendship, is doing the same thing. I don't think I'll ever change in the way I feel about him—the funny thing is I'm always supposed to be the one who changes, but at the bottom I'm the most solid of the lot.

I don't think he *consciously* wants me to fail or come to grief, but it's almost as if *unconsciously,* by some kind of *wishful* desire, he wants me

---

[1] Bacchus Westall was a half-brother of Wolfe's grandfather, Thomas Casey Westall. The three Westall descendants whom Wolfe had looked up were Albert Westall and his sister Marjorie, the grandchildren of Bacchus Westall, and Lonnie Harris, a nephew of Wolfe's grandmother, Martha (Penland) Westall.

to come to grief, as a kind of sop to his pride and his unyielding conviction that he is right in everything—the tragic flaw in his character
that keeps him from admitting that he has wronged anybody or made
a mistake. That is really his great weakness, and I believe it is at the root
of his failure—his growing reaction, his sense of defeat. . . . I shall
always remember him as one of the most wonderful people I ever knew
—but I have neither time nor energy to cope with this thing in him now;
all that I know is that it is against me, and against my work and I
can't give it any sort of break. As much as I can, I want to sever the
connection entirely. Some day, perhaps, if he is willing, I'll take it
up again—but meanwhile, let's not play with fire. Tell him nothing
about me or what I'm doing: that's the only way, believe me, to avoid
trouble. Anyway, it's not a matter of personalities any more: if I'm wrong
it will show in my work: if he's wrong it's going to show in his life. . . .

To end on a more cheerful note, I know a lot of swell people, and I
think you are one of them, and I am proud to know you are my friend.
I won't be back in Portland, and soon from now on I'll be travelling
all the time. I don't know at present what to tell you about mail or
how to reach me. Anyway, I'll write you later and I hope to see you in
about three weeks.

To ELIZABETH NOWELL

[Postcard: Crater Lake from Rim Drive, Crater Lake National Park, Oregon]

Fort Klamath, Oregon
Monday, June 20, 1938

We're off! Stop No 1, and no postcard can ever do justice to the color
and magnificence. 7500 feet up and ten feet of snow, but on to California
to-night.

To ELIZABETH NOWELL

[Postcard: The Three Brothers, Yosemite Valley]

Camp Curry, Cal
June 22, 1938

The one on the left is Canby, the middle one De Voto, with Whitney
Darrow on the right. (I'm getting a swell story out of this.)

To ELIZABETH NOWELL

Hotel Baxter
Bozeman, Mont.

Wednesday morning [June 29, 1938]

Dear Miss Nowell:

We're on the last leg of our trip.—We've gone over 3300 miles in eight days and "seen" nine national parks. We'll do 4500 in all and two more parks by the time I leave my two companions Friday night at Rainier and head in to Seattle. It has been furious, hectic, crowded and wildly comical, but I've seen a whole lot of the country and a lot of people and things. Furthermore I've got it all down—in a huge notebook—the whole thing smacked down with the blinding speed and variety of the trip.[1]

I'm going into Seattle to sleep a day or two—and perhaps to get the whole thing more or less in its present form (the whole trip from the beginning six weeks ago, I mean) typed down. Also, I've got to get some sleep before I start East. I'm ready and able to sleep now, but no time for it.

Am sending this to you air mail and want you to write or wire me Hotel New Washington, Seattle, to let me know if everything is O.K. and if it's all right if I stay a little longer to get the whole thing written and typed up. This is all now. We're on our way today to Glacier Park 400 miles away on the Canadian border—it's 6:45 A.M. and I can't dawdle, dearie, any longer.

To HAMILTON BASSO

[Postcard: Old Faithful Geyser, Yellowstone Park]

Yellowstone, Wyo.

June 30, 1938

Portrait of the author at the two million word point.

[1] This journal, considerably cut, appeared under the title of "A Western Journey" in the summer, 1939, issue of *The Virginia Quarterly Review,* and was published in book form under the title of *A Western Journal* in 1951 by the University of Pittsburgh Press. Wolfe used both titles for it, evidently not having decided which was better.

To EDWARD C. ASWELL

[Postcard: Two Medicine Lake, Glacier National Park]

June 30, 1938

Dear Ed: It has been a wonderful trip and at last I feel I know something about my country.

To ELIZABETH NOWELL

New Washington Hotel
Seattle, Wash.
Sunday, July 3, [1938]

Dear Miss Nowell:

I got here late yesterday afternoon and found telegrams from you and Ed,[1] and your air mail was delivered this morning: all of which relieves me and boosts me up no end. The trip was wonderful and terrific—in the last two weeks I have travelled five thousand miles, gone the whole length of the coast from Seattle almost to the Mexican border, inland a thousand miles and northward to the Canadian border. The national parks, of course, are stupendous, but what was to me far more valuable were the towns, the things, the people I saw—the whole West and all its history unrolling at kaleidoscopic speed. I have written it all down in just this way—with great speed—because I had to do most of it at night before going to bed, usually when we had driven four or five hundred miles and I was ready to drop with sleep. I've filled a big fat notebook with thirty thousand words of it [2] and looking some of it over, it occurs to me that in this way I may have got the whole thing —the whole impression—its speed, variety, etc.—pretty well.

At any rate, I've got a pretty clear record of the whole thing since I left New York six weeks or so ago, and after two or three days rest out on Puget Sound somewhere—(this is a country fit for Gods—you've never seen anything like it for scale and magnificence and abundance: the trees are as tall as the Flatiron Building and yet so much in scale that you simply cannot believe, until you measure them, they are as

---

[1] Aswell's wire of July 1, 1938, said: "Dear Tom: Your new book is magnificent in scope and design, with some of the best writing you have ever done. I am still absorbing it, confident that when you finish you will have written your greatest novel so far. Hope you come back full of health and new visions." Miss Nowell's wire and airmail letter merely told Wolfe of Aswell's enthusiasm, as repeated in a conversation with her.

[2] Wolfe always over-estimated the length of things he'd written. The actual length of the notes found in his suitcase after his death was only about 11,400 words.

big; and you throw a hook into some ordinary looking creek and pull out a twelve pound salmon. I assure you these things are literally true: you feel there's no limit, no end to anything. The East seems small and starved and meagre by comparison, and yet I'm glad there is the East, too—we've got to have the East: there's something in the East they don't have here.)

Anyway, I'd like to loaf and rest for a few days, and then get it typed, revising as much as I can but not taking too much time, and putting it down from the beginning like a spool unwinding at great speed. Perhaps it's not ready to use yet or won't be for a year or two, but I'll have it *down*—and you know what that means to me, and I thought I'd call it "A Western Journal."

Anyway, if that's O.K. by you and Ed, that's my present idea. I really feel ready to *go* again. I've had no rest, but this movement—the sense of life and discovery, the variety—has renewed and stimulated me. Writing thirty thousand words under the circumstances of the past two weeks was an accomplishment and proved to me that I am getting ready again, because I *wanted* to write them—couldn't keep from it.

Anyway, use this hotel as an address for the present. If I go to Puget Sound I'll leave an address here, and anyway I'll keep you posted. Now get some rest yourself—and thanks for everything.

P.S. I'm thinking of buying some firecrackers and spending to-morrow in H.M.'s Canadian town of Victoria, B.C.

To MARGARET ROBERTS

New Washington Hotel
Seattle, Washington

[July 4, 1938]

Dear Mrs. Roberts:

Your letter was forwarded on to me here. I think you are grand to go to so much trouble for me, and if I blow off clouds of volcanic steam, don't think I don't appreciate all you have done and are doing. I was ready to drop when I left New York six weeks ago, but I've seen a whole new continent, the entire West, and now I'm writing thousands of words a day again. I'll be back in N.Y. some time this month: meanwhile I'm trying to rewrite and put the fifty thousand words or more I've written on this trip in a typed manuscript. When I arrived here last night, after 25,000 miles around the whole West in the past 14 days, . . . I found a telegram from my editor at Harper's telling me he had read the 2,000,000 word rough draft I had left with him of the new book, that it was "magnificent in scope and design"—and far and away the best thing I'd ever done. With this wonderful assurance I'm going back and try to live up to it until it's finished as I want it. All your help is gratefully appreciated. Best wishes to you and Mr. R.,

To ELIZABETH NOWELL

[Postcard: C.P.R.S.S. *Princess Kathleen*]

Postmarked Vancouver, B.C.

July 6, 1938

I've just left Victoria B.C. on this ship on my way to Vancouver. Will be back in Seattle tomorrow or day after, and then to work.

It was on this boat trip to Victoria and Vancouver that Wolfe shared a pint of whiskey which he had bought with "a poor, shivering wretch," who probably had influenza, and from whom Wolfe is believed to have contracted the respiratory infection which finally resulted in his death. By the afternoon of July 6, Wolfe was seriously ill with high fever, pains in his lungs, and protracted chills. However, instead of going to a hospital in Vancouver, he took a train back to Seattle and remained, still desperately ill, in the New Washington Hotel there for five more days. Finally, on July 11, he was examined by Dr. E. C. Ruge, who found him to have pneumonia and hospitalized him at Firlawns Sanitarium at Bothell, Washington. By July 15th, Wolfe seemed to have passed the crisis of his pneumonia, and was able to send the following wire to Edward Aswell.

To EDWARD C. ASWELL

[Telegram]

Seattle, Wash.

July 15 (?) [1938]

Doctors say I'm out of danger now. Will write when I feel stronger.

However, during the period of his convalescence, Wolfe began to have recurrent fever and other disquieting symptoms. By the first week of August, Dr. Ruge had him taken to Providence Hospital in Seattle so that X-rays

of his lungs could be made. These revealed an unresolved condition of the upper lobe of the right lung, which the X-ray specialist and Dr. Ruge diagnosed as an old tubercular lesion, but which other doctors considered to be only the result of his pneumonia.

Wolfe remained at Providence Hospital until September 4th, by which time he was suffering from violent headaches and moments of slight irrationality. On the recommendation of the physicians who had succeeded Dr. Ruge when Wolfe entered Providence Hospital, Mabel Wolfe Wheaton, who had come to Seattle to be with Wolfe during his illness, took him by train to Johns Hopkins Hospital in Baltimore. There, on September 12, Dr. Walter E. Dandy performed an exploratory operation on his brain. It was found that germs of tuberculosis, released from an old lesion on Wolfe's lung by his recent pneumonia, had entered his blood stream and been carried to his brain. He died of this cerebral infection three days later, on September 15, 1938.

The following note, written to Maxwell Perkins on August 12, 1938, when Wolfe first had intimations of death, was the last letter which he was ever to write.

To MAXWELL E. PERKINS

Providence Hospital
Seattle, Washington

August 12, 1938.

Dear Max:

I'm sneaking this against orders, but "I've got a hunch"—and I wanted to write these words to you.

I've made a long voyage and been to a strange country, and I've seen the dark man very close; and I don't think I was too much afraid of him, but so much of mortality still clings to me—I wanted most desperately to live and still do, and I thought about you all a thousand times, and wanted to see you all again, and there was the impossible anguish and regret of all the work I had not done, of all the work I had to do—and I know now I'm just a grain of dust, and I feel as if a great window has been opened on life I did not know about before—and if I come through this, I hope to God I am a better man, and in some strange way I can't explain, I know I am a deeper and a wiser one. If I get on my feet and out of here, it will be months before I head back, but if I get on my feet, I'll come back.

Whatever happens—I had this "hunch" and wanted to write you and tell you, no matter what happens or has happened, I shall always think of you and feel about you the way it was that Fourth of July day three years [1] ago when you met me at the boat, and we went out on the café on the river and had a drink and later went on top of the tall building, and all the strangeness and the glory and the power of life and of the city was below.

Yours always,

Tom

[1] The fourth of July, 1935, was the day on which Wolfe had returned to America to find *Of Time and the River* a great success.

INDEX